Semantic Technologies for Business and Information Systems Engineering:

Concepts and Applications

Stefan Smolnik
EBS Business School, Germany

Frank Teuteberg
University of Osnabrueck, Germany

Oliver Thomas
University of Osnabrueck, Germany

Managing Director:	Lindsay Johnston
Book Production Manager:	Sean Woznicki
Development Manager:	Joel Gamon
Development Editor:	Michael Killian
Acquisitions Editor:	Erika Carter
Typesetters:	Jennifer Romanchak, Adrienne Freeland
Print Coordinator:	Jamie Snavely
Cover Design:	Nick Newcomer

Published in the United States of America by
Business Science Reference (an imprint of IGI Global)
701 E. Chocolate Avenue
Hershey PA 17033
Tel: 717-533-8845
Fax: 717-533-8661
E-mail: cust@igi-global.com
Web site: http://www.igi-global.com

Library of Congress Cataloging-in-Publication Data

Semantic technologies for business and information systems engineering: concepts and applications / Stefan Smolnik, Frank Teuteberg and Oliver Thomas, editors.
    p. cm.
  Includes bibliographical references and index.
  Summary: "This book investigates the application of semantic technologies to business and information systems engineering"-- Provided by publisher.
  ISBN 978-1-60960-126-3 (hardcover) -- ISBN 978-1-60960-128-7 (ebook) 1. Semantic computing. 2. Semantic networks (Information theory) 3. Management information systems. I. Smolnik, Stefan, 1970- II. Teuteberg, Frank, 1970- III. Thomas, Oliver, 1971- IV. Title.
  QA76.5913.S47 2012
  005.7--dc23
                                2011031983

British Cataloguing in Publication Data
A Cataloguing in Publication record for this book is available from the British Library.

All work contributed to this book is new, previously-unpublished material. The views expressed in this book are those of the authors, but not necessarily of the publisher.

Editorial Advisory Board

Table of Contents

Section 1
Models and Methods

Daniela Lucas da Silva, Universidade Federal do Espírito Santo, Brazil
Renato Rocha Souza, Fundação Getúlio Vargas, Brazil
Maurício Barcellos Almeida, Universidade Federal de Minas Gerais, Brazil

José M. González and Vázquez, OFFIS – Institute for Information Technology, Germany
Mathias Uslar, OFFIS – Institute for Information Technology, Germany

Peter Fettke, German Research Center for Artificial Intelligence, Germany
Peter Loos, German Research Center for Artificial Intelligence, Germany

Section 2
Data and Knowledge Management

Farid Bourennani, University of Ontario Institute of Technology, Canada
Shahryar Rahnamayan, University of Ontario Institute of Technology, Canada

Section 3
Semantic Technologies in Conceptual Modeling

Section 4
Semantic Process Description

Andreas Bögl, Johannes Kepler University Linz, Austria
Michael Karlinger, Johannes Kepler University Linz, Austria
Michael Schrefl, Johannes Kepler University Linz, Austria
Gustav Pomberger, Johannes Kepler University Linz, Austri

Yun Lin, Agresso, Norway
Darijus Strasunskas, Norwegian University of Science and Technology, Norway

Witold Abramowicz, Poznań University of Economics, Poland
Agata Filipowska, Poznań University of Economics, Poland
Monika Kaczmarek, Poznań University of Economics, Poland
Tomasz Kaczmarek, Poznań University of Economics, Poland

Section 5
Services and Workflows

Tariq Mahmoud, Carl von Ossietzky University of Oldenburg, Germany
Jorge Marx Gómez, Carl von Ossietzky University of Oldenburg, Germany
Timo von der Dovenmühle, Carl von Ossietzky University of Oldenburg, Germany

Rainer Telesko, Fachhochschule Nordwestschweiz, Switzerland
Simon Nikles, Fachhochschule Nordwestschweiz, Switzerland

Marwane El Kharbili, University of Luxemburg, Luxemburg
Elke Pulvermueller, University of Osnabrueck, Germany

Preface

There are increasing opportunities to consider the application of semantic technologies for business information systems. Semantic technologies are expected to improve business processes and information systems, and lead to savings in cost and time as well as improved efficiency. However, the degree of automation in enacting business processes and monitoring information systems and value chains is still unsatisfying. Current problems are representational heterogeneities between the various modeling notations used, the various (subjective) perspectives of the modelers on the application domains, or the different stages in the life-cycles of business processes. Interoperability and integration of advanced business information systems is concerned with the application of semantic technologies. These technologies allow for annotating meaning to business concepts and processes, and allow for automatically monitoring business systems and processes without human interactions. The book at hand explores the potential of semantic technologies for business and information systems engineering and provides an overview of applying semantic technologies for business and information systems engineering.

The first section, *Models and Methods,* covers fundamental aspects of creating and applying knowledge structures. At first, methodologies are compared by Daniela Lucas da Silva, Renato Rocha Souza, and Maurício Barcellos Almeida. The authors conduct an analytical study compiled by the analysis of literature about methodologies for building ontologies and controlled vocabularies as well as by the analysis of international standards for software engineering. The application of an ontology-based method is then described by José González and Mathias Uslar. The authors develop an approach for constructing a domain specific reference model catalogue for the energy sector. In doing so, the authors consider both modeling requirements in the fields of ontology and reference model design. In the last chapter of this section, Peter Fettke and Peter Loos illustrate the use of ontology to evaluate Scheer's reference model for production planning and control systems. The authors use ontology as a tool or theory and thus complement the dominating view on ontologies as design artifacts by a view on ontology in line with the philosophical discipline.

The second section provides an overview of the plethora of applications of semantic technologies in the field of *Data and Knowledge Management*. A fundamental problem in this area is how to process data originating from heterogeneous data sources and in diverse data formats such as text, numerical data, multimedia and others. Farid Bourennani and Shahryar Rahnamayan propose a unified approach for representing and processing data of heterogeneous types which ultimately should augment the interpretation of qualitative and quantitative data with use cases in business and financial sectors. Further, Liane Haak presents new ways for the integration of structured and unstructured data focusing on the application to data warehousing and knowledge management. The chapter introduces a solution for generating an ontology from a data warehouse system and integrating it with a knowledge management systems ontology. The integrated ontologies are subsequently used for semantic navigation.

The last chapter of this section, by Alexey Alishevskikh and Tatiana Emshanova, demonstrates how personal knowledge management can be improved by semantic desktop technologies. It describes theoretical aspects as well as the implementation of a supportive technology and framework integrating several aspects such as content aggregation, search, natural language processing, metadata management, and tagging. The synthesis of these different techniques aims at augmenting the experience of knowledge workers when working with digital information assets.

The third section, *Semantic Technologies in Conceptual Modeling,* focuses on applying semantic technologies to support conceptual modeling. The improved construction and analysis of semi-formal models on a general level is targeted by an approach for conceptual model analysis contributed by Patrick Delfmann, Sebastian Herwig, Łukasz Lis, and Jörg Becker. The approach integrates semantic standardization and structural pattern matching, hence enabling an unambiguous analysis of the models' contents. It is intended for a number of purposes such as revealing syntactical errors, model comparison, model integration or the identification of business process improvement potentials.

Regarding the semantic verification of business process models, an ontology-based approach making use of background knowledge encoded in formal ontologies and rules is proposed by Michael Fellmann, Frank Hogrebe, and Oliver Thomas. The authors develop a model for the ontology-based representation of process models which is used in conjunction with machine reasoning for process model verification. The approach is demonstrated using real-life administrative process models taken from a capital city.

Whereas the two previous approaches aim at improvements regarding the construction and validation or verification of conceptual models and hence stick to more traditional ways of conceptual modeling, a more fundamental shift in the way of modeling is accompanied by the idea of a fully automated model construction. In the domain of process modeling, first results are shown by Bernd Heinrich, Mathias Klier, and Steffen Zimmermann, who present an algorithm and accompanying method for the automated planning of process models.

At the end of this section, the use of semantic technologies from a practical perspective is reported by Hans-Georg Fill and Ilona Reischl. Their chapter describes how semantic technologies can be combined with conceptual models to support management executives in the distribution of knowledge and the analysis of compliance. The approach is based on a stepwise semantic enrichment of conceptual models with formal semantic schemata and has been implemented on the ADONIS meta-modeling platform in the context of a real-life project with the Austrian competent authority in regard to safety in healthcare.

The fourth section of the book, *Semantic Process Description,* is dedicated specifically to the semantically enhanced representation and annotation of semi-formal process models. A detailed model how to annotate semi-formal process models both with lexical and semantic labels bridges the gap between human understandability and machine interpretability. This is introduced by Andreas Bögl, Michael Karlinger, Michael Schrefl, and Gustav Pomberger. Amongst other purposes, it can be applied for the automated refactoring of model elements and automated semantic annotation. The latter is also addressed by Yun Lin and Darijus Strasunskas, albeit they suggest annotating processes on a more coarse-grained level of process model templates. The annotation consists of the three basic parts: meta-model, domain, and goal annotation. It may be used to facilitate the retrieval and reuse of process knowledge.

In the last chapter of this section, the semantically enhanced business process modeling notation is introduced by Witold Abramowicz, Agata Filipowska, Monika Kaczmarek and Tomasz Kaczmarek. This "ontologized" version of the Business Process Modeling Notation is formalized in the sBPMN ontology, which is consequently suggested as a serialization format for BPMN modeling tools. In such a way, annotations can be created invisible to the users and directly embedded into the models leading to advanced machine interpretability which facilitates and mechanizes the task of transforming semi-formal process models into executable workflows.

The last section of the book provides insights on how to use semantic technologies to support *Services and Workflows*. The first contribution in this part by Tariq Mahmoud, Jorge Marx Gómez and Timo von der Dovenmühle offers a Semantic Web services based reference model. This model relies on the idea of applying lightweight semantics to web services targeted at improved service advertisement, service composition, and service validation. While this chapter mainly focuses on the description and composition of services, the check whether such processes comply with regulations or policies is the main concern of the contribution by Rainer Telesko and Simon Nikles. They describe a concept for the semantics-based configuration of service packages with respect to service level agreements thereby capitalizing on the principles and use cases of the EU-project plugIT and additionally reporting on the economic benefits. With similar intentions, semantic policies for modeling regulatory process compliance are envisioned by Marwane El Kharbili and Elke Pulvermueller. They also motivate the need for automation in compliance management and propose the use of policies as a modeling concept for regulations. The authors introduce the CASE model and the corresponding policy modeling ontology. Both are used to support automated compliance checking of enterprise processes to regulations. The utilization of the CASE method as well as the policy ontology is showcased using an example of resource access control in business processes.

In the last chapter of the book, Barbara Thönssen and Daniela Wolff take a broader view on context models with the intent to support business process agility. They present dimensions of change concentrating on a specific ability of an enterprise to deal with change and propose a semantically enriched context model based on a well-known enterprise architecture. Finally, a context aware workflow engine is presented which leverages these concepts and rules which trigger process adaptations during run time.

We hope that this book will receive widespread recognition both from practitioners and the scientific community.

Stefan Smolnik
EBS Business School, Germany

Frank Teuteberg
University of Osnabrueck, Germany

Oliver Thomas
University of Osnabrueck, Germany

Acknowledgment

First and foremost, the editors wish to thank all authors for their excellent contributions to this volume and for shouldering the bulk of the efforts it took to realize this project. Without their effort and cooperation, we could not have finished this book. The high quality of all papers included here was assured by a double blind review process (each submitted chapter was reviewed at least twice). All articles are part of the rapid progress that we are currently witnessing in scientific research on Semantic Technologies for Business Information Systems Engineering.

Furthermore, we would like to thank IGI Global, especially Beth Ardner, and Mike Killian, Editorial Content Department, who have both supported this project at all phases of development in a constructive, professional, dedicated, friendly, and open manner.

This book could not have been completed without professional preparation and organization. Therefore, we would particularly like to thank Ms. Anja Grube for her assistance in coordination and communication as well as for proofreading and translating services.

We hope that this book provides valuable insights for the reader and will encourage the adoption of semantic technologies for business and information systems engineering.

As for the contents of this volume, the editors are always open to any suggestions for improvement and are looking forward to the readers' comments and fruitful discussions.

Stefan Smolnik
EBS Business School, Germany

Frank Teuteberg
University of Osnabrueck, Germany

Oliver Thomas
University of Osnabrueck, Germany

Section 1
Models and Methods

Chapter 1
Ontologies and Controlled Vocabulary:
Comparison of Building Methodologies

Daniela Lucas da Silva
Universidade Federal do Espírito Santo, Brazil

Renato Rocha Souza
Fundação Getúlio Vargas, Brazil

Maurício Barcellos Almeida
Universidade Federal de Minas Gerais, Brazil

ABSTRACT

This chapter presents an analytical study about methodology and methods to build ontologies and controlled vocabularies, compiled by the analysis of a literature about methodologies for building ontologies and controlled vocabularies and the international standards for software engineering. Through theoretical and empirical research it was possible to build a comparative overview which can help as a support in the defining of methodological patterns for building ontologies, using theories from the computer science and information science.

INTRODUCTION

The organization of information has increasingly became a crucial process as the volume of information available has exponentially increased, sometimes resulting in the chaotic information collections. In this sense, a lot of research has been made (Lancaster, 1986; Gruber, 1993; Berners-Lee, Hendler & Lassila, 2001) aiming at the construction of mechanisms for the organization of information with the sole objective of improving the efficacy of the information retrieval systems.

This fact contributes to the attention paid to the ontologies, which are originated in the theoretical field of Philosophy (Corazzon, 2008) and are researched and developed as a tool for the representation of knowledge in Computer and Information Sciences. For the Information Science, the ontologies are of interest because of their potential to organize and represent information

DOI: 10.4018/978-1-60960-126-3.ch001

(Vickery, 1997). According to Almeida & Barbosa (2009), the ontologies can improve the information retrieval processes as they organize the content of the data sources in a specific domain.

Gruber (1993) presents a definition which is widely accepted by the ontology community: "an explicit specification of a conceptualization" (Gruber, 1993, p. 2), where "explicit specification" would be related to concepts, properties and explicitly defined axioms; and "conceptualization" regards an abstract pattern of any real world phenomenon. As components of ontology (Gómez-Pérez, Fernández, & Vicente, 1996; Gruber, 1993), there are: a) conceptual classes which organize the concepts of a domain in a taxonomy; b) class attributes, which are relevant properties of the concept; c) instances, which are used to represent objects specific to a context; d) attributes of instances, which are relevant properties used to describe the instances of a concept; e) relationships between classes, which represent the type of interaction between the concepts of a domain; f) invariants, which always have the same values and are generally used in standards or formulations to infer knowledge in ontology; g) terms, which design the concepts of a domain; h) formal axioms, which limit the interpretation and usage of the concepts involved in the ontology; and i) standards, which determine conditions to the domain besides inferring values for attributes.

This chapter proposes an analytical study on methodologies and methods used for ontology building more commonly found in the literature and methodologies and standards designed to build controlled vocabulary, in order to delineate a comparative overview about the construction of such instruments. Such panorama can contribute to the definition of methodological standards for the construction of ontologies through the integration of theoretical and methodological principles from the Information and Computer Sciences as well as from contributions of known methodologies and methods employed to build ontologies and controlled vocabularies.

In order to accomplish the task proposed, the methodological steps taken in the research were the following: i) the identification and selection of documents referring to the subject methodologies for ontology building; ii) the identification and selection of methodologies for ontology building discussed in them; iii) the identification and selection of standards for the construction of controlled vocabulary; iv) the definition of content analysis categories in order to collect data relevant to the research; and v) the comparative analysis of the methodologies, methods and standards.

Background

Within the domain of ontologies development, the approaches for their building are, invariably, specific and limited. One problem, from the methodological point of view, is that there are neither patterns nor wide accepted methodologies for its building (Fernández et al., 1999; Uschold, & Gruninger, 1996). Despite the fact that great quantities of ontologies have already been developed by different communities – chemistry (Gómez-Pérez, Fernández & Vicente, 1996) and in business process modelling (Gruninger & Fox, 1995), just to give a few examples – under different approaches and using different methods and techniques, there is no consensus about a "gold standard" for the development process (Fernández, Gómez-Pérez & Juristo, 1997). The consequence is the absence of rigorous standardized techniques. Besides that, it is verified the lack of a systematic explanation on how and where the theoretical approaches will be used within their elaboration process.

Information Science researchers (Vickery, 1997; Soergel, 1997; Soergel, 1999; Gilchrist, 2003) often present similarities in their ideas about controlled vocabulary used in Library Science, like the thesauri, taxonomies and tools used in Artificial Intelligence, such as ontologies. The similarities lay especially in the way the structures of these tools are devised, which demands the organization of concepts into processes that include the categorization and classification of concepts, the definition of the relationships between these concepts and the treatment of the terminology employed in the concepts and structure relations.

Soergel (1999) highlights the lack on the communication among the many fields which work with conceptual structures, like ontologies. Silva (2008) corroborated this vision showing how many ontology engineering methodologies are available whilst no true standard is accepted. This may explain why, according to the words of Gómez-Pérez et al (2004), methodologies for ontology engineering are never used in practice

Literature Analysis

The first methodological step in the research was the identification and selection of the available literature on methodologies for ontology building and engineering. We have chosen to search in the knowledge bases that were available, as Citeseer[1], ACM Portal[2] and Google Scholar[3], being all of them references in the Information Science and Computer Science Fields. We have sought also the main references from these articles, in order to enhance the results.

After selecting the knowledge bases, we have performed the following steps: i) selection of articles with the keywords "ontology" or "ontologies" associated to "building", "methodology" and/or "engineering"; ii) selection of the most commonly cited sources from the previously found articles, adding those to the selected documents; iii) identification of the methodologies for building ontologies in the selected documents; iv) frequency analysis of the citations to the methodologies, to choose the most preeminent; and v) definition of the set of methodologies to be used in the research.

The process of analysis and interpretation of retrieved documents took place through the usage of bibliometrics and content analysis (Bardin, 1977) techniques, which enabled the selection of the relevant documents. Content analysis includes

a set of communication analysis techniques which aim at obtaining indicators (quantitative or not) that allow the inference of knowledge present in the messages.

According to the criteria, we have obtained 25 relevant documents from the survey. When we applied citation analysis, we found that the TOVE was the most cited methodology (68%), followed by the Enterprise Ontology (60%), Methontology (56%), Cyc (36%), Kactus (24%), Sensus and On-To-Knowledge (20% each), method 101 (12%) and KBSI IDEF5 (4%). Then we have analysed which of these methodologies aimed to build domain ontologies, discarding the On-To-Knowledge and KBSI IDEF5.

The methodologies and methods used for the construction of ontologies chosen for the comparative analysis were: a) Gruninger and Fox's TOVE methodology; b) Uschold and King's Enterprise Methodology; c) the Methontology methodology; d) the Cyc method; e) the Kactus method; f) the Sensus method; and g) the 101 method. It was assumed that, by analyzing the most discussed methodologies in the literature, it would be possible to achieve a reasonable result regarding a comparative study of methodologies used in ontology engineering.

Throughout the activity to identify methodologies for the building of controlled vocabulary, the existence of standards and manuals created by nationally and internationally acknowledged institutions was also verified. As a main reference, this research used one standard, which is justified by the following criteria: a) it is the most current standard (from 2005), accepted and consolidated in the Information Science community; and b) it is the standard which presents an interdisciplinary approach of the theories derived from Information Science and from Terminology – The Theory of Faceted Classification; the Concept Theory; and Terminology Theory – in the building of controlled vocabulary. This standard, named ANSI/NISO Z39.19-2005 (ANSI, 2005), was built based on several American and international standards concerning the creation of thesauri, including the ISO 2788. Besides the standard, the manual available in the Librarianship, Information and Information Technology site - BITI (Campos, Gomes & Motta, 2004), about thesauri elaboration, was used. The manual, even though focusing on a specific type of controlled vocabulary, proved to be coherent as regards the recommendations given in standard ANSI/NISO Z39.19-2005.

During the preliminary content analysis carried out in the materials regarding the ontology building and controlled vocabulary development, we noticed a similarity between some stages of development of these instruments and other similarities derived from the development of software process. Some similarities were identified especially throughout domain analysis activities and in the technical approaches devised for the creation of conceptual patterns. Therefore it was decided we would use, under this study perspective, the internationally accepted standard for the development of software (IEEE1074-1997), to define the categories of analysis. This choice is justified by the fact that this standard describes a structured and methodical way for product development (Pressman, 2004), and because it derives from Software Engineering, a discipline considered mature in the sense it possesses widely accepted methodologies (Fernández et al., 1999, p.1). As ontologies are considered components of software products (Fernández et al., 1999), the utilization of the standard as instrument for data qualitative analysis was deemed pertinent.

THE CATEGORIES FOR ANALYSIS

The content analysis categories of the empirical material were defined from principles elucidated by Bardin (1977), who advocates the use of categories for procedures of qualitative analysis. According to the author, the choice of categories may involve several criteria: i) semantic; ii) syntactic (verbs, adjectives, pronouns); iii)

lexical (group according to the meaning of the words, group synonyms and antonyms); and iv) expressions and phrases. In this study, the chosen criterion for the categories was the semantic one, that is, it was carried out according to the standard IEEE1074 (1997) and to the literature from the ontologies field. The categories were then adapted to the processes extracted from the standard and from the characteristics particular to ontologies (formalization and integration). They are: i) project management; ii) pre-development; iii) requirements specification; iv) conceptual modelling; v) formalization; vi) implementation; vii) maintenance; viii) integration; ix) evaluation; and x) documentation. Afterwards, each category is established according to standard IEEE-1074 (1997) and methodological principles designed for the building of ontologies (Fernández, Gómez-Pérez, & Juristo, 1997; Uschold, & Gruninger, 1996).

- **Project management:** activities related to the initial stage of a project, such as the software creation and life-cycle; to the monitoring and control of the software project in its entire life-cycle.
- **Pre-development:** consists of analyzing ideas or concepts of a system and, due to problems observed in the environment, allocate the system requirements before the beginning of the software development. This stage includes feasibility study activities and the analysis of the system requirements
- **Requirements specifications:** encompasses restrictions or standards that the software must abide by according to the definitions of the requestor needs. The requirements must serve as an initial document for the realization of modelling and prototyping tasks, and the process is normally interactive.
- **Conceptual modelling:** aims at developing a well organized and coherent repre-

sentation of the system, able to comply with the software requirements specified in the requirements activities.

- **Formalization:** consists of transforming the ontology conceptual model (or conceptualization) into a formal model in order to accurately define its meaning. The professional involved in the ontology building focus on the computer modelling of the problem, using, for example, first-order logic and its extensions (representation systems based on frames, semantic webs, descriptive logic, etc). The techniques used in this stage derive from the Artificial Intelligence area.
- **Implementation:** results in the transformation of the software's engineering project version into a programming language. In the case of ontologies, the implementation consists of mapping the formal model into a language able to respond to the demand, such as the Web Ontology Language – OWL (Van Harmelen et al., 2003).
- **Maintenance:** regarded as a post-development stage consisting of identifying problems and improvements in the products. It can result in new versions of the same products.
- **Integration:** an alternative to facilitate the building of ontologies is to integrate the ontology being created to existing ontologies. This stage considers the reutilization of existing concepts in other ontologies. The proposal is to examine the conceptualization of meta-ontologies (called high level ontologies) and to select (partially or completely) the ones that better fit into the model being constructed. In the integration process the activities can be carried out during the conceptual modelling and ontologies implementing stages. As a result, it is regarded as an integral process.
- **Evaluation:** the activities are carried out at the same time as the activities of processes

turned to the software development, such as: revision and auditing of the processes, development of testing procedures, testing and result assessment.

- **Documentation:** development and distribution of documentation for developers and users involved in the processes, in order to provide, in due time, information on the software.

The next step was the development of a comparative chart depicting the development stages presented in the methodologies and methods used for the building of ontologies and controlled vocabularies. This scope was devised through a matrix structure representing the objects investigated in its columns and each phase of its life cycle on the lines. Based on the treatment and organization of the content in the structure, it was possible to comparatively analyze every methodology, method and standard, making theoretical and empirical conclusions about the ontologies and controlled vocabulary building processes.

METHODOLOGIES ASSESSED

This section presents the methodologies and methods used in the building of ontologies as well as the methodology and standard used for the building of controlled vocabulary. Their analysis is described in detail in Silva (2008, p.132). Hence, the section *The Cyc Method* introduces the Cyc Ontology and the method used for its development. The section *Gruninger and Fox's Methodology* presents a few considerations on the Tove Project and the procedures of Gruninger and Fox's methodology. The section *Uschold and King Method* introduces the Enterprise Ontology Project, regarding the procedures of Uschold and King's method. The section *Kactus Method* presents this method. The section *Methontology Methodology* introduces the methods and techniques of Methontology. The section *Sensus*

Method presents the SENSUS ontology and the method that was based on it, the Sensus Method. The section *101 Method* presents this method. Finally, the section *Methodology and Standard for the construction of controlled vocabulary* ponders about the standard used in the building of controlled vocabulary and demonstrates the methodological procedures in the BITI manual which are used for the building of thesauri.

The Cyc Method

In the 1980's, the company Microelectronics and Computer Technology – MCC began creating Cyc, a broad knowledge base which considers the consensual knowledge on the world, including standards and heuristics for deductions about quotidian objects and events (Reed, & Lenat, 2002). Cyc's language of representation is the CycL, which is considered hybrid because it merges frames to predicate calculus. The language has got an inference machine which allows multiple heritages, automatic classification, maintenance of inverse links, restrictions verification, ordinate search, detection of contradictions and resolution module. The Cyc knowledge base was developed in 1990 by Douglas Lenat and Ramanathan Guha (Fernández, Gómez-Pérez, & Corcho, 2004), and three processes were considered: i) extraction of knowledge from the common sense; ii) extraction helped by computers; and iii) extraction managed by computers. In the first process, the knowledge required for the building of the ontology was manually obtained from different sources, such as articles, books and newspapers. The second process was carried out automatically, with the use of computational tools for the processing of natural language and machine learning capable of using common sense knowledge sufficient to investigate and discover new knowledge. Finally, the third process was carried out by a larger number of tools in order to manage the knowledge extraction from the common sense (parts which are deemed difficult to be interpreted in the knowledge sources involved) in the Cyc base.

Gruninger and Fox's Methodology

The methodology was proposed by Michael Gruninger and Mark Fox in 1995 (Gruninger, & Fox, 1995), having as groundwork for its development the experience gained in the Toronto Virtual Enterprise project, known as the Tove project (Fox, 1992), whose theoretical and methodological principles are found in the field of Artificial Intelligence. Project Tove's goal is to create a common sense model about the company, namely a shared knowledge regarding the business, able to lead to the deduction of answers to the questions concerning the domain (Fox, 1992). In order to accomplish that, ontologies are created to specify models for public and private organizations, taking under consideration the following characteristics: a) the capacity to provide a shared terminology for organizations, which can be understood and used by each application, that is, by every kind of business; b) the definition of the semantics of every term through a logical theory; c) the implementation of the semantics into a set of axioms which allows the ontology to automatically deduce the answers to the questions common in the organizations scope; and d) the definition of a simbology used to graphically represent terms or concepts (Gruninger, & Fox, 1996). Gruninger and Fox's methodology was used in the University of Toronto Enterprise Integration Laboratory for the project and assessment of integrated ontologies, including propositions for the building of new ontologies and extensions of existing ontologies. The following procedures were proposed in the methodology: i) the devising of motivational frameworks which aim at identifying problems in the current environment; ii) the specification of informal questions, which aim at specifying, in natural language, the requirements that the ontology should be able to meet; iii) the devising of the formal terminology in which, through first-order logic statements, the concepts and their properties are organized in a taxonomy; iv) the specification of formal questions, in which problems are consistently defined before the axioms in the ontology; v) the specification of formal axioms which restrict the interpretation of the terms involved in formal questions; and vi) the verification of complete theorems, which determine the conditions under which the solutions to the questions are completed.

Uschold and King Method

The method was initially proposed by Mike Uschold and Martin King in 1995 (Uschold, & King, 1995) and expanded in 1996 by Mike Uschold and Michael Gruninger (Uschold, & Gruninger, 1996) in the development experience of the *Enterprise Ontology*. Such ontology was developed as part of the project *Enterprise* by the Artificial Intelligence Applications Institute of the University of Edinburgh and partners such as IBM, Unilever, among others.

Uschold and King (1995) consider the following stages necessary for a comprehensive methodology: i) identification of the ontology objective, aiming at identifying the need of construction, the degree of formality (from the informal, using natural language, to the strictly formal, employing logic declarations) and the classes of users of the ontology, including developers, maintainers and users of applications; ii) the ontology construction, which is divided in: a) capture or conception of the conceptualization of the ontology; b) codification or implementation through a language of representation of ontologies and c) integration with existing ontologies; iii) ontology evaluation through specified requirements; and iv) documentation concerning the ontology intentions and the primitives used to express definitions in ontology.

Kactus Method

The emphasis of the European project, *Esprit Kactus,* is in the organization of knowledge basis which can be shared and reused in different knowledge based systems. In order to do that, domain ontologies are used to organize knowledge independently from the software application which will be built.

Based on the Kactus Project, Amaya Bernaras and colleagues (Bernaras, Laresgoiti, & Corera, 1996) investigated the viability of reusing knowledge systems of technical complexity, such as the domain of electric networks, and the role of ontologies as a support for such systems. This investigation resulted in an ontology construction method in which the processes involved would be conditioned to the development of the application, i.e., every time an application is built, the ontology that represents the knowledge required for that application would be refined. These processes would involve the: i) development of a list or requirements or prerequisites which have to be fulfilled by the application; ii) identification of relevant terms for the application domain based on such requirements, building, therefore, a preliminary model, iii) refinement and structuring of the ontology in order to achieve a definite model; iv) search for ontologies already developed by other applications so as to reuse them. The reused ontologies would demand refinement and extension to be employed in the new application.

Methontology Methodology

The Methontology was developed in the laboratory of Artificial Intelligence of the Polytechnic University of Madrid between 1996 and 1997 by the group of researchers (Fernández, Gómez-Pérez, & Juristo, 1997; Gómez-Pérez, Fernández, & Vicente, 1996).

Methontology involves a set of development stages (specification, conceptualization, formalization, integration, implementation and maintenance), a life cycle based on prototypes evolution (Pressman, 2004) and techniques to carry out planning, development and support activities. The planning activity includes task echeloning and control, aiming at reaching the desired quality. The support activities involve knowledge acquisition, documentation and evaluation, and they take place throughout the ontology's life cycle. The initial development stages (specification and conceptualization) demand a great effort within the support activities, such as knowledge acquisition and evaluation. This is due to many reasons: a) most of the knowledge is acquired in the beginning of the ontology construction process; and b) the conceptual model should be correctly evaluated to avoid future errors in the life cycle of the ontology. Finally, the detailed documentation should be produced at the end of each stage anticipated in the life cycle.

Sensus Method

The SENSUS ontology was developed by the group of natural language *Information Sciences Institute* – ISI aiming to be used in the processing of natural language. The SENSUS ontology comprehends approximately 70.000 concepts, organized hierarchically according to their abstraction level, which ranges from medium to high. However, its structure does not contemplate domain-specific terms (Swartout et al., 1996); to do so, the domain-specific terms are linked to the comprehensive SENSUS ontology, in order to build ontologies for private domains.

The Sensus method, based on the SENSUS ontology, presents some procedures to establish links among the specific terms and the high-level ontology terms (Swartout et al., 1996). The result of such process is a structure of a new ontology, which is automatically generalized through the OntoSaurus tool (Fernández, Gómez-Pérez, & Corcho, 2004; Swartout et al., 1996). According to the method, the procedures involved in the building of specific domain ontology would be: i) to identify the relevant concepts in the domain; ii) to link manually the concepts to the SENSUS ontology; iii) to add paths to the concept of SENSUS top hierarchy; iv) to add new domain concepts; and v) to complete the hierarchies.

101 Method

The 101 method (Noy, & McGuinness, 2001) was conceived based on the experience in the development of wine and food ontology, using the ontology-editing environment *Protégé-2000* (Horridge et al., 2004).

The 101 method proposes basically four activities for the development of an ontology: i) define classes in the ontology; ii) organize the classes in a taxonomy; iii) define slots (or properties) for the classes and describe their allowed values (called facets); and iv) fill the slots values for the instances. Such activities imply in modelling decisions, which the method tries to emphasize, besides being an iterative process of an ontology life cycle.

Methodology and Standard for the Construction of Controlled Vocabulary

The standard proposed by the *National Information Standards Organization* (NISO, 2005) sets the general guidelines for the construction, formatting and maintenance of controlled monolingual vocabulary. Concerning the construction standards, the ANSI/NISO Z39.19-2005 standard allows the construction of various kinds of controlled vocabulary, including thesauri, taxonomies, lists and synonyms rings, in a known and structured order, aiming at making clear the equivalence, associative and hierarchical relationships, when applicable to each type (see appendix B of the standard, page 135). This flexibility is important, as it allows a better adaptation of the instrument to the needs of the informative environment, as, for example, the Web.

An innovation of the ANSI/NISO Z39.19-2005 in relation to the previous standards is the inclusion of the faceted analysis, whose basis is concentrated in the work of Ranganathan (Ranganathan, 1967) and in the refinements made by the *Classification Research Group* – CRG (Campos, Gomes & Motta, 2004), in England, for the elaboration of thesaurus in specific areas of knowledge. Another important question is the orientation regarding the interoperability among controlled vocabularies.

Finally, the ANSI/NISO Z39.19-2005 standard recommends special treatment in relation to the term with regards to activities involved in the construction process. Yet, the BITI manual (Campos, Gomes & Motta, 2004) on the elaboration of a type of controlled vocabulary, the thesauri, describes in details and in sequence the necessary procedures to its construction. In this way, the BITI manual is more efficient than the ANSI/NISO Z39.19-2005 standard as regards methodological principles explicitly defined for the building of controlled vocabularies. The procedures proposed in the manual can be summarized in: i) planning, which consists in delimitating the subject area to be covered by the specialized vocabulary, define the target public to whom the instrument is destined to and elaborate the planning for future maintenances which become necessary; ii) vocabulary survey, which consists in selecting the terms representing the subject and define them according to the nature of the subject; iii) concept organization, consisting in grouping the terms of the same nature in categories or facets, aiming at allowing a better understanding of the concept and organization of the relationship between the concepts; iv) final presentation, including the kinds of exhibition (simple alphabetic lists or graph visualizations) and the format which can be printed or electronic; and v) evaluation criteria, which determines if the controlled vocabulary is giving satisfactory search results, implying in a good relationship between precision and revocation. After presenting the investigated objects, the content is classified within each category, denominated, from this point on, process building phases. The phases are shown in Table 1, below, summarizing the analysis of the methodologies, methods and norms. The phases

which were not proposed in the investigated objects had their cells filled in with "Absent", when contemplated, the cell was filled in with the adopted methodological principles.

COMPARATIVE ANALYSIS

In order to carry out the comparative analysis, it was necessary to understand the methodological procedures of the investigated objects, presented in the previous section. Such understanding was possible through content analysis conducted in empirical materials by means of the categories of analysis explained in particular section.

Based on the information displayed in the Table 1, some considerations were drawn about the methodologies and methods for the building of ontologies and about the methodology and standard for the construction of controlled vocabularies which were analyzed here. Such considerations are listed below:

- There are several strategies for the development of ontologies, proving the hypothesis that different groups present diverse approaches and characteristics, for different aims and applications (Fernández et al., 1999).
- In the ontologies context, some approaches follow a life cycle model, whereas others do not. In this aspect, the one that stands out is the Methontology as it is almost complete regarding a development cycle, since it does not propose only a pre-development phase. Such remark can be confirmed in Table 1.
- Regarding details of the activities and procedures to carry them out, some methodologies and methods prove to be superficial in the elucidation of the steps to be followed in construction of ontologies. This is the case of the Cyc, Kactus and Sensus

Table 1. *Synoptic table of the methodologies, methods and standards with respect to the categories of pre-defined analysis*

Lifecycle phases		Cyc	Gruninger e Fox		Uschold and King	Kactus	Methontology	Sensus	101 Method	Z39.19-2005	BTI Manual
Project Management		Absent	Absent		Absent	Absent	Staggering of activities; task control and quality guarantee.	Absent	Absent	Recommends characteristics necessary to management systems	Project planning activities.
Guided Projects	Pre-development	Absent	Motivation Scenarios		Absent	Absent	Absent	Absent	Absent	Recommends a construction feasibility study	Absent
	Development	Requirements Specification	Manual knowledge extraction	Informal competency questions.	Determine ontological aims.	Requirements list.	Definition of ontological scope	Absent	Competency questions definition	Absent	i) Area delimitation; and ii) target public definition.
		Conceptual Modelling	Absent	Formal terminology conception.	Consensual vocabulary construction.	Identification of relevant terms.	Activities involving the construction of conceptualization of the ontology.	Identification of the domain key-terms	Definition of classes, *slots*, facets (restrains) and instances.	Recommends the facet analysis in the organization of knowledge; organization of relationships in hierarchical, associative and equivalent.	Terms selection; definition of concepts and relationships (logic and ontological); facets classification.
		Formalization	Absent	Formalization of competency questions. Axioms specifications.	Absent	Absent	Formalize the conceptual model in a formal language as descriptive logic.	Through the semantic network.	Representation language based on *frames*.	Absent	Absent
		Implementation	Knowledge codification and extraction with computer-supported tool	Axioms specifications are implemented in Prolog.	Requires a language representation such as Prolog and Ontolingua.	Absent	Recommends developing environments that fits to meta-ontologies and ontologies selected in the integration phase.	Uses the OntoSaurus tool for development.	Interactive use of the language through the *Protégé* tool.	Absent	Absent

continued on following page

Table 1. Continued

Lifecycle phases		Cyc	Gruninger e Fox	Uschold and King	Kactus	Methontology	Sensus	101 Method	Z39.19-2005	BITI Manual
	Post-development	Maintenance	Absent	Absent	Absent	Orientation concerning the necessary adjustments in the conceptualization activities.	Absent	Absent	Recommends procedures related to the addition, alteration and exclusion of terms.	The inclusion of new terms should be done in a specific spreadsheet.
Integrative processes	Integration	Integration of computer systems to Cyc micro theories.	Integration of common core ontologies.	Integration with existing ontologies.	Search for already existing ontologies.	Integration document with meta-ontologies.	Manual integration to SENSUS ontology.	Considers the reuse of ontologies.	Absent	Absent
	Evaluation	Absent	Through complete theorems.	Can be done through competency questions.	Absent	Divided in ontology verification and validation.	Absent	Absent	Recommends the use of usability testing.	Criteria adopted for the adoption or not of a thesaurus.
	Documentation	Absent	Absent	Claims and primitives.	Absent	Recommended in each phase.	Absent	Via *Protégé*	Recommendations on the documentation content.	Data records in spreadsheets.

methods, which seem to assume that the ontologist already dominates the subject of ontology construction and does not need details about the activities and procedures involved. Yet, the Methontology stands out in supplying, most of the times, details concerning how to proceed in conducting a given activity.

- Some approaches emphasize the development activities, specially the ontology implementation (Cyc method and 101 method), disregarding important aspects related to project management, feasibility studies, and maintenance and evaluation of ontologies.

- The BITI manual presented a virtually complete life cycle according to the IEEE-1074 (1997) standard, as shown in Table 1. The formalization, implementation and integration phases were not taken into consideration as they did not belong to the controlled vocabularies purpose. In this way, the maturity of the methodology in relation to a life cycle model can be checked.

- Finally, it is worth saying that the thesaurus construction methodology stood out in relation to the other methodologies and methods for building ontologies in the theoretical and methodological aspect, for the identification, definition and organization of concepts. Although these indicate methods to identify concepts, present resources to define concepts and organize them in taxonomy, they do not explain clearly the theoretical principles which govern the classification theory (Ranganathan, 1967) neither the concept theory (Dahlberg, 1978) in the specification of their elements. Such principles would be relevant in methodologies for ontology constructions, since both tools, ontologies and thesaurus, present semantic and conceptual relationships.

FUTURE RESEARCH DIRECTIONS

The ontology development, in spite of many works being presented in the last decade, is still a relatively unexplored field, in which much work is still needed. The authors are working at the moment in compiling the gold standard pieces of each methodology, along with some novelty research, to propose an integrated framework for ontology building. For the moment, it is known that it would be less likely that a general framework would work for any ontology type, in any domain, but the different approaches must be integrated in order to an adequate process to take place. We also acknowledge the fact that we have not analyzed the potential influences that each software tool and formal language, chosen to build ontologies, can have. They potentially interferes with the final steps of the process, given the extent in which those tools and languages can represent entities, relationships, instances, constraints, etc.

CONCLUSION

This chapter proposed an assessment of the most representative methodologies and methods for ontology construction in literature, and also pointed out similarities between standards of construction of software (IEEE-1074) and methodological principles used in the elaboration of ontologies and controlled vocabularies. Such similarity was evident in the analysis of methodologies, methods and norms investigated, presented in section *METHODOLOGIES ASSESSED*. The methodology presented in the BITI manual for the construction of thesaurus is mature as a life cycle model, since the construction processes fit most categories of analysis based on IEEE-1074 standard (1997). Although the recommendations of the ANSI/NISO Z39.19-2005 standard were classified in the categories of analysis, such norm does not aim at proposing an activity cycle for the construction of controlled vocabularies, but to recommend a series of treatments concerning the term in activities that fit the building process. Regarding the methodologies for ontology construction, the Methontology was prominent in the maturity aspect according to the IEEE-1074 (1997) standard, as only the pre-development category was not taking into consideration in its development process.

The chapter also confirmed some problems related to the lack of a standard for ontology construction and the lack of systematic explanations of how, where and under which limits the theoretical approaches can be used within the elaboration process. This fact was verified in the methodology analysis and the ontology building methods investigated in the research, which, in most cases, were not efficient in explaining clearly the construction procedures. Thus, the solution for these problems would be centred on a methodological proposal based on theoretical and methodological principles which would give scientific support to the ontology building process. Finally the presentation of a comparative analysis as a preliminary step can be used to define methodological standards for ontology building.

REFERENCES

Almeida, M. B., & Barbosa, R. R. (2009). Ontologies in knowledge management support - A case study. *Journal of the American Society for Information Science and Technology, 60*(10), 2032–2047. doi:10.1002/asi.21120

Bardin, L. (1977). *L'analyse de contenu*. Paris, France: Presses Universitaires de France.

Bernaras, A., Laresgoiti, I., & Corera, J. (1996). Building and reusing ontologies for electrical network applications. In W. Wahlster, (Ed.), *The European Conference on Artificial Intelligence* (pp. 298-302). Chichester, UK: John Wiley & Sons.

Berners-Lee, T., Hendler, J., & Lassila, O. (2001). The Semantic Web. *Scientific American, 284*(5), 34–43. doi:10.1038/scientificamerican0501-34

Campos, M. L. A., Gomes, H. E., & Motta, D. F. (2004). Tutorial de Tesauro. UFF. Retrieved February 8, 2009, from http://www.conexaorio.com/biti/tesauro

Corazzon, R. (2008). *What is ontology? Definitions by leading philosophers. Ontology: A resource guide for philosophers*. Retrieved November 9, 2008, from http://www.formalontology.it/section_4.htm

Dahlberg, I. (1978). A referent-oriented, analytical concept theory for interconcept. *International Classification, 5*(3), 142–151.

Fernández, M., Gómez-Pérez, A., & Corcho, O. (2004). Methodologies and methods for building ontologies . In Gómez-Pérez, A., Fernández-López, M., & Corcho, O. (Eds.), *Ontological engineering* (pp. 107–153). London, UK: Springer.

Fernández, M., Gómez-Pérez, A., & Juristo, H. (1997). *Methontology: From ontological art towards ontological engineering*. Retrieved April 16, 2009, from http://www.aaai.org/Papers/Symposia/Spring/1997/SS-97-06/SS97-06-005.pdf

Fernández, M., Gómez-Pérez, A., Sierra, J. P., & Sierra, A. P. (1999). Building a chemical ontology using methontology and the ontology design environment. *Intelligent Systems, 14*(1), 37–46. doi:10.1109/5254.747904

Fox, M. S. (1992).*The TOVE Project: Towards a common-sense model of the enterprise*. Retrieved December 20, 2005, from http://www.eil.utoronto.ca/enterprise-modelling/papers/fox-tove-uofttr92.pdf

Gilchrist, A. (2003). Thesauri, taxonomies and ontologies - An etymological note. *The Journal of Documentation, 59*(1), 7–18. doi:10.1108/00220410310457984

Gómez-Pérez, A., Fernández-Lopez, M., & Corcho, O. (2004). *Ontological engineering: With examples from the areas of knowledge management, e-commerce and the Semantic Web.* Springer.

Gómez-Pérez, A., Fernández-Lopez, M., & Vicente, A. J. (1996).*Towards a method to conceptualize domain ontologies.* Retrieved March 24, 2005, from http:// webode. dia. fi. upm. es/ Asun/SSS97.ps

Gruber, T. (1993). *What is an ontology?* Retrieved April 16, 2009, from http://www-ksl. stanford. edu/kst/what-is-an-ontology.html

Gruninger, M., & Fox, M. S. (1995). *Methodology for the design and evaluation of ontologies.* Retrieved January 9, 2007, from http:// citeseerx. ist. psu. edu/ viewdoc/ summary? doi=10.1.1.44.8723

Gruninger, M., & Fox, M. S. (1995). Methodology for the design and evaluation of ontologies. In D. Skuce (Ed.), *Proceedings of the Workshop on Basic Ontological Issues in Knowledge Sharing, International Joint Conference on Artificial Intelligence (IJCAI 1995)* (pp. 1–10). Montreal, Canada: AAAI Press.

Horridge, M., Knublauch, H., Rector, A., Stevens, R., & Wroe, C. (2004). *Pratical guide to building OWL ontologies using the Protégé-OWL plugin and CO-ODE tools.* Retrieved June 30, 2006, from http://www.co-ode.org/resources/tutorials/ ProtegeOWLTutorial.pdf

Institute of Electrical and Electronics Engineers. (1997). *IEEE 1074 standard for developing software life cycle processes.* Retrieved February 10, 2006, from http:// ieeexplore. ieee.org/ Xplore/ login.jsp?url=/ iel4/5984/16018/00741936. pdf?temp=x

Lancaster, F. W. (1986). *Vocabulary control for information retrieval.* Richmond, VA: IRP.

NISO. (2005). *ANSI/NISO Z 39.19: 2005 - Guidelines for the construction, format, and management of monolingual controlled vocabularies.* Retrieved April 20, 2008, from http://www.niso.org/kst/reports/standards/ kfile_download?id%3Austring%3Aiso-8859-1=Z39-19-2005.pdf

Noy, F. N., & Guinness, D. L. (2001). *Ontology development 101: A guide to create your first ontology.* Stanford University, 2001. Retrieved February 15, 2003, from http:// protege. stanford. edu/ publications/ ontology_development/ontology101.pdf

Pressman, R. S. (2004). *Software engineering: A practitioner's approach.* New York, NY: McGraw-Hill.

Ranganathan, S. R. (1967).*Prolegomena to library classification.* Bombay, India: Asia Publishing House.

Reed, S. L., & Lenat, D. B. (2002). *Mapping ontologies into Cyc.* Retrieved February 12, 2005, from http://www.cyc.com/doc/white_papers/ mapping-ontologies-into-cyc_v31.pdf

Silva, D. L. (2008). *A proposal for a methodology of building ontologies: Interdisciplinary perspective between the Information Science and the Computer Science.* Master Thesis, Universidade Federal de Minas Gerais, Belo Horizonte, Minas Gerais, BR, School of Information Science.

Soergel, D. (1997). *Functions of a thesaurus / classification / ontological knowledge base.* Retrieved August 2, 2005, from http://dl.lib.brown. edu/intranet/ws/userx/docs/Soergel--Functions% 20of%20a%20thesaurus%20%20classification%20%20ontological%20knowledge%20base. pdf

Soergel, D. (1999). The rise of ontologies or the reinvention of classification. *Journal of the American Society for Information Science American Society for Information Science, 50*(12), 1119–1120. doi:10.1002/(SICI)1097-4571(1999)50:12<1119::AID-ASI12>3.0.CO;2-I

Swartout, B., Patil, R., Knight, K., & Russ, T. (1996). *Toward distributed use of large-scale ontologies.* Retrieved February 2, 2004, from http:// ksi. cpsc. ucalgary. ca/ KAW/ KAW96/ swartout/Banff_96_final_2.html

Uschold, M., & Gruninger, M. (1996). Ontologies: Principles, methods and applications. *The Knowledge Engineering Review, 11*(2). doi:10.1017/S0269888900007797

Uschold, M., & King, M. (1995). *Towards a methodology for building ontologies.* Retrieved July 20, 2002, from http://citeseerx.ist.psu.edu/viewdoc/summary?doi=10.1.1.55.5357

Van Harmelen, F., Hendler, J., Horrocks, I., Mc-Guinness, D. M., Patel-Schneider, P. F., & Stein, L. A. (2003). *OWL Web ontology language 1.0 reference.* Retrieved January 21, 2004 from http://www.w3.org/TR/2003/WD-owl-ref-20030221/

Vickery, B. C. (1997). Ontologies. *Journal of Information Science, 23*(4), 277–286. doi:10.1177/016555159702300402

ENDNOTES

[1]   http://citeseer.ist.psu.edu

[2]   http://portal.acm.org/portal.cfm

[3]   http://scholar.google.com/

Chapter 2

An Ontology–Based Method to Construct a Reference Model Catalogue for the Energy Sector

José M. González and Vázquez
OFFIS – Institute for Information Technology, Germany

Mathias Uslar
OFFIS – Institute for Information Technology, Germany

ABSTRACT

Within this contribution we will introduce a first approach on an ontology-based method for constructing a domain specific reference model catalogue for the energy sector. First of all we will motivate and introduce a reference model catalogue for the energy sector as well as requirements for building such a catalogue. Based on the requirements, we will focus on describing a method which meets these requirements and show how to apply the method.

INTRODUCTION TO SMART GRIDS

The German energy industry is undergoing a process of structural changes due to changing regulations and technical advancements (see e.g. Appelrath & Chamoni, 2007; Brinker, 2009; Kurth 2009; Haas, Redl, & Auer, 2009; Starace, 2009). On the one hand, laws have been approved to encourage competition in the German energy sector like the legal unbundling as described in the German Energy Industry Act (Energiewirtschaftsgesetz EnWG) (Deutscher Bundestag, 2005). On the other hand, technical advancements lead to new products and services like Demand Side Management (DSM) and Automated Meter Reading (AMR). With the upcoming distributed generation, the legal requirements imposed by federal regulation and the resulting unbundling, things have changed a lot. Due to new generation facilities like wind power plants or fuel cells, energy is fed into the grid at different voltage levels und by different

DOI: 10.4018/978-1-60960-126-3.ch002

producers – former customers having their own generation can now both act as consumers and producers (also referred to as prosumer) which feed into the utilities' grid. Therefore, the communication infrastructure has to change.

Current application landscapes for utility companies were built to address requirements of the past de facto monopoly environment. Today, companies in the energy industry face more competition and have to provide new products and services at lower costs. This requires current application landscapes to become more flexible and to be able to adapt faster to the evolving requirements resulting in structural business changes. Therefore, adequate IT-infrastructures supported by appropriate architectures, like service-oriented architecture, are needed (Uslar et al., 2009). Both utility companies as well as software manufacturers have to deal with these changes and need to adapt their application landscapes or software products. In this context, requirements analysis plays an important part.

The energy sector comprises several activities like generation of electricity, gas, fuel or district heating. To reduce the complexity within this contribution, we only address electricity and gas when referring to the energy sector, as they form a major part of the German energy sector (45% of the energy consumption), see BMWi (2008b). In addition, electricity and gas have (with regard to business transactions) several processes in common despite of their physical differences.

Current national (like E-Energy, see www.e-energy.de) and international (like the European Technology Platform on Smart Grids, www.smartgrids.eu) initiatives and discussions in the energy sector reveal that the network is developing towards a so called "Smart Grid" with multiple devices and actors continuously exchanging data to provide user-oriented flexible services and products while operating a self-healing, economic, ecologically friendly and secure network. According to Electric Power Research Institute's report to the US National Institute of Standards and Technology (NIST) the term "Smart Grid" is defined as a process of the modernization of the electricity distribution system to monitor, protect and automatically optimize the operation of its interconnected elements (EPRI, 2009). The drivers for Smart Grid are the same for most of the developed countries, however, implementations differ. Within this contribution, we use the NIST definition (EPRI, 2009) and its application in the US which is different form the European one of the Smart Grids European Technology Platform (ETP), see ETP (2009).

Smart Grid requires the application of standards for being able to cope with heterogeneity and enable interoperability in an economic and technically feasible way. In addition, existing knowledge, often described in functional and standards reference models, should be used to design efficient processes and identify required functionality.

Identifying suitable reference models as well as standards is not easy as a variety of models and standards exists. Here reference model catalogues as defined by (Fettke & Loos, 2002) provide an overview on existing models and support the identification of relevant sources.

The main contribution of this work is to provide an ontology-based method for constructing such a domain specific reference model catalogue for the domain of the electric Smart Grid.

The remainder of this chapter is structured as follows: After describing the background of our research in the next section, the energy reference model catalogue with its components, construction process, modeling requirements and implementation will be introduced. The following section will describe in detail our ontology-based construction method and show examples of its application. Then, we outline the evaluation of our methods and give an overview of related work before we conclude the chapter presenting our conclusion and future research issues.

Background

In 2009, the EPRI has conducted a study for the National Institute of Standards and Technology for developing a study on the technical requirements in terms of standardization for the interoperable Smart Grid of the future (NIST, 2010). With this project, the standardization of the Smart Grid has gained national and international momentum. In Europe, Germany (DKE, 2010; DIN, 2010), Spain (FutuRed, 2009) and Austria (FEEI, 2010) have developed their own roadmaps and the IEC being an international standardization body completed their own standards roadmap (IEC SMB SG3, 2010). All those roadmaps have things in common. First of all, the Smart grid is mainly driven by the increased use of ICT technologies and automation technology within the power grid management. This should lead to an increased uptime, safety, security and efficiency.

The Smart Grid is no new infrastructure since it relies on the old one, mainly being defined as a transition process to the new control paradigm (NIST, 2010). The new generation and storage options, mostly driven by carbon dioxide reduction and distributed small generation and electric mobility are one of the main drivers and core aspects of the electric grid of the future. The consumer gets a bigger and more active role within those new grids which have load balancing and demand response programs along the so called Smart Meters. The intelligent devices no longer reside with the utility but are integrated within the households and companies of the customers which become prosumers.

These core aspects show that the Smart Grid is a complex infrastructure which has a lot of stakeholders, viewpoints and requirements. Unfortunately, it is driven by an unknown transition process which has no single authority. Therefore, the problem itself must be considered somehow being a wicked problem with a large exploration solution space. The complex problem must be structured. Our approach is therefore to develop a reference model catalogue for the Smart grid for both technologies, processes and requirements which can be used by different stakeholders for the work with their part of the Smart Grid. To solve different integration problems of technologies within the Smart Grid, we focus on a Design science based approach (Hevner, March, Park, & Ram, 2004) with prototypes for the different interoperability issues identified within the reference model catalogue. One aspect is the interoperability of data models which will be introduced later by our approach. Here the use of the Common Information model CIM: IEC 61970 / 61968 (IEC, 2007b; 2008) being the core data model for the Smart Grid and providing most of the information needed to model all the objects for the electric grid is recommended. Other data models have to be mapped onto the CIM to efficiently enable interoperability. This is one important aspect also identified by NIST to achieve interoperability for the Smart Grid (NIST, 2010). The integration of the data models will be achieved using ontologies of the data models of each individual standard being mapped by our COLIN (CIM Ontology Alignment Methodology) described later, see (Uslar, 2009).

Reference models have been proved to be useful within development of information systems for years (Scheer, 2000). Several reference models exists for different industries, like the Y-CIM (Scheer, 1994) and a reference model for retail enterprises, see (Becker & Schütte 1998; Becker, Rotthowe, Rosemann, & Schütte 1998). The term reference model is not clearly defined within literature (see Fettke & Loos, 2007; Thomas, 2006a). Within this contribution, a reference model is regarded as a blueprint that can be used in the context of information system development or evolution.

In the energy industry, several models exists but they either focus on one area of the supply chain (like generation) for several viewpoints (like data, processes or function) in detail or one viewpoint for several areas (like generation and distribution) (González, 2009). There is no overview of reference models for the energy industry available. Identifying a suitable model for use within requirement analysis is therefore difficult and time consuming.

Fettke and Loos (2002) introduce the concept of a reference model catalogue providing an overview on reference models. According to Fettke and Loos (2002) a reference model catalogue is typically structured as a table composed of three columns, the first column providing a structure for classifying the reference models (structure part), the second containing the names and authors (main part) and the third one listing several attributes (like modeling language) of the reference model (access part).

Ontologies as building block of semantic technologies are used more and more in a number of important aspects to modern IT, from interoperability to sharing knowledge (Simperl, Mochol, Bürger, & Popov, 2009). An ontology is the specification of a conceptualization (Gruber, 1993). Ontologies are often designed to achieve semantic interoperability, model knowledge and especially to derive new knowledge (reasoning) from existing conceptualizations. A formalization of a reference model catalogue as an ontology seems reasonable to make use of these properties.

In this chapter, the energy reference model catalogue (Energy-RMC) concept a domain specific reference model catalogue for the energy industry formalized as ontology and a method for construction of the catalogue are introduced.

THE ENERGY REFERENCE MODEL CATALOGUE: ENERGY-RMC

Components

The Energy-RMC aims at supporting the identification of suitable models within software development processes in the energy industry, especially regarding requirement analysis. Hereby the Energy-RMC should support business analysts, architects and application system responsible

(within vendor and utility companies) in finding answers to the following questions:

- Which functions are provided in which areas of the energy supply chain by which market role?
- Which sources provide further information on the different functions available in the energy sector?
- Which logical applications support which functions of the energy sector?
- Which products, processes, terms and business objects relate to the areas and activities of the energy sector?

The Energy-RMC consists of five components and two methods see Figure 1. Regarding the components of the catalogue the three main components *functional reference model (FRM)*, *sources* and *criteria* relate to the *structure*, *main* and *access* part of the reference model catalogue (rmc) concept defined by Fettke and Loos (2002). In addition core and additional elements extend the rmc concept of Fettke and Loos (2002).

The FRM forms the main part of the catalogue providing a hierarchical structure composed by supply chain elements and sectors, activities, function groups and functions. A functional reference model is considered according to Närman (2006) as a list of functions that span a certain functional area.

Sources and related classification criteria play a major role within the Energy-RMC. In contrast to Fettke and Loos (2002), not only reference models but also other sources containing valuable domain knowledge for requirement analysis, like for example IT-standards, regulations, enterprise specific models and specifications, are considered for classification and hereby accessible through the Energy-RMC. Sources are linked to the FRM and if needed can be modeled within the catalog at different levels of detail as hierarchical structure consisting of function groups and functions (function groups could contain other function

Figure 1. Overview of components, methods and rules of the Energy-RMC based on González & Appelrath (2010)

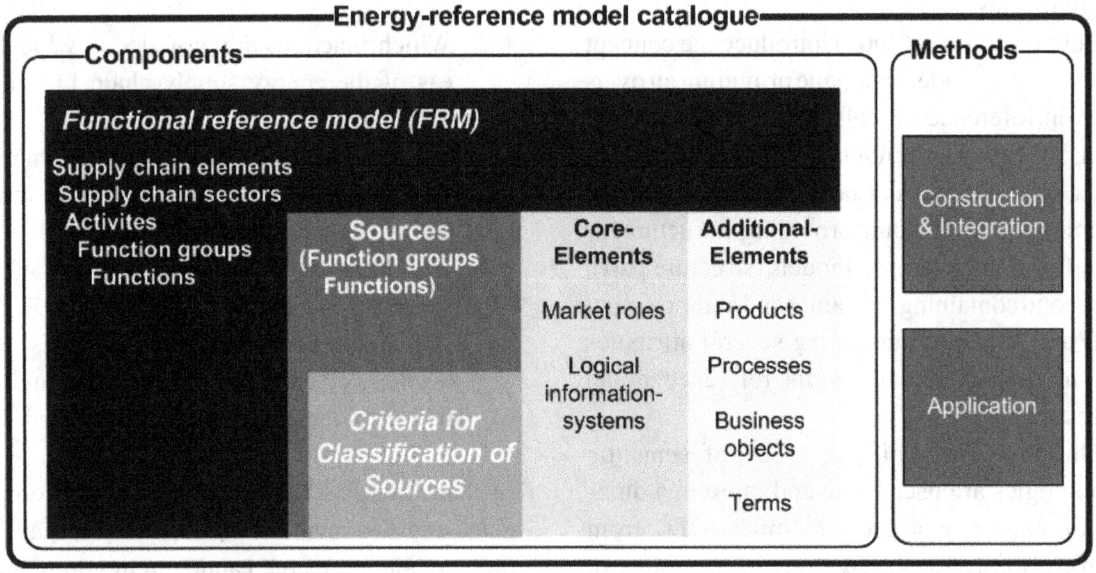

groups). Modeling sources as hierarchy within the Energy-RMC is of great help to identify sources or when comparing different sources regarding functional coverage. The adequate level of detail should be chosen depending on the relevance of the source for the users of the catalog.

Apart from the three main components *FRM*, *sources* and *criteria* the Energy-RMC consists of core elements and additional elements. Following the principles of the ARIS (Architecture of Integrated Information Systems) eEPC (enhanced Event Process Chain) functions cannot be regarded in isolation, they are part of processes which are executed by actors (market roles), often supported by applications exchanging information via business objects in order to provide products or services (Scheer, 1999). Therefore, the Energy-RMC is enhanced through core elements (market roles and logical applications) and additional elements (products, processes, business objects and terms). As the goal of the Energy-RMC is to support the requirement analysis for application system development in the energy sector and regulations in Germany impede companies to fulfill several

market roles at the same time (e.g. independent power producer and transmission system operator), market roles and logical applications are described in detail. Additional elements in contrast to core elements are only modeled on an abstract level of detail without striving for completeness

The three main components together with the core and additional elements build the reference model catalogue. Furthermore, methods for the construction and continuously enhancement (integration of new sources) as well as for using the reference model catalogue are provided. In addition to the methods, a rule framework is described to secure quality of the catalogue and support the methods. On the one hand, rules should support modelers when modeling to obtain similar models which obey the specified rules. On the other hand, they should help identifying elements that are not modeled according to the rules, this is realized through implementation of these rules into the Energy-RMC. Both methods and rules will be described in the subsequent chapters.

In Figure 2, extracts of the components of the Energy-RMC are presented in more detail.

Figure 2. Functional reference model matrix based on González & Appelrath (2010).

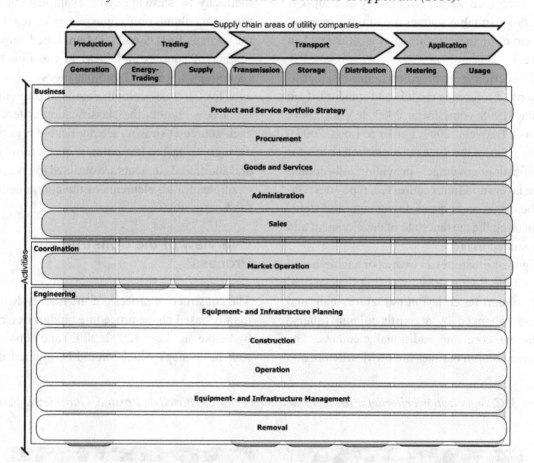

As modeling of functions is an important part within information system development, functions are considered key modeling artifacts within the Energy-RMC too. Therefore a functional reference model is built to structure (structure part) the Energy-RMC. As the energy sector comprises different companies providing several functions, structuring of functions is necessary for the purpose of clarity. After analyzing the energy sector cash flow on the one hand and power / gas flow on the other as well as coordination between both of them were identified as specific activities of this sector. Therefore to support navigation and clarity as well as to facilitate comprehension of the FRM a functional reference model matrix was developed. This matrix provides a sector specific supply chain (production to application) and details corresponding areas of the supply chain (generation to usage), see Figure 2. Further on it groups functions of utility companies by business (cash flow), coordination and engineering (power / gas flow) activities and links them to areas of the supply chain. Within the three main activities business, coordination and engineering further functions where identified which can be considered as function patterns relevant in each supply chain element. With regard to business and engineering these function patterns represent internal supply chains addressing product and service (strategy to sales) as well as technical equipment (planning to removal) life cycle management.

Criteria (access part) to classify and support identifying suitable sources are of main interest. An extract of the classification is illustrated in Figure 3.

These criteria are based on traditional classifications of reference models and standards (see Schütte, (1998; vom Brocke, 2003; de Vries, 2006; Braun & Esswein, 2007; Fettke & Loos, 2003). Figure 3 shows the three main characteristics for classification: coverage – providing information on the layers and fields addressed, type - describing the origin and type of documents, and status – indicating the current state of development and the assumed usage.

Figure 4 illustrates an extract of a table-based view on the Energy-RMC showing the classical three column-based layout (structure, main and access) enhanced by a fourth column (query) containing core and additional elements. The structure column outlines the FRM structure and

hierarchy by showing some examples. Next in the main column only some examples regarding the sources EnWG and CIM are listed showing linking of sources and FRM at function level (paragraph for EnWG and packages / subpackages for CIM, see column details). Following in the access column the classification criteria for each source is shown (see applicable criteria in dark grey). In the last column query some core and additional elements are outlined to give some examples for all elements of the components of the Energy-RMC.

Overview of the Construction Process

The construction process of the Energy-RMC is mainly based on the procedure models described by Fettke and Loos (2002; 2003) and consists of four basic steps which should be applied itera-

Figure 3. Categorization criteria for the identification of sources based on Postina, González & Seychin (2009)

Figure 4. Extract of the Energy-RMC based on González & Appelrath (2010)

Structure				Main		Access											Query				
Functional Reference Model				Sources		Classification											Elements				
						Coverage								Type	Status	Core		Additional			
Levels				Name	Details																
1 Supply Chain	2 Activity	3 Function group	4 Function			Layer addressed	Viewpoints	Granularität	Functional reference model	Political region	Document type	Usage	Development			Market roles	Logical information systems	Products	Processes	Business objects	Terms
Generation	Product and Service Portfolio Strategy															Powerplant operator	Trading-system / generation of electricity				
	Procurement	Operational procurement	procure resources for securing energy supply	EnWG	§ 50													Procure fossil fuels	fossil fuel contracts		fossil fuels
	Goods and Services																				
	Administration																				
	Sales																				
	Market operation																				
	Equipment- and Infrastructure Planning																				
	Construction																				
	Operation	Operation of plants	operate power station	CIM	IEC61970.Generation												EMS				
	Equipment- and Infrastructure Management																				
	Removal																				
Energy-Trading	Product and Service Portfolio Strategy															Energy-Trader	Trading-system				
	Procurement	Operational procurement	buy energy contracts	CIM	Informative.MarketOperations													Energy contracts	Trade		Energy contracts
	Sales	Operational sales	sell energy contracts	CIM	Informative.MarketOperations																
	Market operation																				
Distribution	Construction	Planning of network	calculate network	CIM	IEC61970.Topology IEC61970.Wires IEC61970.OperationalLimits											Distribution System Operator	DMS				
	Operation	Operation of network	operate electrical network	CIM	IEC61970.Wires IEC61970.OperationalLimits IEC61970.Outage																

tively and an additional parallel process focusing on analysis and refinement of the catalog which should be performed at each step, see Figure 5.

Step 1: First Version of the RMC and Rules

The first step comprises the initial development of a first version of the FRM, the classification of sources, the definition of rules and formalizing the catalogue as ontology.

As starting point a first version of the Energy-RMC needs to be worked out for a continuously development and refinement of the catalogue. This first version of the Energy-RMC was developed top-down by identifying key activities and functional supply chain areas of utility companies. For this purpose an analysis of specific functions within the energy sector identifying core supply chain elements and functions regarding core activities (e.g. function patterns, see previous section)

were necessary. In addition a first identification of potential sources to include in the catalogue was performed. On this basis the Energy functional reference model matrix, introduced in the previous chapter, was constructed and used as structure part of the Energy-RMC. Additionally, further function groups and functions were modeled in more detail to complete a first version of the functional reference model.

On basis of the first identified relevant sources and through literature based analysis on classification criteria for (reference) models a first classification should be developed.

To continuously track development of the catalogue rules should be defined for observing quality and coverage of the catalog, see next section for details on rules.

As last task within this step the preliminary catalogue structure and elements should be formalized as ontology specifying classes, properties and individuals as well as first rules. As languages

Figure 5. Overview procedure model for the construction of the Energy-RMC based on González & Appelrath (2010)

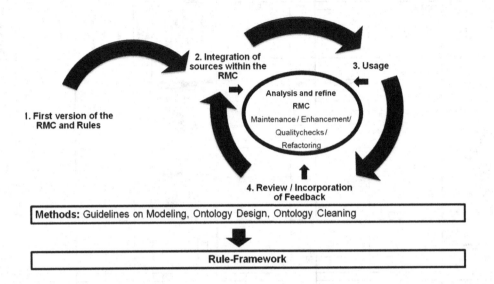

the Web Ontology Language (OWL) (content) and the Semantic Web Rule Language (SWRL) (rules) are proposed.

Based on this first version subsequent versions shall be developed according to the rough iterative procedure model illustrated in Figure 5.

Step 2: Integration of Sources within the RMC

In the second step domain knowledge available as sources should be identified and assigned to functions of the FRM. Sources are classified according to the criteria shown in the previous section. The focus of this step is to add new sources to the catalog and enhance its classification criteria as well as refine and detail the FRM to allow for linking sources and FRM. A procedure model regarding this step is described in section "Usage of COLIN for the enhancement of the Energy-RMC".

In a first iteration of the procedure model shown in Figure 5 current German laws and international standards describing functions in the energy sector were selected and linked to the FRM, taking into account the German laws

assured to cover regulation requirements. Following the recommendations of Uslar et al. (2009), the international standards defined by the International Electrotechnical Commission (IEC) in particular the IEC 61970 and 61968 series were identified as relevant for the Energy-RMC (IEC, 2007b; 2008). Both standard series build the IEC Common Information Model (CIM), an abstract information data model proven and recognized by industry which defines a common vocabulary and basic ontology for aspects of the electric power industry. In addition, the IEC 61968 Part 1 (IEC, 2007a) provides a functional reference model for the field of distribution management. These sources helped to derive and identify further functions. Within the construction of the catalogue, it proved to be helpful to describe functions and link them to other elements like market roles, logical applications, business objects or products to better understand the meaning and context of them and hereby offering more possibilities to identify relevant information through queries. This led to enhancing the Energy-RMC by adding further core and additional elements.

Step 3: Use

The third step addresses the application of the catalogue for identifying relevant sources or comparing different sources.

Here mainly two different scenarios of use can be distinguished, first using the catalogue as knowledgebase and second linking the Energy-RMC to company specific models.

When using the catalogue as knowledgebase, like to identify sources of interest or to compare different sources, the problem to be solved and an appropriate query (for example using the SPARQL Query Language for RDF (SPARQL)) have to be defined based on the vocabulary of the catalogues elements (FRM, core and additional elements and sources classification criteria). After processing the query against the ontology of the catalogue the results could be further analyzed. This represents a generic use case where many queries are imaginable.

When linking the catalogue to company specific models, like to perform impact analysis or to perform queries based on company specific vocabulary, these models need to be formalized as ontology in OWL first. Afterwards the FRM and the specific model have to be linked. On this basis queries using the vocabulary and structure of the company specific model could be defined and executed to identify potential sources of interest based on the own model. When adding other sources, like regulations, impact analysis regarding the own model could be performed, of course this requires the sources and the own model to be described in a certain level of detail for obtaining valuable information.

Step 4: Review / Incorporation of Feedback

Finally, the fourth and last step deals with improving the catalogue on basis of feedback and reviews of users. This step is suggested to be performed within the use of the catalogue as here users are

most willingly to provide feedback. Further on regular review processes (like, for example, interviews) regarding key concepts of the catalog are recommended to improve quality and acceptance of the catalogue.

Parallel Process: Analysis and Refine the Energy-RMC

Continuous analysis, refinement and refactoring of the Energy-RMC within each step are regarded as key points for improving quality and acceptance and hereby increase usefulness of the catalogue.

Analysis should concentrate on applying methods to comply with modeling requirements for (reference) models as well as ontology design and cleaning. This should be achieved by implementing a rule framework and measures to achieve the rules as described in the next section.

The construction of the Energy-RMC is regarded as a never-ending task consisting in iterating four steps and parallel applying analysis and refinement tasks during each of them to enhance the structure and content as well as the quality of the catalogue. Within our contribution, we focus on the second step especially on the integration of sources into the Energy-RMC.

Modeling Requirements for the Energy-RMC

When constructing a reference model catalogue, providing an overview on reference models, formalized as ontology several requirements have to be considered regarding reference models and ontology design.

This contribution bases on the assumption that the subjective position of the modeler is decisive for the result of the modeling process, see also Schütte & Rotthowe, (1998). For this purpose, application of conventions and standards during modeling is necessary. Schütte (1998) introduced the following six principles to enhance the quality of models. These guidelines are often used and referenced in academia when constructing models and are explained briefly in this contribution.

The *Principle of Construction Adequacy (P1)* aims at constructing correct models which represent reality according to defined syntactic and semantic rules.

The *Principle of Language Adequacy (P2)* focuses on modeling only relevant elements regarding the needed level of detail. Therefore, an adequate modeling language and method should be employed.

The *Principle of Economic Efficiency (P3)* considers costs for construction of information models. Every modeling effort or task requires a positive cost-benefit ratio, otherwise if the expected value does not exceed the related costs no modeling should be done.

The *Principle of Clarity (P4)* emphasizes on building comprehensible information models recommending the usage of simple constructs and redundancy when suitable.

The *Principle of Comparability (P5)* aims at constructing models which follow certain conventions and rules, enabling different modelers to model reality in a similar way and develop consistent information models.

The *Principle of Systematic Design (P6)* focuses on coping with complexity regarding modeling as only selected parts of reality can be described. The principle claims to provide an adequate structure with interfaces to different reference models focusing on different views (like between functional reference models and data reference models). A frequently used architecture in this context is ARIS providing the eEPC as central modeling language to link the different views.

The principles of Schütte (1998) lack of concrete implementations and provide high-level recommendations which have to be interpreted and refined. Furthermore, some principles like P2 and P4 are conflictive (concerning redundancy) here a trade-off is necessary, others support each other like P4 and P6 (clarity supports systematic design).

Apart from the principles defined by Schütte (1998) other criteria regarding reference model construction are considered relevant too and presented below.

In general reference models should conform to *universal validity* (G1) and *recommendation character (G2)*. More precisely reference models should be applicable within several use cases or enterprises and for constructing enterprise or project specific models.

In addition, Scheer (1999) defines the following additional requirements:

Syntactic completeness and correctness (S1) – aims at ensuring that models comply with used procedure models, methods and modeling languages.

Semantic completeness and correctness (S2) – require at least one use case for which the reference model provides all needed information to be used as applicable information model.

Ability to adapt (S3) – claims at enabling adaption of the reference model elements to individual requirements of the users for constructing specific models.

As the Energy-RMC is represented as ontology, ontology specific criteria and methods are considered relevant too. With regard to ontology development (Gomez-Perez, Fernandez-Lopez, & Corcho, 2004) define the following six evaluation criteria:

- Verification (O1) – ontology complies with specification.
- Validation (O2) – ontology represents reality correct.
- Assessment (O3) – usability and usefulness regarding reuse and sharing within applications.
- Consistency (O4) – ontology is consistent and lacks contradictions.
- Completeness (O5) – ontology models part of reality complete.
- Conciseness (O6) – ontology lacks of redundancies.

Table 1. Requirements and measures for the Energy-RMC grouped by GOM

Requirements (origin and interactions) grouped by GOM			Supporting measures
Reference model principles	Ontology principles	Trade-off	
P1: Principle of Construction Adequacy			
S1: Syntactic completeness and correctness S2: Semantic completeness and correctness G1: universal validity G2: Recommendation character	O1: Verification O2: Validation O4: Consistency O5: Completeness	Completeness vs. economic efficient level of detail (P1 vs. P3)	• Naming conventions • Usage of Energy-RMC-Schema as specification • Usage of function patterns / types to classify functions • Integration of existing models, laws and standards to achieve completeness • Use of Protégé consistency functions and SWRL rules to avoid contradictions and support completeness
P2: Principle of Language Adequacy			
S1: Syntactic completeness and correctness	O1: Verification O6: Conciseness	Conciseness vs. redundancy supporting clarity (P2 vs. P4)	• Focus on functional modeling • Use of SWRL rules to avoid contradictions • Additionally provide content in Excel sheet for business analyst and people without knowledge of ontology design
P3: Principle of Economic Efficiency			
S3: Ability to adapt G2: Recommendation character	O6: Conciseness	Economic efficient level of detail vs. completeness (P3 vs. P1)	• Focus on important sources • Different level of detail when modeling core and additional elements and according to relevance of information provided by the source • Only allow composition of functions up to three hierarchies (RM-Activity, RM-Functional Group and RM-Function) • Usage of proven open source tools like Protégé • Modeling as ontology in OWL to enable multiple queries
P4: Principle of Clarity			
	O3: Assessment O6: Conciseness	Redundancy supporting clarity vs. conciseness (P4 vs. P2)	• Naming conventions • Function patterns / types • Description of every function identified
P5: Principle of Comparability			
S3: Ability to adapt	O3: Assessment		• Naming conventions • Reference existing models, laws and standards
P6: Principle of Systematic Design			
S3: Ability to adapt	O2: Validation		• Definition of relations between core and additional elements • Only allow composition of functions up to three hierarchies (RM-Activity, RM-Functional Group and RM-Function)

Both ontology and reference model requirements have to be considered integral connected. The GOM as abstract principles offer a good basis for classifying both requirements. In Table 1, ontology and reference model requirements are grouped by the GOM, as they provide more precise criteria and refine the GOM. Some of the GOM principles require a trade-off when coming to application, this is shown as well.

Formalization and Implementation

As stated previously the Energy-RMC is formalized as ontology in OWL (Web Ontology Language), thus providing a technology independent representation, easy access, several capabilities for querying the knowledge base and reasoning through open source software like Protégé (see protege.stanford.edu). Additionally, this formalization offers high flexibility and facilitates semantic integration with other models but requires strict application of conventions and standards to keep the model manageable.

Figure 6 bottom shows the schema of the Energy-RMC describing the basic relationships between its building elements: functional reference model (bottom), core and additional elements (top left) as well as sources and model criteria (top right). The elements of the schema are modeled as OWL-Classes and the relationships as data or object properties, see for an extract of the Energy-RMC ontology Figure 6 (top). Functions (RM-Function) are the central components acting as connectors between the functional reference model and core elements and sources. Functions are additionally assigned to task types (task type), acting as function patterns. Function patterns represent typical activities in the fields of management (like plan, implement or check) as well as product (like procure, produce or trade), services and equipment (like construct or supervise) life cycle management within utility companies. The functional reference model matrix comprised of the assignment of activities to supply chain sectors connects to additional elements and RM-Function Groups. Another important aspect is the modeling of sources and the corresponding assignment to functions of the functional reference model. Sources are modeled in a hierarchical structure (Source-Function groups and Source-Function) and linked at bottom hierarchy level with the RM-Function of the functional reference model.

Figure 6 (top) shows an extract of the ontology derived from the scheme in Figure 6 (bottom) focusing on the linkage of functions and sources (bottom) and outlining the different elements (top left) and model criteria (top right). As stated in the previous chapter, several requirements related to reference model construction and ontology design have to be considered within the development of the Energy-RMC. Table 1 presents measures for each principle within the Energy-RMC.

Formalization and implementation of the Energy-RMC as OWL ontology enhanced by SWRL rules was done with the open source tool Protégé. Furthermore a prototype based on Excel was developed to provide table based visualizations of the functional reference model, elements and sources in several Excel sheets. This allows people without skills in ontology design or Protégé to access the content of the Energy-RMC (see also P2).

ONTOLOGY-BASED METHOD FOR THE CONSTRUCTION OF THE ENERGY-RMC

CIM Ontology Alignment Approach (COLIN)

The CIM Ontology Alignment (COLIN) approach consists of five basic steps to align different ontologies (Uslar, 2009). COLIN tries to overcome all the fallacies in previous integration efforts by establishing a methodology for integrating utility standards taking the domain requirements and current research trends into account.

The approach taken to account as the scientific method was the design science approach by Hevner, March, Park, and Ram (2004). Our aim is to provide meaningful artifacts to evaluate the use of ontology-based integration and mediation in the context of IEC standards. The artifacts e.g. the created mediation ontologies have to be rigorously evaluated and put into different contexts and use cases. We have to distinguish between harmonization on schema level or at instance level, for example. The relevance of each design science artifact being developed must be clear. Furthermore, the transfer of the solution found into practice and showing the importance to both scientific audience and managerial audience is of high importance.

First of all, there are some prerequisites for the proposed approach. We take the CIM as the basic

Figure 6. Energy-RMC Schema and Ontology extract

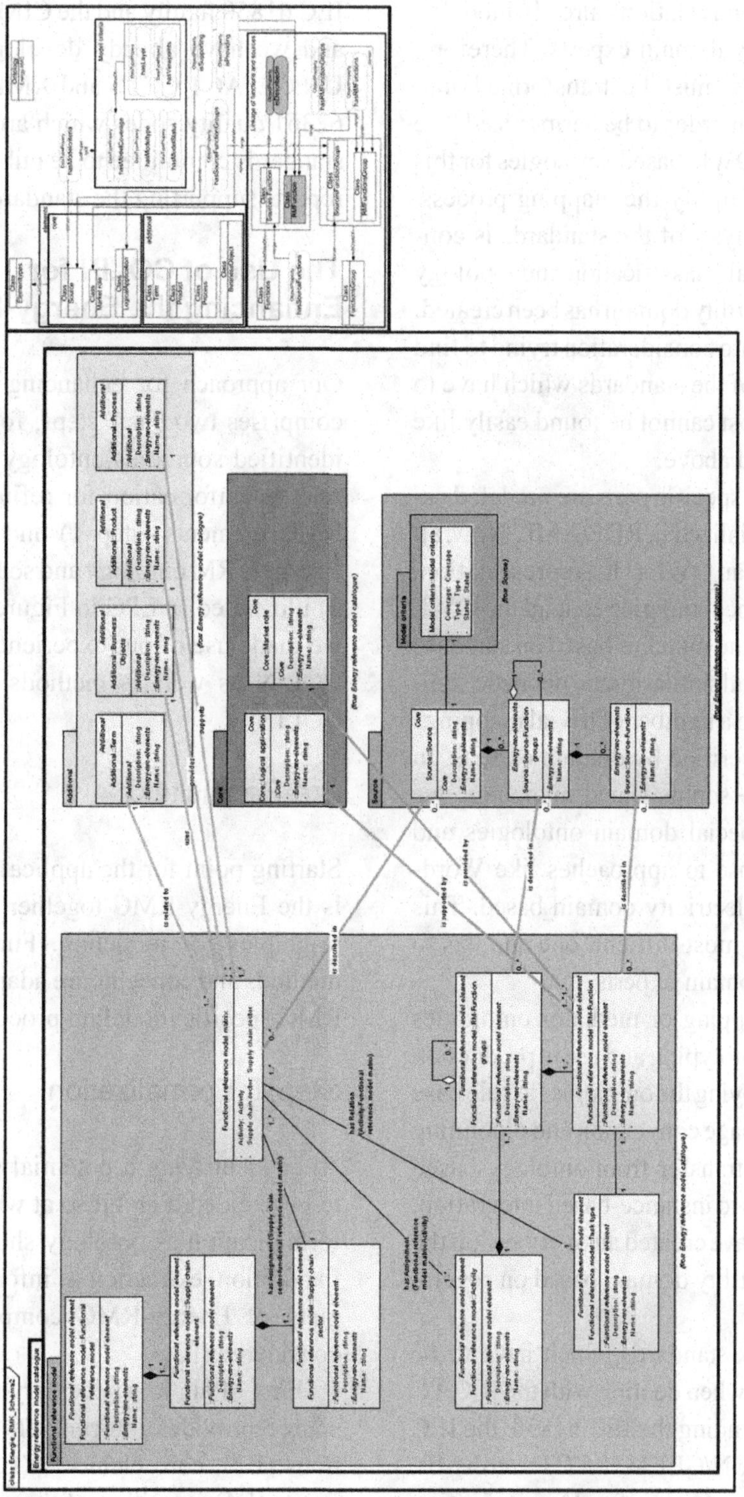

domain ontology due to its overall size and the objects, attributes and relations already modeled and agreed upon by domain experts. Therefore, the other standards must be transformed into electronic models in order to be harmonized. We propose the use of OWL-based ontologies for this task. In order to simplify the mapping process, quantity-based analysis of the standards is conducted and an overall classification and typology of standards in the utility domain has been created. This data is taken into consideration trying to find overlapping parts of the standards which have to be integrated as most cannot be found easily like the ones mentioned above.

Afterwards, the specific parts are modeled using Protége and serialized in RDF/XML. Now, all the standards have an OWL (DL) representation. We use our developed mapping to load the OWL models and try to find matches based on standard algorithms (structural similarity and phonetic similarity). This leads to a number of trivial mappings which have to be verified by domain experts. In order to find more sophisticated mappings, we have developed special domain ontologies and glossaries very close to approaches like Word-Net – but purely electricity domain based. This process step is the most difficult one and has to be supported by domain experts.

Finally, the mapping or mediator ontologies are validated by prototyping and use in production environment, deploying the ontologies as rule base for EAI based message conversion and pipelining – this leads to the transfer from ontology-based schema integration to instance-based integration.

Currently, we have created an overview on the standards for the utility domain based on several taxonomies.

This lead to six standards which have to be taken into account when dealing with the IEC TC 57 framework, including the IEC 61850, the IEC 61970 family, the UN/CEFACT CCTS, ebXML, IEC 62361 Quality Codes for Harmonization and the German national grid standard codes. We have developed ontologies for each standard and therefore, all electronic models exist. Currently, the IEC 61850 family and the CIM are being mapped and we have already developed mappings for UN/CEFACT CCTS and XML naming and IEC 62361 quality codes which are now given to the standards committee to be published as technical reports supporting the standards family.

The Use of COLIN for Enhancing the Energy-RMC

Our approach for enhancing the Energy-RMC comprises two basic steps, formalization of the identified source as ontology and extraction of relevant information for refinement of Energy-RMC elements (step 1) and alignment of the Energy-FRM ontology and source ontology (step 2) illustrated as EPC in Figure 7. In this context we made use of our experiences when applying COLIN as well as methods developed within COLIN.

Pre-Requisites

Starting point for the application of our method is the Energy-RMC together with its rules and principles for modeling. Furthermore COLIN methods and concepts are adapted to the Energy-RMC specific modeling processes.

Step 1: Formalization

After identifying a potential source (E1) it has to be decided if and if so at which level of detail formalization as ontology should be done (F2). In addition, extraction of information for refinement of Energy-RMC components should be considered (F3).

First of all, it is necessary to determine if the source provides information relevant for functions (E2), core elements (E3), additional elements (E4) or neither of them (E5). If E2, E3 or E4 proves true then relevant information should be extracted to refine Energy-RMC elements

Figure 7. Ontology-based construction and integration method for the Energy-RMC

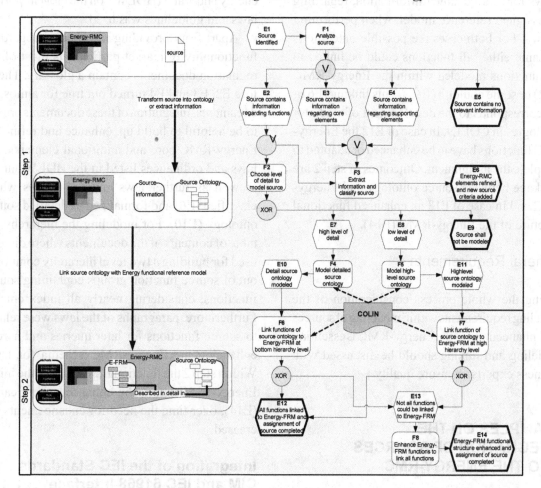

and the source should be classified according to the Energy-RMC criteria. Otherwise if only E5 evaluates true the source is of no interest for the catalogue. In case E2 is true the level of detail concerning the ontology representation of the source needs to be determined, either the source ontology should be modeled with a high (E7 and E10), low (E8 and E11) level of detail or no modeling is required (E9). This differentiation regarding level of detail addresses principle P3 as only relevant sources are modeled with a respective level of detail. Formalization of the source ontology comprises extraction of information of the source into a functional hierarchy composed of function groups and functions. Depending on the processed source possible outcomes of step

1 are a detailed or high-level formalization of the source as ontology and a refinement of the Energy-RMC components. During modeling of the sources in functions F4 and F5 an OWL representation is developed, as proposed by COLIN, taking the Energy-RMC modeling requirements and measures into account.

Step 2: Linkage

Step 2 focuses on linking energy functional reference model and source ontology.

Based on the decision in step 1 concerning the level of detail for modeling the source ontology linking is done on lower (F6) or higher (F7) hierarchy level. A linkage on lower hierarchy level allows for more detailed information, regarding the assigned reference model, when performing queries. For both cases the possible outcome is the same either all functions could be linked to the functions modeled within the Energy-RMC (E12) or some couldn't (E13). This linking (F6 or F7) corresponds to the development of mediator ontologies in COLIN. In case of E12 the Energy-RMC functions have to be enhanced or adapted to complete the assignment. Outcomes of step 2 are a linkage between source ontology and Energy-RMC and in case of E13 an enhanced functional structure of the Energy-RMC (E14).

General Requirements

During the whole process consideration of the modeling requirements within modeling of sources and enhancement of the Energy-RMC is essential. Modeling and linking should be discussed with business experts to ensure quality.

EXAMPLES ON THE INTEGRATION OF SOURCES INTO THE ENERGY-RMC

In this section some examples for the application of the ontology-based construction and integration method of the Energy-RMC are shown.

Integration of Legal Documents

Within the initial development of the Energy-RMC German laws concerning gas and power, like the EnWG (Deutscher Bundestag, 2005), were selected for integration, as they provide information regarding functionality market participants have to provide to assure that at least all regulated functions are covered by the Energy-RMC functional reference model. For identifying relevant regulation documents the survey (BDEW 2008), carried out by the German business association for

energy and water (BDEW), on the most important laws and guidelines was used.

Apart from providing information regarding functionality of market participants most of the regulation documents contain a glossary. Therefore E2, E3 and E4 turned out true for almost all documents. Integration of these documents proved to be helpful to build up, enhance and refine the Energy-RMC core and additional elements. All laws and ordinances listed in the BDEW survey as well as further laws and ordinances where classified (E6) and formalized as detailed source ontology (E10). For modeling the hierarchy the table of contents of the documents where directly used for building a two level hierarchy composed out of source function groups containing source functions, considering nearly all index entries. Furthermore, paragraphs of the laws were related to source functions for later queries and hereby enhancing the Energy-RMC schema for laws. Within step 2 the functional structure of the initial Energy-RMC had to be enhanced significantly (E14), over time the need for enhancements decreased.

Integration of the IEC Standards CIM and IEC 61968 Interface Reference Model IRM

As described previously the well-proven and accepted IEC CIM data model was selected for alignment too.

In contrast to the legal documents, the CIM as data model focuses on data and business objects. Therefore, mainly information for the enhancement of the Energy-RMC additional elements (E3), especially regarding business objects covering nearly the whole supply chain, was extracted. In addition, the CIM was classified according the Energy-RMC criteria (E6). Functions were derived using the descriptions about objects and a high-level source ontology was modeled out of them (E11).

Apart from the IEC CIM standard the interface reference model for distribution management (IRM) described in IEC 61968 Part 1 (IEC, 2007a) providing a functional reference model was chosen for integration.

The IEC 61968 IRM is already structured as hierarchy of functions and could easily be formalized as detail ontology (E10). Because of its focus on distribution management it was very helpful for enhancing the Energy-RMC in the area of distribution and helped to derive similar functionality for the area of transmission (E14).

EVALUATION OF THE METHODS USING DESIGN SCIENCE

One crucial part in developing an Energy-RMC and the COLIN methodology was the overall evaluation of both the methods applied and the artifacts generated by the two approaches. As for the COLIN methodology, the artifacts used and the overall methodology have been evaluated. For each ontology integration scenario developed, the guidelines for Design Science by Hevner, March, Park, and Ram (2004) have been applied. Furthermore, a risk assessment has been done using the framework of Baskerville et al.(2008). The methods applied include evaluation of the artifacts through field studies, case studies, static analysis, architecture analysis, controlled experiments, argumentation and scenario analysis. Especially for the COLIN methodology, an excessive overview is provided by Uslar (2009). As for the Energy-RMC, it is evaluated in a project with a local utility where it is used to analyze their current and design their future application landscape. So far, is has shown to provide an excellent overview for the software and process architects getting an overview on the whole utility domain with ICT impact. The evaluation is done with several case studies and especially dedicated artifacts. First extracts of the Energy-RMC where also presented

to vendors and utility companies at the CIM User Group, see González (2010).

Related Work

The work presented here considers several topics regarding design of reference models, reference model catalogues and ontologies.

Regarding the construction of the reference model catalogue, our contribution is based on the work of Fettke and Loos (2002; 2003) and enhances it. On the one hand, we extended the concept by adding core and additional elements, including also other sources than reference models, refining the procedure model and formalizing the catalogue as ontology. On the other hand, we narrow the concepts application by focusing on the energy sector. In addition the criteria for classification of sources is based on traditional classifications of reference models and standards (Schütte, 1998; vom Brocke, 2003; de Vries, 2006; Braun & Esswein, 2007; Fettke & Loos, 2003). Furthermore, for the structure part of our domain specific reference model catalogue we use a functional reference model, here me made use of research made by Närman, Gammelgard, and Nordström (2006), Gunaratne, Chenine, Ekstedt, and Närmann (2008), as well as Gammelgard, Närman, Ekstedt, and Nordström (2006), where a functional reference model is used for building an own reference model, evaluation of reference models and evaluation of the business value of information systems within the energy sector.

For modeling of the catalogue and its bundle of ontologies proven requirements concerning the construction of reference models and ontologies are relevant. Within our contribution we rely on proven methods like the GOM (Schütte, 1998; Schütte & Rotthowe, 1998) and requirements within reference model modeling as described by Scheer (1999). These requirements are mostly abstract and need to be specialized; hence the method-specific interpretation of the GOM principles was adapted, which Becker and Schütte (2004) and Becker, Rotthowe, Rosemann, and Schütte (1998) applied for the construction of a reference model for use within retail information system development. In addition, we take also evaluation criteria in the field of ontology design as defined by Gomez-Perez, Fernandez-Lopez, and Corcho (2004) into account. In this context several other methods exists for construction of reference models and ontologies, for an overview see vom Brocke (2003; 2006), Thomas (2006b) or Fernández López (1999) respectively.

The representation of structural and hierarchically organized artifacts as ontology as proposed within our method is also applied within other approaches, for example in the field of product management (Hahn, 2005; Häusler, große Austing, & Hahn, 2008), information retrieval (Kuropka, 2004;, 2005a; 2005b), knowledge management (Zelewksi, Alan, Alparslan, Dittmann, & Weichelt, 2005) or semantic enrichment of business process modeling (Thomas & Fellmann, 2009).

Methodically, our contribution is based on Design Science as described by Hevner, March, Park, & Ram (2004).

However, this contribution is based on former own research, too, especially regarding the COLIN method (Uslar, 2009) as well as the reference model catalogue construction (see González & Appelrath, 2010) and application (see Beenken, González, Postina, & Appelrath, 2009, as well as Postina, González, & Seychin, 2009). For first extracts of the Energy-RMC see González (2010).

CONCLUSION AND FUTURE RESEARCH DIRECTIONS

In our contribution, we introduced the Energy-RMC and presented an ontology-based approach to construct a reference model catalogue for the energy sector.

On the one hand our approach provides a systematic process for integration of several sources and continuously enhancement of the Energy-RMC knowledge base which can be used within software development processes in the energy sector, especially for the Smart Grid.

In this context we use the characteristics of ontologies for integration of different sources and to provide a knowledgebase for queries and reasoning.

Furthermore our approach considers proven modeling requirements in the fields of ontology and reference model design, especially regarding the modeling effort (modeling granularity) with respect to relevance.

On the other hand knowledge regarding ontology design, querying and reasoning is necessary to make use of the several capabilities of the Energy-RMC. For this purpose an Excel based prototype for users is provided which overcomes the need for detail knowledge regarding ontologies. Furthermore expert knowledge in the energy sector is required to link several sources to the Energy-RMC functional reference model.

A first evaluation of the methodology proposed was done based on action research within an industry funded research project in cooperation with employees of a utility company and a software vendor which are involved in projects dealing with the enhancement of current applications as well as the procurement and developing of new applications in the energy sector. Adding the sources to the Energy-RMC and linking them to the FRM was mainly done by the authors and later on presented and discussed to the other team members in workshops. Within this project step 2 of the method *Usage of COLIN for the enhancement of the Energy-RMC* especially the linking of FRM and sources proved to be time consuming and error-prone. Here analyze of semi-automatic mapping support will be part of future research to speed up integration of the different sources.

Applying the rules and guidelines proposed in section *Formalization and Implementation* proved helpful especially to increase clarity of the catalogue. Within the process of ontology design and analysis open source tools like Protégé were used and proved to be helpful to support development of the ontology for an ontology engineer. Nevertheless Protégé don't seem to be the tool of choice when making enhancements/modifications to the ontology by somebody not familiar with technical ontology concepts (like business analysts) or when presenting content of the Energy-RMC. In this case an integrated development environment providing support for construction, refactoring and use of the Energy-RMC ontology would be helpful to support non ontology expert users. For presenting the Energy-RMC to non ontology experts and to facilitate the formalization of sources custom development for visualization of the ontology (export to Excel sheets) and import of csv-Files, where sources could be hierarchical modeled by e.g. tools supporting spreadsheets, was done. To establish construction of a reference model catalog in industry collaborative construction and enhancement of the catalogue is recommended were a Energy-RMC catalogue manager takes care of the consistency and quality of the catalogue, supervises refactoring processes and decides on modifications.

Our work on the reference model catalogue is still work in progress. Future research is planned to focus on evaluation and application of the Energy-RMC, especially to define evaluation criteria and metrics which should enhance the construction and integration method presented here. In this context, methods for ontology evaluation seem relevant, as e. g. OntoClean, which is described by Gomez-Perez, Fernandez-Lopez, and Corcho (2004). The further development of the prototype is planned to support users in the usage of the Energy-RMC.

REFERENCES

Appelrath, H. J., & Chamoni, P. (2007). Veränderungen in der Energiewirtschaft-Herausforderungen für die IT (Changes in the energy sector – Challenges for IT). *Wirtschaftsinformatik, 49*(5), 329–330. doi:10.1007/s11576-007-0076-8

Baskerville, R., Pries-Heje, J., & Venable, J. (2008). Evaluation risks in design science research: A framework. In R. Baskerville (Ed.), *Proceedings of the Third International Conference on Design Science Research in Information Systems and Technology*, Georgia State University.

Becker, J., Rotthowe, T., Rosemann, M., & Schütte, R. (1998). A framework for efficient information modeling - Guidelines for retail enterprises. In *Proceedings of the Third Informs Conference on Informations Systems and Technology* (pp. 442-448).

Becker, J., & Schütte, R. (2004). *Handelsinformationssysteme: Domänenorientierte Einführung in die Wirtschaftsinformatik* (2nd ed.) (Retail information systems: Domain orientated introduction to business information systems). Frankfurt am Main, Germany: Redline Wirtschaft.

Beenken, P., González, J. M., Postina, M., & Appelrath, H. J. (2009). S*icherheitsorientierte Gestaltung von Anwendungslandschaften in der Energiewirtschaft* (Security based design of application landscapes in the energy sector). In Internationaler ETG-Kongress 2009. Intelligente Netze. 27—28 Oktober 2009.

Braun, R., & Esswein, W. (2007). Classification of reference models. In R. Decker & H.-J. Lenz (Eds.), *Studies in classification, data analysis, and knowledge organization. Advances in data analysis, Proceedings of the 30th Annual Conference of the Gesellschaft für Klassifikation e.V.,* Freie Universität Berlin, March 8-10, 2006 (pp. 401–408). Springer.

Brinker, W. (2009). The changing structure of the utility industry from its own perspective . In Bausch, A., & Schwenker, B. (Eds.), *Handbook utility management* (pp. 207–222). Berlin, Germany: Springer.

Bundesministerium für Wirtschaft und Technologie (Federal ministry of economics and technology) - Arbeitsgemeinschaft Energiebilanzen. (2008). *Endenergieverbrauch nach Energieträgern: Deutschland* (Consumption of end-use energy: Germany). Quelle: Arbeitsgemeinschaft Energiebilanzen, Stand. Aug. 2008; last Update: 08.10.2008. Retrieved January 02, 2009, from http:// www. bmwi. de/ BMWi/Redaktion/Binaer/ Energiedaten/energiegewinnung-und-energieverbrauch4-eev-nach-energietraegern, property=blo b,bereich=bmwi,sprache=de,rwb=true.xls.

Bundesverband der Energie- und Wasserwirtschaft (BDEW). (German Federal Association for Energy and Water). (Ed.). (2008). *Survey of the most important laws, ordinances, specifications, guidelines and recommended action on the subject of electricity business processes.*

de Vries, H. J. (2006). IT standards typology . In Jakobs, K. (Ed.), *Advanced topics in information technology standards and standardization research* (pp. 1–26). Hershey, PA: Idea Group Pub.doi:10.4018/978-1-59140-938-0.ch001

Deutsche Kommission Elektrotechnik Elektronik Informationstechnik (DKE). (2010). *The German standardization roadmap e-energy/smart grid.* Retrieved from www. dke. de/ de/ std/ Kompetenzzentrum E-Energy/Seiten/Links.aspx

Deutscher Bundestag. (2005). *Gesetz über die Elektrizitäts- und Gasversorgung* (Energiewirtschaftsgesetz – EnWG, German industry act): EnWG.

Deutsches Institut für Normung (DIN). (2009). *Die deutsche Normungsstrategie aktuell* (The current German Standardization Strategy). Retrieved from www.din.de/sixcms upload/ media/ 2896/ DNS 2010d akt.pdf

Electric Power Research Institute (EPRI). (2009). *Report to NIST on the smart grid interoperability standards roadmap.* (Contract No. SB1341-09-CN-0031—Deliverable 10). Post Comment Period Version Document.

Fachverband der Elektro- und Elektronikindustrie (FEEI) & Österreichs E-Wirtschaft. (2010). *Roadmap smart grids Austria: Der Weg in die Zukunft der elektrischen Stromnetze* (Pathway to the future of electrical power grids).

Fernández López, M. (1999). Overview of methodologies for building ontologies. In V. R. Benjamins, B. Chandrasekaran, A. Gomez-Perez & M. Uschold (Eds.), *Proceedings of the IJCAI-99 Workshop on Ontologies and Problem-Solving Methods* (KRR5) Stockholm, Sweden, August 2 (pp. 4-1– 4-13).

Fettke, P., & Loos, P. (2002). Der Referenzmodellkatalog als Instrument des Wissensmanagements - Methodik und Anwendung (The reference model catalogue a knowledge management tool - Methodology and Application) . In Becker, J., & Knackstedt, R. (Eds.), *Wissensmanagement mit Referenzmodellen. Konzepte für die Anwendungssystem- und Organisationsgestaltung* (pp. 3–24). Berlin, Germany: Springer.

Fettke, P., & Loos, P. (2003). Classification of reference models - A methodology and its application. *Information Systems and e-Business Management, 1*(1), 35-53.

Fettke, P., & Loos, P. (Eds.). (2007). *Reference modeling for business systems analysis* (pp. vi–xii). Hershey, PA: Idea Group Pub.

FutuRed. (2009). *FutuRed - Spanish electrical grid platform, strategic vision document.* Retrieved from www.futured.es

Gammelgård, M., Närman, P., Ekstedt, M., & Nordström, L. (2006). Business value evaluation of IT systems: Developing a functional reference model. In *Proceedings of the Conference on Systems Engineering Research.*

Gómez-Pérez, A., Fernández-López, M., & Corcho, O. (2004). *Ontological engineering: With examples from the areas of knowledge management, e-commerce and the Semantic Web* (3rd ed.). London, UK: Springer.

González, J. M. (2009). Gestaltung nachhaltiger IT-Landschaften in der Energiewirtschaft mit Hilfe von Referenzmodellen (Design of sustainable IT landscapes in the energy sector using reference models) . In Eymann, T. (Ed.), *Bayreuther Arbeitspapiere zur Wirtschaftsinformatik* (*Vol. 40*, pp. 35–44). Tagungsband zum Doctoral Consortium der WI.

González, J. M. (2010). *The energy reference model catalog – Energy-RMC.* CIM Users Group Meeting, 2010 Milan, Italy. Retrieved from http:// www. offis. de/ uploads/ tx_useroffis/ 20100714014920_CIMUg_energy _rmc _Gonzalez .pdf

González Vázquez, J. M., & Appelrath, H.-J. (2010). Energie-RMK - Ein Referenzmodellkatalog für die Energiewirtschaft (Energy-RMC – A reference model catalogue fort he energy sector). In G. Engels, D. Karagiannis, & C. M. Heinrich (Eds.), *LNI: Vol. 161. Modellierung 2010*, 24.-26. März 2010, Klagenfurt, Österreich (pp. 319–334). GI.

Gruber, T. R. (1993). A translation approach to portable ontology specifications. *Knowledge Acquisition, 5*(2), 199–220. doi:10.1006/knac.1993.1008

Gunaratne, D., Chenine, M., Ekstedt, M., & Närman, P. (2008). *A framework to evaluate a functional reference model at a Nordic distribution utility.* In Nordic Distribution and Asset Management 2008.

Haas, R., Redl, C., & Auer, H. (2009). The changing structure of the electric utility industry in Europe: Liberalisation, new demands and remaining barriers . In Bausch, A., & Schwenker, B. (Eds.), *Handbook utility management* (pp. 169–192). Berlin, Germany: Springer.

Hahn (2005). Integration verteilter produktmodelle durch semantic-web-technologien (Integration of distributed product models by semantic web technologies). *Wirtschaftsinformatik, 47*(4), 278-284.

Häusler, S., Große Austing, S., & Hahn, A. (2008). A framework for empirical analysis by product development data integration. *Proceedings of the International Product Development Management Conference,* 2008.

Hevner, A. R., March, S. T., Park, J., & Ram, S. (2004). Design science in Information Systems research. *Management Information Systems Quarterly, 28*(1), 75–105.

International Electrotechnical Commission (IEC). (2007a). *IEC 61968-1: IEC 61968-1: Application integration at electric utilities - System interfaces for distribution management – Part 1: Interface architecture and general requirements.*

International Electrotechnical Commission (IEC). (2007b). *IEC 61970-301 Ed. 1: Energy management system application program interface (EMS-API) - Part 301: Common information model (CIM) base.*

International Electrotechnical Commission (IEC). (2008). *IEC 61968-11 Ed. 1: System interfaces for distribution management - Part 11: Distribution information exchange model.*

International Electrotechnical Commission (IEC). (2010). *IEC smart grid standardization roadmap*, edition 1.0. Smart grid strategic group (SMB) (SG3).

Kuropka, D. (2004). *Modelle zur Repräsentation natürlichsprachlicher Dokumente (Models to represent natural language documents)*. Berlin, Germany: Logos.

Kuropka, D. (2005a). Formal proof of adequacy of document pre-processing in IF and IR. In *Proceedings of the 8th International Conference on Business Information Systems,* Poznan, Poland, 2005.

Kuropka, D. (2005b). Uselessness of simple co-occurrence measures for IF&IR - A linguistic point of view. In *Proceedings of the 8th International Conference on Business Information Systems,* Poznan, Poland, 2005.

Kurth, M. (2009). The changing structure of the utility industry from the perspective of regulation authorities. In Bausch, A., & Schwenker, B. (Eds.), *Handbook utility management* (pp. 193–206). Berlin, Germany: Springer.

Närman, P., Gammelgard, M., & Nordström, L. (2006). *A functional reference model for asset management applications based on IEC 61968-1*. In Nordic Distribution and Asset Management Conference.

National Institute of Standards and Technologies (NIST). (2010). *NIST special publication 1108: NIST framework and roadmap for smart grid interoperability standards*.

Postina, M., González, J. M., & Sechyn, I. (2009). On the architecture development of utility enterprises with special respect to the gap analysis of application landscapes. In U. Steffens, J. S. Addicks, M. Postina, & N. Streekmann (Eds.), *MDD, SOA und IT-Management* (MSI 2009). Workshop, Oldenburg, October 2009 (pp. 17–31). Gito.

Scheer, A.-W. (1994). *Business process engineering: Reference models for industrial enterprises* (2nd ed.). Berlin, Germany: Springer.

Scheer, A.-W. (1999). *ARIS - Business process frameworks* (3rd ed.). Berlin, Germany: Springer. doi:10.1007/978-3-642-58529-6

Scheer, A.-W. (2000). *ARIS - Business process modeling* (3rd ed.). Berlin, Germany: Springer. doi:10.1007/978-3-642-57108-4

Schütte, R. (1998). Grundsätze ordnungsmäßiger Referenzmodellierung: Konstruktion konfigurations- und anpassungsorientierter Modelle (The Guidelines of Modeling: Constructing configurable and adjustable models). *Neue betriebswirtschaftliche* [Wiesbaden, Germany: Gabler. PhD-Thesis.]. *Forschung, 233*.

Schütte, R., & Rotthowe, T. (1998). The guidelines of modeling - An approach to enhance the quality in information models. In T. W. Ling (Ed.), *Conceptual modeling - ER '98. Proceedings 17th International Conference on Conceptual Modeling,* Singapore, November 16-19, (pp. 240–254). Berlin, Germany: Springer.

Simperl, E., Mochol, M., Bürger, T., & Popov, I. (2009). Achieving maturity: The state of practice in ontology engineering in 2009. In *On the Move to Meaningful Internet Systems* (pp. 983–991). OTM. doi:10.1007/978-3-642-05151-7_17

Smart Grids European Technology Platform (ETP). (2009). *Smart Grids - Strategic deployment document for Europe's electricity networks of the future*.

Starace, F. (2009). The utility industry in 2020. In Bausch, A., & Schwenker, B. (Eds.), *Handbook utility management* (pp. 147–167). Berlin, Germany: Springer.

Thomas, O. (2006a). *Understanding the Term reference model in information systems research: History, literature analysis and explanation.* In Business Process Management Workshops (pp. 484–496).

Thomas, O. (2006b). *Management von Referenzmodellen: Entwurf und Realisierung eines Informationssystems zur Entwicklung und Anwendung von Referenzmodellen (Management of reference models: Design and Implementation of an information system to design and use reference models).* Berlin, Germany: Logos-Verl. PhD-Thesis.

Thomas, O., & Fellmann, M. (2009). Semantic process modeling – Design and implementation of an ontology-based representation of business processes. *Business & Information Systems Engineering, 1*(6), 438–451. doi:10.1007/s12599-009-0078-8

Uslar, M. (2009). *Ontologiebasierte Integration heterogener Standards in der Energiewirtschaft (Ontology-based integration of heterogeneous standards).* Germany: PhD-Thesis, University of Oldenburg.

Uslar, M., Rohjans, S., Schmedes, T., Gonzalez, J., Beenken, P., Weidelt, T., ... Hein, F. (2009). *Untersuchung des Normungsumfeldes zum BMWi-Foerderschwerpunkt E-Energy - IKT-basiertes Energiesystem der Zukunft,* (Survey on standards for the E-Energy projects prepared for the federal ministry of economics and technology) (BMWi).

Vom Brocke, J. (2003). Referenzmodellierung: Gestaltung und Verteilung von Konstruktionsprozessen, (Reference modeling: design and distribution of construction processes). In *Advances in information systems and management science,* vol. 4. Berlin, Germany: Logos. PhD-Thesis.

vom Brocke, J. (2006). Design principles for reference modelling. Reusing information models by means of aggregation, specialisation, instantiation, and analogy. In Fettke, P., & Loos, P. (Eds.), *Reference modelling for business systems analysis* (pp. 47–75). Hershey, PA: Idea Group Publishing. doi:10.4018/978-1-59904-054-7.ch003

Zelewski, S., Alan, Y., Alparslan, A., Dittmann, L., & Weichelt, T. (2005). *Ontologiebasierte Kompetenzmanagementsysteme (Ontology-based competence Management Systems).* Berlin, Germany: Logos.

Chapter 3

Ontological Evaluation of Scheer's Reference Model for Production Planning and Control Systems

Peter Fettke
German Research Center for Artificial Intelligence, Germany

Peter Loos
German Research Center for Artificial Intelligence, Germany

ABSTRACT

Within the information systems field, reference models have been known for many years. A reference model is a conceptual framework and may be used as a blueprint for information systems development. Despite the relevance of reference model quality, little research has been undertaken on their systematical analysis and evaluation. In this chapter, we evaluate Scheer's reference model for production planning and control systems from an ontological point of view. The evaluation is based on the Bunge-Wand-Weber ontology. Several ontological anomalies are found in Scheer's reference model. The obtained knowledge is useful for selecting, applying, and extending the reference model.

INTRODUCTION

Within the information systems field, information modeling is a vital instrument for developing information systems (Mertins & Bernus, 1998; Mišic & Zhao, 2000; Scheer & Nüttgens, 2000;

Schütte, 1998). However, the modeling process is often resource-consuming and faulty. As a way to overcome these failures and to improve and to accelerate the development of enterprise-specific models, the concept of reference modeling has been introduced (Mertins & Bernus, 1998; Mišic & Zhao, 2000; Scheer & Nüttgens, 2000; Schütte, 1998).

DOI: 10.4018/978-1-60960-126-3.ch003

In the meantime, several reference models have been developed (Fettke & Loos, 2003a). One of the most fundamental issues in conceptual modeling is to define what "quality" means or, to put it more specific, what constitutes good modeling practice. Since some time past, various authors use the Bunge-Wand-Weber model (BWW model, cf. Section II, and the BWW meta-model in (Evermann & Wand, 2001a, 2001b; Opdahl & Henderson-Sellers, 2002; Shanks, Tansley, & Weber, 2003; Wand, Storey, & Weber, 1999)) for evaluating modeling *grammars* (Fettke, 2006; Fettke & Loos, 2003c). In this paper, we apply the BWW model to evaluate a reference model as a special kind of a modeling *script*.

The objective of this piece of research is to evaluate Scheer's reference model for production planning and control systems (so-called Y-CIM model, cf. Section II). Therefore, we propose a method that is based on the BWW model. This study follows the approach of (Wand & Weber, 1993) in at first identifying ontological deficiencies of the grammar (Wand & Weber, 2002, p. 364) which is used to represent a reference model and in identifying afterwards ontological anomalies of the reference model itself.

Our reasoning is not based on empirical observations. Instead we use theoretic arguments and critical discussions to come to our findings. We neither argue that empirical research strategies are useless in the area of conceptual modeling nor that our approach is superior to other approaches. However, we believe our approach can give some interesting insights into Scheer's reference model. From our point of view, this kind of research strategy is adequate in the domain of conceptual modeling because reference models are information products that are primarily produced and interpreted by humans — and not by machines. Nevertheless, we prefer formal investigation methods because they allow precise and clear examinations. Other than with the Design Science approach, we do not develop an information systems artefact.

The paper unfolds as follows: After this introduction we describe the theoretical background of this study. Section III introduces a method for the ontological evaluation of reference models. In Section IV, the proposed method is used to evaluate Scheer's reference model from an ontological point of view. The results of the ontological evaluation are critically discussed in Section V. Finally, Section VI draws some conclusions and points to some further research directions.

THEORETICAL BACKGROUND

Terminology

There is a great deal of terminological confusion in the modeling literature. For example, the term "model" is often used for different purposes. To avoid confusion, we use the following definitions:

A *grammar* "provides a set of constructs and rules that show how to combine the constructs to model real-world domains" (Wand & Weber, 2002, p. 364). In the remainder of this paper, we solely refer to analysis grammars, e.g. the Entity-Relationship Model (ERM) or the Unified Modeling Language (UML). And while a *modeling method* "provides procedures by which a grammar can be used" (Wand & Weber, 2002, p. 364), *scripts* are the product of the modeling process. "Each script is a statement in the language generated by the grammar" (Kruse, Hars, Heib, & Scheer, 1993, pp. 48f.). A script is a representation of a real-world domain using a particular grammar.

A *reference model* is a script representing a class of domains. It is a conceptual framework which may be used as the blueprint for information systems development (Fettke & Loos, 2003a). Reference models are also called universal models, generic models, or model patterns. To use reference models, they must be adapted to the requirements of a specific enterprise. We refer to such adapted models as application models. An overview of reference models is given by (J.-P. W. G. D. Van

Belle, 2003) and (Hay, 1996). Concrete instances of reference models are, e.g., Hay's data model patterns (Fowler, 1997), Fowler's analysis patterns (Scheer, 1994), and Scheer's reference model that is introduced next.

Scheer's Reference Model for Production Planning and Control Systems

Scheer's reference model (the so-called Y-CIM model) (Scheer, 1998a) provides a blueprint for production planning and control systems from a conceptual point of view. It includes both business administration functions, such as customer order processing and order release, as well as technical engineering functions, such as product design and numerical control (NC) programming. The Y-CIM model is based on the "Architecture of Integrated Information Systems" (ARIS, (Scheer, 1997)). Scheer uses mainly five modeling grammars for representing the application domain: the ERM for the data view, event-driven process chains respectively process chain diagrams for the control view, function trees for the function view, and organizational unit diagrams for the organization view. In total, the reference model consists of almost 200 different diagrams (Table 1).

In this study, we select this reference model for several reasons:

- It can be assumed that the Y-CIM model is widely accepted nationally and internationally. The model was first published in a German book that is in its seventh edi-

tion (Scheer, 2004). The English translation of the original book is in its second edition. Numerous courses on information systems application at German universities teach this model. In addition, according to (Fettke & Loos, 2003a; Scheer & Hars, 1992), the model has also found many applications in industry.

- As all reference models, the model does not cover a particular enterprise but a class of similar enterprises.
- The model is — compared to other models — detailed and extensive (Wand & Weber, 1990, 1993, 1995; Weber, 1997).
- To the knowledge of the authors, this is the first evaluation of Scheer's reference model.
- Scheer uses different perspectives to describe an enterprise. This is an interesting challenge for an ontological evaluation.

Bunge-Wand-Weber Model

In this subsection, we recapitulate some concepts of the BWW model that are needed to understand the remainder of our study. This overview cannot replace the original work on the BWW model (Bodart, Patel, Sim, & Weber, 2001; Evermann & Wand, 2001a; Green & Rosemann, 2000; Milton, 2000; Opdahl & Henderson-Sellers, 2001; Rohde, 1995; Wand & Weber, 1989, 1993; Weber & Zhang, 1991). The term "ontology" always refers to the ontology defined by the BWW model. In the following, for reasons of clarity, each term of the vocabulary of the BWW model is attached

Table 1. Overview of modeling grammars used by Scheer's reference model

View	Modeling grammar	Number of diagrams
Organizational view	Organizational unit diagrams	21
Data view	Entity-Relationship Model	93
Function view	Function trees	22
Control view	Event-driven process chains & process chain diagrams	37 & 11

with a BWW prefix. Every BWW term refers to a construct of the BWW ontology.

There are other ontologies aside from the BWW model. However, we chose this model as a basis for analysis for a number of reasons:

- The BWW model is general, does not depend on a particular domain of knowledge, and closely relates to system concepts that are used in information systems development.
- It is well formalized in terms of set theory.
- It has been successfully adapted to information systems modeling, e.g. (Green, 1996; Weber, 1996).
- Empirical studies show the usefulness of this ontology, e.g. (Bodart, et al., 2001; Green & Rosemann, 2001) (Bunge, 1977, 1979).

The BWW model is based on Bunge's ontology (Fettke & Loos, 2003b). The elementary construct of this ontology is a BWW thing. The world is made up of substantial BWW things. A BWW thing, e.g. a person or a book, possesses BWW properties, e.g. name, color, weight, etc. A BWW composite thing can be decomposed into a set of BWW things, e.g. a production system can be decomposed into several working places. There exist basic BWW things that cannot be decomposed. Composite BWW things possess BWW emergent properties that are not possessed by any of their components, e.g. the throughput time of a production system is a BWW emergent property. A BWW class is a set of things that possess a common property.

BWW properties cannot be observed directly; instead, BWW attributes are representations of the BWW properties of a BWW thing as perceived by an observer. A BWW attribute is a function that maps a BWW thing onto a BWW value at some point time. The set of BWW attributes of a BWW thing forms a BWW functional schema. The BWW state of a BWW thing is represented by the vector of all BWW values that are associated with the BWW functional schema of this BWW thing. The set of all BWW states in which a BWW thing can be is called BWW state space. A BWW transformation is a function from the state space into the same state space. Stable states cannot be left without some external interaction while unstable states are intermediate states that a BWW thing can transition out of by itself. A BWW event is a change of the BWW state of a BWW thing; e.g. "the manufacturing machine of a production system is repaired" is a BWW event. Two things are coupled if at least one of them acts on the other (BWW coupling).

So far, the terms "ontology" and "construct of ontology" have been introduced. Additionally, we use the terms "ontological model" and "construct of an ontological model". An "ontological model" is a set of constructs of an ontology that represents reality as perceived by an observer. The term "construct of an ontological model" refers to a specific construct of the ontology used in the ontological model.

Related Work

A recent discussion of known approaches to the evaluation of reference models and their strengths and limitations can be found in (Krogstie, 1995; Lindland, Sindre, & Sølvberg, 1994; Moody & Shanks, 2003). There exist several approaches to conceptual (data) models' quality in general, e.g. (Schuette & Rotthowe, 1998; Schütte, 1998). However, the reference models' quality in particular is just discussed in some work: (Mišic & Zhao, 2000) propose six so-called "principles for reference modeling". Each principle can also be used to conduct an ex-ante evaluation of a reference model. However, we are not aware of such investigations. An alternative framework for reference modeling evaluation is proposed by (Lindland, et al., 1994). Their framework is influenced by (Fettke & Loos, 2003a) and based on semiotic theory. The usefulness of this framework is demonstrated by the evaluation of reference models for electronic commerce. Several criteria for the analysis and evaluation of reference models are introduced by (J.-P. W. G. D. Van Belle, 2003). Using these criteria, the authors characterize several reference models. However, usefulness and purpose of the criteria proposed are not discussed in detail. (J.-P. Van Belle & Price, 2000) constructs a framework for the analysis and evaluation of reference models (a prior version of his framework is discussed by (J.-P. W. G. D. Van Belle, 2003, p. 258)). This framework is applied to several reference models. One characteristic of this framework is that the proposed metrics are operationalized. The interpretation and meaning of specific metrics is sometimes unclear, e.g. both SAP's and Baan's reference models genericity is measured as "16" (Scheer, 1994). For the user, the practical meaning and consequences of this measurement are not straightforward.

METHOD FOR ONTOLOGICAL EVALUATION

Overview of Method

This section introduces our approach to the ontological evaluation of reference models. The main idea of our approach is the ontological normalization of a reference model. An ontological normalization is comparable with the normalization of a database schema. The objective of both techniques is to represent the domain of interest in a normalized way by applying specific transformation patterns. Normalization of a database schema aims at eliminating problems of information representation and processing in database management systems (e.g. avoiding data redundancies, update anomalies, etc.). In contrast, the ontological normalization aims to achieve a unified representation of facts represented by a reference model with respect to the structure of reality. Compared to other representations, such

as UML or ERM, an ontological representation of a reference model has the advantage that it is more general and not influenced by technical aspects. The ontological normalization of a reference model consists of four steps:

- Developing a transformation mapping,
- Identifying ontological modeling deficiencies,
- Transforming the reference model, and
- Assessing the results.

The following subsections discuss each step in more detail.

Developing a Transformation Mapping

Until now, various grammars have been used to represent reference models. For instance, (Scheer, 1998a, 1998b) uses the Architecture of Integrated Information Systems (ARIS) (Hay, 1996), (Fowler, 1997) employs some kind of an ERM, and (Wand & Weber, 1993) uses an object-oriented approach. In the first step of our method, it is necessary to develop a transformation mapping for the grammar used for in order to represent the reference model. This transformation mapping allows us to map the constructs of the grammar used onto the constructs of the BWW model. The term "construct of a grammar" refers to, e.g., a relationship type (when using the ERM) or a class (when using the UML). The first step is based on the method for ontological evaluation of grammars proposed by (Bodart, et al., 2001; Evermann & Wand, 2001a; Green & Rosemann, 2000; Milton, 2000; Opdahl & Henderson-Sellers, 2001; Rohde, 1995; Wand & Weber, 1989, 1993; Weber & Zhang, 1991). The transformation mapping introduces an ontological meaning for each construct of the grammar used by the reference model. The explicitly ontological definition of the transformation mapping has a beneficial effect on the objectivity of the evaluation. Without this definition it would be impossible to criticize — in an intersubjective way — a particular evaluation of a reference model conducted.

The transformation mapping consists of two mathematical mappings: First, a representation mapping describes whether and how the constructs of the BWW model are mapped onto the grammatical constructs. Second, the interpretation mapping describes whether and how the grammatical constructs are mapped onto the constructs of the BWW model. With respect to both mappings, four ontological deficiencies can be distinguished:

- **Incompleteness:** Can each ontological construct be mapped onto a construct of the grammar? A grammar is incomplete if the representation mapping is not defined in total. If otherwise a grammar is complete.
- **Redundancy:** Can each ontological construct be mapped onto exactly one or onto more than one grammatical construct? A grammar is redundant if the representation mapping is ambiguous.
- **Excess:** Can each grammatical construct be mapped onto an ontological construct? A grammatical construct is excessive if it cannot be mapped onto an ontological construct. A grammar is excessive if at least one of its constructs is excessive.
- **Overload:** Can each grammatical construct be mapped onto exactly one or onto more than one ontological construct? A grammatical construct is overloaded if it can be mapped onto more than one ontological construct. A grammar is overloaded if at least one of its constructs is overloaded.

We refer to the term "grammar" as "ontologically clear" if it is neither incomplete nor redundant. A grammatical construct is adequate if it is neither excessive nor overloaded, so that it is defined unambiguously with respect to the interpretation mapping. A grammar is adequate if each of its grammatical constructs is adequate.

The first evaluation step just refers to the grammar used and, therefore, is independent of the reference model being evaluated. This allows such evaluations to be carried out in advance and to reuse the developed transformation mappings for ontological evaluations of various reference models. This paper does not aim to propose transformation mappings for known grammars and to identify their ontological deficiencies. Instead, we refer to the approaches of ontological evaluations of grammars found in literature, e.g. (Wand & Weber, 1993, p. 227).

The fact whether a grammar has ontological deficiencies is independent of the ontological evaluation of the constructs used in the reference model. In other words: the first evaluation step analyzes the used grammar in general. In the second step of the evaluation, the used constructs of the reference model are analyzed with respect to the grammatical evaluation in particular.

Identifying Ontological Modeling Deficiencies

To prepare the ontological normalization of the reference model, all ontological deficiencies of the reference models have to be identified. This is the objective of the second step. The second step is based on the previously constructed general transformation mapping. It is possible that one ontological deficiency is resolvable in various ways or even not resolvable at all. Hence, it is useful to separate the identification of ontological modeling deficiencies from the transforming step of the reference model (which is the next step).

To identify the ontological deficiencies of the reference model all, constructs of the reference model must be reviewed. Each construct of the reference model must be examined with respect to whether the construct is used correctly regarding the interpretation mapping. One of the following situations can arise:

- **Adequacy:** The grammatical construct is ontologically adequate. Nevertheless, an ontological deficiency can emerge by applying the grammatical construct to build the reference model. Therefore it must be examined whether the construct of the reference model is used correctly with respect to the interpretation mapping. The construct of the reference model is used adequately if it is used correctly with respect to the interpretation mapping. Otherwise it should be marked as inadequate. For instance, a reference model contains an entity type "color". Furthermore, using the ERM, an entity type should be mapped onto a BWW class with regard to an appropriate interpretation mapping. So, the entity type "color" has to be mapped onto a BWW class. But this mapping is inadequate because the entity type "color" represents a BWW property and not a BWW class. So, the entity type "color" is not used correctly with respect to the interpretation mapping.

- **Excess:** Construct excess is a modeling deficiency in general and needs a special handling in the transformation step. As a consequence, this construct should be marked as excessive in the reference model. Construct excess occurs if implementation-specific aspects are represented in the reference model, e.g. the technical concepts of message passing or polymorphism cannot be represented with ontological constructs.

- **Overload:** Construct overload is a modeling deficiency in general and needs a special handling in the transformation step. Therefore, this construct should be marked as overloaded in the reference model. For instance, using UML, an UML object can represent a BWW thing (UML object "Mr. Miller" is an instance of the UML class

customer) or a BWW class (UML objects "a-class journal", "b-class journal" etc. are instances of the UML class "journal categories"). So, the construct UML object is ontologically overloaded.

The described step of identification of modeling deficiencies relies on the interpretation mapping. In addition, the representation mapping supports an indirect means to identify modeling deficiencies. With the representation mapping as basis, it can be decided whether the used grammar is incomplete or redundant. An incomplete grammar leads to inadequate representation of specific facts of reality in the reference model. This deficiency appears in models as representation of facts that cannot be adequately represented by a grammatical construct. This case shall be illustrated by an example (Scheer, 1994, pp. 90-197): BWW events cannot be represented by grammatical constructs of the ERM. Hence, persons applying the ERM grammar tend to represent BWW events by using entity types. This leads to a situation in which entity types are not used adequately with respect to the interpretation mapping.

Transforming the Reference Model

In the third step, the reference model will be transformed to an ontological model. The outcome of this step is an ontologically normalized reference model. More formally, an ontologically normalized reference model is a mapping from the constructs of the reference model onto the constructs of an ontological model. While mapping a construct of the reference model onto an ontological construct, four cases can arise:

- **Adequacy:** The construct of the reference model is marked as adequate. It is possible to map this construct in a straightforward way onto a construct of the ontological model.

- **Inadequacy:** The construct of the reference model is marked as inadequate. It is necessary to interpret the representation in the reference model in a sensible manner. The result of this interpretation may be that it is possible to represent this construct by a specific construct of the ontological model.
- **Excess:** The construct of the reference model cannot be mapped onto a construct of the ontological model with respect to the interpretation mapping. Nevertheless it should be examined whether it is possible to represent this construct by a specific construct of the ontological model in particular.
- **Overload:** The construct of the reference model can be mapped onto several constructs of the ontological model with respect to interpretation mapping. It is necessary to decide which interpretation mapping is preferable regarding the interpretation of the representation in the reference model. The result of this decision may be that it is possible to represent this construct by exactly one construct of the ontological model.

The resolution of the ontological deficiencies of constructs should be guided by the intension of these constructs. This step relies on the subject's interpretation performing the evaluation. The result of this transformation is an ontological model representing the reference model in an ontologically normalized way. The ontologically normalized model is assessed with respect to different aspects in the next step.

Assessing the Results

In the last step, the reference model can be evaluated with respect to the results of the three steps mentioned above:

- Assessing the transformation mapping in general,
- Assessing the ontological deficiencies of constructs in particular, and
- Assessing the ontologically normalized reference model.

First, the transformation mapping can be assessed in general. With the representation and interpretation mappings as a basis, it is possible to determine the ontological clarity and adequacy of the grammar used. This assessment gives an idea whether or how this grammar is suitable to represent the facts of reality regarding the intended application in general.

Second, in particular the ontological deficiencies of constructs of the reference model can be assessed. While the ontological deficiencies excess and overload have their roots in the definition of the grammar, the cause of an ontologically inadequate construct of the reference model is the specific application of a grammatical construct employed by the person who developed the model. An ontologically adequate construct of the reference model is not equivalent to a correct modeling (in a syntactical sense). Instead, the high usage of inadequate constructs may be a sign of representing a lot of implementation aspects in the reference model.

Third, the ontologically normalized reference model can be assessed. In this case, three different evaluation aspects are reasonable:

- **BWW completeness:** It can be analyzed whether the normalized reference model specifies a BWW system. This property is called BWW completeness.
- **Isolated assessment:** Different metrics can be used for an isolated assessment of the ontological model. Individual and comparative metrics can be distinguished. For reasons of brevity, we give just two examples. First example: The number of BWW

things can be used to measure the size of the reference model (individual metric). Second example: The complexity of events can be defined as the number of BWW events in relation to the number of theoretically possible BWW events represented in the reference model (comparative metric). The number of theoretically possible BWW events can be calculated as the square of the number of BWW states represented in the reference model. Formally:

$$complexity\ of\ events \underset{def}{=} \frac{number\ of\ BWW - events}{(number\ of\ BWW - states)^2}$$

- **Comparative assessment:** Comparative evaluations of reference models can be undertaken if further ontological models of the application domain are given. In this manner, it is possible to evaluate a reference model with respect to its completeness. Such an evaluation is possible only with respect to another ontological model.

RESULTS

In the following, we present the results of the ontological evaluation of Scheer's reference model. First, we will analyze each individual view. Finally, our evaluation will focus on some inter-grammar issues. For brevity, we cannot provide an ontological evaluation of the whole reference model, but present some interesting results evaluating the functions "Primary Requirements Management" and "Requirements Planning" (Wand, et al., 1999, p. 506) which constitute one major part of a production planning and control system. Primary requirements are requirement figures for end products, independently salable intermediate products and spare parts. The objective of the requirements planning is to determine the in-house and outsourced parts needed to satisfy the primary requirements, to manage the inventories and to procure the outsourced parts.

Data View

Figure 1 depicts a reference data model for primary requirements planning. First, an interpretation mapping has to be introduced. We propose to map an ERM entity onto a BWW thing (Wand, et al., 1999, p. 506). But we do not follow to map an ERM entity type onto a BWW class as proposed by (Evermann & Wand, 2001b, p. 359). Instead, we apply the interpretation mapping for UML classes proposed by (Scheer, 1994, p. 91) to ERM entity types. According to this argumentation, an ERM entity type is mapped onto a BWW functional schema. We do not discuss interpretation mappings for further constructs of the ERM because our evaluation just focuses on entities and entity types.

According to the reference model, articles are identified by article numbers (attribute PNO). Note that these article numbers should not be confused with serial numbers or something like that: a serial number allows one to unambiguously identify a single specific article, e.g. the CPU with the serial number 1000 that is bought by customer X. Instead, the entity type "article" describes a set of articles of a specific type. Possible entities of this type are, e.g., "CPU 1GHz", "CPU 2GHz", etc. Figure 2 depicts this interrelation between the entity type "article", its possible instances and substantial articles. In other words: instances of the entity type "article" cannot be interpreted as BWW things but as sets of BWW things. Hence, instances of this entity type represent specific types of articles. This leads to several implications:

- The reference model implies that articles are discrete or at least made in discrete quantities. This assumption may be problematic in process industries (Scheer, 1994, p. 94).
- Specific articles must be grouped into types or classes. This assumption is not problematic in mass production but may

Figure 1. Reference model to determine primary requirements (Hay, 1996, p. 187)

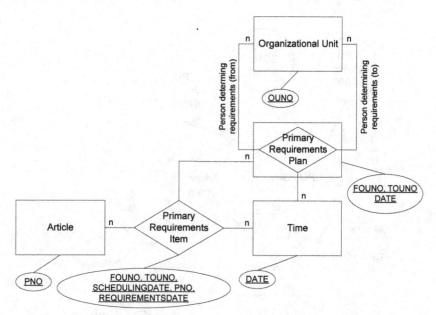

be problematic in customer-oriented manufacturing.

- Specific articles cannot hold specific attributes that must be represented in the information system (e.g. inventory place of a specific article).

Possible entities of the entity type "Organizational Unit" are sales planning or production planning. One possible ontological interpretation of the representation chosen is that these entities represent a specific BWW thing of a specific enterprise. For instance, the organizational unit "production planning" of a specific enterprise may consist of a set of employees, specific machines and other substantial working resources. If this interpretation is agreed upon, then the user of the reference model has to define which things of the enterprise refer to specific entities of this type during the application of the reference model. On the other hand, it can be argued that these entities do not have a factual reference, but have just a formal character. The ontological ambiguity of the reference model cannot be resolved here in general,

but it has important methodological consequences, in particular: following the first interpretation, it is possible to conduct empirical investigations ("Does the organizational unit 'production planning' consist of machine X, employee Y etc. ?"). Such verifications are meaningless if the second interpretation is followed.

Possible entities of the entity type „Time" are date stamps which can represent concrete dates, such as "2003-05-20", or specific periods (period 1, period 2 etc.). The entities are not BWW things. Instead, temporal aspects address a different ontological category. We argue that Scheer's conceptualization of time is caused by the fact that the ERM grammar does not provide sufficient concepts to represent temporal aspects explicitly. Hence, this conceptualization may be problematic.

Organization View

Scheer's reference model for organizational units involved in requirements planning is depicted in Figure 3. Each bubble in the model represents an

Figure 2. Possible ERM entities and possible BWW things

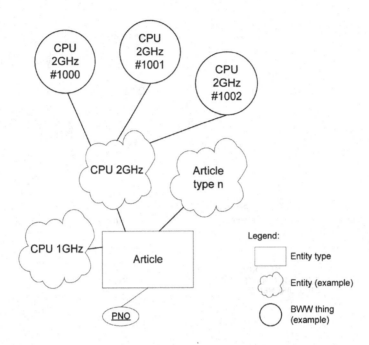

organizational unit. The ontological interpretation of an organizational unit is ambiguous (Scheer, 1998b, pp. 53f.). On the one hand, an organizational unit can be mapped onto a BWW thing of a specific enterprise, e.g. the organizational unit "Production planning" of a specific enterprise may consist of a set of employees, specific machines and other substantial working resources (cf. the evaluation of the data view above). On the other hand, it can be argued that an organizational unit represents a class of BWW things and, therefore, represents a BWW class. Following the second interpretation, the organizational unit "production planning" represents all organizational units of an enterprise that are responsible for the planning of the production, e.g. production planning in plant 1, plant 2, etc. These different ways of interpretations have the following consequences: organizational charts in conjunction with EPC are used to assign responsibilities to organizational units. So, if the second interpretation is followed, it is not possible to exactly assign some responsibilities to a specific organizational unit, e.g. the responsibility of the

function "estimate gross requirements" cannot be assigned to the organizational unit "production planning in plant 1" because the organizational chart represents classes of organizational units but not specific instances. We admit that such assignments can be made in further textual descriptions or annotations of the model. But it is not possible to express such assignments by using this modeling grammar. Scheer is aware of this interpretation ambiguity and distinguishes organizational diagrams on the type level and on the instance level (Scheer, 1994, p. 160). However, the intended interpretation is not stated explicitly in the reference model and may result in confusion.

Function View

Figure 4 depicts a part of Scheer's reference function model for requirements planning. From an ontological point of view, each function can be interpreted as a BWW transformation. However, function trees are only able to define a small portion of the semantic of BWW transformations: the do-

Figure 3. Reference model for organizational units involved in requirements planning (Green & Rose-mann, 2000, pp. 81)

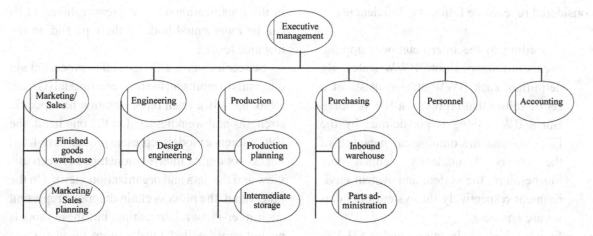

main and co-domain of the BWW transformation, the mapping between domain and co-domain, and the BWW thing to which the BWW transformation belongs are not deducible from the function tree. So, the function model has only a vague ontological meaning. Furthermore, the interrelations between the functions represented in one function tree are unclear. Do the sub-functions of one function complement each other or are they substitutable? For example, the functions "ABC analysis" and "Time series analysis" seem to be substitutable, but the functions "Primary requirements management" and "Inventory management" are clearly not substitutes. For a user of the reference model, this information is quite important because, in a

specific implementation environment, it is not necessary to implement all functions of a reference model but rather those functions that are essential for the application intended. This information is not represented in the function tree.

Control View

The control view describes the relationships between data, function, and organization view. Figure 5 depicts an EPC for the requirements explosion process (Scheer omits the relationships to the data and organization view for reasons of clarity). Events of an EPC can be ontologically interpreted as BWW states, and functions as

Figure 4. Part of the reference function model for requirements planning (Scheer, 1994, pp. 190f.)

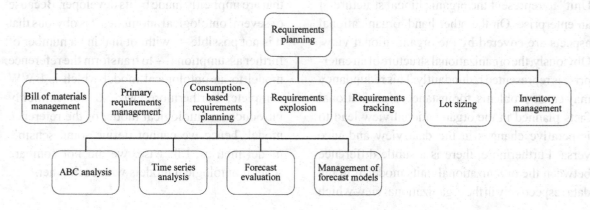

BWW transformations (see discussion above). An ontological evaluation of the reference model considered reveals the following deficiencies:

- According to the interpretation mapping, events are mapped onto BWW states. By definition, each BWW state consists of a set of values that represent a BWW thing. But a BWW thing is not defined by the EPC, so that the ontological meaning of the events is unclearly defined too. Furthermore, the system and system environment respectively the system boundaries are not clear.
- Events which can be interpreted as a BWW stable event do not exist. So, there is no clear-cut condition when or whether the depicted process terminates.
- Obviously, some functions require some user interaction, for instance the functions "Lot sizing" or "Forward Scheduling" can run interactively (Scheer, 1994, p. 129). However, these BWW couplings are not stated in the reference model.

Inter-Grammar Evaluation

This subsection analyzes some interrelations between constructs of different grammars used to represent the reference model. First, we focus on interrelations between the data and the organization view. On the one hand, in the data view, Scheer uses the entity type "Organizational Unit" to represent the organizational structure of an enterprise. On the other hand, organizational aspects are covered by the organizational view. Obviously, the organizational structure of an enterprise is represented redundantly. This redundancy may cause problems, for instance, organizational facts planned in the organizational view lead to imperative changes in the data view and vice versa. Furthermore, there is a subtle difference between the organizational units modeled in the data respectively in the organizational view which

should be considered: in the data view, organizational units are represented on the type level, but in the organizational view, organizational units can be represented both on the type and on the instance level.

Scheer uses both EPC as well as process chain diagrams to represent the reference model (Green, 1996, pp. 85f.). Each representation has specific strengths and weaknesses. On the one hand, the EPC reference models represent processes in detail but do not define interrelationships between this view and the data and organization views. On the other hand, the process chain diagrams represent such inter-view relationships, but these models are not very detailed. Furthermore, the use of two modeling grammars which are almost equally expressive from an ontological point of view causes some inconsistencies, e.g. some functions in EPC models are not represented in process chain diagrams. This is a clear indication that the principle "minimal ontological overlap (MOO)" (Schütte & Zelewski, 2001, p. 3) — when using several modeling grammars — is violated.

CRITICAL DISCUSSION

In the prior section an ontological evaluation of Scheer's reference model is conducted. The evaluation focuses on the identification of ontological deficiencies, on possible ways to transform the reference model to an ontological model, and on explicating assumptions of the reference model that are implicitly made by its developer. Because of several ontological anomalies it is obvious that it is not possible — without making a number of further assumptions — to transform the reference model to an ontological model which is BWW complete. Furthermore, we did not explicitly introduce an ontological model of the reference model; hence we cannot define some sensible model metrics. Likewise, we did not compare several ontological models with each other.

Figure 5. Reference process for requirements explosion (Scheer, 1994, p. 129 & 176)

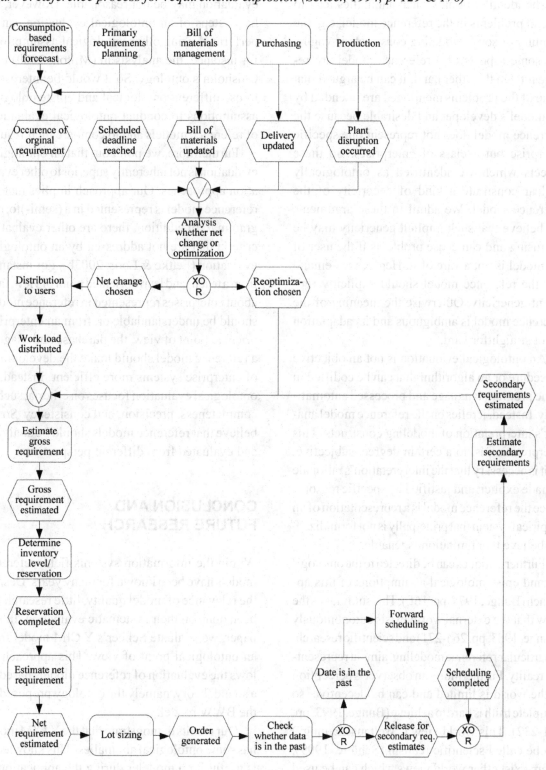

The identified ontological anomalies lead to several problems in the reference model, e.g. the meaning of some modeling constructs is vague, and some aspects of a reference model are redundant. On the other hand, it can be argued that some of the problems mentioned are intended by the model's developer and desirable because the reference model does not represent one specific enterprise but a class of enterprises. So these aspects which we identified as ontologically unclear constitute a kind of genericity of the reference model. We admit to these arguments but believe that such implicit genericity may be confusing and can cause problems if the user of the model is not aware of it. Hence, we demand that the reference model should explicitly represent genericity. Otherwise the meaning of the reference model is ambiguous and its adaptation is not straightforward.

An ontological evaluation is not an objective procedure or an algorithm that can be codified in some program language and processed automatically. Instead, it relies on the reference model analyst's interpretation of modeling constructs. This interpretation is, to a certain degree, subjective. So it is necessary that the interpretation's rationale is made explicit and justified by specific reasons. Since the reference model is a representation of an empirical system that principally is not formalized, we believe this limitation is tenable.

Further critiques can be directed to the ontological and epistemological assumptions of this approach (Bunge, 1977, pp. 16f.). This study takes the view that the external world exists autonomously (Bunge, 1983, pp. 264-271) and scientific research, in particular reference modeling, aims at representing reality. Furthermore, an observer's perception of the world is limited and can be deceptive, so complete truth is hard to achieve (Bunge, 1993, pp. 231-232). This world view ("Weltanschauung") can be called scientific realism (Schütte, 1999). There exist other world views which can be used as a foundation for conceptual modeling (Milton, 2000). From other worldviews, an ontological

evaluation may be not reasonable. However, the basic steps of an ontological evaluation can be performed using other ontological assumptions; for instance, the analysis in (Milton, 2000) uses Chisholm's ontology. So it would be interesting to use different ontological and epistemological assumptions to conduct ontological evaluations of reference models and to compare their results.

Furthermore, we point out that an ontological evaluation is not inherently superior to other evaluation approaches. Our approach implies that the reference model is represented in a (semi-)formal grammar. In addition, there are other evaluation criteria that are not addressed by an ontological evaluation (Fettke & Loos, 2003b). For instance, from a teach- and learn-oriented point of view, facts about enterprises represented in reference models should be understandable or, from an enterprise-oriented point of view, the purchase and usage of a reference model should make the development of enterprise systems more efficient. Instead, an ontological evaluation focuses on criteria, such as completeness, precision, and consistency. So we believe that reference models should be analyzed and evaluated from different perspectives.

CONCLUSION AND FUTURE RESEARCH

Within the information systems field, reference models have been known for many years. Despite the relevance of model quality, little research has been done on their systematic evaluation. In this paper, we evaluate Scheer's Y-CIM model from an ontological point of view. This approach allows the evaluation of reference models based on a sound theory, namely the ontology proposed by the BWW model.

Our results demonstrate that the Y-CIM model has some ontological anomalies. This knowledge is useful for a modeler during the application of the reference model, e.g. the anomalies draw the modeler's attention to "critical" constructs of the reference model. Furthermore, we explicate some implicit assumptions of Scheer's reference model. For example, it assumes implicitly an industrial company producing large quantities of specific product types where each product is made in discrete quantities. The knowledge of these assumptions supports the selection of an appropriate reference model and points out possible extensions of the reference model in the future.

We see several areas for further research. First, the ontological evaluation should be complemented with evaluations from other perspectives (for other perspectives see (Fettke & Loos, 2003b)). By doing so, models' quality can be studied and guaranteed in a broader sense. Second, our approach is based on the BWW model. Further investigations should examine the usefulness of other ontological assumptions. Third, the proposed method should be applied to evaluate further reference models. To conclude, we believe that these studies provide both a better understanding of reference model quality and insights that lead, in the long term, to a theory of conceptual enterprise modeling.

ACKNOWLEDGMENT

This paper is based on results of the research project "Reference modeling with reference model catalogs" funded by the Deutsche Forschungsgemeinschaft (DFG, German Research Foundation). Grant number: LO 752/2-1.

REFERENCES

Bodart, F., Patel, A., Sim, M., & Weber, R. (2001). Should optional properties be used in conceptual modelling? A theory and three empirical tests. *Information Systems Research, 12*(4), 384–405. doi:10.1287/isre.12.4.384.9702

Bunge, M. (1977). *Ontology I: The furniture of the world*. Dordrecht, Holland: D. Reidel.

Bunge, M. (1979). *Ontology II: A world of systems*. Dordrecht, Holland: D. Reidel.

Bunge, M. (1983). *Epistemology & methodology II: Understanding the world*. Dordrecht, Holland: D. Reidel.

Bunge, M. (1993). Realism and antirealism in social science. *Theory and Decision, 35*, 207–235. doi:10.1007/BF01075199

Evermann, J., & Wand, Y. (2001a, December, 15-16). *An ontological examination of object interaction in conceptual modeling*. Paper presented at the Workshop on Information Technologies and Systems (WITS), New Orleans, Louisiana, USA.

Evermann, J., & Wand, Y. (2001b). Towards ontologically based semantics for UML constructs. In H. S. Kunii, S. Jajodia & A. Sølvberg (Eds.), *Conceptual modeling - ER 2001 - 20th International Conference on Conceptual Modeling, Yokohama, Japan, November 27-30, 2001, Proceedings* (pp. 354-367). Berlin, Germany: Springer.

Fettke, P. (2006). *Referenzmodellevaluation - Konzeption der strukturalistischen Referenzmodellierung und Entfaltung ontologischer Gütekriterien*. Berlin, Germany: Logos-Verlag.

Fettke, P., & Loos, P. (2003a). Classification of reference models - A methodology and its application. *Information Systems and e-Business Management, 1*(1), 35-53.

Fettke, P., & Loos, P. (2003b). Multiperspective evaluation of reference models - Towards a framework . In Jeusfeld, M. A., & Pastor, Ó. (Eds.), *Conceptual modeling for novel application domains - ER 2003 Workshops ECOMO, IWCMQ, AOIS, and XSDM, Chicago, IL, USA, October 13, 2003* (pp. 80–91). Berlin, Germany: Springer.

Fettke, P., & Loos, P. (2003c, August 4 - 6). *Ontological evaluation of reference models using the Bunge-Wand-Weber model.* Paper presented at the Americas Conference on Information Systems (AMCIS), Tampa, FL, USA.

Fowler, M. (1997). *Analysis patterns: Reusable object models.* Menlo Park, CA: Addison-Wesley.

Green, P. (1996). *An ontological analysis of Information Systems analysis and design (ISAD) grammars in upper case tools.* PhD Thesis, University of Queensland, Brisbane, Australien.

Green, P., & Rosemann, M. (2000). Integrated process modeling: An ontological evaluation. *Information Systems, 25*(2), 73–87. doi:10.1016/S0306-4379(00)00010-7

Green, P., & Rosemann, M. (2001). Ontological analysis of integrated process models: Testing hypotheses. *Australian Journal on Information Systems, 9*(1), 30–38.

Hay, D. C. (1996). *Data model patterns - Conventions of thought.* New York, NY: Dorset House.

Krogstie, J. (1995). *Conceptual modeling for computerized information systems support in organizations.* PhD Thesis, University of Trondheim, Trondheim.

Kruse, C., Hars, A., Heib, R., & Scheer, A.-W. (1993). Ways of utilizing reference models for data engineering in CIM. *International Journal of Flexible Automation and Integrated Manufacturing, 1*(1), 47–58.

Lindland, O. I., Sindre, G., & Sølvberg, A. (1994). Understanding quality in conceptual modeling. *IEEE Software, 2*, 42–49. doi:10.1109/52.268955

Mertins, K., & Bernus, P. (1998). Reference models. In Bernus, P., Mertins, K., & Schmidt, G. (Eds.), *Handbook on architectures of Information Systems* (pp. 615–617). Berlin, Germany: Springer.

Milton, S. (2000). *An ontological comparison and evaluation of data modelling frameworks.* PhD Thesis, University of Tasmania, Hobart, Australien.

Mišic, V. B., & Zhao, J. L. (2000). Evaluating the quality of reference models. In A. H. F. Laender, S. W. Liddle & V. C. Storey (Eds.), *Conceptual modeling - ER 2000 - 19th International Conference on Conceptual Modeling, Salt Lake City, Utah, USA, October 9-12, 2000 Proceedings* (pp. 484-498). Berlin, Germany: Springer.

Moody, D. L., & Shanks, G. G. (2003). Improving the quality of data models: Empirical validation of a quality management framework. *Information Systems, 28*, 619–650. doi:10.1016/S0306-4379(02)00043-1

Opdahl, A. L., & Henderson-Sellers, B. (2001). Grounding the OML metamodel in ontology. *Journal of Systems and Software, 57*(2), 119–143. doi:10.1016/S0164-1212(00)00123-0

Opdahl, A. L., & Henderson-Sellers, B. (2002). Ontological evaluation of the UML using the Bunge-Wand-Weber Model. *Software and Systems Modeling, 1*(1), 43–67.

Rohde, F. (1995). An ontological evaluation of Jackson's system development model. *Australian Journal of Information Systems, 2*(2), 77–87.

Scheer, A.-W. (1994). *Business process engineering - Reference models for industrial enterprises* (2nd ed.). Berlin, Germany: Springer.

Scheer, A.-W. (1997). *Wirtschaftsinformatik - Referenzmodelle für industrielle Geschäftsprozesse* (7. ed.). Berlin, Germany: Springer.

Scheer, A.-W. (1998a). *ARIS - Business process frameworks* (2. ed.). Berlin, Germany: Springer.

Scheer, A.-W. (1998b). *ARIS - Business process modeling* (2. ed.). Berlin, Germany: Springer.

Scheer, A.-W. (2004). 20 Jahre Gestaltung industrieller Geschäftsprozesse. *Industrie Management, 20*(1), 11–18.

Scheer, A.-W., & Hars, A. (1992). Extending data modeling to cover the whole enterprise. *Communications of the ACM, 35*(9), 166–172. doi:10.1145/130994.131007

Scheer, A.-W., & Nüttgens, M. (2000). ARIS architecture and reference models for business process management. In W. v. d. Aalst, J. Desel & A. Oberweis (Eds.), *Business process management - Models, techniques, and empirical studies* (pp. 376-389). Berlin, Germany: Springer.

Schuette, R., & Rotthowe, T. (1998). The guidelines of modeling - An approach to enhance the quality in information models. In T. W. Ling, S. Ram & M. L. Lee (Eds.), *Conceptual modeling - ER '98 - 17th International Conference on Conceptual Modeling, Singapore, November 16-19, 1998, Proceedings* (pp. 240-254). Berlin, Germany: Springer.

Schütte, R. (1998). *Grundsätze ordnungsmäßiger Referenzmodellierung - Konstruktion konfigurations- und anpassungsorientierter Modelle.* Wiesbaden, Germany: Gabler.

Schütte, R. (1999). Architectures for evaluating the quality of information models - A meta and object level comparison. In J. Akoka, M. Bouzeghoub, I. Comyn-Wattiau & E. Métais (Eds.), *Conceptual modeling - ER '99 - 18th International Conference on Conceptual Modeling, Paris, France, November 15-18, 1999 Proceedings* (pp. 490-505). Berlin, Germany: Springer.

Schütte, R., & Zelewski, S. (2001). *Epistemological problems in working with ontologies.* Essen, Germany: Universität Essen, Institut für Produktion und Industrielles Informationsmanagement.

Shanks, G., Tansley, E., & Weber, R. (2003). Using ontology to validate conceptual models. *Communications of the ACM, 46*(10), 85–89. doi:10.1145/944217.944244

Van Belle, J.-P., & Price, B. (2000). A proposed framework for evaluating generic enterprise models. *South African Computer Journal, 26*, 69–76.

Van Belle, J.-P. W. G. D. (2003). *A framework for the analysis and evaluation of enterprise models.* Thesis Submitted for the Degree of Doctor of Philosophy, University of Cape Town, Cape Town, South Africa.

Wand, Y., Storey, V. C., & Weber, R. (1999). An ontological analysis of the relationship construct in conceptual modeling. *ACM Transactions on Database Systems, 24*(4), 494–528. doi:10.1145/331983.331989

Wand, Y., & Weber, R. (1989). An ontological evaluation of systems analysis and design methods . In Falkenberg, E. D., & Lindgreen, P. (Eds.), *Information systems concepts: An in-depth analysis* (pp. 79–107). North-Holland, Elsevier Science Publishers.

Wand, Y., & Weber, R. (1990). An ontological model of an information system. *IEEE Transactions on Software Engineering, 16*(11), 1282–1292. doi:10.1109/32.60316

Wand, Y., & Weber, R. (1993). On the ontological expressiveness of information systems analysis and design grammars. *Journal of Information Systems, 3*(4), 217–237. doi:10.1111/j.1365-2575.1993.tb00127.x

Wand, Y., & Weber, R. (1995). On the deep structure of information systems. *Information Systems Journal, 5*, 203–223. doi:10.1111/j.1365-2575.1995.tb00108.x

Wand, Y., & Weber, R. (2002). Research commentary: Information systems and conceptual modeling - A research agenda. *Information Systems Research*, *13*(4), 363–377. doi:10.1287/isre.13.4.363.69

Weber, R. (1996). Are attributes entities? A study of database designer's memory structures. *Information Systems Research*, *7*(2), 137–162. doi:10.1287/isre.7.2.137

Weber, R. (1997). *Ontological foundations of information systems*. Melbourne, Australia: Coopers & Lybrand.

Weber, R., & Zhang, Y. (1991, December 16-18). *An ontological evaluation of NIAM's grammar for conceptual schema diagrams*. Paper presented at the International Conference on Information Systems, New York, NY, USA.

Section 2
Data and Knowledge Management

Chapter 4

Heterogeneous Text and Numerical Data Mining with Possible Applications in Business and Financial Sectors

Farid Bourennani
University of Ontario Institute of Technology, Canada

Shahryar Rahnamayan
University of Ontario Institute of Technology, Canada

ABSTRACT

Nowadays, many world-wide universities, research centers, and companies share their own data electronically. Naturally, these data are from heterogeneous types such as text, numerical data, multimedia, and others. From user side, this data should be accessed in a uniform manner, which implies a unified approach for representing and processing data. Furthermore, unified processing of the heterogeneous data types can lead to richer semantic results. In this chapter, we present a unified pre-processing approach that leads to generation of richer semantics of qualitative and quantitative data.

INTRODUCTION

There is much interest from the industry in Heterogeneous Data Mining (HDM). This interest seems to be proportional to the heterogeneity level of the data, i.e., the more heterogeneous the data types are, the greater interest is in automatic data processing. This interest is likely due to the availability and abundance of data which potentially offers richer information when they are combined. However, especially due to Internet expansion, information access is virtually unlimited. Therefore, the amount of available data can exceed human data processing capacity in a reasonable

DOI: 10.4018/978-1-60960-126-3.ch004

time. That is why there is much interest in *automatic* extracting of richer patterns and coincident classification and clustering, of the combined heterogeneous data types. For example, business intelligence sectors and financial institutions are extremely eager to extract coincident clustering results from textual (e.g., business reports) and numerical (especially financial) data based on the content (Bourennani et al., 2009). In a similar manner, many other sectors are attracted by the HDM with the intent of extracting richer patterns from the processing of two or even more combined data types. In brief, the HDM is of importance in many industrial fields. However, it is complex to extract coincident classification results based on the content of heterogeneous data types, likely because of the difficulty of combining the results (Bourennani et al., 2009b). The problem is that, most of the times, non-overlapping research communities work on mining *homogeneous* data types. Therefore, these dissimilar data types are usually pre-processed or represented using completely different techniques. Nevertheless, from a user point of view, these heterogeneous data types should behave and reflect information in a similar way. To respond to this need, several research groups have been working, in the last couple of years, to solve this challenging HDM problem.

In this chapter, different perspectives for mining heterogeneous data types are reviewed. Particularly, by focusing on the pre-processing phase, it is shown how similar representations of heterogeneous data types generate more convergent clustering results (Bourennani et al., 2009c). Self-Organizing Maps are used as clustering methods in our experiments.

LITTERATURE REVIEW ON HETEROGENEOUS DATA TYPES MINING

Based on our best knowledge, Back et al.. (2001) were the first researchers to start working on the HDM in 2001. Their project focused on the

HDM of texts and numerical data for benchmarking activities. The same researchers worked on the HDM for financial and business report data (Ecklund et al., 2001), (Kloptchenko et al., 2004), (Magnussona et al., 2005). The reason for using data mining in those kinds of projects is that the tremendous amount of available financial data simply exceeds the interest of the managers and investors to analyze the data (Adriaans and Zantinge, 1996). Furthermore, "the purpose of benchmarking is to compare the activities of one company to those of another, using quantitative or qualitative measures, in order to discover ways in which effectiveness could be increased" (Ecklund et al., 2001). In these works, the qualitative data are actually from the companies' respective CEOs reports, Business reports depending on the project. The quantitative data are nine financial ratios, namely, Return on Total Assets (ROTA), Return on Equity (ROE), and others. The number of companies was from 3 to 76 depending on the projects. The Self-Organizing Map (SOM) which is an unsupervised clustering algorithm was used for processing the heterogeneous data types. The selection of SOM is judicious because it permits the clustering of the data without knowing the expected number of clusters prior to the data mining operations. In addition, the SOM's trained map facilitates the visual exploration of the clusters and the data relationships. The SOM was successfully applied to purely quantitative data (homogenous data) (Back et al., 2001); however, the clustering results were *divergent* when SOM was applied to heterogeneous textual and numerical data. A couple of inappropriate configurations contributed to divergent clustering results.

Firstly in these works, the heterogeneous textual and numerical data types were mined separately using SOM, then they were combined (their respective heterogeneous trained maps) to form a unified map which was divergent. Actually, matching of the SOM maps is very complex because even with the same input data, the results can be different after every training. It would be more appropriated, in our opinion, to process the heterogeneous data types *simultaneously* by using, for example, Unified Vectorization (UV) (Bourennani et al., 2009), as an alternative solution. Also, other reasons are mentioned for those divergent clustering results such as the CEOs tendency to exaggerate the performances in the text reports when compared to the financial quantitative values of the company. Certainly, these reasons can be secondary factors that cause divergence in the clustering results; however, the separate processing of heterogeneous data types seems to be the main reason for the divergence because these works used other text documents such as quarterly reports which also lead to divergency.

In another work (Fung et al., 2002), a regression analysis of financial data is used to detect price trends while Support Vector Machine (SVM) analysis of text-based news articles is used for performing a binary classification in two predefined classes: stock price rise and drop. Basically, they use several algorithms to train their system based on historical numerical and textual data. In fact, they tried to associate historical text news information with their correspondent stock price trends. Once their system is trained, they try to predict stock price variation based on purely textual data which were news. In the cases where conflicting classification results, i.e., rise and drop were determined to be positive, the system did not provide any recommendation. By having used 350,000 financial news articles, and having simulated a Buy-Hold stratagem based upon their SVM classification results, they showed that their SVM classification approach was *mildly* profitable.

Qui and et al.. (Qiu et al., 2007) worked also on the HDM for assessing companies' financial prospects based on annual reports and financial data. They used SVM-based predictive models by feature selecting methods from ten years annual reports of 30 companies. Each company had 10 consecutive years of data ranging between 1990 and 2003. They explored the use of textual content from annual reports combined with financial per-

formance (numerical) such as Return On Equity (ROE) ratio to predict the company's financial performance in the following year. Each industry had on average about 100 documents for one fold of training and testing the models, while each year had only on average about 20 documents for training and testing of one fold. The results were not adequate for long term assessment; however, they achieved an accuracy of 52-58% depending on the sector of activity for short term previsions. Nevertheless, it remains that the main target of these researches is to attain proper *long term* predictions because that is the main use of these financial reports for investors.

In other works (Shumaker & Chen, 2009); (Shumaker & Chen, 2009b), a learning approach was used for the HDM of financial news articles and stock market prices. They investigated 9,211 financial news articles and 10,259,042 stock quotes covering the S&P 500 stocks during a five-week period. Different machine learning techniques were used, such as, Genetic Algorithm, Naive Baise, and SVM for analyzing several different textual representations. In fact, the research focused on estimating a discrete stock price twenty minutes after a news article was released. The system speculates on the stock price movement and predicts the prices as well. The results show that using both article terms and the stock price at the time of article release, had a dominating performance in all three metrics; measures of Closeness at 0.04261, Directional Accuracy at 57.1% and Simulated Trading at a 2.06% return. This work is a valuable contribution to the HDM applied to investments; however, the results are speculative because the forecasts are only 20 minutes into the future which is a very short period.

Heterogeneous Data Mining by Unified Modeling

All the previously described works were about processing of heterogeneous data types separately. But, some research groups worked on developing unified modeling for heterogeneous data types. It is important to mention that these types of projects did involve training, clustering, or classification as such. Rather, they built more exploratory types of tools as described below.

Cammarano and et al.. (Cammarano et al., 2007) opted for processing heterogeneous data types such as texts, geo-locations, and others together by unifying the modeling. This philosophy of incorporating the heterogeneous data permits users to have a unified visual view of the data. However, opposite to previous works which the data were representing *similar* kinds of information by heterogeneous textual and numerical data types, in this work (Cammarano et al., 2007) the heterogeneous data types represent *complementary* information. Also, the scope of the work is different; it focuses on automatic methods for mapping data attributes (schema matching) to visualization attributes. The Resource Description Framework (RDF) which is used in a semantic web was used for integrating the heterogeneous data types. Several applications were investigated; one of them was the plotting of countries inflation versus GooDs Produced (GDP) per capita. Obviously, there was no data training (learning) process involved in this work; however, the integration of the heterogeneous data types modeling allowed a unified data visualization as an easier way to explore the data.

In a similar manner, another research group (Dua & Mannava, 2005) worked on the development of unified data model for building a search tool. Text and images were combined for searching data in a unified computational framework. The search tool can respond to similarity queries of data mining more accurately and efficiently.

Birkland and Yona (2006) used a graph model to represent heterogeneous data types (DNA sequences, proteins, interactions and cellular pathways). The resulting unified framework spans multiple data types and fuzzy searches could be utilized for many similarity relations.

Heterogeneous Data Mining by Unified Vectorization

In brief, we have reviewed two different approaches for achieving more convergent HDM results. The first approach separates the heterogeneous data types right from the beginning in order to process them separately; then, the data mining results are combined together at the end. The advantage of this approach is that it permits selecting and using of an appropriate machine learning algorithm to every data type for classification or clustering purpose. Also, the same machine learning algorithm could be applied to the heterogeneous data types. The main challenge with this approach is the combination of the heterogeneous data mining results. It is not only complex to combine the heterogeneous classification or clustering results, also, generally speaking, the *unification* of the data is complex after data mining. For example, it is not possible or hard to have a unified visual view of heterogeneous data types. As explained in the beginning of this chapter, from the user point of view, heterogeneous data types should be accessed in the same fashion.

The other approach focuses on the construction of a unified model for the heterogeneous data types which makes it more efficient for providing a unified view of the heterogeneous data types. Consequently, the user is able to access the heterogeneous data types from the same portal in a unified manner. In addition, the user can have a unified visual view of the data, and can perform complex queries over these heterogeneous data types. However, the problem with this approach is that it is purely based on software design which seems to be appropriate for unified architectural modeling but it fails in providing a unified algebraic model. A unified algebraic model serves to train the heterogeneous data types simultaneously as if it was a single data type for a unified clustering result. Therefore, it is still impossible or hard to apply machine learning algorithms to these heterogeneous data types in a unified manner. In this chapter, we propose the use of Heterogeneous Data Mining by Unified Vectorization (HDM-UV) (Bourennani et al., 2009) (Bourennani et al., 2009b) as an alternative solution to the mentioned problems. The proposed HDM-UV permits the construction of a unified algebraic model for processing *simultaneously* heterogeneous data types by a machine learning algorithm. In addition, the heterogeneous data types can be processed faster because the data is processed simultaneously by a same machine learning algorithm. Also, the complex task of combining heterogeneous data mining results is avoided because the data is processed simultaneously. Furthermore, the user can have a unified view of the heterogeneous data types and can perform data exploration in a unified manner or conduct complex data queries.

PROPOSED APPROACH: HETEREGENEOUS DATA MINING USING UNIFIED VECTORIZATION

As a result of the evolution made in hardware technology and networking, never before data has been generated at such high volumes. Nowadays, it is not uncommon to have databases containing terabytes of data. Merging or integrating these repositories can significantly enhance the data richness. However, data analysis of these vast volumes of data for data integration purposes becomes increasingly difficult. For example, discovering similar or semantically equivalent attributes located in different databases is essential toward the definition of data integrity constraints such as Foreign-Key. Due to different business practices, these semantically similar database attributes might have been named differently. Consequently, these attributes very time consuming to detect by the user. In order to preserve high data integrity level of consolidated database, it is important to

identify the equivalent database attributes. Detecting them automatically would be ideal. However, these attributes are of heterogeneous data types such as text, numbers, multimedia, and others. Consequently, a unified approach is required to process them together. In this book chapter, it is described how the heterogeneous data mining (HDM-UV) (Bourennani et al., 2009) (Bourennani et al., 2009b) can solve the challenge of integrating heterogeneous databases composed heterogeneous data types. Furthermore, HDM-UV could be an alternative solution for other applications which require the processing of heterogeneous data types. As a result, the heterogeneous data types could be clustered or classified simultaneously by a same machine learning algorithm, viewed uniformly, and also queried in a unified manner.

Several automatic schema matching techniques have been proposed by researchers to facilitate data integration; some surveys can be found in Ref. (Rahm & Bernstein, 2001) and ref. (Schvaiko & Euzenat, 2007). However, these tools are not fully automated. The developers still need to identify similar or semantically equivalent database attributes over different data sources manually. Due to the basic nature of the problem, it is unavoidable that mistakes will be made in addition to the amount of time required to complete this task. Therefore, an automated tool would be definitely more suitable.

In the following subsections, a visualization approach is proposed to aid end-users to identify automatically the semantically similar data attributes by using the Self Organizing Map (SOM). The same SOM map is used for exploring relationships among data attributes of heterogeneous data types. The algebraic unification of the heterogeneous data types is done by focusing on the pre-processing phase. Therefore, it becomes possible to process heterogeneous data types simultaneously to achieve more convergent clustering results.

PRE-PROCESSING

The pre-processing phase is important; it may even be the most important part of the whole process (Pyle, 1999). In data integration context, the pre-processing phase is necessary because of the large size of the database which contains noisy, missing, and inconsistent data.

There are several pre-processing methods used in data mining, the best-known ones are data cleaning, data integration, data transformation, and data reduction (Han & Kamber, 2006). The data cleaning operations serve to correct the data that may have inconsistencies (discrepancies), incompleteness (e.g. missing values), and noise (errors). The data integration or schema re-consolidation serves to join data from heterogeneous data sources into unique data repositories such as data warehouses. The data transformation improves the data mining results; for example, normalization can be used to prevent features with a large range like "salary" to out-weigh features with smaller ranges like "age". Finally, the data reduction is used to shrink large datasets into smaller ones so that they can be easily processed.

All the pre-processing methods described earlier are used in order to build the SOM-based HDM tool as shown in Figure 1. First, by using the *data cleaning* method, the non-alphanumerical characters are eliminated such as "();.". Furthermore, the short textual terms having less than three characters are eliminated. Second, through the *data transformation* step, the heterogeneous data types are combined using the Unified Vectorization method, and they are normalized using a linear method. Thirdly, the data is reduced using the Random Projection method for the facilitation of the data training process.

Data Representation

In order to implement any clustering technique, the input data is required to be transformed into an algebraic model, so then it can be processed. The standard practice in information retrieval is to represent input documents as vectors in t-dimensional Euclidean space where every dimension corresponds to a word (term) of the vocabulary (Salton, 1989). As a main problem, it is hard to obtain accurate semantic relatedness automatically from textual information only (Lagus, 2000). Therefore, HDM-UV is used for processing textual and numerical data considered from different database entities. In other words, the input documents are from relational database entities. Hence, every document is a column which is extracted from a relational database table. In some literature, the term *field* is used to refer to a column. To illustrate how the input documents are obtained, consider the following example. Suppose a table named **student** represents student-related information, and it has the following columns: id, name, dateBirth, *etc.* For the extracted documents, assuming the naming convention filename.dat are: student@id.dat, student@name.dat, student@dateBirth.dat, *etc.*

The database may contain several data types; however, the processing of two heterogeneous data types is already challenging. This work focuses on two heterogeneous data types, namely, textual and numerical data. Let us start with the pre-processing of textual data followed by the numerical data. Then as shown in Figure 2, the two heterogeneous data representations are combined by unified vectorization in order to process them *simultaneously* using the SOM algorithm. The UV unification bypasses the difficult task

Figure 1. Utilized data pre-processing techniques in the proposed approach

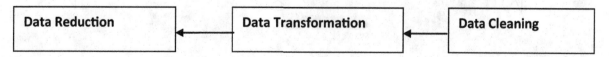

| Data Reduction | ← | Data Transformation | ← | Data Cleaning |

of combining the heterogeneous data processing outputs, and offers the potential to obtain better co-occurring semantic clustering results.

Text Tokenization

The Vector Space Model (VSM) is the most commonly used approach for representing text data (Amine et al., 2008). Every text token is denoted by a numerical vector obtained by counting the most relevant lexical elements. The process of breaking a text up into its constituent tokens is known as tokenization. Let us consider a couple of the text *tokenization* methods.

Bag of Words

The most common tokenization method, within the VSM framework, is the *bag of words* (Amine et al., 2008). The text portions of the document are transformed into vectors where every term is simply a word from the set of terms *T* (Sahami, 1999). This representation offers the advantage of being simple and fast to implement. However, the problem with this tokenization method does not consider the grammatical structure, or etymological analysis of the terms such as between "peace" and "peaceful". The following example illustrates that how *bag of words* works.

Suppose we have a document with the sentence: "Today is a nice day".

There are five extracted tokens: "today", "is", "a", "nice", and "day".

It is important to mention that all the tokens are lower cased in order to avoid duplicating the same term because of capital letters.

N-Grams

Another popular text tokenization method used by text search engines is the N-grams. The N-grams are a substring or a window of *N* consecutive characters along a text word. N-gram offers several advantages; it is an easy and fast way to solve syntax related issues such as misspelling. In addition, it finds common patterns between words having the same root but different morphological forms (e.g., peace and peaceful) without treating them as equal which happens with word stemming (Sebastiani, 2002). Let us illustrate the use of N-grams through an example.

Suppose that we have a document with the following text portion: "Stable economy".

Let us tokenize this portion into 3-grams: Sta, tab, abl, ble, eco, con, ono, nom, omy.

After alphabetical ordering, it gives abl, ble, con, eco, nom, omy, ono, sta, tab.

Figure 2. The proposed chain of pre-processing steps

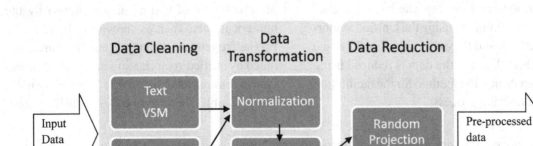

Assume now another phrase portion: "stability in the economy"

After 3-gram tokenization, we get these tokens: sta, tab, abi, bil, ili, lit, ity, the, eco, con, ono, nom, omy.

After reorganizing alphabetically, we get abi, bil, con, eco, ili, ity, lit, nom, omy, ono, sta, tab, the.

When the 3-gram tokenizations of the two sentences are compared, it can be found there are 7 common tokens (highlighted in bold below). The number of common terms reflects the similar content between the two different phrases. In addition, the algorithm is easy to implement. Furthermore, it is faster than stemming, which uses words etymologies, that is why it is less demanding on machine processing resources.

Stable economy: abl, ble, **con, eco, nom, omy, ono, sta, tab**

Stability in the economy: abi, bil, **con, eco,** ili, ity, lit, **nom, omy, ono, sta, tab,** the

Vectorization of the Textual Data

After determining the terms (tokens) of the corpus through different tokenization methods described earlier, their respective weights need to be vectorized in order to construct the VSM matrix as shown in Table 1. All the text data portions of the columns (documents) d_i are transformed into a vector as follows:

$$d_i = (w_{j1}, w_{j2}, ..., w_{jn}).$$

where n is the number of terms in the whole set of terms (or descriptors) T, and w_{kj} represents the weight of the term t_k in the document d_j.

Finally, the VSM matrix, also called document-term matrix, is built by putting together all the document vectors as shown in Table 1.

Table 1. VSM matrix for the textual data

Documents	Terms $t_1 t_2 ... t_n$
d_1	$w_{11} w_{12} ... w_{1n}$
d_2	$w_{21} w_{22} ... w_{2n}$
$\vdots$ d_m	$w_{m1} w_{m2} ... w_{mn}$

Term Frequency-Inverse Document Frequency (TF-IDF) Weighting

Most textual vectorization approaches (Eklund et al., 2002) are based on a vectorial representation of texts using the Term Frequency - Inverse Document Frequency (TF-IDF) measure. The TF-IDF function weights each vector component which represents a vocabulary token in a document as follows:

$$\text{TF IDF}(t_k, d_j) = \frac{Freq(t_k, d_j)}{\sum_k Freq(t_k, d_j)} \times Log \frac{N_{doc}}{N_{doc}(t_k)} \geq 0$$

(1)

where $Freq(t_k, d_j)$ denotes the number of times the term t_k occurs in the document (column) d_j, $\sum_k Freq(t_k, d_j)$ denotes the total occurrences of all the terms in the same document d_j, and N_{doc} is the total number of documents in the corpus, while $N_{doc}(t_k)$ is the number of documents in the corpus with the term t_k.

Let us decorticate the TF-IDF because we will need that in the following subsections. The Term Frequency (TF) gives a measure of the importance of the term t_k within a particular document d_j. Thus, the more a word appears in a document, the higher is its TF score because it is considered to be more significant in this document. The term frequency is defined as follows:

$$\text{TF IDF}(t_k, d_j) = \frac{Freq(t_k, d_j)}{\sum_k Freq(t_k, d_j)} \leq 1$$

Suppose that we have a document d_l which contains 30 words. Among these words, the word "computer" is repeated 4 times. Therefore, its TF is calculated as follows:

TF ("computer", d_1) = 4/30 = 0.13.

The inverse document frequency (IDF) serves for the calculation of the term importance in the *corpus*. Accordingly, if a word is highly frequent in the text collection, it is not considered to be particularly representative of a document because it has been occurred in most or a high number of documents. For instance, stop words such as "the, a, an" usually will receive very low scores. In contrast, if a word is rare in the text collection, it is believed to be very relevant in the host document. Therefore, the second portion of the formulas is:

$$IDF(t_k, d_j) = Log \frac{N_{doc}}{N_{doc}(t_k)}.$$

The 'log' in this formula has a smoothing effect. Let us consider an example with collection of 1000 documents in order to illustrate the IDF calculation and the use of the *log* function.

Example: In order to illustrate the TF-IDF calculation and the smoothing effect of the *log* function, suppose that one of the documents has 4 words, where one of these terms is repeated twice. For example, the document contains this sentence: "Very very nice weather". To compare the results, the TF-IDF is calculated using the *log* function and without using that is shown in the Table 2.

This example shows that how the *log* function avoids the rarity of a word in a document to outweigh the VSM matrix. In the first scenario, the TF-IDF passes from 500 to 1.5. In addition, the example clarifies how the IDF portion for the formulas reflects the rarity of token in the corpus.

Numerical Data Representation

Because of the different nature of numerical data, its pre-processing is done differently from text data. As an illustration of this dissimilarity, suppose we have two numbers 1978 and 1981, representing years of birth or financial values, in two different documents. Their similarity will not be detected by using either "bag of words" nor N-gram representations because they do not possess enough text similarities. That is why it is necessary to pre-process numeric input data differently so it becomes easier to detect semantic similarities among the numerical tokens.

Several data methods can be used to specify concept hierarchies for numerical attributes such as binning, histogram analysis, entropy-based discretization, Z2-merging, cluster analysis, and discretization by intuitive partitioning (Han & Kamber, 2006). In some financial related research projects, pre-processing for SOM was done using histogram equalization, a method for mapping rare events to a small part of the data range, and spreading out frequent events (Kloptchenko et al., 2004). Other Business Intelligence projects, similar to our work, tried to process heterogeneous textual (qualitative) and numerical (quantitative)

Table 2. Examples of TF-IDF calculation

Scenarios	TF-IDF with *log*	TF-IDF without *log*
Out of 1000, there is 1 document only with the word "very".	(2/4) * *log* (1000 / 1) = 0.5 * 3 = 1.5	(2/4) * (1000 / 1) = 0.5 * 1000 = 500
Out of 1000, there are 100 documents with the word "very".	(2/4) * *log* (1000 / 100) = 0.5 * 1 = 0.5	(2/4) * (1000 / 100) = 0.5*10 =5

data, but the results were divergent (Back et al., 2001), (Wang, 2003). In the first work (Back et al., 2001), histograms were utilized to pre-process text data. In the second one (Wang, 2003), they standardized the numerical data by scaling the variables according to the variance. In our proposed approach, also histograms are used for representing numerical data.

Using Histograms for Numerical Data

In this work, histograms are used to ease the SOM neural network's learning process and to improve the quality of the SOM's map. Histogram is an unsupervised discretization technique, because it does not use class information. It partitions the numerical values of a document d_j from the corpus into disjoint ranges called buckets or bins.

In particular, the *Equal-Frequency (Equal-Depth)* histogram is used in the current work because of its good scaling properties and simplicity in implementation. The values are partitioned so that, ideally, each partition contains identical number of tuples (Han & Kamber, 2006). Another benefit for using the histogram is that it reduces the dimensionality of the VSM at least by s times, where s is the size of the bin. However this being said, the size of the bins can be bigger than s in order to avoid cutting a cluster of the same value. For example, if a number x is repeated 200 times in the corpus, then exceptionally the size of the bin to whom x belongs will have a size of at least 200.

The equal-depth histograms are built by extracting all numerical tokens n_i from the document d_j and transforming them into a vector as follows:

Table 3. Numerical portion of the VSM matrix

Documents	Bins $b_1 \ b_2 \dots b_n$		
d_1	v_{11}	$v_{12} \dots$	v_{1l}
d_2	v_{21}	$v_{22} \dots$	v_{12}
...	....		
d_m	v_{m1}	$v_{m2} \dots$	v_{mk}

$$n_i = (v_{1j}, v_{2j}, \dots, v_{|N|j})$$

where N is the total number of histogram bins, and v_{lj} represents the number of observations that fall into disjoint bin b_l.

Finally, the VSM matrix for the numeric data is built by putting together all the document vectors n_i as illustrated in the Table 3.

Example: Let us assume that we have the following group of numbers in the corpus which are ordered: 0.5, 1, 5, 7, 9, 17, 2000, 3500, 3500, 50000. Suppose the histogram's bin size is 4.

$b_1 = \{0.5, 1, 5, 7\}$

$b_2 = \{9, 17, 2000, 3500, 3500\} \rightarrow$ This bin has 5 numbers in order to not cutting the cluster and separating the number 3500 into two different buckets.

$b_3 = \{50000\}$

Combination of Textual and Numerical Mining by Unified Vectorization

Now, we have the numerical and the text VSM matrixes constructed, we propose the use of the Unified Vectorization (UV) method for combining the numerical and textual data in order to process them simultaneously. This combination permits to meet the challenge of extracting more convergent data mining results from these heterogeneous data types (Bourennani et al., 2009c). The two VSMs are combined together as shown in Table 4.

Normalization

Before processing the combined heterogeneous text and numeric data types, the data should be normalized in order to avoid an unjustified outweighing of one of the two data types over the other during the SOM training phase.

There are many methods for data normalization; the most commonly used in data mining are Min-Max normalization, Z-Score normalization,

Table 4. Unified vectorization of textual and numerical data

Docucments	Terms $t_1 \, t_2 \, \cdots \, t_n$	Bins $b_1 \, b_2 \, \cdots \, b_n$
d_1 d_2	$w_{11} \, w_{12} \ldots w_{1n}$ $w_{21} \, w_{22} \ldots w_{2n}$	$v_{11} \, v_{12} \ldots v_{l1}$ $v_{21} \, v_{22} \ldots v_{l2}$
... d_m	... ... $w_{m1} \, w_{m2} \ldots w_{mn}$	... ... $v_{m1} \, v_{m2} \ldots v_{mk}$

and normalization by Decimal Scaling (Han & Kamber, 2006). In the literature, a normalization according to a variance, e.g., was applied to pre-process of financial data furing benchmarking by the SOM (Wang, 2003).

In our proposed approach, the Min-Max normalization was applied because of its simplicity and efficiency; a linear transformation of the original input range into a newly specified data range, typically [0, 1].

$$y' = \frac{y - \min}{\max - \min}(\max' - \min') = \min',$$

where the old min value is mapped to new *min*: *min'*. The old max is mapped to a new *max*: *max'*. Let *y* be the original value, *y'* be the new value. The min and max are the original *min* and *max* values. The *min'*, *max'* are the new *min* and *max*.

All the values of the unified VSM matrix were normalized similarly in a range of [0, 1] through linear operation described above.

Dimensionality Reduction

In many cases, a *high dimensionality* of the data leads to heavy computations and even restricts the choice of data mining methods. As an example, in text mining context, the high dimensionality is due to having a large vocabulary. Therefore, the data dimension preferably should be reduced by preserving the information for the data mining phase. A statistical optimal dimensionality reduction is the data projection onto a lower-dimensional

orthogonal subspace that captures a maximum data variation.

The most widely used method to reduce data dimensions is the Principal Component Analysis (PCA); it is known to give good results and has a lot of useful properties. However, it is computationally expensive and that is not feasible to apply on a large, high dimensional data (Bingham & Mannila, 2001). Therefore, another method should be selected for this project.

Random Projection

Another powerful method for reducing data dimension is the Random Projection (RP) method which is simple, offers clear computational advantages, and preserves similarity (Bingham & Mannila, 2001). The RP was successfully tested with the SOM algorithm on several applications using textual data and images. RP appears to be a good alternative to traditional methods of dimensionality reduction that are computationally infeasible for high dimensional data, in contrast to RP that does not suffer from the curse of dimensionality. It was shown that RPs work well with the Nearest Neighbor methods, and they also combine well with the SVM.

Another good reason for using the Random Projection with textual application is that it is useful for query matching if the query is long, or if a set of similar documents instead of one particular document were searched for (Kohonen, 1982).

In brief, the RP works as follows: given a matrix X, the dimensionality of the data can be reduced by projecting it through the origin onto a lower-dimensional subspace, formed by a set of random vectors R:

$$A_{[m \times k]} = X_{[m \times k]} \cdot R_{[m \times k]}$$

where the variable k is a desired reduced dimension, X is the original matrix, A is the reduced matrix, and R is the random matrix.

Challenges of Heterogeneous Data Mining by Unified Vectorization

The histogram weighting measure for numerical data types enhanced the clustering results if the HDM-UV of numerical and textual data. However, the results were not as good as desired (Bourennani et al., 2009). The reason is that TF-IDF weighting measure for text data does not have the same meaning and representation as the histogram measure for numerical data. More precisely, the histogram measure does not reflect the weight of a numerical term (token) within the corpus as the IDF portion of the TF-IDF does. Therefore, this shows how important can be the impact of the pre-processing phase on the final clustering or classification results. Consequently, when the Unified Vectorization is used for processing heterogeneous data types, their respective vectorization measures or weights should represent the same kind of information. Consequently, another measure similar to TF-IDF is proposed for numerical data types; it is called Bin Frequency – Inverse Document Bin Frequency (BF-IDBF) (Bourennani et al., 2009) (Bourennani et al., 2009b). Let us examine the new measure which is based on both histograms and TF-IDF measures. Furthermore, similar to the TF-IDF measure, the BF-IDBF measure is a combination of the BF and the IDBF measures as illustrated bellow.

Bin Frequency (BF) Measure

The BF is calculated in a similar way as the TF measure; it serves to estimate the importance of a

bin, rather than the importance of a number, in a document d_j. In other words, both measures - the histogram and the TF - are combined together to form the BF measure. The BF is estimated as follows:

$$BF(b_l, d_j) = \frac{Freq(b_l, d_j)}{\sum_k Freq(b_l, d_j)} \qquad (2)$$

where $Freq(b_l, d_j)$ denotes the number of times the bin b_l occurs in the document (column) d_j, while $\Sigma_k Freq(b_l, d_j)$ is the total number of all the bin occurrences in the same document d_j

Other variances of histograms could be used as well to form the BF-IDBF measure; however, because of obtained satisfactory results in ref. (Bourennani et al., 2009b), the "equal depth" histogram was kept for the current project.

Inverse Bin Document Frequency (IDBF) Measure

After calculating the BF, the following step is taken to calculate the IDBF weight which mainly serves to reduce the weight of the bins which is insignificant in the corpus. In other words, if a number or certain range of numbers is common to a large number of documents, the weight is decreased in order to reflect the insignificance of these numbers in their respective documents. The IDBF is calculated through a similar formula to IDF as follows:

$$IDBF(b_l, d_j) = Log \frac{N_{doc}}{N_{doc}(b_l)},$$

where N_{doc} is the total number of documents in the corpus, while $N_{doc}(b_l)$ is the number of documents in the corpus with bin b_l.

Combination of the BF and the IDBF

Finally, the BF-IDBF is calculated by multiplying the two measures BF and IDBF. Therefore, the global formula, as recapitulated in the Table 5, is as follows.

$$\text{BF IDBF}(b_l, d_j) = \frac{Freq(b_l, d_j)}{\sum_k Freq(b_l, d_j)} \times Log \frac{N_{doc}}{N_{doc}(b_l)},$$

As explained previously when illustrating the usage of TF-IDF, the log serves to smooth the results.

Example: Suppose there is a series of numbers, which have been ordered, in a corpus C: 0.5, 1, 5, 7, 9, 17, 2000, 3500, 3500, 50000…

Let us have a bin size of 4 for this example.

$b_1 = \{0.5, 1, 5, 7\}$, $b_2 = \{9, 17, 2000, 3500, 3500\}$, $b_3 = \{50000,…\}$,…, b_n.

In this example, b_2 has 5 elements in order to keep the number 3500 in the same bin (same cluster).

Assume that the document d_1 contains 15 numbers which are distributed among 9 bins. Among these 15 numbers, there are these three $\{0.5, 1, 5\}$.

Suppose that in a corpus of 1000 documents, there are two documents each of which contains one instance of the number 7. In other words,

the bin b_1 can be found in only three documents: d_1, d_2, d_3.

$C = d_1, …, d_{1000}$

$\{9, 17, 2000\} \in d_1$

$\{3500\} \in d_2$

$\{3500\} \in d_3$

Therefore; the BF-IDBF of the bin b_2 in the document d_1 is calculated as follows:

$$\text{BI-IDBF }(d_1, b_2) = (3/9) * log (1000/3) = 0.33*2.52 = 0.84$$

DATA MINING

Unsupervised classification or clustering is one of the fundamental data mining techniques. Furthermore, Self Organizing Map (SOM) (Kohonen, 2001), (Lin, 1997) is an unsupervised learning neural network that produces a topologically clustering map on a plane (2D). In this chapter, the unsupervised clustering property of SOM serves to classify completely unfamiliar databases entities for automated schema matching operations. In essence, despite the unknown databases schemas,

Table 5. Comparison of TF-IDF and BF-IDBF measures

TF-IDF	BF-IDBF
$TF(t_k, d_j) = \dfrac{Freq(t_k, d_j)}{\sum_k Freq(t_k, d_j)}$	$BF(b_l, d_j) = \dfrac{Freq(b_l, d_j)}{\sum_k Freq(b_l, d_j)}$
$IDF(t_k, d_j) = Log \dfrac{N_{doc}}{N_{doc}(t_k)}$	$IDBF(b_l, d_j) = Log \dfrac{N_{doc}}{N_{doc}(b_l)}$
$TF\text{-}IDF(t_k, d_j) = \dfrac{Freq(t_k, d_j)}{\sum_k Freq(t_k, d_j)} \times Log \dfrac{N_{doc}}{N_{doc}(t_k)}$	$BF\text{-}IDBF(b_l, d_j) = \dfrac{Freq(b_l, d_j)}{\sum_k Freq(b_l, d_j)} \times Log \dfrac{N_{doc}}{N_{doc}(b_l)},$

the different database respective technologies, and the dissimilar naming standards (e.g., client vs. customer), it is expected that SOM determines similar database entities based on their semantic content.

Self Organizing Map

The most remarkable SOM capability is that it produces a mapping of high-dimensional input space on to a low-dimensional (usually 2-D) map, where the similar input data can be found on nearby regions of the map. Furthermore, SOM offers all the advantages of visual display for information retrieval listed below (Baeza-Yates & Ribeiro-Neto, 1999).

- The ability to convey a large amount of information in a limited space.
- The facilitation of browsing and the perceptual inferences on retrieval interfaces.
- The potential to reveal semantic relationship of terms and documents.

These SOM qualities facilitate the user to explore a huge amount of database entities, and discover similar columns based on their semantical content, which is practically impossible by traditional ontology based integration tools.

SOM-Based Visualization

A simple way to visualize the clustered database's columns is to match every column d_j to its respective Best Matching Unit (BMU) node (Lin, 1997) on the trained SOM's map. This will result in having semantically similar documents grouped on the same Map's node. In addition, the topological distribution of clusters on the map will reflect their semantical content-based similarities. The closer the nodes are on the map, the stronger is their semantical similarity. Figure 3 illustrates a resulted trained map.

In addition, the graphical interface can offer several visual options. It is possible to zoom the map, enlarge it, flip it, and rotate it. Every node groups semantically similar documents (database entities) which facilitates the database user to detect similar database entities very easily.

Experimental Verifications

The main objective of these experiments, taken from (Bourennani et al., 2009b), is to demonstrate the impact of the different proposed methods, such as, the UV, and the BF-IDBF measure on the heterogeneous data mining. We use the SOM-based clustering. In order to measure clustering performance, F-measure is used. It is calculated with respect to the known classes for each document, and it is based on Precision and Recall weights (Baeza-Yates & Ribeiro-Neto, 1999). Every class is the expected clustering result. The tests are run by using the Northila database, which is a combination of two available online, namely, Northwind and Sakila.

The Table 6 shows the composition of the Northila database. Roughly, ¾ of the database are numerical tokens, while ¼ are textual tokens. The Table 7 presents the number of Northila database classes, which are the expected clusters. It can be observed that the majority of the classes, as well as the majority of files (columns), are numerical data type.

In order to measure the contribution of the BF-IDBF weight and the UV to the data mining results, the F-measure is used.

Precision assesses the predictive power of the algorithm by estimating the ratio of the true positives among the cluster.

$$P = Precision\ (i,\ j) = N_{ij}\ /\ N_j \qquad (3)$$

= number of relevant items retrieved / number of items retrieved

Figure 3. Trained SOM Map

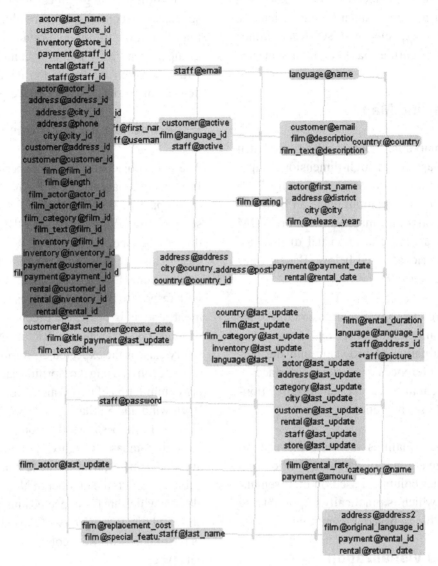

where N_{ij} represents the number of true positives, and N_j is the number of members in the cluster j.

Recall is a function of its correctly classified examples (true positives) and its misclassified examples (false negatives).

$$R = \text{Recall}(i, j) = N_{ij} / N_i \qquad (4)$$

= number of relevant items retrieved / *nb relevant* collection items

where N_{ij} represents the number of true positives, and N_i is the number of elements belonging to the class *i*.

F-measure distinguishes the correct clustering of documents within different classes. In essence, it assesses the effectiveness of the algorithm on a single class, and the higher it is, the better is the clustering. it is defined as follows:

$$F(i) = 2PR / P + R$$

Table 6. The Northila database

Data Set	Columns	Terms (tokens)	Textual tokens	Numeric tokens	Classes
Northila	165	26785	7086	19699	34

Table 7. The Northila database's entities

Types	Textual	Numerical	Alphanumerical	Unclassed	Total
Classes	11	20	2	1	34
Columns	40	94	9	22	165

As shown in Table 8, the highest precision measure, when using SOM, is with the proposed combination of BF-IDBF and TF-IDF measures by UV. It is interesting to observe that the exclusive processing of numerical files using BF-IDBF results are almost as good as the combination of TF-IDF and BF-IDBF. N-grams tokenization were expected to perform better than "bag of words" tokenization; hence, it is not really the case as recapitulated on Figure 4.

Regarding the Recall measure (Table 9, Figure 5), the best observed performance was with the exclusive usage of TF-IDF or BF-IDBF vectorizations. However, the TF-IDF's precision measure performed poorly, that is why the F-measure is a more objective way for evaluating the performance of a clustering algorithm. In other words, the F-measure takes into account the recall and precision measures at the same time, that is why is a more objective performance measure.

As shown in Table 10, the best overall performance is achieved by the combination of the TF-IDF and the BF-IDBF measures, and the exclusive use of the BF-IDBF. However, it is unexpected to see the performance of the exclusive use of the BF-IDBF that high. To some extent, it can be explained by the fact that the majority of the classes and the files are of numerical data type. Therefore, it is normal to see a numerical vectorization measure to have the highest score. The problem is that when the BF-IDBF is combined with TF-IDF, the scores should be higher than the exclusive usage of BF-IDBF. A reason for the higher performance of the BF-IDBF over the combination of TF-IDF and BF-IDBF is that when only BF-IDBF is used for vectorization measure, all the text documents are assigned a vector of zeros, because there are no numerical data inside. In other words, all the text documents are *attracted* to one cluster which could decrease the

Table 8. Precision measures

	TF-IDF	TF-IDF&Histo	TF-IDF & BF-IDBF	Histogram	BF-IDBF
Bag of words	31.01	38.05	49.97		
3-Gram	32.25	35.68	46.83		
4-Gram	29.63	39.15	46.70		
5-Gram	31.62	37.15	48.09		
Numeric				38.19	48.37

Figure 4. Precision measures

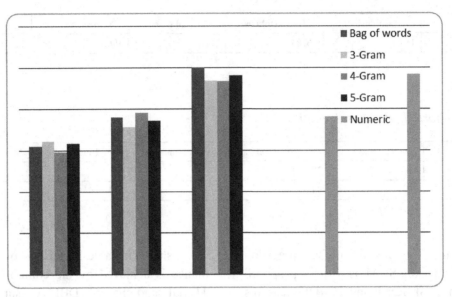

clustering results to a certain degree because the number of text files is smaller. However, this last explanation does not justify everything. Another hypothesis is that the linear normalization is not the most suitable one for the HDM-UV. Consequently, the future research should focus on improving the normalization operations when combining together the VSMs of heterogeneous data types. The normalization operation is very important because the VSMs are normalized three times. The first time, the VSM is normalized before the dimension reduction. Then, the VSM is re-normalized after the dimension reduction. Finally, when the different VSMs, in our case two,

are combined, they are re-normalized for the last time before being sent to the processing phase.

Moreover, it can be observed that (see Figure 6) the BF-IDBF seems to work better than the histogram. It is not the purpose of this research to process purely numerical data; however, it is an interesting observation that should be investigated in the future. It should be reminded that the size of the buckets in our experiments is set to 10 because we found that this size gives the best results. However, we did not do extensive tests to find the optimal bucket size because it is not the real scope of the current book chapter.

Table 9. Recall measure

	TF-IDF	TFIDF+Histogram	TFIDF+BFIDBF	Histogram	BFIDBF
Bag of words	84.77	65.40	77.78	-	-
3-Gram	84.98	69.14	73.21	-	-
4-Gram	84.57	69.93	72.63	-	-
5-Gram	84.57	69.83	72.31	-	-
Numeric				70.37	84.98

Figure 5. Recall measures

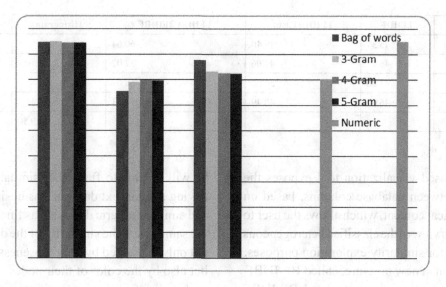

Figure 6. F-Measure

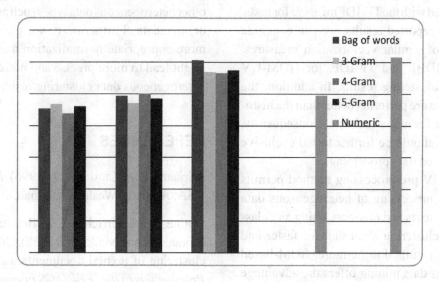

CONCLUSION

In this chapter, different methodologies for processing heterogeneous data types were reviewed specially textual and numerical data types. Furthermore, we have presented the Heterogeneous Data Mining by Unified Vectorization (HDM-UV). The Unified Vectorization permits the simultaneous processing of heterogeneous data types which

is faster than processing the data in sequence by data types, and also it is simpler than combining the data mining results. Furthermore, the user can have a unified view of the heterogeneous data types which are organized based on the semantic similarities. Self Organizing Map was used for data mining. It appeared to be an efficient way to integrate automatically unfamiliar heterogeneous textual and numerical database entities.

Table 10. F-measure

	TF-IDF	TFIDF+Histo	TFIDF+BFIDBF	Histogram	BFIDBF
Bag of words	45.39	49.40	60.64		
3-Gram	46.75	47.06	57.07		
4-Gram	43.86	50.06	56.67		
5-Gram	46.02	48.49	57.53		
Numeric				49.50	61.64

The SOM-based visualization tool exposes the similarity between database columns, based on their semantical content, which allows the user to have a *unified* view of the classified heterogeneous data entities for similarity exploration purposes.

In addition, a new measure, called BF-IDBF, for numerical data types was presented. BF-IDBF improves the Heterogeneous Data Mining results when combined with the TF-IDF measure for texts. According to reported results, we can conclude that the use of similar vectorization measures, such as BF-IDBF and TF-IDF, for HDM-UV offers better clustering results. In addition, the BF-IDBF measure performs better than the histogram measure for numerical data. Consequently, the BF-IDBF should be further tested exclusive numerical-based data processing.

In brief, UV pre-processing method permits simultaneous processing of heterogeneous data types, such as texts and numbers, using any classification or clustering algorithm for faster and more precise results. Furthermore, SOM-based heterogeneous data mining offers the advantage of presenting a visual semantic map classification of the data which is practical for exploration purposes. HDM-UV is especially interesting for applications with consistent heterogeneous data types such as business applications (financial data are numerical, and business reports are of text type) or medical application (doctor reports are text based, blood work are of numerical type, and x-rays are images). In a business case, the user could be interested to find similar companies to a specific company. By exploring the SOM's map,

he will be able to find other similar companies having similar text data such as business reports and similar numeric data such as financial data at the same time. The similarity of the documents is not only expressed by their closeness on the map but also by the color of their nodes.

In our future work, we aim to apply the proposed pre-processing approach for processing of other heterogeneous data types such as multimedia or metadata. Furthermore, we plan to explore more appropriate normalization methods which might lead to more precise and more convergent heterogeneous data clustering results.

REFERENCES

Adriaans, P., & Zantinge, D. (1996). *Data mining*. USA: Addison-Wesley Longman.

Amine, A., Elberrichi, Z., & Bellatreche, L. Si-Monet, M., and Malki, M. (2008). Concept-based clustering of textual documents using SOM. In *Proceedings of the IEEE/ACS International Conference on Computer Systems and Applications*, Doha, Quatar.

Back, B., Toivonen, J., Vanharanta, H., & Visa, A. (2001). Comparing numerical data and text information from annual reports using self-organizing maps. *International Journal of Accounting Information Systems, 2*(4), 249–269. doi:10.1016/S1467-0895(01)00018-5

Baeza-Yates, R., & Ribeiro-Neto, R. (Eds.). (1999). *Modern information retrieval.* Addison Wesley Longman.

Bingham, E., & Mannila, H. (2001). *Random projection in dimensionality reduction: Applications to image and text data.* Seventh ACM SIGKDD International Conference on Knowledge Discovery and Data Mining, San Francisco, USA, (pp. 245-250).

Birkland, A., & Yona, G. (2006). BIOZON: A system for unification, management and analysis of heterogeneous biological data. *BMC Bioinformatics, 7*(1), 70–119. doi:10.1186/1471-2105-7-70

Bourennani, F., Pu, K. Q., & Zhu, Y. (2009). Unified vectorization of numerical and textual data using self-organizing map. *International Journal On Advances in Systems and Measurements, 2*(2&3), 142–155.

Bourennani, F., Pu, K. Q., & Zhu, Y. (2009b). Visual integration tool for heterogeneous data type by unified vectorization. *Proceedings of the 10th IEEE International Conference in Reuse and Integration* (IRI'09), Las Vegas, USA, (pp. 132-137).

Bourennani, F., Pu, K. Q., & Zhu, Y. (2009c). *Visualization and integration of databases using self organizing maps.* International Conference on Advances in Databases, Knowledge, and Data Applications (DBKDA'09), Cancun, Mexico, (pp. 155-160).

Cammarano, M., Dong, X. L., Chan, B., Klingner, J., Talbot, J., Halevy, A., & Hanrahan, P. (2007). Visualization of heterogeneous data. *IEEE Transactions on Visualization and Computer Graphics, 13*(6), 1200–1207. doi:10.1109/TVCG.2007.70617

Dua, S., & Mannava, V. (2005). Towards integrating text and images for multimedia retrieval in heterogeneous data mining. *Multimedia Systems and Applications VIII, LNCS, 6015,* 365–376.

Eklund, T., Back, B., Vanharanta, H., & Visa, A. (2001). *Benchmarking international pulp and paper companies using self-organizing maps. (TUCS Technical Report No 396).* Turku, Finland: Turku Centre for Computer Science.

Eklund, T., Back, B., Vanharanta, H., & Visa, A. (2002). *Assessing the feasibility of self-organizing maps for data mining financial information.* 10th European Conference on Information Systems (ECIS), Gdansk, Poland, (pp. 528-537.)

Fung, G. P., Yu, J. X., & Lam, W. (2002). News sensitive stock trend prediction. In *Proceedings of the 6th Pacific-Asia Conference Advances in Knowledge Discovery and Data Mining,* PAKDD 2002, Taipel, Taiwan.

Han, J., & Kamber, M. (2006). *Data mining: Concepts and techniques* (2nd ed., pp. 72–97). San Francisco, CA: Morgan Kaufmann.

Kloptchenko, A., Eklund, T., Karlsson, J., Back, B., Vanharanta, H., & Visa, A. (2004). Combining data and text mining techniques for analysing financial reports. *Intelligent Systems in Accounting Finance & Management, 12*(1), 29–41. doi:10.1002/isaf.239

Kohonen, T. (1982). Self-organizing formation of topologically correct. *Biological Cybernetics, 43*(1), 59–69. doi:10.1007/BF00337288

Kohonen, T. (2001). *Self-organizing maps.* Berlin, Germany: Springer-Verlag.

Lagus, K. (2000). *Text mining with the WEBSOM.* PhD thesis, Department of Computer Science and Engineering, Helsinki University of Technology.

Lin, X. (1997). Map displays for information retrieval. *Journal of the American Society for Information Science American Society for Information Science, 48*(1), 40–54. doi:10.1002/(SICI)1097-4571(199701)48:1<40::AID-ASI6>3.0.CO;2-1

Magnussona, C., Arppea, A., Eklund, T., & Back, B. (2005). The language of quarterly reports as an indicator of change in the company's financial status. *Information & Management, 42,* 561–574. doi:10.1016/S0378-7206(04)00072-2

Pyle, D. (1999). *Data preparation for data mining.* San Francisco, CA: Morgan Kaufman Publishers.

Qiu, X. Y., Srinivasan, P., & Street, N. (2007). Exploring the forecasting potential of company annual reports. *American Society for Information Science and Technology, 43*(1), 1–15. doi:10.1002/meet.14504301168

Rahm, E., & Bernstein, P. A. (2001). A survey of approaches to automatic schema matching. *The VLDB Journal, 10*(4), 334–350. doi:10.1007/s007780100057

Sahami, M. (1999). *Using machine learning to improve information access.* PhD thesis, Computer Science Department, Stanford University.

Salton, G. (1989). *Automatic text processing.* Addison-Wesley.

Schumaker, R. P., & Chen, H. (2009). Textual analysis of stock market prediction using breaking financial news: The AZFinText system. *ACM Transactions on Information Systems, 27*(2), 12. doi:10.1145/1462198.1462204

Schumaker, R. P., & Chen, H. (2009b). A quantitative stock prediction system based on financial news. *Information Processing & Management, 45*(5), 571–583. doi:10.1016/j.ipm.2009.05.001

Sebastiani, F. (2002). Machine learning in automated text categorization. *ACM Computing Surveys, 34*(1), 1–47. doi:10.1145/505282.505283

Shvaiko, P., & Euzenat, J. (2007). A survey of schema-based matching approaches. *Journal on Data Semantics, 4,* 146–171.

Wang, J. (2003). *Data mining: Opportunities and challenges* (pp. 323–349). Hershey, PA: Idea Group Publishing.

ADDITIONAL READING

Aas, K., & Eikvil, L. (1999). *Text categorization: a survey.* Oslo, Norway: Norwegian Computing Center.

Fradkin, D., & Madigan, D. (2003) *Experiments with Random Projections for Machine Learning.* Ninth ACM SIGKDD International Conference on Knowledge Discovery and Data Mining, Washington, D.C, USA, pp. 517 - 522.

Chapter 5
Semantic Integration of Structured and Unstructured Data in Data Warehousing and Knowledge Management Systems

Liane Haak
University of Oldenburg, Germany

ABSTRACT

Nowadays, increasing information in enterprises demands new ways of searching and connecting the existing information systems. This chapter describes an approach for the integration of structured and unstructured data focusing on the application to Data Warehousing (DW) and Knowledge Management (KM). Semantic integration is used to improve the interoperability between two well-known and established information systems in the business context of nowadays enterprises. The objective is to introduce a semantic solution in the field of Business Intelligence based on ontology integration. The main focus of this chapter is not to provide a complete literature review of all existing approaches or just to point put the motivation for such an approach. In fact, it presents, under consideration of the most important research approaches, a solution for how a Semantic Integration could be technically achieved in this specific application area. After pointing out the motivation, a short introduction to Semantic Integration, the problems and challenges occurring from it, and the application area of Knowledge Management and Data Warehousing are given. Besides the basic ideas of ontologies and ontology integration are introduced. The approach itself starts with a short overview on the determined requirements, followed by a concept for generating an ontology from a Data Warehouse System (DWS) to be finally integrated with Knowledge Management Systems (KMS) ontology. Finally SENAGATOR, an exemplarily system for semantic navigation based on integrated ontologies, is shortly introduced.

DOI: 10.4018/978-1-60960-126-3.ch005

INTRODUCTION AND MOTIVATION

The amount of information and the demand is continuously increasing. Due to this fact, information systems become a critical success factor in today's business. Every year, companies invest a large amount of money in their system landscape and infrastructure to retrieve relevant information supporting their decisions. Numerous information systems, inside and outside the company, offer a huge amount of information. Developments in this area vary, ranging from industry software solutions up to standard software often represented as stand-alone solutions. Some of these solutions offer a high adaptation degree towards the business processes and requirements of the enterprise. One example are ERP systems which are also a kind of integrated Business Information Systems. Nevertheless, most of the existing information systems have a deficit regarding their incapability to collaborate with other information systems, especially cross-company systems. This applies especially for systems with different data types and structures and in particular for those with unstructured data and structured data. The data in these kinds of systems is often partially redundant and inconsistent. Users need to have a consolidated knowledge of all systems that contain possibly relevant information. Because of alteration and permanent technological changes of the IT landscape in today's companies, it is challenging for the user to find the proper and accurate information. Therefore employees need effective and efficient ways to find relevant information. Data structures in heterogeneous information systems pose many challenges achieving this objective.

Two exemplars of heterogeneous information systems are Data Warehouse Systems (DWS) and Knowledge Management Systems (KMS). Resulting from different data sources, and because of unequal data stored in these systems, especially DWS and KMS are often not linked to each other (Dittmer & Gluchowski, 2002; Klesse et al. 2003). The main reason for the gap between such

systems is the different kind of data managed by those systems. There is predominantly structured data in Data Warehouses, which means there is an identifiable regularity within the amount of data and hence a dependency in the data set itself. In contrast, the data in the knowledge base of a Knowledge Management System is mainly unstructured and explicit in documents in different formats (for example *.pdf, *.docx or *.txt). This unstructured data eventually has a manually given structure (like an index or similiar) but not an obviously identifiable dependency inside the data itself. Normally these documents are manually categorized or indexed for better searching, but this is less fine granular then the data structures used in DWS.

In large and medium sized companies, these two different kinds of systems usually exist side by side. Semantic Integration offers new possibilities to get information in context. Generally, an employee must know how to find the relevant information in the both different systems. In this case, the quality of the result is depending on his specific knowledge about the information background and about the domain he is searching in. A main benefit from Semantic Integration is that relevant content could be provided automatically. Ontologies could be used to bridge the gap between these two classes of information systems and their different data sets. Ontologies are widely applied in the area of Knowledge Management Systems but rarely used in the area of Data Warehouse Systems.

The approach introduced in this chapter focuses on Semantic Integration of Knowledge Management Systems and Data Warehouse Systems using ontologies. The objective is to show how Semantic Integration can be used to integrate different data sources under consideration of the context (semantics) to allow an overlapping search in the integrated information. The focus is not restricted to a 'pure' technical solution based on a component or layer integration of two different application architectures, for instance done by middleware technologies, mediators or wrappers. And it is not restricted to schema integration. The approach follows the idea of loose coupling, which allows keeping systems side by side for daily use. They stay in there own implemented way and only semantic linking of the information is used to get the complete information benefit (Hahn et al., 2005). This provides much more benefit for the user. The main idea is to create and use ontologies of each system and later to integrate them to achieve a connection between the two separated systems. Therefore a new method for generating ontologies of the data structure of a Data Warehouse is introduced. In a second step the generated ontology will be integrated with other existing ontologies, here the Knowledge Management System ontology. To find an appropriate way for the integration, a study of several integration forms in theory and of several existing, implemented approaches were necessary (Abels et al., 2005). An implemented system of the finally integrated navigation concept is called "SENAGATOR", which easily illustrates the benefits of this approach.

Background

From the perspective of a technical integration, it is only decisive if a complete integration is targeted, which means that one system is entirely merged into another system or a completely new system is created. It seems reasonable to eliminate redundant functions in both systems. But this procedure often causes unwarrantedly high expenditures, particularly for all active systems. In contrast, a new system, even with partial components, appears often uneconomical for companies. Technologies used in this context are, for example middleware technologies like CORBA, Web Services and other technologies in the field of Enterprise Application Integration (EAI). But this requires often a high resource effort (time and budget) most companies are not willing to invest in times of an unsecure economic growth. The aim of an integrated solution is to find information belonging to the same

context in both systems because initially they are used for different purposes, but only by partly different persons. Focusing on the benefits of an integrated solution, we assume the following:

- Improving the information supply by linking of two isolated decision support systems
- Creating an overview about company-own information inside the information systems by using graphs (which information is available in which system and in which form?)
- Presenting and searching of information forces the companies to a higher investment in work and time than it would be the case for a proper categorization
- Improving navigation and reutilization of information stored in different systems through single point of entry
- Common and wide usage of the data and information also for non-experts
- Retrieving knowledge about the context of the information
- Extending Semantic Integration to other information system in the company in the future

At present, companies spend a lot of time in gaining information (in particular related ones) from diverse data and systems sceneries. An integrated solution has to improve this by offering a search of both data supplies for better decision-making. Besides, Semantic Integration offers the possibility to cover both system classes and opens a row of synergies. This could be, for instance, a common interface which could simplify the usage of these systems for users which are normally not dealing with complex systems like Data Warehouses. This is, besides obtaining of a structure off all company-available information and related a higher degree of transparency, an essential capability of the aimed integration. Alongside, a time reduction will occur if only an integrated system is used for data information exchange and so efficiency of information increases. This, linked with the decrease of the temporal expenditure, leads generally to a reduction of costs which is likewise desirable. Nevertheless it is most important that companies do have more and above all exact context information. But before discussing the problems and challenges in detail, we first of all have to define the term "Semantic Integration", which is essential for this chapter.

Semantic Integration and Subsequent Problems

Research in the integration of heterogeneous information systems is not a new field (Hammer et al., 1995; Beneventano & Bergamaschi, 2004; Miller et al., 2001). As mentioned in the introduction to this section there are mature technologies, for instance in the area of Enterprise Application Integration, which have the objective of performing a technical integration of different sources under consideration of various data formats and interfaces. The following figure 1 shows the main differences between Semantical and pure Technical Integration:

Apart from the technical integration of systems, Semantic Integration has been put in perspective for several years, but it is not common in the filed of business data integration. One reason therefore is the high complexity of performing a Semantic Integration of data. Integrating data in a semantic way needs a modality of interpreting data based on its content. The evolution of Semantic Integration approaches was incited by the development of the so called Semantic Web, introduced by Tim Berners Lee in 1999 …" I have a dream for the Web [in which computers] become capable of analyzing all the data on the Web – the content, links, and transactions between people and computers…." (Berners-Lee & Fischetti, 1999). His "dream" was to link available data sources on the web in a way that computer (e.g., agents) could easily find and access it. The approach introduced in this chapter follows mainly his idea not primary using web sources, but rather using intra-company information systems like Data Warehouses and Knowledge Management Systems as sources.

By identifying semantics, model interoperability between participating data models can be performed, which allows the integration of data based on those data models (Hahn et al., 2005). The intention is to integrate or to link given information from the Data Warehouse to the knowledge base of the Knowledge Management System to

Figure 1. Overview about different kinds of integration (Adapted from Lenz, 2006)

	Technical Integration	Semantical Integration	
Data-integration	Syntactical Framework Standards for representing data	Controlled Vocabularies	Instance-Level
		Domain Models Ontologies	Type-Level
			Context-Level
Functional-integration	Middleware: *Standards for Programming Abstractions*	Application Frameworks: *- Interfaces* *- Interaction Protocols*	

enable i.e. retrieval and reasoning based on this information. This has to be reconciled when integrating, and it forms a restriction in the integration process. Concerning this, the kind and depth of the integration is important, because problems derive if there is only an isolated examination and integration limited to the meta level. The following figure 2 point out the different kinds of technical conflicts probably occurring within semantic data integration (Haak, 2008).

Conflicts on the data model level are resulting from a different depth in expression of the data models, which are conditional on varied structure descriptions or the difference in the terms of integrity (cardinality, referential integrity). *Schema conflicts* occur by the degree of liberty in the modeling of the real world using schema constructs i.e., in the description (names or values), in the structure (different schema constructs) or in the semantics (implicit understanding). Furthermore conflicts could appear with the naming of tables (same name for different tables and vice versa) or for attributes. Different granularities and infringement of the terms of integrity also causes schema conflicts.

Conflicts on the instance level cannot be solved by observing the structure. For a proper rectification the object has first to be identified and then the conflict can be resolved. Additional implicit knowledge of the user or metadata from the system is needed to find out which is the correct piece of information if two objects have conflicts during a merge. In this case of unification the original term has to be known to solve the conflict. But considering this conflicts and subsequent problems, Semantic Integration offers a great value for the company to gain context information from their Data Warehouse and Knowledge Management Systems.

Application Areas: Data Warehousing and Knowledge Management

In general, Data Warehouse Systems and Knowledge Management Systems are widely accepted and well-known used information systems in nowadays companies. Many different definitions could be found about these terms in the literature. Within the scope of our work we follow (Devlin, 1997) and define a Data Warehouse as "…simply a single, complete and consistent store of data obtained from variety of sources and made available to end users in a way they can understand and use in business context." and additionally we adopt the essential characteristics from (Inmon, 2002) like subject orientation, non-volatility, integration and time oriented. Both definitions together correspond to the current understanding about

Figure 2. Conflicts on different integration levels

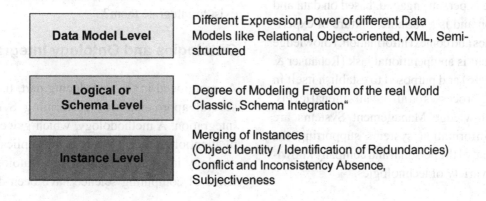

Data Model Level	Different Expression Power of different Data Models like Relational, Object-oriented, XML, Semi-structured
Logical or Schema Level	Degree of Modeling Freedom of the real World Classic „Schema Integration"
Instance Level	Merging of Instances (Object Identity / Identification of Redundancies) Conflict and Inconsistency Absence, Subjectiveness

Data Warehousing in literature and research and constitute the main properties of these systems.

DWS gather data from different operational data sources to allow analysis and conclusions about a wide range of company-wide data. All this data is primary financial oriented, based on numbers and belonging to a well-defined structure with a hierarchy behind. By transforming to the Data Warehouse it is accessible by analytic tools using OLAP (On-Line Analytical Processing) and visualizable, i.e. in form of reports and data charts. Using these techniques offer the possibility for multidimensional data analysis based on information cubes like the one shown in Figure 3 (Haak, 2008):

These data structures have to be considered within the Semantic Integration, which makes integration much more complex, especially to generate an ontology (automatically) from it. The ontology has to represent the same structure and data hierarchy as the Data Warehouse System (Haak, 2008). Additionally there are different views on defining Knowledge Management Systems (for example Davenport & Prusak, 2000; Probst et al., 1999; Rehäuser & Krcmar, 1996 and Nonaka & Takechi, 1997). On one hand this results from different existing attempts (for example human-oriented, organizational or technological) and on the other hand from the different linguistic and cultural areas (Germany / Austria / Switzerland, the USA, Japan) were this domain was invented, formed and discussed. Building up on the definition of (Davenport & Prusak, 2000) knowledge is person engaged, based on data and information and is a variable mixture of experiences, values and context information. Knowledge Management is an operational task (Rehäuser & Krcmar, 1996) and purposed to establish itself in the learning processes on all organizational levels. Today, Knowledge Management Systems are complex information systems supporting the management of the personal and company knowledge by a variety of technologies.

Figure 3. Multidimensional data cube

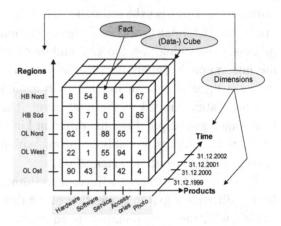

KMS are confronted with the challenge of performing a unified representation of strongly heterogeneous information sources, while managing externalized knowledge. This offers a challenge to integrate as much information as possible from many different information sources into the Knowledge Management System. These information sources are based on different data formats and data models as well but mainly text-based. Additionally, various data qualities have to be considered. Advantages for the Semantic Integration of Knowledge Management Systems occur, because there are different types of systems based on ontologies. For this reason, we could use one of the available ontologies to establish Semantic Integration with the Data Warehouse. But before the approach is described in detail, a short introduction to the term "ontology" is needed; what are ontologies and which methods exist to integrate them?

Ontologies and Ontology Integration

As mentioned in the introducing part, there are several approaches for performing Semantic Integration. A methodology, which gained a lot of attention in recent years, is the application of ontology integration approaches. Ontologies in terms of computing science have been defined very general by Gruber in 1993: "An ontology is an explicit specification of a conceptualization." (Gruber, 1993). Following this, ontologies are formal expressions or formal descriptions of an abstract model and terms, related to it. They model a part of the reality and their relationships, aiming at defining a common understanding. For this purpose, they use an appropriate taxonomy and represent the corresponding relationships between concepts and instances. The result is a common understanding for communication which, as a result of their formalization, is machine readable. Furthermore, the outcome is a semantic model which can be interpreted by systems. Therefore ontologies are an appropriate instrument for the representation of semantic relationships. Following experts in ontology engineering (for example McGuinness, 2003) an ontology is defined by the terms on the right side from the line in the figure 4:

There is more than one way to create ontologies for a specific domain. Hence, there are might even existing different ontologies that express the same or a similar set of information. They might differ in their taxonomic nature or in their terminology. In those cases, ontology integration is necessary (for example Klein, 2001). Regarding to (Sofia & Martins, 2001) "ontology integration is the process of building an ontology in one subject reusing one or more ontologies in different subjects". Furthermore, ontology integration could be differentiated by various integration types, which are depending on the degree of integration. Those types are usually generally known as ontology mapping, aligning or merging. Mapping of ontologies refers to an identification of identical concepts or relations between different ontologies (for example Sofia & Martins, 2001 and Doan et al., 2002). Related to ontology mapping is ontology aligning, which brings two ontologies into a mutual agreement and makes them consistent and coherent (Klein, 2001). In the case of ontology merging, a completely new ontology is built based on two or more existing ontologies. This new ontology combines the existing ones (Klein, 2001). More examples for ontology integration types are given in (Ehrig & Staab, 2004a; Ehrig & Staab, 2004b; Bruijn & Polleres, 2004; Ehrig & Sure, 2004). Available tools are presented for instance in (Noy, 2004) and in the KAON implementation (for example Maedche et al., 2003).

Semantic Integration of Structured and Unstructured Data in DWS and KMS

After introducing the basic idea of ontologies and there integration issues, this section will present a concrete Semantic Integration approach using the concept of ontology integration within the application area of Data Warehousing and Knowledge Management. As mentioned in the introductory

Figure 4. What is an ontology? (Adapted by McGuinness, 2003)

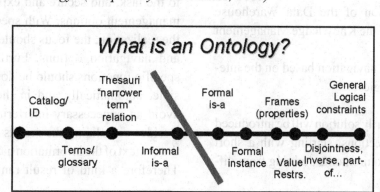

part, the integration of these information systems could generally occur in different varieties. Approaches with focus in the area of Data Warehousing could be found for example in Klesse et al., 2003 and Dittmer & Gluchowski, 2002). Besides, basically the question of integration depth has to be asked and in particular the extent of the Semantic Integration. Next to qualitative aspects of Data Warehouses, context information from the Knowledge Management System should be put in disposal for users. This would reduce the interpretation extent and would provide a better basis for decisive processes. These aspects offer an improvement of the internal information quality for each user.

By identifying semantics, model interoperability between the participating data models can be performed. This allows the integration of data based on those data models to enable for instance retrieval and reasoning of this information. Problematic areas are the different data models, beside structured data, the unstructured data in form of a document archive or a file system, etc. have to be considered. These have to be reconciled during integration and it forms a restriction in the integration process itself. The following figure 5 illustrates the vision of the approach (Haak, 2008).

Mainly this approach of Semantic Integration of structured and unstructured data in Data Warehousing and Knowledge Management Systems consist of three parts:

1. The generation of an ontology from the Data Warehouse
2. The integration of the Data Warehouse Ontology and the Knowledge Management Ontology
3. The semantic navigation based on the integrated ontologies

Each of these partly solution will be introduced in the following sections, starting with a short overview on the requirements deriving from different perspectives.

Figure 5. Semantic integration of DWS and KMS

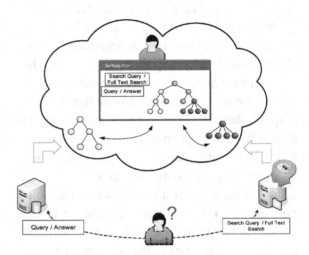

Requirements for Integrating KMS and DWS

In the past sections some general benefits and advantages from a semantically integrated solution were already mentioned. Most of them focus on supporting the user to provide him with all relevant information in a reasonable amount of time to give him an efficient way for accessing. From the perspective of the application areas of Knowledge Management and Data Warehouse Systems the unsophistication of the original content is the most important requirement (Haak, 2008). Additionally, as in other integration approaches, many general requirements to this solution result from the usability: easy access, personalization options, graphical user interface design adequate to the task, and secure and expedient user right management options. With special emphasis on the realization, the focus should be on searching and navigation options. Furthermore, system specific functions should be done, as far as possible, automatically and in the background to avoid an unnecessary interfering with the user. Besides visualizing the results of both systems, the context of the information has to be illustrated. Therefore a kind of result ranking would give the user some important additional background (Haak, 2008). Even though it is not the idea to replace the original system, an external starting point for an extended search in the information of the DWS and the KMS should be given by the integrated platform. The Semantic Integration is based on the concept of loose coupling and allows the untrained employee an efficient way to search information of both systems.

From the perspective of the ontology generation, there are more concrete requirements to be fulfilled. Priority should be given to build up a common understanding of terms for the ontological net for example, based on glossaries for a specific knowledge domain. Furthermore, the parts of the old hierarchy representing parts of the new constructed net have to be defined and the level of abstraction has to be assumed. Therefore the allocation of concepts and instances is necessary which will be quite complicated. Problematic is especially fragmentary and incomplete knowledge, it occurs mismatches within the ontology integration and which have to be solved. The integrated structure has to represent the complete content of both systems whether there are equals on the other side or not. Therefore rules for these mismatches have to be defined. Finally the ontology should be visualized as a graph and to allow navigation in concepts as well as individual customizing passed on the user knowledge to enhance the development of the ontology (Haak, 2008).

Ontology Generation and Integration

Ontologies, based on the data of data warehouse and knowledge management system, are usually quite different. For this concept existing ontologies in the area of Knowledge Management System are used and an ontology of a Data Warehouse System which was generated before from the structure of the DWS. Therefore the definition of rules based on the differences and similarities in formal models in Data Warehousing and in formal ontologies model were necessary.

Before an ontology of a Data Warehouse could be generated a common integration level of the Semantic Integration has to be identified. Therefore some restriction had to be taken into account:

- An ontology for the Semantic Integration has to consider the level to which the information originally belong to in both system, for instance the meta-level
- An ontology has to rebuild the data structure of the Data Warehouse for an integration with the Knowledge Management System, not to define a complete new one
- Any kind of useful mapping or merging is needed to link the different structures of the system

Ontology Generation from the Data Warehouse

To fulfill these requirements an analysis of formal methods for the multidimensional description of Data Warehouse Systems was done to evaluate the main concepts of multidimensional modeling (Haak, 2008). The intention was to find out the coherences in the multidimensional structure to assign them later in the same way to structure of the ontology. Therefore all elements of the hierarchical structure had to be analyzed first as shown in the example in the following figure 6 (Haak, 2008):

In this example from the sales area one data cube (sales) is identified from a set of data cubes and split by his hierarchy elements like dimensions (place, product, time), each of them with an own dimension hierarchy consisting of dimensional level (hardware, software) following a defined dimensional path. A dimensional element (for example Notebook) would represent a concrete data in a dimensional level.

This inherent order (structure) has to be represented by the ontology otherwise it would be impossible to find the correct information in the context of both systems. Therefore it is necessary

Figure 6. From the data cube to the ontology

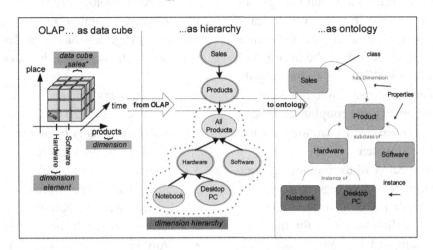

to identify which element of the Data Warehouse structure represents a concept in the ontology and which elements are on an instance level. In a first step, the structures of both systems have to be defined analog to formal methods before, in a second step; rules for the mapping could be applied. For this reason a formal approach of a common multidimensional OLAP model has to be introduced first.

A Formal Approach of a Common Multidimensional OLAP Model

The rapid development in the market of OLAP products over the past years has significantly increased the acceptance and application of multidimensional OLAP models. The available multidimensional OLAP models can be differentiated based on their constructs and operations as well as on their terminology (compare chapter 5.4). To keep interpretation gaps as small as possible a common rigorously defined formal standard model is required. This goal was missed in the past due to different interests of the development companies. This section targets the definition of such a common multidimensional model. This model will be defined on an abstraction level that covers the characteristics of available models and

is detailed enough that the analysis and mapping techniques introduced later can be applied.

The model is derived of the formal model of Pedersen / Jensen (Pedersen / Jensen, 1998) due to its extent and completeness. The model of Pedersen and Jensen is a complete subset of all common elements of multidimensional models without any product dependent aspects. Since not all elements are required to apply the analysis and mapping techniques introduced later the derivation consists primarily in a subset of this model. Elements that are not considered will be discussed in the following text.

According to Pedersen and Jensen the core elements of a multidimensional OLAP model includes fact schemata, dimension types, dimensions, sub-dimensions, and fact-dimension relations to define types and their relationships as wells as multidimensional objects as instances.

Def.: a fact schemata is a pair S=(F, D), consisting of the elements

- F: *the fact type.*
- D: *a set of dimension types.*
  Def.: the dimension type T *is a quad tuple* $(C, \leq_T, \mathbf{T}_T, \perp_T)$, *consisting of*
- C: A set of cate*gory types of* T.

- $\leq_T$: *A partial ordering on* C, *where* $\{\perp_T, \mathbf{T}_T\} \subseteq C$ *and* $\perp_T$ *is the greatest lower border of* C *and* $\mathbf{T}_T$ *lowest upper border of* C.

Let T, T′ *be category types.* T *is called greater then* T′ ($\leq_T$) *if* T *is a superset of* T′.

Def.: Let $T = (C, \leq_T, \mathbf{T}_T, \perp_T)$ *be a dimension type. The function* $\mathrm{Pred}:C \to 2^C$ *computes all direct predecessors of a category type and is defined as follows:*

$$\mathrm{Pred}(c) := \{c' \in C \mid (c', c) \in \leq_T\}$$

Def.: a dimension D *of type* $T = (C, \leq_T, \mathbf{T}_T, \perp_T)$ *is a pair* $D=(C, \leq)$ *consisting of*

- C: *a set of categories, where* $\forall c \in C \exists c \in C : type(c) = c$. *Each category* $c \in C$ *consists of a set of dimension types. The type of all dimension values of a category is equal to the type of category, i.e.:*

$$\forall c \in C \forall e \in c : type(c) = c \Rightarrow type(e) = c$$

- $\leq$: *is the partial ordering of all dimension values with the lowest upper border of their type as upper border, i.e.:* $\bigcup_{e \in c, c \in C} e$ *with* $\forall e \in c : e \leq \mathbf{T}$

Let $D=(C, \leq)$ *be a dimension and* $c \in C$, *then we call* c *a category of dimension* D (*written* $c \in D$). *Let further be* $e \in c$ *a dimension element then* c *is also an element of the dimension* D (*written* $e \in D$).

Def.: Let $D=(C, \leq)$, $D'=(C', \leq')$ *be dimensions.* D′ *is a sub dimension of* D, *if*

$$C' \subseteq C \wedge \forall e_1, e_2 \in D : e_1 \leq' e_2 \Leftrightarrow$$
$$\exists C_1, C_2 \in C' : e_1 \in C_1 \wedge e_2 \in C_2 \wedge e_1 \leq e_2$$

Thus D′ *is a subset of the categories of* D *and* $\leq'$ *is a restriction of* $\leq$ *for all dimension elements.*

In order to differentiate between dimension values and entities of the real world the bijective function group $\mathrm{Rep}:\mathrm{Dom}(C) \leftrightarrow \mathrm{Dom}_{Rep}$ is defined. This function group maps for example between model code of a product and model description like *Code (3)*= "ZJ99" and *Text(3)*= "Notebook for Business Applications."

Def.: Let F *be a set of facts and* $D=(C, \leq)$ *be a dimension. A fact dimension relation between* F *and* D *is the set*

$$R := F \times \bigcup_{e \in c, c \in C} e.$$

For all facts that are not mapped to a dimension value we define (f, T) *avoiding missing values and potential unclear semantics.*

Def.: a multi dimensional object is a quad tuple M=(S,F,D,R), *where* S=(F, D): *is a fact schema.*

- F: *is a set of facts.*
- D: *is a set of dimensions, with* $\forall d \in D:type(d) \in D$.

R: *is a set of fact dimension relations, with*

$$\forall r \in R \forall (f, e) \in r \Rightarrow f \in F \wedge e \in D.$$

The partial order is equivalent to the dimension path and is determined by the highest Æ$_T$ and z$_T$ the lowest element of its specification. The categories C are equivalent to the so-called dimension level or classification level, which are located on these paths. The dimension elements are partial areas of the dimension and arranged on the categories.

Besides, the mentioned elements the formal model of (Petersen / Jensen, 1998) contains algebra, but because of missing relevance it is not further considered in this approach. Essential is that the OLAP data are not manipulated in this way; they will be used to generate an ontology from the structure. The manipulation functions will still be part of the original DWS respectively the OLAP module. It is not necessary to copy these functions and to implement them again in the new system.

Generating Ontology Structure from a Multidimensional Object

Foundations of the ontology generation were the formal ontology model from (Maedche, 2002) and the introduced formal multidimensional model from (Pedersen & Jensen 1998). Following the first author an ontology could be defined as $O = (C,R,H^C,rel,A^O)$ an ontology structure and the quad tuple $\Omega := (C,R,H^C,rel)$ as a mapping relevant part of it. An example from the hardware producing industry should be introduced for better understanding:

Let $KB = ((C,R,H^C,rel,A^O),I,inst_C,instr_R)$ a knowledge base with

- *Concepts C = {description, product, ...}*
- *Relations R = {comes with, explains, ...}*
- *Generalization of concepts H^C = {(hardware, product), (software, product), (operating system, software), ...}*
- *Concept relations rel = {(has, (product, description), explains (description, product)), (described in,(product, article))}*
- *Axioms $A^O = \varnothing$*
- *Instance I = {Dell Latitude, Asus ZJ99, Windows 7}*
- *Concept instantiations $inst_c$ = {(notebook, {Dell Latitude, Asus ZJ99}), (operating system, {Windows 7, Debian Linux}),...}*
- *Relation instantiations $inst_R$ = {(supports, {Asus ZJ99, Windows 7}), tested {(Debian Linux}), described in {Linux, "The new Debian ..."}),...}*

A lexicon of the ontology structure $L^O = (L^L, R^R, F, G)$

- $L^L = \{laptop\}$
- $L^R = \{explains, describes\}$
- $F = \{laptop, notebook\}$
- $G = \{(explains, illustrates), (describes, illustrates), (describes, writes about)\}$ (that G(describes)={explains, writes about})

and a lexicon of the knowledge base $L^{KB} = (L^I,J)$, with

- $L^L = \{DRXJ67\}$
- $J = \{(DRXJ67, Dell Latitude)\}$

This formal description of knowledge base and lexica is visualized in the following figure 7 with the same example from the sales area: the concepts within their concept hierarchy, the instances of the concept (concept instances) and the relations and generalizations between them (Haak, 2008):

In order to achieve the ontology integration, the concepts, their hierarchy and relations are the most relevant objects because the concrete instances vary with the information in the knowledge base and get their relevance later in the concrete search or navigation of a user. According to the knowledge base of the KMS the structure of the multidimensional data model of the DWS has to be defined:

Let M=(S,F,D,R) be a multidimensional object, with

- *Fact schemata S = (product, {hardware, software}), with*
  - *Hardware = ({multimedia hardware, notebook, PDA, graphic card, monitor, hardware component},{(multimedia hardware, $T_{Hardware}$),(notebook, $T_{Hardware}$), (PDA, $T_{Hardware}$), (MP3 player, multimedia hardware), (DVD player, multimedia hardware), (hardware component, MP3 player), (hardware component, DVD player), (hardware component, notebook), (hardware compo-*

Figure 7. Exemplarily visualization of the formal knowledge base and lexica

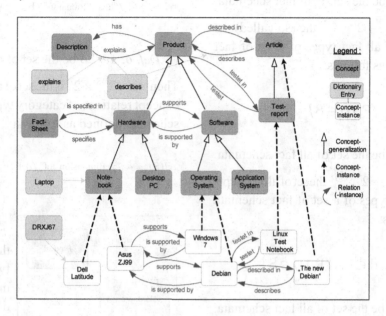

nent, PDA)} (hardware component, $T_{Hardware}$))

° *Software ({operating system, application system, games, software component}, {(operation system, $T_{Software}$), (application system, $T_{Software}$), (game, $T_{Software}$)}, (software component, operating system), (software component, application system), (software component, game)}, (Software Component, $T_{Software}$))*

° *Sales, country, date ...*

Let ...

• *facts $F=(p_1,...,p_2)$ with $n \in N$*
• *dimensions $D= (\{hardware, software\}, \leq_D)$, with*
  ° *Hardware = {HP Presario, Mac Mini, Dell Latitude, Asus JZJ99, Treo 755p, TungstenE2, IPod nano, Philips DVP 5160}*
  ° *Software = {Windows 7, Mac OSX, MS Office, SAP R/4, WoW, Civilization}*
  ° *Sales, country, date ...*

° *and $\leq_D$ assigned according to the partial orderings of the categories of the fact schemata.*

Let further the fact dimension relation exemplarily for product p_1 be {(notebook, Dell Latitude), (operating system, Windows 7), monitor, 15" True Life Display)}.

In the next step both formal models are mapped on each other. The multidimensional elements are mapped on the ontology elements to generate rules that allow an automatic generation by the system itself. Therefore the OLAP elements belonging to concept or instance of the ontology are shown.

Representing an Ontology Based on a Formal OLAP Model

This section defines rules to successively map a set of multidimensional objects (for example their fact schemata) on an ontology structure. These rules will illustrate the mapping of the elements on concepts, relations, and generalizations. The following definitions state the concepts of an ontology structure.

Def. 1: Let ΣS *be the set of all fact schemata.*
Then is $\overset{ft}{con} : 2^{\Sigma S} \rightarrow 2^{\{a,\dots,Z\}^*}$ the (so called) set of all concepts of all fact types of a set of fact schemata defined as follows:

$$\overset{ft}{con}(\bar{S}) := \{ \ F \ | \ (F,D) \in \bar{S}\}$$

Def. 2: Let ΣS *be the set of all fact schemata.*
Then is $\overset{dt}{con} : 2^{\Sigma S} \rightarrow 2^{\{a,\dots,Z\}^*}$ the set of all concepts of all dimension types of a set of fact schemata defined as follows:

$$\overset{dt}{con}(\bar{S}) := \{ \ d \ | \ d \in D \wedge (F,D) \in \bar{S}\}$$

Def. 3: Let ΣS *be the set of all fact schemata.*
Then is $\overset{ct}{con} : 2^{\Sigma S} \rightarrow 2^{\{a,\dots,Z\}^*}$ the set of all concepts of all category types of a set of fact schemata defined as follows:

$$\overset{ct}{con}(\bar{S}) := \{ \ c \ | \ c \in C \wedge d = (C, \leq_T, \bot_T, \mathbf{T}_T) \in D \wedge (F,D) \in \bar{S}\}$$

The sets $\overset{ft}{con}, \overset{dt}{con}$ and $\overset{ct}{con}$ identify fact, dimension and category types as concepts of an ontology, or formally:

Def. 4: Let ΣS *be the set of all fact schemata.*
Then is $\overset{fs}{con} : 2^{\Sigma S} \rightarrow 2^{\{a,\dots,Z\}^*}$ the set of all concepts of all in a fact schemata defined fact, dimension und category types defined as follows:

$$\overset{fs}{con}(\bar{S}) := \overset{ft}{con}(\bar{S}) \cup \overset{dt}{con}(\bar{S}) \cup \overset{ct}{con}(\bar{S})$$

The union set of the concepts represents the first step towards the union of the fact types in the context of the ontology structure.

Def. 5: Let ΣS *be the set of all fact schemata.*
Then is $\overset{ft2dt}{rel} : 2^{\Sigma S} \times 2^R$ is the set of all "has dimension" concept relations of category types of a set of fact schemata defined as follows:

$$\overset{ft2dt}{\overrightarrow{rel}}(\bar{S}) := \{ \ (\text{"has dimension"},(F,d)) \ | \ d \in D \wedge (F,D) \in \bar{S}\}$$

Def. 6: Let ΣS *be the set of all fact schemata.*
Then $\overset{ft2dt}{rel} : 2^{\Sigma S} \times 2^R$ is the set of all „is dimension" concept relations of category types of a set of fact schemata defined as follows:

$$\overset{ft2dt}{\overleftarrow{rel}}(\bar{S}) := \{ \ (\text{"is dimension of"},(d,F)) \ | \ d \in D \wedge (F,D) \in \bar{S}\}$$

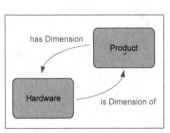

The relations $\overset{ft2dt}{\overrightarrow{rel}}, \overset{ft2dt}{\overleftarrow{rel}}$ determine the connections between fact schemata (e.g., "product") and dimensions (e.g., "hardware"), usually expressed as "has dimension" and "is dimension of".

Def. 7: Let ΣS *be the set of all fact schemata.*
Then is $\overset{ct2ct}{\overrightarrow{rel}} : 2^{\Sigma S} \times 2^R$ the set of all concept relations "aggregates" of category relations of category types of a set of fact schemata defined as follows:

$$\overset{ct2ct}{\overrightarrow{rel}}(\bar{S}) := \{ \ (\text{"aggregates"},(c,c')) \ | \ c,c' \in C \wedge (C, \leq_T, \bot_T, \mathbf{T}_T) \in D$$
$$\wedge (F,D) \in \bar{S} \wedge c' \in \text{Pred}_T(c) \wedge c \neq \mathbf{T}_T\}$$

Def. 8: Let ΣS *be the set of all fact schemata.*
Then is $\overset{ct2ct}{\overleftarrow{rel}} : 2^{\Sigma S} \times 2^R$ the set of all concept relations "is aggregated from" of category relations of category types of a set of fact schemata defined as follows:

$$\overset{ct2ct}{\overleftarrow{rel}}(\bar{S}) := \{ \ (\text{"is aggregated from"},(c',c)) \ | \ c,c' \in C \wedge (C, \leq_T, \bot_T, \mathbf{T}_T) \in D$$
$$\wedge (F,D) \in \bar{S} \wedge c' \in \text{Pred}_T(c) \wedge c \neq \mathbf{T}_T\}$$

The sets $\overrightarrow{rel}^{\,ft2dt}$, $\overleftarrow{rel}^{\,ft2dt}$, $\overrightarrow{rel}^{\,ct2ct}$ and $\overleftarrow{rel}^{\,ct2ct}$ together form the relations between fact and dimension types. They define also the partial order relationships oft the category types from the fact schemata of ontology relationships.

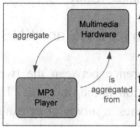

Def. 9: Let ΣS be the set of all fact schemata. Then is $rel^{fs} : 2^{\Sigma S} \times 2^{R}$ the set of all relations of all concepts of all in a fact schemata defined fact, dimension und category types defined as follows:

$$rel^{fs}(\bar{S}) := \overrightarrow{rel}^{\,ft2dt} \cup \overleftarrow{rel}^{\,ft2dt} \cup \overrightarrow{rel}^{\,ct2ct} \cup \overleftarrow{rel}^{\,ct2ct}$$

The union set of the concepts relationships represents the second step towards the union of the fact types in the context of the ontology structure.

Def. 10: Let ΣS be the set of all fact schemata. Then is $gen^{dt2ct} : 2^{\Sigma S} \rightarrow 2^{\{a,...,Z\}^*} \times 2^{\{a,...,Z\}^*}$ the set of all concept generalizations of a set of fact schemata defined as follows:

$$gen^{dt2ct}(\bar{S}) := \{ \ (c,d) \mid c \in C \wedge d = (C, \leq_{T}, \perp_{T}, \mathbf{T}_{T}) \in D \wedge (F, D) \in \bar{S}\}$$

The mapping uses inheritance relationships that exist due to the unique id between dimension element (for example "hardware") and dimension (for example "product"). Previously a so called "sub dimension" was defined. A sub dimension checks if all categories of a dimension (including their partial order relationships) form a subset of the categories of another dimension. If this is the case, the kind of relationship is called "generalization relation". Nevertheless, in this case the mapping between the structures or type definitions of a multidimensional object and an

ontology is shall be defined, thus it is required to change the definition:

Def. 11: Let

$$T = (C, \leq_{T}, \perp_{T}, \mathbf{T}_{T}), T' = (C', \leq_{T'}, \perp_{T'}, \mathbf{T}_{T'})$$

be dimension types. We say T' is a G *Generalization Type of* T , if

$$C \subseteq C' \wedge \forall c \in C : \mathrm{Pred}_{T}(c) \subseteq \mathrm{Pred}_{T'}(c)$$

Therefore T' is a subset of category types of T and $\leq'$ is a restriction of $\leq$ for all category types according to the defined partial order of both dimension types. It is written T'⇒T, if T' is a sub dimension type of T.

Now, we can extend the set of generalization relations in the following way:

Def. 12: Le ΣS be the set of all fact schemata. Then $gen^{dt2dt} : 2^{\Sigma S} \rightarrow 2^{\{a,...,Z\}^*} \times 2^{\{a,...,Z\}^*}$ is the set of "identified" concept generalizations a set of fact schemata defined as follows:

$$gen^{dt2dt}(\bar{S}) := \{ \ (T,T') \mid T' \Rightarrow T \wedge T', T \in D \wedge (F,D) \in \bar{S}\}$$

Since the set of generalizations could contain redundancies (i.e. there are redundant ways in the transitive closure of a generalizations) we need further restrictions to avoid them.

Def. 13: Let g be a generalization set. Then $gen : \{a,...,Z\}^* 2^{\{a,...,Z\}^*} \rightarrow \times 2^{\{a,...,Z\}^*}$ it the set of all children of one element of the generalization hierarchy defined as follows:

$$gen(g,G) := \{k|(g,k) \in G\} \cup \{ek \mid ek \in gen(k,G) \wedge k \in \{k \mid (g,k) \in G\}\}$$

Def. 14: Let ΣS be the set of all fact schemata. Then $gen^{fs} : 2^{\Sigma S} \rightarrow 2^{\{a,...,Z\}^*} \times 2^{\{a,...,Z\}^*}$ is the set of all concept generalizations of a set of fact schemata defined as follows:

$$\overset{fs}{gen(\overline{S})} := \overset{dt2dt}{gen(\overline{S})} \cup \{(v,k) \in \overset{dt2ct}{gen(\overline{S})} \mid k \notin \overset{dt2dt}{gen(v, gen(\overline{S}))}\}$$

The union set of the generalizations represents the third step towards the union of the fact types in the context of the ontology structure. Finally, the mapping of the fact schemata onto the ontology structure can be defined.

Def. 15: Let ΣS be the set of all fact schemata and $\Sigma \Omega$ be the set of all mapping-relevant parts of the ontology structure. The $os : 2^{\Sigma S} \overset{fs}{\to} \Sigma \Omega$ is the mapping between the set of fact schemata onto the ontology structure defined as follows:

$$\overset{fs}{os(\overline{S})} := (C, R, H^C, rel), \text{ with}$$

- $C = \overset{fs}{con(\overline{S})}$: the set of concepts consisting of the set union of fact, dimension, and category types.
- $R=$ {has dimension", "is dimension of", "aggregates", "is aggregated from"}:the set of concept relations consisting of the relation types of all fact schemata.
- $H^C = \overset{fs}{gen(\overline{S})}$: the set of concept relations consisting of the dimension types in relation to category type relationships and identified generalization types of the set of dimension types.
- $rel = \overset{fs}{rel(\overline{S})}$: the relations consists of fact type to dimension type relation and the relations within the dimension types.

The result of these operations is an ontology that can be seen as a semantic net, consisting of concepts and relationships including a hierarchy. Due to the strong hierarchical structures of the sources, they are also part of the ontology for instance between documents. The hierarchical structures are often inheritance relationships that are realized by determining predecessor elements. Figure 8 shows an example of a created ontology (Haak, 2008).

This section defines how to generate an ontology of a general common formal OLAP model of a Data Warehouse System. It will be necessary in several cases to do be some additional manual work in a concrete application scenario because of a mismatch between the identified common formal OLAP Model and the reality.

Ontology Integration for DWS and KMS

In order to get a reference between the two ontologies, the integration is the next step. To find applicable approaches, a survey of existing methods and approaches was done (Abels et al., 2005). It includes an examination the methods, used in ontology integration approaches to apply them in the area of DWS and KMS integration. Therefore some necessary and some optional criteria considering the application area were defined to classify the different solutions:

Necessary requirements are basic criteria for the selection of the tools. They are obligatory for the Semantic Integration and needs to be fulfilled:

- **Availability:** because the tools will be used in an implementation, the source code should be available and not only described in theory
- **OWL support:** OWL (Web Ontology Language) should be supported
- **Interactivity:** the user should be able to interact with the system to make changes
- **Support of matching algorithms:** these algorithm support the manual integration
- **Consideration of label information:** for this application case unique identifier for the class names are needed. Additional information is stored in the labels.

Optional requirements are criteria which are useful and nice to have:

Figure 8. Example of a generated ontology from an OLAP model

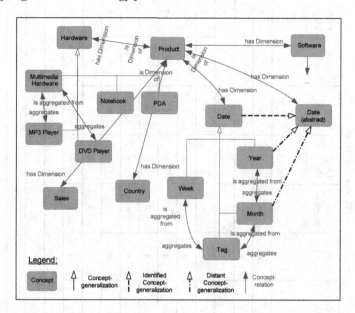

- **Interactions:** affect in this contexts the visualization of ontologies and the graphical user interface
- **Matching methods:** these methods have a important influence on the results and therefore they need to be analyzed
- **Combination of algorithm:** a combination of matching algorithm often allows a more adequate adoption of the algorithm
- **Reuse of mappings:** mappings contain valuable information about the integration process. There reuse could improve the results and extend the basis of the integration

Based on these criteria it is possible to classify the different approaches as shown in following Table 1 (Haak, 2008).

As a result from this analysis, three alternatives for the ontology integration could be discussed:

Alternative I: Merging Tools

None of the analyzed merging tools fulfills the requirements of the integration. PROMPT is eventually a candidate because it is open source and necessary adjustments could be done. Especially the consideration of the label instead of the classes and the extension of the mapping results need to be improved. An additional advantage of PROMPT is the usage of the results from existing mergings which could be used for further integrations. Finally PROMPT is a merging tool that is, with some modifications, applicable for the integration of the Data Warehouse and Knowledge Management Systems ontology.

Alternative II: Graphical Mapping Tools

None of the graphical mapping fulfills the requirements of the integration as well. Positive from this analysis are the findings of the different advantage and disadvantages of graphical user interfaces which could be helpful with a later development of an implementation. Another result from these tools is the knowledge which form of visualization could be useful, for instance the static net structure of VisOn is getting confusing and complex with a bigger amount of data as well as the dynamic

Table 1. Classification of ontology integration approaches

Tool	Type			Properties					Relevant methods					
	Merging	Mapping (graphical)	Mapping (automatic)	Availability binary, source, online	OWL-Support (OWL-Lite)	Usability	Label information	Choice of methods	String-based	Language-based	Ling. Resources	Constraint-based	Graph-based	Reuse Mappings
PROMPT	a			b&s	a	a	-	-	a	a	a	a	a	a
Chimaera	a			O	a	-	-	-	a	a	-	-	-	-
ODEMerge	a			O	a	-	-	-	a	a	-	-	-	-
OntoMerge	a			O	-	O	-	-	-	-	-	-	-	a
Vision		a		s	(a)	--	a	a	a	a	a	a	a	a
COMA++		a		b	(a)	a	a	(a)	a	a	a	a	a	a
MAFRA		a		b&s	-	O	-	-	a	a	a	-	a	a
OntoMap		a		b	a	aa	-	-	-	-	-	-	-	a
FOAM			a	b&s	a	-	a	(a)	a	a	-	a	a	a
OLA			a	b&s	(a)	-	a	a	a	a	a	a	a	a
CMS			a	b&s	a	-	a	a	a	a	a	a	a	a

Legend

Availability:	b = binary; s = source; O = online
OWL-Support:	(a) = OWL-Lite; a = OWL-DL; - = OWL-DL; -- = OWL-Support not possible
Usability:	aa = very good; a = good; O = o.k.; -- = problematic; --- = inapplicable
Choice of methods:	a = detailed; (a) = restricted; - = none

elements of the MAFRA tool. Tree structures appear useful in COMA++ and OntoMap and drag-and-drop functions are easier to handle. Consequently the visualization of OntoMap seems to be a beneficial tool, but although from the overall result it is not applicable for this case.

Alternative III: (Fully) Automatic Mapping-Tools

The group of these (fully) automatic mapping tools seems to have some applicable candidates because of the used methods but a final evaluation in a field test was unfortunately not possible because of missing or not accessible information. That why they could not been finally practically evaluated, just in theory.

Despite from some difference in the procedure the difference of the methods (merging and aligning) are not as huge as it appears in the first moment. Both methods use mappings to connect the concepts. Because of the amount of available tools and approaches, it also seems not reasonable to develop a new integration approach. Finally, the evaluation and tests show that the CMS (CROSI Mapping System) is a proper tool for the integration of the ontologies in this case. It considers label information of the concepts and offers a variety of matching possibilities for our case. More details about the evaluation of the tools could be found (Haak, 2008) or in (Abels et al., 2005). Finally in this chapter, a first implementation called "SENAGATOR" should be shortly introduced to show the practicability of this approach.

SENAGATOR: SEmantic NAviGATOR

The so-called SENAGATOR (SEmantic NAviGATOR) is the first implementation of a Semantic Integration of structured and unstructured data in a Data Warehouse and a Knowledge Management Systems using ontologies. The SENAGATOR is a system a small java-based software tool that combines all advantages of the described approach. The architecture of the software contains three levels:

the graphical user interface (GUI), the generating and the data access component. The GUI allows an easy access even for not trained users to the information in the both systems (DWS and KMS) behind by search and navigation functions. Within the generating component the ontology from the DWS is automatically, based on the described formalization, generated and integrated with the existing KMS ontology. In the background is a semantic similarity search with a term extension implemented that is used to identify the semantic within the ontology concepts and instances. The third component manages the connection to the data and information in the both original systems represented by a loose coupling. It will be for instance used to read out the hierarchy from the Data Warehouse System to generate the DWS ontology.

The system offers the user integrated ontologies based on the generated ontology from the DWS following the described ontology generation concept in this chapter. Additionally, a semantic navigation environment on the integrated information of both systems is implemented. The realization as a typical graph and / or search parameter (5) is user friendly and supports the different search methods of different users. The following Figure 9 shows the graphical user interface of the solution (Haak, 2008).

In this initial screen you find the menu in the top (1), additional properties for the visualization below (3=zoom and 4=rotate) and the search option (full text search in 2). Additionally a search by parameter is implemented (5). Therefore the user could mark a term in the graph of the ontology (main frame in the middle) and add it to the search parameter. The colors used in the ontology visualize to which original data source the information belongs (here red = KMS, blue = DWS, yellow =information in both systems). By using the parameter search the user gets extended information about the results shown in a split screen below the ontology (Figure 10), (Haak, 2008):

In these screens (6 and 7) the results are listed by there original data source, on the left side the

Figure 9. SENAGATOR

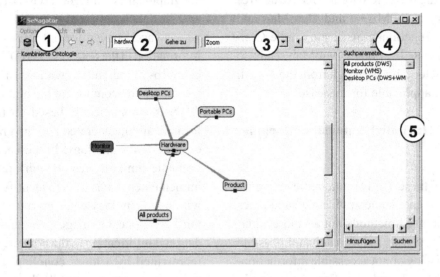

OLAP queries from the Data Warehouse System (6) and on the right side the documents in the Knowledge Management Systems (7). The results are ranked by relevance which is calculated with semantic similarity methods in the generating component of the SENAGATOR (Haak, 2008). The documents are referred with their file types and could be opened directly from the list using the corresponding viewer (for example, *.pdf with Adobe Acrobat Reader). Furthermore, the OLAP results offer the possibility to get deeper into the OLAP data by using predefined dimensions from the data cubes which are actually included in the Data Warehouse ontology. Therefore additional functions and screens are implemented (not included in the figure). Finally an ontology editor

Figure 10. SENAGATOR: The results

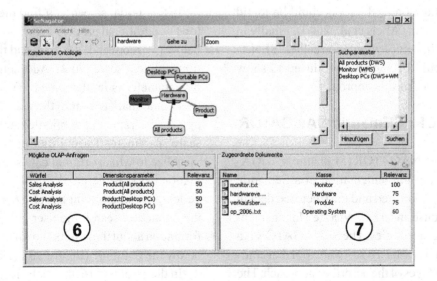

was implemented to give the user the possibility to edit the automatic generated ontology mappings if he has more experience within the domain (extra screen, not included in the figure).

FUTURE RESEARCH AND CONCLUSION

With the implementation of SENEGATOR it could be shown that the idea of a Semantic Integration of structured and unstructured data based on ontologies and applied to the area of DWS and KMS could quite work. Nevertheless there are actually some limitations of the approach, which has to be considered for future research work. Most of them come from the practical usage of the system. For example, one derives from the environment: SENEGATOR was test with a given (static) ontology from a KMS developed during this research and with an Oracle Data Warehouse. In that case the performance was sufficient, but this has to be tested in a more variable and alternating environment. Open research questions are: what happens if there are other ontologies which changes more often and what occurs to the performance if there are more than two systems and ontologies connected? Also the approaches of ontology integration and the algorithm develop fast and a combination of two or more approaches could improve the quality of the generated ontology in the future. Another interesting point derives from the impact for other solutions: because of the loose coupling, it is easily possible to connect other systems to SENEGATOR for example a Customer Relationship Management. But how could an ontology generated from such a system or are there existing ontologies? As mentioned before, the (automatic) generation of the ontology is a critical success factor for such solutions, because the effort to do it manually is too high and therefore not applicable. The introduced approach shows a formal approach how to do this in the case of

a Data Warehouse System and offers in order to that a starting point for other integration projects.

Actual research ideas deal for instance with the usage of ontologies in a bigger context of enterprise systems, for instance using ontologies for Very Large Business Applications (VLBA) (Haak & Brehm, 2008). A VLBA is a business application which is able to be implemented as both different types of business application systems or system landscapes. VLBAs are similar to business information systems in the way that they are able to support several business application areas. In this case they are based on several types of business application systems. They can be found in different departments inside organizations independently of their size. Systems of Enterprise-Resource-Planning (ERP), Supply-Chain-Management (SCM) and Customer-Relationship-Management (CRM) are examples of a VLBA (Grabski, 2007).

These systems are integrated systems based on a technological integration for example with middleware. By contrast, a semantic integration approach allows another (new) level of integration especially in the case of:

- The construction of new VLBAs based on stand alone applications,
- The integration with other applications and
- To support their information processes.

Ontologies offer many possibilities for VLBAs, i.e., they represent a domain specific model which allows semantic conclusions on the base of the process information. The idea is to abstract from the "normal" data processing through interfaces under using for instance middleware. The aim is not to substitute this technical integration; in fact the consideration of semantics is a kind of add-on which could provide many advantages to the user as shown in this approach.

This chapter introduced an approach for Semantic Integration of Data Warehousing and Knowledge Management using ontologies. After an introduction to the motivation in section 1, the technology in section 2 were described and the application area and the problems occurring in the field of ontology integration were explained. The main part of the chapter focuses on the realization of the Semantic Integration, starting with the explanation of the requirements to such a solution in section 3.1. This was followed in section 3.2.1 by the ontology generation based on the data of the Data Warehouse. Therefore a formal approach was pointed out to show how an ontology could be generated from the Data Warehouse without changing the initial structure. Examples from the electronic industry were used to visualize the formal concept.

Based on the Data Warehouse ontology the Semantic Integration with the Knowledge Management ontology is possible, which is shown in section 3.2.2. Based on a survey of the author an evaluation of the different approaches of ontology integration was done. The result of the analysis is presented in Table 1. In section 3.3 an implementation of the concept, called SENAGATOR was introduced, before the chapter closes with some future research aspects using ontologies for VLBA.

REFERENCES

Abels, S., Haak, L., & Hahn, A. (2005). Identification of common methods used for ontology integration tasks. In *Proceedings of the First International ACM Workshop on Interoperability of Heterogeneous Information Systems (IHIS05)*, (p. 13). ACM, Sheridan Publishing.

Beneventano, D., & Bergamaschi, S. (2004). The MOMIS methodology for integrating heterogeneous data sources. In *Proceedings of the IFIP World Computer Congress*. Boston, MA: Kluwer Academic Publishers.

Berners-Lee, T., & Fischetti, M. (1999). *Weaving the Web*. San Francisco, CA: Harper.

Bruijn, J. D., & Polleres, A. (2004). *Towards an ontology mapping specification language for the Semantic Web. (DERI Technical Report: DERI-TR-2004-06-30), University of Innsbruck: Digital Enterprise Research Institute*. DERI.

Davenport, T. H., & Prusak, L. (2000). *Working knowledge. How organizations manage what they know*. New York, NY: McGraw-Hill, Harvard Business School Press.

Devlin, B. (1997). *Data warehouse – From architecture to implementation*. Reading, MA: Addison-Wesley.

Dittmer, C., & Gluchowski, P. (2002). Synergiepotenziale und Herausforderungen von Knowledge Management und Business Intelligence . In Hannig, U. (Ed.), *Knowledge management und business intelligence* (pp. 27–42). Berlin, Germany: Springer. doi:10.1007/978-3-642-55950-1_2

Doan, A., Madhavan, J., Domingos, P., & Halevy, A. (2002). Learning to map between ontologies on the Semantic Web. In *Proceedings of the Eleventh International WWW Conference*. Hawaii, US.

Ehrig, M., & Staab, St. (2004a). *Efficiency of ontology mapping approaches*. In International Workshop on Semantic Intelligent Middleware for the Web and the Grid at ECAI 04. Valencia, Spain.

Ehrig, M., & Staab, S. (2004b). QOM – Quick ontology mapping. In *Proceedings of the Third International Semantic Web Conference*. Berlin, Germany: Springer.

Ehrig, M., & Sure, Y. (2004). Ontology mapping - An integrated approach. In C. Bussler, J. Davis, D. Fensel, & R. Studer (Eds)., *Proceedings of the First European Semantic Web Symposium, LNCS 3053*, (pp. 76-91). Berlin, Germany: Springer.

Grabski, B., Guenther, S., Herden, S., Krueger, L., Rautenstrauch, C., & Zwanziger, A. (2007). Very large business applications. *Informatik Spektrum*, *30*(4), 259–263. doi:10.1007/s00287-007-0171-7

Gruber, T. R. (1993). Toward principles for the design of ontologies used for knowledge sharing. In *Proceedings of the International Workshop on Formal Ontology*. Padova, Italy.

Haak, L. (2008). *Semantische Integration von Data Warehousing und Wissensmanagement*. Berlin, Germany: Dissertation.de.

Haak, L., & Brehm, N. (2008). Using in ontologies in VLBAs. In *Proceedings of IEEE International Conference on Information & Communication Technologies: from Theory to Applications - ICTTA'08*. Damascus, Syria.

Hahn, A., Abels, S., & Haak, L. (2005). Semantic interoperability among models. In Althoff, K.-D., Dengel, A., Bergmann, R., Nick, M., & Roth-Berghofer, T. (Eds.), *Professional knowledge management – Erfahrungen und Visionen, LNCS 3782*. Berlin, Germany: Springer.

Hammer, J., Garcia-Molina, H., Ireland, K., Papakonstantinou, Y., Ullman, J., & Widom, J. (1995). Information translation, mediation, and mosaic-based browsing in the TSIMMIS system. In *Exhibits Program of the Proceedings of the ACM SIGMOD International Conference on Management of Data*. San Jose, CA: ACM Press.

Inmon, W. H. (2002). *Building the data warehouse* (3rd ed.). New York, NY: John Wiley & Sons Verlag.

Klein, M. (2001). Combining and relating ontologies: An analysis of problems and solutions. In A. Gomez-Perez, M. Gruninger, H. Stuckenschmidt & M. Uschold (Eds.), *Workshop on Ontologies and Information Sharing, IJCAI'01*. Seattle, USA.

Klesse, M., Melchert, F., & von Maur, E. (2003). Corporate knowledge center als Grundlage integrierter Entscheidungsunterstützung. In U. Reimer, A. Abecker, S. Staab & G. Stumme (Eds.), *Professionelles Wissensmanagement - Erfahrungen und Visionen* (p. 115-126). Luzern, Switzerland: GI-Edition - Lecture Notes in Informatics (LNI).

Lenz, R. (2006). Technische Grundlagen einer interoperablen sektorenübergreifenden Elektronischen Patientenakte. *Workshop Einrichtungsübergreifende Elektronische Patientenakte (e-EPA)*. 11. KIS-Fachtagung. Frankfurt. Retrieved from http:// www. informatik. fhmannheim. de/ KIS2006/ daten/ vortraege_kis2006/KIS2006_ eEPA_Lenz_3 1052006.pdf

Maedche, A. (2002). *Semantikbasiertes Wissensmanagement - Eine Anwendung im Human Resource Bereich*. Karlsruher Transfer. Retrieved from http:// www. fzi. de/ ipe/ publikationen. php? id= 809

Maedche, A., Motik, B., & Stojanovic, L. (2003). Managing multiple and distributed ontologies in the Semantic Web. *The VLDB Journal, 12*(4), 286–302. doi:10.1007/s00778-003-0102-4

McGuinness, D. L. (2003). Ontologies come of age. In D. Fensel, J. Hendler, H. Lieberman, & W. Wahlster (Eds.), *Spinning the Semantic Web: Bringing the World Wide Web to its full potential*. MIT Press.

Miller, R. J., Hernández, M. A., Haas, L. M., Yan, L., Ho, C. T. H., Fagin, R., & Popa, L. (2001). The Clio Project: Managing heterogeneity. [ACM Press.]. *SIGMOD Record, 30*(1), 78–83. doi:10.1145/373626.373713

Nonaka, I., & Takechi, H. (1997). *Die Organisation des Wissens - Wie japanische Unternehmen eine brachliegende Ressource nutzbar machen*. Frankfurt, Germany.

Noy, N. F. (2004). Tools for mapping and merging ontologies. In Staab, S., & Studer, R. (Eds.), *Handbook on ontologies*. Berlin, Germany: Springer International Handbooks on Information Systems.

Pedersen, T. B., & Jensen, C. S. (1998). Multidimensional data modeling for complex data. In *Proceedings of IEEE International Conference on Data Engineering (ICED)*. Sydney, Australia: IEEE Computer Society Press.

Probst, G., Raub, S., & Romhardt, K. (1999). *Wissen managen. Wie Unternehmen ihre wertvollste Ressource optimal nutzen,* 3rd ed. Frankfurt (Main), Germany.

Rehäuser, J., & Krcmar, H. (1996). Wissensmanagement in Unternehmen . In Schreyögg, G., & Conrad, P. (Eds.), *Managementforschung 6* (pp. 1–40). Berlin, Germany.

Sofia, H., & Martins, J. P. (2001). A methodology for ontology integration. In *Proceedings of the International Conference on Knowledge Capture.* ACM SIGART.

ADDITIONAL READING

Abelló, A., Samos, J., & Saltor, F. (2000). *A Data Warehouse Multidimensional Data Models Classificaton.* Technical Report LSI-2000-6, Dept. Llenguages y Sistemas Informáticos, Universidad de Granada: http://www-lsi.upc.es/~aabello/publications/00.comparison.ps.gz.

Abels, S., Haak, L., & Hahn, A. (2005). An approach to automatic analysis and classification of unstructured data. In: M. Khosrow-Pour (Ed.), *Managing Modern Organizations with Information Technology.* Proceedings of the 2005 Information Resources Management Association International Conference: IRMA 2005. San Diego, California, USA: IGI Publishing.

Bange, C. (2004). *Business Intelligence aus Kennzahlen und Dokumenten. Integration strukturierter und unstrukturierter Daten in entscheidungsunterstützenden Informationssystemen.* Hamburg, Germany: Dr. Kovac Verlag.

Bauer, A., & Günzel, H. (2007). *Data Warehouse Systeme – Architektur, Entwicklung, Anwendung.* 3. Edition. Heidelberg, Germany: dpunkt.

Calvanese, D., Giuseppe, D. G., & Lenzerini, M. (2001). Ontology of integration and integration of ontologies. In: *Proceedings of the 2001 Description Logic Workshop.* Aachen, Tilburg: CEUR-Workshop Proceedings.

Chamoni, P., & Gluchowski, P. (2000). On-Line Analytical Processing (OLAP). In Mucksch, H., & Behme, W. (Eds.), *Das Data Warehouse Konzept – Architektur – Datenmodelle - Anwendungen. 4. Edition.* Wiesbaden, Germany: Gabler.

Chandrasekaran, B., Josephson, J. R., & Benjamins, V. R. (1999). What are ontologies, and why do we need them? *IEEE Intelligent Systems, 14,* 20–26. doi:10.1109/5254.747902

Euzenat, J., Stuckenschmidt, H., & Yatskevich, M. (2005). Introduction to the Ontology Alignment Evaluation 2005. In: Ashpole, B.; Ehrig, M.; Euzenat, J.; Stuckenschmidt, H. (Eds.), *Proceedings of the KCAP'05 Workshop on Integrating Ontologies.* Aachen / Tilburg: CEUR-Workshop Proceedings.

Giunchiglia, F., & Shvaiko, P. (2004). Semantic Matching. *The Knowledge Engineering Review, 18*(3), 265–280. doi:10.1017/S0269888904000074

Guarino, N. (1998). Formal ontology and Information Systems. In: Guarino, N. (Hrsg.): *Formal Ontology in Informationsystems.* Proceedings of the 1st International Conference, Trento, Italy: IOS Press.

Haak, L., & Hahn, A. (2005). An approach to semantic integration of structured and unstructured data to improve the interoperability between decision support systems. In: Khosrow-Pour, M. (Hrsg.): *Managing Modern Organizations with Information Technology.* Proceedings of the 2005 Information Resources Management Association International Conference: IRMA 2005, San Diego, California, USA: IGI Publishing.

Kemper, H.-G., & Mehanna, W., & Unger, C.: *Business Intelligence - Grundlagen und praktische Anwendungen*. Wiesbaden, Germany: Vieweg Verlag.

Kimball, R., Reeves, L., Ross, M., & Thornthwaite, W. (1998). *The Data Warehouse Lifecycle Toolkit - Expert Methods for Designing, Developing and Deploying Data Warehouses. New York*. Wiley.

Maier, R. (2002). *Knowledge Management Systems*. Berlin, Heidelberg, Germany: Springer.

Mertens, P. (2002). Business Intelligence – ein Überblick. Arbeitspapier an der Universität Erlangen-Nürnberg. In: *Information Management & Consulting 17, 2002*.

Priebe, T., & Pernul, G. (2003). Towards Integrative Enterprise Knowledge Portals. In: *Proceedings of the 12. International Conference on Information and Knowledge Management* (CIKM 2003), New Orleans, LA, USA: ACM Press.

Studer, R., Benjamin, V. R., & Fensel, D. (1998). Knowledge Engineering: Principles and Methods. *Data & Knowledge Engineering, 25*, doi:10.1016/S0169-023X(97)00056-6

KEY TERMS AND DEFINITIONS

Business Intelligence: Contains a variety of different approaches for an analysis of business processes and their relevant comprehensible coherences, for example tools and applications with decision supporting character, which allow a better view to the main business and therefore a better understanding of the relevant mechanism to manage it.

Data Warehouse System: Characterizes all technical solutions belonging to the Data Warehouse environment in form of application system and contain the complete system inclusive the additional functions and programs with the aim to apply the data of the operational system to a new logical coherence.

Knowledge Management: Used for the sustainable and efficient transformation from implicit to explicit knowledge with concentration to the company and process objectives.

Interoperability: Allows the seamless cooperation of two software applications without modification of the data organization.

Multidimensional Model: Models data for analysis reasons in along Facts and dimensions and the possibility to concentrate the data.

Ontology: Allows the representation of the real world using a model (ontology) to build up taxonomy to represent knowledge.

Semantic Integration: The summarization of all approaches, which are dealing with the integration of heterogeneous information system based on their content and context.

Chapter 6
Enhancing the Personal Knowledge Management with Semantic Desktop Technologies:
SCAN Approach

Alexey V. Alishevskikh
ViceVersa Technologies, Russian Federation

Tatiana V. Emshanova
ViceVersa Technologies, Russian Federation

ABSTRACT

This chapter introduces the general Semantic Desktop approach that has emerged last year as a researchers' response to necessity of the effective comprehensive personal knowledge management solution. It describes the theoretical foundation and implementation of a supportive technology in the context of the SCAN (Smart Content Aggregation and Navigation) framework that integrates semantic content aggregation, search, natural language processing, metadata management and tagging. It is asserted that synthesis of different techniques will provide new, improved experience for knowledge workers based on intelligence of document management, increasing their productivity, which in turn will have a favourable effect on organizational business outcomes.

DOI: 10.4018/978-1-60960-126-3.ch006

INTRODUCTION

The term *"knowledge worker"* describes a new type of workers that is valued for their ability of productive use of knowledge in the workplace. In 1968 Peter Drucker claimed: "Today the center is the knowledge worker, the man or woman who applies to productive work ideas, concepts, and information rather than manual skill or brawn… knowledge is now the main cost, the main investment, and the main product of the advanced economy and the livelihood of the largest group in the population" (Drucker, 1968, p.264). Since then organizational practitioners and researchers have become increasingly concerned with the management of knowledge and, in particular, with providing the organizational socio-technological environment for knowledge workers to increase their productivity.

While today's working environment becomes more and more heterogeneous (that includes not only formal structure of organizations but also informal, looser, work groupings) new increasing numbers of information deliveries, exchanges and interactions are seen not only as opportunities but also as obstacles. "The old information types never seem to go away – paper forms, documents, drawings, database output, emails, faxes, files and records, and phone messages. Meanwhile, new forms have sprouted, from text and instant messages to blogs, wikis, social networks, podcasts, digital images and sounds, and even digital "stickies" (Gantz et al., 2009, p.4). To be effective today a knowledge worker has to tackle one of the key problems of our time - *information overload*.

An abundance of information in files of different formats, e-mail messages, web-pages and news feeds leads to lack of control over information flows and decreased productivity of a knowledge worker. According to Basex[1], a knowledge economy research firm, information overload costs the U.S. economy $900 billion per year (Spira, 2008). Xerox Information Overload Hub[2] gives the following remarkable statistics: 28% of typical workdays wasted by interruptions caused by unnecessary information, 53% of people who believe that less than half of the information they receive is valuable, 42% of people who accidentally use the wrong information at least once per week. But, information overload is not just about the growing mountain of information. Overcoming the issues related to personal and shared information overload would also help to cope with such important tasks of knowledge workers as effective decision making, problem solving, new ideas generation, knowledge dissemination, and others.

Thus, there is a clear need to seek new intelligent ways to handle information and to integrate them into organizational business processes, as well as to use new technological approaches and tools, supported by automation and intelligence. During last years a number of business management paradigms as well as technological solutions have emerged as a researchers' response to issues mentioned above (Solution-Oriented Management, Creativity Management, Time-Management, Collaboration Management etc.). As one of the most promising concepts we consider *Personal Knowledge Management,* which is conceived as "a conceptual framework to organize and integrate information that we, as individuals, feel is important so that it becomes part of our personal knowledge base" (Frand and Hixon, 1999).

In this chapter we present our vision of the Personal Knowledge Management and the SCAN Semantic Desktop approach that allows knowledge workers to gain a new, based on intelligence of document management, experience, increasing their productivity, which in turn will have favourable effect on organizational business outcome.

PERSONAL KNOWLEDGE MANAGEMENT

Following Drucker (1999), Amar (2002), Pauleen (2009) and many other researchers interested in "what is the knowledge work" and "how to help individuals to be more effective in personal, organizational and social environments", one will agree that organizational knowledge management (OKM), crucially important in our knowledge society (Senge, 1994), would hardly be successful without providing a sufficient support to individual knowledge workers in their daily routines.

Origin of the term "*personal knowledge management*" (PKM) can be traced in the university environment, in a working paper "Personal Knowledge Management: Who, What, Why, When, Where, How?" written by the UCLA's researchers J. Frand and C. Hixon in 1999. Founded on the Davenport and Prusak's (1998) description of knowledge management, authors understand PKM as a conceptual framework that enables individuals to organize and integrate significant information so that it becomes part of their personal knowledge base. They also suggest considering PKM as a strategy for transforming what might be random pieces of information into something that can be systematically applied and that expands individual's personal knowledge (Frand and Hixon, 1999). Their approach covers both the individual skills and technological aspects. It is suggested, at first, to develop a mental map for individuals to describe in detail the knowledge with which they work. Then, an organisational structure needs to be created to facilitate the finding and relating of both personal and professional information. And finally, appropriate computer-based technologies are needed as tools for organizing and storing the results and widening the personal memory.

For some time, PKM has been an isolated concern of universities, but subsequently it has been re-interpreted as valuable in any environment, including the enterprise. Behind Frand and Hixon (1999) many of the researchers and practitioners consider PKM to be an integration of personal information management (PIM), focused on individual skills, with organisational knowledge management (OKM) in addition to input from a variety of disciplines such as cognitive psychology, management, and philosophy.

Our vision of PKM is closely related to Dave Pollard's (2006) point of view that rather than trying to impose new processes and infrastructure on people, PKM should support and reflect the ways knowledge workers intuitively learn and share what they do. It should adapt technology to people's behavior, rather than forcing people to adapt to new technology.

Oren (2006) investigates issues in personal information management, human-computer interaction and information retrieval in an effort to consider how people organize their work and use their desktop. He makes the following resulting lessons, helping to understand better the requirements to socio-technological PKM system:

- **Focus on the individual:** give individual users incentive and benefit before focusing on the social network,
- **Forget rigid classifications:** leave users their freedom and do not constrain them into rigid schemas (i.e. do not use constraint-based semantics),
- **Follow the links:** exploit the interlinked nature, do not rely only on search, and allow people to associate freely,
- **Remember the context:** work to understand the notion of context, capture it together with the information and use it to enhance recall and understanding,
- **Value the power of paper:** find ways to use the computer together with paper, or prepare for non-exclusive usage (people will not easily give up paper),
- **Keep it simple:** focus on simply capturing and representing the things that the user wants to store, before doing any reasoning with it.

Thus, summarizing stated above findings, one can assert that what knowledge workers really need is the hands-on help using the information and technology at their disposal more effectively in the context doing their own unique jobs. Pollard (2006) suggests some mechanisms to provide such a help:

- Mechanisms to enable peer-to-peer expertise finding and connectivity.
- Mechanisms to facilitate peer-to-peer content-sharing with others inside and outside the organization.
- Mechanisms to enhance meaning and context of information content so that it "makes more sense" and has more value to users.

From our side we would add some more propositions that seem to be important in today's collaboration and heterogeneous information environment:

- Mechanisms to seamlessly integrate and consolidate information from different local and global sources on a single workspace.
- Mechanisms to retrieve information intelligently basing on its semantics.
- Mechanisms to augment users' information automatically using a body of data available in their working environment.

Pollard's "bottom-up, peer-to-peer, just-in-time, reintermediated, context-connection-and-sensemaking" PKM approach is clearly involves the exploitation of existent personal and enterprise information assets, including their search and retrieval, gathering, classifying, storing, exchanging, combination and alignment of different people's contributions by innovative methods to an innovative results. It is obvious that special tools and technologies should be used to support these methods. However, some studies (Malone, 1983; Lansdale, 1988; Barreau and Nardi, 1995; Jones et al., 2001) indicate that PKM is poorly supported by current technology, and that many

users struggle to handle, classify and retrieve the information that they accumulate over time in tools such as the file system, the desktop and email (Boardman, 2004). Obviously, knowledge workers need a novel intuitive way of information handling that are not limited by employed applications' boundaries and can be supported by technology being above the underlying applications currently in force.

In resent years some new concepts of a middleware system that seamlessly integrates data from different heterogeneous sources both within a single personal workspace and between workspaces of some users has being well developed. The most promising of them is commonly referred to as the "*Semantic Desktop*", because it represents a semantic layer upon the underlying operating systems.

SEMANTIC DESKTOP CONCEPT

Historical Background

The first personal information system was invented long before personal computers, knowledge management and World Wide Web. In 1945 Vannevar Bush published his famous "As we may think" article, where he introduced an imaginary device, called "memex": "A memex is a device in which an individual stores all his books, records, and communications, and which is mechanized so that it may be consulted with exceeding speed and flexibility. It is an enlarged intimate supplement to [human] memory" (Bush, 1945. pp.106-107). At the heart of invention there were two all-important ideas: the first one is about associative links related pieces of information together and the second one is about semantic annotations that a user can add to items. Thus, the "memex", being able to connect one thing to many others, including connections to one's own annotations, could augment users' memory helping grasping and remembering, as well as quickly extracting relevant information.

Later Douglas C. Engelbart from the Stanford Research Institute continued working on the Bush's ideas developing the Hypothetical Description of Computer-Based Augmentation System, which was aimed to "improving the intellectual effectiveness of the individual human being" (Engelbart, 1962). The great result, in our view, has been found then: "…we do not have to wait until we learn how the human mental processes work, we do not have to wait until we learn how to make computers more intelligent or bigger or faster, we can begin developing powerful and economically feasible augmentation systems on the basis of what we now know and have" (Engelbart, 1962, p.131).

In 1965 Ted Nelson presented "a file structure for the complex, the changing and the indeterminate" (Nelson, 1965). In this publication he introduced the term "hypertext" and a technique called "transclusions" that allows users to virtually include some parts of existing documents into new ones without duplicating the originals. At that a visible link to the source of the transclusion is provided, making a reference note. Ted Nelson's approach has been realizing in a system named Xanadu (Nelson, 1981). Over the forty years, over one hundred people have been involved with the project, trying to represent the world of ideas correctly and clearly. There is no room in our chapter to discuss the project's progress and practical importance for computer science. What is interesting from the PKM perspective is an idea of reference system where moderate structured data can be linked with large often unstructured information body.

A subsequent evolution and implementation of forefathers' findings resulted in the "semantic desktop" paradigms (Decker and Frank, 2004). It is presumed that on the analogy of the "memex" the semantic desktop would support individuals in their daily activities and augment their memory and intellect. Thanks to several research streams and resulting technologies showing up in the recent years it became quite possible to imple-

ment invented theoretical frameworks into real practical solutions.

Semantic Desktop Approach

The *desktop operating system* is the platform that is running on the computers that a person uses for day-to-day tasks. On the analogy of a real desktop where one can find different kinds of objects an individual works with, a computer desktop is a work environment provided by a graphical user interface that represents a number of objects such as folders, documents, phonebooks, calendars, web links, dynamic information areas, taskbars and programs icons so that an user could have a quick access to them. It is also possible to have multiple desktops (e.g. for different projects or applications) and switch between them.

Traditionally in a desktop architecture "applications are isolated islands of data – each application has its own data, unaware of related and relevant data in other applications" (Groza et al., 2007). Till recently there were not approaches to provide interoperability and exchange of data between desktop applications. As well as there were not ways of seamless communication from an application used by one person on their desktop to an application used by another person on another desktop.

The *Semantic Desktop* approach (SD) is aimed to solve these problems by extending the operating system's capabilities to be able to seamlessly integrate, store and handle all users' digital information such as documents, emails, messages, multimedia files and web-resources. According to (Möller and Handschuh, 2007) a central idea of the Semantic Desktop is the linking of data in a number ways. First of all, it is important to link data within the desktop, so that data from different isolated applications can be integrated and connected into a unified information space. Second, data on the particular user's desktop should be linked to things outside a desktop, e.g. data of vocabularies, taxonomies and ontologies existent on the Web. And third, data between desktops should be linked as well.

Thus, the Semantic Desktop represents a seamless, networked working environment that contributes to an effective PKM handling. In such environment borders between individual applications and users' workspaces become loose and invisible. Groza et al. (2007) suggest the following basic functionalities of the Semantic Desktop, divided into five aspects:

- **Desktop:** Annotation, Offline Access, Desktop Sharing, Resource Management, Application Integration, Notification Management
- **Search:** Search, Find Related Items
- **Data Analysis:** Reasoning, Keyword Extraction, Sorting and Grouping
- **Profiling:** Training, Tailor, Trust, Logging
- **Social:** Social Interaction, Resource Sharing, Access Rights Management, Publish / Subscribe, User Group Management

Summarizing our findings we give the following working definition of the Semantic Desktop – it is *a technology to organize, search, share and augment personal information on a basis of it's meaning and associative links between information items.* We suggest to see the Semantic Desktop paradigm as a meeting-point of different time-proved and emerging technologies, which could be used in applications depending on its' particular destination.

SCAN SEMANTIC DESKTOP

To address the described above issues and to bring intelligence in personal information management the SCAN (Smart Content Aggregation and Navigation) technology has been developed at the ViceVersa Technologies software laboratories. Currently the technology is implemented in

the SCAN Semantic Desktop solution[3] aimed to help knowledge workers to handle, classify and retrieve the information they use.

Smart Content Aggregation and Navigation Technology Integrated Approach

The Smart Content Aggregation and Navigation (SCAN) is a technology platform that combines *semantic integration, search, metadata functions, natural language processing and text mining* to build the content management frameworks strongly focused on the semantics of data in diverse areas like distributed digital libraries, knowledge bases and enterprise document stores in which there is a clear need to integrate information from different heterogeneous sources and organize it into a seamless semantic space.

Content Aggregation

SCAN erases the boundaries put on information by different storage systems. It links the information items from multiple sources and of different formats into a seamless digital library, where they can be categorized, annotated, navigated and searched by a uniform way. This provides a homogeneous searchable and explorable semantic information space where files, web-pages, emails, other content items are equal documents organized by their natural semantic properties.

The component architecture makes the technology agnostic of specific types of sources (local or network file systems, web-sites etc.) and of the document formats (MS Office, PDF, HTML). A number of those types of sources and formats can be supported via integration of the components for a specific business application.

SCAN provides a rich set of metadata properties associated with the documents, including document title, description/annotation, author, creation date and others. The properties are set automatically on a document adding and can be edited later. Metadata properties can be used in the structured search to find the documents matching specified criteria. In addition, some properties (e.g., document source path, author or creation date) are used as navigation facets to browse the documents collection.

As it is shown on Figure 1, a document collection comprises a number of heterogeneous data sources (listed in the top left corner). Metadata facet tabs (Path, Author, Date and Language, in the bottom left corner) provide navigation through the items, displayed in the main screen area.

Tagging

A cornerstone of the SCAN system is a concept of tags. Tags are generally understood as keywords or text labels freely attached to items to identify them for quick navigation and finding. Tagging is the easiest and intuitive way of information modeling and organization of the documents collection according to a unique user's mental model and his/her cognitive abilities; it provides a *user-centric approach* to categorizing information.

Tags can be assigned to the items either manually, or automatically, as a result of autotagging

– a process of text analysis and extraction of key words, representing semantic features of item content. It can still be complemented with manual procedure, when users check tags assigned to the document and make changes if it needs. The tag operations like renaming, merging, splitting and deletion are provided.

We consider a combination two methods – text analysis and user input – would bring to the golden mean between restricted effectiveness of text analysis due to the complexity of natural language parsing, from the one side, and lack of sufficient time of users to distill right set of keywords from the content, from the other one. With autotagging it is possible to perform a content analysis in the background, taking none of the users' time, and then make a suggestion about resulting tags to users letting them to edit the given set according human understanding.

All tags together form a taxonomy representing the semantics of the documents collection that are close to user's comprehension in contrast to e.g. corporative classification schemes, generated without the user's participation and dictated from outside or above. The taxonomy can be viewed as a "tags cloud" for navigating through the docu-

Figure 1. The screenshot of the SCAN Desktop browsing interface

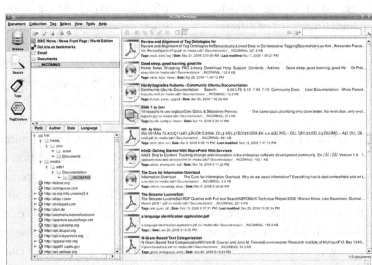

ments (see Figure 2). There is a tag cloud on the left for navigation through the tagged items. A tag size reflects a total number of items associated to a given tag. The tags, relevant to the selected one are highlighted in the cloud to provide hints on topics to see also on a subject.

Text Analysis and Concept Extraction

SCAN brings the power of automated text mining and natural language processing to discover document semantics by extracting the valuable terms and their patterns from the document content. It makes possible to identify what the document is about and how it relates to others. SCAN text analysis functionality is built on top of an operation performed on an inverted index for building a list of terms, relevant to a document or to a broader semantic context. This operation, called *"term-vector extraction"* underlies all SCAN text analysis functions, namely: tag recommendations, auto-tagging, finding documents by similarity and associative search.

In general, the task of retrieval of words, relevant to a given document, consists in building

a list of all document terms (possibly, excluding the stop-words and stem variations) and weighting each term with some weight function, where weight is considered as a measure of relevancy. The resulted list (document term-vector) represents an array of tuples $[t, w(d,t)]$, where t is a term and $w(d,t)$ - a weight function of the term t in the given document d (term relevance). A good weight function must provide values, proportional to specificity of the terms for the documents they are contained in. In other words, the function value increases with significance of a term for a specific document and decreases with general term popularity. The most popular and widely described in IR literature is a weight function based on the ratio of a term frequency in a specific document to its frequency in a whole document corpus. This approach was named "Term Frequency × Inverse Document Frequency" (TFIDF) and its weight function (in variation used in SCAN) is defined as following:

Let t is a term; D is a set of all documents in a corpus; $Dt \in D$ - a set of documents containing the term t. Then the weight of the term t in a document $d \in Dt$ is

Figure 2. The screenshot of the SCAN Desktop tag interface

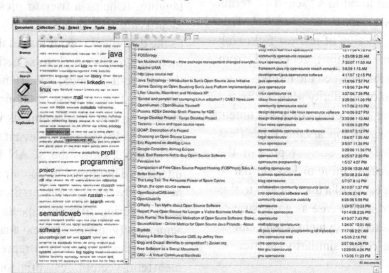

$$w(d,t) = \sqrt{f(d,t) \times \log \frac{|D|}{|D_t|+1}}, \qquad (1)$$

where $f(d,t)$ — term frequency (TF), or a number of occurrences of the term t in the document d; $|D|$ — total number of documents in the corpus; $|Dt|$ — document frequency (DF) of the term t (a number of documents containing the term).

It is obvious that the weight function is context-dependent: the terms of the same document weighted in different semantic context, will have different values of the weight function. TFIDF weight function thus allows to implement efficient procedures of ranking the terms according to their significance for a given document: the important terms (with high TF and low DF) get higher weights against the common words (high DF), as well as the rare terms (low TF and DF).

Search

The *full-text search* and search with *complex, structured queries* both on text and metadata properties are provided by the SCAN technology. It is possible to save the search queries for repeatable use, thus creating the *dynamically populated sets* of the documents grouped by specified criteria.

After any search request is performed, the results are analysed to build a "see also" terms list for *subsequent or similarity searches*. This enables to explore an area of interest following the system recommendations generated from semantic associations between the terms.

The mechanism of similarity search is based upon an interesting side effect of a document term-vector querying: it appears that other (less relevant) results of such query represent the documents with content, more or less similar to the given one. Relevance of a document d to this query is interpreted in this case as a measure of similarity to the pattern document d_0 and can be expressed using the cosine similarity coefficient:

$$s(d_0, d) = \frac{\sum_{t \in T}(w(d_0,t) \times w(d,t))}{\sqrt{\sum_{t \in T} w(d_0,t)^2} \times \sqrt{\sum_{t \in T} w(d,t)^2}}, \qquad (2)$$

where T is a set of terms contained in the term-vector of the pattern document d_0.

As a result a list of semantically related documents is built for a document of interest. The documents in the list represent a semantic context of the pattern document, with the similarity ranged from exact duplication to the specific minimum threshold, found empirically.

Another advanced search technique driven by text analysis is the *pattern search* for finding the documents by similarity. Pattern search explores semantic compatibilities between different documents and allows to find the documents conceptually similar to a subject of a given one. This is useful for finding the exact document duplicates, and the documents with nearly similar semantic characteristics as well.

Tags Suggestion and Auto-Tagging

Text analysis greatly simplifies the process of tagging. It helps a user to pick the key words identifying document semantics and assign them as the document tags. It makes the manual document tagging as simple as selecting the tags from the suggested candidates. If necessary, a user can entrust the process of tagging entirely to the system, so that the documents would be tagged automatically with the relevant terms.

Figure 3 shows the SCAN Desktop tagging interface. The upper box contains a list of existing tags; the lower box represents the tag recommendations featuring different aspects of the document semantics (generated by text analysis algorithm).

Statistical information represented by document term-vectors is essential for implementation of the mechanisms of (semi-)automated document classification and taxonomy generation. Sorted and filtered term-vector can be presented to a user as a list of keywords, recommended to tag the document, or be used in a fully automated tagging procedure. As it has been found empirically, the results of *auto-tagging* can be substantially improved for practical purposes, if a document of interest is analysed together with its semantic context: a cluster of similar documents with the initial document as a centroid. This technique mitigates the value of overrated terms, highly specific to the document in favour of those, specific to a whole subject (an area of knowledge this document belongs to), that generally produces more natural and expectable tag recommendations.

Another technique for improvement of the tag selection algorithm is the *tag novelty* parameter which allows a user to control the growth of the tag vocabulary. This parameter introduces the term

weight normalization depending on whether the term has already been used for tagging the documents. By adjusting the normalization coefficient, a user can select between different tagging strategies ranged from manually controlled vocabulary to free automated tagging.

Thus, the SCAN technology forms a proactive semi-automated semantically-based content environment, which we call as *smart content* or content that *knows something about itself*.

SCAN Desktop Features and Architecture

The SCAN Semantic Desktop application is a personal desktop content aggregator based on the SCAN technology. The goal of SCAN Desktop is to be a solution for major problems of personal content organization and findability in information overload age.

Figure 3. The tagging interface

The SCAN Semantic Desktop is a cross-platform application written in Java. It is designed to be a flexible component framework, easily configurable for specific user needs and extensible by integration the plugins for new document locations and formats, as well as the user interface add-ons. Architecture of the system is presented in Figure 4.

Aggregation Level

On the Aggregation level, the information from external data sources is retrieved. The retrieval framework contains multiple Location Adapter modules to provide access to the sources of different types. Each Location Adapter is designed to work with a specific type of source (a file system, an email store, a web-site, an application-specific database etc.) and knows how to explore its data

structures for document retrieval. The Location Adapters are pluggable components, easily replaceable to create the custom configurations of the retrieval framework, adapted to specific business needs.

Processing Level

After a document is retrieved from a source, it is processed by a Document Parser module, appropriate for a given document format (HTML, MS Word, PDF etc.). The parser generates a uniform internal representation of a document consisting of a set of metadata properties and of a stream of the text tokens representing document content.

Every document parser implements its own strategy of metadata extraction: either mapping the format-specific properties (like PDF and MS Office metadata) to the internal metadata

Figure 4. SCAN semantic desktop architecture

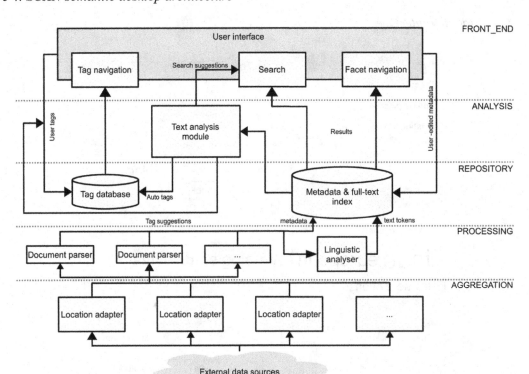

vocabulary, or extending that vocabulary with new property descriptions. The parsers are free to guess the property values if they are not defined explicitly: for instance, it is a common strategy to take the first document paragraph as a document title, if that property is not set in the document. In addition, there is a number of generic, format-independent metadata properties (like document URL's or file modification dates) for which the common extraction procedures are existed. If the document language is identified, the text token stream extracted from a document is additionally post-processed by a Linguistic Analyser module for that language. The linguistic analyser implements a number of text normalization procedures according to a specific language rules, like filtering the common words and stems extraction.

Repository Level

The document repository is based on an inverted text index where metadata values and text tokens are stored in a way, optimized for fast data search, retrieval and analysis. The repository index accepts a broad range of different query types, including free full-text queries, structured metadata queries and their combinations. Another part of the repository is a tag database which relates the documents to the assigned tags. A user can modify information stored in the repository to edit annotation metadata and document tags.

Analysis Level

On the Analysis level, the text data from the index is processed to extract valuable semantic information about the documents or document groups. The results of text analysis procedures underlay a number of automated functions of document management: autotagging; tag suggestions; search suggestions; similar documents finding.

Front-End Level

On the front-end level, the user interface is provided for interaction with the system. The user interface provides a broad range of end-user functions, such as repository administration, navigation, search and results visualization.

Implementation

The SCAN approach presented in this chapter requires a minimum of change and effort from a user's side, what makes the technology good accepted and used. Currently the SCAN Desktop is a full-featured stable platform-independent product available for free under an open source license. Analysis of users' feedback we regularly conducted shows that for the most part it meets the requirements of knowledge workers, providing them individualized help to gather, organize, find and use information quickly, powerfully, and effectively.

Yet we see a spacious room for improving and broadening functionality of the system.

FUTURE RESEARCH DIRECTIONS

Our current R&D efforts are focused on design and development of the SCAN server version. It brings more universality of the technology and raises possibilities to use it in various business-oriented applications as well as in small and medium enterprise networks aimed to integrate and handle information in more intelligent ways.

Besides we are going to investigate some issues that would enable us to add new powerful functionality to existent technology:

- *Context-based retrieval*

Context data such as time, date, task, project's name, geo-location, etc. allows humans to remember information better and then to elicit it from memory faster. Elsweiler et al. (2005), based on results of their memory lapses' study, draw a conclusion that context data help people to recall, renew and reconstruct information in their memory. By analogy with the human recovering processes it would be quite useful to develop mechanisms and tools for retrieving information by the context – a semantic representation of circumstances an information item has getting involved with.

- *Groups' management*

Supporting users in finding expertise and collaborating with each other according to shared interests is one of the major tasks of knowledge management. Following mentioned above Nonaka (1994) who says ideas are developed in social interactions, one could continue that knowledge growths in communities. Networking of personal Semantic Desktops provides a new social dimension in the SD paradigm, while demands a technology to manage users' access rights and to organize users' groups, where people could be able to share information between trusted group's members.

- *Machine-learning algorithms implementing*

While users with their unique mental models and cognitive skills are the core element of our people-centric approach of the Semantic Desktop, some machine-learning algorithms implementation would increase effectiveness of automatic concept extraction and retrieval. Research and technology development should focus on automatically recognizing patterns and making supporting actions based on users' metadata and semantic annotation handling behavior.

Related Projects

Methods and technologies to organize, search, share and augment personal information effectively are studied by a number of research projects last years. They all attempt to go beyond the traditional hierarchical directory model of storing data and present a unified user interface for personal data (Dong and Halevy, 2005).

An early and important reference for systems in which files are organized and can be found by their metadata, instead of their location in a hierarchical system, is a paper by Gifford et al. (1992) that is widely acknowledged as an initial design document to the Spotlight metadata file index system (Apple, 2005). Spotlight is a desktop search system of the Apple's Mac OS X operating system, which creates a virtual index of all items and files on the system, including documents, pictures, music, applications etc. After this the indexes are updated continuously in the background as files are created or modified. As a result users have got a quick access to files within the local computers and moreover they are able to search networked computers and to share files between them.

Another good example of desktop semantic search system is Beagle++, whose main characteristic is metadata generation and indexing information on-the-fly. Metadata are either extracted directly (e.g. email subject, body, sender etc.) or generated automatically using the association rules and some additional background knowledge (Brunkhorst et al., 2006). All metadata are exported in RDF and stored in a metadata index. Then it is used along with a usual full-text index by a search application.

MyLifeBits project (Gemmell et al., 2006) aims to view personal data as a graph of information in which the nodes represent resources and metadata; and the edges represent the 'annotates' relationship. Annotation is made by a user who links a file to another one (that represents metadata) and manually adds text or audio annotation.

Haystack system (Quan et al., 2003; Quan and Karger, 2004) also supports annotations and collections. It focuses on working with the information itself, rather then with an associated application. The solution allows users to create, manipulate and visualize the metadata, defining their own semantic connections between different content items. Haystack creates the data model in a graph structure using the concept of semantic network, which essentially represents the metadata of the archived documents. The users can then interact with this data model through a set of client services that visualize the metadata.

One of the existing approaches of SD is the Gnowsis Semantic Desktop that supports distributed data management with several Desktop Services. It uses a central information server which allows users to administer, link and directly access all the information on their computers based on four-level ontology according to user-defined PIMOs (Personal Information Model Structures) (Sauermann et al., 2009). In addition, data adapters are used to extract metadata from desktop objects automatically, similarly to the Spotlight system. One of the main goals of the Gnowsis project is to complement established desktop applications and the desktop operating system with Semantic Web features, rather than replacing them.

Among other Semantic Desktop projects one could mention IRIS (Cheyer et al, 2005), Deepa-Meetha (Richter et al., 2005), Semex (Dong and Halevy, 2005), SWAP (Ehrig et al., 2003). All of these projects were generally aimed to enable browsing personal information by semantically meaningful associations and to increase users' productivity by leveraging the personal information space in the spirit of the Memex vision.

Some of these projects' findings were adopted and developed in the following NEPOMUK project (Groza et al., 2007). Aiming to build the common Semantic Desktop standard, comprising software architecture, ontologies, etc., the project

is a major step toward a comprehensive approach to personal information handling. It enables users to build, maintain, and employ inter-workspace relations in large scale distributed scenarios. New knowledge can be articulated in semantic structures and be connected with existing information items on the local and remote desktops. Knowledge, information items, and their metadata can be shared spontaneously without a central infrastructure. The main underlying thesis of the Social Semantic Desktop has been derived that the semantics added to personal information management tools will significantly improve productivity and enable new forms of cooperation and interaction which were not previously possible (Bernardi et al., 2008).

Each of presented above systems has both common and distinctive features, complementing others to form an overall Semantic Desktop system vision.

CONCLUSION

In a knowledge economy, the value of an organization derives from the intellectual capital of its knowledge workers. Maximizing the intellectual capital, which consists of human capital (experience and expertise), structural capital (practices and systems) and social capital (networks and relationships), on a personal level is a key objective of Organizational Knowledge Management initiatives. Taking a Personal Knowledge Management approach provides each worker the content, context and connections s/he needs to act more efficiently and productive. An appropriate adaptive knowledge management solution placed at knowledge workers' disposal would help them to tackle with their every-day tasks effectively, increasing their productivity, as well as to leverage organizational knowledge body at a whole through semantic linking both concepts and people.

REFERENCES

Amar, A. D. (2002). *Managing knowledge workers: Unleashing innovation and technology*. Westport, CT: Quarum Books.

Apple. (2005). *Apple to ship Mac OS X Tiger on April 29* [Press Release]. Retrieved December 26, 2009, from http://www.apple.com/pr/library/2005/apr/12tiger.html

Barreau, D., & Nardi, B. A. (1995). Finding and reminding: File organization from the desktop. *ACM SIGCHI Bulletin, 27*(3), 39–43. doi:10.1145/221296.221307

Bernardi, A., Decker, S., van Elst, L., Grimnes, G., Groza, T., & Handschuh, S. ... Sauermann, L. (2009). The social semantic desktop: A new paradigm towards deploying the Semantic Web on the desktop. In J. Cardoso & M. Lytras (Eds.), *Semantic Web engineering in the knowledge society* (pp.290-314). Hershey, PA: IGI Global.

Bibikas, D., Kourtesis, D., Paraskakis, I., Bernardi, A., Sauermann, L., & Apostolou, D. ... Vasconcelos, A. C. (2008). A sociotechnical approach to knowledge management in the era of Enterprise 2.0: The case of OrganiK. In D. Flejter, T. Kaczmarek, & M. Kowalkiewicz (Eds.), *Scalable computing: Practice and experience. Scientific International Journal for Parallel and Distributed Computing, Special Issue: The Web on the Move (SCPE), 9*(4), 315-327.

Boardman, R. (2004). *Improving tool support for personal information management*. PhD thesis, Department of Electrical and Electronic Engineering, Imperial College, London University of London.

Brunkhorst, I., Chirita, P.-A., Costache, S., Gaugaz, J., Ioannou, E., & Iofciu, T. ... Paiu, R. (2006). *The Beagle++ toolbox: Towards an extendable desktop search architecture*. Paper presented at the Semantic Desktop Workshop (SemDesk), Athens, GA, USA.

Bush, V. (1945). As we may think. *The Atlantic Monthly, 176*(1), 101–108. Retrieved December 26, 2009, from http://www.theatlantic.com/doc/194507/bush

Cheyer, A., Park, J., & Giuli, R. (2005). *IRIS: Integrate. Relate. Infer. Share*. Paper presented at the 1st Workshop on the Semantic Desktop at ISWC2005, Galway, Ireland.

Davenport, T. H., & Prusak, L. (1998). *Working knowledge: How organizations manage what they know*. Cambridge, MA: Harvard Business School Press.

Decker, S., & Frank, M. (2004). *The social semantic desktop*. Paper presented at the WWW2004 Workshop on Application Design, Development and Implementation Issues in the Semantic Web, Manhattan, NY, USA.

Dong, X., & Halevy, A. Y. (2005). *A platform for personal information management and integration*. Paper presented at the 2nd Conference on Innovative Data Systems Research (CIDR 2005), Asilomar, CA, USA.

Drucker, P. (1968). *The age of discontinuity: Guidelines to our changing society*. London, UK: Transaction Publishers.

Drucker, P. (1999). Knowledge-worker productivity: The biggest challenge. *California Management Review, 41*(2), 79–92.

Ehrig, M., Tempich, C., Broekstra, J., van Harmelen, F., Sabou, M., & Siebes, R. ... Stuckenschmidt, H. (2003). *SWAP - Ontology-based knowledge management with peer-to-peer technology*. Retrieved December 26, 2009, from http://www. swap. semanticweb. org/ public/ Publications/ ehrig03swapb_wiamis03.pdf

Elsweiler, D., Ruthvan, I., & Jones, C. (2005). *Dealing with fragmented recollection of context in information management.* Paper presented at the Context-Based Information Retrieval (CIR-05) Workshop in Fifth International and Interdisciplinary Conference on Modeling and Using Context (CONTEXT-05), Paris, France.

Engelbart, D. C. (1962). *Augmenting human intellect: A conceptual framework.* Summary Report, (Contract AF 49-638-1024, SRI Project 357B), Stanford Research Institute, Menlo Park, California, AD 289565. Retrieved December 26, 2009, from http://sloan. stanford. edu/ mousesite/ EngelbartPapers/ B5_F18_ConceptFrameworkInd.html

Frand, J., & Hixon, C. (1999). *Personal knowledge management: Who, what, why, when, where, how?* Working paper, UCLA Anderson School of Management. Retrieved December 26, 2009 from http://www.anderson.ucla.edu/faculty/jason. frand/researcher/speeches/PKM.htm

Gantz, J., Boyd, A., & Dowling, S. (2009). *Cutting the clutter: Tackling information overload at the source.* IDC White Paper. Retrieved December 26, 2009, from http://www. xerox. com/ downloads/ usa/en/n/nr_IDC_White_Paper_on_Information_Overload.pdf

Gemmell, J., Bell, G., & Lueder, R. (2006). MyLifeBits: A personal database for everything. *Communications of the ACM, 49*(1), 88-95. Retrieved December 26, 2009, from http://research. microsoft. com/pubs/64157/tr-2006-23.pdf

Gifford, D. K., Jouvelot, P., Sheldon, M. A., & O'Toole, J. W. (1992). Semantic file systems. In *Proceedings of 13th ACM Symposium on Operating Systems Principles* (pp. 16–25). New York, NY: ACM Press.

Groza, T., Handschuh, S., Möller, K., Grimnes, G., Sauermann, L., & Minack, E. … Gudjonsdottir, R. (2007). The NEPOMUK project – On the way to the social semantic desktop. In T. Pellegrini, S. Schaffert (Eds.), *Proceedings of I-Semantics 2007* (pp. 201–211). JUCS. Retrieved December 26, 2009, from http://siegfried-handschuh.net/ pub/2 007/ nepomuk_isemantics2007. pdf

Grundspenkis, J. (2007). Agent based approach for organization and personal knowledge modelling: Knowledge management perspective. *Journal of Intelligent Manufacturing, 18*(4), 451–457. doi:10.1007/s10845-007-0052-6

Jones, W., Bruce, H., & Dumais, S. (2001). Keeping found things found on the Web. In H. Paques, L. Liu, & D. Grossman (Eds.), *CIKM'01: Proceedings of the 2001 ACM CIKM 10th International Conference on Information and Knowledge Management* (pp.119-134). New York, NY: ACM Press.

Kidd, A. (1994). The marks are on the knowledge worker. In *Proceedings of CHI 94: Human Factors in Computing Systems* (pp.186-191). New York, NY: ACM Press.

Lansdale, M. (1988). The psychology of personal information management. *Applied Ergonomics, 19*(1), 55–66. doi:10.1016/0003-6870(88)90199-8

Malone, T. W. (1983). How do people organize their desks? Implications for the design of office information systems. *ACM Transactions on Information Systems, 1*(1), 99–112. doi:10.1145/357423.357430

Möller, K., & Handschuh, S. (2007). *Towards a light-weight semantic desktop.* Paper presented at the SemDesk Design 2007 at ESWC2007, Innsbruck, Austria.

Nelson, T. H. (1965). Complex information processing: a file structure for the complex, the changing and the indeterminate. *ACM/CSC-ER Proceedings of the 20th National Conference* (pp.84-100). New York: ACM Press.

Nelson, T. H. (1981). *Literary Machines*. Sausalito, CA: Mindful Press.

Nonaka, I. (1994). A dynamic theory of organizational knowledge creation. *Organization Science, 5*(1), 14–37. doi:10.1287/orsc.5.1.14

Oren, E. (2006). *An overview of information management and knowledge work studies: Lessons for the semantic desktop*. Paper presented at the ISWC Workshop on the Semantic Desktop and Social Semantic Collaboration (SemDesk 2006), Athens, GA, USA.

Pauleen, D. (2009). Personal knowledge management: putting the person back into the knowledge equation. *Online Information Review, 33*(2), 221–224. doi:10.1108/14684520910951177

Pollard, D. (2006). *The PKM-enabled organization*. Retrieved December 26, 2009, from http://blogs.salon.com/0002007/2006/09/27.html#a1657

Quan, D., Huynh, D., & Karger, D. (2003). Haystack: A platform for authoring end user semantic web applications . In Fensel, D., Sycara, K., & Mylopoulos, J. (Eds.), *The Semantic Web - ISWC 2003 Proceedings* (pp. 738–753). Berlin, Germany: Springer. doi:10.1007/978-3-540-39718-2_47

Quan, D., & Karger, D. (2004). *How to make a semantic web browser*. Paper presented at the 13th International WWW Conference, Semantic Interfaces and OWL Tools Section, New York City, NY, USA.

Richter, J., Völkel, M., & Haller, H. (2005). *Deepamehta - A semantic desktop*. Paper presented at the 1st Workshop on the Semantic Desktop at ISWC2005, Galway, Ireland.

Sauermann, L. (2009). *The Gnowsis semantic desktop approach to personal information management. Weaving the personal Semantic Web*. Doctoral dissertation, University of Kaiserslautern (German Technische Universität Kaiserslautern), Germany.

Senge, P. M. (1994). *The fifth discipline: The art & practice of the learning organization* (2nd ed.). New York, NY: Currency Doubleday.

Spira, J. (2008). *Information overload: Now $900 Billion – What is your organization's exposure?* Retrieved December 26, 2009, from http://www. basexblog. com/ 2008/ 12/ 19 /information -overload-now-900-billion-what-is-your-organizations-exposure/

ADDITIONAL READING

Abdoullaev, A. (2008). *Reality, universal ontology, and knowledge systems: toward the intelligent world*. Hershey, PA: IGI Publishing. doi:10.4018/978-1-59904-966-3

Alexiev, V., & Breu, M. (2005). *Information integration with ontologies: experiences from an industrial showcase*. Chichester, UK: Wiley.

Breslin, J. G., Passant, A., & Decker, S. (2009). *The social semantic web*. Heidelberg, New York: Springer. doi:10.1007/978-3-642-01172-6

Brusilovsky, P., Kobsa, A., & Nejdl, W. (2007). *The adaptive web: methods and strategies of web personalization*. Berlin, New York: Springer.

Choo, C. W. (2002). *Information management for the intelligent organization: the art of scanning the environment. Published for the American Society for Information Science*. Medford, N.J.: Information Today.

Cortada, J. W., & Woods, J. A. (Eds.). (2000). *The Knowledge Management Yearbook 2000 – 2001*. Boston, Oxford: Butterworth-Heinemann.

Davenport, T. H., & Prusak, L. (1998). *Working knowledge*. Boston, Mass: Harvard Business School Press.

Davies, J., Grobelnik, M., & Mladenić, D. (2008). *Semantic Knowledge Management*. Eastbourne, UK: Gardners Books.

Drucker, P. F., & Garvin, D. A. (1998). *Harvard business review on knowledge management*. Boston, Mass.: Harvard Business School Press.

Gorman, G. E., & Pauleen, D. J. (2010). *Personal Knowledge Management: Individual Organisational and Social Perspectives*. Farnham, UK: Ashgate Publishing.

Greenberg, J., & Klas, W. (2008). *Metadata for semantic and social applications: proceedings of the International Conference on Dublin Core and Metadata Applications, DC 2008*. Gottingen, Germany: Universoittsverlag Gottingen.

Ichijo, K., & Nonaka, I. (2007). *Knowledge creation and management: new challenges for managers*. New York, NY: Oxford University Press.

Jacko, J. A., & Sears, A. (2008). *The Human-Computer Interaction Handbook: Fundamentals, Evolving Technologies, and Emerging Applications*. New York, NY: Taylor & Francis Group.

Ma, Z., & Wang, H. (2009). *The Semantic Web for knowledge and data management: technologies and practices*. Hershey, PA: Information Science Reference.

Pauleen, D. J. (2009). *Personal knowledge management*. Bingley, UK: Emerald.

Raedt, L., & Siebes, A. (2001). *Principles of data mining and knowledge discovery: proceedings of the 5th European conference, PKDD 2001*. Berlin; London: Springer.

Stuckenschmidt, H., & van Harmelen, F. (2005). *Information sharing on the semantic Web*. Berlin, New York: Springer.

Sugumaran, V. (2008). *Intelligent information technologies: concepts, methodologies, tools, and applications*. Hershey, PA: Information Science Reference.

ENDNOTES

[1] http://www.basex.com

[2] http://www.xerox.com/information-overload/enus.html#TOP

[3] http://www.viceversatech.com/products/scan-desktop/

Section 3
Semantic Technologies in Conceptual Modeling

Chapter 7
Supporting Conceptual Model Analysis Using Semantic Standardization and Structural Pattern Matching

Patrick Delfmann
University of Münster, Germany

Sebastian Herwig
University of Münster, Germany

Łukasz Lis
University of Münster, Germany

Jörg Becker
University of Münster, Germany

ABSTRACT

Analysis of conceptual models is useful for a number of purposes, such as revealing syntactical errors, model comparison, model integration, and identification of business process improvement potentials, with both the model structure and the model contents having to be considered. In this contribution, we introduce a generic model analysis approach. Unlike existing approaches, we do not focus on a certain application problem or a specific modeling language. Instead, our approach is generic, making it applicable for any analysis purpose and any graph-based conceptual modeling language. The approach integrates pattern matching for structural analysis and linguistic standardization enabling an unambiguous analysis of the models' contents.

DOI: 10.4018/978-1-60960-126-3.ch007

INTRODUCTION

Conceptual models are a common way of documenting requirements and system design in projects addressing the reorganization and development of information systems (IS) (Kottemann & Konsynski 1984). As IS projects are often large-scaled, the required models are increasingly developed in a distributed way in order to increase the efficiency of modeling (vom Brocke & Thomas, 2006). In such cases, different modelers participate in the modeling process developing sub-models – potentially at different places and at a different time. Empirical studies show that such models can vary heavily concerning naming and structure (Hadar & Soffer, 2006). However, even models developed by a single person might include semantic and structural ambiguities if s/he does not follow any explicit modeling conventions (Delfmann, Herwig & Lis, 2009b). Trying to analyze such models, comparison conflicts can occur, which are commonly divided into *naming (semantic) conflicts* and *structural conflicts* (Batini & Lenzerini 1984).

In Figure 1, we present examples of a semantic and a structural conflict as well as a combination of both of them. (1a) depicts two structurally equivalent models, which include different vocabulary and phrasing. Two interpretations are possible. On the one hand, both models might depict the same real-life situation with structurally corresponding element names being semantically equivalent. The differences could result from the lack of semantic standardization. In this case, the terms "bill" and "o.k." would be synonyms of "invoice" and "valid" correspondingly. On the other hand, the two models could depict different issues and the structurally corresponding names could represent semantically different things. The only chance to find out which situation is the case is to discuss the differing semantics with the modeler(s) involved. Thus, an automated analysis is not possible. (1b) depicts two models, which already apply standardized corporate vocabu-

lary disallowing for naming conflicts. However, although these models potentially represent the same real-life issue, they involve different but in this case synonymous modeling structures. When trying to analyze (and compare) these models, we need to take account of the relation between synonymous structural patterns, such as the two depicted here. In (1c), two models involving both semantic and structural conflicts are presented. Besides using proprietary vocabulary (e.g., "component" vs. "part"), the model on the right-hand side has a higher level of detail than the left one, although both depict the same real-life situation. To sum up, due to semantic and structural conflicts performing a consistent analysis might pose an extremely laborious task.

The analysis of conceptual models addresses different goals. For example, single conceptual models are analyzed using typical error patterns in order to check for syntactical errors or potential problems (Mendling, 2007). In the domain of Business Process Management (BPM), process models' analysis helps identifying process improvement potentials (Vergidis, Tiwari & Majeed, 2008). For example, applying structural model patterns to process models can help revealing changes of the data medium during process execution (e.g., printing and subsequently retyping a document), redundant execution of process activities, or application potentials of software systems. In most cases, where modeling is conducted in a distributed way, subsequent integration is necessary to obtain a coherent model. To find corresponding fragments and to evaluate integration opportunities, multiple models – generally of the same modeling language – are compared with each other applying structural model pattern matching (Gori, Maggini & Sarti, 2005). Semantically equivalent (or at least similar) structures are defined as corresponding patterns, which allows for identifying related model fragments. This way, structural pattern matching provides decision support in model analysis and, in particular, integration. Model patterns have already been

Figure 1. Examples of semantic and/or structural conflicts in conceptual models

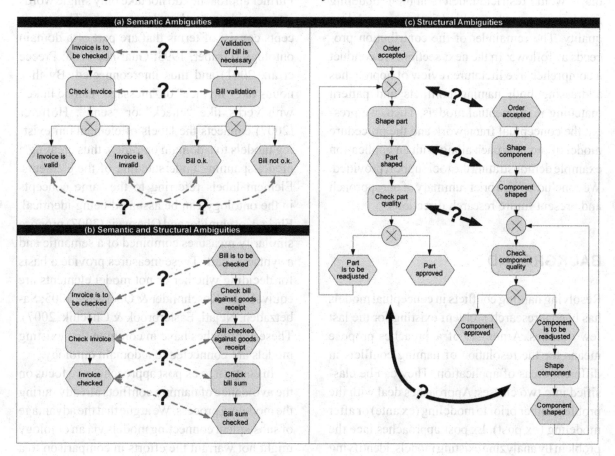

subject of research in the fields of database schema integration (cf. Rahm & Bernstein, 2001 for an overview) and workflow management (e.g., Hidders, Dumas, van der Aalst, ter Hofstede & Verelst, 2005) to give some examples. However, our literature review reveals that existing pattern matching approaches are limited to a specific domain or restricted to a single modeling language. Moreover, before a structural analysis can be performed, all naming conflicts have to be resolved. We argue that the modeling community would benefit from a holistic approach, which coherently addresses both naming and structure and is applicable in multiple model analysis scenarios.

In this contribution, we present a combined approach, which (1) disallows naming conflicts

by enforcing linguistic standardization already during modeling and (2) allows for flexible pattern specification and matching in the model base. This integrated approach is based on our previous research on naming conventions (Delfmann, Herwig & Lis, 2009a) and generic pattern matching (Delfmann, Herwig, Lis, Stein, Tent, & Becker, 2010; Becker, Delfmann, Herwig, & Lis, 2009). For (1), our approach facilitates capturing the corporate language in naming conventions prior to modeling and automatically enforcing these conventions during modeling. For (2), we provide a generic pattern matching environment, which allows the specification of structurally corresponding patterns and automated matching to support model analysis. Although some structural standardization might also be possible, we believe that it would restrict modelers in their modeling freedom too much resulting in lower modeling quality. The remainder of the contribution proceeds as follows: In the next section, we conduct a comprehensive literature review of approaches addressing both naming conflicts and pattern matching in conceptual models. Then, we present the conceptual framework and the procedure model of our approach along with an application example demonstrating the tool support provided. We conclude with a brief summary of our approach and present future research directions.

BACKGROUND

Resolving naming conflicts in conceptual models has been a research problem existing for the last few decades. A number of approaches propose means for the resolution of naming conflicts in different areas of application. They can be classified into two classes: Approaches deal with the problem either prior to modeling (ex ante) or after modeling (ex post). Ex post approaches face the problem by analyzing existing models, identifying naming conflicts and trying to solve them. Ex ante approaches aim at preventing the emergence of naming conflicts by guiding the modeler.

In the 1980s and 1990s, the resolution of naming conflicts was discussed related to the problem of integrating company databases using the underlying schemas as a starting point (cf. Batini & Lenzerini, 1984; Bhargava, Kimbrough & Krishnan, 1991; Lawrence & Barker, 2001; cf. Batini, Lenzerini & Navathe, 1986 and Rahm & Bernstein, 2001 for an overview). Hence, these approaches focus on data modeling languages, mostly dialects of the Entity-Relationship Model (ERM) (Chen, 1976). They analyze given schemas and identify possibly matching fragments. Commonly, the intensity of correspondence is represented by a numerical measure. However, the necessity to involve domain experts to judge on the actual correspondence is explicitly stated.

Further approaches do not take only single words into consideration, but also *concepts*. These concepts consist of terms that are part of a domain ontology (Gruber, 1993; Guarino, 1998; Preece et al., 2001) and thus interconnected. By this, nouns like "invoice" or "message" can be linked with verbs like "check" or "send". Höfferer (2007) connects the labels of elements in existing models to a domain ontology, thus creating a model-spanning understanding of the elements. Element labels referring to the same concepts in the ontology can be assumed being identical. Ehrig, Koschmider and Oberweis (2007) propose similarity measures combined of a semantic and a syntactic part. These measures provide a basis for deciding whether or not model elements are equivalents (Koschmider & Oberweis, 2005; Sabetzadeh, Nejati, Easterbrook & Chechik, 2007). These approaches have in common that existing models are connected to a domain ontology.

In contrast to ex post approaches, we focus on the avoidance of naming conflicts already during the modeling process. We argue that the advantage of subsequent connecting models via an ontology might not warrant the efforts in comparison to a conventional manual analysis.

Such ex ante approaches make use of naming conventions to limit the probability of using ambiguous terminology during the modelling project in advance. Commonly, naming conventions are provided as written glossaries, as semantic wikis (Völkel, 2006), or as ontologies (Gruber, 1993; Guarino, 1998; Preece et al., 2001), containing single terms or multiple terms treated as one concept, which are suitable for the regarded domain. A general understanding of annotating conceptual models with ontological concepts is provided by Ahlemann, Teuteberg and Brune (2006). Greco, Guzzo, Pontieri and Saccà (2004) propose manually adapting ontology terms for process models. Born, Dörr and Weber (2007) take a step forward by providing means for a semi-automatic adoption of model element names from a domain ontology. There, only those terms are allowed, which are part of the ontology. The authors focus on BPMN models (White & Miers, 2008). It also generates proposals for the naming of a given activity based on previous activities and the order of matching domain actions defined in the ontology. This way, it exploits the advanced semantic capabilities of ontologies. Users can choose other labels on their own and thus abandon the convention provided by the ontology. Automated approaches are provided by Rizopolous and McBrien (2005) and Bögl, Kobler and Schrefl (2008), who propose the use of online dictionaries like for example WordNet (Fellbaum, 1998). Model elements are then connected to the corresponding entries of those dictionaries. Thomas and Fellmann (2009) annotate business process models with information taken from ontologies that describe both the modeling language constructs and the semantics of the business process. The statements made in the process models are completely contained in the ontology (e.g., the activity concept "check order" is treated as a whole and semantically related to other ones). An enterprise system-related approach is proposed by Abramowicz, Filipowska, Kaczmarek, and Kaczmarek (2007) and Hepp and Roman (2007). They enhance business process models with ontological information focusing on the suitability of web services for business process model activities.

Mainly originating from the German speaking area during the 1990s, approaches related to linguistics provide standardized phrase structures as means for the generation of consistent model element names. Rosemann (1996) and Kugeler (2000) use this as guidelines for the labelling of process activities in Event-Driven Process Chains (EPCs) (Scheer, 2000). The rule <verb, imperative> <noun, singular> restricts the label to terms like "check invoice". Thus, only those phrases are allowed, that can be built in conjunction with the terms of a technical term model (Rosemann, 2003). The latter has to be generated before the beginning of the modelling project. Although the term rules involve phrase structures, the technical term model is limited to nouns.

To achieve semantic unambiguity in conceptual models, two aspects are crucial: First, compliance with semantic standards – either defined in an ontology or linguistically – has to be enforced. Thus, it has to be assured that modelers follow the standards during modeling. Second, the semantic standards have to consider not only single terms, but also combinations of terms (either represented as complex concepts in ontologies (Thomas & Fellmann, 2009) or phrase structures to be instantiated with predefined terms (Delfmann, Herwig & Lis, 2009a)), since sentences with a different order of terms may have different meanings.

In this paper, we make use of an ex ante linguistic approach (Delfmann, Herwig & Lis, 2009a). It provides the modeler with a domain vocabulary and syntactic conventions restricting the possibilities of building naming phrases. During the modeling process, the modeler is guided by a software wizard in order to assure compliance with the conventions.

Comparing the linguistic strategy to ex ante approaches based on ontologies shows some pros and cons. On the one hand, the semantic richness of the linguistic approach is restricted, compared to ontologies. It is not possible to conduct advanced automatic reasoning only from domain vocabularies. On the other hand, the ontology approach requires presetting every possible concept, instead of only single terms and phrase structure conventions. Hence, persons responsible for developing the ontology have to possess a thorough knowledge of the whole modeling problem (e.g., the business processes of a whole company). Every additional model may require changing the ontology. In the linguistic case, it is only necessary to preset the corporate terms and phrase structure conventions. The semantics of the modeling scenario are defined during the modeling process and not during the presetting of terms or phrase structure conventions. A change of the models does not imply a change of the linguistic standards, as models and standards are independent of each other. Therefore, the development of actual models can be easily distributed. Nevertheless, the models stay comparable as they all rely on linguistic standards. Thus, we favor the linguistic approach in this contribution.

Supporting the structural analysis of conceptual models, fundamental work has been done in the field of graph theory addressing the problem of graph pattern matching (Gori et al., 2005; Fu, 1995; Varró, Varró & Schürr, 2006; Valiente & Martínez, 1997). Based on a given graph, these approaches discuss the identification of structurally equivalent (homomorphous) or synonymous (isomorphous) parts of a given graph in other graphs. To identify such parts, several pattern matching algorithms are proposed, which make use of a pattern definition as comparison criteria to find corresponding parts in other graphs. The algorithms compute walks through the graphs in order to analyze the nodes and the structure of the graphs. As a result, they identify patterns representing corresponding parts of the compared graphs. Thus, a pattern is based on a particular labelled graph section and is not predefined independently. Some approaches are limited to specific types of graphs (e.g., the approaches of Fu (1995) and Varró et al. (2006) are restricted to labeled directed graphs).

In the context of process models, so-called behavioural approaches have been proposed to identify equivalence in process models (Hirschfeld, 1993; de Medeiros, van der Aalst & Weijters, 2008; Hidders et al., 2005). Two process models are considered equivalent if they behave identically during simulation or execution. This implies that the respective modelling languages possess formal execution semantics. Therefore, the authors focus on Petri Nets and other workflow modelling languages (van Dongen, Dijkman & Mendling, 2008). Moreover, due to the requirement of model simulation, these approaches generally consider process models as a whole. Patterns as model subsets are only comparable if they are also executable. Hence, not every pattern – even

if provided with formal execution semantics – can be used for matching.

In the domain of database engineering, various approaches have been presented, which address the already mentioned problem of schema matching. Two input schemas (i.e., descriptions of database structures) are taken and mappings between semantically corresponding elements are created (Rahm & Bernstein, 2001). These approaches operate on single elements only (Li & Clifton, 2000) or assume that the schemas have a tree-like structure (Madhavan, Bernstein & Rahm, 2001). Recently, the methods developed in the context of database schema matching have been applied in the field of ontology matching as well (Aumueller, Do, Massmann & Rahm, 2005). Additionally, approaches explicitly dedicated to matching ontologies have been presented. They usually utilize additional context information (e.g., a corresponding collection of documents (Stumme & Maedche, 2001)), which is not given in standard conceptual modeling settings. Moreover, as schema-matching approaches operate on approximation-basis, similar structures – and not exact pattern occurrences – are addressed (Shvaiko & Euzenat, 2005). Consequently, these approaches lack the opportunity of including explicit structure descriptions (e.g., paths of a given length or loops containing given elements) in the patterns.

Patterns are also proposed as an indicator for possible conflicts typically occurring during modelling and the model integration process. Hars (1994) proposes a collection of general patterns for ERMs (Chen, 1976). On the one hand, these patterns depict possible structural errors that may occur. For such error patterns corresponding patterns are proposed, which provide correct structures. On the other hand, a number of model patterns is discussed, which possibly lead to conflicts while integrating such models into an overall model. Similar work in the field of process modelling is done by Mendling (2007). Based on the analysis of EPCs, he detects a collection of general patterns, which depict syntactical errors in EPCs. However, these two approaches focus on particular structural patterns for specific modelling languages rather than a pattern definition and matching approach for arbitrary modelling languages.

To sum up, we identify the following need for development towards supporting the analysis of conceptual models: To assure linguistic standardization, methodical support for the formal specification and enforcement of naming conventions is required. Concerning the structural analysis, we need methodical support allowing for pattern matching in conceptual models of any modeling language and for any type of patterns (i.e., patterns with a predefined or unlimited number of elements). For this purpose, we make use of a generic pattern matching approach based on set operations (Delfmann, Herwig, Lis, Stein, Tent, & Becker, 2010; Becker, Delfmann, Herwig, & Lis, 2009). Furthermore, to enable an unambiguous analysis of the content of a model base, a methodical approach is needed combining linguistic standardization and structural pattern matching.

A GENERIC MODEL ANALYSIS APPROACH

Procedure Model

Since a precondition for unambiguous models is a unified understanding of terms, the first step in order to enable proper model analysis is to define the corporate language (cf. Figure 2). As a basis, decision makers have to agree on the vocabulary considered valid in the regarded company. Based on the selected modeling languages to be used in the modeling project, the next step is to define valid phrase structures for each of the modeling languages' element types. Based on these definitions, the models are developed. Since the natural language used to denote the model elements is standardized, ambiguities in the denotation should not occur. Hence, single model analysis – even concerning structure – should cause no ambiguity problems at all. Model comparison is supported through structural model analysis as mentioned in the introduction.

First, according to the procedural model, we introduce a framework allowing for standardizing the natural language used in conceptual models and for enforcing the use of this language during modeling. Second, we develop a formal approach to define structural model patterns and to match these patterns in the model base. Third, we show what a particular model analysis could look like based on four application examples.

Linguistic Standardization Framework

In order to standardize a corporate language, we make use of basic linguistic concepts. A natural language, as it is used for model element names, consists of terms (i.e., natural language words) and syntax (e.g., the English syntax). Consequently, standardization of a natural language means defining considered valid terms and considered valid syntax. Therefore, we restrict the terms of

Figure 2. Procedure model

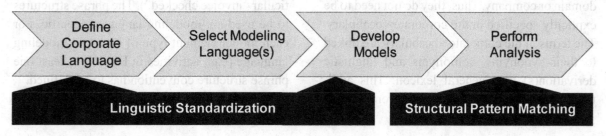

Figure 3. Establishing a corporate language

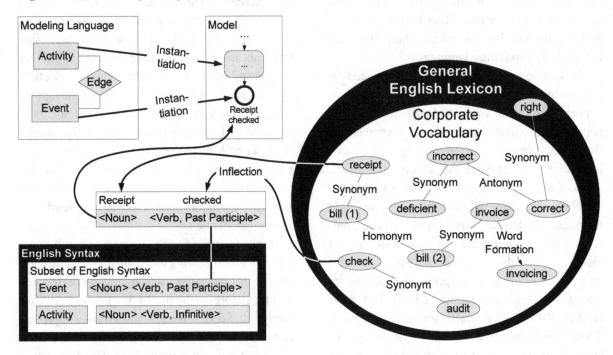

a natural language to a subset – the corporate vocabulary. At the same time, we restrict the natural language's syntax. This means that we restrict the sentence structures that are allowed to be used in model element names to a subset of the natural language's syntax. Thus, we establish so-called phrase structure conventions. Filling in a valid phrase structure with valid terms from the corporate vocabulary leads to a particular phrase representing a valid model element name (cf. Figure 3).

The corporate vocabulary can be created from scratch, or by reusing possibly existing thesauri or glossaries. It includes nouns, verbs, adjectives, and adverbs being interrelated. Other word classes are generally independent from a special domain or company. Thus, they do not need to be explicitly specified in the corporate vocabulary. The terms in the corporate vocabulary are linked to their synonyms, homonyms and linguistic derivation(s) in a general lexicon. This additional information can be obtained from linguis-

tic services, which already exist for different natural languages (e.g., WordNet (2009)). In case of a violation of the corporate language by the modeler, synonymous or derived valid terms can be automatically identified and recommended this way. The terms specified should be provided with textual descriptions, allowing modelers for looking up the exact meaning of a term.

The corporate language has to be specified once for a company or domain, whereas already existing standards can be reused. For example, in the context of process modeling, activities like such in BPMN are labeled with actions (e.g., <verb, imperative> <noun, singular>; in particular "check invoice") and events are labeled with states (e.g., <noun, singular> <verb, past participle>; in particular "invoice checked"). The phrase structures to be used are modeling language-specific. For each model element type of a certain modeling language (e.g., activities in BPMN) at least one phrase structure convention has to be defined.

Figure 4. Validation and suggestion of model element names

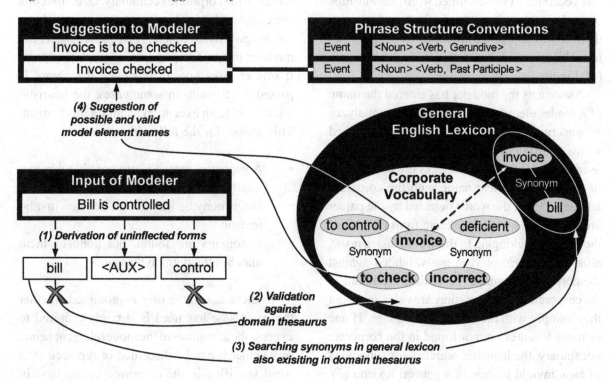

During modeling, the model element names entered by a modeler are verified simultaneously against the specified corporate language. On the one hand, the structure of an entered model element name is validated against the corporate language syntax specification. On the other hand, an automatism checks whether the used terms are allowed. Nouns, verbs, adjectives, and adverbs (i.e., word classes covered by the corporate vocabulary) are validated against it. Other word classes are validated against the general lexicon.

In case of a positive validation, the entered model element name is declared as valid against the corporate language. In case of a violation of one or both criteria, alternative valid phrase structures and/or terms are suggested based on the user input.

To assure the correctness of both specified phrase structure conventions and the structure and words of model element names, we make use of linguistic syntax parsing. According parsing

methods detect the syntax of a given sentence. For example, an according parsing method analyzes the phrase "invoice checked" and returns the phrase type *<noun, singular> <verb, past participle>* as well as the lexemes "invoice" and "check". For reasons of clarity, we do not introduce these methods in detail (cf. (Kaplan, 2003) for an overview). Given a phrase structure convention, according parsing methods are able to determine whether the convention complies with the syntax of a natural language. Furthermore, given a model element name, they determine whether the syntax of the name complies with the phrase structure conventions. This way we check the convention-related correctness of model element names concurrently.

In our approach, we parse sentences against the corporate vocabulary and the restricted English syntax. If the terms used within model element names do not comply with the conventions, we search alternative but valid lexemes in the corporate vocabulary via the defined word relationships or in the general language lexicon and propose them in the appropriate inflection form for proper use. This process is automated through a heuristic (cf. Figure 4).

As soon as the modeler has entered the name of a model element, a linguistic parser analyzes it concerning the phrase structure and the used words. Starting from the phrase structure and the used words, the heuristic checks the compliance of the model element name with the corporate language. First, the words detected by the parser are re-inflected to their lexeme form (1). All of the lexemes belonging to the word classes *noun, adjective/adverb,* or *verb* are validated against the corporate language (2). If they are found in the corporate vocabulary, they are valid, meaning they comply with the corporate language. If one or more lexemes are not found in the corporate vocabulary, the heuristic searches for synonyms of each invalid lexeme in a general lexicon (3). The synonyms found are matched against the corporate vocabulary. If one of the synonyms matches the vocabulary entry, the original lexeme is replaced with the valid synonym (e.g., the invalid lexeme "bill" is replaced with the valid lexeme "invoice").

Second, the phrase structure used as model element name is validated against the phrase structure conventions. If the phrase structure and all of the original lexemes are valid the original phrase as a whole is marked as valid and the heuristic terminates. If the phrase structure is valid, and the original lexemes had to be replaced by synonyms, the synonyms are inflected automatically according to the phrase type, and the new phrase is proposed to the modeler as an alternative to his original suggestion (e.g., "The name 'bill is controlled' you entered violates the naming conventions. Did you mean 'invoice checked'?") (4).

If the phrase structure entered by the user is invalid, the heuristic calculates all possible phrases complying with both the phrase structure conven-

tions and the corporate vocabulary. Of course, this can cause multiple phrase alternatives, which are not necessarily complete. As a consequence, the modeler has to complete an incomplete phrase, if s/he chooses one. In this case, the phrase is parsed once again. In some cases, the heuristic must provide an exception handling mechanism. This applies for the following situations:

- A synonym search is not possible due to a totally unknown original lexeme
- No synonyms are found for an invalid lexeme
- Synonyms are found, but none of them matches the domain thesaurus

In these cases, the user is prompted whether the word s/he has used is strongly required to express the semantics of the model element name, or whether it can be discarded or replaced by a word specified in the corporate vocabulary. In the latter case, the user can search the corporate vocabulary for an appropriate word. If the original term is strongly required and cannot be replaced by an alternative one, the user can propose the term as a new entry for the corporate vocabulary (like it is done similarly with distributed ontology development editors (e.g., Sunagawa, Kozaki, Kitamura, and Mizoguchi, 2003). Then the modeling expert committee has to decide whether or not the term is added to the corporate vocabulary. In this case, the model element name is marked as preliminary until the decision of the committee. Once a decision has been made, the domain thesaurus is either updated accordingly, and the model element marked as preliminary is finally accepted, or the model element name marked as preliminary is changed by the modeling expert committee according to the corporate language. In both cases, the modeler is informed. Accepting a new term requires a preceding synonym analysis of the corporate vocabulary to prevent ambiguities.

Structural Pattern Matching Framework

The structural analysis of models requires recognizing model sections that match structural patterns. We define a structural model pattern as a template for a set of model objects being interrelated. This means that a model section matches a pattern as soon as its model objects belong to the types defined in the pattern and the structure established by their relationships matches the structure preset in the pattern. Therefore, we regard a conceptual model as a set of model elements. Here, we further distinguish between objects representing nodes and relationships representing edges interrelating objects. Starting from this set, pattern matches are searched by performing set operations on this basic set. By combining different set operations, the pattern is built up successively. Given a pattern definition, the matching process returns a set of model sections representing the pattern matches found. Every match found is put into an own subset. The following example illustrates the general idea.

An exemplary pattern definition consists of three objects of different types that are interrelated with each other by relationships. A pattern match within a model is represented as a set containing three different objects and three relationships that connect them. To distinguish multiple pattern matches, each match is represented as a separate subset. Thus, the result of a pattern matching process is represented by a set of pattern matches (i.e., a set of sets, cf. Figure 5).

Combining both linguistic standardization of models and structural pattern matching, structural, semantic and combined model analysis is made possible due to unambiguous naming and ability to find arbitrary structures.

Conceptual Specification

The conceptual specification of a generic model analysis approach has to consider three main aspects. Since the approach is generic, the specification must allow for using arbitrary modeling languages: As a specification basis, we use a generic meta-meta model for conceptual modeling languages, which is closely related to the Meta Object Facility (MOF) specification (OMG, 2009). Here, we use a subset, which is represented in the Entity-Relationship notation (Chen, 1976) with (min,max)-cardinalities (ISO, 1982).

Figure 5. Representation of pattern matches through sets of elements

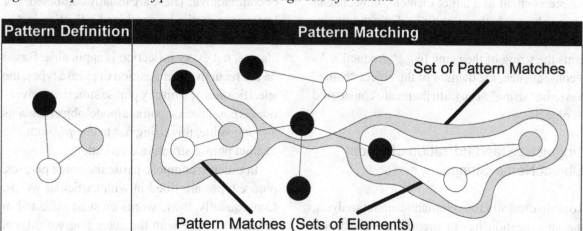

Generic Specification Environment for Modeling Languages

Modeling languages typically consist of modeling objects that are interrelated through relationships (e.g., vertices and edges). In some languages, relationships can be interrelated in turn (e.g., association classes in UML Class Diagrams (OMG 2009b)). Hence, modeling languages consist of element types, which are specialized as object types (e.g., nodes) and their relationship types (e.g., edges and links) (cf. Figure 6, constructs shaded black). In order to allow relationships between relationships, we define the relationship type as a specialization of the element type. (E.g., n-ary relationship types can be specified in two different manners: Either they are represented by object types like it is usual in entity-relationship models or they are represented by multiple interrelated binary relationship types.) Each relationship type has a source element type, from which it originates, and a target element type, to which it leads. Relationship types are either directed or undirected. Whenever the attribute directed is FALSE, the direction of the relationship type is ignored. The instantiation of modeling languages leads to models, which consist of particular elements. These are instantiated from their distinct element type. Elements are specialized into objects and relationships. Each of the latter leads from a source element to a target element. Objects can have values, which are part of a distinct domain. For example, the value of an object "name" contains the string of the name (e.g., "product"). As a consequence, the domain of the object "name" has to be "string". Thus, attributes are considered as objects.

Linguistic Standardization of Model Object Name Strings

To realize unambiguous semantic model analysis, the specification has to incorporate constructs realizing linguistic standardization for model ele-

ment names (cf. Figure 6, constructs shaded grey). These constructs have to consider both the domain vocabulary and phrase structure conventions: Since different modeling languages imply different requirements towards model element naming (e.g., activities in process models are named differently to objects in data models), we allow for specifying different phrase structure conventions for different object types of modeling languages. Therefore, we define phrase structure conventions (PSC) depending on distinct object types.

Phrase structure conventions consist of phrase types or word types. A phrase type specifies the structure of a phrase used as a model element name. Therefore, a phrase type can be composed recursively of further phrase types or word types. Representing atomic elements of a phrase type, word types are acting as placeholders for particular words. An example of a word type is <noun, singular>, an example of a phrase type is <verb, imperative> <noun, singular>. The composition of phrase types is defined by the phrase type structure. At this, we define the allocation of sub phrase types or word types to a phrase type and their position in the superordinate phrase type.

A word type consists of a distinct word class (noun, verb, adjective, adverb, article, pronoun, preposition, conjunction, or numeral) – and its inflection. Inflections modify a word according to its case, number, tense, gender, mood, person, or comparative. These are usually combined. For instance, a particular combined inflection is <3rd person, singular>. In respect to specific word classes, not every inflection is applicable. Based on the recursive composition of phrase types, the specification of arbitrary phrase structure conventions is possible. As soon as a model object contains a *string* value, this string has to *comply* with one distinct phrase structure convention.

In order to compose particular name phrases, phrase types are filled in with particular words. Consequently, those words must be inflected in order to comply with the according word type. These inflected words are called word forms (e.g.,

Figure 6. Conceptual specification of the generic model analysis approach

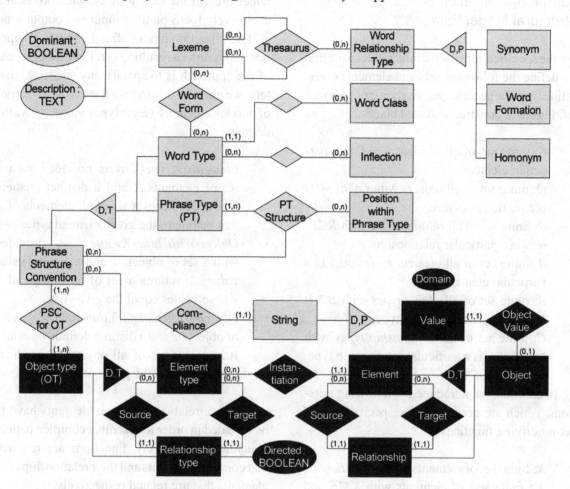

past participle "checked"). Independent from their corresponding word class, particular uninflected words are called lexemes (e.g., the verb "check").

To specify the domain thesaurus, words are stored in the form of lexemes being related by different word relationship types. These are homonym, synonym, and word formation relations. Word formation means that a lexeme originates from (an)other one(s) (e.g., the noun "control" originates from the verb "to control"). In case of synonym relations, one of the involved lexemes is marked as *dominant* to state that it is the valid one for the particular modeling context. Homonym relations are necessary to distinguish lexemes that consist of the same string but have a different

meaning and to prevent errors during modeling. Word formation relations are used to search for appropriate alternatives when a modeler has used invalid terms and phrase structures. For instance, if the phrase "order clearance" violates the conventions, the alternative phrase "clear order" can be found via the word formation relation of "to clear" and "clearance". Based on the word relationship types, lexical services are connected to the domain thesaurus. To specify what is actually meant by a lexeme, a semantic *description* is added at least to each dominant lexeme. This way, modelers are enabled to check whether the lexeme they have used actually fits the modeling issue.

Formal Specification of Structural Model Patterns

For the specification of structural model patterns, we define the following sets and elements originating from the generic specification environment (cf. Figure 6, constructs shaded black):

- E: finite set of all *elements*; $e \in E$ is a particular element.
- O: finite set of all *objects* with $O \subseteq E$; $o \in O$ is a particular object.
- R: finite set of all *relationships* with $R \subseteq E$; $r \in R$ is a particular relationship.
- A: finite set of all *element types*; $a \in A$ is a particular element type.
- B: finite set of all *object types* with $B \subseteq A$; $b \in B$ is a particular object type.
- C: finite set of all *relationship types* with $C \subseteq A$; $c \in C$ is a particular relationship type.

In addition, we introduce the following notations, which are needed for the specification of set-modifying functions:

- X: finite set of elements with $x \in X \subseteq E$.
- X_k: finite sets of elements with $X_k \subseteq E$ and $k \in N_0$
- Y: finite set of objects with $y \in Y \subseteq O$.
- Z: finite set of relationships with $z \in Z \subseteq R$.
- n_X: positive natural number $n_X \in N_1$

Building up structural model patterns successively requires performing set operations on the basic sets. In the following, we introduce predefined functions on these sets in order to provide a convenient specification environment dedicated to conceptual models. However, in order to make the approach reusable for multiple purposes, the formal specification of these functions is based on *predicate logic*. For clarity reasons, we will not present the detailed formal specifications here (for a detailed formal specification, cf. Delfmann, Herwig, Lis, Stein, Tent, & Becker, 2010). We

rather present the functions as black boxes and exclusively focus on their input and output sets.

Each function has a defined number of input sets and returns a resulting set. First, since a goal of the approach is to specify any structural pattern, we must be able to reveal specific properties of model elements (e.g., type, value, or value domain):

- *ElementsOfType(X,a)* is provided with a set of elements X and a distinct element type a. It returns a set of all elements of X that belong to the given element type.
- *ObjectsWithValue(Y,value$_Y$)* is provided with a set of objects Y and a distinct value $value_Y$. It returns a set of all objects of Y whose values equal the given one.
- *ObjectsWithDomain(Y,domain$_Y$)* takes a set of objects Y and a distinct domain $domain_Y$. It returns a set of all objects of Y whose domains equal the given one.

Second, relations between elements have to be revealed in order to assemble complex pattern structures successively. Functions are required that combine elements and their relationships and elements that are related respectively.

- *ElementsWithRelations(X,Z)* is provided with a set of elements X and a set of relationships Z. It returns a set of sets containing all elements of X and all undirected relationships of Z, which are connected. Each occurrence is represented by an inner set.
- *ElementsWithOutRelations(X,Z)* is provided with a set of elements X and a set of relationships Z. It returns a set of sets containing all elements of X that are connected to directed, outgoing relationships of Z, including these relationships. Each occurrence is represented by an inner set.
- *ElementsWithInRelations(X,Z)* is defined analogously to *ElementsWithOutRelations*.

In contrast, it only returns incoming relationships.

- *ElementsDirectlyRelatedInclRelations(X₁,X₂)* is provided with two sets of elements X_1 and X_2. It returns a set of sets containing all elements of X_1 and X_2 that are connected directly via relationships of R, including these relationships. The directions of the relationships given by their "Source" or "Target" assignment are ignored. Furthermore, the attribute "directed" of the according relationship types has to be FALSE. Each occurrence is represented by an inner set.

- *DirectSuccessorsInclRelations(X₁,X₂)* is defined analogously to *ElementsDirectlyRelatedInclRelations*. In contrast, it only returns relationships that are directed, whereas the source elements are part of X_1 and the target elements are part of X_2.

Third, to construct model patterns representing recursive structures (e.g. a path of an arbitrary length consisting of alternating elements and relationships) the following functions are defined:

- *Paths(X₁,Xₙ)* takes two sets of elements as input and returns a set of sets containing all sequences, which lead from any element of X_1 to any element of X_n. The directions of the relationships, which are part of the paths, given by their "Source" or "Target" assignment, are ignored. Furthermore, the attribute "directed" of the according relationship types has to be FALSE. The elements that are part of the paths do not necessarily have to be elements of X_1 or X_n but can also be of $E \backslash X_1 \backslash X_n$. Each path found is represented by an inner set.

- *DirectedPaths(X₁,Xₙ)* is defined analogously to *Paths*. In contrast, it only returns directed paths leading from X_1 to X_n.

- *Loops(X)* takes a set of elements as input and returns a set of sets containing all sequences, which lead from any element of X to itself. The directions of the relationships, which are part of the loops, given by their "Source" or "Target" assignment, are ignored. Furthermore, the attribute "directed" of the according relationship types has to be FALSE. The elements that are part of the loops do not necessarily have to be elements of X, but can also be of $E \backslash X$. Each loop found is represented by an inner set.

- *DirectedLoops(X)* is defined analogously to *Loops*. In contrast, it only returns loops, the relationships of which have the same direction.

To avoid infinite sets, only finite paths and loops are returned. As soon as there exists a complete sub-loop on a loop or a path, and this sub-loop is passed the second time, the search aborts. The path or loop that was searched for is excluded from the result set. To provide a convenient specification environment for structural model patterns, we define some additional functions that are derived from those already introduced:

- *ElementsWithRelationsOfType(X,Z,c)* is provided with a set of elements X, a set of relationships Z and a distinct relationship type c. It returns a set of sets containing all elements of X and relationships of Z of the type c, which are connected. Each occurrence is represented by an inner set.

- *ElementsWithOutRelationsOfType(X,Z,c)* is defined analogously to *ElementsWithRelationsOfType*. In contrast, it only returns outgoing relationships.

- *ElementsWithInRelationsOfType(X,Z,c)* is defined analogously to *ElementsWithOutRelationsOfType*.

- *ElementsWithNumberOfRelations(X,nₓ)* is provided with a set of elements X and a distinct number n_X. It returns a set of sets containing all elements of X, which are connected to the given number of relationships of R, including these relationships. Each occurrence is represented by an inner set.

- *ElementsWithNumberOfOutRelations(X,n_x)* is defined analogously to *ElementsWithNumberOfRelations*. In contrast, it only returns outgoing relationships.
- *ElementsWithNumberOfInRelations(X, n_x)* is defined analogously to *ElementsWithNumberOf OutRelations*.
- *ElementsWithNumberOfRelationsOfType(X,c,n_x)* is provided with a set of elements X, a distinct relationship type c and a distinct number n_x. It returns a set of sets containing all elements of X, which are connected to the given number of relationships of R of the type c, including these relationships. Each occurrence is represented by an inner set.
- *ElementsWithNumberOfOutRelationsOf Type(X,c,n_x)* is defined analogously to *ElementsWithNumberOfRelationsOfType*. In contrast, it only returns outgoing relationships.
- *ElementsWithNumberOfInRelationsOf Type(X,c,n_x)* is defined analogously to *ElementsWithNumberOfOutRelations OfType*.
- *PathsContainingElements(X_1,X_n,X_c)* is provided with three sets of elements X_1,X_n, and X_c. It returns a set of sets containing elements that represent all paths from elements of X_1 to elements of X_n, which each contain at least one element of X_c The directions of the relationships, which are part of the paths, given by their "Source" or "Target" assignment, are ignored. Furthermore, the attribute "directed" of the according relationship types has to be FALSE. Each such path found is represented by an inner set.
- *DirectedPathsContainingElements (X_1,X_n,X_c)* is defined analogously to

PathsContainingElements. In contrast, it only returns directed paths containing at least one element of X_c and leading from X_1 to X_n.

- *PathsNotContainingElements(X_1,X_n,X_c)* is defined analogously to *PathsContaining Elements*. It returns only paths that contain no elements of X_c.
- *DirectedPathsNotContainingElements(X_1,X_n,X_c)* is defined analogously to *DirectedPathsContainingElements*. It returns only paths that contain no elements of X_c.
- *LoopsContainingElements(X,X_c)* is defined analogously to *PathsContainingElements*.
- *DirectedLoopsContainingElements(X,X_c)* is defined analogously to *LoopsContainingElements*. In contrast, it only returns directed loops containing at least one element of X_c.
- *LoopsNotContainingElements(X,X_c)* is defined analogously to *LoopsContainingElements*. It returns only those loops that contain no elements of X_c.
- *DirectedLoopsNotContainingElements(X,X_c)* is defined analogously to *DirectedLoopsContainingElements*. It returns only loops that contain no elements of X_c.

Nesting the functions introduced above, it is possible to build up structural model patterns successively. The results of each function can be reused adopting them as an input for other functions. In order to combine different results, the basic set operators union ($\cup$), intersection ($\cap$), and complement ($\setminus$) can be used generally. Since it should be possible to combine not only sets of pattern matches (i.e., sets of sets) but also the pattern matches themselves, that is the inner sets, we define additional set operators. These operate on the inner sets of two sets of sets respectively (cf. Table 1).

Table 1. Set operators for sets of sets

Basic Sets	Operator Definition	Operator Symbol
$F,G \subseteq P(E)$, $f \in F$, $g \in G$	$Join(F,G)=\{f \cup g \mid \exists e \in E: e \in f \wedge e \in g\}$	$F \sqcup G$
$F,G \subseteq P(E)$, $f \in F$, $g \in G$	$InnerIntersection(F,G)=\{f \cap g\}$	$F \sqcap G$
$F,G \subseteq P(E)$, $f \in F$, $g \in G$	$InnerComplement(F,G)=\{f \setminus g \mid \exists e \in E: e \in f \wedge e \in g\}$	$F \searrow G$
$F \subseteq P(E)$, $f \in F$	$SelfUnion(F)=\cup_{f \in F} f$	$\sqcup F$
$F \subseteq P(E)$, $f \in F$	$SelfIntersection(F)=\cap_{f \in F} f$	$\sqcap F$

The *Join* operator performs a *Union* operation on each inner set of the first set with each inner set of the second set. Since we regard patterns as cohesive, only inner sets that have at least one element in common are considered. The *Inner-Intersection* operator intersects each inner set of the first set with each inner set of the second set. The *InnerComplement* operator applies a complement operation to each inner set of the first outer set combined with each inner set of the second outer set. Only inner sets that have at least one element in common are considered.

As most of the functions introduced above expect simple sets of elements as inputs, we introduce further operators that turn sets of sets into simple sets. The *SelfUnion* operator merges all inner sets of one set of sets into a single set performing a union operation on all inner sets. The *SelfIntersection* operator performs an intersection operation on all inner sets of a set of sets successively. The result is a set containing elements that each occur in all inner sets of the original outer set.

Application

A precondition for a successful model analysis is the enforcement of a corporate language directly during modeling as described above. Models with unambiguous naming can be then analyzed in any suitable way. In the following, we introduce particular examples showing the feasibility of our model analysis approach.

Single Models

An exemplary semantic analysis of a single model base could be used to reveal all sections of a process model being related to a specific process object, for example "invoice" (cf. Figure 7, left hand side).

Hence, all model objects accessing an "invoice" should contain the term "invoice". An according pattern looks like the following:

ObjectsWithValue(ObjectsWithDomain (O,STRING),"*invoice*")

The inner function returns all objects of the analyzed model containing a string value. The outer function examines the values of these objects and returns only those containing "invoice" as part of the string.

Purely structural analyses can for example be used for syntactic checks. The following example depicts a syntactic check of EPCs. Regarding their object types and relationship types, EPCs are defined as follows:

$B=\{Function, Event, XOR, OR, AND\}$ is the set of object types.

$C=\{Control\_Flow\}$ is the set of relationship types, whereas $directed(Control\_Flow)=TRUE$

$A=B \cup C$ is the set of element types.

$E=O \cup R$ is the set of particular elements.

For instance, loops containing only connectors represent a syntactic error in EPCs. The following

Figure 7. Purely semantic and purely structural analysis of conceptual models

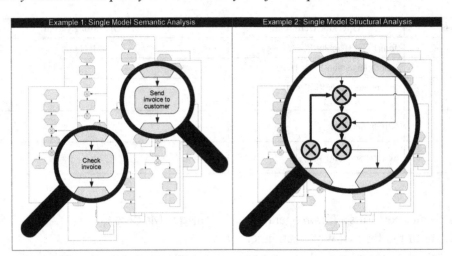

pattern returns all connector loops in a given EPC model base and therefore can be used to reveal syntax errors (cf. Figure 7, right hand side):

The first argument of the outer function defines the element types with that a loop starts and ends, that is only connectors. The second one restricts the element types being allowed to be part of a loop to anything but function and events – meaning only connectors (see Exhibit 1).

Combined semantic and structural analyses reveal model sections showing a special structure and at the same time contain specific textual information. For example, in ERMs, so-called receipt structures are quite popular. These are commonly used to relate positions of a receipt to its header. Regarding their object types and relationship types, ERMs are defined as follows:

- *B={EntityType (ET), RelationshipType (RT), RelationalEntityType (RET)}* is the set of object types.

- $C=\{ET{\rightarrow}RT,\ ET{\rightarrow}RET,\ RET{\rightarrow}RET,\ RET{\rightarrow}RT\}$ is the set of relationship types, whereas *directed(c)=FALSE* $\forall\ c{\in}C$
- $A=B{\cup}C$ is the set of element types.
- $E=O{\cup}R$ is the set of particular elements.

A possible subject of analysis could be to find all receipt structures in ERMs containing elements related to the business object "invoice" (cf. Figure 8). As a first step, all receipt structures are recognized by the pattern $\mathcal{K}$ (see Exhibit 2).

As a second step, the resulting pattern sets are restricted to those containing at least one object containing "invoice" in a string value (see Exhibit 3).

Model Comparison

For example, receipt structures and ternary relationships are regarded as equivalent in ERMs. An exemplary semantic and structural analysis

Exhibit 1. Loops not containing elements

LoopsNot containing elements
    ElementsOfType(O,OR) UNION ElementsOfType(O,XOR) UNION ElementsOfType(O,AND),
    ElementsOfType(O,Function) UNION ElementsOfType(O,Event)
)

Figure 8. Combined structural and semantic analysis of conceptual models

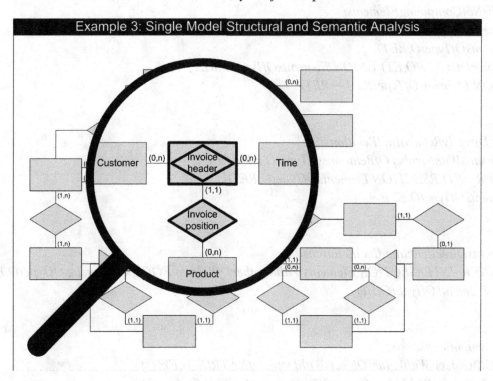

Exhibit 2. Pattern Ж

Ж*= PathsNotContainingElements(*
     ElementsOfType(O,ET),
     ElementsOfType(O,RET),
     (ElementsOfType(O,ET) UNION ElementsOfType(O,RET) UNION ElementsOfType(R,ET→RET)
)
JOIN
ElementsDirectlyRelatedInclRelations(
     (ElementsWithNumberOfRelationsOfType(O,ET→RET,2)
     INNER_INTERSECTION ElementsOfType(O,RET)),
     ElementsOfType(O,ET)
)

Exhibit 3. String value

Ж*'={X∈Ж|ObjectsWithValue(ObjectsWithDomain(X,STRING),"*invoice*")≠{}},*
Ж,Ж*'⊆P(E)*

Exhibit 4. Structural analysis and semantic analysis1ˢᵗ step: structural analysis:

Ж= *PathsNotContainingElements(*
   ElementsOfType(O,ET),
   ElementsOfType(O,RET),
   (ElementsOfType(O,ET) UNION ElementsOfType(O,RET)
   UNION ElementsOfType(R,ET→RET)
)
JOIN
ElementsDirectlyRelatedInclRelations(
   (ElementsWithNumberOfRelationsOfType(O,ET→RET,2)
   INNER_INTERSECTION ElementsOfType(O,RET)),
   ElementsOfType(O,ET)
)

Φ=ElementsDirectlyRelatedInclRelations(
   O INNER_INTERSECTION ElementsWithNumberOfRelationsOfType(ElementsOfType(O,RT),ET
→RT,3), ElementsOfType(O,ET)
)

2ⁿᵈ step: semantic analysis:
Ж'*={X∈*Ж*|ObjectsWithValue(ObjectsWithDomain(X,STRING),F)≠{}},*
Φ'={X∈Φ|ObjectsWithValue(ObjectsWithDomain(X,STRING),G)≠{}},
F=G,
Ж,Ж'*,Φ,Φ'⊆**P***(E)*

Figure 9. Structural and semantic model comparison

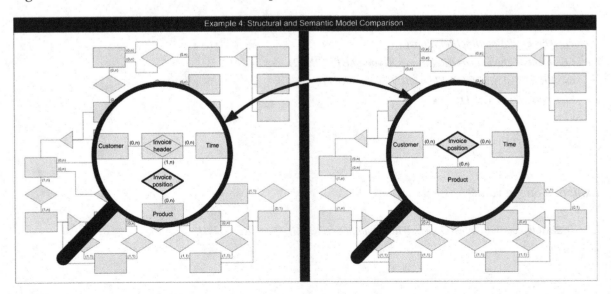

(see Exhibit 4) could be used to find all receipt structures in the first model base and all ternary relationships in the second model base that contain elements named the same (cf. Figure 9).

EXPERIENCES, CONCLUSION AND OUTLOOK

To show general feasibility and applicability of our presented approach, we developed a software prototype based on a modeling tool resulting from previous research projects. The functionalities of both the enforcement of naming conventions and the pattern matching support have been realized in a modular plug-in architecture allowing for flexible coupling of different linguistic services and other components. Although various software modules were integrated into the modeling software, the achieved performance seems promising for a successful application in real life settings. Thus, the prototype shows the technical feasibility of our approach.

Future research will continue focusing on further evaluating the proposed approach in certain dimensions. In the short-term, we will instantiate the approach for different modeling languages, different natural languages, and different application scenarios. In particular, we are going to evaluate the capability of our approach to increase the efficiency of model analysis and its acceptance. For this, the efficiency of the approach will be observed in a laboratory experiment by comparing three different modeling groups. Given the same business case, each group has to model it in a distributed way and consolidate the models afterwards. One group has to model it without any guidance, the second one with paper-based glossaries, and the third one with the software support through our prototype. The insights from this experiment should help revise the approach in a manner that its applicability in general and its responsiveness in particular may prove themselves in a real life scenario.

Moreover, the user acceptance of our approach needs to be evaluated in a wide application scenario. In particular, it has to be proven whether our pattern specification framework is sufficient to analyze conceptual models of arbitrary type. Furthermore, we will focus on increasing the usability of our approach and the software prototype itself by, for example, providing an integrated graphical model analysis environment. An interesting alternative to the here shown formal specification of patterns might be an intuitive graphical notation.

With respect to related work in the field of ontologies and semantic wikis, further future work will address the relation of linguistic-based and ontology-based semantic standardization supporting model analysis. Based on the pros and cons discussion briefly brought up on the Background Section, it will be an exciting task to reveal synergies of both standardization strategies and identify integration potentials.

REFERENCES

Abramowicz, W., Filipowska, A., Kaczmarek, M., & Kaczmarek, T. (2007). Semantically enhanced business process modelling notation. In M. Hepp, K. Hinkelmann, D. Karagiannis, R. Klein, & N. Stojanovic (Eds.). *Semantic business process and product lifecycle management. Proceedings of the Workshop SBPM 2007, Innsbruck, April 7, 2007* (pp. 88-91). Innsbruck, Austria: CEUR Workshop Proceedings.

Ahlemann, F., Teuteberg, F., & Brune, G. (2006). Ontologie-basierte Attributierung von Informationsmodellen: Grundlagen und Anwendungsgebiete . In Teuteberg, F., & Ahlemann, F. (Eds.), *ISPRI-Arbeitsbericht, Nr. 01/2006*. Osnabrück, Germany: Universität Osnabrück.

Aumueller, D., Do, H.-H., Massmann, S., & Rahm, E. (2005). Schema and ontology matching with COMA++. In *Proceedings of the 2005 ACM SIGMOD international Conference on Management of Data (SIGMOD '05)* (pp. 906-908) New York, NY: ACM Press.

Batini, C., & Lenzerini, M. (1984). A methodology for data schema integration in the entity relationship model. *IEEE Transactions on Software Engineering, 10*(6), 650–663. doi:10.1109/TSE.1984.5010294

Batini, C., Lenzerini, M., & Navathe, S. B. (1986). A comparative analysis of methodologies for database schema integration. *ACM Computing Surveys, 18*(4), 323–364. doi:10.1145/27633.27634

Becker, J., Delfmann, P., Herwig, S., & Lis, L. (2009). A generic set theory-based pattern matching approach for the analysis of conceptual models. In A. H. F. Laender, S. Castano, U. Dayal, F. Casati, J. Palazzo, & M. de Oliveira (Eds.), *Proceedings of the 28th International Conference on Conceptual Modeling (ER 2009), Gramado, Brazil, 2009 LNCS 5829,* (pp. 41-54). Berlin, Germany: Springer.

Bhargava, H. K., Kimbrough, S. O., & Krishnan, R. (1991). Unique name violations, a problem for model integration or you say tomato, I say tomahto. *ORSA Journal on Computing, 3*(2), 107–120.

Bögl, A., Kobler, M., & Schrefl, M. (2008). Knowledge acquisition from EPC models for extraction of process patterns in engineering domains. In M. Bichler, T. Hess, H. Krcmar, U. Lechner, F. Matthes, A. Picot, … P. Wolf (Eds.), *Proceedings of the Multi-Conference on Information Systems [in German: Multikonferenz Wirtschaftsinformatik] 2008 (MKWI 2008)*. Munich, Germany: GITO.

Born, M., Dörr, F., & Weber, I. (2007). User-friendly semantic annotation in business process modeling. In M. Weske, M.-S. Hacid, C. Godart (Ed.), *Proceedings of the International Workshop on Human-Friendly Service Description, Discovery and Matchmaking (Hf-SDDM 2007) at the 8th International Conference on Web Information Systems Engineering (WISE 2007)* (pp. 260-271). Nancy, France: Springer.

Chen, P. P.-S. (1976). The entity-relationship model: Toward a unified view of data. *ACM Transactions on Database Systems, 1*(1), 9–36. doi:10.1145/320434.320440

de Medeiros, A. K. A., van der Aalst, W. M. P., & Weijters, A. J. M. M. (2008). Quantifying process equivalence based on observed behavior. *Data & Knowledge Engineering, 64*(1), 55–74. doi:10.1016/j.datak.2007.06.010

Delfmann, P., Herwig, S., & Lis, L. (2009a). Unified enterprise knowledge representation with conceptual models - Capturing corporate language in naming conventions. In *Proceedings of the 30th International Conference on Information Systems (ICIS 2009)*, Phoenix, Arizona, USA.

Delfmann, P., Herwig, S., & Lis, L. (2009b). conflictual naming practice in event-driven process chains - Linguistic analysis and proposal for a method of resolution [In German: Konfliktäre Bezeichnungen in Ereignisgesteuerten Prozessketten - Linguistische Analyse und Vorschlag eines Lösungsansatzes]. In M. Nüttgens, F. Rump, J. Mendling, N. Gehrke (Ed.), *Proceedings of the 8th GI-Workshop EPK 2009: Geschäftsprozessmanagement mit Ereignisgesteuerten Prozessketten.* Berlin, Germany.

Delfmann, P., Herwig, S., Lis, L., Stein, A., Tent, K., & Becker, J. (2010). Pattern specification and matching in conceptual models. A generic approach based on set operations. *Enterprise Modelling and Information Systems Architectures, 5*(3).

Ehrig, M., Koschmider, A., & Oberweis, A. (2007). Measuring similarity between semantic business process models. In *Proceedings of the 4th Asia-Pacific Conference on Conceptual Modelling (APCCM)*. Ballarat, Australia: Australian Computer Society.

Fellbaum, C. (Ed.). (1998). *WordNet: An electronic lexical database*. Cambridge, MA: The MIT Press.

Fu, J. (1995). Pattern matching in directed graphs. In Z. Galil, & E. Ukkonen (Eds.). *Proceedings of the 6th Annual Symposium on Combinatorial Pattern Matching* (pp. 64-77). Helsinki, Finland: Springer.

Gori, M., Maggini, M., & Sarti, L. (2005). The RW2 algorithm for exact graph matching. In S. Singh, M. Singh, C. Apté, & P. Perner (Eds.), *Proceedings of the 3th International Conference on Advances in Pattern Recognition* (pp. 81-88). Bath, UK: Springer.

Greco, G., Guzzo, A., Pontieri, L., & Saccà, D. (2004). An ontology-driven process modeling framework. In F. Galindo, F., Takizawa, M., & R. Traunmüller (Ed.). *Proceedings of the 15th International Conference on Database and Expert Systems Applications (DEXA 2004)* (pp. 13-23). Zaragoza, Spain: Springer.

Gruber, T. R. (1993). A translation approach to portable ontology specifications. *Knowledge Acquisition, 5*(2), 199–220. doi:10.1006/knac.1993.1008

Guarino, N. (1998). Formal ontology and Information Systems. In N. Guarino (Ed.), *Proceedings of the 1st International Conference on Formal Ontologies in Information Systems* (pp. 3-15). Trento, Italy: ACM Press.

Hadar, I., & Soffer, P. (2006). Variations in conceptual modeling: Classification and ontological analysis. *Journal of the AIS, 7*(8), 568–592.

Hars, A. (1994). *Reference data models: Foundations of efficient data modeling* [In German: Referenzdatenmodelle. Grundlagen effizienter Datenmodellierung]. Wiesbaden, Germany: Gabler.

Hepp, M., & Roman, D. (2007). An ontology framework for semantic business process management . In Oberweis, A., Weinhardt, C., Gimpel, H., Koschmider, A., Pankratius, V., & Schnizler, B. (Eds.), *eOrganisation: Service-, Process-, Market-Engineering. Proceedings der 8th Internationalen Tagung Wirtschaftsinformatik* (*Vol. 1*, pp. 423–440). Karlsruhe, Germany: Universitätsverlag.

Hidders, J., Dumas, M., van der Aalst, W. M. P., ter Hofstede, A. H. M., & Verelst, J. (2005). When are two workflows the same? In M. Atkinson, & F. Dehne (Eds.), *Proceedings of the 11th Australasian Symposium on Theory of Computing* (pp. 3-11). Newcastle, NSW, Australia.

Hirschfeld, Y. (1993). Petri nets and the equivalence problem. In E. Börger, Y. Gurevich, & K. Meinke (Eds.). *Proceedings of the 7th Workshop on Computer Science Logic (CSL'93)* (pp. 165-174). Swansea, UK: Springer.

Höfferer, P. (2007). Achieving business process model interoperability using metamodels and ontologies. In H. Österle, J. Schelp, & R. Winter (Ed.). *Proceedings of the 15th European Conference on Information Systems (ECIS 2007)* (pp. 1620-1631). St. Gallen, Switzerland.

ISO(1982). ISO/TC97/SC5/WG3: Concepts and terminology for the conceptual schema and the information base.

Kaplan, R. M. (2003). Syntax . In Mitkov, R. (Ed.), *The Oxford handbook of computational linguistics* (pp. 70–90). Oxford, UK: Oxford University Press.

Koschmider, A., & Oberweis, A. (2005). Ontology based business process description. In *Enterprise Modelling and Ontologies for Interoperability. Proceedings of the Open Interop Workshop on Enterprise Modelling and Ontologies for Interoperability, Co-located with CAiSE'05 Conference.* Porto, Portugal: Springer.

Kottemann, J. E., & Konsynski, B. R. (1984). Information Systems planning and development: Strategic postures and methodologies. *Journal of Management Information Systems, 1*(2), 45–63.

Kugeler, M. (2000). *Organisational design with conceptual models. Modelling conventions and reference process model for business process reengineering* [In German: Informationsmodellbasierte Organisationsgestaltung. Modellierungskonventionen und Referenzvorgehensmodell zur prozessorientierten Reorganisation]. Berlin, Germany: Logos.

Lawrence, R., & Barker, K. (2001). Integrating relational database schemas using a standardized dictionary. In *Proceedings of the 2001 ACM Symposium on Applied Computing (SAC)*. Las Vegas, NV: ACM.

Li, W., & Clifton, C. (2000). SemInt: A tool for identifying attribute correspondences in heterogeneous databases using neural network. *Data & Knowledge Engineering, 33*(1), 49–84. doi:10.1016/S0169-023X(99)00044-0

Madhavan, J., Bernstein, P. A., & Rahm, E. (2001). Generic schema matching with Cupid. In P. M. G. Apers, P. Atzeni, S. Ceri, S. Paraboschi, K. Ramamohanarao, & R. T. Snodgrass (Eds.), *Proceedings of the 27th International Conference on Very Large Data Bases* (pp. 49-58). Rome, Italy: Morgan Kaufmann Publishers Inc.

Mendling, J. (2007). *Detection and prediction of errors in EPC business process models*. Unpublished doctoral dissertation, Vienna University of Economics and Business Administration, Austria.

Object Management Group (OMG). (2009). *Meta object facility (MOF) core specification. OMG available specification,* version 2.0. Retrieved December 4, 2009, from http://www.omg.org/spec/MOF /2.0/PDF

Object Management Group (OMG). (2009b). *Unified modeling language (OMG UML), infrastructure,* v2.1.2. Retrieved December 4, 2009, from http://www. omg.org/docs /formal/07-11-04 .pdf

Preece, A., Flett, A., Sleeman, D., Curry, D., Meany, N., & Perry, P. (2001). Better knowledge management through knowledge engineering. *IEEE Intelligent Systems, 16*(1), 36–42. doi:10.1109/5254.912383

Rahm, E., & Bernstein, P. A. (2001). A survey of approaches to automatic schema matching. *The International Journal on Very Large Data Bases, 10*(4), 334–350. doi:10.1007/s007780100057

Rizopolous, N., & McBrien, P. (2005). A general approach to the generation of conceptual model transformations. In *Proceedings of the 17th Conference on Advanced Information Systems Engineering (CAiSE'05)*.

Rosemann, M. (1996). *Complexity management in process models. Language-specific modeling guidelines* [in German: Komplexitätsmanagement in Prozeßmodellen. Methodenspezifische Gestaltungsempfehlungen für die Informationsmodellierung]. Wiesbaden, Germany: Gabler.

Rosemann, M. (2003). Preparation of process modeling . In Becker, J., Kugeler, M., & Rosemann, M. (Eds.), *Process management – A guide for the design of business processes* (pp. 41–78). Berlin, Germany: Springer.

Sabetzadeh, M., Nejati, S., Easterbrook, S., & Chechik, M. (2007). A relationship-driven framework for model merging. In *Proceedings of the Workshop on Modeling in Software Engineering (MiSE'07) at the 29th International Conference on Software Engineering*. Minneapolis, MN: IEEE Computer Society.

Scheer, A.-W. (2000). *ARIS - Business process modelling* (3rd ed.). Berlin, Germany: Springer. doi:10.1007/978-3-642-57108-4

Shvaiko, P., & Euzenat, J. (2005). A survey of schema-based matching approaches. [Berlin, Germany: Springer.]. *Journal on Data Semantics, 4*, 146–171.

Stumme, G., & Maedche, A. (2001). FCA-merge: Bottom-up merging of ontologies. In B. Nebel (Ed.), *Proceedings of the 17th International Joint Conference on Artificial Intelligence, IJCAI 2001* (pp. 225-230). Seattle, WA: Morgan Kaufmann Inc.

Sunagawa, E., Kozaki, K., Kitamura, Y., & Mizoguchi, R. (2003). An environment for distributed ontology development based on dependency management. In D. Fensel, K. Sycara, & J. Mylopoulos (Eds.), *The Semantic Web - ISWC 2003. Second International Semantic Web Conference. Sanibel Island, FL, USA, October 20-23, 2003, Proceedings LNCS 2870* (pp. 453–468). Berlin, Germany: Springer.

Thomas, O., & Fellmann, M. (2009). Semantic process modeling – Design and implementation of an ontology-based representation of business processes. *Business & Information Systems Engineering, 1*(6), 438–451. doi:10.1007/s12599-009-0078-8

Valiente, G., & Martínez, C. (1997). An algorithm for graph pattern-matching. In R. Baeza-Yates, & N. Ziviani (Ed.), *Proceedings of the 4nd South American Workshop on String Processing* (pp. 180-197). Valparaíso, Chile: Carleton University Press.

van Dongen, B. F., Dijkman, R., & Mendling, J. (2008). Measuring similarity between business process models. In Z. Bellahsene, & M. Léonard (Eds.), *Proceedings of the 20th International Conference on Advanced Information Systems Engineering* (pp. 450-464). Montpellier, France: Springer.

Varró, G., Varró, D., & Schürr, A. (2006). Incremental graph pattern matching: Data structure and initial experiments. In T. Margaria, J. Padberg, & G. Taentzer (Ed.). *Proceedings of the 2nd International Workshop on Graph and Model Transformation*. Brighton, UK: Electronic Communications of EASST.

Vergidis, K., Tiwari, A., & Majeed, B. (2008). Business process analysis and optimization: Beyond reengineering. *IEEE Transactions on Systems, Man, and Cybernetics, 38*(1), 69–82. doi:10.1109/TSMCC.2007.905812

Völkel, M. (Ed.). (2006). *Proceedings of the 1st Workshop on Semantic Wikis – From Wiki to Semantics (SemWiki2006)*, held at ESWC 2006, June 11–14, Budva, Montenegro.

vom Brocke, J., & Thomas, O. (2006). Designing infrastructures for reusing conceptual models. A general framework and its application for collaborative reference modeling. In W. Abramowicz, & H. C. Mayr (Eds.), *Proceedings of the 9th International Conference on Business Information Systems (BIS2006)* (pp. 501-514). Klagenfurt, Austria: Lecture Notes in Informatics (LNI).

White, S. A., & Miers, D. (2008). *BPMN modeling and reference guide. Understanding and using BPMN*. Lighthouse Point, FL: Future Strategies Inc.

WordNet. (2009). *WordNet. A lexical database for the English language*. Retrieved May 4, 2009, from http://wordnet.princeton.edu

Chapter 8
Semantic Verification of Business Process Models:
Prospects and Limitations

Michael Fellmann
University of Osnabrueck, Germany

Oliver Thomas
University of Osnabrueck, Germany

Frank Hogrebe
University of Hamburg, Germany

ABSTRACT

This chapter presents an ontology-driven approach that aims at supporting semantic verification of semi-formal process models. Despite the widespread use of these models in research and practice, innovative solutions are needed in order to address the verification of process model information. But what are the prospects and limitations of semantic verification? In order to investigate this issue we suggest an ontology-driven approach consisting of two steps. The first step is the development of a model for ontology-based representation of process models. In the second step, we use this model to support the semantic verification based on this representation and on machine reasoning. We apply our approach using real-life administrative process models taken from a capital city.

INTRODUCTION

Motivation

Models are important to manage complexity. They provide a means for understanding the business process, and understanding already is a benefit.

DOI: 10.4018/978-1-60960-126-3.ch008

This is indicated by a study from Gartner revealing an increase in efficiency of 12 percent gained solely by documenting actions and organizational responsibilities using process models (Melenovsky 2005, p. 4). Moreover, process models serve for optimization, reengineering, and implementation of supporting IT systems. Due to the importance of process models, model quality is important. According to ISO 8402, quality is "the totality of characteristics of an entity that bear on its ability to satisfy stated and implied needs". Facets of quality are – amongst others – adequate coverage of the domain or system to be modeled, appropriateness in respect to the abstraction level of the representation (scale), detail of representation (granularity) and the correctness of a model. We concentrate on correctness as the most fundamental quality aspect. Among the aspects of correctness are: (a) syntactical correctness, (b) correctness in regard to the formal semantics, (c) correctness in regard to linguistic aspects focusing on the labels used in models, (d) correctness in regard to the coherence of connected models and (e) compliance to rules and regulations focusing on the correctness of the model's content and thus on semantic correctness. While there are numerous verification approaches available to ensure (a-d), only a few approaches focus on (e) in the sense of the verification of the semantic correctness. With the term "verification", we denote criteria targeting the internal, syntactic and semantic constitution of a model. In contrast to that, validation means the eligibility of a model in respect to its intended use (Desel 2002, p. 24) – in other words: if the criteria is something outside the model (Chapurlat & Braesch 2008; Mendling 2009, p. 2). Following this distinction, we call the procedures to ensure semantic correctness "semantic verification".

A major problem regarding semantic verification is how to automate it. This problem is rooted in natural language being used for labeling model elements, thus introducing terminological problems such as ambiguity (homonyms, synonyms) and other linguistic phenomena. Model creators and readers do not necessarily share the same understanding as the concepts they use are usually not documented and mix both discipline-specific terminology and informal, ordinary language. Therefore, it is hard for humans to judge if a model is semantically correct and almost impossible for machines (apart from using heuristics) because the model element labels are not backed with machine processable semantics. The result

is that the machine cannot interpret the contents of model elements. Our solution approach is to encode the model element semantics in a precise, machine readable form using ontologies. Further, we then use rules to encode constraints used for verifying aspects of semantic correctness.

Prospects of Semantic Verification

The proposed approach of semantic verification allows performing additional checks on process models. Such checks are possible by annotating process models with instances of a formal ontology containing terminological knowledge of the domain under consideration. The ontology in conjunction with an inference engine can then be used to automatically verify several aspects of models based on the semantics of the individual model elements. This decoupling from human labor makes semantic verification scalable even in incremental approaches to model construction where a model has to be re-verified repeatedly. An important additional benefit thereby is that the semantic verification rules can be formalized on a more abstract and generic level and the inference engine interprets them with the help of both explicitly encoded and inferred knowledge from the ontology. Therefore, it is possible to formulate semantic verification rules in a more natural and understandable way that accommodates to the nature of generic rules such as guidelines, best practices, conventions, recommendations or laws being rather abstract in order to ensure broad applicability.

The paper is organized as follows. In the related work section, we provide an overview of approaches and tools in the state-of-the-art of model verification. In the next section, we present a case study that motivates our approach. In the section "Ontology-driven Approach for Semantic Verification" we present our approach of semantic verification along with a rule classification and examples illustrating the application of such rules to the real-world problems of the case study. In the section "Limitations of Semantic Verification", we describe the limitations of semantic verification and in the last section we look at future research.

RELATED WORK

Procedures and methods for the verification of semi-formal process models partly originate from *software engineering* (Gruhn 1991) where they are discussed under the terms "model checking" and "theorem proving" (Clarke 2008; Chapurlat & Braesch 2008). These approaches mainly concern dynamic aspects of model execution which are verified using finite state automata (FSM). A major problem to be tackled here is the explosion of the state space which is solved or alleviated by symbolic representations (Xiang, Bultan & Su 2002) or reduction procedures (Awad, Decker & Weske 2008). Approaches that aim at the verification of software-related systems and processes (Gruhn 1991; Cobleigh, Clark & Osterweil 2000; Dong, Alencar & Cowan 2004; Barjis 2008) are sometimes also transferred to conceptual modeling (Varró 2003). Clearly, as we are engaged in verifying conceptual models, software processes are out of scope.

Another research area is the *verification of workflows* (van der Aalst 1997; Sadiq & Orlowska 2000; Sadiq, Orlowska & Sadiq 2005; Salomie et al. 2007; Touré, Baïna & Benali 2008) where notions such as "soundness" (Dehnert & van der Aalst 2004) and "relaxed soundness" (van der Aalst 1998) have been developed. Recent research extends workflow management to the verification of web services orchestrations (Nakajima 2002; Xiang, Bultan & Su 2002; Foster et al. 2003; Geguang et al. 2004; van Breugel & Koshkina 2006; Kovacs & Gönczy 2008; Touré, Baïna & Benali 2008; Okika 2009; Abouzaid & Mullins 2009). In general, workflow management emphasizes the instance level of processes, i.e. the process execution, whereas our semantic verification approach targets the type level of processes, i.e. the process schema.

In the area of the *verification of conceptual process models*, formal criteria developed in the workflow management community have been adapted and extended resulting in independent criteria and definitions of e.g. „soundness", „relaxed soundness" or „well-structuredness" which are used to detect shortcomings such as deadlocks, livelocks, missing synchronisations and other defects regarding the formal semantics (van der Aalst 1999; Dijkman, Dumas & Ouyang 2007; Mendling & van der Aalst 2008; Dijkman, Dumas & Ouyang 2008; Mendling 2009). The verification in this sense abstracts from the individual semantics of model elements which is given by natural language and concentrates on formal procedures. Therefore, the formalization of the semantics of semi-formal process models is suggested (Kindler 2006) and formal languages such as Petri Nets are heavily used. There are some tools supporting these verifications such as the bflow*-Toolbox (www.bflow.org) (Gruhn & Laue 2009) or the EPC-Tools (wwwcs.uni-paderborn. de/cs/kindler/research/EPCTools).

Research regarding *formal verification of conceptual models* in general is still an active field. New approaches consider e.g. the verification of access constraints in semi-formal models (Wolter, Miseldine & Meinel 2009), the verification in the context of hierarchical models (van der Aalst 2003; Salomie et al. 2007; Gruhn & Laue 2007b), the consistency of related models which is discussed mainly in the realm of the Unified Modeling Language (UML) (Engels, Heckel & Küster 2001; Varró & Pataricza 2002; Heckel, Küster & Taentzer 2002; Koehler, Tirenni & Kumaran 2002; Chanda, Kanjilal & Sengupta 2010), lightweight approaches which do not rely on a formal language such as Petri Nets (Pons & Garcia 2008) as well as the verification of aspects related to the context of models. Such contextual aspects range from access rights (Wolter, Miseldine & Meinel 2009) to process artifacts such as business objects which participate in a process (Xinhua, Weida & Wenjian 2007; Koliadis & Ghose 2007; La Rosa et al. 2008; Deutsch et al. 2009; Gerede & Su 2009) or goals and outputs produced by a process (Soffer & Wand 2004; Lu, Bernstein & Lewis 2006). Also, metrics are studied mainly for error prediction and evaluation purposes (Aguilar et al. 2006; Mendling, Neumann & van der Aalst 2007). Further aspects include the quality of the model construction process (Nelson & Monarchi 2007) and interactive approaches for verification based on reduction rules (van Dongen, van der Aalst & Verbeek 2005; van Dongen et al. 2007). Whereas we address the semantics of individual model elements which is expressed using natural language labels, these approaches do not consider this sort of semantics.

Verification of the labels of conceptual process model elements has gained substantial research interest during the last few years, mainly in respect of improving the model quality and comprehensibility (Mendling, Reijers & Recker 2010; Friedrich 2009). This might be achieved by conforming to specific naming conventions (Leopold, Smirnov & Mendling 2009) or using glossaries (Becker et al. 2009; Peters & Weidlich 2009). Although this stream of research is addressing the natural language labels of model elements, in contrast to our approach it does not try to formalize the semantics of model elements using formal knowledge representations such as ontologies. Instead, most of such approaches are concerned with purely linguistic analysis and tools such as word stemming, part-of-speech tagging and other approaches belonging to the field of computational linguistics.

Verification beyond formal semantics and linguistic aspects is discussed e.g. in the context of compliance. Compliance can be understood as the conformity of something such as a process model to the entirety of relevant legal liabilities, directives and rules as well as to the internal guidelines and best practices of an enterprise (Wecker & van Laak 2008). This clearly goes beyond syntax and

formal semantic and requires also checking the individual model elements and their semantics often expressed using natural language. We call approaches in this direction "semantic verification approaches" as they touch the content or the subject matter of individual model elements in a process model, i.e. "what happens". Whereas most approaches aim at detecting compliance violations caused by the model structure or execution semantics (Speck, Pulvermüller & Heuzeroth 2004; Goedertier & Vanthienen 2006; Liu, Müller & Xu 2007; Awad, Decker & Weske 2008) or by violating a prescribed modeling style (Gruhn & Laue 2007; Gruhn & Laue 2007c) and hence enforce compliance prior to model implementation or execution, some approaches also aim at verifying running processes and to cope with changes of the conceptual model (i.e. the process schema) (Ly, Rinderle & Dadam 2008) or process instances (Ly, Rinderle & Dadam 2010) as well as analyzing already finished processes ex ante on the basis of process logs (van der Aalst, de Beer & van Dongen 2005). Although these approaches address aspects of semantic correctness and partly make use of machine reasoning (esp. Ly, Rinderle & Dadam 2008), they are in contrast to our work as they do not make use of a knowledge structure such as an ontology expressed in a description logic or fragment of first order logic and the deductions which are made possible by using such representations in conjunction with an inference engine.

First approaches to *ontology-based semantic verification* can be found in the context of Semantic Web Services. Semantically annotated process models are verified with an emphasis on logical preconditions and effects which are specified relative to an ontology (Drumm et al. 2007; Weber 2009; Weber, Hoffmann & Mendling 2010). These approaches usually require both the annotation of preconditions and effects and hence enable to check if the model is consistent. They do not build upon a formal representation of the (intentional) semantics of individual model elements (i.e. what is "inside the box" of a model element). Following this argument, a function "receive guest" and "welcome guest" in a hotel service process may have the same preconditions and effects, but differ considerably. Our approach enables capturing such differences by using a single annotation of a model element in order to associate it with its intended meaning explicitly specified in a formal ontology. Semantic verification rules then allow to check if a model complies with a set of requirements using this explicitly specified meaning along with the deductions that are possible due to its formal representation. Our approach is therefore orthogonal to approaches considering preconditions and effects (i.e. what is "outside the box" of a model element). So far, there are only a few researchers expressing initial ideas of using rules together with semantic process descriptions (Happel & Stojanovic 2006; Thomas & Fellmann 2009) as well as frameworks for semantic verification related to compliance (El Kharbili & Stein 2008; El Kharbili et al. 2008).

The *dynamics of verification rules* is a major problem of semantic verification approaches in general. On the one hand, rules are required being detailed enough in order to be useful for verification of concrete models describing specific processes and on the other hand, rules are required to be generic enough in order to be applicable for a set of such processes. In contrast to rules and procedures for formal verification, e.g. to detect deadlocks, rules for semantic verification more often change. This is the case since the subject matter is not (in contrast to formal semantics) the relatively stable modeling language and its use, but rather the content of the models expressed in a modeling language. As such, it is exposed to frequent changes due to the dynamics of the contemporary economic and legislative world (e.g. minimum age for customers of a product may change due to law). Some efforts address this problem area of changing rules and suggest graphical modeling languages such as BPSL (Business Property Specification Language) (Liu,

Müller & Xu 2007) or to capture the required rules implicitly by providing negative examples (Simon & Mendling 2006). Also, patterns are sometimes discussed in this context (Speck, Pulvermüller & Heuzeroth 2004; Namiri & Stojanovic 2007). However, despite such improvements in rule capturing a fundamental problem is still that most approaches require a fine grained specification of rules conflicting with the rather abstract nature of compliance rules in the sense of guidelines, best practices and general principles. We extend the state-of-the-art by showing that ontology-based representations of process models provide for the formulation of generic verification rules which are applied to concrete process models using an inference engine in order to automate semantic verification. We apply our approach to real-world problems and therefore demonstrate that semantic verification is not only feasible, but also useful to solve real-world problems.

CASE STUDY

The municipality we chose for our case is one of the biggest cities in our country (regional capital city). It has about 580,000 inhabitants and the public administrative authorities are employing about 9,100 employees, distributed over about 440 administration buildings. The structure is decentralized and subdivided into seven departments, each with 48 assigned offices and institutes. Based on a Fat Client Server architecture, the 6,000 IT-jobs are workplace-based and completely linked with each other via a communication system throughout the city. In view of the increasing international competition, the city is requested to rearrange its product and process organization, particularly, as the support of enterprise-related activities increasingly becomes a competitive factor. In the city, about 99% of the enterprises have less than 500 employees and can be considered as small or medium-sized enterprises. These are about 40,000 enterprises. The strategic objective of the city is to make the place even more attractive for enterprises in terms of their competitiveness with a long-lasting effect. This shall be achieved by making the enterprise-related offers and services of the city even easier for enterprises to access, in terms of a One-Stop eGovernment. To reach this goal, the city has to model about 550 enterprise-related administrative processes. The process setting is highly relevant for the capital city, because several of the procedures are used about 15,000 to 25,000 times per year by the companies.

After starting the project we detected several inconsistencies in the collected data. The problems of the city in process modeling can be subdivided into two problem areas, which are applicable as a basis to generalize the findings towards the public sector at all. Subsequently, we show the core modeling problems that we encountered, classified into *terminology problems* and *verification problems*.

Terminological Problems

- (T1) Due to the fact that laws and regulations are regularly made by jurists and not by IT-experts, terms and facts of cases often are differently named, although the meaning of two terms is the same. For example, the terms "admission" and "permission" were found in 334 administrative process models, but the terms always had the same meaning and the same process-related consequence.
- (T2) Another terminology problem occurs concerning the fact that in the city no rules were arranged to allow only one certain term for one correspondent meaning. For example, some modelers (14) used "address" and some (8) "mailing address". Or modelers use abbreviations, like "doc" instead of "document".

So, there is a lack of *terminological modeling rules*. These terminology problems hindered the identification, comparison and further use of the administrative process models (e.g. in process automation) in the city we focused on.

Verification Problems

The administrative process models had several errors regarding the correct sequence processing. Subsequently, we show the core modeling errors of process sequence conflicts (V1-V4) and in process sequence conformance (V5-V7):

- (V1) In 64 process models, the event "admission free of charge" was followed by the (wrong!) function "start payment process".
- (V2) As part of a preliminary check, which is executed in every application process at the beginning, the civil servants check the completeness of the submitted documents. In 41 of these process models, we found after the event "documents uncompleted" the (wrong!) event "preliminary check complete", although documents were still missing.
- (V3) In 32 process models we found after the event "application is not licensable" the (wrong!) function "send admission".
- (V4) The next step after the preliminary check is an in-depth check of the admission case. This row is strictly followed. But in 13 of the administrative process models, we found the two checks reversed.

So, there is lack of *element flow rules* like: After X must (must not) follow Y.

- (V5) If a process contains the event "procedure is billable", the same process must contain also a function "calculate charge". But in 21 of the relevant process models no such function was found.

So, there is lack of *element occurrence rules* like:

If a process contains X, the process must (must not) contain Y.

- (V6) Usually, process activities are executed by certain organization divisions. For example, the function "check the application of business registration" can only be executed by the civil servants of the business registration office. But in 44 of the relevant process models, a wrong department was modeled or the organization unit was missing completely.

So, there is lack of *resource usage rules* like:
If a process uses an activity X, the process must (must not) use the resource Y.

- (V7) Companies often combine several application cases. For example, in 24% of the cases the companies combine both the application of business registration and the application of business building permission. In these cases, two different organization units are responsible, the business registration office and the building authority. But in 13% of the cases, one of the responsible organization units was missing.

So, there is lack of *resource occurrence rules* like:

If a process demands the resources X and Y, the process must contain X and Y.

ONTOLOGY-DRIVEN APPROACH FOR SEMANTIC VERIFICATION

Ontology-Based Representation of Process Models

A first step towards semantic verification of semi-formal process models is the representation of the process models using a formal ontology language such as the Web Ontology Language (OWL) standardized by the World Wide Web Consortium (http://w3.org/2004/OWL). We use this ontology language, as it has gained a broad acceptance both inside and outside the Artificial Intelligence and Semantic Web community. The use of the ontology-based representation is two-fold. On the one hand, it allows the connection of process models with domain knowledge in order to improve the interpretation and derive new facts not explicitly specified by the modeler but relevant for verification. On the other hand, it provides for a machine processable representation enabling the automation of such derivations and therefore using logic and reasoning to automate verification tasks. The ontology-based representation of process models consists of creating a model representation in the ontology (step 1) and the annotation of domain knowledge to that representation (step 2) (cf. Figure 1) which are described subsequently.

The creation of a process model representation in the ontology is done by considering its graph structure. For each node, an instance is created and for each arc, a property is added connecting the two nodes which are at the end of the arc. This step can be executed automatically using the capabilities of a transformation language such as XSLT. The instances created in the ontology are instances of the classes shown in the left part of Figure 1 which reflect the well known Workflow Patterns. The properties having their domain and range on the p:ProcessGraphNode Class are used to represent direct connections between model elements (property p:connectsTo being a sub-property of p:flow) as well as the set of following elements which can be reached without traversing an exclusive decision point such as an XOR-Gate (transitive property p:followedBy) or which can be reached by an arbitrary path along the flow in the process model (transitive property p:flow). We use the namespace-prefix p: for indicating the process space in general and ex: for indicating

Figure 1. Ontology-based representation of process models

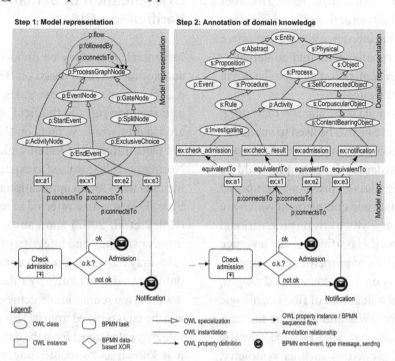

example data that is strongly intertwined with the concrete process fragment being used for illustrative purposes. Due to space limitations, we have omitted the translation of BPMN-lanes into organizational units in Figure 1, but this is possible using a property p:assignedTo connecting each node in a lane with the responsible organizational unit (as it is shown e.g. in Figure 4). Currently, we also omit pools for the sake of simplicity.

The annotation of the process model representation with domain knowledge via the p:equivalentTo-properties shown in the right part of Figure 1 provides for the semantic specification of the model elements with machine processable semantics. Domain ontologies can be built by leveraging existing ontologies, using reference models, ontologizing industrial standards or extracting structures out of IT-systems such as database schemas (see e.g. Thomas & Fellmann 2009 for an overview of relevant ontologies and approaches). Also, top-level or upper ontologies

may be used as a basic backbone structure that helps bootstrap ontology development and reaching ontological commitment on how to think about the world in the sense of a shared "contract" between the different involved stakeholders.

In the example of Figure 1, we have used the Suggested Upper Merged Ontology (SUMO) (Pease, Niles & Li 2002) as a backbone structure providing basic distinctions such as between abstract and physical entities forming the basis of the subsumption hierarchy. This hierarchy does not only serve for disambiguation purposes (e.g. *Service* as subclass of *ComputerProcess* vs. subclass of *Product*). It also provides for the specification of semantic verification rules on varying levels of generality. This enables the specification of rather generic verification rules such as guidelines and best practices and letting an inference engine do the work of verifying whether a specific model is compliant or not. So, for example, a government agency could have the guideline that immediate feedback should be given on each application. If a process model starts with a citizen having filed her tax return and contains an activity "send feedback via e-mail", then the inference engine can prove that this process complies with that guideline as the tax return is an application and feedback via e-mail is a form of feedback.

Beyond such simple subsumption reasoning, an inference engine can also be used to automatically derive more complex conclusions. Automatic classification of instances for example could be achieved by using class expressions composed of intersection, union and complement which are available in OWL and which rely on propositional logic. Also, automatic classification can leverage existential restrictions of properties on classes as well as restrictions on their domain and ranges, thereby relying on a fragment of first order logic (FOL). Moreover, OWL and most of the current ontology languages also provide specific characteristics of properties such as symmetry, transitivity, reflexivity etc. leading to additional conclusions in regard to the structure of a process graph represented in the ontology. Whereas we use an ontology for both, representing a process graph and inferring new facts about it, we use rules to express constraints for semantic verification. Before we show the application of such rules to solve the case problems described in the section "Verification Problems", we will introduce them in the next section.

Classification of Semantic Verification Rules

In general, rules may be divided into deductive and normative rules based on Boley et al. (2007, p. 273 et sqq.). Deductive rules, also referred to as derivation rules in the field of business rules, are used to win new facts on the basis of existing facts through the use of logical implications. Normative rules are used to express conditions for the data used for an application or the logic used by it. They are also referred to as structural rules (Boley et al. 2007) and can be further divided into consistency and integrity rules. Consistency rules may be used to prevent contradictions in the ontology, whereas integrity rules may be used to maintain the semantic correctness of the ontology and the facts derived from it. This understanding of integrity rules stems from the database field where it is known as "semantic integrity constraints". This understanding implies that the ontology is either entirely true or contains incorrect facts. As we also want to express constraints which – when violated – result merely in warnings and thus leave it up to human judgment to decide whether a model construct is correct or not, we do not call our rules "integrity rules". Instead, we prefer the term "verification rules".

According to the IEEE 1012-1998 definition (IEEE 1998) "verification" means to check whether an artifact and/or its creation comply

Figure 2. Semantic verification rules

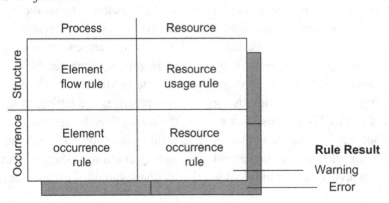

to a set of given requirements, thus focusing on artifact-internal aspects (is the artifact correct?). Due to the fact that our approach suggests also using terminological and domain knowledge (encoded in ontologies) for verification, we call our verification rules "semantic verification rules". Semantic verification rules for process models can be characterized fundamentally according to rule matter, rule focus and rule result (cf. Figure 2).

The rule matter specifies the subject of a rule which is either the process, i.e. the set of nodes and arcs which constitute the core process graph, or the resources which are involved in the process and which appear as additional nodes and edges, e.g. in the form of organizational units assigned to tasks. The rule focus is either the structure of a process graph involving several nodes connected by edges or the occurrence of specific nodes anywhere in the process graph. The result of the execution of a semantic verification rule may be a warning, if a human finally has to judge the correctness or an error message, if the knowledge formalized in the ontology is sufficient to definitely identify it as an error.

The rule types portrayed by the classification of verification rules are to be understood as basic rule types. In practical applications, any combination of the four types may be combined in a single rule. For example, if an organizational unit "government representative" is present anywhere in the process (resource occurrence), then an additional sequence of activities such as "report results to head of administration" has to be performed (element flow rule) involving at least one information system for archiving the results (resource usage rule).

APPLICATION TO THE CASE PROBLEMS

In this section, we provide practical examples for each of the four basic semantic verification rule types introduced in the previous section by illustrating how our approach of semantic verification can be applied to the case problems given in the section "Verification Problems". Figure 3 illustrates the application of an element flow rule (on the left side) and an element occurrence

Figure 3. Element flow rule and element occurrence rule

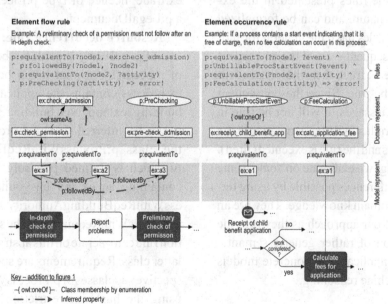

rule (on the right side). At the bottom layer, fragments of a process described by using BPMN are displayed, whereas model elements targeted by the verification rules are highlighted. Above the model layer, the ontology is displayed consisting of a model representation part and a domain representation part. The semantic verification rules using the classes and instances of the ontology are displayed above the ontology. The rules are displayed in an informal notation with variables prefixed by question marks, class memberships written as functions with one argument and predicates (properties in the OWL-terminology and edges in the graph-terminology) as functions with two arguments. To improve comprehensibility, the rules have additionally been paraphrased using natural language at the topmost layer.

Regarding rules, there are a number of non-web-based ontology languages, such as OCML and Ontolingua, which make it possible to formulate rules without an extension. The ontology language OWL, used in this article, only supports the formulation of rules via extensions (apart from simple property chains in OWL 2.0). Such an extension is the Semantic Web Rule Language (SWRL) (Horrocks et al. 2004) which extends OWL with IF-THEN-rules in the form of a logical implication. The rules presented in the examples are of this nature and can be formalized using SWRL. The rules have the general form of antecedent -> consequent – i.e. if the antecedent (body) of the rule is true, then the consequent (head) must also be true. Since the consequent consists of error messages, it will not be true in a literal sense, it rather will be generated if the antecedent matches and the rule is executed (fired).

In the following, we elaborate on some of the abstractions and inferences possible by using terminological and domain knowledge. They are an important merit of our approach as they provide for the formulation of rather generic semantic verification rules applicable to concrete models by automated machine reasoning.

Element flow rule: Terminological knowledge is used in stating that ex:check_permission is the same as ex:check_admission. Hence, the p:equivalentTo property between ex:a1 and ex:check _admission can be inferred. Moreover, as p:followedBy is a transitive property, the triple ex:a1 p:followedBy ex:a3 can be inferred. As ex:a3 is annotated with an ontology instance that belongs to the class of p:PreChecking activities, the antecedent of the rule is satisfied and the rule fires.

Element occurrence rule: The example makes use of a class definition by enumeration resulting in ex:receipt_child_benefit_app being classified as an individual of p:UnbillableProcStart Event. The rule fires because there is another node in the process that is annotated with an individual belonging to the class p:FeeCalculation. Obviously, the rule is specified rather generic and will fire if two nodes are annotated with instances classified as members of the two classes p:UnbillableProcStartEvent and p:FeeCalculation.

Resource usage rule: The rule in the given example (Figure 4) fires, if any activity node assigned to an organizational node being an individual of p:ConsultingUnit produces a legal document as output. The example makes use of subsumption reasoning so it can be inferred that ex:trade_licence of type p:LicenceDocument is a p:LegalDocument.

Resource occurrence rule: The rule makes use of a property p:contains being the inverse of p:occursIn, so that it can be concluded that ex:process contains the application of business building ex:app_bus_building. Based on this, it can be inferred that this process belongs to the class p:ProcessWithReqBuildingAuthori ty which is defined precisely as all processes containing an ex:app_bus_building. As p:Proc essWithReqBuildingAuthority is subsumed by p:ProcessWithRequirement, the semantic verification rule can operate on this abstract level using the latter class. Requirements are specified on the respective subclasses of p:ProcessWithRequirement using the hasValue-restriction of OWL which

Figure 4. Resource usage and resource occurrence rule

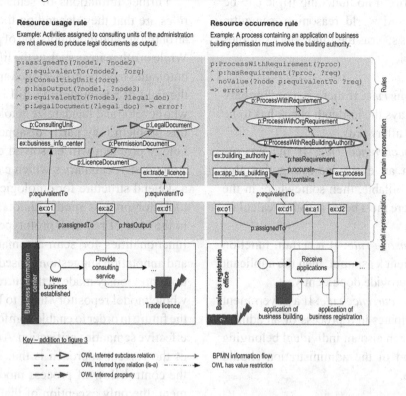

allows specifying a value of the requirement, i.e., an instance that must be present in the process that should be annotated to at least one of the process nodes. The rule checks if there is not a single node in the process graph being annotated with that instance by using the noValue()-extension of the Jena built-in rule engine ARQ (jena.sourceforge. net/ARQ/).

The examples presented to exemplify the four rule types have in common, that they use facts that are explicitly known (either explicitly declared or implicitly inferred). The general pattern of this is a ^ b -> error. However, all of the four rules can also be modified to the form of a ^ ¬b -> error, i.e. if some facts a (fragments of a process graph) are known, some other facts b (again fragments of a process graph) should not be present in the knowledge base and the failure to derive them should be treated as a form of (weak) negation. This implies closed world reasoning (as opposed

to open world reasoning) and negation as failure (NAF). Ontologies in the Sematic Web adhere to the open world assumption (OWA), which makes sense in an open and networked environment such as the web. According to the OWA, facts that are not explicitly stated in the knowledge base are not false but instead unknown or undefined. In contrast to that, to verify process models it would be useful to at least temporarily assume to know all the facts and hence switch to closed world reasoning. This sort of reasoning requires negation as failure (NAF) and can be introduced using the Jena built-in rule engine which provides this feature using procedural built-in primitives which can be called by the rules. Each primitive is implemented by a Java object and additional primitives can be created and registered by the user. To achieve closed world reasoning using NAF, the primitive noValue(?subject, ?predicate, ?object) can be embedded in a rule which will cause a rule to fire if no matching triple can be found. With closed world reasoning, semantic verification rules such as the following examples would be possible:

- *Element flow rule*: If there is a preliminary check, always the in-depth check has to be performed afterwards.
- *Element occurrence rule*: If the process starts with an event indicating that this process is billable, then somewhere in the process there must be an activity "calculate fee".
- *Resource usage rule*: If a certain function has document x as input, then the applicant must also provide document y.
- *Resource occurrence rule*: If a government unit participates in a process of an administration, then also an individual belonging to the head of the administration should participate.

Furthermore, tools such as Jena or the SQWRL query language implemented in the Protégé-editor also provide built-ins for counting, geo-related reasoning and many other possibilities which enhance the power of semantic verification rules.

LIMITATIONS OF SEMANTIC VERIFICATION

Clearly, semantic verification rules have some limitations. To begin with, they should not be regarded as a surrogate for verifications related to the meta-model or the grammar of the used modeling language. They are rather complementary to such verifications and correct models form the basis for additional semantic verification checks. Also, aspects regarding the execution semantics of models such as soundness, relaxed soundness etc. dealing mainly with the absence of deadlocks, livelocks and other anomalies are not covered by our approach.

Further limitations of semantic verification rules are that they depend on the availability of an ontology and the annotation of process models. While in other areas such as the life sciences huge ontologies have been developed and standardized, the field of administration still lacks authorities who develop and standardize ontologies. However, this problem may partly disappear if the terminology problem will be solved e.g. by defining structured vocabularies which can well serve as a skeletal structure for ontologies. Also, current tools for process model annotation are mostly in the state of research prototypes. In particular, functionalities for semi-automated annotations and annotation suggestions based e.g. on annotations previously made in the current model or the whole model repository have to be developed in the future in order to enable comfortable and cost-effective semantic verification. A major limitation of the current approach is that it is agnostic to the control flow of process models. At the moment, the only exception of that is the property p:followedBy connecting only nodes which form a sequence when the model will be executed and so it provides for rules such as "b should not be executed after a".

CONCLUSION AND FUTURE RESEARCH

The approach presented in this paper showed how to use ontologies, rules and reasoning for the semantic verification of process models. The role of ontologies is to describe elements of semi-formal process models with machine processable semantics. In conjunction with an inference engine, the model elements can be classified thereby using facts automatically derived from the ontology. Based on these classifications of model elements, abstract semantic verification rules are used to decide whether the model conforms to rules and regulations.

Future versions of our approach will tackle some of the described limitations. As a next step, we plan to integrate a further pre-processing step which will mark the nodes in the graph according to their succession of logical connectors such as AND, XOR and OR. The capturing of information on such local contexts of parallelism or exclusivities to the ontology based representation of process models will allow advanced semantic verification rules such as "resource x must not be used in parallel branches" or "activity x should always be executed exclusively with activity z".

REFERENCES

Abouzaid, F., & Mullins, J. (2009). Model-checking Web services orchestrations using BP-calculus. *Electronic Notes in Theoretical Computer Science*, *255*, 3–21. doi:10.1016/j.entcs.2009.10.022

Aguilar, E. R., Ruiz, F., García, F., & Piattini, M. (2006). Evaluation measures for business process models. In *Proceedings of the 21st Annual ACM Symposium on Applied Computing* (pp. 1567-1568). New York, NY: ACM.

Awad, A., Decker, G., & Weske, M. (2008). Efficient compliance checking using BPMN-Q and temporal logic. In M. Dumas, M. Reichert, & M.-C. Shan (Eds.), *Proceedings of the 6th International Conference on Business Process Management* (pp. 326–341). Berlin, Germany: Springer.

Barjis, J. (2008). The importance of business process modeling in software systems design. *Science of Computer Programming*, *71*(1), 73–87.

Becker, J., Delfmann, P., Herwig, S., Lis, L., & Stein, A. (2009). Towards increased comparability of conceptual models – Enforcing naming conventions through domain thesauri and linguistic grammars. *Arbeitsberichte der Universität Münster*. Retrieved from http://www.wi.uni-muenster.de/is/studieren/vorlesung/inmo_ss-2009/

Boley, H., Kifer, M., Patranjan, P. L., & Polleres, A. (2007). Rule interchange on the Web. In G. Antoniou, U. Aßmann, C. Baroglio, S. Decker, N. Henze, P.-L. Patranjan, R. Tolksdorf (Eds.), *Reasoning Web: Third International Summer School 2007, Dresden, Germany, September 3–7* (pp. 269–309). Berlin, Germany: Springer.

Chanda, J., Kanjilal, A., & Sengupta, S. (2010). UML-compiler: A framework for syntactic and semantic verification of UML diagrams. In *Proceedings of the Distributed Computing and Internet Technology Conference* (pp. 194–205). Berlin, Germany: Springer.

Chapurlat, V., & Braesch, C. (2008). Verification, validation, qualification and certification of enterprise models: Statements and opportunities. *Computers in Industry*, *59*(7), 711–721. doi:10.1016/j.compind.2007.12.018

Clarke, E. M. (2008). The birth of model checking. In *Proceedings of the 15th International Conference Tools and Algorithms for the Construction and Analysis of Systems* (pp. 1–26). Berlin, Germany: Springer.

Cobleigh, J. M., Clark, L. A., & Osterweil, L. J. (2000). Verifying properties of process definitions. *ACM SIGSOFT Software Engineering Notes*, *25*(5), 96–101. doi:10.1145/347636.348876

Dehnert, J., & van der Aalst, W. M. P. (2004). Bridging the gap between business models and workflow specifications. *International Journal of Cooperative Information Systems*, *13*(3), 289–332. doi:10.1142/S0218843004000973

Desel, J. (2002). Model validation – A theoretical issue? In J. Esparza, & C. Lakos (Eds.), *Proceedings of Application and Theory of Petri Nets 2002*, (pp. 23–43). Berlin, Germany: Springer. Retrieved from http://dx.doi.org/ 10.1007/3-540-48068-4_2

Deutsch, A., Hull, R., Patrizi, F., & Vianu, V. (2009). Automatic verification of data-centric business processes. In *Proceedings of the 12th International Conference on Database Theory* (pp. 252–267). New York, NY: ACM.

Dijkman, R. M., Dumas, M., & Ouyang, C. (2007). *Formal semantics and automated analysis of BPMN process models*. In (Technical Report Preprint 5969). Retrieved from http://eprints.qut.edu.au/ archive/00005969/

Dijkman, R. M., Dumas, M., & Ouyang, C. (2008). Semantics and analysis of business process models in BPMN. *Information and Software Technology, 50*(12), 1281–1294. doi:10.1016/j.infsof.2008.02.006

Dong, J., Alencar, P. S. C., & Cowan, D. D. (2004). A behavioral analysis and verification approach to pattern-based design composition. *Software and Systems Modeling, 3*(4), 262–272.

Drumm, C., Filipowska, A., Hoffmann, J., Kaczmarek, M., Kaczmarek, T., Kowalkiewicz, M., … Zyskowski, D. (2007). *Dynamic composition reasoning framework and prototype*. In (Project IST 026850 SUPER, Deliverable 3.2, SAP, 2007).

El Kharbili, M., & Stein, S. (2008). Policy-based semantic compliance checking for business process management. In P. Loos, et al. (Eds.), *Modellierung betrieblicher Informationssysteme (MobIS 2008), CEUR Workshop Proceedings 420* (pp. 165–177). Bonn, Germany: Köllen.

El Kharbili, M., Stein, S., Markovic, I., & Pulvermüller, E. (2008). Towards a framework for semantic business process compliance management. In *Proceedings of the 1st International Workshop on Governance, Risk and Compliance (GRCIS2008), CEUR Workshop Proceedings 339* (paper 1).

Engels, G., Heckel, R., & Küster, J. (2001). Rule-based specification of behavioral consistency based on the UML meta-model . In *UML 2001 – The Unified Modeling Language. Modeling Languages, Concepts, and Tools* (pp. 272–286). Berlin, Germany: Springer. doi:10.1007/3-540-45441-1_21

Foster, H., Uchitel, S., Magee, J., & Kramer, J. (2003). Model-based verification of web service compositions. In *Proceedings of the 18th IEEE International Conference on Automated Software Engineering (ASE 2003), October 6–10* (pp. 152–161). Montreal, Canada: IEEE Computer Society.

Friedrich, F. (2009). Measuring semantic label quality using WordNet. In M. Nüttgens, et al. (Eds.), *8th Workshop der Gesellschaft für Informatik e.V. (GI) und Treffen ihres Arbeitskreises Geschäftsprozessmanagement mit Ereignisgesteuerten Prozessketten (WI-EPK)* (pp. 7–21). Berlin, Germany: Springer.

Geguang, P., Xiangpeng, Z., Shuling, W., & Zongyan, Q. (2004). Towards the semantics and verification of BPEL4WS. In *Proceedings of the International Workshop on Web Languages and Formal Methods (WLFM2005)*.

Gerede, C., & Su, J. (2009). Specification and verification of artifact behaviors in business process models . In *Service-Oriented Computing – ICSOC 2007* (pp. 181–192). Berlin, Germany: Springer.

Goedertier, S., & Vanthienen, J. (2006). Designing compliant business processes with obligations and permissions . In Eder, J., & Dustdar, S. (Eds.), *Business Process Management Workshops* (pp. 5–14). Berlin, Germany: Springer. doi:10.1007/11837862_2

Gruhn, V. (1991). Validation and verification of software process models. In *Proceedings of the European Symposium on Software Development Environments and CASE Technology* (pp. 271–286). Berlin, Germany: Springer.

Gruhn, V., & Laue, R. (2007). Checking properties of business process models with logic programming. In *Proceedings of the 5th International Workshop on Modelling, Simulation, Verification and Validation of Enterprise Information Systems (MSVVEIS 2007)*, Madeira, Portugal (pp. 84–93).

Gruhn, V., & Laue, R. (2007b). Forderungen an hierarchische EPK-Schemata. In M. Nüttgens, F.-J. Rump, & A. Gadatsch (Eds.), *Geschäftsprozessmanagement mit Ereignisgesteuerten Prozessketten; 6. Workshop der Gesellschaft für Informatik e.V. (GI) und Treffen ihres Arbeitskreises Geschäftsprozessmanagement mit Ereignisgesteuerten Prozessketten (WI-EPK), CEUR Workshop Proceedings 303* (p. 59 ff.).

Gruhn, V., & Laue, R. (2007c). What business process modelers can learn from programmers. *Science of Computer Programming, 65*(1), 4–13. doi:10.1016/j.scico.2006.08.003

Gruhn, V., & Laue, R. (2009). Ein einfaches Verfahren zur Erkennung häufiger Fehler in EPKs. In M. Nüttgens et al. (Eds.), *8th Workshop der Gesellschaft für Informatik e.V. (GI) und Treffen ihres Arbeitskreises Geschäftsprozessmanagement mit Ereignisgesteuerten Prozessketten (WI-EPK), CEUR Workshop Proceedings 554* (p. 74 ff.).

Happel, H.-J., & Stojanovic, L. (2006). *Ontoprocess – A prototype for semantic business process verification using SWRL rules*. In 3rd European Semantic Web Conference. Retrieved from http://www.eswc2006.org/demo-papers/FD40-Happel.pdf

Heckel, R., Küster, J., & Taentzer, G. (2002). Towards automatic translation of UML models into semantic domains. In A. Corradini, H. Ehrig, H.-J. Kreowski, & G. Rozenberg (Eds.), *Proceedings ICGT 2002 – First International Conference on Graph Transformation (ICGT2002)* (pp. 11–22). Berlin, Germany: Springer

Horrocks, I., Patel-Schneider, P. F., Boley, H., Tabet, S., Grosof, B., & Dean, M. (2004, May 21). *SWRL: A Semantic Web rule language: Combining OWL and RuleML*. W3C member submission. Retrieved from http://www.w3.org/Submission/SWRL/

IEEE. (1998). *IEEE 1012–1998*. Retrieved from http:// www. techstreet. com/ standards/ IEEE/ 1012_1998? prod-uct_id=31920

Kindler, E. (2006). On the semantics of EPCs: Resolving the vicious circle. *Data & Knowledge Engineering, 56*(1), 23–40. doi:10.1016/j.datak.2005.02.005

Koehler, J., Tirenni, G., & Kumaran, S. (2002). From business process model to consistent implementation: A case for formal verification methods. In *6th International Enterprise Distributed Object Computing Conference (EDOC 2002)* (pp. 96–107).

Koliadis, G., & Ghose, A. (2007). Verifying semantic business process models in inter-operation. In *Proceedings of the International Conference on Services Computing (SCC 2007), Salt Lake City, USA* (pp. 731–738).

Kovacs, M., & Gönczy, L. (2008). Simulation and formal analysis of workflow models. In *Electronic Notes in Theoretical Computer Science: Proceedings of the Fifth International Workshop on Graph Transformation and Visual Modeling Techniques (GT-VMT 2006)* (pp. 221–230).

La Rosa, M., Dumas, M., ter Hofstede, A., Mendling, J., & Gottschalk, F. (2008). Beyond control-flow: Extending business process configuration to roles and objects. In *Proceedings of the Conceptual Modeling 2008 (ER2008)* (pp. 199–215). Berlin, Germany: Springer.

Leopold, H., Smirnov, S., & Mendling, J. (2009). On labeling quality in business process models. In M. Nüttgens, et al. (Eds.), *8th Workshop der Gesellschaft für Informatik e. V. (GI) und Treffen ihres Arbeitskreises "Geschäftsprozessmanagement mit Ereignisgesteuerten Prozessketten (WI-EPK), CEUR Workshop Proceedings 554* (pp. 42–57).

Liu, Y., Müller, S., & Xu, K. (2007). A static compliance-checking framework for business process models. *IBM Systems Journal, 46*(2), 335–361. doi:10.1147/sj.462.0335

Lu, S., Bernstein, A., & Lewis, P. (2006). Automatic workflow verification and generation. *Theoretical Computer Science, 353*(1–3), 71–92. doi:10.1016/j.tcs.2005.10.035

Ly, L. T., Rinderle, S., & Dadam, P. (2008). Integration and verification of semantic constraints in adaptive process management systems. *Data & Knowledge Engineering, 64*(1), 3–23. doi:10.1016/j.datak.2007.06.007

Ly, L. T., Rinderle-Ma, S., & Dadam, P. (2010). Design and verification of instantiable compliance rule graphs in process-aware Information Systems. In *Proceedings of CAiSE'10, Hammamet, Tunisia. LNCS 6051* (pp. 9–23). Berlin, Germany: Springer.

Melenovsky, M. J. (2005). *Business process management's success hinges on business-led initiatives*. Stamford, CT: Gartner Research.

Mendling, J. (2009). Empirical studies in process model verification. In Jensen, K., & van der Aalst, W. M. P. (Eds.), *Transactions on petri nets and other models of concurrency II* (pp. 208–224). Berlin, Germany: Springer. doi:10.1007/978-3-642-00899-3_12

Mendling, J., Neumann, G., & van der Aalst, W. (2007). On the correlation between process model metrics and errors. In *Proceedings of the 26th International Conference on Conceptual Modeling (ER2007), Auckland, New Zealand, Australia* (pp. 173–178). Berlin, Grmany: Springer.

Mendling, J., Reijers, H. A., & Recker, J. (2010). Activity labeling in process modeling: Empirical insights and recommendations. *Information Systems, 35*(4), 467–482. doi:10.1016/j.is.2009.03.009

Mendling, J., & van der Aalst, W. (2008). Advanced reduction rules for the verification of EPC business process models. In *Proceedings of the Third AIS SIGSAND European Symposium on Analysis, Design, Use and Societal Impact of Information Systems, Marburg, Germany* (pp. 129–140). Bonn, Germany: Köllen.

Nakajima, S. (2002). Model-checking verification for reliable web service. In *Proceedings of OOWS'02, satellite event of OOPSLA'02, Seattle, USA*. Berlin, Germany: Springer.

Namiri, K., & Stojanovic, N. (2007). Pattern-based design and validation of business process compliance. In Meersman, R., & Tari, Z. (Eds.), *On the move to meaningful Internet systems 2007: CoopIS, DOA, ODBASE, GADA, and IS – OTM Confederated International Conferences CoopIS, DOA, ODBASE, GADA, and IS 2007 Vilamoura* (pp. 59–76). Berlin, Germany: Springer. doi:10.1007/978-3-540-76848-7_6

Nelson, H. J., & Monarchi, D. E. (2007). Ensuring the quality of conceptual representations. *Software Quality Journal, 15*(2), 213–233. doi:10.1007/s11219-006-9011-2

Okika, J. C. (2009). Analyzing orchestration of BPEL specified services with model checking. In *Proceedings of the PhD Symposium of the 7th International Joint Conference on Service Oriented Computing*, Stockholm, Sweden.

Pease, A., Niles, I., & Li, J. (2002). The suggested upper merged ontology: A large ontology for the Semantic Web and its applications. In *Proceedings of the 2002 AAAI Spring Symposium, March 25–27, Stanford University, Palo Alto, California*. Retrieved from http://ontologyportal.org

Peters, N., & Weidlich, M. (2009). Using glossaries to enhance the label quality in business process models. In M. Nüttgens, et al. (Eds.), *8th Workshop der Gesellschaft für Informatik e.V. (GI) und Treffen ihres Arbeitskreises "Geschäftsprozessmanagement mit Ereignisgesteuerten Prozessketten (WI-EPK)", CEUR Workshop Proceedings 554* (pp. 75–90).

Pons, C., & Garcia, D. (2008). A lightweight approach for the semantic validation of model refinements. *Electronic Notes in Theoretical Computer Science, 220*(1), 43–61. doi:10.1016/j.entcs.2008.11.005

Sadiq, S. W., Orlowska, M. E., & Sadiq, W. (2005). Specification and validation of process constraints for flexible workflows. *Information Systems, 30*(5), 349–378. doi:10.1016/j.is.2004.05.002

Sadiq, W., & Orlowska, M. E. (2000). Analyzing process models using graph reduction techniques. *Information Systems, 25*(2), 117–134. doi:10.1016/S0306-4379(00)00012-0

Salomie, I., Cioara, T., Anghel, I., Dinsoreanu, M., & Salomie, T. I. (2007). A layered workflow model enhanced with process algebra verification for industrial processes. In *Proceedings of the 2007 IEEE International Conference on Intelligent Computer Communication and Processing, Cluj-Napoca, Romania* (pp. 185–191). Montreal, Canada: IEEE Computer Society.

Simon, C., & Mendling, J. (2006) Verification of forbidden behavior in EPCs. In H. C. Mayr, & R. Breu (Eds.), *Proceedings of the GI Conference Modellierung (MOD2006), Innsbruck, Austria* (pp. 233–242). Berlin, Germany: Springer.

Soffer, P., & Wand, Y. (2004). Goal-driven analysis of process model validity. In A. Persson & Stirna (Eds.), *Advanced Information Systems engineering* (pp. 229–319). Berlin, Germany: Springer

Speck, A., Pulvermüller, E., & Heuzeroth, D. (2004). Validation of business process models. In L. Cardelli (Ed.), *Proceedings of the 17th European Conference on Object-oriented Programming (ECOOP)*. Berlin, Germany: Springer.

Thomas, O., & Fellmann, M. (2009). Semantic process modeling – Design and implementation of an ontology-based representation of business processes. *Business & Information Systems Engineering, 1*(6), 438–451. doi:10.1007/s12599-009-0078-8

Touré, F., Baïna, K., & Benali, K. (2008). An efficient algorithm for workflow graph structural verification. In *Proceedings of the OTM 2008 Confederated International Conferences, CoopIS, DOA, GADA, IS, and ODBASE 2008* (pp. 392–408). Berlin, Germany: Springer.

van Breugel, F., & Koshkina, M. (2006). *Models and verification of BPEL*. In Technical Report, York University, Toronto, Canada. Retrieved from http://www.cse.yorku.ca/franck/research/drafts/ tutorial.pdf

van der Aalst, W. M. P. (1997). Verification of workflow nets. In G. Balbo & P. Azema (Eds.), *Proceedings of the 18th International Conference on Application and Theory of Petri Nets* (pp. 407–426). Berlin, Germany: Springer.

van der Aalst, W. M. P. (1998). The application of Petri nets to workflow management. *Journal of Circuits Systems and Computers, 8*, 21–66. doi:10.1142/S0218126698000043

van der Aalst, W. M. P. (1999). Formalization and verification of event-driven process chains. *Information and Software Technology, 41*(10), 639–650. doi:10.1016/S0950-5849(99)00016-6 van der Aalst, W. M. P. (2003). Inheritance of business processes: A journey visiting four notorious problems . In Ehrig, H., Reisig, W., Rosenberg, G., & Weber, H. (Eds.), *Petri net technology for communication-based system* (pp. 383–408). Berlin, Germany: Springer. doi:10.1007/978-3-540-40022-6_19

van der Aalst, W. M. P., de Beer, H. T., & van Dongen, B. F. (2005). Process mining and verification of properties: An approach based on temporal logic . In Tari, Z. (Ed.), *On the move to meaningful Internet systems 2005: CoopIS, DOA, and ODBASE* (pp. 130–147). Berlin, Germany: Springer. doi:10.1007/11575771_11

van Dongen, B. F., Jansen-Vullers, M. H., Verbeek, H. M. W., & van der Aalst, W. M. P. (2007). Verification of the SAP reference models using EPC reduction, state-space analysis, and invariants. *Computers in Industry*, *58*(6), 578–601. doi:10.1016/j.compind.2007.01.001

van Dongen, B. F., van der Aalst, W. M. P., & Verbeek, H. M. W. (2005). Verification of EPCs: Using reduction rules and Petri nets . In Pastor, O., & Falcáo e Cunha, J. (Eds.), *advanced information systems engineering* (pp. 372–386). Berlin, Germany: Springer. doi:10.1007/11431855_26

Varró, D. (2003). Towards symbolic analysis of visual modeling languages. *Electronic Notes in Theoretical Computer Science*, *72*(3), 51–64. doi:10.1016/S1571-0661(04)80611-X

Varró, D., & Pataricza, A. (2002). Metamodeling mathematics: A precise and visual framework for describing semantics domains of UML models. In *«UML» 2002 – The Unified Modeling Language* (pp. 449–456). Berlin, Germany: Springer.

Weber, I., Hoffmann, J., & Mendling, J. (2010). Beyond soundness: On the verification of semantic business process models. *Distributed and Parallel Databases*, *27*(3), 271–343. doi:10.1007/s10619-010-7060-9

Weber, I. M. (2009). Verification of annotated process models . In Weber, M. (Ed.), *Semantic methods for execution-level business process modeling* (pp. 97–148). Berlin, Germany: Springer. doi:10.1007/978-3-642-05085-5_4

Wecker, G., & van Laak, H. (Eds.). (2008). *Compliance in der Unternehmenspraxis: Grundlagen, Organisation und Umsetzung*. Wiesbaden, Germany: Gabler.

Wolter, C., Miseldine, P., & Meinel, C. (2009). Verification of business process entailment constraints using SPIN. In *Proceedings of the 1st International Symposium on Engineering Secure Software and Systems* (pp. 1–15). Berlin, Germany: Springer.

Xiang, F., Bultan, T., & Su, J. (2002). Formal verification of e-services and workflows. In *Proceedings of Web Services, E-Business, and the Semantic Web: CAiSE 2002 International Workshop, WES 2002, Toronto, Canada* (pp. 180–202). Berlin, Germany: Springer.

Xinhua, L., Weida, W., & Wenjian, L. (2007). An intelligent methodology for business process model verification. In *Proceedings of the IEEE International Conference on Control and Automation (ICCA2007), Frankfurt* (pp. 2381–2385).

Chapter 9
Automated Planning of Process Models:
Towards a Semantic–Based Approach

Bernd Heinrich
University of Innsbruck, Austria

Mathias Klier
University of Innsbruck, Austria

Steffen Zimmermann
University of Innsbruck, Austria

ABSTRACT

Companies need to adapt their processes quickly in order to react to changing customer demands or new regulations, for example. Process models are an appropriate means to support process setup but currently the (re)design of process models is a time-consuming manual task. Semantic Business Process Management, in combination with planning approaches, can alleviate this drawback. This means that the workload of (manual) process modeling could be reduced by constructing models in an automated way. Since existing, traditional planning algorithms show drawbacks for the application in Semantic Business Process Management, we introduce a novel approach that is suitable especially for the Semantic-based Planning of process models. In this chapter, we focus on the semantic reasoning, which is necessary in order to construct control structures, such as decision nodes, which are vital elements of process models. We illustrate our approach by a running example taken from the financial services domain. Moreover, we demonstrate its applicability by a prototype and provide some insights into the evaluation of our approach.

DOI: 10.4018/978-1-60960-126-3.ch009

INTRODUCTION

In times of dynamically shifting markets, companies, especially those integrated in electronic supply chains, have to adapt or even restructure their processes frequently. First, regarding the sales market of a company, changing customer needs and new offers of emerging competitors need to be considered and demand for quick reactions in the form of enhanced services and innovative products. Second, a national and international network of business partners gets more and more important in order to be able to offer best-of-breed-products and customized solutions instead of commodities. Such approaches, along with an efficient design of the supply chain, constitute distinguishing factors between competitors. Third, the market of suppliers for a company, especially of IT suppliers, is expanding. Only ten years ago, the share of proprietary and individual software has been considerably higher than today. In the future, it should be possible to design and modify company specific applications by composing Web Services provided by external software suppliers according to predefined business processes. In any of these three "market views" processes constitute the starting point for dynamic modifications along the value chain.

In order to counter the above mentioned requirements of a dynamic and flexible (re)design, traditional techniques and tools for process modeling and optimization seem to be insufficient or inadequate to some extent. Reasons are that traditional modeling techniques for process (re)design imply a significant degree of manual work (e.g. Becker & Kahn, 2003; Borges et al., 2005; Ma & Leymann, 2008) or result repeatedly in a high demand for communication and clarification because of different terminologies (Becker et al., 2000; Thomas & Fellmann, 2006).

According to the ongoing research in the area of Semantic Business Process Management (SBPM), a higher degree of automation concerning the use of process models can contribute to a solution (cf.

Hepp et al., 2005; Thomas & Fellmann, 2006). More precisely, we envision the automated design of process models. As this task can be regarded as a kind of planning problem (cf. Ghallab et al., 2004; Henneberger et al., 2008; Heinrich et al., 2009), we speak of an automated planning of process models. One basis for the automated planning of process models constitute Semantic Web standards like the Web Ontology Language (OWL) that enables a semantically enriched description of process models and their elements (e.g. Betz et al., 2006; Drumm et al., 2006). These standards have already been used for Semantic Web Service Composition. Yet, in contrast to Semantic Web Service Composition approaches, the planning of process models is conducted on a conceptual level independent from the underlying technology. The composition of Web Services is accomplished for a specific problem, that means a number of Web Services is arranged together to deliver one distinct and previously defined output. For the planning of process models, however, we abstract from one individual process execution and its implementation. Thus, process models are initially technology independent and may partially be realized by different combinations of available Web Services (from different providers) that may be chosen afterwards by means of economic aspects like cost and risk. This two-step approach is advantageous as it increases flexibility and bears optimization potential. It is moreover reasonable to assume that the step from descriptions of process models and process actions to concrete implementations using Web Services is relatively small (e.g. Drumm et al., 2006).

Yet, the automated planning of process models – in the sense of an automated design of entire new process models – is hardly discussed in the scope of SBPM, if at all. Doubtlessly the conceptual and technological basis for an automated planning of process models is to a certain extent already present in the areas of Artificial Intelligence (AI) planning and Semantic Web Service Composition. Several approaches in both domains indeed exist, but the planning problem and particularly the planning of process models is far from being solved (cf. Heinrich et al., 2009). For instance, Semantic Web Service Composition approaches are often restricted to a manageable number of sequentially executed Web Services and do normally not focus complex compositions, including vital control structures in process models like parallel split.

Therefore, the aim of our paper is to introduce an approach, called SEMPA (SEMantic-based Planning Approach) that supports and enables the automated planning of process models using semantically described process actions. Figure 1 clarifies the problem setting and specifies some terms and concepts used. Based on a semantic description of the domain (in terms of the OWL ontology) and the description of actions which

are available in a library, the planning algorithm is supposed to find process models for a given problem definition. The problem definition includes, besides the library and the ontology, an initial state that characterizes the overall inputs of the process and one to many goals. Goals are representing process outputs.

We organized the chapter as follows: In the next section we introduce a running example. Afterwards, we elaborate the fundamental requirements for the planning of process models and give a short review of the relevant literature. Based on that, the planning algorithm SEMPA which is conceptually divided into three steps is elaborated. We then briefly discuss the evaluation of our approach before we finally summarize the main results and define further research.

Figure 1. The basic idea of automated planning of process models

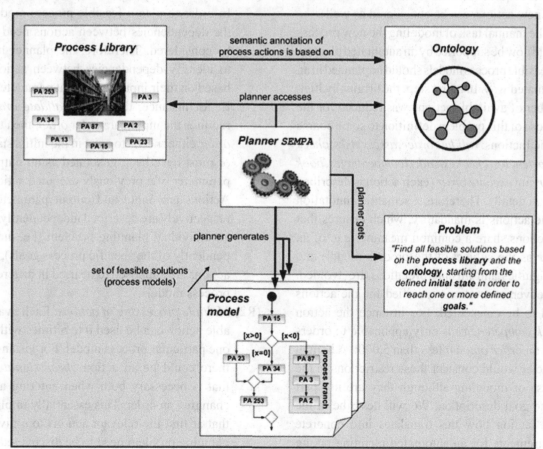

Running Example

The basic idea will be illustrated by a running example originating from the financial services industry. The problem definition of this use case is inspired by a project with a financial services provider. We consider a situation where a new process model for the execution of an order (e.g. stock order) is needed. In the initial state there is the order that has been entered by a customer. The goal is to execute the order (executed and entered are two feasible values of the order status). At the same time the guidelines of the financial services provider require a risk assessment for each order to be executed. Based on this, a process modeler would try to develop a new process model reusing existing actions that are already part of similar models. This complies with the frequently appearing case for financial products that new process models require established actions (at the same time new actions can be considered as well).

The manual task of modeling the new process should now be supported by an automated planner, i.e. feasible process models should be planned in an automated way. In a first step, the originally high number of available actions was reduced for the purpose of this problem definition to some coarse grained actions: *validate order, assess risks, check competencies, check extended competencies, book order* and *execute order* (each action is described later in detail). Therefore, a semantic annotation of the actions is mandatory, which ensures that all actions share a common meaning (e.g. of an *order* as the subject of the process model) and ambiguities and misinterpretations are avoided. Moreover, restrictions specified for the actions need to be considered. For instance the action *check competencies* is only applicable to orders with an *order amount* less than 5,000[1]. A human modeler would consider these restrictions in the course of modeling although they are not part of the goal description. We will describe in the next section how this translates into concrete requirements for an automated planning taking the running example into account.

REQUIREMENTS FOR PROCESS PLANNING AND RELATED WORK

In a first step, we elaborate the basic requirements for the planning of process models. Then, we give a review of selected existing approaches with respect to these requirements.

Requirements for Planning Process Models in the Context of SBPM

Firstly, we give an overview of the requirements a process planner needs to meet in detail. They constitute criteria to evaluate existing approaches as well as the planner we suggest. The following requirements derived from literature (cf. e.g. Constantinescu et al., 2004; Meyer & Kuropka, 2006) need to be considered:

(R1) *Input and output parameters of actions*[2]: In order to plan a feasible process model, the dependencies between actions need to be considered. Therefore, the planner has to identify dependencies between actions based on their input and output parameters. If, for instance, the action *validate order* requires the input parameter *order,* then the *order* either needs to exist in the initial state or must have been generated as an output parameter of a previously executed action. Actions and input and output parameters respectively are described independently of an individual planning problem (i.e. independently of the specific process goals), as actions are supposed to be used in different process models.

(R2) *Multiple processing of actions*: Each available action can be used 0 to n times within one particular process model. For instance, there could be an action *check signature* that is necessary both when entering and changing an order. This essentially implies that at first the relevant actions to a given planning problem need to be discovered in a potentially large library.

(R3) *Composite input and output parameters*: In other approaches oftentimes rather simple input and output parameters are assumed (see below). However, this is not sufficient for the planning of realistic process models. Instead, the planner needs to handle composite parameters, i.e. actions may require or generate composite parameters which consist of at least two atomic parameters. An *order* (composite parameter) in our example for instance consists of the atomic parameters *orderState*, *orderAmount* and *orderType*.

(R4) *Numerical and alphanumerical data types*: It must be possible to assign numerical and alphanumerical data types (cf. Biron & Malhotra, 2004) to each atomic parameter in the ontology (in contrast to other approaches that for the sake of simplicity assume only Boolean variables). For example the *orderAmount* may be of the data type *positiveInteger*. This definition applies for any action in the library that has the parameter *orderAmount*. However, some actions may require certain ranges of values of an input parameter for instance. As already mentioned the action *check competencies* is only reasonable for *orders* with an *orderAmount* less than 5,000. Such restrictions have to be considered, i.e. it should be possible to specify the range of values an action accepts for an input parameter and the range of values it produces for an output parameter.

(R5) *Non-deterministic planning*: Due to restrictions the input and output parameters of two consecutive actions may not match completely. This happens for instance if the action *check competencies* succeeds an action that produces an output parameter *order* and the *orderAmount* can also adopt a value higher than 5,000. As the concrete realizations of values of input and output parameters (of a single process run) are not determined at the moment of planning, the planner needs to consider all possible real-

izations. This requirement is referred to as non-deterministic planning (cf. Henneberger et al., 2008).

(R6) *Semantic-based Reasoning:* The planner has to use a given ontology that contains all input and output parameters and their data types and describes relations between them (such as the subclassof relation). Input and output parameters of actions have to be compared based on the ontology in order to identify dependencies between actions. For the analysis of the dependencies, inference mechanisms have to be applied by the planner to detect identities, equivalences and specialization relations etc. If, for instance, an action requires an input parameter *order* and it can be deduced from the ontology that a *stock order* is a specialization of *order*, then a *stock order* can be processed as an input parameter as well.

(R7) *Control structures in process models:* A planner must be able to plan control structures in process models in an automated way. Van der Aalst et al. (2003) provide a comprehensive description of the various control structures (workflow patterns) that may be part of a process model and workflow respectively. They moreover analyze how these structures are represented in different process modeling languages (like for instance UML activity diagrams (Russel et al., 2006)). A process planner needs to consider for example the following basic and advanced structures (cf. van der Aalst et al., 2003): exclusive choice, parallel split, synchronization, simple merge, and arbitrary cycles.

(R8) *Set of feasible solutions:* Besides control structures there are often many feasible solutions (alternative process models) for one given problem definition. A feasible solution is any process model, where all goal states can be reached starting in the initial state. For example, different feasible solutions occur when two or more process actions do not have any input/output dependencies and therefore a sequential as well as a parallel composition may be possible. This applies for instance to the actions *assess risks* and *check extended competencies* in our example, that can be executed sequentially (starting with either of the two) or in parallel, which results into three feasible solutions. The planner has to construct such feasible process models in an automated way.

After specifying the requirements to a process planner in general, we will give a review of existing approaches related to this issue.

Related Work

The automated planning of process models – in the sense of an automated design of entire new process models – is hardly discussed in the research strand of SBPM. Related work can be mainly found in the fields of AI and Web Service Composition. In the following, we will discuss approaches related to these research areas.

Automated Planning

The task of finding a number of actions that transform an initial state into a goal state is called planning (Ghallab et al., 2004). In this respect, a process model can be regarded as an abstract plan. Each action, when executed, results into a new state (thereby a state is constituted by the output parameters produced by the actions). However, an important characteristic is that for the planning of process models we abstract from an individual process execution and therefore the individual realizations of parameter values (and thus the current state in a single process run) are not determined at the moment of planning. In fact a process model should be more general and hold for different possible process runs. This conforms to so-called *non-deterministic* planning problems (Ghallab et al., 2004). Non-deterministic planning

approaches are oftentimes further differentiated depending on the extent to which concrete values can be observed at execution time, i.e. when the plan (or in our case the process depicted by the model) is executed. Assuming limited knowledge at execution time seems to be odd – although for example the *order amount* of a particular order is not determined at the moment of planning, there is no reason, why it should be unknown at process execution time, too – but it makes perfectly sense for traditional automated planning domains such as robotics. For instance, a robot may have limited sensors and thus may be not able to capture its current position in a room exactly. This has to be accounted for when actions are planned for the robot. Thus, non-deterministic planning approaches are further differentiated into non-deterministic planning approaches under full observability, under partial observability (also called planning with sensing), and under no observability (no sensors at all). Existing approaches to the mentioned problem domains will be analyzed in the following with respect to our problem setting.

Considering our requirements and in particular requirement (R4), *non-deterministic planning approaches under no observability* can be omitted here because they generally build sequential plans (Bonet & Geffner, 2000). Process models should, however, contain control structures (e.g. exclusive choices).

Plans in *non-deterministic planning domains under full observability* may contain branches. Several approaches have been introduced in this area (cf. Cimatti et al., 1998; Kabanza et al., 1997). However, these approaches explicitly enumerate all states that may occur after applying an action. This is not practicable in our case, since parameters and their data types may have a nearly infinite domain (e.g. real number). Therefore, approaches for planning under full observability do not contribute to a solution, as well.

Non-deterministic planning approaches under partial observability are for instance Bertoli et al. (2001), Bonet & Geffner (2001), and Hoffmann & Brafman (2005). They build so-called conditional plans that branch at the conditions of certain variables which are tested by pre-defined sensing actions. Most of these approaches accomplish a search in the space of belief states, where a belief state encapsulates the set of states that are conceivable at a certain point in planning. Petrick & Bacchus (2002), in contrast, introduce a knowledge based approach to planning, where knowledge bases provide means to describe possible states of the world without enumerating them explicitly (which is advantageous for the reasons outlined above). Again, however, an important problem with most of these approaches is that they do not support numerical data types (requirement (R4)). Or if numbers are integrated then they are regarded as resources, which is not appropriate for planning process models. A prominent example of a resource is time; another example maybe fuel (e.g. in a car driving scenario). Actions are consuming (or producing) proportions of a resource, i.e. they are increasing or decreasing the value of the corresponding numerical variable. Resources are considered as constraints to the planning problem or they are part of a goal specification. For instance, the challenge may be to find a plan that reaches a goal with minimum consumption of time and fuel, which is obviously quite different to our problem setting. An additional drawback of most planning approaches is related to requirement (R7). Although non-deterministic planning approaches under partial observability build conditional plans, the conditions at the branches are in general given in advance (by the planning domain) and are restricted to most often binary variables. In process modeling, which is our problem context, such conditions are not given as this would simplify planning process models to a great extent (detailed in Heinrich et al., 2009).

In summary, we can state that because of these differences none of the existing approaches in AI planning reaches out for the planning of process models.

Web Service Composition

In fact, the approaches with the closest similarity to the specified problem setting are automated Web Service Composition approaches because they employ to some extent planning techniques as well. Additionally, automated Web Service Composition approaches make similar assumptions. For instance, several approaches assume that Web Services are semantically described applying for example SAWSDL or OWL-S. These languages are based on semantic Web standards (RDF, OWL) and Web Service standards respectively (SOAP, WSDL, WS-BPEL) and have in common, that they enable the semantic specification of input parameters, output parameters, preconditions and effects. As already mentioned actions can be described in a similar fashion. Preconditions and effects were not mentioned so far. In a process modeling context they most often refer to the input and output of actions and can therefore be modeled as restrictions (as we will see later on). Henceforth there are analogies between the planning of process models and Web Service Composition, which justifies analyzing them in more detail with regard to the requirements stated above.

Few papers so far try to categorize the nearly unmanageable amount of Web Service Composition approaches (cf. Berardi et al., 2006; ter Beek et al., 2006). In the following paragraphs we briefly discuss the approaches which are – to the best of our knowledge – the ones with the highest similarity to the problem setting described above.

In Lang & Su (2005) the Web Service Composition problem is regarded as a search problem in a so called AND/OR graph. This approach contains several ideas that are interesting in our context. The authors select and compose Web Services based on their input/output dependencies ((R1), (R2)), even considering composite input and output parameters, as demanded by requirement (R3). However, the approach does not account for data types of input and output parameters (R4). Semantic based reasoning capabilities are mentioned, but not elaborated in detail (R6). Moreover, non-deterministic planning (R5) and control structures (R7) are not considered at all. But the approach at least theoretically enables the extraction and subsequent evaluation of all feasible solutions to their composition problem (see (R8)).

The next two approaches we consider are SHOP2 and Golog, which both are employed for Web Service Composition (cf. Sirin et al., 2004; McIlraith & Son, 2002). Given a list of tasks that have to be achieved and a set of Web Services that accomplish these tasks, these planners build a plan representing an ordered sequence of Web Services that needs to be executed. The basis for planning is the description of input and output parameters as well as preconditions and effects, which is in accordance with (R1). However, the tasks to be accomplished are specified in advance, which simplifies the selection of appropriate Web Services to a great extent (R2). Input and output parameters are neither complex, nor do they have data types ((R3), (R4)). Moreover, at the moment of planning, all necessary values are fully determined and a deterministic plan can be constructed. Consequently, both planner do not consider requirements (R5) and (R8), and give therefore no idea or solution. Control structures may be part of the given problem definition but are not constructed in an automated way (R7). Semantic based reasoning capabilities (R6) are not reported in these approaches. However, it seems the authors are still working on this issue.

Pathak et al. (2006) propose a framework for modeling Web Service Composition and Execution based on symbolic transition systems. Compared to the approaches discussed before, they focus additionally on non-functional requirements (e.g. Quality of Service-parameters like cost). The composition algorithm then chooses Web Service Compositions based on these requirements. That means a set of feasible solutions (alternative Web Service Compositions) with the same functionality but different non-functional properties can be constructed. Thus in contrast to Shop2 and Golog, requirement (R8) is fulfilled.

The algorithms analyzed so far lack the capability to construct more complex plans that is considered by the next approaches. A planner that has already been employed for Web Service Composition is MBP, as described in Pistore et al. (2005). When we face this approach with our requirements, apparently (R1) is met, since the input and output parameters are considered for planning. As in the current solution only two Web Services are orchestrated, it is difficult to assess how the selection and multiple use of component Web Service works (R2). Composite input and output parameters and numerical data types are not supported ((R3), (R4)). However, the MBP support non-determinism (R5). Accordingly, plans can include the control structure exclusive choice (R7), but no other control structure like parallel split. Semantic based reasoning is not employed as the authors concentrate on a syntactical composition (R6). Moreover it is not the intention to generate all feasible solutions to their planning problem or even to evaluate them (R8).

In Meyer & Weske (2006) a heuristic search algorithm for automated Web Service Composition is presented. Considering the requirements specified above, we observe that some, but still not all requirements are fulfilled. Planning is accomplished using the input and output parameters as well as preconditions and effects (R1). The paper does not go into detail whether the chosen Web Services are the only available ones and whether a Web Service might be used more than once (R2). The authors mention that the composition will be extended in future versions by numerical state properties, but currently the requirements (R3) and (R4) are not met. Moreover, the composition does not consider semantic descriptions so far (R6).

The requirements (R5) and to a certain extent also (R7) are fulfilled, since the planning graph supports simply alternative and parallel process flows. As only one plan is returned, requirement (R8) is not met.

Constantinescu et al. (2004a, b) propose a type-based approach for Web Service Composition. Their approach meets only parts of the claimed requirements. The approach fulfills (R1), as input and output parameters are used as a planning basis. Requirement (R2) is also met, because the same Web Service may occur in several paths of the presented solution. The approach supports primitive data types including numerical values (R4) but no composite parameters (R3). Requirement (R5) is met, since partially matching Web Services lead to different branches in the composite solution. Semantic descriptions and appropriate reasoning mechanisms (R6) are considered only elementary as matching parameters need to be semantically equal. Furthermore, only exclusive choices and the corresponding simple merges can be deduced from the result (R7). The extraction of different feasible solutions (R8) is not supported.

After all, we summarize that none of the discussed approaches meets all of the requirements for process planning (see Table 1). Non-deterministic planning, the construction of control structures, the ability to handle composite input and output parameters and numerical data types as well as the usage of appropriate inference mechanisms seem to be most challenging. Yet, especially these issues provide interesting questions for the planning of process models: How can we derive dependencies between actions by means of a semantic analysis considering numerical data types as well as restrictions on these data types? How can we account for composite parameters in this context? How can the identified dependencies be used for non-deterministic planning? These questions are addressed in the following section.

SEMANTIC-BASED PLANNING OF PROCESS MODELS

In the following, the SEMPA algorithm for the planning of process models will be introduced. Therefore the defined requirements constitute the starting point for the design. To be able to address these requirements, the algorithm is conceptually divided into three steps:

1. To identify dependencies between actions originating from their input and output parameters, we create an Action Dependency Graph (ADG). The ADG includes actions and corresponding parameters (as nodes). We use semantic reasoning in this step of SEMPA, i.e. we analyze the classes of input and output parameters and their relations defined in the ontology.

2. The ADG describes no direct sequences of actions, yet. Hence, in the next step of SEMPA we employ a forward search algorithm to determine all sequences of actions leading from the initial state to the goals. As result, we obtain an Action State Graph (ASG) that comprises all feasible solutions to the corresponding planning problem.

3. In the third step, we design the control structures in the ASG and build syntactically correct process models. These process models are finally presented to the user.

Figure 2 illustrates the three steps of the algorithm. They are described below in detail.

The division of the algorithm into three steps has a couple of advantages:

As already mentioned in requirement (R2) the number of available actions may be significantly large. The division allows us to reduce complexity while efficiency can be increased. Actions that can never be part of a feasible solution of a specific problem definition are separated out

Table 1. Selected approaches for Web Service composition

Authors	Approach	(R1) Input and output parameters of actions	(R2) Multiple processing of actions	(R3) Composite input and output parameters	(R4) Numerical and alphanumerical data types	(R5) Non-deterministic planning	(R6) Semantic-based Reasoning	(R7) Control structures in process models	(R8) Set of feasible solutions
Lang and Su 2005	AND/OR-graph	✓	✓	✓	-	-	✓	-	✓
Sirin et al. 2004	SHOP2 (HTN Planning)	✓	✓	-	-	-	✓	-	-
McIlraith and Son 2002	Golog language (situation calculus)	✓	✓	-	-	-	✓	-	-
Pathak et al. 2006a, b	Symbolic Tran-sition Systems	✓	✓	-	-	✓	-	✓	✓
Pistore et al. 2005	State Transition Systems	✓	✓	-	-	✓	-	✓	-
Meyer and Weske 2006; Kuropka and Weske 2008	Heuristic Search via Hill Climbing	✓	✓	-	-	✓	-	✓	-
Constantinescu et al. 2004	Type-based Composi-tion	✓	✓	-	✓	✓	✓	✓	-

Figure 2. The three steps of the SEMPA approach.

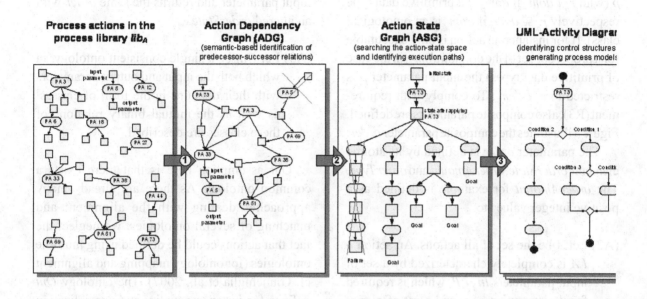

in the ADG (step one) and are not processed in further steps. Accordingly, by means of the ADG the search space for the following forward search (step two) can be significantly reduced. Moreover, dependencies analyzed once in the ADG can be reused for further planning problems.

Semantic reasoning – demanded by requirement (R6) – is a complex and thus time-consuming task, especially in the presence of composite parameters with different data types and restrictions (cf. requirements (R3) and (R4)). Therefore, semantic reasoning is accomplished mainly once (in the first step). This avoids redundant analysis during the following steps of the algorithm.

The ASG forms a (language independent) basis for the extraction of process models. Characteristics of process modeling languages concerning for instance control structures are only considered in the last step (cf. requirement (R7)). This gives us the flexibility to consider different process modeling languages at a time without adapting the fundamental search algorithm. On the other hand it provides the possibility to develop different search algorithms generating the ASG without affecting the extraction of process models.

Assumptions and Definitions

Before we introduce the three steps of the algorithm with a focus on the first step, we will provide essential assumptions and definitions.

(A1) Let P be the set of all input and output parameters. A parameter p (with $p \in P$) is either an atomic or a composite parameter. An atomic parameter is a triple (l_p, dom_p, r_p) which consists of an identifier l_p, its domain $dom_p \in Dom$, and the restriction r_p on the domain. A composite parameter $(l_p, \{(l_{p1}, dom_{p1}, r_{p1}), ..., (l_{pn}, dom_{pn}, r_{pn})\})$ is a tuple containing an identifier l_p and a set of $n \geq 2$ atomic parameters, with $n \in N$.

Parameters establish the basis for planning. For reasons of simplicity, we focus on atomic parameters in the formal descriptions. They have a (global, unchangeable) domain dom_p that is defined in an ontology (cf. (A3)). This domain is either a primitive data type (cf. data types in XML-Schema (Biron et al., 2004)) or an ontological class. Additionally, each action can define an individual restriction r_p for each of its parameters p (with $r_p \in dom_p$ if dom_p is a primitive data type respectively $r_p \nsubseteq dom_p$ if dom_p is an ontological class). If for instance an action is only executable for a proper subset of the domain dom_p (in the case of primitive data types) the input parameter p is restricted to $r_p \in dom_p$. To comply with requirement (R3), also composite parameters are defined. Figure 3 illustrates the composite parameter *order*.

The parameter *order* is defined by its atomic elements *orderState*, *orderAmount* and *orderType*. The *orderAmount* for example is defined as a positive integer value etc.

(A2) Let A be the set of all actions. An action $a \in A$ is completely characterized by a set of input parameters $In_a \in P$, which is required for the execution of a and a set of output parameters $Out_a \in P$, which is provided by a after execution. All actions a are stored as a triple (a, In_a, Out_a) in a library lib_A.

An action a is characterized by its input In_a and its output Out_a. In contrast to proposed standards like OWL-S, WSDL-S or WSMO, we do not distinguish between the information space used by the actions (often referenced to as inputs and outputs of a Web Service) and the state (of the world) that might be changed due to the execution of an action (often referenced to as preconditions and effects). Here, we assume that the (world-)state is modeled – together with the information-space – by a set of parameters and especially their restrictions.

Figure 4 illustrates the specification of process actions with an example of our use case. The action *validate order* requires an arbitrary *order* as input parameter and returns the same *order* with an altered *orderState*.

(A3) Let *Ont* be a single consistent ontology, in which both the input and output parameters with their domains in the form of classes[3] as well as the mutual binary relations of these classes are described.

Our assumption here is that there exists a common ontology. As there are already many approaches dealing with the alignment and matching of several ontologies, we neglect the fact that actions could be defined using multiple ontologies (for ontology mapping and alignment cf. Giunchiglia et al., 2007). The ontology *Ont* defines for instance equality and specialization relations between parameters (represented by relations between ontological classes). These relations and their usage in the course of the semantic analysis will be described below in detail.

An ontology for the introduced running example is illustrated in Figure 5.

(A4) The objective of the algorithm is the planning of feasible solutions (in the sense of process models) for the problem defined as $Prob = (Ont, Init, Goals, lib_A)$. *Ont* is the reference ontology and *Init* $\in P$ the initial set of parameters (initial state). In addition, $Goals = \{G_1, G_2, ..., G_k\}$ defines the set of $k \in N$ different (sets of) parameters $G_x \in P$ (with $x = 1, ..., k$), which shall all be met in each feasible solution. lib_A is the given library containing all existing actions.

Figure 3. The parameter order

```
(order, ⟨(orderState, state, {checked}), (orderAmount, int+, int+),
        (orderType, {buy order, sell order}, {buy order, sell order}) ⟩)
```

Figure 4. The action validate order

```
(validate order,
    {(order, ⟨(orderState, state, {entered}), (orderAmount, int+, int+),
    (orderType, {buy order, sell order}, {buy order, sell order}) ⟩}},
    {(order, ⟨(orderState, state, {valid, invalid}), (orderAmount, int+, int+),
    (orderType, {buy order, sell order}, {buy order, sell order})⟩ )})
```

According to requirement (R8) the algorithm should provide the set of feasible solutions so that in a further step the optimal solution can be chosen. For each feasible solution and for each G_x Î *Goals*, there exists a certain path in the resulting process model so that G_x can be reached.

In the following, we will describe our approach in detail starting with the first step of SEMPA.

Generation of the Action Dependency Graph (ADG)

First, we determine the dependencies among actions. It is crucial to mention that dependencies do not determine a concrete sequence of actions. The following example illustrates this statement: As an input parameter can possibly be provided by alternative actions, dependencies do not necessarily translate into direct predecessor-successor-relationships. The dependencies between actions are stored in the ADG and are provided as basis for further steps.

To determine the dependency between two actions a, b Î A, we have to analyze if there is an output parameter p Î Out_a of a that can be used as an input parameter q Î In_b of b or vice versa, i.e. if input and output parameters match. In the simplest case, all input parameters of one action are identical to the output parameters of another action. But not every dependency is the result of a simple comparison of all input and output parameters of exactly two actions. First, input parameters may be provided by the output parameters of more than one action. Additionally,

Figure 5. Ontology used for the running example

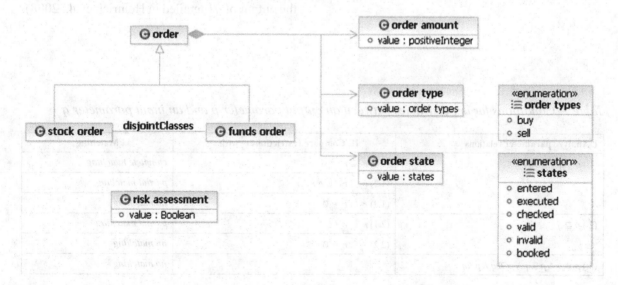

it might be necessary to compare the parameters not only syntactically, but also use their semantics to identify dependencies, as the input parameters might be deduced from the available output parameters (of one or several actions) through semantic-based reasoning. For instance, an input parameter q of b could be non-identical to an output parameter p of a, but nevertheless being associated by an equivalence or a specialization relation. This causes a dependency of b from a, which is not directly obvious from the syntax of the individual parameters. Such dependencies can be deduced from the ontology using semantic-based reasoning (cf. (R4) and (A3)). We therefore consider the relations *identity* ($=$), *equivalence* ($^\circ$) and *specialization* ($\sqsubseteq$) between parameters. Two parameters are *identical* ($= \acute{I} P \ ' P$), if identifier and domain are identical (with no consideration of the associated restrictions). The *equivalence* ($^\circ$ $\acute{I} P \ ' P$) associates two parameters analogously to the *specialization* ($\sqsubseteq \acute{I} P \ ' P$), if and only if a reasoner can deduce an *equivalentClasses* relation respectively a *subClassOf* relation between the classes from the ontology that represent the parameter.

The matching between an output parameter p of a and an input parameter q of b proceeds in two steps and uses the semantic relations to identify dependencies (cf. Table 2).

Analyze Parameter Relations

First, we analyze, if there exists a relation between the two parameters. Besides the simple relations *identity* $(p = q)$ and *equivalence* $(p \ ^\circ q)$, the *specialization* relation needs closer consideration. If a returns a parameter p that is a *specialization* of the parameter q $(p \sqsubseteq q)$, then b can be executed, as each occurrence of p is also an occurrence of q. Therefore, the constellations $p = q$, $p \ ^\circ q$ or $p \sqsubseteq q$ constitute the first case (1.) of Table 2. In the second case (2.), if $p \sqsupseteq q$ holds, there might arise the situation that a returns p which at the same time is not an occurrence of the *specialized* parameter q and thus b is not executable. Consequently, a complete dependency cannot be asserted. Only a partial dependency may exist. For example, if a produces an *order* as output parameter p and b is able to process only *stock orders* as input parameter q (with *stock order* $\sqsubseteq$ *order, fund order* $\sqsubseteq$ *order* and *stock order* is different from *fund order* according to at least one atomic parameter) then a can return *stock orders* as well as *fund orders* although the latter one cannot be handled by b. So a partial dependency will be determined, if the set of possible instances of an output is a superset of the processible set of input instances. The last case (3.) with $p \ ^1 q \wedge p \not\equiv q \wedge p \not\sqsubseteq q \wedge p \not\sqsupseteq q$ results into no dependency, because b can never handle the output of a (detailed in Heinrich et al., 2008).

Table 2. Conditions for dependencies between an output parameter p and an input parameter q

I. Analyze parameter relations	II. Compare restrictions r_p with r_q		Matching
(1.) $p = q \vee p \ ^\circ q \vee p \sqsubseteq q$	(1.1) $r_p \subseteq r_q$		*complete matching*
	(1.2) $r_p \cap r_q \ ' \emptyset \wedge r_p \setminus r_q \ ' \emptyset$		*partial matching*
	(1.3) $r_p \cap r_q = \emptyset$		*no matching*
(2.) $p \sqsupseteq q$	(2.1) $r_p \cap r_q \ ' \emptyset$		*partial matching*
	(2.2) $r_p \cap r_q = \emptyset$		*no matching*
(3.) $p \not\equiv q \wedge p \not\sqsubseteq q \wedge p \not\sqsupseteq q \wedge p \ ^1 q$			*no matching*

Compare Restrictions

As actions may restrict the domain of input and output parameters, we additionally need to consider restrictions. Even if the input parameter q matches with the output parameter p, restrictions still can prevent action b to be executed and a partial respectively no dependency is asserted. No dependency occurs if the restrictions do not match at all, i.e. the intersection of both restrictions is empty (1.3 and 2.2). A partial dependency is possible, if the restrictions match partially. Thus, restriction r_p contains both, values that are also values of restriction r_q and values that exist in r_p but not in r_q (1.2 and 2.1). Finally, both restrictions may also match completely respectively all values of r_q are also values in r_p (1.1). So a complete dependency is not avoided by them and depends on the result of I.

As an outcome of this matching procedure, we obtain either no dependency or a dependency that might be complete or partial. These identified dependencies are represented in the ADG. Therefore, each action is connected with the parameters it provides as output and with the parameters it uses as input. To enable semantic relations, we have to distinguish between an available output parameter and the parameter used as input in the following steps of SEMPA. Therefore, we store the input parameter as label of an input edge which connects the available output parameter (as node) with the action. Based on this, the ADG is defined as a directed, bipartite graph $G_{ADG} = (V_{ADG}, E_{ADG})$ with the set of nodes V_{ADG} and the set of edges E_{ADG}.

(D1) The set of nodes V_{ADG} consists of the two partitions $Part_a^{ADG} \hat{I} \ lib_A$ containing the actions identified by the planning algorithm and $Part_p^{ADG} \hat{I} \ P$ containing the input and output parameters corresponding to the identified actions ($V_{ADG} := Part_a^{ADG} \cup Part_p^{ADG}$).

(D2) The set of edges E_{ADG} is the union of input edges E_{in} and output edges E_{out} ($E_{ADG} := E_{in} \cup E_{out}$).

(D3) E_{in} is defined as a set of input edges $((p, a), p_{in})$ consisting of a directed edge (p, a) and an edge label p_{in}. $p \ \hat{I} \ Part_p^{ADG}$ denotes a parameter that is required as an input parameter $p_{in} \ \hat{I} \ In_a$ by the action $a \ \hat{I} \ Part_a^{ADG}$. Here, p_{in} does not necessarily have to be identical to p, but needs to be associated by a semantic relation implicating a dependency. If such a relation exists between the involved process actions, we write $p \sim p_{in}$.

$$E_{in} := \{((p, a), p_{in}) \mid p \ \hat{I} \ Part_p^{ADG}, \ p_{in} \ \hat{I} \ In_a, \ a \ \hat{I} \ Part_a^{ADG}, \ p_{in} \sim p\}$$

(D4) The set of output edges E_{out} consists of all directed edges (a, p_{out}), where $p_{out} \ \hat{I} \ Part_p^{ADG}$ is an output parameter of the action $a \ \hat{I} \ Part_a^{ADG}$.

$$E_{out} := \{(a, p_{out}) \mid a \ \hat{I} \ Part_a^{ADG}, \ p_{out} \ \hat{I} \ Part_p^{ADG}, \ p_{out} \ \hat{I} \ Out_a\}$$

To briefly illustrate the ADG, we take an action *check competencies* that provides the parameters *exchangeOrder* (an order that is routed directly to a stock exchange) and *riskAssessment* as output. Another action *execute order* is able to process arbitrary *orders* and a *riskAssessment* as input parameter. Besides the obviously complete dependency based on the *riskAssessment* parameter, we detect a further dependency of *execute order* from *check competencies*. Due to the semantic reasoning, we can determine that *exchangeOrder* is a *specialization* of *order* (step I.1.) and that the relevant restrictions are either identical (step II.1.1.) or that the restriction of the provided parameter is a non-empty, strict subset of the restriction of the required parameter (step II.1.2.). An excerpt of the ADG is shown in Figure 6.

The algorithm constructs the ADG starting with the goals G_x. It identifies at first all actions in lib_A delivering at least one of the parameters,

Figure 6. Excerpt of the ADG illustrating the dependency, based on a semantic matching

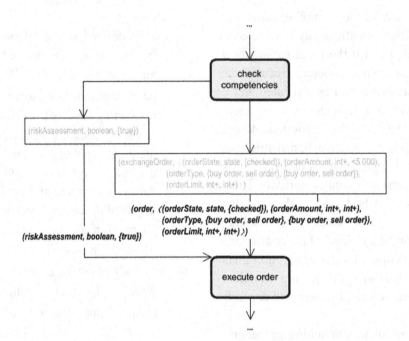

the goal parameters can be deduced from, and adds them to the graph. Afterwards, the algorithm searches iteratively actions, on which already added actions depend. Those actions are added to the graph as well. This procedure is continued until either all input parameters of the graph (that are not given in the initial state) are provided by at least one action or until there are no more actions in the library that could provide the required input parameters. Here, the ADG contains only those actions that might be required to reach the goals. Actions, whose inputs are never needed by any of the actions being part of the ADG, are not considered in the graph. Also actions that are required to receive only *Init* will be ignored and not added to the ADG.

Subsequently, a post-processing takes place. Some of the actions in the current ADG may have input parameters that cannot be delivered by other actions. These actions (and their input parameters as well as the output parameters that are only provided by these actions) are iteratively removed from the graph. Afterwards, each remaining output parameter is removed if it is not needed as input inside the ADG. If all output parameters of an action are deleted, we also delete the providing action, because such actions do not contribute to reach one of the goals. Both steps – removing input parameters and output parameters (with their requiring/providing actions) – are executed recursively until no more parameter can be removed and we obtain a stable ADG. Thus, we increase efficiency in the subsequent steps of the algorithm. Note that the situation may occur that some goals could not be achieved completely. This happens, if there is a parameter as element of the goals, which is not provided by any action or the initial state. Those goals are reported to the user as they cannot be fulfilled and a further consideration during the planning process is not reasonable.

Generation of the Action State Graph (ASG)

The subsequent order of actions is far from being determined by the ADG. In the second step of SEMPA, we therefore apply an algorithm that searches the action-state space in order to bring actions in a feasible order. We define a state in this context as the current set of parameters that are available at a certain point in the plan:

(D5) A state s is a subset of the set of parameters P, $s \subseteq P$.

After applying an action a to a state s, a new state is determined by a so called state-transition function (cf. Heinrich et al., 2009). To put it in a nutshell: Output parameters that already existed in s are updated considering the new restrictions, output parameters that did not exist before are added to the new state, and parameters that existed before are deleted to the new state.

In this context it has to be pointed out, that our notion of a state differs slightly from the definitions usually applied for planning problems. Whereas classical planning approaches in general rely on the definition of a state as a set of propositions or first-order literals and logical connectives (cf. Ghallab et al., 2004), we consider a state as a kind of knowledge base containing the (available) output parameters of the previously executed actions. Defining a state as a set of parameters conforms to a state-variable representation of a planning problem, where parameters are considered as variables adopting ranges of values within their specified domain. This is advantageous, as it constitutes a more intuitive representation in comparison to classical planning approaches and simplifies the usage of numerical data types. At the same time this notion of a state conveys the non-deterministic character of the planning problem as a state is not constituted by the individual values of parameters but by the restrictions that currently hold for the parameters (cf. requirement (R5)).

An appropriate (non-deterministic) planning algorithm must be able to handle composite input and output parameters with various data types (cf. requirements (R3) and (R4)). Moreover the result of planning should be a suitable basis to extract different feasible solutions (R8) and to design control structures (R7) in the third step of SEMPA. For the further understanding of our algorithm, we need to contemplate on the relationship between actions and states first, taking into account these requirements. This essentially comprises two issues: First, it has to be defined under which circumstances an action is regarded to be applicable in a state, and second, the transformation of states through actions has to be examined.

An action a is called to be applicable in a state s, if for each input parameter of a there is at least one parameter in s matching this input parameter. In this respect, complete as well as partial matches are considered, i.e. for each input parameter of a there must be at least one completely or partially matching parameter in s. Input and output parameters of actions have already been matched in the first step of the algorithm. The corresponding information – represented by the ADG – is now used to identify applicable actions (for a technical definition cf. Heinrich et al., 2009). After considering an action in the plan, a new state is determined. The new parameters generated by the action are added and changes regarding the restrictions of already existing parameters are updated.

With these prerequisites we can now turn our attention to the search algorithm itself. The algorithm implements a forward search in the action-state space. Starting with the initial state *Init*, it identifies applicable actions by means of the ADG. After each action a new state is determined. As a state in general can be followed by several executable actions, this procedure results into a branched structure we call ASG. More precisely, the ASG is a directed graph, which consists of two kinds of nodes, action nodes and state nodes that appear in alternating order, starting with the initial state *Init:*

(D6) An ASG is an acyclic, bipartite, directed graph $G_{ASG} = (V_{ASG}, E_{ASG})$, with the set of nodes V_{ASG} and the set of edges E_{ASG}.

(D7) The set of nodes V_{ASG} consists of two partitions, the set of action nodes $Part_a^{ASG}$ and the set of state nodes $Part_s^{ASG}$. Each state node $s \hat{I} Part_s^{ASG}$ is representing one distinct state in the ASG. An action node $n \in Part_a^{ASG}$ is defined as $n: = (a, j)$, with an action $a \in Part_a^{ADG}$ and $j \hat{I} N$ (index).

We use the index j to be able to differentiate action nodes containing identical actions (an action may be planned more than once according to assumption (A2)).

Figure 7 shows a part of the ASG in our example. In the initial state only the action *validate order* is applicable. This leads to a new state, where the element *orderState* being part of the composite parameter *order* changes its value either to *valid* or *invalid*. In this state three different actions can be applied.

As in each state a potentially high number of actions may be applicable, a large action-state space needs to be explored. Thus, there are measures included in the algorithm to avoid unnecessary searching (orientated at the ideas of Bertoli et al., 2001). We will give a short overview of these measures in the following paragraphs (cf. Henneberger et al., 2008).

1. Planning is conducted by a depth-first search. Backtracking takes place, if a state s is encountered that meets at least one of the specified goals, i.e. $s \subseteq G_x \hat{I} Goals$. The depth-first search guarantees fast results, if only a limited number of alternative feasible solutions is needed (if for instance the user only wants to choose from a limited number of solutions) and the solutions comprise only a few branches. At the same time the algorithm ensures that all paths are explored and all feasible solutions are found.

2. The algorithm includes a simple loop checking schema: It stops exploring a current state, if an identical state has already occurred. Consider for instance the case that a state t' after applying an action a is identical to a state t before a. Theoretically the action a

Figure 7. Extract of the ASG in the example

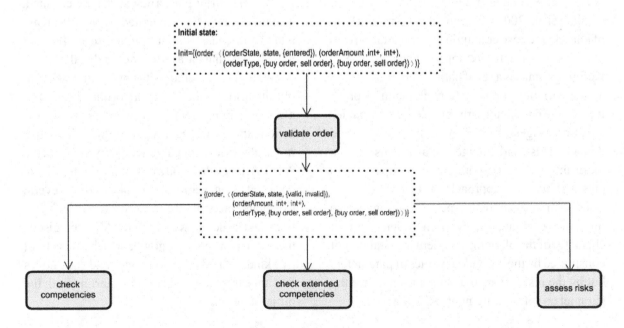

could be applied in *t'* again, which eventually would result in an infinite loop. The algorithm detects that *t'* is identical to *t* and initiates a backtracking.

3. States leading to at least one of the specified goals are saved. New states are compared to these states. If there is an identical state in an already explored path leading to one of the specified goals, then a link is established to this state. Further analysis of the current path is not necessary anymore and a backtracking takes place. This case occurs for instance, when there are two actions *a* and *b*, that can be put in either order *a* before *b* or *b* before *a* after a state *s* and both alternatives result into an identical state *s'*. If there is at least one path from *s'* reaching a goal, then this path is explored just once by the algorithm. In this respect it is an advantage of the depth-first search that a path is completely explored before the next path is analyzed.

4. Likewise, the algorithm tries to determine (as far as possible in advance), whether it is impossible to reach a goal from the current state. In this case the algorithm does not have to explore this state any further and again backtracking takes place. To this end, the information about failures during the search (i.e. situations where no action can be applied anymore or where the search resulted into an infinite loop) is saved in a failure log. Whenever a newly created state meets the conditions specified in the failure log, processing of the current state is stopped and again a backtracking is initiated.

Generation of Process Models

In the third step of SEMPA control structures are constructed within the ASG and process models (feasible solutions) are created. In the following, we illustrate the fundamental ideas and techniques of this step of SEMPA omitting the underlying technical definitions (cf. Heinrich et al., 2009 for a technical description).

The construction of both control structures and process models have not yet been regarded by traditional planning approaches so far (cf. Meyer & Kuropka, 2006). Therefore, it is a widely novel challenge. Up to now we are able to consider the control structures *sequence, parallel split, synchronization, exclusive choice,* and *simple merge.* The control structure *exclusive choice* indicates different branches of a process model that are merged by the corresponding control structure *simple merge. Parallel split* and *synchronization* are used to allow concurrent execution of actions that are independent in terms of input and output parameters for example. These control structures in fact constitute a subset of the control structures defined in (R7). Future versions of the algorithm are supposed to handle additional control structures.

In order to construct control structures, the third algorithm within SEMPA analyzes the alternating state and action nodes in the ASG as well as the partial and complete dependencies between actions defined in the ADG. The design of *sequences* is straight forward as all actions in the (acyclic) ASG are already in a feasible order. If there is a state node in the ASG with one preceding action node *a* and exactly one succeeding action node *b*, then we can build a *sequence b* following *a*.

Generally a state node may have more than one succeeding action node in the ASG. Yet, not every branching indicates an *exclusive choice* as the following considerations will show: An ASG comprises all possible paths from the initial state to the goals. Let there be two actions that can alternatively be applied as they deliver identical output parameters for instance. In the ASG this entails a branching with two different paths ultimately leading to the same goal. Obviously the two paths belong to two different feasible solutions, i.e. two different process models. In this case one feasible solution is only a sub graph of the ASG. In order to represent single feasible solutions in the form of process models we need to separate them in the ASG. Accordingly, we need to clearly distinguish branches in the ASG resulting into *different branches within* a process model from branches that are ultimately leading to *alternative process models* representing different feasible solutions. But how can we construct *exclusive choices* under these circumstances? Consider a state *s* with a number of succeeding actions $a_1...a_n$. The algorithm analyzes the sets of input parameters of these actions (considering as well the set of parameters provided by state *s*):

- If restrictions are mutually exclusive for at least one input parameter, then obviously no feasible combination of values of the parameters in *s* exists, so that more than one action can be executed.

- If restrictions are identical for all input parameters, then all of the actions $a_1...a_n$ can be executed at a time. They can be regarded as alternatives that may belong to different feasible solutions. We mark the state node representing *s* with a delimiter symbol in order to separate out different feasible solutions. For scalability reasons we keep on working with one overall ASG and extract different feasible solutions later on.

- If neither of these cases applies, the algorithm determines disjoint (concerning parameter restrictions) sets of actions. We will describe the basic principle with an example in our example. Consider the state after *validate order* in the ASG in Figure 7. In this state the ASG branches into three different process actions: *check competencies*, *check extended competencies* and *assess risks*. Restrictions are neither identical nor mutual exclusive. However, in this case, the restrictions for all input parameters of the actions *check extended competencies* and *assess risks* are identical (both requiring *orderAmount > 5,000*). This indicates they are alternatives and a delimiter

symbol is needed. Additionally, regarding the input parameter *orderAmount* there is no overlap with the remaining action *check competencies* (requiring *orderAmount ≤ 5,000*). Thus, the algorithm adds a decision node distinguishing between the cases *≤ 5,000* and *> 5,000*. By this, we demonstrated the idea considering exactly one input and output parameter at a time (here: *orderAmount*). The idea remains the same, even when there are several input and output parameters. The main difference is that analysis and decomposition get more complex (cf. Heinrich et al., 2009).

- The algorithm also tests if there are feasible combinations of values of the output parameters in a state *s*, so that no action can be executed at all. In order to get a syntactically correct activity diagram, we then add a decision node branching directly *to* a UML final node. In our example this applies in the state after the action *validate order*. All of the preceding actions require an input parameter *orderState = valid*. In the case *orderState = invalid*, which is also a reasonable *result of validate order*, no action can be executed. Thus, the process *needs to terminate* (in a final *node)*.

*After constru*cting *exclusive choices* the algorithm *tries to find simple merges*. Here, the information about prior *exclusive choices* is needed. Therefore, this information is passed to all subsequent state nodes along the ASG, i.e. for each state node n_i we save a cumulative, ordered set M_i of (distinguishable) control structures that occurred along the way from the initial state to this node. We need the sets M_i to realize branches that can be merged (in contrast to branches belonging to alternative solutions). Starting with the state nodes in the ASG representing goals we now identify state nodes where we can merge different branches of the ASG.

Finally, we test for cases where we can parallelize actions using the control structures *parallel split* and *synchronization*. For that reason, we analyze all state nodes n_k in the ASG marked with a delimiter symbol before. For instance, when a number of *l* actions following n_k in each branch are identical but in another order and at the same time the sequence of *l* actions in all branches is completed with a state node representing identical states, then we can place a parallelization. Again we demonstrate our approach with our example. As determined before, in the state after *validate order*, we have to differentiate two feasible solutions. As we can see, the actions *check extended competencies* and *assess risks* are independent from each other. We could either execute *check extended competencies* before *assess risks* or the other way around and furthermore we could parallelize both actions.

With the considerations above we can finally construct syntactically correct UML activity diagrams which are graphical representations of our feasible solutions. State nodes in the ASG representing a goal are replaced by final nodes. The initial state is replaced by a start node.

How does the process model – planed by SEMPA – now finally look like in our running example? A conceivable planning result is depicted in Figure 8. The financial services provider receives a *stock order* which is validated at first. If the *stock order* is "*invalid*" (e.g. because of lack of data), the process is aborted. If we have a "*valid*" *stock order,* it is differentiated, whether the *order amount* is greater than or equal *5,000* or less than *5,000*. In the latter case, competencies are checked. Otherwise (≥ *5,000*), an extended check of competencies is required and a separate risk assessment takes place. Having finished these actions, the *stock order* can finally be executed.

Evaluation

SEMPA has been evaluated in several ways. First, it has been prototypically implemented. Second, SEMPA and its prototypical implementation have been evaluated with regard to the requirements and have been applied to various process mod-

Figure 8. UML activity diagram in the process modeling tool AgilPro[4]

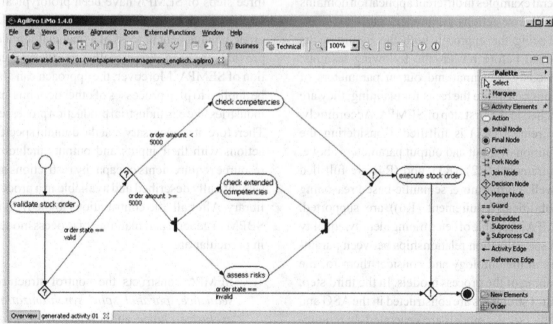

eling problems in practice. Third, the SEMPA algorithm and the outcome of planning, namely the process models, have been analyzed theoretically including formal criteria (e.g. termination of the planning algorithm). In the following, we will describe selected aspects of the evaluation starting with the prototypical implementation.

SEMPA has been realized as a plug-in for the open-source process modeling tool AgilPro. Using AgilPro, processes can be modeled, displayed in different views or simulated. We use OWL 2 to define ontologies, because of the higher expressive power in comparison to OWL 1.0. For the processing of ontologies, the OWL API (OWL Application Programming Interface) is used. The OWL API is a Java interface and implementation for the handling of ontologies in OWL. It supports OWL Lite and OWL DL and offers an interface for inference engines such as Pellet. The latter is employed for the semantic-based reasoning in the prototypical implementation. Since Pellet as well as the OWL API implement the DIG-interface, other Semantic Web frameworks (such as KAON2) could be used as well. The prototypical implementation has been subject to an evaluation. It has been tested with jUnit tests and the algorithm has been applied to several examples in different application domains with diverse actions, parameters, etc.

Facing the approach with the requirements outlined before reveals the following insights: Obviously, the input and output parameters of actions constitute the basis for planning; they are matched in the first step of SEMPA. Accordingly, requirement (R1) is fulfilled. Considering the definition of input and output parameters above, requirements (R2), (R3), and (R4) are fulfilled as well. Furthermore, semantic-based reasoning capabilities (requirement (R6)) are supported. SEMPA is capable of determining identity, equality and specialization relationships between parameters in the ontology and consider them for the planning of the process models. In the third step, control structures are constructed in the ASG and finally process models are generated. In require-

ment (R7) different control structures have been outlined that should be recognized: *exclusive choice*, *parallel split*, *synchronization*, *simple merge*, etc. The previous sections described how those can be recognized, focusing particularly on *exclusive choices*. Since feasible solutions are represented as valid UML activity diagrams, moreover, requirement (R8) is fulfilled.

From a theoretical perspective, we can show that the planned process models are *valid* with respect to certain criteria like completeness, minimality, termination and computational complexity regarding time. In this respect, we have to refer to Heinrich et al. (2009) due to length restrictions.

RESULTS AND FURTHER RESEARCH

In this chapter we introduced the SEMPA approach for the automated planning of process models. The idea of SEMPA was motivated by a real world problem, which means the high effort for the manual modeling of processes. Our search for an algorithm for the automated planning of process models was guided by a set of requirements. The three steps of SEMPA have been prototypically implemented. From different test scenarios an order management process of a financial services provider has been chosen to illustrate the application of SEMPA. Moreover, the approach can also be applied to plan processes of other domains and industries like e.g. industrial production processes. Therefore, it is necessary that the domain specific actions with their inputs and outputs including resource requirements or capacity restrictions are semantically described and available in a process library. After all, the contributions to the field of SBPM in general and planning of process models in particular are:

1.   SEMPA constructs the control structures *sequence*, *parallel split*, *synchronization*, *exclusive choice* and *simple merge* in an

automated way. In comparison to existing planners there is a particular improvement e.g. regarding the structures *exclusive choice* or *parallel split*.

2. Currently manually designed process models are suffering from inconsistently used terms which restricts their economically reasonable application, i.e. before using or adapting process models terms have to be clarified, coordinated and adjusted (especially if modelers are altering). The specification of an ontology together with semantic reasoning can sustainable contribute to a reduction of costs for clarification and adjustment. In contrast to many existing planners, SEMPA is creating added value here. A faster and more flexible construction of process models seems possible. The added value of a semantic description applies also to the implementation of processes with Web Services. It enables an automated search (cf. Drumm et al., 2006) for (semantic) Web Services based on the semantic description of the actions. This is of particular interest, as the number of new Web Services that are offered, will probably increase significantly. Thus a continuous and cost-effective valuation of such new offers regarding their application in process models is gaining importance.

3. Existing planning approaches mainly focus on the generation of a single feasible solution for a problem definition with a start point and exactly one single end point (one goal). With SEMPA process models with multiple end points (set of goals) can be generated. This is of particular importance, because today and in the near future it seems to be unrealistic that a planner generates a model for a business-critical process (e.g. an order process) isolated for exactly one goal and that this process can be realized in an automated way afterwards without (further) discussions of other processes.

4. Another important aspect is the generation of a set of feasible solutions for a given goal specification. It is the starting point to derive the set of efficient solutions (those that are not dominated by other feasible solutions) and finally an optimal solution for a specific company considering economic aspects. For this purpose not only a mapping of available Web Services realizing the feasible solutions, but also economic evaluation parameters and the Quality of Service properties of a Web Service have to be available.

Alongside also critical points have to be mentioned which define our further research. Currently not all control structures that could be part of process models are supported by the algorithm. Furthermore, information such as resources, execution time and cost are not considered for planning in the current version of SEMPA. We intend to advance especially the planning algorithm in the second step. To this end established planning approaches with time and resources provide an appropriate starting point. The SEMPA approach forms an appropriate fundament for this as well as for the aforementioned enhancements and thus serves as a suitable basis for further research.

REFERENCES

Becker, J., & Kahn, D. (2003). The process in focus . In Becker, J., Kugeler, M., & Rosemann, M. (Eds.), *Process Management. A guide for the design of business processes* (pp. 1–12). Berlin, Germany: Springer.

Becker, J., Rosemann, M., & von Uthmann, C. (2000). Guidelines of business process modeling . In van der Aalst, W. M. P., Desel, J., & Oberweis, A. (Eds.), *Business process management, models, techniques and empirical studies* (pp. 30–49). Berlin, Germany: Springer.

Berardi, D., De Giacomo, G., Mecella, M., & Calvanese, D. (2006). Automatic Web service composition: Service-tailored vs. client-tailored approaches. In *Proceedings of the 4th International Workshop on AI for Service Composition (AISC) 2006*. Retrieved February 15, 2010, from http://ftp.dis.uniroma1.it/~degiacom/papers/2006/bera-calv-degi-mece-AISC-2006.pdf

Bertoli, P., Cimatti, A., Roveri, M., & Traverso, P. (2001). Planning in nondeterministic domains under partial observability via symbolic model checking. In B. Nebel (Ed.), *Proceedings of the 17th International Joint Conference on Artificial Intelligence (IJCAI) 2001* (pp. 473-478). San Francisco, CA: Morgan Kaufmann.

Betz, S., Kling, S., Koschmider, A., & Oberweis, A. (2006). Automatic user support for business process modeling. In K. Hinkelmann, D. Karagiannis, N. Stojanovic & G. Wagner (Eds.), *Proceedings of the Workshop on Semantics for Business Process Management at the 3rd European Semantic Web Conference (ESWC) 2006* (pp. 1-12). Berlin, Germany: Springer.

Biron, P. V., & Malhotra, A. (2004). *XML schema part 2: Datatypes,* 2nd ed. Retrieved February 15, 2010, from http://www.w3.org/TR/xmlschema-2

Bonet, B., & Geffner, H. (2000). Planning with incomplete information as heuristic search in belief space. In S. Chien, S. Kambhampati & C. A. Knoblock (Eds.), *Proceedings of the 5th International Conference on AI Planning and Scheduling (AIPS) 2000* (pp. 52-61). Madison, WI: AAAI Press.

Bonet, B., & Geffner, H. (2001). GPT: A tool for planning with uncertainty and partial information. In B. Nebel (Ed.), *Proceedings of the 17th International Joint Conference on Artificial Intelligence (IJCAI) 2001* (pp. 82-87). San Francisco, CA: Morgan Kaufmann.

Borges, M. R. S., Pino, J. A., & Valle, C. (2005). Support for decision implementation and follow-up. *European Journal of Operational Research, 160*(2), 336–352. doi:10.1016/j.ejor.2003.09.005

Cimatti, A., Roveri, M., & Traverso, P. (1998). Automatic OBDD-based generation of universal plans in non-deterministic domains. In *Proceedings of the 15th National Conference on Artificial Intelligence (AAAI) 1998* (pp. 875-881). Madison, WI: AAAI Press.

Constantinescu, I., Faltings, B., & Binder, W. (2004a). Large scale, type-compatible service composition. In [ICWS]. *Proceedings of the IEEE International Conference on Web Services, 2004*, 506–513. Retrieved February 15, 2010. doi:10.1109/ICWS.2004.1314776

Constantinescu, I., Faltings, B., & Binder, W. (2004b). Type-based composition of information services in large scale environments. In N. Zhong, H. Tirri, Y. Yao & L. Zhou (Eds.), *Proceedings of the IEEE/WIC/ACM International Conference on Web Intelligence (WI) 2004* (pp. 306-312). Retrieved February 15, 2010, from http://ieeexplore.ieee.org/servlet/opac?punumber=9689

Drumm, C., Lemcke, J., & Namiri, K. (2006). Integrating Semantic Web services and business process management: A real use case. In K. Hinkelmann, D. Karagiannis, N. Stojanovic & G. Wagner (Eds.), *Proceedings of the Workshop on Semantics for Business Process Management at the 3rd European Semantic Web Conference (ESWC) 2006* (pp. 1-12). Berlin, Germany: Springer.

Ghallab, M., Nau, D., & Traverso, P. (2004). *Automated planning*. San Francisco, CA: Elsevier.

Giunchiglia, F., Yatskevich, M., & Shvaiko, P. (2007). Semantic matching: Algorithms and implementation. *Journal on Data Semantics, 9*, 1–38.

Heinrich, B., Bewernik, M., Henneberger, M., Krammer, A., & Lautenbacher, F. (2008). SEMPA - A semantic business process management approach for the planning of process models. [formerly WIRTSCHAFTSINFORMATIK]. *Business & Information Systems Engineering, 50*(6), 445–460.

Heinrich, B., Bolsinger, M., & Bewernik, M.-A. (2009). Automated planning of process models: The construction of exclusive choices. In H. Chen & S. A. Slaughter (Eds.), *Proceedings of the 30th International Conference on Information Systems (ICIS) 2009* (Paper 184). Berlin, Germany: Springer.

Henneberger, M., Heinrich, B., Bauer, B., & Lautenbacher, F. (2008). Semantic-based planning of process models. In M. Bichler, T. Hess, H. Krcmar, U. Lechner, F. Matthes, A. Picot, B. Speitkamp & P. Wolf (Eds.), *Proceedings of the Multikonferenz Wirtschaftsinformatik (MKWI) 2008* (pp. 1677-1689). Berlin, Germany: Gito.

Hepp, M., Leymann, F., Domingue, J., Wahler, A., & Fensel, D. (2005). Semantic business process management: A vision towards using Semantic Web services for business process management. In W. Tsai, J. Chung & Y. Muhammad (Eds.), *IEEE International Conference on e-Business Engineering (ICEBE) 2005* (pp. 535-540). Retrieved February 15, 2010, from http://ieeexplore.ieee.org/servlet/opac?punumber=10403

Hoffmann, J., & Brafman, R. I. (2005). Contingent planning via heuristic forward search with implicit belief states. In S. Biundo, K. Myers & K. Rajan (Eds.), *Proceedings of the 15th International Conference on Automated Planning and Scheduling (ICAPS) 2005* (pp. 71-80). Menlo Park, CA: AAAI Press.

Kabanza, M., Barbeau, M., & St-Denis, R. (1997). Planning control rules for reactive agents. *Artificial Intelligence, 95*(2), 409–438.

Lang, Q. A., & Su, S. Y. W. (2005). AND/OR graph and search algorithm for discovering composite web services. *International Journal of Web Services Research, 2*(4), 46–64.

Ma, Z., & Leymann, F. (2008). A lifecycle model for using process fragment in business process modeling. In S. Nurcan, R. Schmidt, P. Soffer, E. Hunt, X. Franch & R. Coletta (Eds.), *Proceedings of the 9th Workshop on Business Process Modeling, Development, and Support held in conjunction with the CAiSE '08 Conference* (pp. 1-9). Aachen, Germany: Sun SITE Central Europe.

McIlraith, S., & Son, T. C. (2002). Adapting Golog for composition of Semantic Web services. Retrieved February 15, 2010, from www.cs.nmsu.edu/~tson/papers/kr02gl.pdf

Meyer, H., & Kuropka, D. (2006). Requirements for automated service composition . In Eder, J., & Dustdar, S. (Eds.), *Business Process Management Workshops, Lecture Notes in Computer Science* (*Vol. 4103*, pp. 439–450). Vienna, Austria: Springer.

Meyer, H., & Weske, M. (2006). Automated service composition using heuristic search. In S. Dustdar, J. L. Fiadeiro & A. Sheth (Eds.), *Proceedings of the 4th International Conference on Business Process Management (BPM) 2006* (pp. 81-96). Berlin, Germany: Springer.

Pathak, J., Basu, S., & Honavar, V. (2006). Modeling Web service composition using symbolic transition systems. In P. Doshi, R. Goodwin & A. Sheth (Eds.), *Papers from the AAAI Workshop on AI-Driven Technologies for Service-Oriented Computing 2006*. Menlo Park, CA: AAAI Press.

Petrick, R. P. A., & Bacchus, F. (2002). A knowledge-based approach to planning with incomplete information and sensing. In M. Ghallab, J. Hertzberg & P. Traverso (Eds.), *Proceedings of the Sixth International Conference on Artificial Intelligence Planning Systems (AIPS) 2002* (pp. 212-221). Menlo Park, CA: AAAI Press.

Pistore, M., Traverso, P., Bertoli, P., & Marconi, A. (2005). Automated synthesis of composite BPEL4WS Web services. In *Proceedings of the 3rd International Conference on Web Services* (pp. 293-301). Retrieved February 15, 2010, from http://klase.itc.it/paper_firb_astro_klase/additional/AM_ICWS05.pdf

Russell, N., van der Aalst, W. M. P., ter Hofstede, A. H. M., & Wohed, P. (2006). On the suitability of UML 2.0 activity diagrams for business process modeling. In J. F. Roddick & A. Hinze (Eds.), *Proceedings of the 3rd Asia-Pacific Conference on Conceptual Modeling (APCCM) 2006* (pp. 95-104). Hobart, Australia: Australian Computer Society.

Sirin, E., Parsia, B., Wu, D., Hendler, J., & Nau, D. (2004). HTN planning for Web service composition using SHOP2. *Journal of Web Semantics, 1*(4), 377–396. doi:10.1016/j.websem.2004.06.005

Smith, M. K., Welty, C., & McGuinness, D. L. (2004). *OWL Web ontology language guide.* Retrieved February 15, 2010, from http://www.w3.org/TR/owl-guide/

Ter Beek, M. H., Bucchiarone, A., & Gnesi, S. (2006). *A survey on service composition approaches: From industrial standards to formal methods.* (Technical Report 2006-TR-15, ISTI, Consiglio Nazionale delle Ricerche). Retrieved February 15, 2010, from http://fmt.isti.cnr.it/WEBPAPER/TRWS-FM06.pdf

Thomas, O., & Fellmann, M. (2006). Semantische Integration von Ontologien und Ereignisgesteuerten Prozessketten. In M. Nüttgens, F. Rump & J. Mendling (Eds.), *Geschäftsprozessmanagement mit Ereignisgesteuerten Prozessketten EPK 2006* (pp.7-23). Bonn, Germany: GI.

Van der Aalst, W. M. P., ter Hofstede, A. H. M., Kiepuszewski, B., & Barros, A. P. (2003). Workflow patterns. *Distributed and Parallel Databases, 14*(3), 5–51. doi:10.1023/A:1022883727209

ENDNOTES

[1] Units may be Dollars or Euros respectively. For the sake of simplicity we omit units in the following text.

[2] In this chapter, we use the terms input and output parameters instead of the terms *preconditions* and *effects*, which are well-established in the field of AI planning. Following this, we use the term *input parameter* for everything an action needs in order to be performed and the term *output parameter* for everything an action provides after it was performed. This also includes e.g. also resource requirements or capacity restrictions.

[3] Besides simple classes, an OWL ontology can also define complex classes by constructors like union, intersection and complement or by enumerating its individuals as class extension (cf. Smith et al., 2004).

[4] The notation of the tool is based on UML activity diagram although there are minor differences concerning the form of the symbols (e.g. decision node).

Chapter 10
Stepwise Semantic Enrichment in Health–Related Public Management by Using Semantic Information Models

Hans-Georg Fill
University of Vienna, Austria & Stanford University, USA

Ilona Reischl
AGES PharmMed, Austria

ABSTRACT

The use of semantic technologies in practical scenarios requires carefully balancing the tradeoff between costs and benefits in order to gain acceptance. In this chapter we report on a project conducted together with the Austrian competent authority in regard to safety in healthcare. It is described how semantic technologies can be combined with conceptual models to support management executives in the distribution of knowledge and the analysis of compliance. The approach is based on a step-wise semantic enrichment of conceptual models with formal semantic schemata in order to support human analyses. It has been implemented on the ADONIS meta modeling platform and applied to a scenario dealing with the management of applications for clinical trials.

INTRODUCTION

Over the past years significant effort and money has been invested into research and industrial projects dealing with semantic technologies by funding organizations such as Darpa, the European

Commission, and Asian funding organizations (Bussler, 2008), (Bertolo, 2005). As a result, a large number of technologies, standards, and research prototypes are today available which permit to easily implement semantic functionalities and apply them to concrete use cases. Thereby, the unique value propositions of semantic technologies in

DOI: 10.4018/978-1-60960-126-3.ch010

order to meet critical real world challenges can be directly assessed cf. (Cardoso, et al., 2007). In the area of information systems, the process to introduce semantic technologies to practical scenarios is governed by the principles of design science. By building and evaluating artifacts in the form of constructs, models, methods, and instantiations (March and Smith, 1995) it can be shown how technologies can be implemented in a working system, thus allowing for the assessment of the suitability of the artifacts for their intended purpose (Hevner et al., 2004). As a consequence, the relevance of the technology for the constituent community, i.e. the practitioners who deal with information systems and their technologies can be estimated (Hevner et al., 2004). With the following elaborations we report on a research project that has been undertaken by the University of Vienna in cooperation with AGES PharmMed as the Austrian Competent Authority in regard to safety in health care. The main objective of the project was to develop IT-based solutions for supporting executives in the area of health-related public management, in particular for the approval of clinical trial applications. The methodology that has been elaborated for this purpose is based on the concept of *semantic information models*. It allows for the combination of visual conceptual models and semantic technologies on the basis of a meta modeling approach and follows a design-oriented research objective. The particular benefit of the approach lies in the facilitation of human analyses of complex visual conceptual models and their alignment to internationally used semantic schemata by using a step-wise approach. The purposes are to support knowledge distribution and compliance management, as well as to establish a basis for performance and resource management in health-related public management. The chapter is structured as follows: The next subchapter will give a brief introduction to the foundations used for our approach and describe the linkages to existing work. Thereafter we will present the details of the approach and how it influenced the distribution of knowledge in the organization and the assurance of the performance and compliance of the processes. The chapter is concluded with an outlook on future research directions.

BACKGROUND

To provide the foundations for our approach we will briefly give some background information to outline the challenges in the domain of health-related public management, the use of conceptual modeling and meta modeling concepts to represent conceptual visual models and on the currently available semantic technologies in the area of health.

Health-Related Public Management

The development of new medical treatments and products at a high quality and an affordable price is today one of the central challenges in the area of health-related public management. In particular, the research for new drugs involves a large number of resources and imparts considerable risks that have to be taken on by pharmaceutical companies (Sauer and Sauer, 2007). Of every 5,000 molecules tested, about 250 substances enter preclinical testing, 10 enter clinical development and just one will be finally approved by the regulatory authorities and receive the marketing authorization (EFPIA, 2010). For the parties involved in this process it is therefore essential to ensure the efficient use of resources as well as the compliance to legal regulations. On the side of pharmaceutical companies, the findings from basic laboratory research have to be translated into new methods for diagnosis, therapy, and prevention. Despite the large number of tests that can already be conducted during this pre-clinical stage, the crucial data are accumulated during the clinical trial stage, where the substances are applied to humans. Depending on the phase of the clinical trial this involves either healthy volunteers or voluntary patients.

The compliance with established standards of manufacturing and laboratory practice and the consideration of relevant scientific guidelines is required to ensure the safety of substances before their first human application.

In all these stages *public authorities* play a major role. They are responsible for ensuring the completeness of the dossier, the verification of the use of state-of-the-art scientific methods and procedures, and the compliance with the legal framework. The application for clinical trials has to be approved by the authorities before they can be initiated. This involves the assessment of the dossier with respect to manufacturing, preclinical and clinical aspects. Parallel to the evaluation by the competent authorities, ethics committees have to assess the ethical impact of the trial, as well as pre-clinical and clinical aspects and the standard of care. The basis for all these activities is a number of national and international legal regulations and guidelines. This framework is continuously adapted to the advancement of science and technology and with a view of international harmonization.

In Europe, the approval of new medicinal substances or products has to be based on a licensing application that can either be submitted on a national level, in the course of a mutual recognition procedure (MRP) in case a substance has already been approved in another member state, by a decentralized procedure (DCP) to gain approval in several countries in parallel or, for a defined group of medicinal products, via a centralized procedure by the European Medicines Agency (EMA). Both during the clinical trial stage and at the time of an application for marketing authorization, the interaction between the applicant and the authorities, and amongst the authorities and the European Medicines Agency, relies on several IT systems and databases. In order to allow for an efficient and effective processing of applications for the clinical testing of new substances and their introduction to the market, the procedures executed by the regulatory authorities need to be constantly

updated and adapted to new legal and scientific requirements. The effective communication of information about these updates and adaptations both to the staff of the authorities as well as to all external stakeholders participating in these activities is therefore a crucial task. In addition, the assurance of the legal compliance and the efficient use of resources requires a continuous analysis and optimization by the responsible executives.

Conceptual Modeling and Meta Modeling

One way to deal with the complexity involved in the above outlined tasks is to use models that represent necessary parts of reality for the purposes of a human user cf. (Stachowiak, 1973). Modeling methods in general can be described according to a framework set up by (Karagiannis and Kühn, 2002). In this framework modeling methods are composed of a modeling technique and mechanisms and algorithms. The modeling technique is again composed of a modeling language and a modeling procedure. The modeling procedure defines the steps and results in the course of the application of the modeling language. The modeling language is composed of a syntax, semantics, and notation. In contrast to other approaches, e.g. as described in (Harel and Rumpe, 2000), the notation is separated from the syntax and stands for the visual representation of the elements of the modeling language cf. (Fill, 2009). This allows to modify the visual representation independently of the syntax. The semantics of the syntax elements is defined by applying a semantic mapping to a semantic schema. This semantic schema may either be formally defined or expressed in natural language. Based on the modeling language, mechanisms and algorithms can be implemented and used for the modeling procedure. The mechanisms and algorithms can either be generic, in the sense that they are independent of a specific modeling language. Or they can be specific, i.e. they are applicable only to one or a selected number of modeling languages or hybrid, i.e. they contain parameters that allow specific parts to be adapted to other modeling languages.

An example for a modeling paradigm that can serve as the basis for realizing modeling methods and that is capable of dealing with complex static and dynamic phenomena are conceptual models cf. (Wand and Weber, 2002). Modeling languages in this paradigm are characterized by a formal syntax that allows capturing the essential aspects of a given phenomenon and depicting them in the form of a visual notation (Fill, 2009). In contrast to knowledge representation approaches, conceptual modeling is directed towards the use by humans for purposes of understanding and communication and not towards the use by machines (Mylopoulos, 1998). Therefore, the semantics of conceptual modeling languages are usually not formally specified but given in natural language.

However, as has been shown by many applications of conceptual modeling techniques in science and practice, the formal definition of conceptual models may also be extended in order to allow for a technical implementation (Fill, 2004) or to support mathematical analyses such as verifications (Mendling and van der Aalst, 2007) and the application of algorithms, e.g. for the purpose of simulation cf. (Kühn and Junginger, 1999).

The implementation of conceptual model editors and processing tools requires a solid formal basis. This basis can either be realized by reverting to existing platforms and frameworks for implementing modeling languages such as EMF (McNeill, 2008) or can be performed from scratch in any kind of higher programming language. An established approach in this context is the use of meta modeling techniques (Karagiannis and Höfferer, 2006). Meta modeling techniques provide concepts to define the formal syntax of a modeling language together with their visual representation. Thereby, they enable the creation of mechanisms and algorithms working on the abstract and concrete syntax of the modeling language. They are available in the form of inter-

national standards such as the meta-object facility (OMG, 2006) or in proprietary formats (Junginger et al., 2000), (Gunderloy, 2004). In the terminology of meta modeling, a meta model defines the model of a modeling language cf. (Karagiannis and Höfferer, 2006). The meta model itself is again described in a particular meta modeling language that defines the syntax, semantics, and notation for the composition of meta models. The semantics of meta models is usually defined by mapping the elements of the meta model to natural language descriptions. Thereby, the semantics of the elements of the abstract syntax of the modeling language are described, which shall be denoted as *type semantics* cf. (Höfferer, 2007). This type semantics remains constant for all instances of the meta model and can therefore be directly used for implementing mechanisms and algorithms. However, a second kind of semantics is assigned to the instances of a particular meta model: To describe the content of a particular instance element and thus make it distinguishable from other instance elements, attributes such as a name are assigned to the instance. The content of these attributes is though not pre-determined but is assigned by a user during modeling. Therefore, the semantics described by this content – which we will denote according to (Höfferer, 2007) as *inherent semantics* – is not made explicit but described in natural language and therefore not directly accessible to machine processing.

To process the inherent semantics of conceptual models, several proposals have been made in the area of business process management that can be subsumed under semantic business process modeling cf. (Thomas and Fellmann, 2009), (Höfferer, 2007), (Ehrig et al., 2007), (Lautenbacher et al., 2008). A common aspect of these approaches is the introduction of annotations for the instances of a business process modeling language in order to apply formal semantic techniques. An extension to these approaches for other model types in the context of business process management has been discussed recently in (Fill and Reischl, 2009). In this work, the approach of *semantic information models* has been described that stands for the combination of arbitrary types of conceptual models and formal semantic schemata. As will be shown in the main section of this chapter, this approach can be extended to achieve an alignment to shared semantic schemata and thus realize a step-wise semantic enrichment of conceptual models (Figure 1).

Semantics in Health-Related Public Management

As a foundation for expressing semantics in the area of health-related public management three areas have been identified that provide particular knowledge and technologies. These are: general biomedical ontologies, data interchange standards as issued by the Clinical Data Interchange Standards Consortium (CDISC), cf. (CDISC, 2010), and international harmonization initiatives by the International Conference on Harmonization of Technical Requirements for Registration of Pharmaceuticals for Human Use (ICH), cf. (ICH, 2010).

Biomedical ontologies are today used to search and query heterogeneous biomedical data, exchange data among applications, integrate information, process natural language, represent encyclopedic knowledge or apply computer reasoning to data (Rubin et al., 2008). They come in various types of formality ranging from controlled vocabularies, glossaries and thesauri to fully-fledged ontologies – for a good overview see (Rubin et al., 2008). Most of them are available for public use. The NCI BioPortal currently provides access to sixteen different terminologies including BiomedGT, the Gene Ontology, HL7, NCI Thesaurus, and SNOMED-CT (NCI, 2010). An ontology specialized on clinical research data has been recently presented by (Tu et al., 2009). A well known example for a controlled vocabulary in this area is the gene ontology (GO) that provides information about gene and protein roles in cells (Ashburner et al., 2000). It allows researchers to search for gene products that are either involved in particular biological processes, have certain molecular functions or that are located in a specific cellular component (Rubin et al., 2007). Furthermore, it can be used to gain insight into experimental results by annotating the results with

Figure 1. Components of modeling methods (Karagiannis and Kühn, 2002)

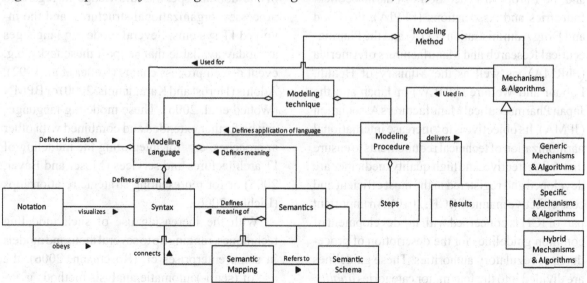

concepts from the GO and then executing analyses based on these annotations. Another example for a biomedical ontology is the NCI thesaurus developed by the National Cancer Institute. It is a biomedical terminology that contains about 80,000 concepts from several controlled vocabularies (De Coronado and Fragoso, 2009). Several formats are available for the NCI thesaurus including the common OWL DL ontology format.

CDISC is a global, open, multidisciplinary, and non-profit consortium that established standards to support the acquisition, exchange, submission and archive of clinical research data and metadata (CDISC, 2010). Its aim is to develop platform-independent data standards to enable the interoperability of information systems in medical research and related areas of healthcare. Currently, CDISC maintains primarily data standards in formats such as XML. However, also semantic definitions such as the CDISC glossary are available – but so far not in a technically processable format.

In the area of health-related public management an important organization in regard to the standardization of terminologies is the ICH. It is a joint initiative of regulators and research-based industry representatives of the European Union, the USA, and Japan (ICH, 2010). Currently the members of the ICH are the European Union and the European Federation of Pharmaceutical Industries and Associations (EFPIA), the Food and Drug Administration (FDA) and the Pharmaceutical Research and Manufacturers of America (PhRMA), as well as the Ministry of Health, Labour and Welfare (MHLW) in Japan and the Japan Pharmaceutical Manufacturers Association (JPMA). Its objective is to "increase international harmonization of technical requirements to ensure that safe, effective, and high quality medicines are developed and registered in the most efficient and cost-effective manner" (ICH, 2010). An important part of ICH is concerned with the development of common guidelines for the description of procedures of regulatory authorities. These guidelines are divided into the four major categories *quality,*

safety, efficacy, and multidisciplinary. Although these guidelines follow an informal approach described in natural language they contain classifications of terms and detailed glossaries about the domain specific understanding of the terms and the procedures related to them. This makes them a valuable source of reference for the regulatory authorities that is continuously updated and approved by all member organizations.

AN APPROACH FOR A STEPWISE SEMANTIC ENRICHMENT OF CONCEPTUAL MODELS

As has been outlined above, the management tasks in the area of health-related public management are characterized by complex relationships between professional knowledge in the area of medical research, continuously changing compliance requirements and the need for an efficient use of resources. Additionally, several actors and IT systems are involved that need to communicate with each other and exchange information. To master these challenges, the use of conceptual modeling techniques has been found to be an appropriate solution (Fill and Reischl, 2009). In particular, conceptual models allow for the representation of the domain specific knowledge in regard to processes, organizational structures, and the involved IT systems. Several modeling languages are today available that support these tasks, e.g. event driven process chains (Keller et al. 1992), Adonis (Herbst and Karagiannis, 2000) or BPMN (Wohed et al. 2006). These modeling languages can be further extended and combined with other approaches, e.g. for integrating the modeling of IT architectures and services (Moser and Bayer, 2005) or for representing strategic relationships (Lichka, 2006).

With the increasing use of such modeling techniques, ranging up to several thousand models in some enterprises cf. (Rosemann, 2006), the use of (semi-)automatic analysis methods gains importance. This concerns not only the evaluation of traditional *process performance indicators* such as time, cost, and quality attributes but also the inspection in regard to *compliance requirements* or the *distribution of knowledge* to the different stakeholders. To support these analyses from a technical point of view, the conceptual models thus need to be extended. One way to enable such analyses of conceptual models is to use annotations with concepts from formal semantic schemata such as ontologies. In this way, semantic functionalities such as the provision of background knowledge for query expansion or rewriting, the facilitation of natural language processing, the retrieval and integration of information from different, distributed sources or the provision of navigation structures can be realized and directly employed for advanced analysis tasks cf. (Van Elst and Abecker, 2002).

The use of such semantic annotations for concrete practical scenarios has so far been described for some cases in the area of business process management e.g. (De Francisco, 2009). When bringing these approaches to practice, the tradeoff between costs and benefits of a particular approach has to be well argued in order to gain acceptance. Especially, when aiming for a high level of formality of semantic schemata, large efforts may be required including specially trained personnel and high costs for the time consuming, ambiguous and error-prone process of formalization (Van Elst and Abecker, 2002). Therefore the degree of formality has to be carefully chosen. In contrast, conceptual modeling approaches are characterized by the use of intuitive, visual elements that need not obey formal constraints. When the processing of the conceptual models becomes necessary, they can be gradually enriched with the formal concepts required for the processing.

Based on these considerations, we developed an approach that is based on conceptual models and allows for a step-wise semantic enrichment of these models. This shall be described in the following sections.

Meta Modeling as a Basis

As a basis for our approach we used the concepts of meta modeling to define the formal syntax of the involved modeling languages. The intuitive concepts of meta models proved particularly useful to communicate the concepts also to non-technical users and thus receive early feedback on the approach. By using meta modeling as the foundation for all involved modeling languages, particular advantages for the implementation of algorithms can be gained as the technical environment for the modeling languages remains the same and thus all information is available in a coherent format and structure. Therefore, application programming interfaces and tools supporting meta modeling can be easily re-used. To realize the step-wise semantic enrichment we defined three phases (see Figure 2):

The first phase only contains traditional conceptual models that are derived from a common meta model. The expression of semantics in this phase is conducted by creating conceptual visual models based on the modeling language as defined by the meta model. As the meta model itself is described by natural language, e.g. in the way of a manual explaining the concepts and relations, and the conceptual models do not contain formal semantics at this stage, formal analyses of the models can only be performed on the syntax and the type semantics of the modeling elements. The inherent semantics of the model elements cannot be processed at this stage. An example could be a conceptual model of a business process containing elements for activities, decisions, and relations that express a flow between these two elements. Thus, the type semantics of the elements is given, i.e. a creator of an algorithm could use the knowledge that the model can be used to express a flow of activities and decisions and implement her algorithm accordingly. However, the inherent semantics of the elements, e.g. the name of an activity, is given in natural language and thus not formally defined in semantic terms.

Figure 2. Phases of the semantic enrichment of conceptual models

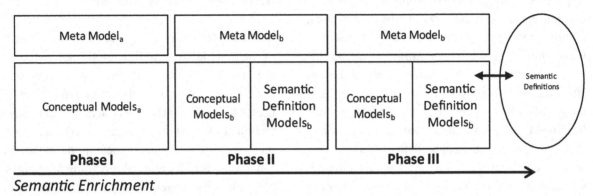

Semantic Enrichment

In the second phase, semantic definition models are added. They are also defined based on a common meta model and can be used to express the inherent semantics of the conceptual models. The semantic definition models may contain any type of elements that serve the purpose of describing the inherent semantics of the conceptual models. Examples could be formal semantic schemata but also models of documents or other types of conceptual models taking the role of a semantic definition. By linking elements of the conceptual models to elements of the semantic definition models, semantic annotations can be created. Thereby, it becomes possible to assign, for example, to the name of an activity "Write approval letter" elements from the semantic definition model that detail the semantics of "Write" and "approval letter". Carrying on with the example, the semantic definition model may thus contain a controlled vocabulary with an entry for "approval letter" that defines in natural language what is understood by an approval letter. The purpose of semantic definition models in this phase is therefore to provide a common semantic reference to the conceptual models. The concrete composition and the modeling language of the semantic definition models are left open and may range from strictly formal to primarily syntactic forms.

For the third phase, the semantic definition models are synchronized with externally available semantic definitions. In contrast to the second phase, the semantic definitions in the third phase are not static, in the sense that they can only be modified within the framework of conceptual models and semantic definitions models. Rather, they can now be updated and aligned to external semantic definitions. An example could be a shared ontology or a wiki that is maintained as a web resource. From this resource, either parts or the complete resource can be integrated as semantic definitions. In case the resource is updated, corresponding mechanisms have to ensure the consistency with the conceptual models that have been annotated with semantic definitions from the resource. The advantage of integrating external semantic definitions is on the one hand the re-use of existing definitions and on the other the facilitation of semantic interoperability. A concrete instantiation of this three-phase framework will be described in the following section by reverting to the approach of *semantic information models*.

Instantiation Using Semantic Information Models

As has been described above, the conceptualization of semantic definition models can be performed in various ways, ranging from formal semantic schemata to primarily syntactic model definitions. The choice for the composition of the definitions depends on factors such as the goal of the annotation and the expected advantages of a formal definition, the familiarity of the users with certain semantic definition languages, and the technical support in regard to the available tools for processing semantic definitions.

For the application in the area of health-related public management, we used the concept of semantic information models to create semantic definition models based on formal semantic schemata. As has been shown in previous work, semantic schemata that are suitable for this approach are for example controlled vocabularies and ontologies based on the web ontology language (OWL) specification (OWL, 2009), cf. (Fill and Reischl, 2009), (Fill and Burzynski, 2009). In the approach presented here, we developed an extension to the controlled vocabulary definitions in (Fill and Reischl, 2009). The conceptual model types are based on a common business process modeling language with extensions to allow for simulations of the business processes and to represent document models and organizational models. All model types have been specified in an integrated meta model as shown in Figure 3: The business process model type contains elements to define the control flow and the information flow of business processes. *Variable* elements can be used to further detail decisions taken in the process flow and thereby provide formal definitions of the *decisions* for executing the simulation. The organizational model type is based on role concepts. *Roles* can be assigned to actors for expressing their skills and qualifications. By further assigning *roles* to *activities* in the process flow, business process models and organizational models can be linked. In the same way, elements of the document model type can be linked to *activities*. To integrate semantic definitions, the semantic definition model type provides *term* elements. Term elements can be linked to each other by using *is broader term* relations. Additionally,

relationships between terms can also be defined using the *related term* property. With this property three qualified relations can be expressed: *synonyms*, *comments*, and arbitrarily *related* terms. Thereby, basic semantic relations between terms of a controlled vocabulary can be defined which proved sufficient for providing solutions in the context of health-related public management so far. The *term* elements can be linked to elements in the business process model type, the document model type, and the organizational model type to express semantic annotations. For the creation of user-centric visualizations, a *view definition* element is available in the business process and the organizational model type. Through references to terms it can thus be defined, which elements have been annotated with a specific term. This is then used to derive a visualization that can visually highlight these elements.

In detail, these model definitions and the linkages to the semantic definition model allow for the following analyses to be conducted: By annotating *role* elements, *activity* elements and *document* elements with the *term* elements, analyses of the *compliance* to specific regulations can be supported. For example, this allows to easily identify activities that are related to a specific term and need to be updated due to a change of the regulations of this term as indicated through a link to the corresponding legal document. In the same way, not only a search for specific roles and thus actors who are responsible for certain activities can performed, but this search can also be done using semantic relationships, e.g. by using the *related term* or *synonym term* properties. This applies also to the search for documents that are relevant for the execution of activities in the process.

As all elements of the models are formally defined, the implementation of the meta model on a concrete technical platform can be directly performed. For our approach we used the ADONIS[1]

Figure 3. Excerpt of the meta model used for the scenario of health-related public management

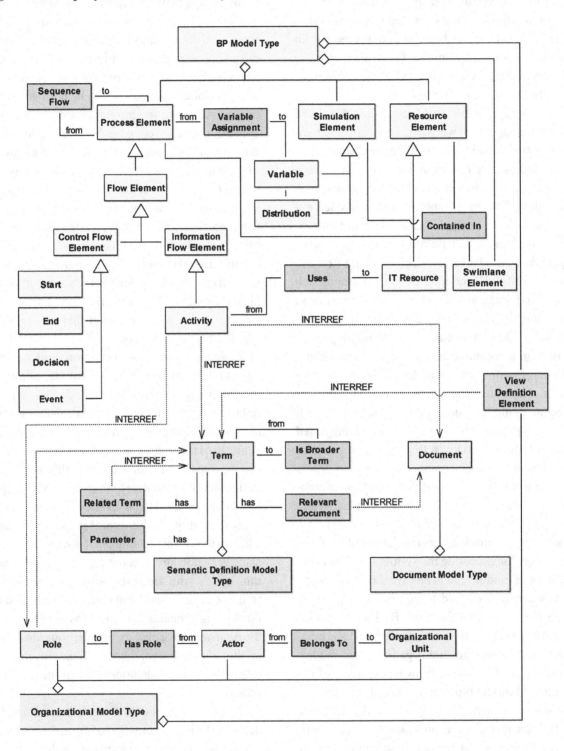

meta modeling platform to implement the meta models and define the visual representations of the model elements. This also permits to easily distribute the knowledge contained in the models in other formats, e.g. for the distribution in the form of HTML pages that can be stored on a website and made accessible to all internal and external stakeholders. With the formal definitions based on a meta model mechanisms and algorithms working on these models can be immediately realized. In particular, algorithms for the simulation of the contained business processes can be applied to generate information about cycle times and the usage and requirements of resources for executing the processes. Furthermore, the annotation of the model elements can be used as input to advanced visualization functionalities (Fill, 2009). These can highlight for example particular parts of a complex model based on a set of given terms and semantically related terms to directly support the user in analyzing the structure of the model based on the view definitions.

Concerning the above described phases of semantic enrichment, the presented meta model is able to support all three phases. For the traditional use of conceptual modeling the semantic definition models can be left out and the use restricted to the business process model, organizational model and document model type. For the second phase, semantic definition models can be added based on user-defined semantic terms and their relationships. This ensures already a consistent terminology by linkages to the semantic terms throughout the various conceptual models. It also permits to conduct several semantic analyses. By integrating semantic definitions from external sources, the semantic capabilities of the approach can be even further extended. In this phase, even more powerful semantic definitions can be used for the analyses, including large ontologies and thesauri that can be mapped to the semantic definition models.

Application at AGES PharmMed

The above described approach has been applied in a practical scenario at AGES PharmMed. AGES PharmMed and the Federal Office for Safety in Health Care (BASG), the Austrian Competent Authority, went operative on January 2, 2006 following a reorganization and out-sourcing from the Federal Ministry of Health. Legal responsibilities of the BASG center on issues pertinent to drug development and licensing. The purpose of AGES PharmMed, which is fully owned by the Republic of Austria, is to support BASG by providing services, personnel, and location. The tasks of AGES PharmMed can be described by nine categories: (1) the approval of clinical trials with medicinal products and/or medical devices; (2) the approval of pharmaceuticals; (3) pharmacovigilance, i.e. the systematic logging of adverse reactions of medicinal products; and the vigilance of medical devices (4) the monitoring of the market of medicinal products; (5) the inspections of pharmaceutical companies; (6) haemovigilance, i.e. the monitoring of blood donations and transfusions; (7) the provision of scientific advice for pharmaceutical companies; (8) the official medicines control laboratory; and (9) the official international representation of Austria in European organizations such as the European Medicines Agency (EMA).

The focus of the scenario was the management of clinical trial applications with medicinal products. These applications are subject to European Directives that have been introduced to harmonize the different work practices in regard to clinical trials. European Directives have been translated into National Law and are applicable to all member countries (Heerspink et al., 2008). In particular, the clinical trials directive Dir/2001/20/ EC clearly defines the role of central and local ethics committees and how they should interact in the procedures for the application of clinical trials cf. (European Parliament and the Council, 2001). For example, it is thus stated that an application for a clinical trial has to be submitted to a central ethics committee and the member state's competent authority in parallel and that both parties have to give an opinion on the trial application within 60 days from the receipt of the application. In addition, competent authorities have to provide mechanisms for the access of regulatory information by investigators and the general public and to evaluate and improve standards in clinical trials according to the recent scientific advancements. This constant adaptation to national and international procedures according to the legal framework requires a high degree of flexibility on the side of the competent authorities.

To apply the approach of semantic information models at AGES PharmMed the following steps were taken: In preliminary workshops the processes relevant for the administration of clinical trials were identified. These processes were then modeled in detail in ADONIS using mainly the business process model type together with the organizational model type and the document model type. As a next step, a controlled vocabulary was added using the semantic definition models. This controlled vocabulary contained terms that are central to the management of clinical trial applications and allowed to create first user-centric visualizations of the process models in order to highlight specific process parts. The last step so far comprised the integration of the CDISC glossary in the form of a semantic definition model. The CDISC glossary is freely available in a textual format and contains 400 terms from the area of clinical research. In contrast to most of the available biomedical ontologies it contained a large number of terms relevant for the management of clinical trial applications and did not require knowledge about formal semantic definitions. The textual format was parsed using a Java application and transformed into a model instance of the semantic definition model type - see Figure 4 for a screenshot showing the ADONIS meta modeling

platform with a business process model on the left, the semantic definition model of the CDISC glossary on the right, another semantic definition model from the second phase at the bottom and a document model.

The terms contained in the CDISC glossary are explained in natural language. In addition, the glossary provides references to synonym terms, related terms, and relevant ICH and FDA guidelines. This information was also transferred to the semantic definition model and the links between the terms were established automatically in the model in case they were defined in the CDISC file. Finally, the elements of the conceptual models were partly annotated by hand using the terms from the CDISC glossary. Thereby it turned out that some of the terms and concepts were only applicable to a specific type of organization or even only to specific countries with particular regulations. Although some of the terms defined in the CDISC glossary are based on the ICH guidelines – which ensure a common understanding between all member countries – several terms are specific to the US way of handling certain procedures. For example the entry for "action letter" defines it as "…an official communication from FDA to an NDA sponsor…" (CDISC, 2010). Therefore, a direct annotation with these concepts was not possible as it would mislead a potential investigator of this term. However, it was found that the usage of terms from the CDISC glossary together with the conceptual models proved helpful in order to understand the origin of the meaning of a specific term and its embedding in a particular process.

Based on the annotations of the models with terms from the CDISC glossary, the user-centric visualizations of the process models could thus also be performed using an internationally established terminology standard - see Figure 5 for an example. In this screenshot, three activities in the process are shown that deal with the applications for "Substantial amendments" and "Non-substantial amendments" and the report-

Figure 4. Screenshot of the implementation on the ADONIS meta modeling platform

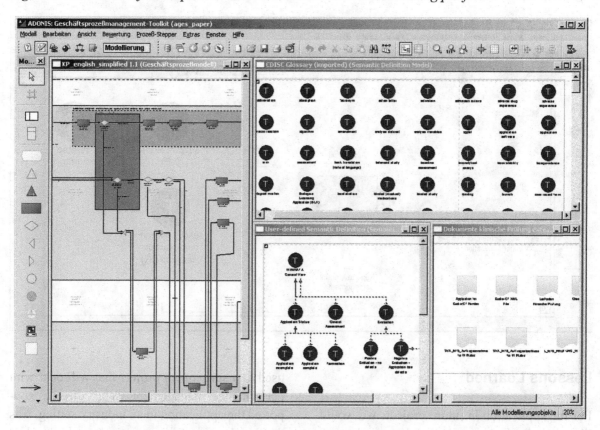

ing of SUSARs (Suspected Unexpected Serious Adverse Reaction). The activity "SUSAR reporting" has been annotated with the CDISC term "serious adverse drug reaction (serious ADR)". In the CDISC glossary this term contains a relation to the term "adverse experience" via the *related* property. The term also has another relation to the term "adverse event (AE)", again with the *related* property. At the same time, a view definition element has been defined for the process model (not visible on the screenshot) that contains a reference to the term element "serious adverse drug reaction (serious ADR)" of the semantic definition model containing the CDISC glossary. It was therefore possible to adapt the visualization of the process model based on these relationships, so that in this view, only activities that have been annotated with the terms defined by the view definition element are highlighted and all others with lower contrast.

By additionally using the semantic information of the *related* properties, it is also possible to expand the visualization semantically, in the way that any terms transitively related to "adverse event (AE)" can be found and used for highlighting correspondingly annotated activities.

As a consequence of these functionalities, it is possible to support the distribution of knowledge in the way that commonly used terms of the CDISC glossary can be used to find the related information in the process model. Furthermore, the management of compliance to legal frameworks can be supported by identifying process parts that are related to terms that have undergone a change in scientific or legal procedures. An example could be a change in the handling of activities related to adverse events that require new reporting measures and that can be found via the above outlined mechanisms.

Figure 5. Screenshot of a user-centric visualization using the CDISC glossary

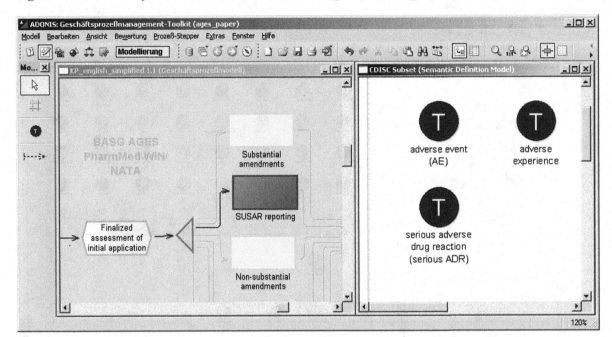

Lessons Learned

For the application in future projects we would like to give a short overview of the main lessons learned through applying the approach in practice. The representation of the business processes using the described modeling language together with the semantic annotations led to several benefits. Among them was the facilitation of the distribution of knowledge about the processes within the organization and the possibility of relating different information sources using a common terminology. This proved particularly helpful for the instruction of new staff members and their understanding of the complex dependencies between the various procedures and the according terminology standards. Furthermore, the separation of the organizational roles from concrete performers using the role concepts and their semantic annotation established a good basis for analyzing resource requirements by applying the described visualization technique. The insights gained by these analyses will be directly

used in a subsequent project that will deal with performance management. What directly supported the application in an industry setting, was the fact that a stepwise approach could be taken for the formalization. Although formalization can offer a large range of additional processing functionalities, the effort for encoding just the basic semantic relationships of real-life business processes and the dependencies on a large number of legal regulations for ensuring compliance in formal terms can quickly outweigh its expected benefits. Especially the semantic technologies that have been reported in approaches for semantic enrichments of models so far still require a considerable amount of manual encoding that requires itself considerable knowledge about the formal foundations and the represented domain knowledge. Although the approach used here does not exempt domain users from dealing with formal issues, the stepwise semantic enrichment greatly smoothed the way towards it. Furthermore, the use of visual models helped to generate results rather quickly by the domain experts themselves.

FUTURE RESEARCH DIRECTIONS

Future work will include the evaluation of the approach in regard to the additional benefits of using semantic information models in the context of health-related public management. This concerns in particular the investigation of the mechanisms necessary to execute (semi-) automatic analyses of the compliance of the processes to legal regulations and the use of semantic schemata with a higher degree of formality such as ontologies. For this purpose it can be reverted both to a number of ongoing work in the area of compliance management of business processes (Karagiannis et al., 2008) and the application of semantic technologies for automated checking (Awad et al., 2008), (El Kharbili and Stein, 2008). However, for the concrete application field of health-related public management the most relevant semantic standards such as the ICH guidelines are currently not available as a formal specification. A fruitful approach to integrate also these guidelines could be to apply techniques of natural language processing in order to generate appropriate formal schemata for the integration as semantic definition models. Furthermore, it will have to be investigated, how the annotation of the conceptual models can be (semi-)automatically performed or at least how humans can be better supported during this task. Possible solutions for this goal might be found in the area of machine learning and artificial neural networks.

CONCLUSION

In this chapter we described an approach for the stepwise semantic enrichment of conceptual models. Our focus area was the field of health-related public management. To support management executives in this field we developed a meta model based approach for creating conceptual models and annotating them with elements from semantic definitions. The goal was to support knowledge distribution and compliance management, as well as to establish a basis for performance and resource management. By using a three-phased approach we showed how conceptual models can be semantically enhanced and related to externally defined semantic schemata. The approach benefits both staff and management in dealing with complex conceptual models. It has been applied and positively evaluated at the Austrian competent authority AGES PharmMed in a practical setting.

ACKNOWLEDGMENT

Parts of the work on this chapter have been funded by the Austrian Science Fund in the course of an Erwin-Schrödinger Fellowship Grant Number J3028-N23.

REFERENCES

Ashburner, M., Ball, C. A., Blake, J. A., Botstein, D., Butler, H., & Cherry, J. M. (2000). Gene ontology: Tool for the unification of biology. *Nature Genetics, 25*, 25–29. doi:10.1038/75556

Awad, A., Decker, G., & Weske, M. (2008). Efficient compliance checking using BPMN-Q and temporal logic. In M. Dumas, M. Reichert, & M.-C. Shan (Eds.), *Proceedings of the 6th International Conference on Business Process Management*, (pp. 326-341). Berlin.

Bertolo, S. (2005). *Funding strategies for the Semantic Web: Current activities and future trends in the European Union*. Retrieved January 15, 2010, from ftp:// ftp. cordis. Europa .eu/ pub/ ist/ docs/ directorate_e/kmcc/funding-strategies-for-the-semantic-web_en.pdf

Bussler, C. (2008). Is Semantic Web technology taking the wrong turn? *IEEE Internet Computing*, (January/February): 75–79. doi:10.1109/MIC.2008.16

Cardoso, J., Hepp, M., & Lytras, M. (2007). *The Semantic Web - Real world applications from industry*. Springer.

CDISC (Clinical Data Interchange Standards Consortium). (2010). *Glossary - Request for comments on CDISC terms*. Retrieved January 15, 2010, from http://www.cdisc.org/glossary

De Coronado, S., & Fragoso, G. (2009). *NCI Edit Tab: Protege 3.4 plugin for editing and maintaining NCI thesaurus*. Paper presented at the 11th International Protégé Conference.

De Francisco, D., & Grenon, P. (2009). *Enhancing telecommunication business process representation and integration with ontologized industry standards*. Paper presented at the 4th International Workshop on Semantic Business Process Management (SBPM2009).

EFPIA (European Federation of Pharmaceutical Industries and Associations). (2010). *Industry in figures - A highly regulated industry*. Retrieved January 15, 2010, from http://www.efpia.eu/content/default.asp?PageID=361

Ehrig, M., Koschmider, A., & Oberweis, A. (2007). Measuring similarity between semantic business process models. In J. F. Roddick & A. Hinze (Eds.), *Proceedings of the Fourth Asia-Pacific Conference on Conceptual Modelling (APCCM 2007)* (vol. 67, pp. 71-80). ACM.

El Kharbili, M., & Stein, S. (2008). Policy-based semantic compliance checking for business process management. In P. Loos, et al. (Eds.), *Modellierung betrieblicher Informationssysteme (MobIS 2008), CEUR Workshop Proceedings 420*, Aachen, (pp. 165-177).

European Parliament and the Council. (2001). *Directive 2001/20/EC of the European Parliament and of the Council of 4 April 2001 on the approximation of the laws, regulations and administrative provisions of the member states relating to the implementation of good clinical practice in the conduct of clinical trials on medicinal products for human use*. Retrieved January 15, 2010, from http://eur-lex. europa. eu/ LexUriServ/ LexUriServ. do?uri= CELEX: 32001L0020: EN: HTML

Fill, H.-G. (2004). UML statechart diagrams on the ADONIS metamodeling platform. *Electronic Notes in Theoretical Computer Science, 127*(1), 27–36. doi:10.1016/j.entcs.2004.12.028

Fill, H.-G. (2009). *Visualization for semantic Information Systems*. Gabler. doi:10.1007/978-3-8349-9514-8

Fill, H.-G., & Burzynski, P. (2009). *Integrating ontology models and conceptual models using a meta modeling approach*. Paper presented at the 11th International Protégé Conference.

Fill, H.-G., & Reischl, I. (2009). *An approach for managing clinical trial applications using semantic information models*. Paper presented at the 3rd International Workshop on Process-oriented information systems in healthcare (ProHealth '09).

Gunderloy, M. (2004). Review: MetaEdit+. *Application Development Trends Magazine, 3*(12).

Harel, D., & Rumpe, B. (2000). *Modeling languages: Syntax, semantics and all that stuff - Part I: The basic stuff (No. MCS00-16)*. Rehovot, Israel: The Weizmann Institute of Science.

Heerspink, H. J., Dobre, D., Hillege, H. L., Grobbee, D. E., & De Zeeuw, D. (2008). Does the European Clinical Trials Directive really improve clinical trial approval time? *British Journal of Clinical Pharmacology, 66*(4), 546–550. doi:10.1111/j.1365-2125.2008.03246.x

Herbst, J., & Karagiannis, D. (2000). Integrating machine learning and workflow management to support acquisition and adaptation of workflow models. *Intelligent Systems in Accounting . Financial Management, 9*(2), 67–92.

Hevner, A. R., March, S. T., Park, J., & Ram, S. (2004). Design science in Information System research. *Management Information Systems Quarterly, 28*(1), 75–105.

Höfferer, P. (2007). *Achieving business process model interoperability using metamodels and ontologies.* Paper presented at the 15th European Conference on Information Systems (ECIS2007), St. Gallen, Switzerland.

ICH. (2010). *ICH guidelines.* International Conference on Harmonization of Technical Requirements for Registration of Pharmaceuticals for Human Use (ICH). Retrieved January 15, 2010, from http://www.ich.org/cache/compo/276-254-1.html

Junginger, S., Kühn, H., Strobl, R., & Karagiannis, D. (2000). Ein Geschäftsprozessmanagement-Werkzeug der nächsten Generation - ADONIS: Konzeption und Anwendungen (German: ADONIS: A next generation business process management tool - Concepts and Applications). *Wirtschaftsinformatik, 42*(5), 392–401.

Karagiannis, D., & Höfferer, P. (2006). Metamodels in action: An overview. In J. Filipe, B. Shishkov & M. Helfert (Eds.), *ICSOFT 2006 - First International Conference on Software and Data Technologies* (pp. IS-27 - IS-36). Setúbal, Portugal: Insticc Press.

Karagiannis, D., & Kühn, H. (2002). Metamodeling platforms. In K. Bauknecht, A. Min Tjoa & G. Quirchmayer (Eds.), *Third International Conference EC-Web 2002 – Dexa 2002* (pp. 182). Aix-en-Provence, France: Springer.

Karagiannis, D., Mylopoulos, J., & Schwab, M. (2008). *Business process-based regulation compliance: The case of the Sarbanes-Oxley Act.* 15th IEEE International Requirements Engineering Conference (RE 2007). IEEE.

Keller, G., Nuettgens, M., & Scheer, A.-W. (1992). Semantic process modeling on the basis of event-driven process chains (in German). *Publications of the Institute of Business Informatics . Saarland University, 89*, 29.

Kühn, H., & Junginger, S. (1999). An approach to use UML for business process modeling and simulation in ADONIS. In H. Szczerbicka (Ed.), *Proceedings of the 13th European Simulation Multiconference (ESM99) - Modeling and Simulation: A Tool for the Next Millenium* (pp. 634-639). Warsaw, Poland.

Lautenbacher, F., Bauer, B., & Seitz, C. (2008). *Semantic business process modeling - Benefits and capability.* Paper presented at the AAAI Spring Symposium, Stanford University, California.

Lichka, C. (2006). *Business scorecarding as model-driven approach for strategy implementation.* PhD thesis, University of Vienna, Austria, Vienna.

March, S. T., & Smith, G. F. (1995). Design and natural science research on information technology. *Decision Support Systems, 15*, 251–266. doi:10.1016/0167-9236(94)00041-2

McNeill, K. (2008). *Metamodeling with EMF: Generating concrete, reusable Java snippets.* Retrieved April 8, 2008, from http://www.ibm.com/developerworks/library/os-eclipse-emfmetamodel/index.html?S_TACT=105AGX44&S_CMP=EDU

Mendling, J., & Van der Aalst, W. M. P. (2007). Formalization and verification of EPCs with OR-joins based on state and context. In J. Krogstie, A. L. Opdahl & G. Sindre (Eds.), *Proc. of the the 19th International Conference on Advanced Information Systems Engineering* (Vol. LNCS 4495, pp. 439-453). Springer.

Moser, C., & Bayer, F. (2005). IT architecture management: A framework for IT services. In J. Desel & U. Frank (Eds.), *Proceedings of the Workshop on Enterprise Modelling and Information Systems Architectures*. Klagenfurt, Austria: Lecture Notes in Informatics - Gesellschaft für Informatik (GI).

Mylopoulos, J. (1998). Information modeling in the time of the revolution. *Information Systems, 23*(3-4). doi:10.1016/S0306-4379(98)00005-2

NCI (National Cancer Institute). (2010). *Bio-Portal*. Retrieved January 15, 2010, from http://bioportal.nci.nih.gov/

Object Management Group OMG. (2006). *Meta object facility (MOF) specification 2.0*. Retrieved January 15, 2010, from http://www.omg.org/spec/MOF/2.0/PDF/

OWL. (W3C OWL Working Group). (2009, October 27). *OWL 2 Web ontology language document overview - W3C recommendation*. Retrieved January 15, 2010, from http://www.w3.org/TR/2009/REC-owl2-overview-20091027/

Rosemann, M. (2006). Potential pitfalls of process modeling: Part B. *Business Process Management Journal, 12*(3), 377–384. doi:10.1108/14637150610668024

Rubin, D. L., Shah, N. H., & Noy, N. F. (2008). Biomedical ontologies: A functional perspective. *Briefings in Bioinformatics, 9*(1), 75–90. doi:10.1093/bib/bbm059

Sauer, C., & Sauer, R. M. (2007). Is it possible to have cheaper drugs and preserve the incentive to innovate? The benefits of privatizing the drug approval process. *The Journal of Technology Transfer, 32*, 509–524. doi:10.1007/s10961-007-9036-0

Stachowiak, H. (1973). *Allgemeine Modelltheorie (German: General Model Theory)*. Springer.

Thomas, O., & Fellmann, M. (2009). Semantic process modeling – Design and implementation of an ontology-based representation of business processes. *Business & Information Systems Engineering, 1*(6), 438–451. doi:10.1007/s12599-009-0078-8

Tu, S., Carini, S., Rector, A., Maccallum, P., Toujilov, I., Harris, S., et al. (2009). *OCRe: An ontology of clinical research*. Paper presented at the 11th International Protégé Conference.

Van Elst, L., & Abecker, A. (2002). Ontologies for information management: Balancing formality, stability, and sharing scope. *Expert Systems with Applications, 23*, 357–366. doi:10.1016/S0957-4174(02)00071-4

Wand, Y., & Weber, R. (2002). Research commentary: Information Systems and conceptual modeling - A research agenda. *Information Systems Research, 13*(4), 363–376. doi:10.1287/isre.13.4.363.69

Wohed, P., Van der Aalst, W. M. P., Dumas, M., Ter Hofstede, A. H. M., & Russell, N. (2006). *On the suitability of BPMN for business process modelling*. Paper presented at the BPM 2006, Vienna, Austria.

ENDNOTE

[1]   ADONIS is a commercial product and trademark of BOC AG. A community edition is available at http://www.adonis-community.com/

Section 4
Semantic Process Description

Chapter 11

EPCs Annotated with Lexical and Semantic Labels to Bridge the Gap between Human Understandability and Machine Interpretability

Andreas Bögl
Johannes Kepler University Linz, Austria

Michael Karlinger
Johannes Kepler University Linz, Austria

Michael Schrefl
Johannes Kepler University Linz, Austria

Gustav Pomberger
Johannes Kepler University Linz, Austria

ABSTRACT

Labels of EPC functions and events are the key to understanding EPC models by humans and by machines. Empirical studies show that the current labeling practice of model elements is conducted rather arbitrarily which inherently causes potential threats for understanding by humans. Thus, refactoring of model element labels is suggested either human-driven or with automated support while semantic annotation using domain-ontologies is well-recognized to approach the understanding of model elements by machines. Current research either focuses on improving the quality of labels or on semantic annotation to facilitate machine interpretability. To the best of our knowledge, there is a significant lack of approaches that facilitate to exploit the potentials and benefits arising from bridging the gap between approaches that improve human understandability and that facilitate machine interpretability. This work introduces a comprehensive, formalized approach that enables the modeling tasks automated refactoring of model elements and automated semantic annotation by bridging the gap between informal and formal representation of model elements.

DOI: 10.4018/978-1-60960-126-3.ch011

INTRODUCTION

Event-driven Process Chains (EPCs) (Keller, Nüttgens, & Scheer, 1992) have gained broad acceptance in industry for designing processes on a business-level with key objectives such as the documentation of processes, the automated translation of process models into enactable workflows (Van der Aalst, Hofstede, & Weske, 2003) or the automated discovery of common modeling practices (Bögl et al. 2008a). Unfortunatley, the achievement of these key objectives is hampered by lack of human understanding and machine interpretability of process models, due to ambiguities in model element labels and lack of behavioral correctness, which has been shown in recent research on process model quality and on guidelines of modeling (GOM) (Schütte & Totthowe 1998; Mendling, Reijers, & Van der Aalst 2009).

To elaborate on understandability and interpretability of EPC models we distinguish between *structural aspects* and *labeling aspects*. From a human perspective, structural aspects are concerned with the size, complexity of EPC models, for example. According to different studies in research and practice (e.g. Gruhn & Laue, 2006), it turned out that well-structured EPC models are easier to comprehend for humans and less error prone. For machines, however, size and complexity of EPC models do not affect the interpretability; it refers to the processability respectively the behavioral semantics of EPC models. The focus is on the semantic correctness to prevent errors at run-time, i.e. that no undesired process behavior occurs such as deadlocks or lack of synchronization (Vanhatalo, Völzer, & Leymann, 2007) or unreachable activities (Van der Aalst, et al., 2002). In this context, *soundness* (Van der Aalst, 1997) defines a minimum correctness criterion that an EPC should fulfill to ensure processability by machines. Structural aspects such as well-structuredness and soundness

of EPC models are well researched and will not be further discussed in the rest of this paper (e.g. Laue & Mendling (2009), Mendling & Van der Aalst (2007), Kiepuszewski, Hofstede, & Bussler (2000), Boudewijn, Mendling, & Van der Aalst (2006), Dehnert & Zimmermann (2005)).

In contrast to structural aspects, *labeling aspects* are associated with natural text clauses in conjunction with some graphical representation. Natural text clauses are used to describe the process meaning of the model elements function and event of EPC models. A function captures an activity and an event describes its pre- and post-conditions. The process meaning of an EPC model element at least refers to the process items task and state each having a relationship to a process object. For example, the function *"Define Software Requirements"* means that the task *"Define"* is *performed on* process object *"Software Requirements"*; the event *"Software Requirements Defined"* means that the state *"Defined"* is *state for* the process object *"Software Requirements"*.

Labeling model elements is inherent with certain subjectivism imposed by process modelers which lead to so-called linguistic or term defects such as synonyms, homonyms or vagueness. The following examples account some practical experiences and do not claim for completeness. If a lexical term of a model element is referred to as *"Invoice"*, a further element in another model as *"Bill"* and both terms represent the same real-world object then a synonymic labeling is at hand which allows much room for interpretation even for humans. Also, model element labels such as *"printing notification"* or *"purchase requisition processing"* are affected by ambiguity. The first label can be interpreted in the sense to *print* a *notification* or to *notify* somebody to carry out a print job, for the second label it is not obviously whether purchase or *processing* reflects an action (Leopold, Sergey, & Mendling, 2009). Apart from linguistic or term defects, different labels may express the same meaning due to freedom of modeling. For example, the functions *"Define SW Requirements"* and *"Define Requirements for Software"* are syntactically different but refer to the same process meaning.

It is evident that labels are the key to understanding EPC models by humans. According to Leopold, Sergey, & Mendling, 2009, *"the use of informative and unambiguous labels improves an overall understanding of a process model"*. However, empirical studies show that the current labeling practice of model elements is conducted rather arbitrarily (Mendling, Reijers, & Recker, 2010) which inherently causes a potential threat for understanding EPC models by human model reader.

A consistent practice of lexical terms and their collocation according to a particular grammatical style significantly improve the quality of labels and thus affects understandability for humans. In fact, model elements should comply with a particular labeling style. A labeling style is an informal guideline for model element labeling implemented by naming guidelines as suggested by the process modeling community (cf. Rosemann (1995), Schütte R., (1998)). If a labeling style or naming convention is constantly applied it significantly contributes to how well or how poorly process models can be understood by human model readers. According to empirical studies conducted by Mendling, Reijers, & Recker, (2010), the *verb-object* style (e.g. "Verify Order") has least impact on affected ambiguity and thereof is recommended as preferred labeling style; it manifests that a task or action should be expressed by a verb and a process object by a noun or noun phrase.

From the perspective of machines, the use of natural language hampers an automated processing or querying of processes since the meaning of model element names is not machine-processable. All together, these problems become obvious when process models are compared, combined, searched, validated or translated (Thomas &

Fellmann, 2007). Actually, labeling of model elements can be regarded as a trade-off between (ambiguous) textual descriptions for human comprehension on the one hand and a formalized, unambiguous encoding for computer systems on the other hand.

Semantic annotation of EPC model elements using domain-ontologies is well-recognized in order to approach the understanding of model element names by machines. From the perspective of a machine, *"ontologies are conceptual models of what exists in some domain, brought into machine-interpretable form by means of knowledge representation techniques."* (Grimm, Hitzler, & Abecker, 2007). The formal representation of the meaning of a model element name in terms of concepts and relationships in an ontology empowers machines to interpret model element names formulated in natural language.

There is a mutual positive impact between the usage of labeling styles to improve human understanding of model element names and the semantic annotation of model elements to improve machine interpretability. For example, if a model element name adheres to a particular labeling style, it is possible to automatically generate the model element's semantic annotation from its name, which is referred to as *automated semantic annotation*. Conversely, if a model element is already semantically annotated, it is possible to reformulate the model element's name such that it conforms to the process vocabulary in the business domain at hand and a manifested lexical naming convention, which is referred to as *automated label refactoring*. In order to facilitate the modeling tasks of automated semantic annotation and automated label refactoring, it is necessary to bridge the gap between model element names and labeling styles on the one hand and the semantic annotation of model elements on the other hand.

Figure 1 illustrates our approach that exploits the potentials and benefits arising from bridging the gap between human understandability and machine interpretability. The idea is to annotate model elements with *lexical labels* and *semantic labels* captured by *label repositories* and to use *bindings for label templates* based on *binding policies* in order to keep lexical knowledge separate from process knowledge.

A lexical label defines an unambiguous model element name to ensure human comprehension and to facilitate the modeling task of automated semantic annotation. It is made up of a sequence of *lexical items* arranged according to a *lexical label template*. Each of the lexical items forming a model element name is linked to a *lexical knowledge base* that provides standardized, commonsense vocabulary. A lexical label template represents a formalized *lexical naming convention* that implements a particular labeling style.

A semantic label encodes the linguistic meaning of a model element name to ensure interpretability by machines and to facilitate the modeling task of automated refactoring of model element names. It is made up of a sequence of process items

according to a *semantic label template*. Each of the process items forming the meaning of a model element is linked to a *process knowledge base*. A semantic label template represents a formalized *semantic naming convention* for a model element; i.e. it prescribes required raw process items and their raw relationships to semantically annotate a model element by a semantic label.

The approach of keeping lexical knowledge separate from process knowledge by introducing lexical labels and semantic labels is a methodologically sound principle (see also Hepp et al. 2008:p 135 et seq.) since this mechanism facilitates to maintain the boundary between lexical and domain knowledge (Pustejovsky & Boguraev 1993). However, lexical and semantic labels are shaped and affected by each other due to following reasons. An automated semantic annotation requires a linguistic analysis of lexical labels while automated refactoring requires to extract a lexical label from a semantic label. To facilitate these analysis tasks we introduce a mechanism

Figure 1. Basic approach to bridge the gap between human understandability and machine processability

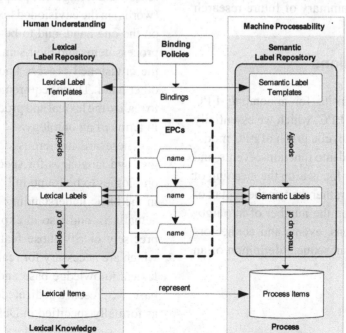

what we call *binding policy* and *bindings* based on binding policies. Binding policies allow to define interdependences between the meaning of lexical items and process items while bindings are used to associate different lexical label templates to a semantic label template. This mechanism facilitates to bridge the gap between alternative lexical labels and a unified process meaning.

This work is an extended and revised version of the studies published by Bögl et al. (2008b) discussed in more detail in the *related work* section. The rest of this paper is organized as follows. In the subsequent section, we introduce some preliminary definitions used throughout this work. Afterwards, we introduce the lexical knowledge base and the notion of lexical labels and lexical label templates followed by the process knowledge base and the notion of semantic label and semantic label templates. Building on this, in section *bridging the semantic gap*, we will show how binding policies and bindings based on binding policies can used for facilitating the modeling tasks automated semantic annotation and automated refactoring of model element labels. Finally, the paper concludes with an analysis of related work and a summary of future research directions.

Preliminary Definitions

The obvious prerequisite for annotating EPC model elements is an EPC, which we essentially define as a directed, acyclic graph of EPC model elements distinguished into functions, events, and connectors. Since our focus is on the meaning of model element labels rather than on the syntax of an EPC, constraints on the number of in/outgoing edges for functions, events and connectors are neglected in the subsequent definition of an EPC model.

Definition 1 (Event-Driven Process Chain)

An *EPC model* $\mathbb{E} = \left(M_E, M_F, M_C, A, i \right)$ consists of

- The disjoint sets of *events* M_E, *functions* M_F, and *connectors* M_C, where the set of all *model elements* is denoted by $M = M_E \cup M_F \cup M_C$;
  - The set of arcs $A \subseteq M \times M$, which connects the model elements in M and is required to form a directed, acyclic graph structure over M;
- Function $i : M \mapsto \left\{ string \right\}$, which assigns to each model element $m \in M$ a string n, called the *name* of m. It is required that for all $m \in M_C$,

$$i(m) \in \left\{ \text{"}and\text{"}, \text{"}or\text{"}, \text{"}xor\text{"} \right\}. \quad \blacksquare$$

To facilitate the automated semantic annotation of EPC model elements and the automated of model element labels, requires to be able to reason about linguistic properties of lexical items (words) in the envisioned lexical knowledge base on the one hand, and to be able to reason about process items and their semantic relationships in the envisioned process knowledge base on the other hand. These requirements make it obvious to realize the lexical and process knowledge bases in terms of an ontology.

There are numerous definitions of ontologies and languages for specifying and querying ontologies to be found in literature, which differ in the basic understanding of what an ontology actually is, and also in expressivity. In order to precisely clarify those features of an ontology which are necessary for realizing the envisioned lexical knowledge base and process knowledge base, we present a dedicated notion of ontologies, as formally specified in Definition 2.

Definition 2 (Ontology)

An ontology $\mathbb{O} = (\mathbb{T}, \mathbb{A}, \mathbb{D}, \acute{o})$ consists of a terminological box T, an assertion box A, a concept definition box Δ, and the symbol assignment .

The *terminological box* $T = (C_P, C_D, \leq_c, R, \hat{o}, \leq_R)$ defines:

- The disjoint sets of *primitive concepts* C_p and *derived concepts* C_D. The set of all concepts is denoted by $C = C_P \cup C_D$;
- The partial order $\leq_C$ over C, called *concept hierarchy*. The set of all *sub concepts* of a concept $c \in C$, denoted by *sub(c)*, is given by $sub(c) = \{c' \in C\# c' \leq_C c\}$.

The set of relationships R;

- The function $\hat{o} : R \mapsto C \times C$, which assigns to each relationship $r \in R$ a pair of concepts $(c, c') \in C \times C$, called the *relationship type* of r;
- The partial order $\leq_R$ over R, called *relationship hierarchy*, which requires that

  $\forall (r, r') \in R \times R$, if $r \leq_R r'$ then $c \leq_C \bar{c}$

  and $c' \leq_C \bar{c}'$, where $(c, c') = \hat{o}(r)$ and $\left[\bar{c}, \bar{c}'\right] = \hat{o}(r')$.

The *assertion box* $\mathbb{A} = (I, \acute{e}, \tilde{n})$ defines

- The set of *individuals I;*
- The function $\acute{e} : I \mapsto C$, which assigns to each individual $1 \in I$ the concept $c \in C_P$ it is an *asserted instantiation* of. The set of all asserted instantiations of a concept $c \in C_P$, denoted by *I(c)*, is given by $I(c) = \{1 \in I | \acute{e}(1) = c\}$;
- The function $\tilde{n} : R \mapsto P(I \times I)$, which assigns to each relationship $r \in R$ a set of pairs of individuals

$\left\{\left(\hat{1_1}, \hat{1_1}\right), ..., \left(\hat{1_n}, \hat{1_n}\right)\right\} \in P(I \times I)$, called *asserted relationship instantiations* of r;

The *concept derivation box* $\mathbb{D} = (D, \ddot{a})$ defines

- The set of *derivation expressions* $D = \{d_1, ..., d_n\}$, which are expressions of the form $d = r, I$ or $d = I, r$, where $\bar{r} \in R$ is a relationship and $\bar{I} \subseteq I$ is a set of individuals;
- The function $\ddot{a} : C_D \mapsto D$, which assigns to each derived concept $c \in C_D$ a derivation expression $d \in D$. The set of all *derived instantiations* of a concept $c \in C_D$, denoted by *I(c)*, is given by

$$I(c) = \begin{cases} \left\{1 \in I \mid \forall 1 \in I, \ (1, 1) \in \tilde{n}(r)\right\} & : \ddot{a}(c) = r, I \\ \left\{1 \in I \mid \forall 1 \in I, \ (1, 1) \in \tilde{n}(r)\right\} & : \ddot{a}(c) = I, r \end{cases}$$

- The extension of a concept $c \in C$, denoted by *ext(c)*, is given by $ext(c) = \{1 \in I\# \exists c' \in sub(c) such that \ \acute{e}(1) \in I(c')\}$. It is required that $\forall r \in R$, if $(1, I') \in \tilde{n}(r)$ then $1 \in ext(c)$ and $I' \in ext(c')$, where $(c, c') = \hat{o}(r)$.
- The *symbol assignment function* $\acute{o} : C \cup R \cup I \mapsto \{string\}$ assigns to each concept $c \in C$, relationship $r \in R$, or individual $1 \in I$ a string s, called its *symbol*. It is required that $\forall \{x, x'\} \in C \cup R$, $\acute{o}(x) \neq \acute{o}(x')$. ∎

In our context, an ontology essentially consists of a terminological box, which specifies the concepts and their relationships in the ontology, and an assertion box, which specifies the individuals in the ontology, the asserted instantiations of concepts by individuals, and the asserted instantiations of relationships between individuals. Concepts, relationships, and individuals are identities on their own, and are strictly separated from their symbolic representation. This separation is especially important for realizing the lexical knowledge base, since a particular string (symbol) may represent different words (individuals). For example, the distinct individuals 'check' as a noun and 'check' as a verb would both be represented by the symbol "check". In contrast to individuals, we apply the unique name assumption for concepts and relationships, which are therefore uniquely identified by their symbolic representations.

The concepts in an ontology form a specialization hierarchy, and are distinguished into primitive concepts, whose instantiation by individuals is asserted in the assertion box, and derived concepts, whose instantiation by individuals is derived according to so-called derivation expression. In our context, it suffices to have derivation expressions which allow to specify a set of individuals by means of requiring that each of these individuals instantiate a particular relationship with each one of a particular set of other individuals. Derivation expressions and their assignments to derived concepts are specified in what we call the derivation box.

An individual which is either an asserted or a derived instantiation of a certain concept is called a direct instantiation of that concept, and an individual is an indirect instantiation of that concept if it is a direct instantiation of any of its sub-concepts. The set of all direct and indirect instantiations (asserted or derived) of a certain concept is what we call the extension of that concept.

Like concepts, also the relationships in an ontology form a specialization hierarchy. Notably, we only require binary relationships for realizing the lexical and process knowledge base, and we therefore restrict relationships to relate exactly two concepts to one another, which we call the type of the relationship. The type of a relationship demands that a pair of individuals must not instantiate the relationship if the individuals are outside the extensions of the respective concepts in the relationship's type.

In order to keep the amount of formal notation within text as small as possible, we now introduce a shorthand notation for referring to concepts, relationships, and individuals in an ontology.

Definition 3 (Shorthand Notation for Ontologies)

Let s be a string and let $\mathbb{O} = (\mathbb{T}, \mathbb{A}, \mathbb{D}, \acute{o})$ be an ontology, where $\mathbb{T} = (C_P, C_D, \leq_C, R, \acute{o}, \leq_R)$, $\mathbb{A} = (I, \acute{e}, \tilde{n})$, and $\mathbb{D} = (D, \ddot{a})$. We use (Table 1). ∎

Further, to simplify comprehension of concepts, individuals and their relationships in the subsequent specifications of the lexical and process knowledge bases, we introduce next a graphical specification language for ontologies.

Definition 4 (Graphical Ontology Specification Language)

Let s_1, s_2, and s_3 be strings and let $\mathbb{O} = (\mathbb{T}, \mathbb{A}, \mathbb{D}, \acute{o})$ be an ontology, where $\mathbb{T} = (C_P, C_D, \leq_C, R, \acute{o}, \leq_R)$, $\mathbb{A} = (I, \acute{e}, \tilde{n})$, and $\mathbb{D} = (D, \ddot{a})$. The language constructs of the graphical ontology specification language L are (Table 2): where the formal semantics of each language construct is specified below the language construct. ∎

Table 1.

«s»	to denote the unique concept $c \in C$ for which $\sigma(c) = s$;
‹s›	to denote the unique relationship $r \in R$ for which $\sigma(r) = s$;
's'	to denote the set of individuals $\{i \in I \mid \sigma(i) = s\}$;

Table 2.

$\exists c \in C_P \mid \sigma(c) = s$	«s»	$\text{«}s_1\text{»} \leq_C \text{«}s_2\text{»}$	$\exists I \in I \mid \sigma(I) = s$
$\exists c \in C_D \# \ \sigma(c) = s$	«s»	$\text{«}s_1\text{»} \leq_C \text{«}s_2\text{»}$	$\iota\left('s_1'\right) = \text{«}s_2\text{»}$
$\exists r \in R \mid \sigma(r) = s_3 \wedge$ $\tau(r) = (\text{«}s_1\text{»}, \text{«}s_2\text{»})$		$\langle s_1 \rangle \leq_R \langle s_2 \rangle$	$\left('s_1','s_2'\right) \in \rho(\langle s_3 \rangle)$

Lexical Knowledge Base

The lexical knowledge base is intended to serve as a commonsense inventory of process vocabulary in a certain domain which is enriched with morphological knowledge, i.e. knowledge about the inflection of words such as the single or plural form of nouns, or the past tense of verbs. Commonsense domain vocabulary represents the inventory of terms, which we call lexical items, used for labeling model elements and also for labeling process items in the process knowledge base.

Whereas publicly available resources like the WordNet lexical database (Miller, 1995) do provide commonsense vocabulary, using them as inventories of domain vocabulary has considerable drawbacks. In general, such resources are open world dictionaries which typically comprise thousands of open world entities and semantic relationships[1] but lack at the same time of organization specific terms and acronyms. Also, the sheer number of terms in an open world dic-

tionary tends to cause needless search efforts or even confusion when looking for the right word in formulating a model element label. Notably, according to our own experiences but also according to several empirical studies (e.g. Malone, Crowston, & Herman, 2003)[2], a domain specific, controlled process vocabulary usually comprises of several hundred shared key terms at most, which are easy to be maintained and used. In order to avoid a knowledge acquisition bottleneck when establishing a lexical knowledge base, one can initialize the lexical knowledge base for example with the terms in an organization's technical term model or with the terms used in element labels of present EPC models.

In designing a lexical knowledge base, it is important to accommodate that the terms in a lexical knowledge base are not only domain specific but also language specific. In addition to the actual terms, also the morphological knowledge in a lexical knowledge base is language specific, and it is therefore illusive to attempt to design *one* lexical knowledge base for all languages. For this reason, the subsequent definition of a lexical knowledge base is dedicated to the representation of English domain vocabulary and English morphological knowledge.

Definition 5 (Lexical Knowledge Base)

A lexical knowledge base $\mathbb{L} = (\mathbb{T}, \mathbb{A}, \mathbb{D}, \delta)$ is an ontology according to Definition 2 which conforms to the following graphical specification in language $\mathcal{L}$

The assignment of derivation expressions to the derived concepts in $\mathbb{L}$ is given by:

$$
\begin{aligned}
\ddot{a}\left(\ll PluralNoun \gg\right) &= \langle noun\_number\rangle, "Plural" \\
\ddot{a}\left(\ll SingularNoun \gg\right) &= \langle noun\_number\rangle, "Singular" \\
\ddot{a}\left(\ll PastParticiple \gg\right) &= \langle part\_tense\rangle, "Past" \\
\ddot{a}\left(\ll ImperativeVerb \gg\right) &= \langle verb\_mood\rangle, "Imperative" \\
\ddot{a}\left(\ll PluralNounPhrase \gg\right) &= \langle np\_number\rangle, "Plural" \\
\ddot{a}\left(\ll SingularNounPhrase \gg\right) &= \langle np\_number\rangle, "Singular"
\end{aligned}
$$

∎

Essentially, the lexical knowledge base for English conceptualizes the parts of speech *noun, verb, preposition, conjunction, adjective,* and *participle,* which is in our context a special form of an adjective. In addition, the lexical knowledge base enables the representation of *abbreviations* (acronyms) and *noun phrases,* i.e. nouns which are composed of a head noun and a prependend or appended adjective or other noun. Regarding English morphological knowledge, the lexical knowledge base allows to assign properties of certain *grammatical categories* to nouns, noun phrases, and verbs. Thereby, inflected nouns, noun phrases, and verbs as well as infinitives and gerunds are related to the base form of the respective word, which is useful for example in deciding whether or not two words basically have the same meaning.

In addition to the parts of speech discussed previously, the English lexical knowledge base also represents so-called *word types,* which are subgroups of words within the parts of speech.

We will require the notion of word types later in our discussion of labeling styles. To shed some light on word types, consider the verb-object style which requires that the labels of conforming EPC functions are composed of a verb in imperative and a noun. In this example, the subgroup of verbs which are in imperative mood are a word type, i.e. a subgroup of words within all verbs.

For the purpose of illustration, consider the representation of words "define" and "Software Requirements" within a lexical knowledge base depicted in Figure 2. The word "define" is represented by the lexical item "define" which is an instantiation of a ‹‹Conjugated Verb››. It is moreover represented that "define" is a conjugation of the infinitive "to define" in the imperative mood. The word "Software Requirements" is represented by the individual "Software Requirements" which is an instantiation of a ‹‹Declined Noun Phrase››. This noun phrase is composed of the head word "Requirements," which is itself a plural declination of noun "Requirement," and the prepended noun "Software," which is an ‹‹Atomic Noun››.

Lexical Label Repository

The idea behind a lexical label repository is to annotate EPC model elements with lexical knowledge. On the one hand, lexical knowledge relates to morphological knowledge about the words in a model element name, and on the other hand it relates to the grammatical surface structure of a model element name.

To tackle the issue of annotating morphological knowledge to model element names, we introduce the notion of lexical labels, which specify the collocation of lexical items in model element names as formally specified in the next definition.

Definition 6 (Lexical Label)

Let $\mathbb{L} = (\mathbb{T}, \mathbb{A}, \mathbb{D}, \delta)$ be a lexical knowledge base, where $\mathbb{T} = (C_P, C_D, \leq_C, R, \hat{o}, \leq_R)$ and $\mathbb{A} = (I, \acute{e}, \tilde{n})$. A *lexical label* $l_L = l_1, \ldots, l_n \subseteq I$

Figure 2. Lexical items in the English lexical knowledge base $\mathbb{L}1$ for the software engineering domain

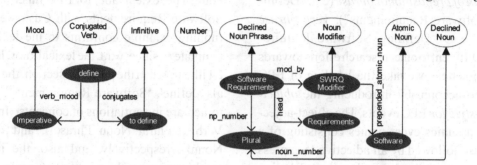

over $\mathbb{L}$ is a sequence of individuals, where for all $i \in \{1,\ldots,n\}$, $l_i \in ext(\text{«}LexicalItem\text{»})$. ∎

It is important to understand that a lexical label does not simply specify a sequence of strings but instead a sequence of lexical items taken from a lexical knowledge base. This way, a lexical label captures morphological knowledge about the name of a model element.

We now illustrate Definition 6 by the lexical label l_{L1} for EPC function "Define Software Requirements with Customer", which is depicted in the middle of Figure 3. The Lexical label l_{L1} is defined over the lexical knowledge base Λ_1, illustrated in the previous section, and is made up of lexical items "Define", "Software Requirements", "with" and "Customer" in exactly this order.

To tackle the issue of specifying the grammatical surface structure of an EPC model element name, we introduce the notion of a lexical label

template. To give an idea of lexical label templates requires some discussion about labeling styles and lexical naming conventions. A labeling style serves as a *"grammatical blueprint"* for naming model elements in a particular language. Reconsider lexical label l_{L1} depicted in Figure 3 which is an example for the verb-object labeling style. Informally, the verb-object style requires EPC function names to be composed of a verb in imperative mood succeeded by a noun or noun phrase which is satisfied by the EPC function "Define Software Requirements with Customer". Another labeling practice for EPC functions is referred to as action-noun style which states the task as a noun. Moreover, according to empirical investigations conducted by Leopold, Sergey, & Mendling (2009), an action-noun style may further be classified into the sub styles *Noun phrase* (e.g. "Software Requirements Definition"), *Noun*

Figure 3. Lexical label l_{L1} and lexical label template t_{L1} in the lexical label repository R_{L1} over $\mathbb{L}1$

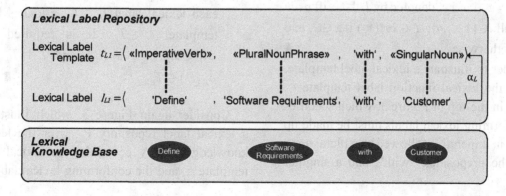

phrase with of prepositional phrase (e.g. "Definition of Software Requirements"), *Verb phrase (gerund)* (e.g. "Defining Software Requirements"). Different to other research efforts towards labeling practices we take the labeling of EPC events into account by introducing the *object-adjective-style for* EPC events. The object-adjective-style assumes event names consisting of a noun phrase followed by an adjective to express a state. To sum up the discussion about labeling styles, it is obvious that labeling styles generally permit to formulate model element names according to different grammatical surface structures to express the same linguisitic meaning.

In this work, a lexical naming convention represents a specification of the grammatical surface structure of a model element name over a given lexical knowledge base that implements a particular labeling style. The formalized description of a lexical naming convention according to the subsequent definition is said to be a lexical label template.

Definition 7 (Lexical Label Template)

Let $\mathbb{L} = (\mathbb{T}, \mathbb{A}, \mathbb{D}, \acute{o})$ be a lexical knowledge base, where $\mathbb{T} = (C_P, C_D, \leq_C, R, \acute{o}, \leq_R)$ and $\mathbb{A} = (I, \acute{e}, \tilde{n})$. A *lexical label template* $t_L = x_1, ..., x_n \subseteq C \cup I$ over $\mathbb{L}$ is a sequence of concepts and individuals, where for all $i \in \{1,...,n\}$, $x_i \in sub(\text{«}WordType\text{»})$ if $x_i \in C$, and $x_i \in ext(\text{«}LexicalItem\text{»})$, otherwise. The lexical label $l_L = l_1, ..., l_n$ *conforms* to the lexical label template $t_L = x_1, ..., x_m$, denoted by $l_L \models t_L$, iff $n=m$ and for all $i \in \{1,...,n\}$, $l_i \in ext(x_i)$ if $x_i \in C$, and $l_i = x_i$, otherwise. ∎

In order to illustrate a lexical label template, consider the lexical function label template t_{L1} depicted in the top of Figure 3, which specifies that conforming lexical labels must be made up of a verb in imperative followed by a plural noun phrase, the preposition "with", and a singular

noun. The lexical label for EPC function "Define Software Requirements with Customer" of our running example conforms to the lexical label template t_{L1} since, w.r.t. the lexical knowledge base $\mathbb{L}1$ illustrated in the previous section, the individuals Define', 'Software Requirements', and Customer' are instantiations of concepts ‹‹Imperative Verb››, ‹‹Plural Noun Phrase››, and ‹‹Singular Noun››, respectively, and also, the individual 'with' appears at the specified position, i.e. position number three.

Definition 8 (Lexical Label Repository)

Let $\mathbb{L}$ be a lexical knowledge base. A *lexical label repository* $\mathbb{R}_L = (L_{LE}, L_{LF}, T_{LE}, T_{LF}, S, \acute{a}_L)$ over $\mathbb{L}$ consists of:

- The disjoint sets of *lexical event labels* L_{LE} and *lexical function labels* L_{LF}, where $\forall l_L \in L_{LE} \cup L_{LF}$, l_L is a lexical label over $\mathbb{L}$. The set of all lexical labels is denoted by $L_L = L_{LE} \cup L_{LF}$;

- The disjoint sets of *lexical event label templates* T_{LE} and *lexical function label templates* T_{FE}, where $\forall t_L \in T_{LE} \cup T_{LF}$, t_L is a lexical label template over $\mathbb{L}$. The set of all lexical label templates is denoted by $T_L = T_{LE} \cup T_{LF}$;

- The set of *labeling styles* $S \subseteq P(T_L)$, for which it is required that $\forall s \in S$, $s \subseteq T_{LE}$ or $s \subseteq T_{LF}$, and $\forall \{s,s'\} \subseteq S$, $s \cap s' = \varnothing$.

- Function $\acute{a}_L : L_L \mapsto T_L$, which assigns to each lexical label $l_L \in L_L$ a lexical label template $t_L \in T_L$. It is required that $\forall l_L \in L_L$, $l_L \models \acute{a}_L(l_L)$ and $l_L \models L_{LE}$ iff $\acute{a}_L(l_L) \in T_{LE}$. ∎

Consider again Figure 3, which illustrates a lexical label repository P_{L1} over the lexical knowledge base Λ_1 containing the lexical label template t_{L1} and the conforming lexical label l_{L1}

introduced in our previous examples. The lexical label template t_{LI} is part of the verb-object style, as indicated by the fact that an imperative verb, i.e. the task of an EPC function, must be followed by a plural noun phrase, i.e. the process object processed by an EPC function. We refer the interested reader to the appendix for more examples of lexical function label templates in the Verb-Object style, but also for lexical function label templates in the Action-Noun style as well as lexical label templates for EPC events.

Process Knowledge Base

The introduced lexical knowledge base and the lexical label repository are the backbone for interpreting lexical knowledge of model element names by machines. The linguistic meaning what we call process meaning in forth however is not accessible by machines; a machine would interpret a lexical label according to its corresponding lexical label template. Referring again to our example depicted by Figure 3, a machine does not recognize that the lexical label conveys that the task is performed on the process object in corporate manner with a and that the process object denotes a specialization of the process object .

To facilitate interpretability of model element names by machines requires to conceptualize the process items forming the process meaning

of a model element independently from domain vocabulary. For this reason, we introduce the process knowledge base that is a domain ontology which stands independently as a logical and computational unit to facilitate interpretability of model elements by machines. With regard to our approach for describing ontologies it is worth to note that domain concepts encode tasks, states and process objects what we call process items while asserted individuals represent real world objects of process instances or business cases.

In what follows, we define the process knowledge base that encodes the process meaning of model element names to facilitate interpretability by machines.

Definition 9 (Process Knowledge Base)

A *process knowledge base* $\mathbb{P} = (\mathbb{T}, \mathbb{A}, \mathbb{D}, \delta)$ is an ontology according to Definition 2, which conforms to the following graphical specification in language L (Table 3).

Essentially, a function describes a ‹‹Task›› that is performed on a ‹‹Process Object››. A task concept represents an action which is performed on a process object expressed by the relationship ‹is_performed_on›(‹‹Task››,‹‹Process Object››). A process object represents a real or an abstract thing being of interest within a process domain. Additionally, a task may refer to a parameter. A

Table 3.

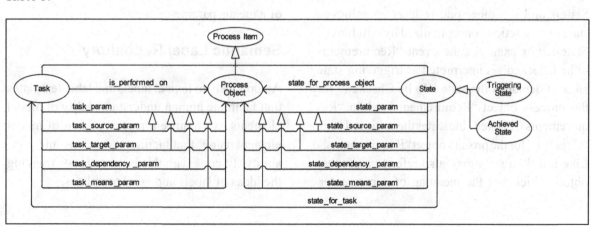

parameter denotes a process object which might be used for defining intentional aspects relevant for executing a task on a process object. The specification of a parameter is stated by the relationship ‹task_param›(‹‹Task››,‹‹Process Object››). We identified the four intentional aspects *source*, *target*, *means*, and *dependency* between a task and a process object each of them expressed by a specialized ‹task_param›(‹‹Task››,‹‹Process Object››) relationship.

A source parameter indicates a process object as non-consumable input required for performing a task. For example, the function "Derive Quality Goal from Specification" states the process object "Specification Document" as a source parameter. A target parameter denotes a recipient process object of a task execution. For example, the function "Send Reworked Specification to Customer" states "Customer" as a target parameter. A means parameter refers to a process object which is consumed by a task execution. For example, the function "Rework Specification with Software Goals" indicates "Software Goals" as a means parameter. A dependency parameter indicates a process object which is necessary input for a decision made by a task. For example, the function "Decide Quality Measure Upon Review Status" specifies "Review Status" as a dependency parameter.

Essentially, an event describes a ‹‹State›› for a ‹‹Process Object››. The state of an event permits two semantic interpretations; one refers to a state to be achieved conceptualized by ‹‹Triggering State›› and the other one reflects an achieved state by a function conceptualized by ‹‹Achieved State››. For example, the event "Requirements to be Checked" is interpreted as triggering state since it demands the state "To be Checked" for the process object "Requirements" while "Requirements Checked" indicates the achieved state "Checked" for the process object "Requirements". Like a task, a state may also refer to a process object which has the meaning of a parameter.

Associated parameters to a state are expressed by specialized relationships of the general relationship ‹state_param›(‹‹State››,‹‹Process Object››).

There is coherence between a performed task and its resulting state expressed by the relationship ‹state_for_task›(‹‹State››,‹‹Task››). For example, the state "Checked" relates to the task "Check".

For the purpose of illustration, consider Figure 4 which depicts a process knowledge base P_1 that contains process items ‹‹TA1››, which is a ‹‹Task››, and ‹‹PO1››, ‹‹PO2››, and ‹‹PO3››, which are ‹‹Process Objects››. Task ‹‹TA1›› is the language independent representation of task "define", and process objects ‹‹PO2››, ‹‹PO3››, and ‹‹PO1››, are the language independent representations of a customer, a requirement, and the special form of a software requirement, as indicated by the specialization of ‹‹PO3›› by ‹‹PO1››, respectively. The relationship ‹TA1_performed_on_PO1› states that the task ‹‹TA1›› ("define") is performed on the process object ‹‹PO1›› ("software requirements"), and the relationship ‹TA1_means_param_PO2› states that a customer is related to the task "define" in terms of a means parameter. We note that relationships ‹TA1_performed_on_PO1› and ‹TA1_means_param_PO2› are specializations of the general ‹is_performed_on› and ‹task_means_param› relationships, and that it is therefore explicitly stated that particularly the task ‹‹TA1›› is performed on process object ‹‹PO3›› as well as that particularly the process object ‹‹PO1›› is related to task ‹‹TA1›› in terms of a means parameter.

Semantic Label Repository

Analogously to lexical labels and label templates that facilitate human understandability of model elements, we require a representation of model element names that facilitates machine interpretability. To cope with this issue suggests reviving the ideas of labels and label templates.

Figure 4. Process items and their relationships in the process knowledge base $\mathbb{P}_1$ for the software engineering domain

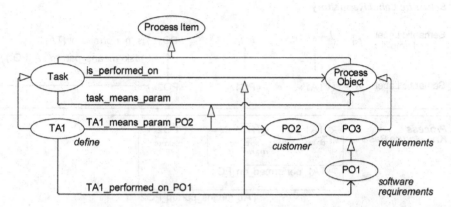

A semantic label acts as a semantic description of model elements which is interpretable by machines. A semantic label is made up of a sequence of concepts in a process knowledge base. In particular these concepts are specializations of a the raw process items ‹‹Task››, ‹‹Process Object›› and ‹‹State››, as formally specified in the next definition.

Definition 10 (Semantic Label)

Let $\mathbb{P} = (\mathbb{T}, \mathbb{A}, \mathbb{D}, \hat{o})$ be a process knowledge base, where $\mathbb{T} = (C_P, C_D, \leq_C, R, \hat{o}, \leq_R)$. A *semantic label* $l_S = c_1, \ldots, c_n \subseteq C$ over P is a sequence of concepts in C. ■

For the purpose of illustration, consider the semantic label 1_{s1} depicted in the middle of Figure 5, which is the machine interpretable representation of EPC function *"Define Software Requirements for Customer"*. In particular, semantic label 1_{s1} is made up of the process items ‹‹TA_1››,‹‹PO_1››, and ‹‹PO_2››, which are the machine interpretable representations of the task "Define", and the process objects "Software Requirements" and "Customer" in the process knowledge base P_1.

In compliance with lexical label templates that specify lexical naming conventions for lexical labels, we introduce next semantic label templates

that specify what we call semantic naming conventions of semantic labels. A semantic label template specifies a sequence of raw process items in terms of variables and raw relationships in terms of constants between variables required for a semantic labeling of model elements. The variables and relationship constants of a semantic label template represent slots for domain concepts which have to be specializations of the referenced variables and relationship constants. This way, a semantic naming convention for annotating model elements with semantic labels is enforced.

Definition 11 (Semantic Label Template)

Let $\mathbb{P} = (\mathbb{T}, \mathbb{A}, \mathbb{D}, \hat{o})$ be a process knowledge base, where $= (C_P, C_D, \leq_C, R, \hat{o}, \leq_R)$. A *semantic label template* $t_S = (V, \phi, G, \tilde{a})$ over P consists of

- The set of *variables* V over the concepts C;
- Function $\phi : V \mapsto C$, which assigns to each variable $v \in V$ a concept $c \in C$, called the type of v.
- The set of relationship constants $G \subseteq R$;
- Function $y: G\gamma : G \mapsto V \times V$, which assigns to each constant $g \in G$ a pair of variables $(v, v') \in V \times V$, called the *type* of g.

Figure 5. Semantic label 1_{S1} and semantic label template t_{S1} in the semantic label repository R_{S1} over P_1

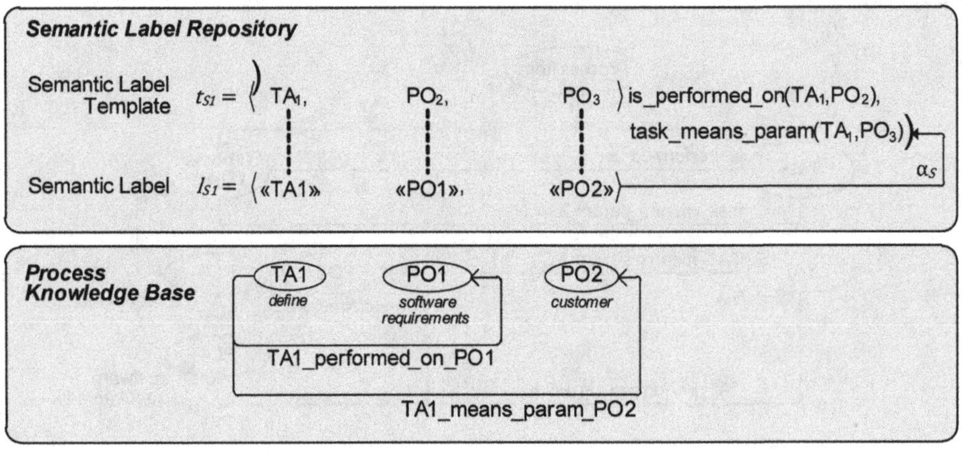

It is required that $\forall g \in G$, if $\gamma(g) = (v, v')$ then $\tau(g) = (\phi(v), \phi(v'))$.

- The semantic label $l_s = c_1, ..., c_n$ *conforms* to the semantic label template $t_S = (v_1, ..., v_m, \phi, G, \gamma)$, denoted by $l_s | = t_s$, iff $n = m$, and $\forall i \in \{1, ..., n\}$, $c_i \leq_C \phi(v_i)$, and $\forall g \in G$, there exists relationship $r \in R$ such that $r \leq_R g$ and if $(v_i, v_j) = \gamma(g)$ then $(c_i, c_j) = \tau(r)$, where $c_i, c_j \in c_1, ..., c_n$. ∎

Before illustrating a semantic label template, we now introduce a shorthand notation for semantic label templates in order to keep the amount of formal notation in text as small as possible.

Definition 12 (Shorthand Notation for Semantic Label Templates)

Let $v_1, ..., v_n$ and $r_1, ..., r_m$ be strings, and let $t_S = (V, \phi, G, \gamma)$ be a semantic label template. Then $(v_1, ..., v_n, r_1(v_{11}, v_{12}), ..., r_m(v_{m_1}, ..., v_{m_1}))$, where for all $i \in \{1, ..., m\}$, $\{v_{i_1}, v_{i_2}\} \subseteq \{v_1, ..., v_n\}$, denotes that:

- $V = v_1, ... v_n$;
- $\forall i \in \{1, ..., n\}$, $\phi(v_i) = «v_i»$;

- $G = \{\langle r_1 \rangle, ..., \langle r_m \rangle\}$;
- $\forall i \in \{1, ..., m\}$, $\gamma(\langle r_i \rangle) = (v_{i1}, v_{i2})$; ∎

For the purpose of illustration, consider the semantic label template t_{S1} over process knowledge base P_1 depicted in the top of Figure 5, which states that conforming semantic labels must be composed of a task and two process objects, such that the task is performed on the first process object and the second process object is related to this task in terms of a means parameter. The semantic label template t_{S1} defines for this purpose variable TA_1 of type «Task», and variables PO_2 and PO_3 of type «ProcessObject». The relationship constants is_performed_on(TA_1, PO_2) and task_means_param(TA_1, PO_3) state that the task bound to variable TA_1 in a conforming semantic label has to be performed on the process object bound to variable PO_2, and that the process object bound to variable PO_3 has to be related to this task in terms of a means parameter.

Also, the semantic label l_{S1} for example, depicted in the middle of Figure 5, conforms to the semantic label template t_{S1}, where task «TA_1» ("define") is bound to variable TA_1 and process objects «PO1» ("Software Requirements") and «PO2» ("Customer") are bound to variables PO_2 and PO_3 due the specific order of process items in l_{s1} and raw process items in t_{S1}. In particular, l_{s1} conforms to t_{S1} because relationships ⟨TA1_performed_on_PO1⟩ and ⟨TA1_means_param_PO2⟩ are specializations of the general ⟨is_performed_on⟩ and ⟨task_means_param ⟩ relationships, as required by the relationship constants is_performed_on (TA_1,PO_2) and task_means_param (TA_1,PO_3). Notably, the semantic label ⟪TA1⟫,⟪PO2⟫, ⟪PO1⟫does not conform to t_{S1} since ⟨is_performed_on⟩(⟪TA1⟫,⟪PO2⟫) is not a relationship in the process knowledge base, which nevertheless meets the intuition that task "define" may not be performed on process object "customer".

A semantic label repository establishes semantic naming conventions for EPC events and functions. Since semantic naming conventions for EPC functions essentially differ from semantic naming conventions for EPC events, both the semantic labels and templates in a semantic label repository are grouped according to whether they are intended for annotating EPC events or functions.

Definition 13 (Semantic Label Repository)

Let P be a process knowledge base. A *semantic label repository* $\mathbb{R}_S = (L_{SE}, L_{SF}, T_{SE}, T_{SF}, \alpha_S)$ over P consists of

- The disjoint sets of *semantic event labels* L_{SE} and *semantic function labels* L_{SF}, where $\forall l_s \in L_{SE} \bigcup L_{SF}$, l_s is a semantic label over P. The set of all semantic labels is denoted by $L_S = L_{SE} \bigcup L_{SF}$;
- The disjoint sets of *semantic event label templates* T_{SE} and *semantic function label templates* T_{SF}, where $\forall t_s \in T_{SE} \bigcup T_{SF}$, t_s is a semantic label template over P. The set of all semantic label templates is denoted by $T_S = T_{SE} \bigcup T_{SF}$;
- Function $\alpha_S : L_S \mapsto T_S$, which assigns to each semantic label $l_s \in L_s$ a semantic label

template $t_S \in T_S$. It is required that $\forall l_S \in L_S$, $t_S \vDash \alpha_S(l_S)$, and $l_S \vDash L_{SE}$ iff $\alpha_S(l_S) \in T_{SE}$. ∎

For example, the semantic label repository P_{S1} over process knowledge base P_1 depicted in Figure **5** contains the semantic label template t_{s1} and the conforming semantic label l_{S1} introduced in previous examples, which are both intended for annotating EPC functions. We refer the interested reader to the appendix for more examples of semantic label templates for both EPC functions and events.

Bridging the Semantic Gap

In this section we introduce a mechanism that facilitates to exploit the complementary benefits of using lexical and semantic labels for the modeling tasks of automated label refactoring and automated semantic annotation. The specific way in which our mechanism contributes to these modeling tasks will be discussed in more detail in the concluding section.

The key to bridge the gap between the lexical and the semantic representation of a model element is a mapping between the respective lexical and a semantic label templates, which we call *template binding*. The binding of a lexical label template to a semantic label template is not arbitrary. Instead it must account for the process meaning of lexical items as specified by the used labeling style. To underpin this claim, reconsider for example the verb-object style which requires function names to be composed of a verb followed by a noun phrase and implicitly expresses that the verb refers to a task as well as that the noun phrase refers to a process object. This labeling style informally defines a mapping of word types to raw process items which has to be met by humans when formulating a model element name in order to enforce this labeling style. Thus, a feasible binding between a lexical and a semantic label template depends on the labeling style of the respective lexical label template. In other words, labeling styles are the foundation to specify the compliance between lexical and semantic label templates, which we call a *binding policy*.

For practical application, we introduce a unified architecture called the EPC repository. Essentially, the EPC repository accommodates a lexical and a semantic label repository over a lexical and a process knowledge base and defines template bindings to achieve both human understandability and machine interpretability of model element names.

In the remainder of this section, we first present our definitions of template bindings based on binding policies to bridge the gap between lexical and semantic representation of model elements. We then present the unifying EPC repository.

Binding Policies for Lexical and Semantic Label Templates

Binding policies are the fundamental perquisite to establish a feasible binding between a lexical and a semantic label template according to a manifested labeling style. The binding between lexical and semantic label templates ensures that each lexical label annotated to a model element has assigned a representation which is interpretable for machines in terms of a semantic label. Conversely, the binding between a semantic and a lexical label ensures that the language independent representation of a model element, i.e. the semantic label, becomes comprehensible for humans.

We now define in a first step the binding of a lexical label template to a semantic label template without taking into account the role of certain binding policies. In a second step, we then show how to use binding policies in order to guideline the binding of templates according to a labeling style.

Definition 14 (Template Binding)

Given a lexical knowledge base $\mathbb{L} = (\mathbb{T}, \mathbb{A}, \mathbb{D}, \sigma)$, where $\mathbb{T} = (C_P, C_D, \leq_C, R, \tau, \leq_R)$, and a process knowledge base P, let $t_L = x_1, ..., x_n$ be a lexical label template over $\mathbb{L}$, and let $t_S = (v_1, ..., v_n, \phi, G, \gamma)$ be a semantic label template over P. A *template binding* $\beta_{(t_L | t_S)} : \{ x_i \in t_L | x_i \in C \} \mapsto \{ v_1, ..., v_m \}$ of t_L to t_s is a bijection between the concepts $\{ x_i \in t_L | x_i \in C \}$ in t_L and the variables $\{ v_1, ..., v_m \}$ of t_s. ∎

For the purpose of illustration, Figure 6 depicts the binding $\beta_{(t_{L1} | t_{S1})}$ of the lexical label template t_{L1} to the semantic label template t_{S1}, where the dashed lines from t_{L1} to t_{S1} show the particular binding of word types in t_{L1} to variables in t_{S1}. We note that $\beta_{(t_{L1} | t_{S1})}$ does not bind the lexical item 'with' to a variable in t_{S1}. The reason for this is that "with" is a preposition which relates the «ImperativeVerb» and the «SingularNoun» in the lexical label template t_{L1} and thus indicates a certain relationship between tasks represented by variable TA_1 and process objects represented by variable PO_3 in the semantic label template t_{S1}. In particular, the relationship constant task_means_param(TA_1, PO_3) in t_{S1}, which has been introduced in a previous example, specifies that there is a task_means_param› relationship between tasks represented by variable TA_1 and process objects represented by variable PO_3. The relationship constant task_means_param(TA_1, PO_3) in combination with the particular binding $\beta_{(t_{L1} | t_{S1})}$ of word types to variables therefore specifies that preposition 'with' is the lexical representation of the ‹task_means_param› relationship within the context of the lexical label template t_{L1}.

A feasible template binding is based on the binding policy of a labeling style. Reconsider the binding $\beta_{(t_{L1} | t_{S1})}$ of the lexical label template t_{L1} to the semantic label template t_{S1} which is based on the verb-object style binding policy. This bind-

Figure 6. Lexical representation of process items, template bindings and a binding policy for the verb-object style in the EPC repository B_1

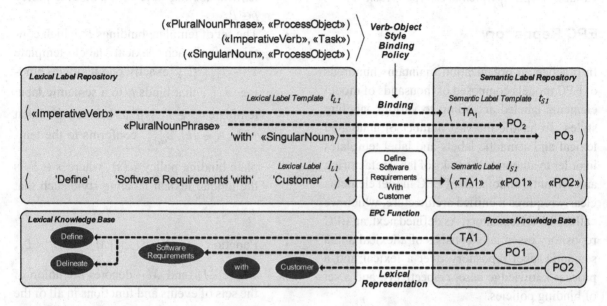

ing policy explicitly demands to bind the word type «Imperative Verb» to a «Task». In contrast, a sub style of the action-noun style for example demands to bind the word type «NounSingular» to a «Task». Such bindings between word types and sub concepts of raw process items are what we call *binding rules*, and in our context a binding policy is essentially a set of such binding rules.

Definition 15 (Template Binding Policy)

Let $\mathbb{L} = (\mathbb{T}_{\mathbb{L}}, \mathbb{A}_{\mathbb{L}}, \mathbb{D}_{\mathbb{L}}, \sigma_{\mathbb{L}})$ be a lexical knowledge base, where $\mathbb{T}_{\mathbb{L}} = (C_{P_{\mathbb{L}}}, C_{D_{\mathbb{L}}}, \leq_{C_{\mathbb{L}}}, R_{\mathbb{L}}, \tau_{\mathbb{L}}, \leq_{R_{\mathbb{L}}})$, and let $\mathbb{P} = (\mathbb{T}_{\mathbb{P}}, \mathbb{A}_{\mathbb{P}}, \mathbb{D}_{\mathbb{P}}, \sigma_{\mathbb{P}})$ be a process knowledge base, where $\mathbb{T}_{\mathbb{P}} = (C_{P_{\mathbb{P}}}, C_{D_{\mathbb{P}}}, \leq_{C_{\mathbb{P}}}, R_{\mathbb{P}}, \tau_{\mathbb{P}}, \leq_{R_{\mathbb{P}}})$. A *template binding policy* $p \subseteq \bar{C}_{\mathbb{L}} \times \bar{C}_{\mathbb{P}}$ over $\mathbb{L}$ and $\mathbb{P}$, where $\bar{C}_{\mathbb{L}} = sub(\text{«}WordType\text{»}) \subseteq C_{P_{\mathbb{L}}} \bigcup C_{D_{\mathbb{L}}}$ and $\bar{C}_{\mathbb{P}} = sub(\text{«}ProcessItem\text{»}) \subseteq C_{P_{\mathbb{P}}} \bigcup C_{D_{\mathbb{P}}}$, is a set of pairs of concepts $\{(c_{\mathbb{L}_1}, c_{\mathbb{P}_1}), \dots, (c_{\mathbb{L}_n}, c_{\mathbb{P}_n})\}$, called *binding rules*.

The template binding $\beta_{(t_L|t_S)}$ of the lexical label template $t_L = x_1, \dots, x_n$ over $\mathbb{L}$ to the se-

mantic label template $t_S = (v_1, \dots, v_n, \phi, G, \gamma)$ over P *conforms* to the template binding policy p over $\mathbb{L}$ and P iff for all $c_j \in \{x_i \in t_L | x_i \in C_{P_{\mathbb{L}}} \bigcup C_{D_{\mathbb{L}}}\}$, $\left(c_j, \phi\left(\beta\left(c_j\right)\right)\right) \in p$. ∎

For the purpose of illustration, consider the template binding policy over the lexical knowledge base L_1 and the process knowledge base P_1 depicted in the top of Figure 6. If we use p_1 to denote this template binding policy then the binding rules of p_1 specify that the word type «Imperative Verb» in lexical label templates must be bound to variables of type «Task» in semantic label templates and analogously that word types «PluralNoun-Phrase» and «Singular Noun» must be bound to variables of type «ProcessObject». For example, the binding $\beta_{(t_{L1}|t_{S1})}$ of the lexical label template t_{L1} to the semantic label template t_{S1} of our running example conforms to the template binding policy p_1. If the binding rule (‹Imperative Verb›, ‹Task›) in p_1 is for example replaced by the binding rule (‹SingularNoun›,‹Task›), which is common for the action-noun labeling style, then binding $\beta_{(t_{L1}|t_{S1})}$ does not conform to p_1, since word type «Imperative Verb» in t_{L1} is bound to variable TA_1 in t_{S1} which is of type «Task».

EPC Repository

In practice an organization maintains hundreds of EPC models composed of thousands of model elements labeled according to various labeling styles. To handle the vast number of annotated lexical and semantic labels and label templates in order to automate the tasks of label refactoring and semantic annotation of EPC model elements clearly requires a unified architecture, which we call the EPC Repository. As defined next, an EPC repository essentially consists of a lexical and a semantic label repository over a lexical and a process knowledge base, respectively, and a set of binding policies.

Definition 16 (EPC Repository)

An EPC Repository $B=(E, \mathbb{L}, \mathbb{P}, \chi, \mathbb{PL}_p, \mathbb{S}_{,p_\omega}, B, \lambda$ *cons*ists of the set of EPC models E;

- A lexical knowledge base $\mathbb{L} = (\mathbb{T}_\mathbb{L}, \mathbb{A}_\mathbb{L}, \mathbb{D}_\mathbb{L}, \sigma_\mathbb{L})$;
- A process knowledge base $\mathbb{P} = (\mathbb{T}_\mathbb{P}, \mathbb{A}_\mathbb{P}, \mathbb{D}_\mathbb{P}, \sigma_\mathbb{P})$;
- Function $\chi : sub(\text{«ProcessItem»}) \mapsto P(ext(\text{«LexicalItem»}))$, which assigns to each concept $c \in sub(\text{«ProcessItem»})$ in T_p a set of individuals $\{l_1, \dots, l_k\} \subseteq ext(\text{«LexicalItem»})$ of A_L, called the *lexical representations* of c.
- A lexical label repository $\mathbb{R}_L = (L_{LE}, L_{LF}, T_{LE}, T_{LF}, S, \alpha_L)$ over $\mathbb{L}$;
- A semantic label repository $\mathbb{R}_S = (L_{SE}, L_{SF}, T_{SE}, T_{SF}, \alpha_S)$ over P;
- The set of template binding policies P, where $\forall p \in P$, p is a binding policy over $\mathbb{L}$ and P;

- Function $\omega : S \mapsto P$, which assigns to each lexical labeling style $s \in S$ a binding policy $p \in P$;
- The set of template bindings B, which contains for each lexical label template $t_L \in T_{LE} \bigcup T_{LF}$ exactly one template binding $\beta_{(t_L|t_S)}$ that binds t_L to a semantic label template $t_S \in T_{SE} \bigcup T_{SF}$. It is required that $\forall \beta_{(t_L|t_S)} \in B$, $\beta_{(t_L|t_S)}$ conforms to the template binding policy $\omega(\bar{s})$, where $\bar{s} \in S$ is the unique lexical labeling style such that $t_L \in \bar{s}$.

- Function $\lambda : \bar{M}_E \bigcup \bar{M}_F \mapsto L_L \times L_S$, where $\bar{M}_E$ and $\bar{M}_F$ denotes the union of the sets of events and functions in all of the EPC models in E, which assigns to each function or event $m \in \bar{M}_E \bigcup \bar{M}_F$ a pair $(l_L, l_S) \in L_L \times L_S$ of a lexical label and a semantic label. It is required that $\forall m \in \bar{M}_E \bigcup \bar{M}_F, \bar{l}_L \in L_{LE}$ and $\bar{l}_S \in L_{SE}$ iff $m \in \bar{M}_E$, and $\beta_{\left(\bar{t}_L | \bar{t}_S\right)} \in B$, where

$$(\bar{l}_L, \bar{l}_S) = \lambda(m), \quad \bar{t}_L = \alpha_L(\bar{l}_L), \quad \text{and}$$

$$\bar{t}_S = \alpha_S(\bar{l}_S). \qquad \blacksquare$$

Essentially, an EPC repository reconciles the lexical and the semantic representations of EPC model elements on the level of the lexical and process knowledge bases and also on the level of the lexical and the semantic label repositories.

In particular, the EPC repository reconciles the process knowledge base and the lexical knowledge base by establishing a connection between the process items in the process knowledge base and distinguished sets of lexical items in the lexical knowledge base, called lexical representations (cf. function χ in Definition Definition 16).

The EPC repository reconciles the lexical and semantic label repository by specifying the particular pairs of a lexical and a semantic label which represent the same EPC model element (cf. function λ in Definition Definition 16). In order to achieve a consistent annotation of EPC model elements with lexical and semantic labels, the EPC repository formulates two constraints. First, it is required that EPC functions are exclusively annotated with lexical and semantic function labels and analogously that EPC events are exclusively annotated with lexical and semantic event labels. Second, it is required that a model element is only annotated with a lexical and a semantic label if their templates are bound to one another.

RELATED WORK

The research reported in this work is related to two major streams of related work: semantic business process management *(SBPM)* and enforcement of naming conventions for model elements.

Core aspect of the *semantic business process management (SBPM)* vision is linking process models and ontologies also referred to as the approach to ontology-based semantic annotation of process models. The SBPM vision is to bridge the semantic gap in business process management that is a better automation of the bi-directional translation between business level and technical level by using a set of ontologies, and to use machine reasoning for carrying out or supporting the translation tasks between the two spheres (Hepp et al. 2005). Ontology-based semantic annotation of process models can be differentiated into *metamodel-annotation* and *model-annotation*. Metamodel annotation is concerned with annotating the metamodel constructs of a specific process modeling language while model annotation aims at an ontology-based attribution of terms used by model elements. Metamodel-level annotation requires process ontologies either designed for a particular process modeling language or process

ontologies used to align the heterogeneous metamodels of process modeling languages such as Business Process Modeling Ontology (BPMO) which provides an universal ontology for the Business Process Modeling Notation (BPMN) and EPC process modeling language (Dimitrov et al. 2007). Model-annotation requires domain ontologies which define concepts and relationships to facilitate a shared common understanding of used terminology in a business domain. One might use domain ontologies defined in the context of the MIT Process handbook (Malone et al. 1999), the TOVE (Toronto Virtual Enterprise) ontologies (Fox 1992) or the Enterprise Ontology (Uschold et al. 1995).

Most approaches target a fully-fledged semantic description of process models by realizing a metamodel and model-annotation. For example, a comprehensive study towards semantic annotation for process models has been conducted by Lin et al. (2006). Based on a broad examination of available annotation approaches, the *Process Semantic Annotation Model (PSAM)* has been developed which abstracts from a certain process modeling language. Other approaches gear towards particular process description languages by providing semantic language extensions. Examples are the approaches by Thomas & Fellmann (2007) (EPC modeling language), by Koschmider & Ried (2005) (Petri-Nets), or by Abramowicz et al. (2007) (BPMN). There exists, however a significant research gap regarding model annotation, in particular the conceptualization of model element names to account the process meaning of terms and their dependencies. To the best of our knowledge, apart from the approach proposed by Born et al. (2007) and the MIT Handbook (Malone et al. 1999), we observed that while most domain ontologies used for model-level annotation are of potential benefit they suffer from an explicit conceptualization of task, process object, and state terminology to specify the process meaning of model elements. The domain ontology introduced in this work explicitly treats this issue in detail.

In essence, it provides a thoroughly formalized foundation for semantic model annotation by introducing semantic labels and semantic label templates captured by a semantic label repository. The idea introducing semantic label templates in a formalized manner is inspired by the work of Rolland & Achour, (1998). They employ so-called *semantic patterns* to extract a use case model from ambiguous textual use case descriptions.

The importance of a standardized labeling of model elements has been recognized as essential impact on understandability for humans and process model quality in general (Mendling & Reijers 2008). Only few approaches especially emerging from German speaking area suggest standardized phrase structures. For example, Rosemann (1995:p.201 et seq.) and (Schütte R., 1998) Schütte (1998:p.189 et seq.) made pioneer contributions to naming conventions. More recently, Mendling, Reijers, & Aalst (2009) introduce informal process modeling guidelines which build on strong empirical insights to ensure the modeling of intuitive and easy to comprehend process models. Such informal guidelines are vital recommendations for novices and non-experts in practice.

A major limitation, however, concerns compliance checking, i.e. there is a lack of mechanisms which support automated compliance verification with manifested naming guidelines to ensure enforcement. A serious approach of methodological support to the definition of naming guidelines and to ensure their enforcement during modeling is addressed by the work of by Becker et al. (2009). They formalize naming conventions by combining domain thesauri and phrase structure conventions based on a linguistic grammar. Textual descriptions for model element labels entered by process modeler are validated against phrase structure conventions via linguistic parsing. In this way compliance with modeling conventions is ensured. In case of violation, the approach suggests valid phrases.

While such approaches tend to enforce naming conventions based on the linguistic perspective,

our approach encounters the enforcement of naming conventions from the semantic perspective. We argue that a process designer should not be burdened with linguistic requirements when labeling model elements to enforce naming conventions. Actually, a process modeler has domain knowledge in terms of tasks, process objects and state information in mind when specifying names for model elements rather than verbs or nouns inflected according to a grammatical category. A major novelty of our approach is to facilitate an automated generation of standardized names to enforce manifested naming conventions. This is achieved by the introduction of bindings for label templates and of binding policies to bridge the gap between linguistic and process knowledge.

The presented approach is a revised and extended version of the studies reported by Bögl et al. (2008). One of the objectives of this work was to introduce a comprehensive formalization to set the foundation for future research directions. Also, this required normative specifications for the lexical and process knowledge base. In realm of this work, some major revisions of the originally proposed process knowledge base have been made. In particular, domain specific process knowledge is encoded in terms of concepts instead of individuals. The reason for this was to attach individuals to concrete process cases or process instances. Further, we adjusted the conceptualization of parameters. We recognized to gain more expressive power of parameters when expressing the meaning between process objects and a task via different relationship types rather than introducing different conceptualizations. Beyond that, we introduced the notions lexical label in conjunction with lexical label templates and semantic label in conjunction with semantic label templates. Semantic labels and templates extend the idea of semantic pattern templates in that relationships between process items can be included when specifying the process meaning of a model element. Finally, the enriched expressive power of semantic label templates motivate to introduce bindings for label templates and binding policies which make the previously proposed concept of analysis rules obsolete.

CONCLUSION

Lexical and semantic labels are of high practical relevance for process designers when facing the tasks of naming model elements from scratch, semantically annotating model elements, or refactoring names of existing model elements. Subsequently, we illustrate how these modeling tasks are supported by our approach towards an EPC repository.

The traditional way of naming model elements from scratch requires a process designer in a first step to keep in mind a certain combination of a process object and a task or state, and to formulate a model element name that conveys the process meaning according to some labeling style in a second step. In contrast to the traditional approach towards naming model elements, the availability of a lexical and semantic label repository eases this modeling task significantly due to the following reason. Semantic labels inspire process designers to use process knowledge rather than lexical knowledge. If a semantic label which expresses the desired process meaning is available in the semantic label repository, a corresponding lexical label and thus the model element name can be automatically generated on basis of one of the lexical label templates in a particular labeling style associated to the semantic labels' template and the lexical representations of process items in the semantic label template.

In case that no semantic label which expresses the desired process meaning is available, the process designer has to create a new semantic label based on a common semantic label template. After selecting a common semantic label template, the process designer has to bind the variables in the template to domain specific process items by exploring the process knowledge base. This task

can be executed very efficiently since process modelers are only confronted with domain specific process items which are automatically preselected on basis of the relationships specified by the semantic label template. Consider for example the labeling of EPC function "Check Requirements". To identify for example the process item ‹‹Requirements››, the process designer may query the process knowledge base for a list of all available tasks and select the task ‹‹Check››. Based on this selection, those process objects which are related to task ‹‹Check›› by the O ‹is_performed_on› relationship will be automatically preselected. The actual generation of the model element name then follows the procedure illustrated before.

We discuss next how the task of automated semantic annotation benefits from bridging the gap between informal and formal representation. To facilitate automated semantic annotation requires the annotation of model elements with lexical labels as a prerequisite. To automatically create a lexical label for a given model element name in turn requires an analysis of the parts of speech used in the model element name in order to determine the applied labeling style. The labeling style a model element name adheres to is the clue for extracting the process meaning of model element names. In particular, the knowledge about the word types of lexical items in conjunction with the knowledge about the correspondence of word types and raw process items specified by binding policies enables to automatically determine the process items that constitute the semantic label to be generated. Consider for example the lexical label with the individuals 'Check' and 'Requirement', and assume that the binding policy associated to this lexical label's template states that 'Check' is bound to a ≪Task≫ and that 'Requirements' is bound to a ≪Process Object≫. Then, it is required to locate sub concepts of a task and a process object whose lexical representations correspond to the individuals 'Check' and 'Requirement'. In the exceptional case where no such concepts can be located, the process knowledge base needs to be populated with new domain concepts.

Recently, the refactoring of model elements has gained great attention in research and practice with the key intention to reformulate model element names potentially affected by ambiguity into a lexical representation that is easy to comprehend by humans. The annotation of model elements with semantic labels establishes a wide range of different refactoring possibilities. We briefly highlight a major objective which is concerned with the enforcement of a preferred labeling style which requires the transformation of model element names into other lexical representations implementing a chosen labeling style. Due to the separation of semantic and lexical representations and the availability of template bindings based on a chosen labeling style, the feasibility of reformulating model element names is given. To give an idea, consider the function "Checking of Requirements" in action-noun style which should be reformulated to "Check Requirements" in verb-object style. Both model element names are represented by the semantic label consisting of the process items ≪Check≫ and ≪Requirements≫. In order to enforce the verb-object style it is solely required to extract a lexical label based on a lexical label template that implements the verb-object style.

In this work, we exploited the complementary benefits for the modeling tasks automated semantic annotation and label refactoring when bridging the gap between approaches for improving human understandability and approaches for achieving machine interpretability of model element names. Based on the introduced approach, future research addresses the specification of algorithms that automate the modeling tasks label refactoring and semantic annotation.

REFERENCES

Aalst, W. (1997). *Verification of workflow nets* (pp. 407–426). ICATPN.

Aalst, W. v., Hee, K. V., Kees, P. D., Hee, M., De, R. R., Rigter, J., et al. (2002). *Workflow management: models, methods, and systems.*

Abramowicz, W., Filipowska, A., Kaczmarek, M., & Kaczmarek, T. (2007). *Semantically enhanced business process modelling notation.* SBPM.

Basili, R., Pennacchiotti, M., & Zanzotto, F. (2005). *Language learning and ontology engineering: An integrated model for the Semantic Web.* 2nd Meaning Workshop. Trento, Italy, February 2005.

Becker, J., Delfmann, P., Herwig, S., Lis, L., & Stein, A. (2009). *Towards increased comparability of conceptual models - Enforcing naming conventions through domain thesauri and linguistic grammars.* 17th European Conference on Information Systems (ECIS 2009).

Bögl, A., Schrefl, M., Pomberger, G., & Weber, N. (2008a). *Semantic annotation of EPC models in engineering domains to facilitate an automated identification of common modelling practices. ICEIS* (pp. 155–171). Springer Verlag.

Bögl, A., Schrefl, M., Pomberger, G., & Weber, N. (2008b). *Semantic annotation of EPC models in engineering domains by employing semantic patterns* (pp. 106–115). ICEIS.

Born, M., Dörr, F., & Weber, I. (2007). *User-friendly semantic annotation in business process modeling* (pp. 260–271). WISE Workshops.

Bornstein, D. D. (1984). *An introduction to transformational grammar. University Press of America.* TM Inc.

Boudewijn, B. F., Mendling, J., & Aalst, W. M. (2006). *Structural patterns for soundness of business process models* (pp. 116–128). EDOC.

Dehnert, J., & Zimmermann, A. (2005). On the suitability of correctness criteria for business process models. *Business Process Management, 3rd International Conference* (pp. 386-391).

Dimitrov, M., Simov, A., Stein, S., & Konstantinov, M. (2007). *A BPMO based semantic business process modelling environment*. SBPM.

Fox, M. S. (1992). *The TOVE Project: Towards a common-sense model of the enterprise* (pp. 25–34). IEA/AIE.

Grimm, S., Hitzler, P., & Abecker, A. (2007). *Knowledge representation and ontologies - Logic, ontologies and Semantic Web languages*. Berlin, Germany: Springer.

Gruhn, V., & Laue, R. (2006). *How style checking can improve business process models* (pp. 47–56). MSVVEIS.

Hepp, M., Leenheer, P. d., Moor, A. d., & Sure, Y. (2008). *Ontology management: Semantic Web, Semantic Web services, and business applications* (p. 7). Springer.

Hepp, M., Leymann, F., Domingue, J., Wahler, A., & Fensel, D. (2005). *Semantic business process management: A vision towards using Semantic Web services for business process management. ICEBE* (pp. 535–540). IEEE Computer Society.

Keller, G., Nüttgens, M., & Scheer, A.-W. (1992). Semantische Prozessmodellierung auf der Grundlage Ereignisgesteuerter Prozessketten. In A.-W. Scheer (Ed.), *Veröffentlichungen des Instituts für Wirtschaftsinformatik, Heft 89, Saarbrücken*. Retrieved from http://www.iwi.uni-sb.de/Download/iwihefte/heft89.pdf

Kiepuszewski, B., Hofstede, A. H., & Bussler, C. (2000). On structured workflow modelling. *Conference on Advanced Information Systems Engineering*, (pp. 431-445).

Koschmider, A., & Ried, D. (2005). Semantische Annotation von Petri-Netzen. *Proceedings des 12. Workshops Algorithmen und Werkzeuge für Petrinetze (AWPN'05)*, (pp. 66-71).

Laue, R., & Mendling, J. (2009). Structuredness and its significance for correctness of process models. *Information Systems and E-Business Management*. 10.1007/s10257-009-0120-x

Lautenbacher, F., Bauer, B., & Seitz, C. (2008). Semantic business process modeling - Benefits and capability. In K. Hinkelman (Ed.), *AAAI 2008 Stanfort Spring Symposium - AI Meets Business Rules and Process Management (AIBR)*. Stanford University, California, USA, March 26-28, (pp. 71-76).

Leopold, H., Sergey, S., & Mendling, J. (2009). On labeling quality in business process models. *Proceedings of the 8th GI-Workshop Geschäftsprozessmanagement mit Ereignisgesteuerten Prozessketten (EPK), Berlin, Germany*.

Lin, Y., Strasunskas, D., Hakkarainen, S., Krogstie, J., & Solvberg, A. (2006). Semantic annotation framework to manage semantic heterogeneity of process models. *CAiSE*, (pp. 433-446).

Malone, T., Crowston, K., Lee, J., Pentland, B., Dellarocas, C., Wyner, G., et al. (1999). Towards a handbook of organisational processes. *Magement Science, 45*, 425-443.

Malone, T. W., Crowston, K., & Herman, G. A. (Eds.). (2003). *Organizing business knowledge: The MIT process handbook* (1st ed.). The MIT Press.

Mendling, J., & Aalst, W. M. (2007). Formalization and verification of EPCs with OR-joins based on state and context. *CAiSE*, (pp. 439-453).

Mendling, J., Reijers, H., & Recker, J. (2010). Activity labeling in process modeling: Empirical insights and recommendations. *Information Systems, 35*, 467–482. doi:10.1016/j.is.2009.03.009

Mendling, J., & Reijers, H. A. (2008). *The impact of activity labeling styles on process model quality* (pp. 117–128). SIGSAND-EUROPE.

Mendling, J., Reijers, H. A., & Aalst, W. v. (2009). Seven process modeling guidelines (7PMG). *Information and Software Technology, 52*(2), 127–136. doi:10.1016/j.infsof.2009.08.004

Miller, G. A. (1995). WordNet: A lexical database for English. *Communications of the ACM, 38,* 39–41. doi:10.1145/219717.219748

Nitzsche, J., Wutke, D., & van Lessen, T. (2007). *An ontology for executable business processes.* SBPM.

Pustejovsky, J., & Boguraev, B. (1993). Lexical knowledge representation and natural language processing. *Artificial Intelligence, 63,* 193–223. doi:10.1016/0004-3702(93)90017-6

Rolland, C., & Achour, C. B. (1998). Guiding the construction of textual use case specifications. *Data & Knowledge Engineering, 25,* 125–160. doi:10.1016/S0169-023X(97)86223-4

Rosemann, M. (1995). *Komplexitätsmanagement in Prozessmodellen.* PhD-thesis.

Schütte, R. (1998). *Grundsätze ordnungsmäßiger Referenzmodellierung. Konstruktion konfigurations- und anpassungsorientierter Modelle.* Wiesbaden, Germany: Gabler.

Schütte, R., & Totthowe, T. (1998). The guidelines of modeling as an approach to enhance the quality of information models. In T. W. Ling, S. Ram, M. L. Lee (Eds.), *Conceptual Modeling - ER '98. 17 th International ER-Conference Singapore, November 16-19, 1998.* (pp. 240-254). Berlin.

Thomas, O., & Fellmann, M. (2007). Semantic EPC: Enhancing process modeling using ontology languages . In Hepp, M., Hinkelmann, K., Karagiannis, D., Klein, R., & Nenad, S. (Eds.), *SBPM. 251. Retrieved from CEUR-WS.org*

Thomas, O., & Fellmann, M. (2007). Semantic EPC: Enhancing process modeling using ontology languages. *SBPM, 251.* Retrieved from CEUR-WS.org

Thomas, O., & Fellmann, M. (2009). Semantic process modeling - Design and implementation of an ontology-based representation of business processes. *Wirtschaftsinformatik,* 51–56, 206–518.

Uschold, M., King, M., Moralee, S., & Zorgios, Y. (1995). The enterprise ontology. *The Knowledge Engineering Review, 13,* 31–89. doi:10.1017/S0269888998001088

van der Aalst, W., Hofstede, A., & Weske, M. (2003). Business process management: A survey. *Proceedings of the 1st International Conference on Business Process Management, LNCS 2678* (pp. 1-12). Springer-Verlag.

Vanhatalo, J., Völzer, H., & Leymann, F. (2007). *Faster and more focused control-flow analysis for business process models through SESE decomposition* (pp. 43–55). ICSOC.

ENDNOTES

[1]   Currently, the WordNet Database includes about 147,000 entries (retrieved from http://wordnet.princeton.edu/wordnet/man/wnstats.7WN.html, 11/2010)

[2]   The MIT-Process handbook defines eight generic verbs: 'Create', 'Modify', 'Preserve', 'Destroy', 'Combine', 'Separate', and 'Mange'. *"The first four are actions that can occur for any object; the next two can occur when multiple objects are involved; the final two verbs are informational actions that could have been included under the earlier verbs."* (Malone T., et al. 1999)

APPENDIX A: ABBREVIATIONS

Process items		Word Types		Relationships		Labeling Styles	
TA:	Task	*VI:*	ImperativeVerb	*ipo:*	is_performed_on	*V:*	Verb-Object
STA:	Achieved State	*NS:*	SingularNoun	*ttp:*	task_target_parameter	*A:*	Action-Noun
STT:	Triggering State		*S:*			Sin-gular-Noun,	SingularNounPhrase
isf:	is_state_for			*PO:*	Process Object	*P:*	
		Plural-Noun,	PluralNounPhrase	*stp:*	state_target_parameter		
		N:	S, P				
		AA:	Adjective				
		AP:	PastParticiple				

APPENDIX B: TEMPLATE BINDING POLICIES

Verb-Object Style	Action-Noun Style	Object-Adjective Style
(«VI», «TA»)	(«VG», «TA»)	(«N», «PO»)
(«N», «PO»)	(«NS», «TA»)	(«AA», «STT»), («AA», «STA»)
	(«N», «PO»)	(«AP», «STT»), («AP», «STA»)
		(«P», «PO»)
		(«S», «PO»)

APPENDIX C: LEXICAL AND SEMANTIC TEMPLATES

Template bindings are stated as sets of pairs of the form (w_i, v_j) which denote that the i-th word type in the lexical label template is bound the j-th variable in the semantic label template stated directly above. Also, unless stated explicitly beneath a lexical label template, the binding of word types to variables in the semantic label template corresponds to the sequence in which the word types and variables are stated.

Lexical and Semantic Label Templates for EPC Functions		
	Template	Example EPC function name
	$t_{SF1} = \left(\mathrm{TA}_1, \mathrm{PO}_2, \mathrm{ipo}\left(\mathrm{TA}_1, \mathrm{PO}_1\right)\right)$	
V	$t_{LF1} = \text{«VI»}, \text{«N»}$	"Identify Requirements"
A	$t_{LF2} = \text{«VG»}, \text{«N»}$	"Identifying Requirements"
A	$t_{LF3} = \text{«NS»}, \text{'of'}, \text{«N»}$	"Identification of Requirements"
A	$t_{LF4} = \text{«N»}, \text{«NS»}$ $\beta_{(t_{LF4}\sharp t_{SF1})} = \{(w_1, v_2), (w_2, v_1)\}$	"Requirements Identification"
	$t_{SF2} = \left(\mathrm{TA}_1, \mathrm{PO}_1, \mathrm{PO}_2, \mathrm{ipo}\left(\mathrm{TA}_1, \mathrm{PO}_1\right), \mathrm{ttp}\left(\mathrm{TA}_1, \mathrm{PO}_2\right)\right)$	
V	$t_{LF5} = \text{«VI»}, \text{«N»}, \text{'for'}, \text{«N»}$	"Define Quality Goal for Project Plan"
A	$t_{LF6} = \text{«VG»}, \text{«N»}, \text{'for'}, \text{«N»}$	"Defining Quality Goal for …"
A	$t_{LF7} = \text{«NS»}, \text{'of'}, \text{«N»}, \text{'for'}, \text{«N»}$	"Definition Of Quality Goal for …"
A	$t_{LF8} = \text{«N»}, \text{«NS»}, \text{'for'}, \text{«N»}$ $\beta_{(t_{LF8}\sharp t_{SF2})} = \{(w_1, v_2), (w_2, v_1), (w_3, v_3)\}$	"Quality Goal Definition for …"
	$t_{SF3} = \left(\mathrm{TA}_1, \mathrm{PO}_1, \mathrm{PO}_2, \mathrm{ipo}\left(\mathrm{TA}_1, \mathrm{PO}_1\right), \mathrm{ttp}\left(\mathrm{TA}_1, \mathrm{PO}_2\right)\right)$	
V	$t_{LF9} = \text{«NS»}, \text{«N»}, \text{'and'}, \text{«N»}$	"Review Risks And Measures"
A	$t_{LF10} = \text{«VG»}, \text{«N»}, \text{'and'}, \text{«N»}$	"Reviewing Risks And Measures"
A	$t_{LF11} = \text{«NS»}, \text{'of'}, \text{«N»}, \text{'and'}, \text{«N»}$	"Review Of Risks And Of Measures"
A	$t_{LF12} = \text{«N»}, \text{'and'}, \text{«N»}, \text{«NS»}$ $\beta_{(t_{LF12}\sharp t_{SF3})} = \{(w_1, v_2), (w_2, v_3), (w_3, v_1)\}$	"Risks and Measures Review"

APPENDIX C: CONTINUED

Lexical and Semantic Label Templates for EPC Events in the Object-Adjective Style	
Template	Example EPC event name
$t_{SE1} = \left(PO_1, STA_2, isf\left(STA_2, PO_1\right)\right)$	
$t_{LE1} = \langle\langle N\rangle\rangle, \langle\langle AA\rangle\rangle$	"Requirements Identified" "Development Risk High"
$t_{LE2} = \langle\langle P\rangle\rangle, \,'are\,', \langle\langle AA\rangle\rangle$	"Requirements are Checked"
$t_{LE3} = \langle\langle S\rangle\rangle, \,'is\,', \langle\langle AA\rangle\rangle$	"Development Risk is High"
$t_{SE2} = \left(PO_1, PO_2, STA_3, isf\left(STA_3, PO_1\right), stp\left(STA_3, PO_2\right)\right)$	
$t_{LE4} = \langle\langle N\rangle\rangle, \,'for\,', \langle\langle N\rangle\rangle, \langle\langle AA\rangle\rangle$	"Goals for Project Plan Defined"
$t_{SE3} = \left(PO_1, PO_2, STT_3, isf\left(STT_3, PO_1\right), stp\left(STT_3, PO_2\right)\right)$	
$t_{LE5} = \langle\langle N\rangle\rangle, \,'for\,', \langle\langle N\rangle\rangle, \,'to\,', \,'be\,', \langle\langle AP\rangle\rangle$	"Goals for Project Plan To Be Defined"

Chapter 12
Semantic Annotation of Business Process Templates

Yun Lin
Agresso, Norway

Darijus Strasunskas
Norwegian University of Science and Technology, Norway

ABSTRACT

Process models represent valuable resources for integration and alignment of business processes. Nowadays, due to networked business and tighter integration along a value chain, the number of enterprises that need to orchestrate their workflows is increasing. These circumstances urge companies to improve management of process models and templates. Machine-readable and interoperable semantics of the process templates facilitate retrieval and reuse. However, the heterogeneity of both model representations and modeling languages makes it difficult to retrieve, comprehend, compare, and reuse the templates. Therefore, in this chapter we elaborate on the semantic annotation of process model templates consisting of three basic parts: meta-model, domain, and goal annotations. For this purpose, we use ontologies representing generic constructs of process models, concepts from a business domain, and business goals. We illustrate application of the approach in OWL and provide a case study with exemplary semantic queries.

INTRODUCTION

Business needs and technology advancement open up for business collaboration and knowledge sharing across different enterprises. Significant efforts are put on aligning and integrating their

DOI: 10.4018/978-1-60960-126-3.ch012

business processes that is typically achieved through workflow integration or Web services orchestration. Process models are often used to model, document, execute and analyze workflows and procedures. Moreover, in business integration, legacy process models are reusable assets, providing a documented knowledge about the processes used by particular organizations.

The legacy models can be retrieved as process templates, thereby facilitating integration of process models. The process templates provide core information about the processes used by organizations. To be useful and usable, retrieval of the process templates should be efficient and effective opening for an easy transformation into target process models across different organizations. One critical issue in this application is the interoperability (Sheth, 1998) of heterogeneous models due to diverse business jargon and different modeling languages. Heterogeneity leads to problems retrieving knowledge about process models and reusing it when integrating them.

The interoperability problem can be decomposed into two levels: a model and a meta-model level. Typically, there are two interoperability problems at the model level: 1) synonyms – different terms are used for the same concept in two models, e.g., 'Client' vs. 'Customer', 'purchase' vs. 'buy'; 2) mismatch of conceptualization, e.g., 'City' as a class vs. 'City' as a property, 'finish' as an action vs. 'finish' as a state. Similar problems also occur at the meta-model level: 1) mismatch of modeling constructs (terminology), e.g., 'agent' in ActionWorkflow (Medina-Mora, Winograd, Flores et al., 1992) vs. 'actor' in CPR (Core Plan Representation) (Pease & Carrico, 1997); 2) mismatch of conceptualization, e.g., 'activity' is an atomic concept in PSL (Process Specific Language) (Schlenoff, Gruninger, Tissot et al., 2000) while it is decomposable in WooRKS (Ader, Lu, Pons et al., 1994).

A common semantic representation of models is needed to solve the above discussed interoperability problems. Therefore, we have developed an approach to annotate process templates with both domain information as well as common process modeling constructs. The underlying assumption is that process modeling languages have sufficient similarities to be sensibly mapped to abstract common constructs. Our approach consists of a common semantic annotation structure for the process templates made of three parts: meta-model annotation, model content annotation and model

goal annotation. Within this structure, semantic heterogeneity at the meta-model level is reconciled by means of mapping the process modeling constructs to the proposed process ontology. The latter is made of the most essential concepts of process modeling languages. At the model level, annotations are made by building semantic relationships between model contents and domain ontologies. The domain ontology is a conceptual model that standardizes the representation of the conceptualization of a certain business domain. The ontology is usually built based on industrial standards of a particular domain. At the pragmatic level, goal annotations are included to encode the purpose and intended use of process models. There business goals are represented in a goal ontology, and linked to fragments of the process model. We have chosen OWL (Web Ontology Language), originally proposed by McGuinness & Harmelen (2004) for semantic annotation. In particular, we have implemented the approach using OWL DL (Description Logic) due to its balanced power of expressiveness and inference.

In the remainder of this chapter we elaborate on our approach. First, we detail an overall structure for the semantic annotation of process templates, where a general process ontology and a set of common process template modeling morphemes are presented. Then, we illustrate application of the semantic annotation structure to a process template transforming the annotated process template into a semantic enriched model in OWL. A case study and exemplary semantic queries are elaborated before we conclude this chapter.

SEMANTIC ANNOTATION STRUCTURE FOR PROCESS TEMPLATES

Semantic annotation of a process model should abstract and communicate (a) the meaning of different modeling constructs, (b) different domain terminology and (c) purpose of the process model. A systematic and comprehensive annotation is a key to enabling semantic interoperability of process templates. Consequently, below we elaborate on meta-model, domain and goal annotations of process model templates.

Meta-Model Annotation

Meta-model annotation provides semantic harmony of modeling languages. Different model constructs are semantically abstracted and mapped to a set of model morphemes for the process template. For example, 'actor' in one process modeling language is semantically equal to 'agent' in another process modeling language. However, in the set of model morphemes for the process template, the construct 'actor' is defined as a common modeling construct. 'Agent' or 'actor' defined in the specific modeling languages are annotated using the agreed construct 'actor'.

As a common reference point, the process ontology provides type level concepts of process modeling. The type level is grounded at the instance-level that provides semantics (Aitken & Curtis, 2002). At the type level, we introduce General Process Ontology (GPO) to provide a common understanding reference of different modeling languages, the meta-model annotation maps the modeling constructs of modeling languages to their concepts in GPO (General Process Ontology).

Typically, a process template is an abstracted form of a specific process model represented in a particular process modeling language. In order to represent templates with common understandable structures, a neutral process template modeling language is derived following our GPO. Comparing with other process modeling languages, the Process Template Modeling Language (PTML) covers the common and core constructs used in most process modeling languages and also simplifies the structures of models with several modeling constructs. Although it may appear to be a new process modeling language, it is not created for that purpose. It is used to represent the retrieval results of process templates independently of specific modeling tools. Application of GPO and PTML are discussed later.

General Process Ontology (GPO) is based on the BWW (Bunge-Wand-Weber) ontology (Wand & Weber, 1995). BWW ontological constructs provide semantic basis of meta-models of conceptual models. The BWW ontology can be used as the upper level ontology since it is initially built from a set of core constructs in the computer science and information systems field (Wand & Weber, 1990), especially the core concepts used in conceptual modeling, namely *Thing, Property, State, Law, Event, Process, Transformation* and *System*. Although it is not initially process-oriented, some concepts are related with dynamic parts of information systems, such as Event, State, Process and Transformation which we call the process concepts. They are major process concepts which can be represented by most process modeling languages (PMLs) such as PSL (Schlenoff, Gruninger, Tissot et al., 2000), TOVE (Fox, 1992), PIF-CORE (Lee, Grunninger, Jin et al., 1996), CPR (Pease & Carrico, 1997), APM (Carlsen, 1997), EEML (Krogstie & Jørgensen, 2004), BPMN (White, 2004), etc. Through investigation of those PMLs, we adapt the BWW ontology into GPO and represent in UML (Figure 1).

Activity is used in most process ontology or modeling languages. In a set of process modeling languages, *Activity* is composed of events or operations. Comparing with *Activity*, construct *Event* is a detailed analysis concept. According to Bunge (1977), processes may be either chains or trees of events. From this perspective, *Activity* is a synonym of *Process*. However, we also observe that *Process* is seldom a construct or just a package construct in most process modeling languages because it is obvious that a process model describes processes. Since in a business or enterprise process template we do not need to concentrate on the detailed sequence of *Event*, hence, a construct *Activity* is used in our general process ontology. An activity may be an atomic activity or a composed activity represented by the aggregation relation between activities, i.e, one

Figure 1. General process ontology

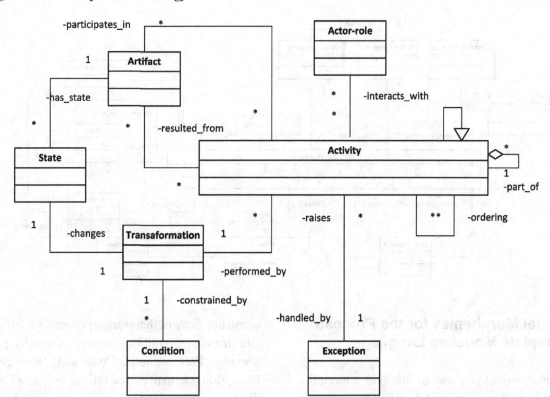

activity can be a part of another activity. Moreover, one activity may be a kind of another activity, e.g. 'swimming' can be a kind of 'exercising'. The relation of the 'kind of' is the hypernym relationship of two concepts, which is often used in ontology representation.

Artifact represents resources used in an activity such as product, information, tool and software. Artifacts are not specified in more details. We only differentiate the direction of the relations between *Artifact* and *Activity*, 'participate_in' and 'resulted_from'. Only inputs and outputs are specified in a model template. *Actor-role* is the one who interacts with the activity. Although actor and role are two different concepts, we combine those into one. *Actor-role* is representation of a class rather than an instance of actor or role in process templates.

State is the core concept in state modeling languages, e.g. statechart. State models are closely related to process models although the two kinds of models are not described in a same modeling language. In (Wand & Weber, 1995), state of a thing is described as "the vector of values for all property functions of a thing" in the BWW ontology. We simplify it by saying that *Artifact* has *State*. In a process model, *State* is usually used together with *Activity*, e.g. 'start', 'finished', 'suspended'. If we consider an activity is also a thing, we can extend the BWW ontology that *Activity* may have *State*. Another concept *Transformation* defined in the BWW ontology is also seldom used as a construct in a process modeling language but it stands for a phenomenon in all processes. *Transformation* can change *State* and *Transformation* is performed by *Activity*. **Condition** represents some context of a process which constrains *Transformation*. **Exception** provides additional information about the failure of the process or any exceptional cases in a process.

Figure 2. Meta-model of the process template modeling language (PTML)

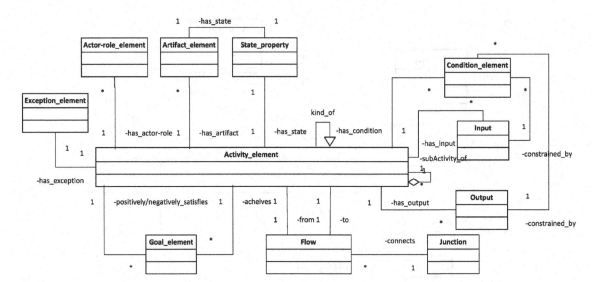

Model Morphemes for the Process Template Modeling Language

A meta-model is a way to interpret a modeling language. The meta-model of the Process Template Modeling Language (PTML) is displayed in Figure 2. The elements in the meta-model of PTML are process template model morphemes.

PTML is derived from GPO and also relates to process modeling languages, e.g., PSL, APM, EEML, BPMN, BPML. Some model morphemes are directly mapped from the concepts in GPO and are distinguished by a postfix '_element' in PTML. Such model morphemes are Activity_element, Actor-role_element, Artifact_element, Condition_element and Exception_element. In the various process modeling languages, the similar constructs to Activity_element are 'Action', 'Task', 'Activity' etc. The possible Actor-role_element in other process modeling languages may be 'Agent', 'Role', 'Actor', 'Object' or 'User'. 'Object', 'Artifact', 'Resource', 'Product' or 'Tool' defined in some process modeling languages can be mapped with Artifact_element in PTML. Since *State* is always described as a state of an artifact or a state of an activity, it is difficult to represent *State* as an independent

construct. *State* is, therefore, a property of *Artifact* and *Activity*. Condition_element is usually presented as 'PreConditon', 'Constraint', 'Rule', etc. Exception_element can be refined as 'Error Handler', 'Fault Handler' in certain process modeling languages.

There are also model morphemes such as Input, Output, Flow and Junction that are commonly used in many process modeling languages. Those model morphemes are seldom used and, therefore, they are not represented in GPO. However, they are necessary elements to build a model. Input and Output are ports of the Activity_element and they provide an interface for parameters in an activity. Flow is used to link activities and shows the sequence of the activities. Junction is a logic connection for joining or splitting flows, inputs or outputs. Combining those model morphemes can represent semantics of GPO. For example, the Activity_element and Flow can present the *ordering* of the *Activities*. If two activities are linked by a flow and the properties of the flow are from and to, the model is represented by *Flow_1*<from> *Activity_1* and *Flow_1* <to> *Activity_2*. Such model discloses the semantics that *Activity_2* follows *Activity_1*.

Transformation does not have corresponding model morphemes in PTML. Since *Transformation* is performed by *Activity* and changes *State*, its meaning can be interpreted by Activity_element together with State_property and other model morphemes. However, *State* can indicate certain goal achievements. Goal_element is introduced in some process modeling languages such as EEML, although the goals can be separately modeled and linked to process models later. Corresponding to the goal ontology definition, Activity_element can be linked with Goal_element to represent how a process achieves/satisfies business goals.

It is impossible to build one-to-one mapping between PTML and a specific process modeling constructs. However, PTML can represent the core of the process by template modeling in order to store and present process templates in a simple and comprehensible way for ordinary end-users.

Domain Annotation

Models (contents) are instances of the meta-model that describe certain domains. We divide the content of a process template into two parts: the process and the domain. The process part is the workflow representation. Any objects participating in the process are defined and represented in a domain model separated from the process part. Locally the semantics of the workflow representation are explicitly represented using the process/workflow modeling languages. The business objects orchestrated by the process model are defined in the logical domain model. In order to understand models from different organizations, we need a common understanding relating both process and content parts. Process concepts and process patterns defined in the reference process ontology are used to annotate the model fragments in the process part.

Domain ontologies are agreed as standard representations and semantic definitions of domain concepts. Semantic heterogeneity in the contents of models can be reconciled by making reference to the ontological concepts represented in domain

ontologies. In the model annotation, the annotation method builds semantic mappings or relationships between model contents and domain ontologies.

Goal Annotation

The aim of goal annotation is to identify the intended use of process models. Goal annotation links process model fragments with a goal ontology, similar to the way in which tasks and goals are linked in i*/GRL (GRL, 2000). i*/GRL is designed as a top-down method for specifying requirements, in which high level goals are broken down into low level tasks. However, no process is depicted in the goal models. Most approaches to modeling processes do not include goal modeling. To fill this gap, goal annotation specifies associations between the processes and their goals. We standardize goal representations by formalizing them into a goal ontology following the meta-model shown in Figure 3.

The goal ontology provides the conceptualization of business objectives and their relationships. In the semantic annotation of process templates, the annotation relationships between model fragments and goal ontologies are specified as "achieves" for hard goals, and "positively satisfies" or "negatively satisfies" for soft goals (Lin & Sølvberg, 2007).

APPLICATION OF SEMANTIC ANNOTATION

Here we demonstrate how to annotate process templates with ontology and describe them using PTML. As discussed, process model templates have two parts: one modeling process logic, and another one representing domain semantics. Typically, objects and actors are directly involved in the process logic. However, they are specific to the domain. The domain model defines the classes, attributes, and relationships of objects and actors from the static perspective. Then objects and actors are linked to the process part. They are referred in the process part through ID defined in the domain model.

A simple example illustrates the structures in Figure 4. There is a process template of a buying process. The specific process modeling language is EEML. In this EEML process template, 'purchase' is a task and 'client' is a personrole. The task 'purchase' is defined in the process part. Although 'client' is used as a personrole in the process part but it is defined as a class in local domain model. Hence the ID of 'client' defined in the local domain model is used for personrole by URI (Uniform Resource Identifier). The process part is in XML and the domain model is in RDFS. The meta-model of EEML is described in a XMLS (XML Schema) file.

Meta-Model Annotation

In the meta-model annotation, we map the original modeling language elements with the reference to the GPO concepts. Then process models are transformed into PTML models based on the mapping. Mapping of two meta-models is alike to ontology mapping considering a meta-model being the ontology of a modeling language. There are already many helpful ontology mapping techniques (cf., Euzenat & Shvaiko, 2007). SKOS Core (Miles, Rogers & Beckett, 2004) was chosen to describe the ontology mapping. SKOS Core is an RDF schema for representing thesauri and similar types of knowledge organization system.

PTML has less constructs than any specific process modeling language, therefore, the mapping from a concrete set to a general set is relatively easier than the reverse mapping. However, it is hard to avoid loss of semantics during the mapping. A process template is not complicated or concrete as a model instance. A general description of the model template represented by a specific construct can be described using a relatively general concept or construct without losing too much of original semantics.

In the EEML buying process example, element 'task' is annotated with concept *Activity* in GPO in SKOS representation. According to the semantic annotation and comparing meta-models of EEML and PTML, construct 'task' in EEML is replaced by 'Activity_element' in PTML (Exhibit 1).

Process model templates can be transformed into intermediate models in PTML that abstracts away heterogeneous representations of different process modeling languages, for instance (Exhibit 2).

Domain Annotation

After the meta-model annotation and the PTML model transformation, we continue to annotate the domain semantics. Again, here we distinguish two steps of model annotation: process part and domain model.

For the process part we annotate instances of PTML model elements, for example the Activity_element 'purchase'. For instance, a domain specific task ontology has a reference concept 'Purchase' that is used in the model annotation. We can still use SKOS mapping to build the reference link between a specific PTML model element and a reference concept in the domain task ontology. The representation of the model annotation for the process part is the following (Exhibit 3).

Since a process template does not contain any instance and all the concepts are on a type-level, the domain model is a local ontology or thesaurus for the project. The concepts used in the local ontology can be annotated with concepts used in a reference domain ontology or thesaurus by mapping two ontologies. 'Client' defined in the local domain model can be annotated with an agreed reference domain ontology. We assume that there is a concept 'Customer', and term 'client' is defined as its synonym in the reference domain ontology. We use SKOS to annotate 'client' appearing in the local domain model for more refined semantics mapping (Exhibit 4).

Figure 3. Meta-model of the proposed goal ontology

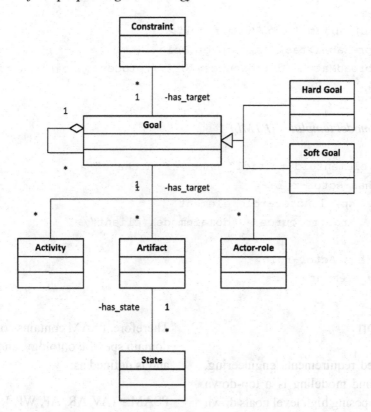

Figure 4. Structures of EEML process template

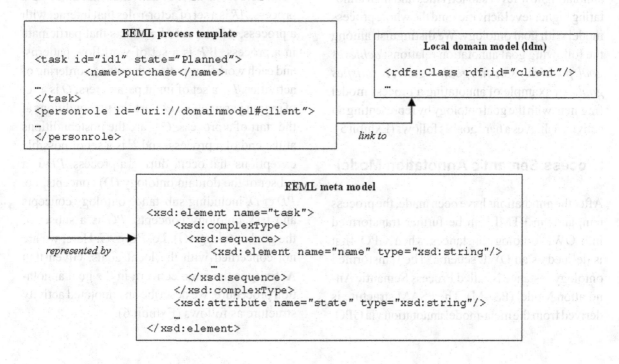

Exhibit 1. EEML buying process example

```
<skos:Concept rdf:about="uri://eeml#task">
        <skos:preLabel>task</skos:preLabel>
        <skos:broadMatch rdf:resource="Uri://processonto#Activity"/>
</skos:Concept>
```

Exhibit 2. Process model templates (PTML)

```
<ptml:Activity_element id = "tid1" name = "purchase" >
        <ptml:has_Actor-role>
                <ptml:Actor-role_element
                 rdf:resource = "domainmodel#client"/>
                ...
        </ptml:has Actor-role>
</ptml:Activity_element>
```

Goal Annotation

In the goal oriented requirements engineering, the goal analysis and modeling is a top-down procedure—decomposing high level goals down to lower level goals and operational activities. The goal annotation is a bottom-up procedure—first annotating low level subactivities and then annotating higher level activities and the whole process model with goal ontology. We distinguish among the following goal annotation relations: *achieves goal, positively satisfies goal, negatively satisfies goal*. An example of annotating a process model fragment with the goal ontology by representing an activity achieves a hard goal as follows (Exhibit 5).

Process Semantic Annotation Model

After the annotations have been made, the process templates in PTML can be further transformed into OWL ontology instances when GPO first is defined as an OWL schema. The transformed ontology instance is called Process Semantic Annotation Model (PSAM). The PSAM structure is derived from the meta-model annotation via GPO.

Therefore, PSAM contains concepts of GPO, the domain specific ontology, and the goal ontology and is defined as:

$$PSAM = (AV, AR, AF, WP, I, O, \Theta^{pre}, \Theta^{pos}, E, PD, PG)$$

Where AV is a set of activities that make up a process, AR is a set of actor-roles that interact with a process, AF is a set of artifacts that participate in a process, WP is a set of workflow patterns, and each workflow pattern denotes an ordering of activities. I is a set of input parameters, O is a set of output parameters. Θ^{pre} are the preconditions at the start of a process, Θ^{pos} are the postconditions at the end of a process, and E is a set of possible exceptions that occur during a process. PD is a subset of the domain ontology (D) concepts, i.e. $PD \subseteq D$, including substance ontology concepts and task ontology concepts. PG is a subset of the goal ontology (G), i.e. $PG \subseteq G$. Here, we are not concerned with the local goals. Given that **Activity** is the main concern in the goal annotation procedure, we describe an annotated activity structure as follows (Exhibit 6).

Exhibit 3. Model annotation

```
<skos:Concept rdf:about="PTMLmodel#tid1">
      <skos:prefLabel>purchase</skos:prefLabel>
      <skos:altLabel>buy</skos:preLabel>
      <skos:exactMatch rdf:resource =
 "uri://domainprocessonto#Purchase">
      ...
      </>
</skos:Concept>
```

Exhibit 4. SKOS example

```
<skos:Concept rdf:about="domainmodel#client">
      <skos:prefLabel>client</skos:prefLabel>
      <skos:altLabel>customer</skos:preLabel>
      <skos:closeMatch rdf:resource = "uri://domainonto#Customer">
          ...
      </>
</skos:Concept>
```

Exhibit 5. Goal annotation

```
<ptml:Activity_element id ="&MODEL_NAMESPACE#MODEL_ID">
      <ptml:achieves>
        <ptml:Goal_element
            rdf:resource="&GOAL_ONTOLOGY#GOAL_ONTOLOGY_CONCEPT"/>
      ...
```

Relationships between the concepts defined in the GPO are represented as properties here. For example, the relationship between an *Activity* and *Actor-role* is specified as a property "*has_Actor-role*", the composition relationship between two Activities (i.e. one Activity is a part of another Activity) is represented as "*subActivity_of*", and the ontological relationship like hypernym is expressed as "*kind_of*" which can be replaced with SKOS representation *skos:broader* or *skos:broadMatch*.

CASE STUDY

A case study has been conducted on the process models in a logistic domain. The process models are originally modeled by different enterprises using different modeling languages, and then annotated by the proposed approach. An industrial standard, SCOR (2005), for logistic process is taken as a reference ontology for model content and goal annotation. OWL DL is used to formalize SCOR, as the logistics domain and goal ontologies.

Exhibit 6. Annotated activity structure

```
AV_i = (id, model_fragment, name, alternative_name, has_Actor-role, has_Arti-
fact, has_Input, has_Output, has_preceedingActivity, has_succeedingActivity,
has_Precondition, has_Postcondition, has_Exception, subActivity_of,
same_as(skos:preLabel, skos:altLabel, skos:exactMatch, skos:closeMatch),
kind_of(skos:broader, skos:broadMatch),
superConcept_of(skos:narrower, skos:narrowMatch),
phase_of(skos:broader, skos:broadMatch),
compositionConcept_of(skos:broader, skos:narrowMatch),
achieves|positively_satisfies|negatively_satisfies_Goal)
```

The annotation results can be used to achieve the semantic retrieval of process templates. We use SWRL (Semantic Web Rule Language, combining OWL and RuleML (Horrocks, Patel-Schneider, Boley et al., 2004)) to formalize the queries of annotation models. The SWRL rules provide the computational capability of the annotation models in OWL.

SCOR Reference Ontology

SCOR is a process reference model that was developed and endorsed by the Supply Chain Council as the industry standard diagnostic tool for supply-chain management. A SCOR reference model has been developed to describe the standard business activities associated with all phases of satisfying a customer's demand. The process element level of the SCOR reference model consists of definitions of process elements, the input and output of information to and from process elements, process performance metrics, examples of best practice and the system capabilities required to support it, and systems/tools (SCOR, 2005).

The SCOR reference model was formalized as the domain ontology by the INTEROP project (Panetto, Scannapieco & Zelm, 2004). We extended this ontology by categorizing the concepts of SCOR_MGM_PROCESS, SCOR_IN-PUT_OUNTPUT and SCOR_ORGANIZATION into 3A (*Activity*, *Artifact*, *Actor-role*) in order to

annotate the PSAM models. The goal ontology is also derived from SCOR. Hard goals are derived from process elements, inputs, and outputs. Soft goals are defined according to performance attributes and their metrics (Soffer & Wand, 2005). The concepts are modeled as OWL Classes and are organized into a subsumption hierarchy. An OWL model of the SCOR ontology is presented in Table 1.

Semantic Reasoning on Process Knowledge

After the annotations have been made, the process knowledge in the models is represented in PSAM models and aligned with the SCOR ontology. The PSAM models are stored in a knowledge repository, which may be used for querying, discovering, and navigating the process knowledge. Due to the fact that ontologies and annotations are all represented in OWL DL, description logic inference can be used for semantic reasoning for both ontological query and annotated models. Using this semantic reasoning, the semantics of queries may be matched with the semantics of annotated models.

The inference services of OWL DL enable semantic reasoning on classes, properties and instances of ontology, such as consistency, subsumption, equivalence, instantiation, and retrieval. The reasoning on the classes and properties of an

Table 1. OWL definition of the SCOR ontology

OWL Ontology Class	Subsumption Relation	OWL Properties	Property Range
SCOR_MGMT_ PROCESS	owl:subClassOf Activity	hasInput	*multiple* SCOR_INPUT_OUTPUT
		hasOutput	*multiple* SCOR_INPUT_OUTPUT
		precedes	*multiple* SCOR_MGMT_PRO-CESS
		isPrecededBy	*multiple* SCOR_MGMT_PRO-CESS
SCOR_INPUT_OUTPUT	owl:subClassOf Activity	isInputTo	*multiple* SCOR_MGMT_PRO-CESS
		isOutputOf	*multiple* SCOR_MGMT_PRO-CESS
		has_state	*(data property inherited from Artifact)*
SCOR_ORGANIZATIONAL	owl:subClassOf Actor-role	-	-
Goal	*has sub-Class* Hard Goal, Soft Goal	has_parts	*multiple* Goal
		part_of	*multiple* Goal
		targetActivity	*multiple* Activity
		targetArtifact	*multiple* Artifact
		targetRole	*multiple* Actor-role
		targetConstraint	*(data property)*

ontology is often called T-Box inference, with A-Box inference being associated with the instances of the classes (Horrocks, 2002). Semantic reasoning is useful in ontology-based querying of process knowledge. A-Box inference is used when retrieving the process model fragments that are represented as the GPO instances in the PSAM model. T-Box inference can be applied when determining the semantic relationships between the ontological concepts that describe the query and domain ontologies.

Two examples of semantic reasoning are selected from the annotation results of the cases described above.

Querying Process Templates Using SWRL

SWRL allows users to write Horn-like rules to reason about OWL individuals and to infer new knowledge about them. SWRL rules take the

form of an implication between an antecedent (body) and consequent (head), i.e. *antecedent → consequent*. The intended meaning may be read as: whenever the conditions specified in the antecedent hold, so must the conditions specified in the consequent. Both the antecedent and the consequent consist of zero or more atoms. Atoms in rules can be of the form $C(x)$ or $P(x,y)$, where C is an OWL description, P is an OWL property, and x, y are either variables, OWL individuals or OWL data values.

SWRL rules can be query rules or inference rules. The inferences are usually built through correlations to OWL properties. For example, besides the Object Property *has_Artifact* of *Activity*, the relationship between *Activity* and *Artifact* can also be inferred through connecting relations among *Activity, Input, Output*, and *Artifact*. Checking the *Artifact*s related to the *Input/Output* of activities is therefore formalized as follows (Exhibit 7).

Table 2. Examples of semantic reasoning

1. Users of the model need to *find model fragments of the process that deals with "Bill" in enterprise systems*. The following steps must be taken (formalized in (i), (ii), and (iii)):
Query: $?x|(x, Bill) \in R$: has_artifact, $x \in Activity$ w.r.t. O^{gpo}, O^{scor} (i)
T-Box inference: $? C |C = Bill$ w.r.t. SCOR ontology ^{Oscor} $? C |C\_Bill$ w.r.t. $O^{scor(ii)}$
A-Box inference: $?y|(x, y) \in R$: has_artifact, $y \in Artifact$ w.r.t. ^{Ogpo} $(y, C) \in R$: same_as· kind_of, part_of w.r.t. $^{Ogpo(iii)}$
2. Users of the model would like to *retrieve the process model fragments that affect the goal of improving delivery performance*. Similar steps are undertaken formalized in (jj), (jj), and (jjj):
Query: $?x|(x, ImproveDeliveryPerformance) \in R$: positively_satisfies, negatively_satisfies, $x \in Activity$ w.r.t O^{gpo}, O^{scor} (j)
T-Box inference: $? C |C = ImproveDeliveryPerformance$ w.r.t. ^{Oscor} $? C |C\_ImproveDeliveryPerformance$ w.r.t. ^{Oscor} $? C	ImproveDeliveryPerformance$ has_parts C w.r.t. $^{Oscor(jj)}$
A-Box inference: $(x, C) \in R$: positively_satisfies, negatively_satisfies w.r.t. $^{Ogpo(jjj)}$

Exhibit 7. Checking the Artifacts

```
IRule-Activity-Input-hasArtifact
        Activity(?x) ^ has_Input(?x, ?y) ^ related_Artifact(?y, ?z) →
Activity(?x) ^ has_Artifact(?x, ?z)
IRule-Activity-Output-hasArtifact
        Activity(?x) ^ has_Output(?x, ?y) ^ related_Artifact(?y, ?z) →
Activity(?x) ^ has_Artifact(?x, ?z)
QRule-Activity-hasArtifact
        Activity(?x) ^ has_Artifact(?x, ?y) → query: select(?x, ?y) ^
query: orderBy(?x)
```

They can be used to infer the fact that if an *Artifact* is related to the *Input* or *Output* of an *Activity*, the *Activity* might have such an *Artifact*. Such inference tasks can be used to find possibly missing annotations of *has_Artifact*.

The SWRL rules and queries are executed on annotation results. Analysis of the results of rule execution helps to check the kind of knowledge that can be derived from the annotation results.

Related Work

Ontology-based semantic annotation is generally considered to be an appropriate technique for achieving semantic interoperability, and is achieved by introducing common means of understanding and standardization. Most semantic annotation work has been developed on and applied to unstructured textual resources (e.g. MnM

(Vargas-Vera, Motta, Domingue et al., 2002), KIM (Popov, Kiryakov, Kirilov et al., 2004) and OntoMat-Annotizer (Handschuh, Staab, & Maedche, 2001)) and structured artifacts (e.g. METEOR-S (Patil, Oundhakar, Sheth et al., 2004), WSMO (Bruijn, Bussler, Domingue et al., 2005), OWL-S (Martin, Burstein, Hobbs et al., 2004), SAWSDL (Kopecky, Vitvar, Bourne et al., 2007) and WSDL-S (Akkiraju, Farrell, Miller et al., 2005) for Web services) to improve interoperability at different levels. A few semantic approaches (including our own) that use semi-structured artifacts (usually enterprise models) have been developed in recent years, such as those reported in the INTEROP project (Panetto, Scannapieco, & Zelm, 2004) and the ATHENA project (Ruggaber, 2006). For the semantic annotation of unstructured and structured artifacts, semantic reconciliation focuses on one level only, that of the data in the text or in the schema. For semi-structured artifacts, semantic heterogeneities are taken into account on more than one level. These are usually either the meta-model (i.e. modeling language) or domain (i.e. model content), or even the intention level (i.e. goal modeling).

Compared with the contemporary projects, INTEROP and ATHENA, we focus mainly on the business process models defined as the CIM (Computation Independent Model), rather than PIM (Platform Independent Model) and PSM (Platform Specific Model)[1] of enterprise models. We herein cover the horizontal mapping between the CIM models used by different organizations, rather than the vertical mappings for model transformation between CIM, PIM, and PSM. We propose a generalized, yet simple, process ontology for modeling language mapping rather than a unified and complex, enterprise modeling language for model exchange and translation. These distinctions are inherent in the purpose of our study.

CONCLUSION AND FUTURE WORK

Interoperability is a very vital issue and a difficult problem in meaning understanding and sharing in many enterprise applications, such as heterogeneous enterprise application integration, e-business, web services, knowledge sharing and information exchanging. In this paper, we addressed an interoperability problem in semantic retrieval of process templates. Since the process templates are reusable knowledge and resources of process modeling, they are required to be comprehensible and adaptable to other enterprise modeling users. We discern two main levels of interoperability of model templates, namely model level and meta-model level. To enhance reuse of process templates, we propose a semantic annotation method to annotate modeling languages, process model fragments and goals.

The main contribution of this approach is the General Process Ontology including goal ontology which is used to annotate common and general process concepts. GPO is used as a reference process ontology in process modeling. A set of process model morphemes in a neutral Process Template Modeling Language is generated from GPO and is used to represent the process template. GPO and PTML are not designed for very specific or detailed models but model templates, so its constructs are more general and simple than other process modeling languages. It can be regarded as an approach allowing generalizing process models to the level of necessary details for templates to be reused. Moreover, the paper presented the semantic annotation structure, procedure and ontological representation with reasoning power. It disclosed the technical possibility and applicability of the approach. With the semantic annotation of process templates, process model designers can retrieve their desired templates and reuse them.

REFERENCES

Ader, M., Lu, G., Pons, P., Monguio, J., Lopez, L., De Micelis, G., ... Vlondakis, G. (1994). *WooRKS, an object oriented workflow system for offices.* ITHACA technical report.

Aitken, S., & Curtis, J. (2002). A process ontology. In Gomez-Perez, A., & Benjamins, V. R. (Eds.), *EKAW 2002, LNAI 2473* (pp. 108–113). Berlin, Germany: Springer-Verlag.

Akkiraju, R., Farrell, J., Miller, J., Nagarajan, M., et al. (2005). *Web service semantics – WSDL-S.* Retrieved October 10, 2010, from http://www.w3.org/Submission/WSDL-S/

Bruijn, J., Bussler, C., Domingue, J., Fensel, D., et al. (2005). *Web service modeling ontology (WSMO).* Retrieved October 10, 2010, from http://www.w3.org/Submission/WSMO/

Bunge, M. (1977). *Ontology I: The furniture of world. Treaties on basic philosophy (Vol. 3).* Boston, MA: Reidel.

Carlsen, S. (1997). *Conceptual modeling and composition of flexible workflow models.* Doctoral dissertation, NTNU, Trondheim, Norway.

Euzenat, J., & Shvaiko, P. (2007). *Ontology matching.* Berlin, Germany: Springer-Verlag.

Fox, M. S. (1992). The TOVE Project: A commonsense model of the enterprise. In Belli, F., & Radermacher, F. J. (Eds.), *Industrial and engineering applications of artificial intelligence and expert systems, LNAI 604* (pp. 25–34). Berlin, Germany: Springer-Verlag. doi:10.1007/BFb0024952

GRL. (2000). *Goal-oriented requirement language.* Retrieved October 10, 2010, from http://www.cs.toronto.edu/km/GRL/

Handschuh, S., Staab, S., & Maedche, A. (2001). CREAM: Creating relational metadata with a component-based, ontology-driven annotation framework. In [ACM Press.]. *Proceedings of K-CAP, 2001,* 76–83.

Horrocks, I. (2002). Reasoning with expressive description logics: Theory and practice. In *Proceedings of Automated Deduction - CADE-18, LNCS 2392* (pp. 1–15). Berlin, Germany: Springer-Verlag.

Horrocks, I., Patel-Schneider, P. F., Boley, H., Tabet, S., Grosof, B., & Dean, M. (2004). *SWRL: A Semantic Web rule language combining OWL and RuleML.* Retrieved October 10, 2010, from http://www.w3.org/Submission/SWRL/

Kopecky, J., Vitvar, T., Bourne, C., & Farrell, J. (2007). SAWSDL: Semantic annotations for WSDL and XML schema. *Internet Computing, 11*(6), 66–67. doi:10.1109/MIC.2007.134

Krogstie, J., & Jørgensen, D. H. (2004). Interactive models for supporting networked organisations. In Persson, A., & Stirna, J. (Eds.), *Advanced information systems engineering, LNCS 3084* (pp. 550–563). Berlin, Germany: Springer Verlag. doi:10.1007/978-3-540-25975-6_39

Lee, J., Grunninger, M., Jin, Y., Malone, T., Tate, A., Yost, G. et al. (1996). *The PIF process interchange format and framework,* version 1.1.

Lin, Y., & Sølvberg, A. (2007). Goal annotation of process models for semantic enrichment of process knowledge. In Krogstie, J., Opdahl, A. L., & Sindre, G. (Eds.), *advanced information systems engineering, LNCS 4495* (pp. 355–369). Berlin, Germany: Springer-Verlag. doi:10.1007/978-3-540-72988-4_25

Martin, D., Burstein, M., Hobbs, J., Lassila, O., McDermott, D., McIlraith, S., et al. (2004). *WL-S: Semantic markup for Web Services.* Retrieved October 10, 2010, from http://www.w3.org/Submission/OWL-S/

McGuinness, D. L., & Harmelen, F. (2004). *OWL Web ontology language overview*. Retrieved June 2, 2004, from http://www.w3.org/TR/owl-features/

Medina-Mora, R., Winograd, T., Flores, R., & Flores, F. (1992). The action workflow approach to workflow management technology. *Proceedings of the Conference on Computer Supported Cooperative Work (CSCW'92)*, (pp. 291-299). ACM Press.

Miles, A. J., Rogers, N., & Beckett, D. (2004). *SKOS-core 1.0 guide*. Retrieved October 10, 2010, from http://www.w3.org/2001/sw/Europe/reports/thes/1.0/guide/

Panetto, H., Scannapieco, M., & Zelm, M. (2004). INTEROP NoE: Interoperability research for networked enterprises applications and software. In Meersman, R., & Tari, Z. (Eds.), *On the move to meaningful Internet system 2004: OTM 2004 Workshops, LNCS 3292* (pp. 866–882). Berlin, Germany: Springer-Verlag. doi:10.1007/978-3-540-30470-8_100

Patil, A. P., Oundhakar, S. A., Sheth, A. P., & Verma, K. (2004). METERO-S Web service annotation framework. *13th International Conference on World Wide Web (WWW 2004)* (pp. 553-562). New York, NY: ACM Press.

Pease, A., & Carrico, T. M. (1997). *Object model working group (OMWG) core plan representation – Request for comment, version 2*. DARPA.

Popov, B., Kiryakov, A., Kirilov, A., Manov, D., Ognyanoff, D., & Goranov, M. (2004). KIM – A semantic platform for information extraction and retrieval. *Natural Language Engineering, 10*(3-4), 375–392. doi:10.1017/S135132490400347X

Ruggaber, R. (2006). ATHENA – Advanced technologies for interoperability of heterogeneous enterprise networks and their applications. In Konstantas, D., Bourrieres, J. P., Leonard, M., & Boudjlida, N. (Eds.), *Interoperability of enterprise software and applications* (pp. 459–460). London, UK: Springer. doi:10.1007/1-84628-152-0_45

Schlenoff, C., Gruninger, M., Tissot, F., Valois, J., Lubell, J., & Lee, J. (2000). *The process specification language (PSL) overview and version 1.0 specification. (NISTIR 6459)*. Gaithersburg, MD: National Institute of Standards and Technology.

SCOR. (2005). *Supply-chain operations reference-model: SCOR version 7.0 overview*. Retrieved August 12, 2006, from http://www.torconsulting.com/downloads/scor7_overview.pdf

Sheth, A. P. (1998). Changing focus on interoperability in Information Systems: From system, syntax, structure to semantics. In Goodchild, M. F., Egenhofer, M. J., Fegeas, R., & Koffman, C. A. (Eds.), *Interoperating Geographic Information Systems*. Kluwer.

Soffer, P., & Wand, Y. (2005). On the notion of soft-goals in business process modeling. *Business Process Management Journal, 11*(6), 663–679. doi:10.1108/14637150510630837

Vargas-Vera, M., Motta, E., Domingue, J., Lanzoni, M., Stutt, A., & Ciravegna, F. (2002). MnM: Ontology driven semi-automatic and automatic support for semantic markup. *Proceedings of the 13th International Conference on Knowledge Engineering and Knowledge Management, LNCS 2473*, (pp. 379-391). Berlin, Germany: Springer-Verlag.

Wand, Y., & Weber, R. (1990). An ontological model for an Information System. *IEEE Transactions on Software Engineering, 16*(11), 1282–1292. doi:10.1109/32.60316

Wand, Y., & Weber, R. (1995). On the deep structure of Information Systems. *Information Systems Journal*, *5*, 203–223. doi:10.1111/j.1365-2575.1995. tb00108.x

White, S. A. (2004). *Introduction to BPMN*. Retrieved October 10, 2010, from http://www. bpmn.org/

ENDNOTE

[1]   CIM, PIM and PSM are three different viewpoint models defined in OMG's MDA (Model-Driven Architecture) (http://www. omg.org/mda/).

Chapter 13
Semantically Enhanced Business Process Modeling Notation

Witold Abramowicz
Poznań University of Economics, Poland

Agata Filipowska
Poznań University of Economics, Poland

Monika Kaczmarek
Poznań University of Economics, Poland

Tomasz Kaczmarek
Poznań University of Economics, Poland

ABSTRACT

Semantic Business Process Management (SBPM) bridges the gap between business and IT by taking advantage of the Semantic Web technologies. The foundation for SBPM is the detailed ontological description of enterprise models. These models encompass also business processes taking place in enterprises. Within this chapter, we show how the process-oriented knowledge may be captured for the needs of SBPM. For this reason, we describe semantically enhanced Business Process Modeling Notation (sBPMN) being a conceptualization of one of the main process modeling notations with the fast growing popularity among the tool vendors, namely BPMN. The sBPMN ontology is based on the BPMN specification and may be used as a serialization format by the BPMN modeling tools, thus, making creation of annotations invisible to users. In this chapter, we also present an example of a process model description.

INTRODUCTION

The growing interest in the Business Process Management (BPM) idea, results from a need to streamline business operations, increase business process efficiency and save costs. To ensure

DOI: 10.4018/978-1-60960-126-3.ch013

availability of desired functionalities and quality level of performed activities, over the years, much research has been devoted to investigate and advance techniques and tools for BPM.

Nowadays, BPM is often combined with the Service Oriented Architecture (SOA) paradigm, as together these two approaches may offer many benefits. BPM focusing on business directions, goals and processes defines how organizational resources (including IT resources) are used in order to support fulfillment of business goals. SOA complements BPM by offering a flexible IT architecture that may be easily adapted to changing business requirements and helps to leverage IT investments through provision of reusable components.

Although combining BPM and SOA offers many benefits, various challenges still are to be addressed. One of them is limited support for automation of the BPM lifecycle. It is especially visible when it comes to the smooth and automated transition from one BPM phase to another. For instance, the automated transition from the modeling to the implementation phase is hardly possible due to an insufficient and non-technical description of a process provided by a business analyst who perceives a business process differently than an IT engineer. This is known as the semantic gap between the business and IT worlds (Dehnert and van der Aalst 2004).

Recently, researchers and practitioners turn their attention to the possibility of combining the BPM domain also with Semantic Web technologies (Hepp, Leymann et al. 2005; Brockmans, Ehrig et al. 2006; Wetzstein, Ma et al. 2007), thus, contributing to the creation of the Semantic Business Process Management (SBPM) approach. Semantic technologies and tools aiming at providing more explicit meaning of the information are considered to be able to help automating the BPM lifecycle and offer new functionalities to business experts. To implement the vision of SBPM, business process models as well as the enterprise context and existing IT infrastructure must be ontologically captured to enable machine reasoning. Thus, the ontologies i.e. formalized descriptions of entities with their properties and relations (Grueninger and Fox 1995), constitute a backbone of the SBPM concept. There are several open questions with regard to this issue: what should be the scope of this representation, what are the scenarios showing advantage of its utilization, what tool support should be provided to facilitate business analysts' interactions with semantics.

Within this chapter we focus on the ontologised version of the Business Process Modeling Notation (BPMN). It was originally created by the BPMI group and has emerged as a standard notation for process modeling, gathering and combining experience from many other modeling notations e.g., UMLADs, IDEF, ebXML and EPCs (BPMN, 2006). BPMN aims at bridging the gap between the business process design and process implementation. It was to allow for the automatic translation from the graphical process diagram into the BPEL process representation (Arkin et al., 2005) that may be then executed using Web services technology. Although the goal of automatic translation is very appealing, the intention failed in practice for a number of reasons. One of them is that BPMN is a graph-oriented language and its mapping to the block-structured BPEL representation is challenging. In addition, BPMN allows designing not well-formed processes that cannot be translated directly into a set of the BPEL executable instructions (Ouyang, 2006).

Application of the ontologized version of BPMN i.e. sBPMN (Semantic Business Process Modeling Notation) intends to add meaning to each of the process elements and make them machine-readable. Thus, it will allow for reasoning on the process description. Once sBPMN is additionally enriched with Semantic Web services (SWS) extensions, it will be also possible to automatically assign Web service (or their compositions) to each task. Having Web services matched to tasks is only one step from generating a BPEL process representation that may be deployed on the execution engine.

The goal of this chapter is to provide an overview of the ontology stack to support SBPM with a special focus assigned to sBPMN being the ontology for process flow description. Therefore, the remaining of this chapter is structured as follows. Next section presents related work on SBPM approaches and process modeling ontologies. Following sections introduce sBPMN ontology, its scope and competency questions against which the ontology was checked for completeness. Then an example demonstrating description of a process using the developed ontology follows. The chapter concludes with final remarks.

BACKGROUND

The aim of the Semantic Business Process Management is to increase the level of automation within the BPM lifecycle and to provide support within the process lifecycle for business users and IT engineers. Four phases of the Business Process Management may be identified, namely: modelling, implementation (also called configuration), execution and analysis. As the application of the semantic technologies does not affect these stages, but rather increases the level of their automation as well as provides new functionalities, the division into the above mentioned phases applies as well to the SBPM concept (Wetzstein et al., 2007). Therefore, the first phase of SBPM is the Semantic Business Process Modelling that produces semantically annotated business process models. The goal of the semantic annotation is to explicitly specify the semantics of tasks and decisions in the process flow. At this stage not only ontology-based modelling is supported, but also the additional functionalities taking advantage of the developed process descriptions are offered e.g. reuse of existing process fragments, autocompletion of processes, validation of processes. Within Semantic Business Process Configuration phase, semantic business process models are transformed to executable process models that may be deployed to a process execution engine. The ontological representation of a model provides complex description of a process. However, as it is not yet ready for deployment, some additional activities within this phase need to be undertaken. The most important one is composition of a process i.e. as-

signing to each task a composition of Semantic Web services able to fulfil the task's goal. After composition the model is validated, transformed to semantically enhanced BPEL process representation and only then, after adequate serialisation, may be finally deployed to the engine. After a semantic business process model is deployed to the process engine, it becomes ready for execution. After execution, the next phase, i.e. Semantic Business Process Analysis starts. It involves analysis of already executed process instances (based on data from monitoring) in order to enable improvement of existing process models. Therefore, the functionalities assuring conformance checking, organization mining, performance analysis and auditing are provided.

Taking into account the above phases as well as reviewing the existing initiatives within the SBPM field, two main groups of supported use cases of applying semantic technologies to BPM can be distinguished, namely (Hepp et al. 2005):

- Applying semantic technologies (especially reasoning) to analyze enterprise models and
- Applying semantic technologies to create entirely new models or to create new parts of enterprise models.

Within the first scenario, semantic technologies are used to discover previously unknown facts relevant to an enterprise and its models. Within the second scenario, semantic technologies are used to generate or partially define new elements of an enterprise model. This encompasses also a semiautomatic construction of business processes, supporting the evolution of a process, and semiautomatic retrieval and reuse of process artefacts.

The above scenarios are possible, as Semantic Business Process Management is based on the assumption that main aspects of an enterprise model can be captured semantically using ontologies. One of the first ontologies, that could be potentially used within SBPM is the Enterprise Ontology presented by (Uschold, King et al. 1998). This Enterprise Ontology provides concepts for organizational, strategy, process and resource modeling. Although being quite comprehensive, the ontology provides neither appropriate support for modeling languages used in industry nor is extensible, i.e., it does not allow replacing or extending parts of it with other ontologies. To address this issue, other approaches were proposed, e.g., TOVE project (Fox 1992), REA ontologies (Lampe 2002) or e3-value (Gordijn 2002).

The second issue concerns providing new meta-models for description of processes, namely process flow. Among such efforts are annotations of Petri Nets (Brockmans, Ehrig et al. 2006), UML activity diagrams (Lautenbacher and Bauer 2006), EPC (Thomas and Fellmann 2007) and formal framework for process description (Greco, Guzzo et al. 2004). The examples of the process ontologies not directly related to any particular existing notations are recently developed GPO (General Process Ontology) (Lin 2008) and BPMO (Business Process Modelling Ontology) (Cabral, Norton et al. 2009).

Up till now, most of the research efforts focused on provision of a detailed meta-model for one process modelling notation only. The SUPER project[1] was the first effort to propose a comprehensive ontology stack to support SBPM (Hepp and Roman 2007, Pedrinaci, Domingue et al. 2008, Filipowska, Kaczmarek et al. 2009). This stack is discussed briefly in the next section, as the sBPMN ontology presented in this chapter is a part of the ontology stack proposed in SUPER.

ONTOLOGIES TO SUPPORT THE SEMANTIC BUSINESS PROCESS MANAGEMENT VISION

In order to realize the SBPM vision as introduced in the previous section, a few requirements need to be addressed. First of all, the main artifacts used within the BPM and SOA life cycle need to be semantically annotated and the adequate interactions taking advantage of these artifacts need to be defined and implemented. The main concept of SOA is a service, thus the Semantic Web services technology is utilized. Similarly, as a process is the core concept of BPM, so the main semantic enhancements of BPM should concern the description of processes, i.e. the description of a control flow of a process as well as description of its content. By process content we understand all artifacts that a process definition may refer to and that specify the business environment and organizational context of the process.

The required semantic representation of a process, utilized during all phases of SBPM, may be divided into three main groups: process, organization-related and domain-specific ontologies. The high-level view on the process description for the needs of the Semantic Business Process Management is depicted in Figure 1.

Process ontologies are created in order to describe the structure of a process (i.e. its control flow), whereas organization related ontologies provide a description of artifacts that are utilized by or involved in the process i.e. description of actors, resources, systems, etc. The domain ontologies provide additional information specific to an organization from a given domain. Thus, the domain ontologies extend the organization related ones. Such an approach allows for future reusability of the developed solutions.

The process ontologies layer includes ontologized versions of popular modeling notations, Event–driven Process Chain (Filipowska et al., 2008) and BPMN. The latter is presented in details within this chapter. The ontologized versions of EPC and BPMN, in order to describe processes, are to use the concepts/instances defined within organization-related ontologies. The organizational ontologies aim at providing vocabulary and constraints for describing an environment in which processes are carried out from the organizations' perspective. Following (Hepp and Roman, 2007), the organizational ontologies provide a basic

Figure 1. SBPM ontology stack

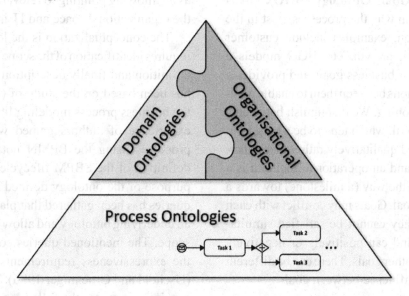

vocabulary and structure for describing organizations, business goals and resources, define common types of divisions, roles and tasks, and define common types of business resources. Thus, the organizational ontologies layer provides a high-level view on the organization and process-related space. They may be logically divided into a few subontologies, each of them describing different part of this space:

1. **Organizational Structure Ontology (OSO).** This ontology focuses on organizational structure (hierarchy) of a company. It provides main structure and relations aiming at achieving domain independency. The OSO shows how elements of organization work together in order to achieve organization's goals. It encompasses such information as: departments, employees, their responsibilities, resources used etc. as well as relations among them.

2. **Organizational Units Ontology (OUO).** This ontology provides specification of typical units that may be found in a company. Along with the other ontologies (Business Functions, Business Roles and Business Resources Ontology) it provides extensions to OSO.

3. **Business Roles Ontology (BROnt).** This ontology provides a common meaning of concepts related to roles featured by organizational members (i.e. actors). Each actor may play more than one role and these roles may change depending on the context. It also allows modeling both internal as well as external roles played by various actors.

4. **Business Functions Ontology (BFO).** This ontology provides a hierarchy of different functions that may be carried out within the company. It is supposed to enable vendor and domain independent classification of company processes and process fragments providing abstraction over single tasks constituting processes.

5. **Business Resources Ontology (BRO).** This ontology describes applications and resources that should be spent when carrying out certain processes or that may be results of certain task within a process.

6. **Business Goals Ontology (BGO).** Goals may explain why the processes exist in the organization; examples include customer satisfaction, growth, etc. BGO models a hierarchy of business goals and provides a set of relations between them to enable goal-based reasoning. We distinguish between a strategic goal, which tend to be a long term and defined qualitatively rather than quantitatively, and an operational goal that is a step along the way (a milestone) towards a strategic goal. Goals may conflict with each other (if they cannot be satisfied simultaneously) and can positively or negatively influence other goals. There can be different levels of influence between goals.

Together the process and organizational ontologies with accompanying ontology instances constitute a powerful knowledge base that may be used to create a detailed and machine understandable description of a process. The following sections focus on the semantically enhanced version of the BPMN standard.

SEMANTICALLY ENHANCED BUSINESS PROCESS MODELLING NOTATION

There exist a few methodologies used to design an ontology. Within the conducted research, we followed the approach suggested by Uschold and Grueninger (1996). They consider the following steps of an ontology design: definition of the ontology purpose, conceptualization, validation, and finally coding.

The ontology model of SBPM ontology presented in this section has been designed following the above-mentioned steps. The onotology purpose was expressed as follows: to define an information model describing elements of a process and control flow compliant with the BPMN notation as well

as all allowing pointing to relevant artifacts from the organizational space and IT infrastructure.

The conceptualization is the longest step and requires identification of the scope of the ontology, definition and finally description of concepts. It has been based on the study of (BPMN, 2006), the business process modeling literature and the experience of authors gained while modeling processes using the BPMN notation. Given a definition of the SBPM lifecycle as well as the purpose of the ontology defined above, a set of queries has been gathered that place demands on an underlying ontology and allow determining its scope. The mentioned queries constitute in fact the expressiveness requirements as defined in (Uschold and Grueninger 1996). The mentioned queries encompass the following questions:

-   What are the elements of a given process?
-   What is the input / output of given process?
-   What is the input / output of each task constituting the process?
-   What are the sequence flow connection rules?
-   What is the execution order of activities within the process?
-   What is the status of the process?
-   What artifacts are used within a given process?
-   Who performs different tasks within the process?
-   Which events and what types of events are part of the process?
-   How a certain type of activity can be triggered?

However, the above mentioned competency questions can be also answered utilizing XPATH and XQuery on the XML serialization format of the BPMN specification, and no semantics is required. The real potential and possibilities offered by the sBPMN ontology become visible when it is combined with other ontologies from the organizational space mentioned in the previous section, as then it should be able to answer also the following exemplary questions:

- Which existing elements of IT infrastructure may be used to implement it?
- Which actors are involved in a certain process?
- Which business goals are associated with a certain process or activity?

Provided that reasoning is applied on the semantic representation of a complex business process models library, also additional questions may be posed. Examples of such questions are given below:

- Are there any conflicts between the higher-level business process goal, and the goals of the subprocesses?
- In what way are the processes belonging to the same functional domain in an enterprise related?
- Are there any processes assigned to an organizational unit that should not belong there given the functions within the organization intended for the unit?

The sBPMN ontology formalizes the main elements of the BPMN notation. The core element of the sBPMN ontology is a Business Process Diagram that presents the process model. According to the BPMN specification four basic categories of elements, used within the BPMN and as a consequence depicted in the sBPMN ontology, are Flow Objects, Connecting Objects, Swimlanes and Artifacts, However, for the sake of clarity and compatibility to the other SUPER process ontologies (e.g., semantically annotated EPC), the Process concept was also introduced on the same level. Therefore, the main concepts of the sBPMN ontology are as follows:

- **Flow Objects:** the main graphical elements defining the behavior of a business process. There are three kinds of Flow Objects: Events, Activities and Gateways.
- **Connecting Objects:** as there are three ways of connecting the Flow Objects to each other or to other information, BPMN utilizes three types of Connecting Objects: Sequence Flow, Message Flow and Association.
- **Swimlanes:** utilized when grouping the primary modeling elements (see above). Two kinds of swimlanes were developed in BPMN, namely: Pools and Lanes.
- **Artifacts:** used to provide additional information about the process. The current set of Artifacts includes: Data Object, Group and Annotation.
- **Process:** used to group flow objects elements into a set of objects.

The concepts presented above represent only a core subset of the sBPMN ontology. Each of them has a number of subconcepts. The current sBPMN ontology has approximately 95 concepts and over 50 axioms (ontology constraints).

During the ontology development, a number of modeling decisions had to be taken. It had to be decided whether specific occurrences of process model elements are to be subclasses or instances of specific concepts. A decision was to use Class to represent a type of entity, i.e. process, task, gateways. Therefore, core business process diagram elements (BPMN, 2006) were modeled as classes having appropriate attributes defined in the BPMN Specification (if the specification defined possible set of values for attribute, appropriate constraints were added). Thus, the annotation of processes with sBPMN means creating instances of its concepts, e.g. a task ObtainLicense will be an instance of the Task class, and not a subclass of it. Another issue concerns the association of the BPMN elements to a specific process. To make

Figure 2. sBPMN class hierarchy

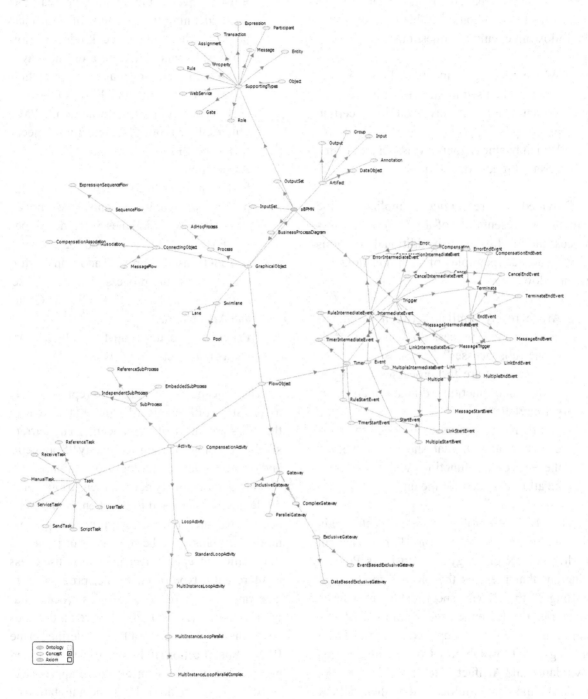

sure that all the elements of a process model refer to it, special property was introduced (named hasProcess) for explicit or implicitly (through recursion) reference.

The sequence flow is modeled using the connection rules attached to the Source and Target properties of the SequenceFlow concepts defining which Flow Objects (e.g. Tasks, Activities, Events, Gateways) may be connected one to another (in line with the BPMN Sequence Flow Connection Rules). The message flow connection rules were implemented analogically.

On the highest level of the class hierarchy, enumeration types such as SupportingTypes and Trigger types were included. They do not fit elsewhere in the hierarchy, but are required for modeling of Events and general properties for the different classes. They are used throughout the BPMN Specification in different contexts. The most controversial may be the Object class, which is often used in the BPMN Specification in a very general meaning, which does not point to any specific class.

Collapsed and Expanded Sub-Processes from the BPMN Specification were omitted as purely graphical elements related to the diagram layout and not its semantics. We assume that the BPMN diagrams will be converted to the sBPMN in the expanded form.

All types of triggers were distinguished as subclasses. This was necessary in order to define events properly. There are three types of events that get additional properties or restrictions depending on the type of trigger that causes the event. Therefore, multiple inheritance was used. Specific event classes are derived from the Event type class and the Trigger type class and so they get all the necessary properties. By creating the subclasses, we ensured that certain conditions imposed on the Event subclass are fulfilled. For example according to the BPMN Specification, there can be no start error event. Consequentially only Intermediate and EndEvent classes has ErrorXXXEvent subclasses.

The following concepts allow for linking the sBPMN to the organizational and domain related ontologies: Pool; Lane; Participant; Role. In addition, the list of attributes of some concepts, resulting from the specification, has been extended in order to allow for their annotation with BusinessGoals and Resources as well as pre and post-conditions.

Figure 2 shows the class hierarchy of the sBPMN ontology. Direction of the arrows shows the superClass dependency. The figure visualizes all classes of the sBPMN ontology. For the meaning of each class, we refer a reader to the BPMN specification[2].

The SUPER ontology framework was represented using the WSML language for which scalable reasoners, repositories, and tools are available (Filipowska, Kaczmarek et al. 2009). Therefore, as a representation language for the SBPMN ontology also the WSML was selected. In order to gain the maximum of expressive power while retaining computational completeness, the WSML Flight subset was applied. WSML-Flight is an extension of WSML-Core which provides a rule language. It adds features such as meta-modeling, constraints and non-monotonic negation.

The developed ontology has been validated against the set of competency questions (some of which were mentioned before). An example of one of the exemplary competency questions represented in the form of a WSML query follows in Table 1.

All queries have been successfully executed on the IRIS reasoning engine. As a result, the domain coverage as well as reasoning possibilities were proved.

The third phase of ontology development introduced further improvements to the ontology based on the annotated examples as well as requirements of the interested parties.

USE CASE SCENARIO

This section provides an example of application of sBPMN. An example is based on a Digital Asset Supply use case scenario from the telecommunication domain. The aim of this scenario is the provision of digital content to end users as shown in Figure 3. The service provider, based on a customer query on the digital content, firstly validates customer checking his eligibility, then specifies URL and digital rights license, finally providing customer with a link and a license for the resource.

The following WSML excerpts show the ontologized representation of the BPMN diagram (Figure 3). The provided excerpts should not be prepared manually by a user, but an appropriate tool support is to be provided.

First, the business process diagram needs to be instantiated (Exhibit 1).

The bgo# is the namespace identifier indicating that the DeliverContent goal is defined within the Business Goal Ontology being a part of the organizational ontologies stack. The organizational ontologies, as already mentioned, provide description of a process space within a

Table 1. Exemplary competency questions

Competency question	WSML Query
Which roles are involved in a given process?	*?y memberOf* BusinessProcessDiagram *and ?y[hasPool hasValue ?x] and ?z[hasParticipant hasValue ?t] and ?t[hasRole hasValue ?x]*

Figure 3. Digital asset management process

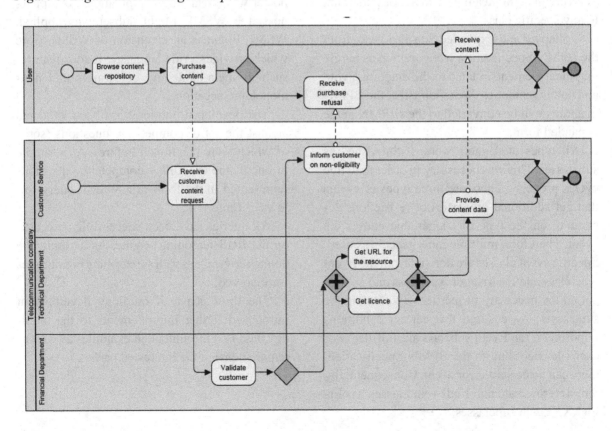

company. Thus, within our use case, the organizational and telecommunication ontologies are used to describe e.g. participants and their roles, goals, and functions realized by tasks.

Once, the business process diagram is instantiated, the definition of the user pool follows encompassing information on inter alia its participant, existing lanes as well as a process it belongs to (Exhibit 2).

Then, the Telecommunication Company Pool definition follows. This pool encompasses three lanes and has three participants (Exhibit 3).

The definition of lanes follows and includes in this case redundant information on its parent pool, e.g (Exhibit 4).

The participants used while defining the pools refer to instances from other ontologies, e.g. UserParticipant points to Digital Content Buyer defined within the telecommunication ontology (telco#)(Exhibit 5).

Finally, the definition of processes follows in Exhibit 6, and the definition of all control and message flow elements, such as:

- Events (Exhibit 7)

Exhibit 1. Instantiating the business process diagram

```
instance DAS memberOf sbpmn#BusinessProcessDiagram
        sbpmn#hasID hasValue "1"
        sbpmn#hasName hasValue " Digital Asset Supply Use Case Scenario Busi-
ness Process Diagram"
        sbpmn#hasPool hasValue {TelecommunicationCompanyPool, UserPool}
        sbpmn#hasBusinessGoal hasValue bgo#DeliverContent
```

Exhibit 2. Definition of the user pool

```
instance UserPool memberOf sbpmn#Pool
        sbpmn#hasID hasValue "2"
        sbpmn#hasName hasValue "User Pool"
        sbpmn#isBoundaryVisible hasValue _boolean("true")
        sbpmn#hasLane hasValue UserLane
        sbpmn#hasParticipant hasValue telcoUser
        sbpmn#hasProcess hasValue UserProcess
```

Exhibit 3. Telecommunication Company Pool definition

```
instance TelecommunicationCompanyPool memberOf sbpmn#Pool
        sbpmn#hasID hasValue "4"
        sbpmn#hasName hasValue " TelecommunicationCompanyPool "
        sbpmn#isBoundaryVisible hasValue _boolean("true")
        sbpmn#hasLane hasValue {FinancialDepartmentLane, TechnicalDepartment-
Lane, CustomerServiceLane}
        sbpmn#hasParticipant hasValue {FinancialDepartmentParticipant, Techni-
calDepartmentParticipant, CustomerServiceParticipant}
        sbpmn#hasProcess hasValue TelecommunicationCompanyProcess
```

Exhibit 4. Definition of lanes

```
instance UserLane memberOf sbpmn#Lane
        sbpmn#hasID hasValue "6"
        sbpmn#hasName hasValue "User Lane"
        sbpmn#hasParentPool hasValue UserPool
```

Exhibit 5. Telecommunication ontology

```
instance UserParticipant memberOf sbpmn#Participant
        sbpmn#hasType hasValue telco#DigitalContentBuyer
while the FinancialDepartment instance points to the Financial Auditor role
defined within the the Business Roles Ontology (bro#).
instance FinancialDepartmentParticipant memberOf sbpmn#Participant
        sbpmn#hasType hasValue bro#FinancialAuditor
```

Exhibit 6. Definition of processes

```
instance UserProcess memberOf sbpmn#Process
        sbpmn#hasID hasValue "10"
        sbpmn#hasName hasValue "User Process"
        sbpmn#isAdHoc hasValue _boolean("false")
        sbpmn#isEnableInstanceCompensation hasValue _boolean("true")
        sbpmn#hasType hasValue "None"
```

Exhibit 7. Definition of all control and message flow elements

```
instance StartEventUserProcess memberOf sbpmn#StartEvent
        sbpmn#hasID hasValue "11"
        sbpmn#hasPool hasValue UserPool
        sbpmn#hasName hasValue "Start Event of the Customer Process"
        sbpmn#hasEventType hasValue "Start"
```

- Tasks, where additional information on assigned goals is also stored and refers to the Business Goals Onotology (bgo#) (Exhibit 8).
- exchanged messages (Exhibit 9),
- gateways, (Exhibits 10, and 11)

Finally, the sequence flows e.g. between Start Event and the Purchase Content Task (1st ex-ample, Exhibit 12) and Parallel Gateway and ProvideContentData (2nd example, Exhibit 13) as well as message flows are defined (Exhibit 14).

The above process description is machine-readable and allow for reasoning. By applying sBPMN, the presented process model may be automatically checked for consistency and well-formness. As all models are described using the same terminology their common understandabil-

Exhibit 8. Business Goals Onotology (bgo#)

```
instance PurchaseContentTask memberOf sbpmn#ServiceTask
        sbpmn#hasID hasValue "13"
        sbpmn#hasPool hasValue UserPool
        sbpmn#hasName hasValue "Purchase content Task"
        sbpmn#hasActivityType hasValue "Task"
        sbpmn#hasStatus hasValue "None"
        sbpmn#hasStartQuantity hasValue 1
        sbpmn#hasLoopType hasValue "None"
        sbpmn#isCompensationActivity hasValue _boolean("false")
        sbpmn#hasTaskType hasValue "Service"
        sbpmn#hasImplementation hasValue "Web Service"
        sbpmn#hasInMessage hasValue PurchaseContentTaskReceiveContentRequest-
TaskMessage
        sbpmn#hasOutMessage hasValue SendLicenseAndUrlTaskPurchaseContentTask-
Message
sbpmn#hasGoal hasValue bgo#purchaseContent
```

Exhibit 9. Exchanged messages

```
instance PurchaseContentTaskReceiveContentRequestTaskMessage memberOf
sbpmn#Message
        sbpmn#hasFromParticipant hasValue UserParticipant
        sbpmn#hasName hasValue "User ID nad Content ID"
        sbpmn#hasToParticipant hasValue CustomerServiceParticipant
```

Exhibit 10. Gateways

```
instance ParallelGateway1 memberOf sbpmn#ParallelGateway
        sbpmn#hasID hasValue "31"
        sbpmn#hasPool hasValue TelecommunicationCompanyPool
        sbpmn#hasName hasValue "Parallel Gateway Split- Get Url and License"
        sbpmn#hasGatewayType hasValue "AND"
        sbpmn#hasGate hasValue {Gate1, Gate2}
instance Gate1 memberOf sbpmn#Gate
        sbpmn#hasOutgoingSequenceFlow hasValue SequenceFlow_Telecommunication-
CompanyProcess3
```

Exhibits 11. SequenceFlow Telecommunication Company Process

```
instance Gate2 memberOf sbpmn#Gate
        sbpmn#hasOutgoingSequenceFlow hasValue SequenceFlow_STelecommunica-
tionCompanyProcess4
```

Exhibit 12. Sequence flows between Start Event and the Purchase Content Task

```
instance SequenceFlow_UserProcess1 memberOf sbpmn#SequenceFlow
        sbpmn#hasID hasValue "14"
        sbpmn#hasTarget hasValue PurchaseContentTask
        sbpmn#hasSource hasValue StartEventUserProcess
        sbpmn#hasConditionType hasValue "None"
        sbpmn#hasQuantity hasValue 1
```

Exhibit 13. Sequence flows between Parallel Gateway and ProvideContentData

```
instance SequenceFlow_TelecommunicationCompanyProcess3 memberOf
sbpmn#SequenceFlow
        sbpmn#hasID hasValue "32"
        sbpmn#hasSource hasValue ParallelGateway1
        sbpmn#hasTarget hasValue ProvideContentData
        sbpmn#hasConditionType hasValue "None"
        sbpmn#hasQuantity hasValue 1
```

Exhibit 14. Message flows

```
instance MessageFlow_1 memberOf sbpmn#MessageFlow
        sbpmn#hasID hasValue "16"
        sbpmn#hasTarget hasValue ReceiveContentRequestTask
        sbpmn#hasSource hasValue PurchaseContentTask
        sbpmn#hasMessage hasValue PurchaseContentTaskReceiveContentRequest-
TaskMessage
```

ity is ensured. It allows for their effective categorization and cataloguing. This facilitates discovery of processes or process fragments and allows for efficient reuse of already modelled processes. In addition, such semantic annotation of the discussed process allows for categorization and clear assignment of roles/tasks/responsibilities and supports more sophisticated process analysis. Indeed, having the semantically annotated model offers entirely new possibilities for querying the model space, thus, a manual task of analysing existing process models may be substituted by querying semantically enabled enterprise models. A business expert defines a query based on a domain ontology used in a company and then a reasoner computes the query as well as the content of the enterprise model to discover relevant facts. Another possibility is a semantic compliance management or compliance checking allowing a business expert to automatically discover all business processes and other elements of the enterprise affected by a new regulation or changed business rules. In addition, a clear representation of process content allows for constant monitoring of the workload of employees, level of resources etc. Finally, once tasks are annotated with pre and post-conditions, it is also possible to automatically assign Web service (or their compositions) to each task.

CONCLUSION AND FUTURE RESEARCH DIRECTIONS

In this chapter we have discussed the Semantic Business Process Management concept. In order to realize its goal, SBPM requires semantically annotated enterprise models. Therefore, one of the issues that arises in this context, is the ontologization of business process modelling notations. In our discussion, we focused on the sBPMN being a semantically enhanced BPMN notation that may be used by tools supporting SBPM. We have provided an in-depth discussion regarding its scope, current structure as well as provided some insights into the modelling decisions that needed to be taken during the ontology development.

By showing the exemplary use case scenario, we argue that together with organisational and domain specific ontologies, sBPMN becomes a powerful tool for querying the process space during the process modelling and analysis. In addition, providing the machine-processable representation of the process models allows for automation of e.g. process implementation. This enables for creation of executable process models based on the process model provided by a business expert. Using semantics within BPM promises machine processability and rich description of process content and involved resources. It should ensure that the developed process models are consistent and are described using the same terminology what facilitates their reuse and common understandability.

Although quite promising, the main challenge here lays in the availability and existence of the common domain description that would be accepted by the process participants and could be used together with the sBPMN ontology. Another challenge is connected with the availability of the appropriate tool support that would facilitate the interactions of users with ontologies.

REFERENCES

Arkin, A., Askary, A., Bloch, B., Curbera, F., et al. (2005). *Web services business process execution language,* version 2.0. Working Draft. WS-BPEL TC OASIS, May 2005

Brockmans, S., Ehrig, M., et al. (2006). Semantic alignment of business processes. In Y. Manolopoulos, J. Filipe, P. Constantopoulos & J. Cordeiro (Eds.), *Eighth International Conference on Enterprise Information Systems* (ICEIS 2006). Paphos, Cyprus, INSTICC Press.

Business Process Modeling Notation Specification (2006). *OMG final adopted specification.*

Cabral, L., Norton, B., et al. (2009). *The business process modelling ontology.* Workshop: Semantic Business Process Management (SBPM 2009) at ESWC 2009, ACM International Conference Proceedings Series. ACM Press.

Dehnert, J., & van der Aalst, W. M. P. (2004). Bridging the gap between business models and workflow specifications. *International Journal of Cooperative Information Systems, 13*(3), 289–332. doi:10.1142/S0218843004000973

Filipowska, A., Kaczmarek, M., et al. (2008). *Semantically annotated EPC within semantic business process management.* Workshop on Advances in Semantics for Web Services (semantics4ws), Milan, Italy.

Filipowska, A., Kaczmarek, M., et al. (2009). *Organisational ontology framework for semantic business process management.* Business Information Systems: 12th International Conference, BIS 2009, Poznan, Poland, Springer Berlin.

Fox, M. (1992). *The TOVE Project: A common-sense model of the enterprise. Industrial and Engineering Applications of Artificial Intelligence and Expert Systems. LNAI 604.* Berlin, Germany: Springer-Verlag.

Gordijn, J. (2002). *E3value in a nutshell. Technical report*. HEC University Lausanne.

Greco, G., Guzzo, A., et al. (2004). An ontology-driven process modelling framework. In F. Galindo, M. Takizawa & T. Traunmueller (Eds.), *Database and Expert Systems Applications: 15th International Conference, DEXA 2004* (pp. 13-23). Zaragoza, Spain: Springer.

Grueninger, M., & Fox, M. S. (1995). *Methodology for the design and evaluation of ontologies. Technical Report*. Toronto, Canada: University of Toronto.

Hepp, M., Leymann, F., et al. (2005). *Semantic business process management: A vision towards using Semantic Web services for business process management*. IEEE International Conference on e-Business Engineering (ICEBE), Beijing, China.

Hepp, M., & Roman, D. (2007). An ontology framework for semantic business process management. *Proceedings of Wirtschaftsinformatik 2007*, Karlsruhe, February 28 - March 2, 2007.

Lampe, J. C. (2002). Discussion of an ontological analysis of the economic primitives of the extended-REA enterprise information architecture. *International Journal of Accounting Information Systems*, 3(1). doi:10.1016/S1467-0895(01)00021-5

Lautenbacher, F., & Bauer, B. (2006). Semantic reference and business process modelling enables an automatic synthesis. In K. Hinkelmann, D. Karagiannis, N. Stojanovic & G. Wagner (Eds.), *Workshop on Semantic Business Process Management, 3rd European Semantic Web Conference*. Budva, Montenegro, (pp. 89-100).

Lin, Y. (2008). *Semantic annotation for process models: Facilitating process knowledge management via semantic interoperability*. Department of Computer and Information Science. Trondheim, Norway, Norwegian University of Science and Technology. PhD Thesis.

Ouyang, C., van der Aalst, W. M. P., Dumas, M., & ter Hofstede, A. H. M. (2006). *Translating BPMN to BPEL*. BPM Center Report BPMcenter. org, 2006. Retrieved from http://is.tm.tue.nl/staff/wvdaalst/BPMcenter/reports.htm

Pedrinaci, C., Domingue, J., et al. (2008). *A core ontology for business process analysis*. 5th European Semantic Web Conference (ESWC), Tenerife, Spain.

Thomas, O., & Fellmann, M. (2007). Semantic business process management: Ontology-based process modelling using event-driven process chains. *IBIS - Interoperability in Business Information Systems, 1*(2), 29-43.

Uschold, M., & Grueninger, M. (1996). Ontologies: Principles, methods and applications. *The Knowledge Engineering Review, 11*, 93–136. doi:10.1017/S0269888900007797

Uschold, M., & King, M. (1998). The enterprise ontology. *The Knowledge Engineering Review*, 13.

Web Service Modelling Language. (n.d.). *Website*. Retrieved from http://www.wsmo.org/wsml/

Wetzstein, B., Ma, A., et al. (2007). Semantic business process management: A lifecycle based requirements analysis. *Proceedings of the Workshop on Semantic Business Process and Product Lifecycle Management* (SBPM 2007) Wien. Retrieved from CEUR-WS.org

KEY TERMS AND DEFINITIONS

BPEL: Business Process Execution Language (BPEL), enabling modeling executable processes using Web services, OASIS Standard.

Business Process: sequence of activities designed to fulfill a certain goal in a company.

Business Process Management: area of research and practice, dealing with all aspects of managing processes within companies i.e. modeling, validation, deployment, execution, analysis.

Business Process Modelling Notation (BPMN): one of the key business process modeling notations, OMG Standard supported by major IT companies.

Ontology: representation of knowledge in a form of concepts and their associations with imposed rules (axioms), fully usable when accompanied with knowledge base consisting of concept instances.

Semantic Web Services: semantically described Web services.

ENDNOTES

[1] http://www.ip-super.org

[2] .http://www.bpmn.org/Documents/
OMG%20Final%20Adopted%20
BPMN%201-0%20Spec%2006-02-01.pdf

Section 5
Services and Workflows

Chapter 14
Functional Components Specification in the Semantic SOA–Based Model

Tariq Mahmoud
Carl von Ossietzky University of Oldenburg, Germany

Jorge Marx Gómez
Carl von Ossietzky University of Oldenburg, Germany

Timo von der Dovenmühle
Carl von Ossietzky University of Oldenburg, Germany

ABSTRACT

Semantic Web Services are providing means for (semi-) automatic discovery, composition, and execution of Web Services. However, these new emerging semantic techniques seem to be inaccurate to be used in terms of semanticizing the capabilities of Web Services and the requests of Web Services consumers. This comes from the blurred representation of their involved ontologies. This chapter presents a semantic Web-Service-based reference model that is mainly relying on the idea of applying lightweight semantics to Web Services in order to have an efficient solution for different business domains. The model advances the reusability of its components and reduces the necessity of data transformation functions in business process descriptions. Furthermore, technical aspects about the core prototypical implementation are described.

INTRODUCTION

Nowadays, it becomes more and more critical and essential for the vendors in the business-related markets to tailor their products and software to suit the Small and Medium Enterprises (SME) needs

since their market share has been enormously raised. The issues related to Business-to-Business (B2B) environment (Bussler, 2003) are becoming important challenges to be considered in such area as well.

Talking about integration within B2B markets, Web Services seem to be one of the powerful techniques to solve the integration problems.

DOI: 10.4018/978-1-60960-126-3.ch014

Enterprises' Service Oriented Architecture (SOA) (Bieberstein, Bose, Fiammante, Jones, & Shah, 2005) solutions are accorded the killing applications to be utilized in the SME market (Armario, Ruiz, & Armario, 2008). However, SOA-based solutions lack (semi)-automatic support in both service discovery and invocation phases. (Semi)-automatic service composition among Web Services supplied by service providers and the queries provided by the consumers together with data and process interoperability, information sharing, finding, extraction, interpreting, maintaining and representation are also not fully considered. This means that nowadays the existing architecture of the enterprise Web has many defects such as lack of interoperability, massive unstructured data and increasing number of various systems that are waiting to be linked (Hu, Sun, Wei, & Yang, 2008). Moreover, SOA solutions also lack the semantic documentation of the Web Services interfaces.

After this brief analysis and to address such problems, new approaches are being proposed and developed. Semantic Web (Berners-Lee, 1998) and in particular Semantic Web Services (Cardoso & Sheth, 2004) seem to be one of the soundest solutions.

Semantic Web Services (Burstein et al., 2005) are one of the promising techniques that emerge from the Semantic Web. They are providing means for (semi-) automatic discovery, composition and execution of Web Services. However, on the one side the new emerging technologies in the world of Semantic Web makes the techniques used in semantic-enabled SOA solutions being inaccurate to be used in terms of semanticizing the capabilities of Web Services (WS) and the requests of WS consumers because of the blurred representation of their involved ontologies. On the other side, traditional SOA-based solutions lack semantic documentation of the Web Service's interfaces (Mahmoud & Marx Gómez, 2008), and that will return inaccurate information to their consumers.

Based on that, our proposed lightweight semantic SOA-based solution tries to overcome

the problems of the traditional SOA solutions and the complexity of the semantic ones by being responsible of splitting the semantic annotation from the core services. This is done in a way where both normal and Semantic Web Services (Studer, Grimm, & Abecker, 2007) can be validated (Maximilien & Munindar, 2004), evaluated, and used. The system will also provide a second level of Web Services classification by grouping these Web Services in higher-level categories named "Web Service assemblages (WS-assemblage)". These assemblages represent the areas of interests (domains) within an enterprise or business. The assemblages will include all the validated Web Services provided by different service providers as registered members. These assemblages entail their concepts from a predefined "WS-assemblage ontology" that represents the whole aspects regarding Web Services. The WS-assemblages are created by semantic Web-Service-based system within the proposed reference model. Their main role is to represent a second level of Web Service classification to enhance the search results within the service discovery phase. Detailed explanation about these WS-assemblages and the underlying ontology will be described later in section three.

In this chapter, we describe the main aspects of our model and initially present the above-mentioned ideas in the following sections. The main aspects and description of the semantic SOA-based reference model components and design aspects are explicated in the second section. In section three we show the Web Service's assemblage ontology specification with the Web Service registration scenario. Moreover, literature review and related work are presented in section four. Section five includes the potential future research directions and the concepts of how this model should be applied in practice. Finally, we conclude the chapter with the main outcomes from using this model and conclusion that summarizes this chapter.

FUNCTIONAL COMPONENTS SPECIFICATION OF THE SEMANTIC SOA-BASED MODEL

The main idea behind this model is to have an ontological-based architecture that has the role of dealing with semantic annotations as well as representing the whole aspects of Web Services; all the services will entail their concepts from pre-defined WS-assemblage ontology. This ontology has category type and generic operations divided into syntactic, semantic, behavioral and qualitative operations. Starting from this point, a new categorizing level is done by the aid of semantic Web-Service-based system (see next paragraph) that has the responsibility of grouping Web Services in "WS-assemblages". The classification is based on the domain of interest. Each of these WS-assemblages is itself a Web Service and the semantic Web-Service-based system advertises them in the semantic service directory.

Service provider system is searching in the semantic service directory via the validation system for its desired WS-assemblage based on its business domain and registering its Web Services in one of these assemblages after annotating them with semantics using the annotation provider in the validation system. The process of adding semantics on Web Service's request and capabilities will take benefits from the resource controller system by submitting semantic goal (a highly defined request) to be fulfilled with specific (semantic) Web Service capability(s).

At the later stages, the architecture will be applied on one of the enterprise systems like Enterprise Resource Planning (ERP) (Robertjacobs & Tedwestonjr, 2007) to have a semi-automated ERP solution. By using a workflow system, we can use the market best practices by storing workflows in an internal database.

The Reference Model

In designing this reference model, we defined the main aspects in designing the service interface and implementation respectively. We firstly specified the overall conceptual architecture that gives the overall view regarding concepts, goals and concerns in this model. In this conceptual architecture, we propose the structure and the overall concepts, the scope of the solution besides the internal and external interactions. Related concepts of what processes, channels, external systems, services and service groups are defined as well. All of this has to conform to the semantic SOA-based model's business model and semantic information model (document schema). Secondly, we modeled the business requirements by having use case diagrams, actors, detailed scenario diagrams (activity and partitioned activity diagrams) and finally defined the service specifications following the information model. This information model describes the elemental entities and the relationships between them and concerns about information, documents and actors to create classes and relationships between them. Service specification has to include service name, description, provided and required interfaces, service protocol, constraints, qualities of services and the policies for using them.

The final step in modeling the service interface was the solution modeling that is a kind of complement to the problem modeling to complete and finalize the enterprise shared information model, design the service model based on the scenarios, identify service definition diagrams, operational procedures, and finally define the document model.

Service implementation design shows that the implementation responsibilities can be split into three divisions namely: service interface, service business and resource access divisions. These divisions (the separation of responsibilities and the separation of data) support the architectural principle of concerns separation, contribute to localization of possible changes and constitute the service implementation model.

In this chapter, we show component-based reference model. In addition, all the aforementioned design aspects are applied through all of the model's components. Figure 1 illustrates the Semantic-SOA-based reference model as component-based model. It has the following components (sub-systems):

Web Service Consumer System (User System)

It implements functions that will be used in the end users interfaces. This sub-system is able to generate user screens at runtime. Its interface has a connection to the workflow system interface that deals with business processes described in an appropriate XML-based workflow language. The user system represents the Web Service consumer system. It contains the necessary schema definitions and functions that are needed for discovering and calling Web Services provided by different service providers (following the semantic information model). It is linked to the resource controller system (see next paragraph) via the semantic user interface that has the responsibility of transforming the requests coming from the consumer system into an appropriate format accepted by the internal model's sub-systems and vice versa.

Resource Controller
This sub-system is controlling the data flow within the reference model components. It receives the consumer's request and forwards it to the semantic Web-Service-based system to find the services that fulfill this request. The latter system will check the semantic service repository to locate the matching services. There are two possible scenarios: realized and unrealized services. While realized services are registered members in the semantic service repository (they can be retrieved at any time), the unrealized services are the ones that are not

registered in this repository (not existing yet in the model). The functionalities of the unrealized services will be announced via the announcement unit in the validation system and later on, this functionality announcement can be accessed by provider system so that it can implement Web Services that fulfill this required functionality. Information about realized services is stored in the semantic service repository. The resource controller sub-system has three main interfaces:

- **Interface to the semantic user interface:** Each user request is tunneled via the semantic user interface and forwarded to the resource controller. If the main system can handle the request then a response to the semantic user interface is generated via the processing system. Otherwise, the system is not able to handle the request and a response via the resource controller is generated back to the user system indicating that the required service is not available.
- **Interface with semantic Web-Service-based system:** to forward a request came from the user system and to get response about finding suitable service for this request (or not).
- **Interface with the validation system:** Absent functionalities that do not exist yet in the system are forwarded to the service providers by using the interface of the validation sub-system's announcement unit. This interface is a unidirectional one, because the result of the validation process will be stored via the semantic service directory in the semantic Web-Service-based system.

Semantic Web-Service-Based System
This sub-system's main task is to handle requests initiated by the resource controller sub-system. It uses (semantic) Web Services that are advertised in the semantic service directory to fulfill a consumer request or to orchestrate new services using the

Figure 1. Semantic SOA-based reference model

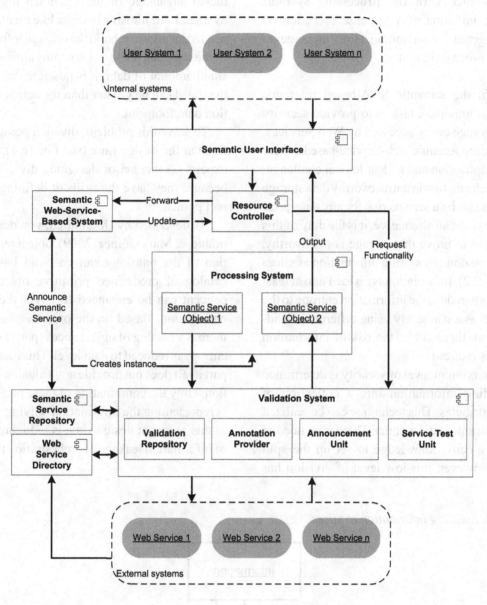

existing ones. It notifies and updates the resource controller about the services' availability in order to reduce the overall response time taking into consideration all the possible responses regardless whether the capability requested by the user is available or not. Moreover, it also informs the consumer system about the start of the response procedure.

This sub-system implements three main interfaces:

- **Interface with the semantic service repository:** Notifications about the status of (semantic) services or the advertisement of newly created services are in the semantic service repository.
- **Interface with resource controller:** The main usage of this interface is to receive requests and notify the resource controller sub-system about the status of the system response.

- **Interface with the processing system:** The initiation of a response procedure is triggered by an initialization message to the processing system.

Within the semantic SOA-based reference model, an important task is to provide security on any storage entity accessed by Web Services. However, the semantic Web-Service-based system has an implication and a clear logical challenge. Storing information in untrustworthy data storage resources can be a serious risk for any enterprise or business. As an alternative, it is the duty of this sub-system to prove that storage is trustworthy. This can be done by storing information as slices (see Figure 2). Information is divided into at least two slices to reduce the information entropy to the data level as a whole. By using different providers to store these slices, the risk of information leaking is reduced.

The maximum level of security is determined by dividing information into a collection of atomic attributes. This technique can be realized fully in an automatic manner. There is no need of domain specific knowledge to set up the split points. However, this low level of division has the disadvantage of having much higher data overhead. Administrative data like identifiers are needed in order to rebuild the original information. In the case that an object contains attributes with small amount of data, it is possible that the data overhead can be greater than the actual information data footprint.

To solve this problem, division points are defined at the design time (see Figure 3). Domain experts do this act of designing division points because they have the skills of defining the correct points.

As described by (Mahmoud, von der Dovenmühle, & Marx Gómez, 2009), object representation of the ontology can be build based on a catalog of predefined primitive objects. This concept can be enhanced to target the goal of obfuscation. Based on the primitive data types, there is a catalog of object slices (parts) where its entropy is reduced to data level. This means, each part itself does not provide any valuable information. Only the combination of these parts (slices) is representing the information. Giving attention to this aspect at design-time is reducing the risk of information leakage at orchestration time. The

Figure 2. Splitting information to slices

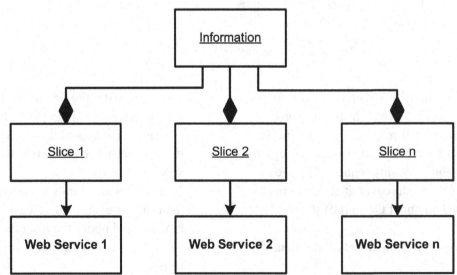

Figure 3.Object with mapped attributes

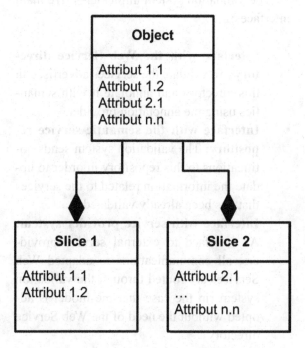

main benefit of splitting information into slices can be seen as follows:

- From the consumer's point of view, the objects look like as they are expected (because the consumer can see these objects as a whole not as individuals).
- From the provider's point of view, there are only data fragments, which have no (informational) values and it is the provider duty to store these slices (it can have just part of information regarding specific service not all the information).

Processing System

The processing system in this model adapts the mechanism of how the services fulfill user requests, and this is done by having the actual services as members of higher-level services called WS-assemblages that are published in the semantic service repository. In this way and from a technical point of view the WS-assemblages and their members (services) will fulfill the functionality requested by the consumer system. Each invocation of a WS-assemblage's member (the matching service) represents an invocation of the WS-assemblage to which this member is belonging.

Web Service Directory

Its interface has the responsibility of the publication and searching for Web Services based on requests provided by the consumer system. It has a link to the validation repository so that it can store data about Web Services to be used for the validation.

Semantic Service Directory

What is stored in this directory does not represent a physical Web Service rather the representation of Web Services enriched with semantic annotation. The semanticized Web Services are advertised in this directory because the typical Universal Description, Discovery and Integration registry (UDDI) (OASIS, 2004) does not handle the semantic representations done by the semantic annotation provider within the validation system. The semantic service directory implements two interfaces:

- **Interface with semantic Web-Service-based system:** To send information about the number of Semantic Web Services that fulfills a consumer request and to advertise new functionalities.
- **Interface with the validation System:** After annotating the Web Services with semantics using the annotation provider in the validation system, they will be advertized in this directory.

Web Service Provider System

It deals with HyperText Transfer Protocol (HTTP) incoming and outgoing user's requests and contains functions required for providing Web Services, and has connection to the Web Service directory to allow service publication. It has also a connection to the validation system to validate its Web Services before being annotated with semantics in order to be advertised in the semantic service directory.

Validation System

The validation system is liable to adapt external Web Services provided by the service provider system and to provide the correct semantic annotation to these services as well. Four sub-components within this system are realizing its functionality. These components are the service test unit, the announcement unit, the semantic annotation provider and the validation repository. The service test unit is responsible of testing the adapted Web Services in quantitative and qualitative terms. Quantitative tests are compatible with the classical availability tests like checking the maximum load, response times and availability of a specific Web Service. Qualitative tests are validating a Web Service's compliance. If a Web Service passes the validation test, Uniform Resource Identifier (URI) (IETF, 2005) of the service is given to the semantic annotation provider in order to annotate the service with semantic concepts entailed from the assemblage ontology. This annotation process is done after validating a Web Service. Unlike other approaches, annotations provided by Web Services themselves will be ignored and the system will deal only with the annotations that are done by the annotation provider within the validation system. The main benefit behind this is to activate the adapted Web Services reusability within the system. Validation repository is used to store information about the validation results. This information is the qualitative and basic quantitative information of a service that is generated at the service adaption stage together with the availability and response time information that is obtained from the regular service operations. Announcement unit is used to expose new functionalities implementation requests to the service providers.

The Validation system implements five main interfaces:

- **Interface with the Web Service directory:** To validate the services advertised in this directory and annotate it with semantics using the annotation provider.
- **Interface with the semantic service repository:** The validation system sends notifications to this repository in order to update the information related to the services that has been already validated.
- **Interface with service provider system:** As interface to external service providers, all communications to adapted Web Services are routed through the validation system (in the case that the model is adopted without the need of the Web Service directory).
- **Interface with the processing system:** While the creation of new members (as semantically annotated Web Services) is initiated by the semantic Web-Service-based system, the communication to the external Web Services that are supplied by the service provider is tunneled through the validation system in order to monitor the Web Services operations.
- **Interface with resource controller system:** If new absent functionality is requested by a consumer system, the validation system will create a new functionality announcement request available to the service provider system using the announcement unit.

Communication within the Reference Model

To have an overall view of the communication flow within semantic SOA-based model, we used the sequence diagram in Figure 4 to illustrate this flow between the model's components.

Figure 4. Communication flow

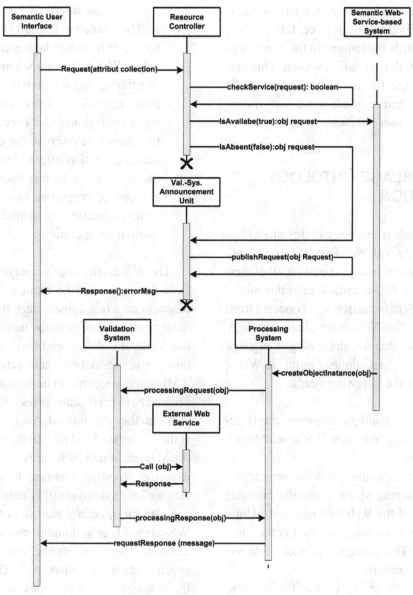

In this figure, we are showing just the main message exchange between some components in the reference model (to reduce the complexity of the overall message exchange for the reader). The communication flow starts from the semantic user interface where a request is sent to the resource controller sub-system. The resource controller receives this request and checks whether this service exists or not. In the case that this service is available, this request will be forwarded to the semantic Web-Service-based system in order to locate the service and then create an object instance request to be sent to the processing system. Processing system sends processing request to the validation system that in turn calls the external service and gets the response from it. Then the validation system generates processing response back to the processing system that in turn responds to the consumer system using the semantic user interface. In the case that the requested functionality is not fulfilled by any service, the resource controller forwards the request to the announcement unit within the validation system. This unit then publishes the functionality request to the provider system and responds to the user system via the semantic user interface.

WS-ASSEMBLAGE ONTOLOGY SPECIFICATION

The WS-assemblage ontology in this model has the role of dealing with Web Services, annotating them with semantics and representing all of their concepts. All the WS-assemblages in this model will entail their characteristic and concepts from this ontology. The WS-assemblage ontology specification is written in Web Ontology Language (OWL) language (McGuinnes, Smith, & Welty, 2004) and it has the following fields:

- **ID:** Contains a unique name and a text description that indicates WS-assemblage's characteristics.
- **Category:** It specifies the WS-assemblage's area of interest within a specific business domain. All the Web Services that belong to the WS-assemblage are having the same category. This category is accessible via several operations.
- **Members:** It refers to the list of WS-assemblage members. By being members of a WS-assemblage, Web Service providers assure that they will implement one or several WS-assemblage's operations.
- **Operations (Properties):** Are abstract operations that depict the main functions that the WS-assemblage members have to specify. Semantic Web-Service-based system has the duty of defining WS-assemblage operations based on the area of interest. Initially, there are no values as-

signed to these operations and this means that only an interface for each operation will be defined to be used and implemented by the WS-assemblage members (i.e., the actual Web Services) whom are interested in offering the functionalities assigned by these operations. Those members import these operations. The execution of operation therefore refers to the execution of an actual operation offered by a member that assigns a value to this operation. The operations or properties can be classified as syntax operations, semantic operations and qualitative operations.

The WS-assemblage's category has a *domain* field that provides the main WS-assemblage's business area (e.g., financing). It takes its value from taxonomy of domain names. It might be that different WS-assemblages adopt different taxonomies to define their category attribute. XML namespaces might be used in this context in order to have prefix categories with the taxonomy in which they are defined. Another category field is the *synonyms* field that contains similar or optional domain names for a WS-assemblage. For example, "funding, business finance and public finance" are synonyms of "financing". Category has also the *specialization* field that is a set the WS-assemblage's domain characteristics. For example, "personal finance" and "employee" are specialization of "financing". This means that the WS-assemblage provides personal financing services for employees. The last field of category is the *imbrications* field. Since WS-assemblages generally have something in common with each other, they are linked to each other through ontology's relationships that are specified in the imbrications attribute. It contains the list of categories that overlap with a WS-assemblage's category. For example, an operation that belongs to a WS-assemblage whose domain is "temporary contract employees" may be composed with another operation that belongs to a WS-assemblage whose domain is "personal finance". This will provide "personal finance" for "temporary contract employees". The semantic Web-Service-based system will have the responsibility of identifying related categories and assign them to this attribute.

Regarding WS-assemblage's operations and as we had mentioned above, they are classified into syntactic, semantic, behavioral, and qualitative operations. Each of these classes has to be specified separately. For the syntactic and semantic operations, they can be seen as messages, operations and as inter- and intra-operations. An important issue to be considered here is to define the responsible entity that can assign the values to these aforementioned operations whether it will be the semantic Web-Service-based system, the service provider or other third parties.

Web Services Registration

Semantic Web-Service-based system will have the responsibility of defining the WS-assemblages to sign up the Web Services in them. This classification is based on the business domain. As we mentioned before, each WS-assemblage is itself a Web Service can be published and advertised in the semantic service repository. At this point the service provider system searches in this repository via the validation system for one or more desired WS-assemblages which meet its business domain and interests, entails the required concepts from them and implements its own Web Services to register them in the desired WS-assemblages after passing the validation process. If there is no WS-assemblage matches with its purposes, the service provider will forward a request to the semantic Web-Service-based system. The latter creates a new assemblage and advertises it in the semantic service repository. All the concepts of the new WS-assemblage are also inherited from the WS-assemblage ontology.

In the case that the service provider will find the desired WS-assemblage and after passing the validation process, it forwards a registration request to a membership operator. This operator is responsible of negotiating another operator called the assemblage operator, update WS-assemblages list that includes the list of assemblages in which the Web Services of this service provider are registered and has a link to the rule database. This database contains the set of rules that enable the membership operator to react to any changes issued by the semantic Web-Service-based system.

The assemblage operator receives the registration request and updates the WS-assemblage's member list, registers the Web Services in the desired WS-assemblage(s) and updates the WS-assemblage's description to be republished in the service discovery.

A full scenario of importing the operations of the WS-assemblage and assign values to Web Services is part of our ongoing research.

RELATED WORK

Nowadays, applications are the major constituents in most of the enterprise IT architecture and all the software engineering processes from design to maintenance are centering upon applications. However, a clear distinction between applications and enterprise SOA has to be taken into consideration. Generally, applications are being built purposefully serving to provide certain functionalities depending on their own data entities and user sets. This results in a kind of isolation among enterprise sectors because each application has its own responsibility of producing its subset of the overall enterprise data almost in isolation regarding what have been processed by other enterprise applications. Adopting SOA solutions is not making it much better; rather it tries to overtake the weak points in the application-centric architectures (Nord & Tomayko, 2006).

By implementing these applications' functionalities as Web Services and annotating them with semantics, following our assemblage's ontology specifications we can provide the following advantages:

- From design and implementation perspectives, our system supports coordination-oriented view in contrast with function-oriented view in application-centric architectures.
- The solution behind our system is resulting in loosely coupled enterprise solution based on semantic message-oriented interactions in comparison with object-oriented interactions in application-centric architectures.
- Semantic SOA-based model provides dynamic and adjustable compositions of enterprise services that can be built at design and runtime following the enterprise requirements.

Comparing to our model, there are many efforts had been done to integrate semantic SOA-based solutions in business applications. Mainly we can find the most of efforts are made in the B2B-integration domain using Semantic Web Services. The Digital Enterprise Research Institute (Digital Enterprise Research Institute, 2009) network tries to address intelligent Web Services upon Semantic Web technologies (Anjomshoaa, Tjoa, Karim, & Shayeganfar, 2006). One of its projects is called Fast and Advanced Storyboard Tools (FAST) project, and the main objective behind it is to facilitate the development of complex front-end gadgets, involving execution of relatively complex business processes that rely on back-end Semantic Web Services (Morfeo Competence Center, 2009). It represents a user-centric approach. Moreover, it is based on the user model and it will visually establish the connection to back-end Web Services going through process execution flows if necessary. The difference between FAST and our proposed model is that we have the WS-assemblage

provider that have the responsibility of supplying the most related business WS-assemblages to the user needs. In this way, we do not have to change the user model to be adapted and being up-to-date to the market needs. Instead, we provide the up-to-date business services wrapped in appropriate WS-assemblage(s).

Another important issue that has to be mentioned in the research domain of business informatics is the process of creating the upper ontologies for a specific problem field. If we take the Enterprise Resource Planning (ERP) domain as a concrete example, we can find that the lack of common comprehensible standards and ontologies has contributed to massive failures (Summer, 2000). That motivates us towards defining a comprehensive Web Service-based ontology to be the main component where all of the business-based WS-assemblages and Web Services in our proposed semantic SOA system are to be implemented and published. So we will be mainly based on the idea of applying lightweight semantics to Web Services in order to have an efficient solution for different business domains.

FUTURE RESEARCH DIRECTIONS

The results from designing our reference model show that different methods to enable semantic annotation to Web Services and to achieve validation on them can be done. On a purely mechanical level, a service validation is feasible. Different measurements such as response time and service availability can be determined using well-founded methods. Based on the information obtained from implementing this model, statements about the likely future system behavior can be estimated.

As a part of the reference model, we defined an ontology model that describes how more complex ontologies can result out of the lower-level ones. On the logical level, the applicability of the overall reference model in practice is depending on the underlying components and objects. Objects must be described very accurately in order to perform and pass meaningful tests. During the distribution of different systems, the data object-context can be lost. This means that a validation cannot be limited to the data rather to objects. A test can verify whether data relevant to a specific object are correct or not. The development of such a test library is very extensive. The goal of the universal validity of the tests that is used in our model has to be done in a very high quality.

The applicability of the validation within this model depends on the definition of applied semantic depth and the underlying ontologies. However, this does not state the correctness of the way in which the ontologies are designed and developed. An implication here can be raised and it resides in the utilization universal properties. Many deployed ontologies are based on the universal formulated models. This approach is in some conflict with the main objective of using semantic distinctions: to give meaning to the data. From the emerged experiments behind using our model's implementation, the main difference between our work and related work is that the validation at both semantic and technical levels is practically excluded.

To apply this model in practice, it has to be placed between the service consumer and provider and all the semantic annotations and service validations will be part of the model responsibilities. Moreover, by adopting this reference architecture small and medium enterprises can benefit from shared resources that can be requested based on Web Services.

The prototypical implementations include the process of implementing ontology to create Web Services assemblages, grouping Web Services in these assemblages, defining semantic goals, performing the matchmaking process between goals and Web Services, creating static and dy-

namic workflows and implementing them using workflow engines.

There is now an ongoing research for testing the quality of Web Services. Trust and security issues also will be part of the future work. In addition, service reputation system and load balancing mechanisms are now also ongoing researches and they will be considered in the future prototypical implementations. A concrete methodology for performing the dynamic Web Service composition will be defined in the future work.

CONCLUSION

In this chapter, the focus was to introduce an ontological SOA-based architecture that deals with Semantic Web Services, in order to be applied later on to one of the enterprise systems. The main outcomes that can be harvested from using this architecture are the high reusability of its components where each component can be seen as a standalone system, the composition of Web Services to support new functionalities, the generation of dynamic workflows in the process of dynamic service composition, designing an applied ontology model, Web Service validation and evaluation. Finally, the proposed solution offers the advertisement of new Web Services based on the consumer requests in the case of functionality absence.

One of the main purposes of this architecture also is to group the Web Services based on the actual domain to which they are related (the area of interest). We had also presented Web Service validation within this model together with explaining the different functionalities provided by its sub-components: the service unit test, announcement unit, validation repository, and annotation provider. Finally, future prototypical implementations will show the practicability of this work.

REFERENCES

Anjomshoaa, A., Tjoa, A., Karim, S., & Shayeganfar, F. (2006). Exploitation of Semantic Web technology in ERP systems. In A. Tjoa, L. Xu & S. Chaudhry (Eds.), *IFIP TC 8 International Conference on Research and Practical Issues of Enterprise Information Systems (CONFENIS 2006)* (pp. 417-427). Vienna, Austria: Springer.

Armario, J. M., Ruiz, D. M., & Armario, E. M. (2008). Market orientation and internationalization in small and medium-sized enterprises. *Journal of Small Business Management, 46*(4), 485–511. doi:10.1111/j.1540-627X.2008.00253.x

Berners-Lee, T. (1998). *Semantic Web road map*. Retrieved October 15, 2009, from http://www.w3.org/DesignIssues/Semantic.html

Bieberstein, N., Bose, S., Fiammante, M., Jones, K., & Shah, R. (2005). *Service-oriented architecture (SOA) compass: Business value, planning, and enterprise roadmap*. IBM Press.

Burstein, M., Bussler, C., Finin, T., Huhns, M. N., Paolucci, M., & Sheth, A. P. (2005). A semantic web services architecture. *IEEE Internet Computing, 9*(5), 72–81. doi:10.1109/MIC.2005.96

Bussler, C. (2003). *B2b integration*. New York, NY: Springer.

Cardoso, J., & Sheth, A. P. (2004). Introduction to semantic web services and web process composition. In J. Cardoso & A. P. Sheth (Eds.), *SWSW-PC04: Proc. of First Intl Workshop on Semantic Web Services and Web Process Composition, San Diego, CA* (pp. 1-13). Berlin, Germany: Springer.

Digital Enterprise Research Institute. (2009). *Home*. Retrieved September 20, 2009, from http://www.deri.ie

Hu, Y., Sun, X., Wei, P., & Yang, Q. (2008). Applying Semantic Web services to enterprise Web. In *ICMR08: Proceedings of the 6th International Conference on Manufacturing Research, Brunel University, UK* (pp. 589-595).

IETF. (2005). *Uniform resource identifier (URI): Generic syntax*. Retrieved November 28, 2009, from http://tools.ietf.org/html/rfc3986

Mahmoud, T., & Marx Gómez, J. (2008). Semantic Web services process mediation using WSMX concepts. In *InterSymo-2008: Proceedings of the 20th International Conference on System Research, Informatics and Cybernetics, Baden-Baden, Germany*.

Mahmoud, T., von der Dovenmühle, T., & Marx Gómez, J. (2009). *Web service validation within semantic SOA-based model. ICT Innovations 2009*. Ohrid, Macedonia: Springer.

Maximilien, E., & Munindar, P. (2004). *Towards autonomic Web services trust and selection*. New York, NY: ACM Press.

McGuinnes, D. L., Smith, M. K., & Welty, C. (2004). *OWL Web ontology language guide*. Retrieved September 20, 2009, from http://www.w3.org/owl-guide/

Morfeo Competence Center. (2009). *Fast and advanced storyboard tools (FAST) project*. Retrieved September 20, 2009, from http://fast.morfeo-project.eu/

Nord, R. L., & Tomayko, J. E. (2006). Software architecture-centric methods and agile development. *IEEE Software, 23*(2), 47–53. doi:10.1109/MS.2006.54

OASIS. (2004). *UDDI Spec TC*. Retrieved November 17, 2009, from http://uddi.org/pubs/uddi-v3.0.2-20041019.htm

Robertjacobs, F., & Tedwestonjr, F. (2007). Enterprise resource planning (ERP) – A brief history. *Journal of Operations Management, 25*(2), 357–363. doi:10.1016/j.jom.2006.11.005

Studer, R., Grimm, S., & Abecker, A. (2007). *Semantic Web services: Concepts, technologies and applications.* Heidelberg, Germany: Springer. doi:10.1007/3-540-70894-4

Summer, M. (2000). Risk factors in enterprise-wide/ERP projects. *Journal of Information Technology, 15*(4).

KEY TERMS AND DEFINITIONS

SOA: Service-oriented architecture represents an architectural style that guides all aspects of creating and using services. These services are made available for all of the key players in an enterprise or even outside it allowing different applications to exchange data regardless of what operating systems and programming languages they use.

Semantic SOA: Is an architectural style that enables the use of Semantic Web Services. Its data structures are expressed with the help of ontologies to constitute distributed knowledge base.

ERP System: An ERP system is a highly integrated software system that represents different types of business application systems.

Ontology: An ontology is defining the information formal semantics. It represents formal explicit specification of a shared conceptualization and links machine and human terminologies.

Chapter 15
Semantic–Enabled Compliance Management

Rainer Telesko
Fachhochschule Nordwestschweiz, Switzerland

Simon Nikles
Fachhochschule Nordwestschweiz, Switzerland

ABSTRACT

A lot of companies are nowadays obliged to follow regulations and to integrate specific policies from these regulations into their business processes. Implementing compliance automation concepts is crucial for companies because of the dependencies between compliance policies, IT-infrastructure and business process management. Nowadays in many companies there exist either no compliance automation concepts at all, or automation is limited to simply integrating hard-coded checks into standard software with no linkage to the business processes. In the scientific community in the past years, some concepts for compliance automation based on business processes, workflow technology, and semantic technologies have been developed. Semantic technologies seem to be a promising approach where implemented regulations are expressed by means of ontologies. In this chapter we present an approach for a semantics-based configuration of a service package with respect to Service Level Agreements, which capitalizes on the principles and use cases of the EU-project, plugIT. This chapter discusses the approach in detail, shows the economical benefits, and concludes with an outlook for the next steps.

DOI: 10.4018/978-1-60960-126-3.ch015

INTRODUCTION

Compliance management is concerned with the implementation of various kinds of regulations and requires an integrated approach covering business process-, risk- and information-management aspects. In this chapter we outline the various approaches for semantic-based compliance management, assess their maturity and show what elements may be part of future commercial compliance management systems. Furthermore we present the EU-project plugIT where a modeling framework for Business-IT Alignment is currently developed. One use case in this project is focusing on the semi-automatic creation of an SLA based on existing models for the business and IT side using case-based reasoning.

Business Cases and Challenges

This section is organized as follows. We start with definitions for compliance automation and motivate the increasing demand for automation concepts. Afterwards we list the main challenges in this field and give an overview about existing approaches. Basically compliance automation approaches can be divided into the two main approaches "compliance by design" and "compliance by detection". We conclude the section by outlining some promising approaches using different technologies.

Why Compliance Automation?

Compliance automation comprises the use of IT for ensuring that business processes and practices are in accordance with prescribed compliance regulations.

There will be an increasing demand for compliance automation concepts in future because of several reasons:

1. The number of regulations which have to be observed will increase in future. Due to the fact that the legislative bodies pass on the costs to the companies, efficient compliance management with IT technologies is mandatory in order to avoid a cost explosion.
2. Time-consuming and cost-intensive manual checking of documents and internal controls can be significantly reduced by using IT.
3. Because of the increasing use of IT for the automation of business processes (e.g. Workflow, SOA etc.) and the necessity to integrate compliance management into business process management concepts for business process-based compliance automation will become more important in future.
4. IT systems provide a lot of information that can be used for compliance validation (e.g. ERP systems etc.).
5. Effective monitoring concepts indicating the actual compliance level need sophisticated IT.

The main challenges for compliance automation can be listed as follows (Sackmann, Kähmer, Gilliot and Lowis 2008) and (Rinderle-Ma, Ly and Dadam 2008):

1. Multi-compliance management: Usually, enterprises have to comply with a multitude of regulations. An automated solution for compliance management has to ensure that different regulations can be handled and redundant controls are avoided. Furthermore such a solution has to guarantee that new releases of regulations are quickly integrated and valid statements about the compliance status are possible even in the case of changed business processes.
2. Promptly delivering information about the actual compliance status.
3. Openness concerning flexible business processes and technological developments.

4. Proper integration into the business process framework and finding the right level of automation. Today, a lot of companies are running automation concepts on the level of integration of hard-coded checks and compliance repositories thus neglecting the integration into the business processes. However, the effort for using such approaches increases dramatically when compliance requirements and business processes are changing rapidly and multi-compliance issues have to be tackled (Sackmann et al. 2008).

Compliance Management is covering all steps from the identification of relevant regulations to the implementation with IT. Identifying the relevant regulations and deriving the policies to be applied usually cannot be automated, thus means there is no generic solution for compliance automation.

"Compliance by Design" vs. "Compliance by Detection"

Basically there are two main approaches for compliance automation, "compliance by design" vs. "compliance by detection". The selection of the appropriate strategy in a company has severe implications for effort, cost and risk management. An in-depth discussion of these two concepts is given in (Sackmann, 2008). We summarize the arguments given in (Sackmann, 2008) and show the implications for the selection of a proper compliance management strategy.

"Compliance by design" is a preventative approach which aims at guaranteeing future conformance to regulations. This approach is top-down oriented and consists of analyzing all the regulation requirements and implementing these requirements into the business processes and IT-systems. The underlying idea is that if no compliance violation within the IT-systems is possible, absolute conformance can be guaranteed and later-on audits and validation procedures are unnecessary. Such an approach requires that all business process activities together with process states and exceptions have to be known in advance. The outcome of the activities has to be assessed if there is a possible non-conformance concerning regulations. Even if a company succeeds in realizing such an IT-based compliance by design approach - what is in reality impossible considering the number of process activities and exceptions together with the number of observable regulations - such an effort is worthless because in the meantime a lot of things on the business process and regulation side have changed which make a modification of the IT-systems indispensable. In other words business reality is in any case faster than a once implemented and tested solution for a 100%-conformance. Also some activities make a "compliance by design" approach simply impossible by their nature. If an activity specifies that certain logging data has to be preserved for the next two years, this can only be verified after the completion of this time period. In this case a retrospective approach is compulsory.

The benefit of implementing a "compliance by design" solution - even if this solution is incomplete - is that the state space of possible violations and the complexity for the compliance validation can be reduced. What activities are selected here depends on the application domain and the implemented risk strategy.

"Compliance by design" can be realized with one of the following strategies:

1. **Prohibiting the execution of "non-compliant" activities:** In this strategy possible violations are defined as rules and implemented in an IT-system. The main advantage of such a solution is the high degree of freedom because all activities besides the specified violations are still possible.

2. **Ensuring the execution of only "compliant" activities:** This strategy is quite the opposite of the strategy above. Based on the regulations to be followed, "compliant"

business processes are defined and realized with IT. For realizing such a strategy the underlying effort is very high, and such a strategy may also interfere with the management goals and daily business. Reducing the effort by allowing no exceptions may lead to a total inflexible business process management system which is of course contradictory to the idea of compliance management. If exceptions are allowed, the effort for designing an efficient business process management system dramatically increases and such a solution also has to be permanently updated and changed in order to guarantee up-to-dateness.

"Compliance by detection" is a retrospective approach which assumes that all relevant activities, events and data are tracked and monitored by an IT-system. If this can be guaranteed there still remains the problem of a "data overflow". Additionally for the analysis of the gathered data an integrated data model spanning all the covered business processes has to be provided. The big advantage of such an approach is the maximum degree of freedom for the business processes, especially with respect to unforeseen events. On the other side a retrospective approach is by nature only reactive which implies that first a violation has to occur in order to trigger compliance-related activities. The technical challenge of this approach here is the provision of tools for an automatic detection of severe violations based on an enterprise-wide data model which are integrated into the business process management system, can handle the very often considerable workload and are robust against false alarms.

From the discussion above it is clear that only an integrated approach balancing "compliance by design"- and "compliance by detection"-elements seems useful. The key to define a successful compliance management strategy is to set up an appropriate risk management. If a company is not willing to take any risks resulting from the violence of regulations, the underlying compliance strategy has to be based on a "compliance by design" approach requiring considerable effort.

On the other side, if risks cannot be assessed or there is no suitable infrastructure for implementing a preventative approach, the reactive "compliance by detection" will be chosen by setting up monitoring and logging procedures. In most cases, an incremental approach is recommended. Here one starts with monitoring compliance violations. Based on the monitoring a classification of the risks can be realized, for example by defining different levels of gravity. In the next step the risks are assessed and prioritized with regard to the feasible implementation of risk avoidance techniques. This is exactly where "compliance by design" comes into play in order to avoid the future occurrence of compliance violations. Such a combined, balanced strategy requires a tight coupling between compliance- risk-, and process management. The precondition that such a strategy really succeeds is the assessment of compliance violations in terms of the implemented risk management system. However, this is very often not the case.

BUSINESS PROCESS COMPLIANCE

We have shown in the previous section that an integrated strategy for compliance-, process-, and risk management is recommended. In the last years, also due to the business process hype, several approaches have been developed for linking business process and compliance management. This is what (Rinderle-Ma et al. 2008) call "Business Process Compliance". (Rinderle-Ma et al. 2008) distinguish three categories for approaches interlinking compliance and business process management (see Table 1). For each category appropriate technologies are listed.

We shortly describe each approach and present specific implementations from literature afterwards.

Table 1. Categories for compliance automation

Approach	Description	Technologies USED
Annotation of process models with regulations	Visualizing regulations in process models	Process modeling techniques, Logic-based expressions for regulations
Compliance assertion during modeling time (compliance by design)	Compliance by generation: Only valid (i.e. compliant) models are generated. Compliance by validation: Existing process models are checked if they are compliant	Concurrent Transaction Logic, Temporal Logic, Formal Contract Language
Compliance assertion during run time	Checking compliance during run time	ECA (Event-condition-action) rules, Temporal Logic, Enforcement points in the process model

- **Approach 1:** Annotating process models with regulations: Here process models are extended with logic-based expressions for regulations. Very often this approach is used for visualizing the regulations in process models and is supported by process management tools of large IT-vendors.

- **Approach 2:** Compliance assertion during modeling time: In this approach only valid process models can be created or if they have already been created in the past, specific components check for compliance and raise alerts in case of missing or non-compliant activities. This is exactly what we have previously described with "compliance by design" in the context of business process modeling.

- **Approach 3:** Compliance assertion during run time: In most cases the granularity on the activity or task level is not sufficient to gain satisfactory information about the actual compliance status. Let us assume that there is a regulation prescribing that a contract has to be signed by two officers if the amount exceeds 100k Euro. The process for concluding the contract itself was designed and automated for example by the use of a workflow system. For being able to check compliant behavior the workflow system has to perform the mapping of the role "Officer" to two existing employees in the company and fill the variable "contract

amount" with a specific value. During runtime the workflow system monitors if the rule was violated or not.

In the following we are going to show exemplary current research work for Business Process Compliance.

Approach 1: Process Annotation

An example for process annotation is described in (Sadiq, Governatori, Naimiri 2007). Enriching process models with control objectives helps to establish a better understanding between the stakeholders, i.e. business process architects/managers and compliance managers. In (Sadiq et al. 2007) the Formal Control Language (FCL) is introduced for expressing normative specifications. FCL-rules are described in the form

$$r: A_1, ..., A_n => B$$

where r is the rule name, $A_1,...,A_n$ are the premises and B is the conclusion of the rule. Propositions of the logic are built from a finite set of atomic propositions and the operators for negation, obligation, permission and violation/reparation. Control objectives derived from various regulations are introduced into business processes via the notion of control tags. In (Sadiq et al. 2007) four types of control tags are introduced:

- **Flow tag:** Tag indicating an impact of a control objective on the flow of the business process.
- **Data tag:** Tag expressing the necessary data to be retained based on a specific control objective.
- **Resource tag:** Tag related to access, role management and authorization.
- **Time tag:** Tag expressing time constraints, e.g. deadline, maximum duration etc.

Sadiq et al. (2007) are using control tags for enhancing business process models in a twofold manner. Propositions related to checking conditions are annotated as "check" (e.g. segregation of duties) and all deontic operations (i.e. negation, obligation, permission etc.) are annotated as "perform" (e.g. Obligation AlertPurchaseManager). Process annotation supports the development of business process models by considering both process and compliance aspects. Analysis tools can furthermore help to identify and solve redundancies and conflicts between the "business process" and "compliance" views. The FCL-approach supports besides a visualization of compliance rules also the assertion of process models during build-time. For that purpose Sadiq et al. (2007) introduce the notion of compliance distance, i.e. the effort in terms of "checks" and "performs" to create a compliance-conformant business process model with regards to a set of predefined control objectives.

Approach 2: Compliance Assertion during Modeling Time

The crucial point for a successful compliance automation solution is the right definition of a policy language. This is also evident from Figure 1 (Sackmann, Kähmer 2008) where it is shown that a policy language links the non-technical and technical levels of compliance management.

The main task when defining such a policy language is to balance between expressiveness

and computability. In most cases current research approaches are expressing this policy layer by means of logic-based modeling (see Rinderle-Ma, Ly, Dadam 2008).

(Sackmann, Kähmer 2008) propose for such a policy layer a language called ExPDT (Extended Privacy Definition Tool) which allows the definition of declarative policies in OWL-DL (Figure 1). The generic form of such an ExPDT rule has the following form:

([r] (User, Action, Data, Purpose)) +, Conditions, (Ruling)

The semantics of the rule elements is as follows:

- **User:** For defining customers, employees and system services
- **Action:** For defining activities like passing on a purchase order etc.
- **Data:** System objects and data items, e.g. purchase order
- **Ruling:** ExPDT defines the modalities permission, prohibition, and order.

Approach 3: Compliance Assertion during Run Time

Agrawal, Johnson, Kiernan and Leymann (2006) describe a solution architecture for checking Sarbanes-Oxley (SOX) compliance during runtime based on a database technology. The approach consists of the following four steps: (1) Modeling of required Workflows (WF), (2) Active enforcement of control activities, (3) Auditing of actual workflows to verify compliance, (4) Discovery-driven on-line analytical processing (OLAP).

In the following the basic ideas of the approach are shortly described:

- **WF modeling:** Here internal processes containing required SOX control activities are modeled. Agrawal et al. (2006) propose an inductive bottom-up approach for build-

Figure 1. Levels of compliance management (Sackmann, Kähmer 2008)

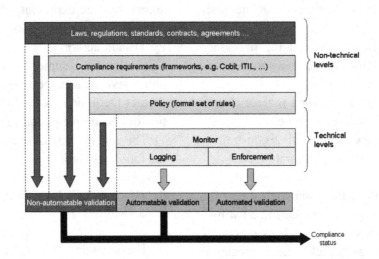

ing such workflows because of company culture reasons.

- **Active enforcement of control activities:** This step is concerned with the enforcement of SOX constraints on workflows during execution time. For that purpose a workflow execution and analysis infrastructure is proposed. Active enforcement can be realized in two ways:
  - Non-compliant transactions are blocked.
  - Non-compliant transactions are allowed and used for a later in-depth analysis. However when implementing such a solution, the management has to take into account that missing or inappropriate internal controls may lead to considerable damage for the company.
- **Workflow auditing:** Workflow auditing implements "compliance by detection" and can be used to assess the maturity of the actual internal control system. Two types of workflow auditing are proposed:
  - *Compliance Verification:* In a first step actual workflows are reconstruct-

ed, e.g. by analyzing activity logs. In a second step theses actual workflows are compared with required, i.e. correct workflows, for example by using graph comparison techniques.
  - *Query-based auditing:* Here logging techniques are used to detect suspicious activities in workflow instances.
- **Discovery-driven on-line analytical processing:** As complementary method to the process-driven analysis of workflow instances, OLAP can be used to detect anomalies in financial reports.

Business-IT-Alignment: The plugIT project

The European Union funded project "Business and IT Alignment using a Model-Based Plug-in Framework", for short plugIT (Nr.: ICT-231430), (Utz, Karagiannis 2009) envisions a kind of IT-Socket where the business may plug in to be provided with adequate IT-Services. With a model based approach, the relevant knowledge to align the business requirements with a suitable IT infrastructure is externalized. By using semantic technologies, the expressivity can be enhanced and the alignment process, which may include several internal and external regulations, can be supported with compliance checks. Thus, the knowledge on both, the IT-Provider and the business side, is captured using graphical modeling languages as a semi formal representation.

plugIT identified eight areas (see Figure 2) to describe the IT-Socket which contain models to describe (1) the business, (2) the business requirements, (3) the alignment competence, (4) the business alignment organization, (5) IT-Service competence, (6) IT-Services, (7) IT-Service organization and (8) the IT-Infrastructure. The expected result of plugIT is the so called NGMF (Next Generation Modeling Framework) that provides the functionality to transform the captured knowledge and support the alignment process. As the knowledge owners, the domain experts usually are not familiar with the difficult task of creating semantic models, graphical modeling languages, e.g. the Business Process Modeling Notation (BPMN) are used and afterwards translated into ontologies. Therefore, first an approach is needed to transform the modeling language into an ontology. Secondly, as different model languages may be used by different experts for the same aspects (e.g. business process), the models may have to be translated between languages to make them comparable. A further point is that the models may have a non-uniform level of abstraction. For example, if the business side expresses certain technical aspects, these will be probably on a far higher abstraction level than the corresponding description of the IT-Provider. For this reason, several mappings and transformations have to be done. To translate between models, plugIT defines a Model Language Ontology (MLO) per language (meta model) to which a concrete model in the corresponding language can be mapped directly. The MLO is mapped to an upper level Conceptual Reference Ontology (CRO) to represent conceptual accordance. Additionally,

Figure 2. IT-Socket

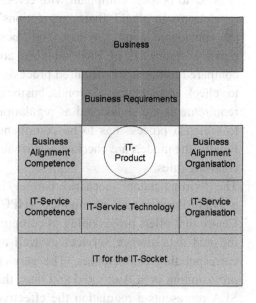

there is a domain ontology, to which the model ontologies are translated in order to interpret the model ontologies and thus support the mapping.

Use-Case Scenarios in plugIT

There are three use cases in the plugIT project dealing with specific governance and compliance issues, first the "certification" scenario, second the "virtualization" and thirdly the "governance" scenario. This section provides an overview on them whilst in the next section we are going to discuss the second use case "virtualization" with respect to SLA compliance and product configuration management in more detail. In this project Service Level Management is regarded as a specific compliance issue, where regulations with regards to IT-Services are defined.

- The use case partner in the "certification" scenario is actually the one closest to the business offering 3rd party software, consulting, customization and system support, mainly to SMEs. They do not certify companies but advice and support them

299

in order to become compliant with certain regulations. In plugIT three "regulations" are considered. First, the so called "best practice" processes of ERP solutions are compared to the actual acquired processes to check compliance. Second, business requirements are considered as regulation to which a process has to be compliant. Finally, the models are checked against accounting rules.

- The "virtualization" scenario partner is a High Performance Computing (HPC) Centre that offers provisioning of computing and data storage services as well as corresponding competences. The service provisioning is SLA ensured and thus, the SLA represents a regulation the effective provided performance and service configuration has to be compliant with. With the NGMF, the decision process of evaluating resource grants of national computing systems has to be supported and to propose SLAs automatically built from blocks for certain types of customers considering the historical and dynamically collected load information. As mentioned, the SLA as constraining specification of compliance is the main focus of this chapter and therefore, the use case will be discussed in more detail later on.

- Finally the third use case partner in the "governance" scenario is an IT-Provider offering a broad number of services like system-, middleware- and application-hosting. In this use-case, the NGMF supports the alignment of weakly and more structured business-request with a corresponding IT-Provision, an improved design of the IT-Infrastructure and dependencies and the comparison of as is processes against reference processes.

Use Case: SLA Compliance and Product Configuration Management

By providing high-performance computing solutions, there exists an almost infinite number of configuration solutions (plugIT deliverable D2.1 2009). A provided service consists of several building blocks, including hardware resources, software components and domain expertise. A simulation service may for example consist of the usage of a resource for pre-processing, one for computation, one for visualization and another for storage. Additionally there may be a need for authorization, support & training as well as configuration of the accounting and billing process.

Offering a solution to a customer requires the identification of adequate services and hardware configurations. The hardware selection and configuration can be seen as a determining factor for the SLA on the one side and the SLA can constrain the hardware setup on the other side. For some customer groups the first, for others, the second possibility will apply. Whilst for certain customers, the requirements may lead to hardware acquisitions, for other customers, the capacity of the available hardware infrastructure represents the scope of possibilities and thus, depending on the capacities and load factors, restricts the level of service which can be offered. Within the plugIT project, five processes concerning business-IT alignment were identified. All processes, as far as the IT-Provider may provide an adequate solution, result in a IT-Solution considered as configuration of a Virtual Organization. The first process starts with a weakly structured business request. The process contains an initial assessment, experiments, prototyping, setups and analysis of possible solutions. The second process is triggered by a research proposal submitted online via the so called OPS (Online Proposal Submission) system. This process contains the evaluation of formal criteria and includes peer-reviews regarding the proposed IT-Infrastructure. In the third process, the alignment is done by a third party within a framework agreement. The fourth process is based on a concrete request (call for tender) based on which the available solutions and possible service mixes are analyzed. Finally, there is an ongoing process, validating the existing alignments, i.e. checking whether the running configurations still cover the business requirements.

The Next Generation Modeling Framework (NGMF)

As mentioned above, the NGMF is a framework that founds on (semi-formal) graphical models which are converted into a formal representation and related to each other and to domain knowledge to support the alignment of business and IT. Overall, the framework is not installable software but an extensible set of distributed services which contribute to modeling and model processing (see Figure 3). In a model oriented view, the alignment can be seen as finding IT products and services out of models which describe them that match the requirements and the given context (e.g. processes, IT infrastructure and business rules). Therefore, formal semantic models have to be compared and mapped. Thus, the framework distinguishes several layers. Beyond the services which provide access to modeling user interfaces and functionality related to graphical models and supporting services which enable data access and exchange the core piece is the semantic kernel that deals with the formal representations. The functionality of the semantic kernel can be divided into three categories: (a) modeling language processing, (b) model processing and (c) semantic processing. The modeling language processing services are responsible for creating modeling language ontologies out of graphical modeling languages and to integrate them in terms of capturing relations between languages (conceptual references). The model processing services generate model ontologies which base upon the language ontologies and relate them to domain ontologies. The

semantic services then use inference and matching approaches to find similarities and relations between different model ontologies to actually support the alignment process.

Semantic Compliance Management

SLA compliance management is the task of measuring the conformance to a contracted SLA. The basic elements of an SLA can be derived for example from (ITIL V3 2009) specification. Furthermore, there exists a variety of ITIL templates which can form the basis of building an SLA-ontology. The basic building blocks of an SLA are the agreement overview, goals and objectives, stakeholders, the service agreement itself with the service scope and the details with regards to the service level management (availability, measurement, maintenance, exceptions etc.).

A challenge is to offer an appropriate service level to certain types of customers while considering historical and dynamically collected load information of resources. Building satisfiable SLAs which reflect the requirements and monitor the adherence of existing agreements is crucial.

An SLA ontology (Green 2006), i.e. a semantic description of a service, has to be matched with the existing IT infrastructure and the available services. Therefore, a semantic description of the services has to be realized and the requirements have to be transformed into a comparable model. For each offered Service, also corresponding system requirements have to be specified. Thus, the whole hardware infrastructure including the configuration and partitioning options have to be documented. From the existing situation i.e. running jobs, services and gathering past data a maximum possible service level can be derived. This maximum service level is either an indicator for the proposed SLA or for the decision, whether the required service level can be fulfilled or not. To assess the available capabilities, not only the mentioned infrastructure information has to be

Figure 3. NGMF architecture

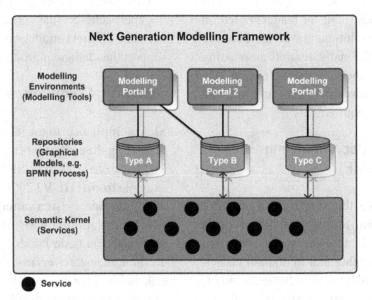

available but also the workload at the time of the offered service execution. Based on this information, we attempt to find an appropriate service package including the SLA and the configuration of hard- and software.

Based on the approach developed in the plugIT project and the identified services of the semantic kernel, our approach supports the SLA compliance management at design time. It is not a fully automatic approach but is considered as a assistant system that assumes validation of proposed solutions by experts. However, the concept is extensible to also support run-time compliance management.

Figure 4 depicts the overall view of our solution. There are four areas where each of them is modeled by means of (graphical) modeling languages: (a) the customers view on the expected service, i.e. business requirements and their context, as for example by means of function trees and business processes which should be supported. (b) The IT providers view on the offered services, i.e. a product catalogue with the required IT technology and the expected context which could be supported with the services, for

example represented by reference processes. (c) SLA templates which provide building blocks for different categories of service levels, e.g. SLA gold and SLA bronze with certain performance indicators. (d) The IT infrastructure of the IT Provider which represents the actual hardware landscape and the configurations.

In the following the OPS (Online Proposal Submission) Use Case is described in detail.

Use Case in Detail: The Online Proposal Submission (OPS)

The following sections describe the online proposal submission process in detail.

Problem and Context

The main idea of the OPS Use Case is to give support for the derivation of an SLA based on the context and historical data. The OPS web application allows a project Manager to enter via a GUI the project requirements. These requirements are composed by project issues (e.g. application area, project description, required software for

Figure 4. Principle of model-based business-IT alignment

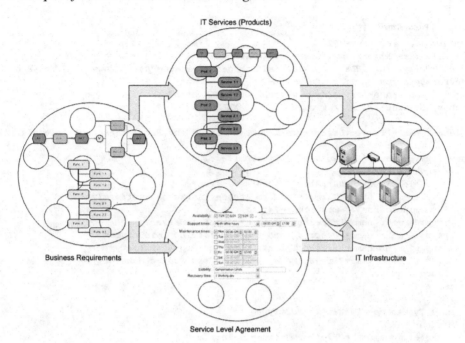

numerical simulation etc.) and technical issues (e.g. disk space, RAM, CPU hours, software stack etc.). The IT socket in the OPS application can be seen as an expert system and creates - based on the context and historical data (see step 4 for details)- a recommendation for the most appropriate SLA. Because an SLA is always the product of negotiations between various parties, the recommendation can be seen as a first step and be overridden if specific issues (e.g. price) are changing. Nevertheless an automatic creation of an SLA speeds up the whole negotiation procedure and leads to shorter projects.

Input Description

In terms of the model based approaches aspired in the plug-IT, the request can be seen as the model of the required solution from the customer's point of view or business perspective respectively. In the given case this is not a graphical model but a web-form which relates to a concrete XML Schema that somehow represents the model type whilst a filled form is regarded as a model of that type. Figure 5 shows an extract of the schema defining the project context and basic requirements: The Application area that could be "Computational Fluid Dynamics" for example. The target platform which consists of a platform name, requested resources like number of CPUs, memory and disk space, and the software, for example a simulation software package described with several properties. Further on, information on the requested permanent storage as well as more detailed project information is provided.

In the given representation, the requirements appear rather concrete but however, also alternative systems with equivalent performance could potentially represent an adequate solution. It is also possible, that customers do not request the optimal system for the given application, e.g. too low or oversized performance indicators. Thus, an expert has to evaluate the request with respect to its adequateness as well as with regard to the available service offer. Both aspects can be basically assessed through a comparison with his-

303

Figure 5. Extract of the OPS input in XML

```
[S] Proposal.xsd  ☒    [X] Proposal.xml
 1<?xml version="1.0" encoding="UTF-8"?>
 2<xs:schema xmlns:xs="http://www.w3.org/2001/XMLSchema"
 3    xmlns:tns="http://www.HLRS.org/Proposal" targetNamespace="http://www.HLRS.org/Proposal"
 4    elementFormDefault="qualified">
 5    <xs:import namespace="http://www.w3.org/2001/XMLSchema"
 6        schemaLocation="http://www.w3.org/2001/XMLSchema.xsd" />
 7
 8    <xs:element name="ProjectDescriptionTemplate" type="tns:ProjectDescriptionTemplateType" />
 9
10    <xs:complexType name="ProjectDescriptionTemplateType">
11        <xs:sequence>
12            <xs:element name="AppArea" type="xs:string" />
13            <xs:element name="TargetPlatform" type="tns:TargetPlatformType"
14                minOccurs="1" maxOccurs="4" />
15            <xs:element name="FileServer" type="tns:FileServerType" />
16            <xs:element name="Description" type="xs:string" minOccurs="0" />
17            <xs:element name="ProjectTitle" type="tns:ProjectTitleType" />
18            <xs:element name="ProjectManager" type="tns:ProjectManagerType" />
19        </xs:sequence>
20    </xs:complexType>
21
22    <xs:complexType name="TargetPlatformType">
23        <xs:sequence>
24            <xs:element name="Platform" type="xs:string" />
25            <xs:element name="Resource" type="tns:ResourceType" />
26            <xs:element name="Software" type="tns:SoftwareType" />
27        </xs:sequence>
28    </xs:complexType>
```

torical cases but also through the comparison with the actual infrastructure, e.g. existing configurations. To enable such comparisons, historical data as well as configuration information has to be available to provide indicators on applications and dependencies. As a great variety of application areas exists, it is very beneficial to classify them. This allows for inferring properties and requirements, even if no historical case is available that matches exactly with a given request. For example, certain application classes may require strong graphics rendering, others are rather hungry for memory. Therefore it is important to manage a domain ontology for simulation that can be related with the infrastructure and the online proposals.

In order to support ontology-enabled case-based reasoning a domain ontology for numerical simulation problems was developed. The following taxonomy shows for reasons of simplicity the key simulation areas for the customers.

- **Natural science:** germ propagation, mutation, genetic engineering, ecological problems
- **Physics:** standard model of elementary physics, phase transformation, fluid dynamics
- **Astronomy:** big bang simulation, nuclear fusion
- **Meteorology:** climate models, climate change
- **Engineering science:**
  - *Civil Engineering:* static strength calculation, dynamic strength calculation

- ◦ *Process engineering:* Combustion processes in gasoline and Diesel systems
- ◦ *Mechanical Engineering:* flight simulators, vibration analysis, crash tests with finite element analysis
- ◦ *Technical physics:* heat conduction processes, processes in fusion reactors and particle accelerators
- **Military:** Plutonium dissolution in intercontinental ballistic missiles

For illustrating the case-based reasoning we shortly discuss a specific numeric simulation problem which has a big importance for automotive suppliers, the simulation of combustion processes in order to calibrate and optimize the engines. If a customer is interested in simulating combustion processes (e.g. fuel injection simulation) for a 4-cylinder gasoline system, relevant parts of the simulation can be reused for SLA purposes and configuration management by taking into account past simulations for a 6- or 8-cylinder gasoline system. The rules in the ontology will also tell that it is not possible to transfer results from a Diesel engine (This is because a Diesel engine works differently).

Output Description

An SLA is a contract between the business customer and the IT provider. In practice there exists a big variety of SLA template for practical use.

The IT socket in the OPS application generates the following output:

- General Overview
- Periodic Review of SLA
- Service Description and Service Scope
- Partner Role and Responsibilities
- Service Scope and Pricing
- Service Management
  - ◦ Service Availability
  - ◦ Availability Restrictions

- ◦ Service Measurement
- ◦ Service Level Reporting
- ◦ Service Requests
- ◦ Service Exceptions

This recommendation forms the basis for further discussions.

SLA Proposition Process

The actual infrastructure and the domain knowledge is a fundamental prerequisite to fulfill business requirements. But, as indicated before, expert knowledge founding on experience is equally important. For example, system requirements of software may be formalized but having experience with certain configurations may lead to better solutions. Thus, a base of historical cases may help to find more reliable or proven offers. Thus, an initial phase in our approach requires formalizing SLAs developed by experts of the IT provider in close cooperation with customers and to relate the schema of the input data with relevant ontologies, especially with the application domain ontology and infrastructure configuration ontology.

The concrete expert system support process works as depicted in Figure 6: The customer fills the online form which results in an XML document. According the previously defined relations between the XML Schema and the relevant ontologies (e.g. the application element with the application ontology), related data from is assigned to the proposal. Based on the enriched information, historical cases are searched and, even if no exact matching case is available, similar cases can be found based on similar application areas. The resulting cases can then be compared with the existing configurations. It is possible, there is not anymore a configuration that exactly matches the historical configuration but one with comparable properties. Taking into account an identified matching configuration, the SLA ontology can be consulted to find an appropriate construct with respect to the business requirements and the system

Figure 6. SLA proposition process

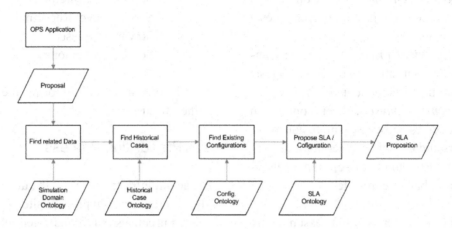

configuration. This finally results in a proposition, which can be reviewed by an expert.

Advantages of the Designed Solution

All models are formalized by a mainly automatic conversion in several steps. First modeling language ontology is created for the used graphical modeling languages. Second conceptual reference ontology is built to represent the relations, similarities and equalities between elements of several languages. Third, the graphical models are converted into model ontologies which correspond to the language ontologies and, as a fourth step, are related to possibly available domain ontologies to discover additional meaning and to interpret and relate models from different sources (e.g. customer and IT Provider).

At this state, we have then a relatively comprehensive formal model of the scenario. The next task in our approach is to find an appropriate product (i.e. set of services) and service level. Finding proper services is done by ontology matching of the requirement model and the service catalogue model. This means to compare required functions and purposes (e.g. the processes) with the available functionality and expected purposes. Similarly, based on performance indicators of the require-

ments specification and maybe additionally based on the customer category (e.g. business customer vs. research customer), matching SLA building blocks are assembled.

SOLUTIONS AND RECOMMENDATIONS

Through a semantic model based approach, the dependencies between the business and IT sides are made transparent. Thus, the consequences for the IT due to changes on the business side become transparent as well as vice versa, when the corresponding models are changed and the alignment mechanisms are applied. Therefore, the business gains flexibility and transparency.

The IT provider can reduce costs through the improved support of finding solutions which comply with agreements required by the business. Furthermore through the collection of best practices improvement potentials of the existing job scheduling process can be detected and described in a formal and transparent manner. These weaknesses in the current job scheduling process can be used as a starting point for process improvement.

Finally we make an assessment of the approach followed in the plugIT project. The model-based approach for aligning the business and IT-side has the following advantages and disadvantages:

- **Advantages:**
  - The approach helps to speed up the business-IT alignment process. This is evident for the SLA creation where the two parties get a list of proposals which can be used for an in-depth negotiation.
  - The approach is model-driven which enables a semi-automatic processing of the contained information objects.
  - The conducted matching and proposals can be used for building up a Lessons Learned database.
- **Disadvantages:**
  - The effort for modeling and a later on updating of the models should not be underestimated. The plugIT approach makes only sense if a company capitalizes on a valid set of business and IT models.
  - So far non-model-based artifacts like text documents, pictures etc. are not considered. In future concepts extending the model-based approach are necessary which manage the (semi)-automatic integration of such artifacts.

FUTURE RESEARCH DIRECTIONS

In this chapter we presented some approaches for semantic-enabled compliance management. All these approaches currently exist on a prototypical level. The main future research directions are the following:

- **Automated multi-compliance management:** Most of the current approaches focus on the formalization of policies of only one regulation (mainly internal control system-related policies). In future research concepts will be required which extend the described semantic-based formalization to an arbitrary number of regulations. In order to achieve that goal a metamodel has to be developed which integrates types of regulations (e.g. process compliance, internal control system etc.).
- **Extended use of Business Intelligence (BI) for Compliance Automation:** As shown in Agrawal et al. (2006) business intelligence will play an important role for compliance automation in future. In future there will be a clear focus on the application of BI techniques within business process management. This research direction is currently called "Business Process Intelligence" and deals with the intelligent analysis of workflow instances supporting the improvement of the implemented compliance management based on detected violations and weaknesses.
- **Integration of Compliance Automation with Business Process Automation:** Nearly all companies dealing currently with Business Process Automation (e.g. SOA, human workflow, Process Mashups etc.) are interested in finding an architectural solution which also covers compliance management.
- **Separation of business and control models:** One big issue concerning the integration of formalized policies into business processes is the danger to reduce the flexibility of the processes (Sackmann 2008). In future this will be one of the hot topics, the most promising research direction currently proposes the segregation of business and control models.
- **Integration of risk management:** One big issue is also to determine the risk level if a specific violation in a business process occurs (Sackmann, Kähmer 2008). The decision to continue or to stop the process has

a big business impact. Currently there are no concepts available which determine the specific risk associated with a business process instance (e.g. workflow) during run-time. For that purpose risk management concepts and context information have to be integrated and analyzed by means of BI-techniques for a further analysis.

CONCLUSION

This chapter described how to realize compliance automation with semantic technologies. An explicit representation of policies to be checked within business processes is a promising approach. The main issue is to find an adequate language for formalizing the policies which balances expressiveness and computability. For the future the main research challenges are the automated multi-compliance management, the integration of risk management during business process execution and the application of BI techniques to a target-oriented analysis of violations supporting the further improvement of the existing compliance management system.

REFERENCES

Agrawal, R., Johnson, C., Kiernan, J., & Leymann, F. (2006). Taming compliance with Sarbanes-Oxley internal controls using database technology. In *Proceedings of the 22nd International Conference on Data Engineering (ICDE'06)*. Washington, DC: IEEE Computer Society.

EU. (2009). *Use case analysis and evaluation criteria specification*. plugIT project (EU 7th FP, ICT-231430) plugIT Deliverable D2.1.

Green, L. (2006). Service level agreements: An ontological approach. In *Proceedings of the 8th International Conference on Electronic Commerce (ICEC)* (pp. 185-194). Fredericton, New Brunswick.

ITIL. (n.d.). *ITIL version 3 core OGC titles*. Retrieved from http://www.itil-officialsite. com/Publications/Core.asp

Namiri, K., & Stojanovic, N. (2007). A formal approach for internal controls compliance in business processes. In *Proceedings of the 8th Workshop on Business Process Modeling, Development, and Support (BPMDS'07)*. Trondheim.

Rinderle-Ma, S., Ly, L. T., & Dadam, P. (2008). Aktuelles Schlagwort business process compliance. *EMISA Forum, 28*(2), 24–29.

Sackmann, S. (2008). Automatisierung von Compliance. *HMD - Praxis der Wirtschafts-informatik, 45*(263), 39-46.

Sackmann, S., & Kähmer, M. (2008). ExPDT: Ein Policy-basierter Ansatz zur Automatisierung von Compliance. *Wirtschaftsinformatik, 50*(5), 366–374. doi:10.1007/s11576-008-0078-1

Sackmann, S., Kähmer, M., Gilliot, M., & Lowis, L. (2008). *A classification model for automating compliance*. In 10th IEEE Conference on E-Commerce Technology and the 5th IEEE Conference on Enterprise Computing, E-Commerce and E-Services. Crystal City, Washington, D.C.

Sadiq, S., & Governatori, G. (2009). A methodological framework for aligning business processes and regulatory compliance. In M. Brocke, J., & Rosemann (Eds.), *Handbook of business process management*. Berlin, Germany: Springer.

Utz, W., & Karagiannis, D. (2009). Towards business and IT alignment in the future Internet: Managing complexity in e-business. In J. Bi (Ed.), *The First International Conference on Advances in Future Internet (AFIN 2009)*. Athens, Greece: Institute of Electrical and Electronics Engineers (IEEE).

ADDITIONAL READING

Bace, J., & Rozwell, C. (2006): "Understanding the Components of Compliance", Gartner, Report G00137902, 2006.

Cannon, J. C., & Byers, M. (2006): "Compliance deconstructed", in: CACM Queue, Vol. 4(7), pp. 30-37.

Dan, A., Ludwig, H., & Pacifici, G. (2003). Web Service Differentiation with Service Level Agreements. White Paper. IBM Corporation. Retrieved December 11, 2009, from http://www.ibm.com/developerworks/webservices/library/ws-slafram/

Giblin, C., Muller, S. & Pfitzmann, B. (2006). From Regulatory Policies to Event Monitoring Rules: Towards Model Driven Compliance Automation. IBM Research Report. Zurich Research Laboratory. Oct. 2006.

IT Policy Compliance Group. (2006): "Actions to Improve Compliance Results: Small Business". http:// www. itpolicycompliance. Com /guidance/ smb_ special_ interests/ read. asp? ID=32, last access: 2008-05-15.

Kabilan, V., Johannesson, P., & Rugaimukamu, D. M. (2003): "Business Contract Obligation Monitoring through Use of Multi Tier Contract Ontology", in: Proceedings of the Workshop on Regulatory Ontologies and the Modelling of Complaint Regulations (WORM CoRe), Springer, 2003, 2889/2003, pp. 690-702.

Kähmer, M., & Gilliot, M. (2008): "Extended Privacy Definition Tool", in: Proceedings of the Multikonferenz Wirtschaftsinformatik (MKWI 2008), Munich.

Lee, J., & Ben-Natan, R. (2002). *Integrating Service Level Agreements: Optimizing Your OSS for SLA Delivery. 1st*. John Wiley & Sons, Inc.

Lu, R., Sadiq, S. W., & Governatori, G. (2007): "Compliance Aware Business Process Design", in: 3rd International Workshop on Business Process Design (BPD'07), Brisbane, 24th September, 2007.

Mahub, K., & Spandoudakis, G. (2007). Monitoring WS-Agreements: An Event Calculus-Based Approach . In *Test and Analysis for Web Services* (pp. 265–306). Springer. doi:10.1007/978-3-540-72912-9_10

Moses, T. (2004): "eXtensible Access Control Markup Language (XACML)", version 2.0, Oasis Standard. http://xml.coverpages.org/xacml.html, last access: 2008-05-15.

Namiri, K., & Stojanovic, N. (2007). A Formal Approach for Internal Controls Compliance in Business Processes. In Proceedings of the 8th Workshop on Business Process Modeling, Development, and Support (BPMDS'07). Trondheim, Norway.

Sackmann, S. (2008): "Assessing the Effects of IT Changes on IT Risk – A Business Process-Oriented View", in: Proceedings of the Multikonferenz Wirtschaftsinformatik (MKWI 2008), Munich.

Sackmann, S., Strüker, J., & Accorsi, R. (2006). "Personalization in Privacy-Aware Highly Dynamic Systems", in . *Communications of the ACM*, *49*(9), 32–38. doi:10.1145/1151030.1151052

Sadiq, S., & Governatori, G. (2009). A methodological framework for aligning business processes and regulatory compliance. In van Brocke, J., & Rosemann, M. (Eds.), *Handbook of Business Process Management*. Berlin: Springer.

Sahai, A., Durante, A., & Machiraju, V. (2002). Towards Automated SLA Management for Web Services, HP Laboratories, Palo Alto, California, HPL-2001-310R1.

Tarantino, A. (2006). *Manager's Guide to Compliance*. Hoboken: Wiley.

KEY TERMS AND DEFINITIONS

Business-IT Alignment: Adjusting IT-services and IT-infrastructure according to predefined business needs and strategies.

Compliance: Set of policy rules form regulations which have to be implemented in a company.

Compliance Automation: Strategy to use IT-technologies for compliance management.

Ontology: An ontology is an explicit specification of a conceptualization. (T. Gruber)

Service Level Agreement (SLA): Contract between the customer and the service provider with respect to the scope, quality and parameters of contracted services.

Chapter 16
Semantic Policies for Modeling Regulatory Process Compliance

Marwane El Kharbili
University of Luxemburg, Luxemburg

Elke Pulvermueller
University of Osnabrueck, Germany

ABSTRACT

Business process management (BPM) as a paradigm for enterprise planning and governance is nowadays a core discipline of information systems management. Growing up from the first process re-engineering initiatives in the 1980's, BPM technologies now seek to span all of the organizational silos of enterprises, and also expand vertically from the strategy layers where visions and goals are defined to the lower data transaction layers. Ensuring the compliance of processes to the guidance and control provided to the business by regulations is an obligation to every enterprise. In this work, we motivate the need for automation in compliance management and propose the use of policies as a modeling concept for regulations. We introduce the CASE model for structuring regulatory compliance requirements as policies. Policies shall allow to model regulations at abstraction levels adequate to implementing platform independent mechanisms for policy verification. We describe the CASE model and explain how it can be used to structure and model policies extracted from regulations. This chapter also defines a policy modeling ontology that we propose as a language for formally modeling CASE policies. The basic CASE model and the corresponding policy modeling ontology support compliance of enterprise processes to regulations by enabling automation to compliance checking (verification). The utilization of the CASE method as well as the policy ontology is showcased using an example of resource access control in business processes.

DOI: 10.4018/978-1-60960-126-3.ch016

INTRODUCTION

Business Process Management (BPM) is the discipline of capturing, modeling implementing, and controlling all activities taking place in an environment defining the enterprise, and this, in an integrated manner (Scheer, 2000). Organizations do not only own business processes, they are also subject to regulations. Not being compliant to regulations diminishes the added-value business processes represent for the organization, e.g. through non-optimal alignment with (i) quality standards, (ii) business partner service agreements or (iii) non-identified security flaws (El Kharbili et al., 2008a). Non-compliance to regulations could also be the cause of judiciary pursuits, as in the case with laws such as the Sarbanes-Oxley Act (SOx, 2002), which, among other aspects, seek to impeach financial manipulations in order to protect stakeholders in a company.

Consequently, non-compliance has both short-term (e.g. cost savings, reduced governance complexity) and long-term (e.g. judiciary pursuits, market confidence) consequences. Compliance management is the term covering all activities and methods to ensure that a company follows all guidance and implements all measures required by an external or internal regulation (El Kharbili et al., 2008a). By extension, compliance management also refers to standards, frameworks, and software used to ensure the company's observance of legal texts. In the context of BPM, compliance management applies on business processes and the related resources like data and systems. Business processes are typically inter-departmental by nature. Similarly, inside organizations, compliance management spans the spectrum of horizontal activities (e.g. IT security or quality standard compliance) that are inter-departmental and inter-organizational by nature. Non-compliance at the level of business processes is critical because business processes control all value adding activities of a company. A comprehensive compliance management framework for Business Process (BP)-centered enterprises should take this aspect into account and permit hiding the complexity of BPs from compliance experts in order to concentrate efforts on what should be checked instead of how it should be checked.

A framework allowing organizations to integrate regulatory compliance tasks with business process management presents many advantages, as we will show. There exists a very high interest in the issues tackled by this work within the scientific community. Large projects like Compas (Compas, 2010) and Master (Master, 2010) illustrate this, for instance.

Requirements on such a framework have already been elicited in (El Kharbili et al., 2008a) and in more systematic and analytical fashion in (Ly et al., 2008) as well as a high-level architecture proposed in (El Kharbili et al., 2008a). Our approach to designing such a framework is based on policies. We argue that policies supported with semantic descriptions of business processes present many advantages for our purpose with regard to modeling, knowledge management and enforcement as well as monitoring.

More than the need for automation and complete coverage of enterprise models in compliance management, formal modeling of compliance is a requirement when considering the need for verification and validation of modeled compliance measures. Also automated compliance management implies compliance checking functionalities. In the following sections of this chapter, we will show how policies and rules as enterprise model artifacts can be used for fulfilling these requirements. In our work, we assume that an enterprise model is process-centered (as with ARIS (Scheer, 2000)), and as such, we seek to model compliance on semantically modeled BPs which are used as the elements connecting enterprise model artifacts. This is for instance the approach taken by the SUPER project (SUPER, 2010a). Our work will also lead us to introduce an extension of the

SUPER BPM ontology stack (SUPER, 2010) with an ontology for modeling policies and rules, thus providing an integrated way of managing compliance in BPM.

In the following, we first introduce the SUPER semantic BPM platform, which constitutes the frame of this work, followed by a section where we give a presentation of our approach to compliance management. In the Approach section, we additionally introduce the policy and the rule ontologies for modeling compliance requirements. Finally, the Related Work and Future Research Direction section contains a review of related research efforts and discusses future tasks in the scope of this work. We conclude by giving remarks criticizing the work in the final section.

BACKGROUND

The idea of the SUPER semantic BPM (SBPM) platform is to support modeling semantic business processes by delivering a stack of ontologies (Pedrinaci et al., 2008) for the domain of BPM as well as an architecture for supporting BPM with semantic web services (SWS), as described in (Hepp et al., 2005) and (Hepp et al., 2007). BPM seeks to bring more automation in enabling business modelers to define inter-organizational applications, while offering a fully-fledged life-cycle for managing the resulting BPs. SUPER builds on previous results from semantic web services research in order to offer automation in composition, execution and analysis of BPs. It also seeks to integrate between the business layers of BPM where mostly conceptual BP models are managed and the execution layers where semantic web services as an Enterprise Application Integration (EAI) paradigm are used to implement BPs.

As stated in (Pedrinaci et al., 2008), the SUPER lifecycle for BPM is composed of four phases: Semantic Business Process (SBP) modeling (design of BP models), SBP configuration (tackles the deployment of SBP models on IT infrastructure, e.g. BP Management System, Web Services, ERP, etc.), SBP Execution for running SBP models and finally SBP analysis for assessing the quality and conformance of executed SBPs to initially drawn expectation in the modeling phase. SUPER defines a stack of ontology specifications which seek to cover various aspects of enterprise modeling while enriching it with semantics. Languages such as sEPC, sBPMN, and SBPEL have been defined as ontologized versions of respectively EPC (Event Process Chains), BPMN (Business Process Modeling Notation) and BPEL (Business Process Execution Language) languages. Also, ontologies for process monitoring, mining, resource, role, strategy and event modeling have been defined. These ontologies are used in order to enrich the description of SBP models with information relevant for both business modelers, and for semantic applications delivered by SUPER such as BP composition using Semantic Web Services (SWS).

Because of this, SUPER allows defining a semantic enterprise model. Formal models for representing enterprise knowledge as enterprise models already exist, e.g. the non-semantic ones such as TOGAF (TOGAF, 2008), ARIS (Scheer, 2000), Zachman framework (Zachman, 1992), as well as semantic approaches such as the Enterprise Ontology by Dietz (Dietz, 2006), by Uschold et al. (Uschold et al., 1998) and the TOVE project (Fox, 1992; Kim, 1999). However, none of these frameworks explicitly tackles the challenge of enterprise-wide corporate compliance management. Although work such as TOVE do consider aspects like quality management in enterprise modeling, no generic ways of modeling and enforcing regulatory compliance is given yet. Compliance management is still a discipline relying heavily on manual, error-prone, sample-based procedures undertaken by auditors, i.e. the level of automation is still very low.

APPROACH: POLICY AND RULE ONTOLOGY FOR COMPLIANCE

A Model for Dealing with Regulatory Compliance

Regulations are defined for a whole enterprise. Rarely do regulations specify exactly which elements of the enterprise they relate to. This would make no sense since such information varies depending on the enterprise, and regulations are made to be as generic as possible. In order to allow for some degree of automation in implementing regulations, we need to offer tools to business experts that will allow them to transform a regulation into something that is verifiable on the enterprise. In this section, we will derive an approach that shall allow business users dealing with textual regulations to structure a regulatory document into compliance requirements. We have designed an approach based on a model called CASE, which allows us to represent compliance requirements specified by a regulatory document in such a way that they can be formally modeled. Only when compliance requirements (as extracted from a regulatory document) are formally structured, we can expect to be able to verify them for a given enterprise.

On another side, enterprises can be represented using enterprise models. In the case of our research, we only consider the information system part of an enterprise model. Information system models allow us to have a precise description of the elements and the static as well as the dynamic elements of an enterprise's information system. For instance, a security service model can represent all the available web services with security functionality available inside a certain enterprise. While a logistics process model can represent some of the logistics processes that create value in a transport company, our approach seeks to combine formally modeled compliance requirements with information system models in order

to verify these requirements on the latter. Our problem transformation is illustrated in *Figure 1*.

In dealing with regulations, a number of aspects need be taken into account. First of all, regulations are abstract, generic documents describing a required or desired state of the world. When applied to information systems, regulations - in the form of a law, a standard, a norm or a contract - specify guidelines as to how the structure, the behavior of aspects of an information system are advised to be like.

Since regulations do not seek to enforce a certain way of respecting the guidance they propose, the concrete implementation of a regulation is not obvious. In fact, the industry usually creates it own sets of standards for describing best practices about how to implement and enforce a given regulation, in a certain domain. This is the result of the experience and work of domain experts who have conducted numerous implementation initiatives of these regulations. COSO (COSO, 2010) is an example of such standards; it seeks to help implementing the SOx regulation (SOx, 2002) (financial regulation). COBIT (ISACA, 2010) is another example, for IT management standards.

In order to tackle the implementation of a regulation, the domain to which it applies, or less formally, the business context, needs to be clearly described. For instance, the same financial regulation may be implemented differently in two companies operating in two different business fields, e.g. logistics and mining.

Additionally to their high level of abstraction, the inner complexity of regulations is due to the fact that the latter are written in natural language. Making their understanding vary depending on the business domain and the experts involved in the compliance management initiative. As such, one of the main areas of optimization in compliance management processes, compliance automation, becomes a hard problem. Compliance automation would mean making the regulatory documents understandable to machines, and by extension, would also mean that the concrete controlling pro-

Figure 1. Transforming the regulatory compliance problem

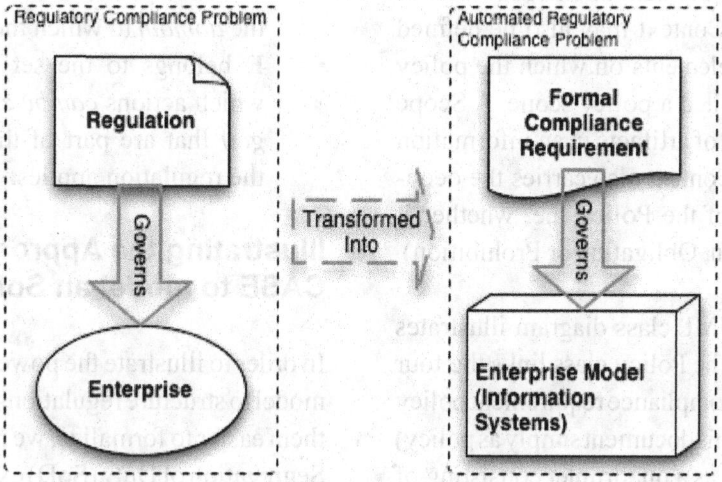

cedures that would ensure keeping compliant with a regulation are also described in the regulatory documents. Unfortunately, in most regulations, this is not the case. HIPAA (medical/healthcare domain) (HHS, 2010), BASEL II (banking domain), SOLVENCY II (insurance domain) or ISO27001 (security domain) are examples of this.

Structuring Regulatory Documents for Formal Modeling: The CASE Model

Having identified the structuring of regulations as the main challenge in building a bridge between a regulatory document and a formal representation of the compliance requirements it expresses, we propose here the use of a structuring model called CASE. CASE has been designed to allow the extraction of policies in an abstract form from a regulatory document. This section defines the CASE model.

CASE stands for (Context, Action, Subject, Entity). This model basically expresses that a compliance policy is built using a CASE quadruplet specifying the following four elements:

- **Subject:** the element of a system to which the policy applies. It can be a whole organization, a service, a business process, a person, a business role or some application. A Subject can execute Actions on an Entity.

- **Entity:** the abstract element of a system on which an Action can be performed by a Subject. An Entity can be some data, a business service, a business process or activity, a resource, a person, etc. The same element of a system can be both at the same time, an Entity and a Subject, i.e. it can execute Actions on other Entities, and can have other Subjects execute Actions on it.

- **Action:** any type of action a Subject can execute on an Entity. An Action can be manual (i.e. a human is involved in doing this Action) or automatic (e.g. performed by an application).

- **Context:** An Action may only be executed by a Subject on an Entity in a given Context. This Context is expressed using logical conditions on the state of the system (i.e. system attributes) where the policies are defined. These conditions may be seen as a kind of "activation" condition of the policy. A Context may also be defined by the set of elements on which the policy may apply, called a policy scope. A Scope can be any set of artifacts in an information system. The Context also carries the deontic modality of the Policy (i.e. whether it is a Permission, Obligation or Prohibition).

In *Figure 2*, a UML class diagram illustrates the CASE model. The Policy class links the four CASE concepts. A compliance requirement policy (referred to later in this document simply as policy) is thus first defined as a quadruplet consisting of four CASE concepts. The reader will notice that only a description of knowledge of the domain targeted by the compliance modeling initiative can allow a meaningful description of a compliance policy. The following Definition 1 summarizes the informal semantics of the CASE model.

Definition 1: CASE Model

A regulatory compliance policy is a quadruplet (C, A, S, E) where:

- **C** is a description of the *context* in which the compliance requirement needs to be ensured (through policy enforcement). Usually, this context is provided by a combination of:
  - The deontic modality of the policy.
  - The logical conditions under which the *action* can be operated by the policy *subject* on the policy *entity* expressed on attributes of the *system* governed by the regulation
  - A selection of the system elements on which the compliance policy acts.
- **A** belongs to the set of *actions* defined in the *domain* on which the regulation applies.

- **S** belongs to the *set of all elements capable* of actions *(action source)* that are part of the *domain* to which the regulation applies.
- **E** belongs to the set of all elements on which actions *can be executed (action target)* that are part of the *domain* to which the regulation applies.

Illustrating the Approach: Using CASE to model an SoD Regulation

In order to illustrate the power of using the CASE model to structure regulations in a form that makes them easier to formalize, we refer to the following Segregation of Duty (SoD) example. We are given the following regulatory paragraph:

*"Accounting must be regularly audited for conformance to the company's financial guidelines. Such an audit shall be conducted one every fiscal year. An **external** auditor must conduct the financial audit. The company may also in special cases **employ** the **auditor**, in order to conduct special pre-official auditing. In this case the **auditor cannot** be **involved** in the **expenses** he is auditing."*

Starting from this regulation, we extract the following compliance requirement:

If the auditor is an employee of the company, he cannot be at the same time one of the accountants of the company, as the latter may be directly or indirectly involved in financial transactions being audited.

We assume we have a description of the environment (i.e. in our case, an information system) in which the policy shall be enforced. This description is given in *Figure 3*.

In our domain example, employees are organizational entities having a business role. Each organizational entity has a segregation of duty policy attached. Each business role has a set of rights.

Figure 2. The CASE model for modeling regulatory compliance policies – UML class diagram

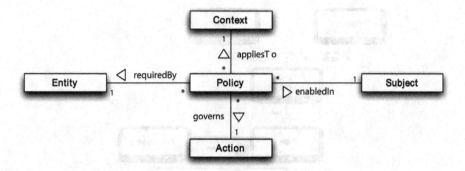

In addition to the model in *Figure 3*, *Figure 4* gives an overview of the concepts of the business domain describing the system in which the policy is to be enforced. A financial responsible is a specific type of roles. The concept of Action refers to actions defined in the system. An Action always has a target Resource. If the target of an Action is a Document, the Action is called a DocumentAction. Two specific instances of FinancialResponsible are defined: the Auditor and the Accountant role instances. A specific type of documents available is called FinancialReportingDocument.

In order to model the compliance requirement specified above, we define the following CASE quadruplet: ((Permission, RoleEquivalence), DocumentAction, Employee, FinancialReportingDocument).

The context is (Permission, RoleEquivalence). The context is formed by the indication that the policy is a permission (deontic modality). The second part of the context is given by a condition expressed by the RoleEquivalence expression.

RoleEquivalence is a first order rule and expresses the strict distinction of roles.

For example, assuming that our business domain model describes the organizational structure of the company, and that each organizational entity has a role that describes some of its functions, we may formalize this Context rule in OCL (Object Constraint Language; Warmer & Kleppe, 2003) as follows:

Figure 3. Example: A domain model describing the policy (in UML)

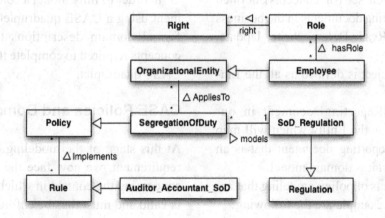

Figure 4. Example: A domain model describing the business domain

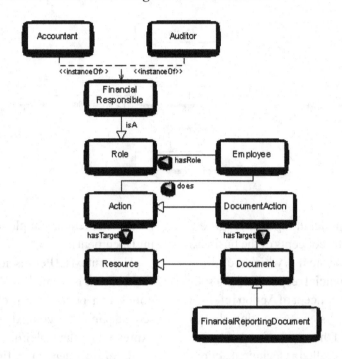

- **Context**: OrganizationalEntity
- **Inv**:this.hasRole.contains(Auditor)implies not (this.hasRole.contains(Accountant)). Note that the Context construct in OCL does not have the same meaning as in a CASE quadruplet.

DocumentAction is any *action* defined for the *environment* where the policy is to be enforced. In our example, AnyAccessAction will map to the following action set (of concepts) defined for financial reporting documents in the business domain model: {Read, Delete, Write, Update, Create, Save}.

The policy Subject is defined as all the Employee instances.

The FinancialReportingDocument in our CASE quadruplet is the Entity which will map to any financial reporting document that is an instance in the business domain model.

The other aspects of policy modeling that are not tackled in this example are the following:

- **Action Model:** The actions for which the policies are defined. For example, the possible access actions allowed by the system environment.
- **Environment/System Model:** We need to describe the environment where the policy is active, by describing for instance the organizational structure, information system resources, etc.

In order to fully model a compliance requirement using a CASE quadruplet, we hence need formal domain descriptions that contain the concepts required to complete the definition of a CASE quadruplet.

CASE Policies and Domain Models

At this stage of the modeling of a compliance requirement, we now face the modeling issues concerning the context in which a certain policy is valid and must thus be enforced, and on post-

Figure 5. The CASE model in combination with domain models for modeling compliance requirements

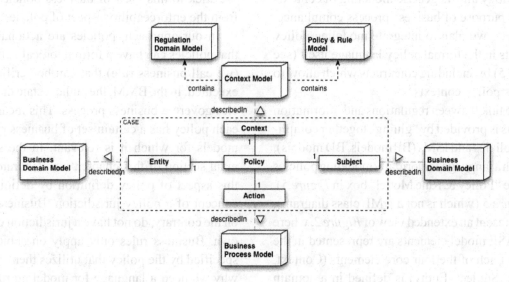

conditions that need to be true once a policy is enforced. The CASE model thus needs to allow us to structure compliance requirements in a clear form amenable to later formalization using a language for modeling policies and rules. This policy and rules language must be able to deal with domain descriptions specifying the Entities and Subjects described by a policy, as well as all the Actions mentioned in a regulation to be formalized.

In our approach, we consider that information system models (ISMs) are capable of providing accurate descriptions of the regulated system, so that we can use these ISMs to model compliance policies. ISMs describe for example the organizational aspects of an enterprise, the strategy models, the service models, the process models, etc. ISMs are widely used in enterprise architecture (EA) to structure and document knowledge about an enterprise. Business process models are a typical example of a type of ISMs. Frameworks have been proposed to capture ISMs as early as the 1980s (the Zachmann framework (Zachman, 1987)). Languages have also been proposed for ISMs such as the Archimate language and framework (Van Buuren et al., 2006).

With this assumption, we consider that in the particular case of business process management compliance, actions are accurately described in the BP models, while Subjects and Entities are accurately described in business domain models (see *Figure 5*). We define BP models as models describing the control flows, actions (also referred to as BP tasks), the resources, the services, and the human entities involved in a process.

In our work, we regard business domain models as the abstractions representing the business or areas of business concerned with a regulation. Business domain models may contain organizational structure descriptions, roles, rights, business duties and responsibilities, etc. In the particular case of a single regulation, a single business domain model (e.g. describing the organizational structure of a department of a company) may be needed. But in more complex cases, several business domain models (BD models) may be required, e.g. a strategy model (using the OMG's business motivation model (BMM, 2008) for example).

Our approach does not consider building a domain specific language for modeling contexts, as this is a whole different area of research, and to our knowledge, no existing standard, model or ontology allows generic modeling of contexts for the purpose of business process compliance. However, we plan to integrate modeling policy contexts in the formal policy language itself (see *Figure 5*) by including constructs which allow to express policy contexts.

The link between regulations and information systems is provided by "gluing" together compliance policies and ISMs (BP models, BD models), through a language for formally modeling policies (see the "Policy & Rule Model" box in *Figure 5*). In *Figure 5* (which is not a UML class diagram), we represent an extended view of *Figure 2*, where the CASE model elements are represented in the center. Each of the four core elements (Context, Action, Subject, Entity) is defined in a domain model. Entities and Subjects are described in business domain models, while Actions are described in a process model. Contexts are defined in context models that contain both (i) a model which is an instance of a language for modeling policies and rules; (ii) and a regulation domain model. The next subsection explains the need for the latter model. The policy modeling language allows formal modeling of CASE quadruplets by specifying the jurisdictions of policies and their enablement conditions, the entities governed, the actions and the subjects concerned. It also expresses the concrete implementation of a policy, by expressing it as a business rule.

Regarding policy and rule domain models, our work is aligned with the view of the OMG on the matter as a policy is defined in the Business Motivation Model (BMM, 2008): a policy is a *"non-actionable directive whose purpose is to govern or guide the enterprise. Business Policies provide the basis for Business Rules. Business Policies also govern Business Processes"*. Whereas a rule is defined as a *"directive, intended to govern, guide, or influence business behavior, in support of Business Policy"*. The BMM standard adds: *"often, a business rule is derived from business policy. Business rules guide business processes"*.

We stick to this view of business policies apart from the enforceability aspect of policies.

In our approach, policies are actionable, in that policies can have a formal logical definition (we call business rule) that can be verified and executed. In the BMM, the authors state that policies govern a business process. This means that each policy has a certain set of business process models for which it is relevant. In the second main section of this chapter, we elaborate upon this aspect of policy definition by defining the concept of a policy jurisdiction. Business rules on the contrary, do not have a jurisdiction of their own. Business rules only apply on subjects as specified by the policy that utilizes them. This is why we need a language for modeling rules, in order to allow formal modeling of policies (see *Figure 5*).

We cannot argue that the CASE model allows covering all types of policies contained in regulations, in fact, there may be some parts of a regulatory document that can hardly be represented using solely CASE. In this research work however, we refer to a regulation as the subset of the original regulatory document obtained by composing all the CASE quadruplets that can be extracted from the latter by a domain expert (see Definition 2).

Definition 2: Regulation

A regulation is a logical set of CASE quadruplets. It can be expressed as a conjunction of disjunctions of CASE quadruplets.

While each of the three elements, Action, Subject and Entity, is described by a domain model, the Context is described using part of a specific language for modeling policies. In order to describe Subjects and Entities for example, we can use organizational ontologies such as the organizational ontology developed in the SUPER research project on semantic BPM (Filipowska, 2008). As for Actions, a domain model describing the existing services or available actions to humans in the information system, such as in a business process, is required. In SUPER, such Actions models can be obtained by using a semantic business process model. Needless to say that such a model can be an ontology, which formally describes the semantics of the domain.

On the Need for a Regulation Domain Model

The structure of a regulation as it is expressed using compliance policies needs to be documented. We need models that express the structure of a regulation, which policies implement which requirements, as well as the regulation's zones of jurisdiction on an ISM (i.e. link regulations or regulatory compliance requirements to parts of the information system (IS) that are governed by the regulation). This is useful when conducting regulation model analysis. We consider in our requirements on a policy modeling language the following useful analysis types:

- **Coverage analysis:** In order to know how much of the compliance requirements of a given regulation are covered by a policy (or a policy set), we need a means to link policies which enforcement/verification fulfill a given compliance requirement to this compliance requirement in the regulation (i.e. to a section of the textual representation of the regulation).
- **Composition analysis:** In cases of complex compliance requirements, which are a composition of (e.g. structural combination, reference to another compliance requirement) several requirements, we need to keep track of how the policy model implements this composition.
- **Impact analysis:** When modifying a regulation, we need to be able to discover which modeled/implemented policies are impacted by this change. Symmetrically, when a change is operated on a compliance policy, compliance requirements must be re-analyzed and experts must validate that the policy model implementing the regulation is still accurate.

- **Conflict analysis:** In scenarios where multiple compliance requirements may lead to conflicting compliance policies (e.g. several regulations with conflicting policy jurisdictions), the policy language must allow linking conflicting policies to parts of the regulation (regulatory compliance requirements) that are responsible for the definition of each of the conflicting policies. This information shall help business experts sort out the reasons why policies conflict and make a decision about it using the mechanisms provided by the policy modeling language. For example, later in this chapter, we discuss the concept of policy prioritization.

Wrap-Up: From a Regulation Text to Formally Modeled Policies

In this section of the chapter, we have proposed the use of the CASE model for approaching and structuring regulations. The goal of this approach is to provide a structured and formal model of regulatory compliance requirements as CASE policies. Each policy is thus initially expressed as a CASE quadruplet.

The goal in the remainder of the approach is to enrich these CASE quadruplets with additional information and finally to develop a policy modeling language (in particular, a policy ontology) incarnating the CASE principles.

The CASE quadruplets are further formally modeled by relaying on a set of domain specific languages. The languages we identified are the following, as summarized in *Figure 6*. Note that each of the domain models is an instance of a metamodel that acts as a language for creating instance descriptions of a given domain. As such, a BP model is an instance of a BP metamodel that is a domain specific language for representing business processes such as the metamodel of the BPMN language (BPMN, 2010):

- Business process metamodel.
- Business domain metamodel.
- Regulation domain metamodel.
- Policy modeling language (PML) that allows expressing: policy contexts and rules.

In this approach, modeling at the compliance level is independent of the:

- **Computing model**: the concrete logics or rule implementation of a compliance requirement is not relevant in modeling CASE policies.
- **System model**: ISMs are separate artifacts in our approach and do not influence the modeling of a regulation.

The boundaries between conceptual modeling and knowledge modeling become fuzzy (Yun, 2008). Formal ontology modeling has the advantage of making knowledge models computable and ready for inference. Whereas domain specific models allow to structure the world in separate domains and allow for reusability and

more flexibility (e.g. using model transformations) in dealing with the produced formal models. We argue that ontologies, with the formal semantic power they provide, constitute a suitable tool for creating these domain specific languages. We propose that each of the four required languages be defined as an ontology. This approach fits in the semantic BPM perspective derived in projects such as the SUPER project (SUPER, 2010), where every asset in process management is defined using an ontology, in order to allow reasoning on the process models.

In the remainder of this chapter, we will solely concentrate on the PML language as a means to create more formal descriptions of CASE quadruplets. More specifically, we will study the part of the PML that allows modeling policies as rules. In the following sub-section we introduce the BPRO ontology as a language for allowing more detailed and system-near modeling of a CASE policy.

A SEMANTIC FRAMEWORK OF POLICIES AND RULES

We now proceed to the definition of an initial integrated approach to model, check and enforce

Figure 6. Models for formalizing regulations as compliance policies

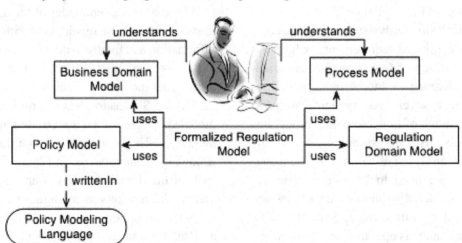

compliance on enterprise models, as summarized in *Figure 7*.

As specified in *Figure 5*, we need a language for creating models of policies and rules. We propose to use ontologies to define this metamodel, just like the other metamodels used in the approach (*Figure 7*). *Figure 7* summarizes the overall approach taken in this research work. Regulatory documents are structured as CASE quadruplets. The definition of the CASE quadruplets is completed using additional domain model descriptions, in order to obtain a formalized regulation.

By means of the proposed ontologies we turn the CASE theory into a format which can be automatically processed by the computer. Structuring the regulations using CASE is a pre-step bridging the large gap between the original regulation document and its corresponding computer format. With CASE and ontologies we propose to approach a computer-readable format for rules in small-steps manner.

Figure 7. An integrated approach for modeling and enforcing BP compliance

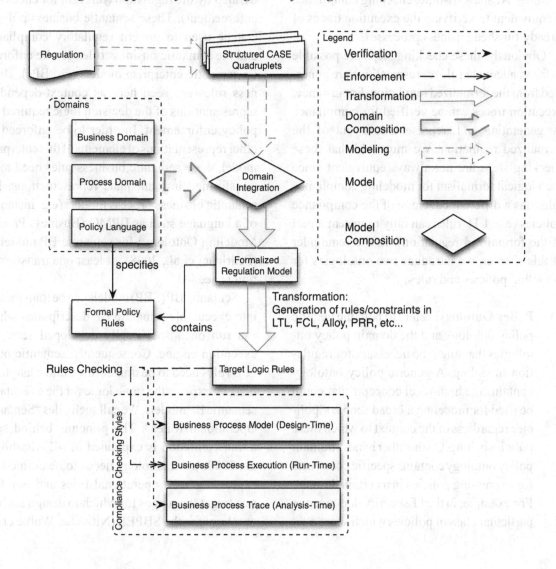

Having derived the CASE quadruplets a following step in the process is the further formalization of the regulation by defining formal policies and rules using the ontology we detail in the next subsection. The formal policies and rules are transformed into target logic languages (e.g. LTL – Linear Temporal Logic) in order to be verified on business process models. Here, we distinguish three types of verification. Design-time business process models can be verified for compliance with the regulation by checking the formal rules on the business process model. Further on, executed business processes can be monitored for compliance with the regulation by enforcing business rules at run-time. At analysis-time, checking compliance is equivalent to verifying the execution traces of already finished business processes.

Obviously, these checking steps are possible as far as adequate rule representations are generated from the formalized regulation. For instance, execution traces can be verified for compliance by generating LTL representations out of the formalized regulation. We must add that these checking steps are not always equivalent since each logical formalism for modeling compliance rules has a different coverage of the compliance policies (e.g. LTL rules can only represent a part of the formalized regulation). In the remainder of this chapter, we introduce two ontologies for modeling policies and rules:

(i) **Policy Ontology:** refers to both the generic policy ontology and the domain policy ontologies that might be necessary for regulation modeling. A generic policy ontology contains the high-level concepts that could be used for modeling a broad scope of policies regardless of the context to which these policies belong. On the other hand, a domain policy ontology contains specific constructs for expressing policies in a certain domain. For example, in the IT security domain, one particular class of policies which share a set of attributes and properties are role-based access control (RBAC) policies.

(ii) **Business Rules Ontology:** refers to the ontology providing constructs needed to express policies as business rules. The business rules ontology will typically allow serializing policies in some kind of mathematical logic (e.g. predicate logic, first order logic, description logic, temporal logic, etc.).

The result of using these two ontologies to model policies and rules is an ontology containing a semantic model of the policies and their further logical specification as business rules defined by the regulation (relevant for checking/enforcement). These semantic business policies can be used to govern regulatory compliance and the semantic business rules can be enforced on semantic enterprise models (i.e. BPs). Business rules are seen here as context-dependent representations of the decision logic required for policy enforcement. In order to be enforced on other representations of elements of this enterprise model, these semantic business rules need to be transformed into adequate representations. For semantic business process models (e.g. instances of a language such as BPMO (Business Process Modeling Ontology) for semantic BP modeling (Pedrinaci et al., 2008), at least one transformation is needed.

Semantic BP (SBP) models can be transformed into executable semantic BP descriptions which can run on a specifically developed semantic execution engine. Consequently, semantic business rules need to be transformed into a language that can express the same logic for the executable semantic BP models. We call such rules "Semantic Operational Rules". The principle behind such a transformation is explained in (El Kharbili et al., 2008b). An ontology needs to be defined for expressing such operational rules and our first two target languages for which to design such an ontology are the SBPEL (Nitzsche, Wutke et al.,

2007) and the BPEL4SWS (Nitzsche, van Lessen et al., 2007) languages. The latter are a semantic representation of the BPEL standard and an extension of the BPEL (WSBPEL, 2007) standard for invoking semantic web services.

In order to check regulatory compliance on process logs, a special transformation of the business rules into constraints verifiable directly on these logs is necessary. This is needed in case of the so-called Backward Compliance Checking, where compliant behavior of the business processes is checked after the concerned BP instances have finished running. Such checking techniques could be used in case some wants to check behavior only for a sub-class of all process instances defined by the BP model.

One of our approaches in realizing this with a prototype relies on defining semantic LTL (Linear temporal Logic) formulae of semantic business rules and using the ProM (Van Dongen, 2005) mining tool for checking if these formulae hold on process logs. As to now, no work provides performance comparison to model checking techniques. But it would still be reasonable to think that such a checking technique can be at least as cheap as the so-called Forward Compliance Checking techniques (El Kharbili et al., 2008a).

Business Policy and Rule Ontology (BPRO)

The BPRO is the ontology stack used to model policies and rules in the SUPER ontology stack. The BPRO incorporates and realizes the CASE theory within ontology languages. The idea for the BPRO is to be independent from the concrete execution of the rules and to bring as much information from the rule language to the policy layers, while keeping the policy definition independent from any rule language. We will start by listing some examples of competency questions that the ontology needs to be able to answer and then proceed to a short description of the main concepts.

Figure 8 and *Figure 9* detail the business policy and the business rule ontologies which we introduced earlier. As already said, these ontologies seek to provide a generic and high level model to be reused by other ontologies for concrete regulatory compliance modeling. In order to later validate the design of the ontology we first need to specify the competency questions it needs to be able to answer. This is not a sufficient validation criterion though, and a well-founded evaluation of the soundness of the ontology still has to be performed.

1. In a given BP model state, which policies are active?
2. Which policies are called by policy P once policy P is activated?
3. What policies apply to BP activity A?
4. To which activities, roles and resources does policy P apply?
5. Policy P1, P2 and P3 are active and need to take a decision on Resource R: Which policy has the highest priority?
6. Policy P took its decision: which rules need to fire in order to implement this decision?
7. Which business goals does policy P fulfill?
8. What is the jurisdiction of policy P?
9. What is the scope of a policy P inside a jurisdiction J?
10. Which regulations is policy P part of?
11. What is the type of policy P?
12. What is the modality of policy P?

The main idea in the business policy ontology is that policies take decisions on whether a state of the business (enterprise model/BP) is allowed or not. In Rei (Kagal, 2004), this is achieved by defining modalities upon actors, actions and targets of these actions. In the business policy ontology, this is achieved by setting modalities for attributes and properties of ontological concepts. These concepts can be concrete actions or be simply the result of these actions. The modalities are combined with condition evaluation that is left for a rule to do.

Figure 8. The business policy ontology

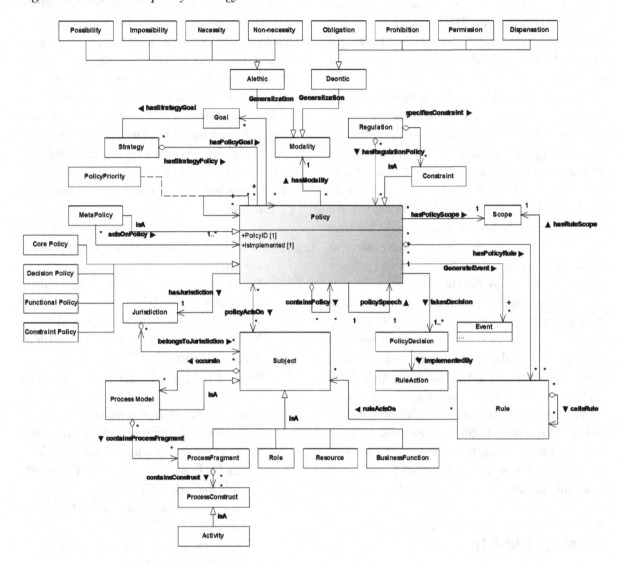

The decision taken by a policy is implemented by executing a rule too, and/or by triggering an event. Events are used to propagate decisions inside the policy framework. For example: to express the policy that a resource of type X cannot be accessed by a business process activity which has a responsible person of Role Y, it is necessary for the policy to check the attribute Responsible of a BP activity which is connected to the resource X on which it applies after having checked that resource X has an attribute type=="X". In this

scenario, both a passive and active approach to compliance checking work.

In the case of passive checking, the policy is modeled in a decision point. In this example, it means that the activation and evaluation of the policy is directly triggered by the element governed by this policy: resource X. Before the concerned BP activity even executes, it checks which policies are active, by evaluating all the conditions to activate policies attached to it. These activation conditions are part of the definition of the business policy. In the case of active checking,

Figure 9. The business rule ontology

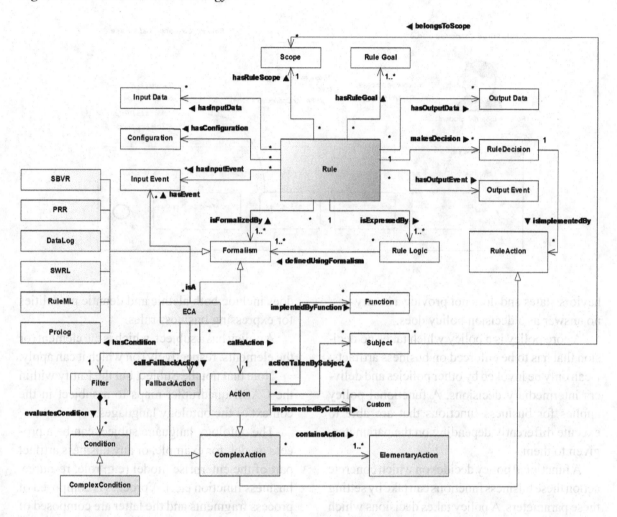

it means that the policy enforcement component actively supervises all states traversed by the BP model and matches these states to policies that need to be activated for the current state. Changes in states are triggered by actions, or, in the case of BP models, of transitions from one activity to the other. Reasoning on the current transition to be made and matching it with policies to activate and then evaluating these policies, leads to the policy taking a yes/no decision about the current state violating the policy (non-compliant) or not.

The policy ontology is represented in *Figure 8* and we will now proceed to a concise description of its concepts. This description ignores both,

relationships constraints and constraints (axioms). The central concept of the ontology is the Policy concept (see *Figure 10* and *Figure 11* for an example). A policy belongs to a regulation together with other policies. A policy also fulfills a goal and belongs to a strategy. Strategies are assigned to a goal. A policy can be a meta-policy, which is a policy acting on other policies. With regard to another policy, a policy has a priority set.

A constraint is one kind of policy, next to decision, functional and core policies. A constraint policy decides on how to constrain a resource in showing some behavior. It delivers one or many of several discrete allowed business artifact be-

Figure 10. Example of a role-based resource access control (RBRAC) policy: Using policies and rules

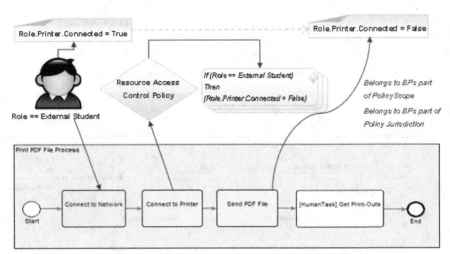

haviors/states and does not provide a binary yes/no answer as a decision policy does.

A core policy is a policy which takes no decision that has to be enforced on business artifacts; it can only be invoked by other policies and delivers intermediary decisions. A functional policy applies for business functions that are able to execute differently depending on the parameters given to them.

A functional policy decides on which concrete action these business functions can take by setting these parameters. A policy takes decisions which can result in rule actions. Rule actions can be implemented outside the BPRO either by another ontology or by being implemented in another system and invoked from the BPRO.

A policy has two kinds of modalities: deontic and alethic. Deontic modalities allow expressing behavioral constraints and are of three types: Prohibition (interdiction), Permission and Obligation. Dispensation is an additional special type which frees a subject from a constraint rather than imposing it. Deontic constraints nap to those modeled in Rei (Kagal, 2004). Alethic modalities allow expressing structural constraints and are of four types: Necessity, Non-necessity, Possibility and Impossibility. The SBVR (SBVR, 2008) standard

does include both alethic and deontic modalities for expressing business rules.

A policy has a subject, which is the element (or the elements, respectively) on which it can apply.

Note that not the Subject but the Entity within the CASE quadruplet maps to a subject in the context of the ontology languages.

The ontology language subject can be a process model, for example, or any business artifact part of the enterprise model (e.g. role, resource, business function etc.). A process is composed of process fragments and the latter are composed of process constructs such as activities. The concepts related to BP modeling have to be mapped to the used BPM ontologies. A policy has a jurisdiction and a scope.

A jurisdiction is the domain in which a policy has the right to take decisions. Outside its jurisdiction, a policy cannot take any decisions, cannot be solicited, and cannot communicate with other policies about subjects not belonging to its jurisdiction. A jurisdiction has a set of subjects. These sets of subjects can be defined in a declarative way, such as using assertions on properties of subjects, e.g. "all roles of type == [engineer | manager] where role.budget >= 1000 units". We do not take into account jurisdiction management (which would

Figure 11. WSML code snippet – Business Policy example

```
instance User_RBAC_obligation memberOf BPRO#Obligation
instance Student_X78651 memberOf oso#OrganisationalPosition
instance Academic_598712 memberOf bronto#AcademicROle
instance BizRule_12_A memberOf BPRO#BusinessRule
        isFormalizedBy "WSML-Flight"
        isExpressedBy "?z memberOf RolePerformsReviewCustomerFinancialDetails (?y
memberOf ReviewCustomerFinancialDetails, ?x) : ?x Customer memberOf
OrganisationalPosition and ?x[CRM_State hasValue TRUE]"
instance BizPolicy_RBAC_1 memberOf BPRO#Policy
        hasID hasValue "zu873928_kuasi09"
        hasModality hasValue User_RBAC_obligation
        isImplemented hasValue TRUE
        hasTextualDescription hasValue "Role-Based Access Control Policy for electronic
institute resources"
        hasSubject hasValue Student_X78651
        hasSubject hasValue Academic_598712
        hasRule BizRule_1_A
instance BizRule_1_A memberOf BPRO#Rule
    isExpressedBy hasValue ⁼ axiom ServiceRequestVeryLowPriority
    definedBy ?y memberOf InstituteIT#Printer and ?x memberOf
    {oso#OrganizationalPosition, bronto#AcademicRole} and
    ?x[InstituteIT#ConnectedToPrinter hasValue ?y] and ?x[HR#Registered
    hasValue False] implies ?x[RBAC#AccessRight hasValue False."

        isFormalizedBy hasValue "WSML-Flight"
        implementsPolicy hasValue BizPolicy_RBAC_1
```

require a dedicated algebra) in order to define these inter-policy relations unambiguously. The latter are those managed by the Rei (Kagal, 2004) framework and make use of speech acts (policy delegation, policy revocation, policy invocation, policy cancellation) and conflict resolution.

Scopes are different from a jurisdiction in that scopes are always strictly included in jurisdictions and define the set of subjects inside a given jurisdiction upon which a policy can take a decision. Scopes introduce additional flexibility in managing policies, by allowing moving a policy's scope inside a given jurisdiction.

Figure 9 displays all concepts of the business rule ontology, which we will briefly describe here. As the figure shows, rules allow modeling action taking, which is triggered by a policy decision. A rule belongs to one or several policies. That means

rules can be composed in order to implement a certain policy, although the BPRO doesn't include concepts for expressing rule composition yet.

A rule is also attached to a business goal and has a scope. A rule has input and output data it processes and an input and output event. Input events can trigger the execution of a rule and output events are generated by a rule to trigger other rules or actions. A rule has configuration data which enables the rule to execute different logics depending on its configuration.

A rule implements a policy decision and produces a rule decision. A rule decision allows modeling chains of rule executions which brings more expressiveness to rule modeling. A parallel to business processes would be that a chain of rule decisions is like a sequence pattern of business process activities, where the activities are all rule executions. A rule contains rule logic that is expressed in a certain formalism. Rule actions support expressing complex actions that use logical operators such as (AND, OR, NOT, XOR) on rule calls.

There is a multitude of formalisms for expressing business rules available. In *Figure 9*, the Event-Condition-Action (ECA) formalism has been used as an example. An ECA rule has a filter (condition), an action which can be a complex expression of actions, and a fallback action which is the action to be taken in case the condition evaluates to false. It is also triggered by one of the input events of the rule. The action taken by the ECA rule is performed on a subject and can be implemented either by an available function (from the business functions ontology in SUPER) or be a custom action which means it is implemented as a concept in an external ontology or an external system.

A Demonstrating Simple Example

To illustrate the concepts we have presented in both the ontologies above, we have taken the following example shown in *Figure 10*.

In this example, a simple role-based resource access control policy is modeled. Upon connecting to the network, an external student is connected by default to all open access printers, which assume that he has necessary credentials since he has signed in into the network. However, the student chooses a special laser color printer with high-definition in order to print his electronic poster of a rock-band.

This laser printer has a resource access policy attached to it (passive compliance checking), which is implemented by several business rules. As the student connects to the printer, the printer activates its policy and evaluates the business rules implementing the policy. One of these rules precisely evaluates the right of an external student to print on the printer to False and for this, sets the credentials of this student on the printer

to False. As the student sends his PDF file to the printer, nothing is printed. The business rule called an action that sends an email to the student explaining that he doesn't have the right to print on the laser printer because he is signed-in as an external student.

This example is usually implemented in systems either by hard-coding it as a set of code snippets distributed on components of the system, or in more elaborated architectures, by making use of a Business Rule Management System (BRMS) which simply outsources business rules modeling and execution but still involves some hard-coding of the rule in system components (e.g. in web services implementing business process activities).

The difference here is that making use of specifically modeled ontologies allows reasoning on all system assets (because they are available as ontology instance individuals). This way the policy can be modeled declaratively without having to cope with details of concrete system components. It practically means that no custom coding in a programming language is necessary. Policy enforcement is done through reasoning by the policy and rule inference engine. *Figure 11* shows how the modeling of the formal policy from the example in *Figure 10* is written in the WSML-Flight language (WSMO, 2010), which is an ontology language with rule modeling capabilities used, among other projects, in the SUPER project.

Another advantage of this approach is reusability as well as being easier to change since changes to policies are done directly on the ontology. It also adds more flexibility in implementing policies by making these independent from the rules used to implement them. For example, if a certain system requires writing a rule differently, the same governance policy that is valid on an enterprise level, can be implemented differently on two different enterprise systems simply by linking two different rules to the same policy, one for each system.

RELATED WORK AND FUTURE RESEARCH DIRECTIONS

In our approach, policy documents in natural language are the initial input. These should be first processed to fit into a pre-defined structured natural language dialect for expressing policies. Business rules are expressed in standardized languages (e.g. standardized English or standardized French – The ISO 639 standard (ISO 639, 2008)) by relying on a pre-defined business vocabulary. An underlying formal model allows a logic-based representation of these natural language business rules. Another prominent approach to structured natural language business rules is the Attempto Controlled English (Fuchs et al., 2008). This has the advantage of making rules understandable to people who are responsible for managing them: business analysts. It also makes it possible to compute machine-processable representations of regulations (provided that the latter be written/transformed into some structured language) thus avoiding multiple and possibly diverging interpretations of regulatory texts. Consequently, changes to regulations can be automatically processed by regenerating adapted representations of the policies than can be enforced on BPs.

In (El Kharbili et al., 2008a) and in (Sackmann, 2008), the authors explain that in order to allow automating some parts of regulations, these need first to be transformed into relevant compliance requirements for a given business domain. Once these compliance requirements are extracted, both approaches propose using declarative and formal means of structuring and modeling these compliance requirements into policies. Enforcing the obtained policies thus guarantees the enforcement of the parts of a regulation these policies cover. The regulatory compliance management problem is thus brought down to the problem of verifying/enforcing compliance policies.

There has been ongoing work on semantic compliance management, as shown in (Namiri, 2007) where an approach for semantic compliance management for BPM is presented. However, the approach used concentrates on implementing internal controls and is restrictive because it relies on the necessary definition of risks. Another approach is presented in (Sadiq, 2007) where the authors introduce the modeling of internal control objectives in business processes as a mean to integrate compliance requirements in business process design. The authors also relate their work to risk analysis and internal control modeling.

In (Karagiannis, 2008; Karagiannis, 2007), another approach for business process-based compliance management is presented. It defines an extension to a business process meta-model for regulatory compliance. However, the approach does not incorporate ontologies and thus, does not profit from the power of semantic technologies. In (Goedertier, 2006; Governatori, 2006), deontic (obligations and permissions) constraints expressible for business processes are modeled using temporal deontic assignments. The latter can also be used in business process design and in expressing business process contracts.

The authors of (Sadiq, 2006) present an approach to formalize contract documents and those aspects of BPs that relate to these business contracts. For this purpose, the semantics of business contracts and their violations are described using a specialized logic. Furthermore, the authors have shown how this formal specification of contracts can be used to generate compliant processes. The work in (Schmidt, 2007) is one of the rare semantic approaches to BP compliance where a compliance ontology is designed and proposed to be integrated in BP models. (Ghose, 2007) proposes an approach based on so-called compliance patterns (i.e., pre-defined BP models proven to be compliant to regulations) where the deviation of a given BP model to a certain compliance pattern is computed.

While relying on the definition of compliance as SWRL rule, (Parameswaran, 2007) recognizes the limited expressiveness of the language and proposes the use of extensions. The authors of

(Liu, 2007) identify the need for separate modeling of compliance and processes. Process models are transformed from BPEL into Pi-Calculus (algebra for modeling concurrent communicating processes) and compliance rules are modeled in temporal logic using a special graphical notation. Model checking techniques are then used to formally check a process pool. In (Milosevic, 2005), policy definitions are integrated into BPs and rely on BP events and transactions for runtime compliance monitoring. In fact, this work poses fundamental questions about architectures for process compliance monitoring integrating events and policies such as the need for a formal definition of events, event triggers, event patterns, message handling as well as state management.

As opposed to our approach none of the previously presented approaches takes a (i) generic approach to regulatory compliance management, (ii) makes use of the advantages of semantic technologies for compliance management, (iii) allows declarative modeling of policies and rules while separating these two concepts and (iv) takes compliance modeling, enforcement and monitoring as a target all at the same time.

The existing related approaches might extend the compliance management framework. Several aspects of the presented work require further research. For instance, further empirical evidence has to be collected as to how well is the CASE model suited for being used by business and legal experts for modeling usability. Neither is there a proof that most of the regulations can be broken down to pieces that can be represented using CASE quadruplets. Generally speaking, one considerable research work that needs to be undergone is to assess the expressiveness and usability of both the CASE model and the PML language. Moreover, computational aspects of inference on PML ontologies are a field of future research. The efficiency will be an important issue in this.

The presented language enabling to model compliance policies (PML) requires in addition a concrete syntax that suits the needs of business users. These are typically non-logicians having a hard time dealing with the textual descriptions of compliance policies. A graphical concrete syntax is a potential direction of further research. Also, the abstract syntax presented in this chapter lacks a logical language that could represent the logic part of a compliance policy, and can thus be used for inferring on policy violations, policy conflicts etc. We plan to extend the PML language in order to add high-level logic modeling functionalities that allow to generate compliance policy rules expressed in a target logic chosen by the business user. Examples of such target languages are linear temporal logics (LTL) (Emerson, 1990; Gabbay, 1994), a graphical extension of a temporal logic language, e.g. CTL (Pulvermueller, 2010), a formal contract language (Governatori, 2006), the rule interchange format RIF (RIF, 2005) or further existing verification technologies for (business) processes (Speck, 2009; Runte, 2009).

Up to now first prototype implementations have shown partial results of our approach, e.g. using a WSML policy representation and related transformation tools or using a combination of ARIS and ProM-based LTL checking (Van Dongen et al., 2005). A fully integrated implementation of our semantic framework of policies and rules including CASE and PML is one of the future tasks.

CONCLUSION

The challenge of regulatory business process compliance management is nowadays of the outmost relevance for businesses, as regulations grow in number and get larger. We motivate the use of policies as an intuitive concept for modeling and enforcing compliance on BP-centered enterprise models. This chapter contributes an approach for dealing with the raw form of regulations. It proposes a semantic framework of policies and rules based on the introduced CASE model for structuring regulatory documents by experts and based on policy ontologies as Policy Modeling Language.

The advantage of the CASE model is that it bridges the regulation document with the formal modeling of compliance requirements as policies. This work makes domain knowledge such as business process knowledge available to policies as ontologies. Hence, it is possible to infer on compliance policy descriptions for reasoning about compliance. CASE policies offer this functionality as assistance to business and legal experts that must implement regulations and assess regulatory compliance.

We have, furthermore, contributed a core ontology for modeling policies and rules incorporating the CASE theory. The ontology seeks to be used as generic top-level ontology in compliance modeling. The metamodel proposed for this ontology defines at the same time the abstract syntax of a language for modeling compliance policies, a so-called policy modeling language (PML). Depending on the end user requirements, the concrete syntax of this language can be defined so that business experts make the best use of it (El Kharbili, Decreus et al., 2010).

REFERENCES

BMM. (2008). *Business motivation model (BMM) version 1.0: OMG business modeling specifications*. Retrieved from http://www.omg.org/spec/BMM/1.0/

BPMN. (2010). *Business process modeling notation*. Retrieved on March 1, 2010, from http://www.bpmn.org/

Compas (2010). Compliance-driven models, languages, and architectures for services. (EU ICT 7FP). http://www.compas-ict.eu/. Retrieved on 01 March 2010.

Congress of the United States. (2002). *Public Company Accounting Reform and Investor Protection Act,* (Sarbanes-Oxley Act). Pub. L. No. 107-204, 116 Stat. 745.

COSO. (2010). *Committee of Sponsoring Organizations of the Treadway Commission*. Retrieved on March 1, 2010, from http://www.coso.org

Dietz, J. (2006). *Enterprise ontology - Theory and methodology*. Berlin, Germany: Springer-Verlag. doi:10.1007/3-540-33149-2

El Kharbili, M., Decreus, K., Poels, G., & Pulvermueller, E. (2010). Policy-enabled goal-oriented requirements engineering for semantic business process management. *International Journal of Intelligent Systems, 25*(8), 784–812. doi:10.1002/int.20431

El Kharbili, M., Stein, S., Markovic, I., & Pulvermüller, E. (2008a). Towards a framework for semantic business process compliance management. In S. Sadiq, M. Indulska& M. zur Muehlen (Eds.), *Proceedings of the workshop on Governance, Risk and Compliance for Information Systems (GRCIS 2008),* CEUR Workshop Proceedings, Montepellier, France, June 2008, 339, (pp. 1-15).

El Kharbili, M., Stein, S., & Pulvermueller, E. (2008b). Policy-based semantic compliance checking for business process management. In *Proceedings of MOBIS Workshops - MOBIS Conference,* Saarbrücken, November 2008.

Emerson, E. A. (1990). Temporal and modal logic. In van Leeuwen, J. (Ed.), *Handbook of theoretical computer science*. Elsevier.

EU. (2010). *Managing assurance, security and trust for services*. (EU ICT 7FP). Retrieved March 1, 2010, from http://www.master-fp7.eu/

Filipowska, A., Kaczmarek, M., Starzecka, M., Stolarski, P., & Walczak, A. (2008). Semantic enterprise description for the needs of business process automation, SemBPM. In. *Proceedings of the COMPSAC, 2008*, 987–992.

Fox, M. S. (1992). The TOVE project: Towards a common-sense model of the enterprise. In *IEA/AIE '92: Proceedings of the 5th International Conference on Industrial and Engineering Applications of Artificial Intelligence and Expert Systems*, (pp. 25–34). London, UK: Springer-Verlag.

Fuchs, N. E., Kaljurand, K., & Schneider, G. (2005). *Verbalising formal languages in attempt to controlled English I.* deliverable I2-D5 of the REWERSE research project. Retrieved August 15, 2008, from http://rewerse.net/deliverables/m18/i2-d5.pdf

Gabbay, D. M., Hodkinson, I., & Reynolds, M. (1994). *Temporal logic (volume 1): Mathematical foundations and computational aspects*. Oxford University Press.

Ghose, A. K., & Koliadis, G. (2007). Auditing business process compliance. In *Proceedings of the International Conference on Service-Oriented Computing* (ICSOC-2007), LNCS 4749 (pp. 169–180).

Goedertier, S., & Vanthienen, J. (2006). *Designing compliant business processes from obligations and permissions*. 2nd Workshop on Business Processes Design (BPD'06).

Governatori, G., Milosevic, Z., & Sadiq, S. (2006). *Compliance checking between business processes and business contracts*. 10th International Enterprise Distributed Object Computing Conference (EDOC 2006), (pp. 221-232). IEEE Press.

Hepp, M., Leymann, F., Domingue, J., Wahler, A., & Fensel, D. (2005). Semantic business process management: A vision towards using Semantic Web services for business process management. In Lau, F. C. M., Lei, H., Meng, X., & Wang, M. (Eds.), *ICEBE* (pp. 535–540). IEEE Computer Society.

Hepp, M., & Roman, D. (2007). An ontology framework for semantic business process management. *Proceedings of Wirtschaftsinformatik 2007*, February 28 - March 2, 2007, Karlsruhe.

HHS. (2010). *United States Department of Health & Human Services, Office for Civil Rights, Health Insurance Portability and Accountability Act, 2003*. Retrieved March 1, 2010, from http://www.hhs.gov/ocr/privacy/

ISACA. (2010). *Control objectives for information and related technology framework*. Information System Audit and Control Association. Retrieved March 1, 2010, from www.isaca.org

ISO. (2008). *ISO 639 standard series*. Retrieved on January 11, 2008, from http://www.iso.org/iso/iso_catalogue/catalogue_tc/catalogue_detail.htm?csnumber=39534

Kagal, L. (2004). *A policy-based approach to governing autonomous behavior in distributed environments*. PhD Thesis, Faculty of the Graduate School of the University of Maryland.

Karagiannis, D. (2008). A business process based modelling extension for regulatory compliance. *Proceedings of the Multikonferenz Wirtschaftsinformatik 2008*, Munich.

Karagiannis, D., Mylopoulos, J., & Schwab, M. (2007). Business process-based regulation compliance: The case of the Sarbanes-Oxley Act. *Proceedings of 15th IEEE International Requirements Engineering Conference*, New Delhi.

Kim, H. M., Fox, M. S., & Gruninger, M. (1999). An ontology for quality management - Enabling quality problem identification and tracing. *BT Technology Journal, 17*(4), 131–140. doi:10.1023/A:1009611528866

Liu, A. Y., Müller, S., & Xu, K. (2007). A static compliance-checking framework for business process models. *IBM Systems Journal, 46*(2), 335–361. doi:10.1147/sj.462.0335

Ly, L. T., Göser, K., Rinderle-Ma, S., & Dadam, P. (2008). Compliance of semantic constraints – A requirements analysis for process management systems. In S. Sadiq, M. Indulska & M. zur Muehlen (Eds.),*Proceedings of the Workshop on Governance, Risk and Compliance for Information Systems* (GRCIS 2008), CEUR Workshop Proceedings, Montepellier, France, June 2008, 339, (pp. 31-45).

Milosevic, Z. (2005). Towards integrating business policies with business processes. In van der Aalst, W. M. P., Benatallah, B., Casati, F., & Curbera, F. (Eds.), *Business process management* (*Vol. 3649*, pp. 404–409). doi:10.1007/11538394_31

Namiri, K., & Stojanovic, N. (2007). *A formal approach for internal controls compliance in business processes.* 8th Workshop on Business Process Modeling, Development, and Support (BPMDS07). Trondheim, Norway.

Nitzsche, J., van Lessen, T., Karastoyanova, D., & Leymann, F. (2007). *BPEL for Semantic Web services (BPEL4SWS). On the Move to Meaningful Internet Systems 2007: OTM 2007 Workshops* (pp. 179–188). Springer-Verlag. doi:10.1007/978-3-540-76888-3_37

Nitzsche, J., Wutke, D., & van Lessen, T. (2007). An ontology for executable business processes. In M. Hepp, K. Hinkelmann, D. Karagiannis, R. Klein, & N. Stojanovic (Eds.), *Semantic business process and product lifecycle management, Proceedings of the Workshop* SBPM 2007. Innsbruck, April 7, 2007, CEUR Workshop Proceedings. ISSN 1613-0073

Object Management Group (OMG). (2008). *Semantics of business vocabulary and rules (SBVR), formal specification* V1.0. Retrieved August 1, 2008, from http://www.omg.org/spec/SBVR/1.0/

Parameswaran, N., Ray, P., & Yip, F. (2007). Rules and ontology in compliance management. In *Proceedings of the 11th IEEE International Enterprise Distributed Object Computing Conference*, (p. 435).

Pedrinaci, C., Brelage, C., van Lessen, T., Domingue, J., Karastoyanova, D., & Leymann, F. (2008). *Semantic business process management: Scaling up the management of business processes.* In 2nd IEEE International Conference on Semantic Computing (ICSC), IEEE Computer Society.

Pulvermueller, E., Feja, S., & Speck, A. (2010). Developer-friendly verification of process-based systems. *Knowledge-Based Systems, 23*.

RIF. (2005). *W3C rule interchange format working group*. Retrieved on March 1, 2010, from http://www.w3.org/2005/rules/

Runte, W. (2009). Modelling and solving configuration problems on business processes using a multi-level constraint satisfaction approach. In *The Young Researchers Workshop on Modeling and Management of Business Processes* (YRWMBP 2009), GI LNI 147, (pp. 237–238).

Sackmann, S., & Kähmer, M. (2008). ExPDT: A policy-based approach for automating compliance. *Wirtschaftsinformatik, 50*(5), 366–374. doi:10.1007/s11576-008-0078-1

Sadiq, S., Governatori, G., & Namiri, K. (2007). Modeling control objectives for business process compliance. *Proceedings of the 5th International Conference*, BPM 2007, (pp. 149-164). Brisbane, Springer.

Sadiq, S., Milosevic, Z., Fiadeiro, J., & Orlowska, M. (2006). Towards a methodology for deriving contract-compliant business processes. In *Proceedings of the 4th International Conference on Business Process Management* (BPM06), Vienna, Austria.

Scheer, A. W. (2000). *ARIS - Business process frameworks* (3rd ed.). Berlin, Germany: Springer. doi:10.1007/978-3-642-57108-4

Schmidt, R., Bartsch, C., & Oberhauser, R. (2007). Ontology-based representation of compliance requirements for service processes. *Proceedings of the Workshop on Semantic Business Process and Product Lifecycle Management* (SBPM 2007).

Speck, A., & Pulvermueller, E. (2009). Verification support for generative system development. In The 8th International Conference on Software Methodologies, Tools and Techniques (SoMeT 2009), (pp. 131 - 147), IOS Press.

SUPER. (2010). *Official ontology stack*. Retrieved March 1, 2010, from http://www.ip-super.org/content/view/129/136/

SUPER. (2010a). *Semantics utilised for process management within and between enterprises*. Retrieved March 1, 2010, from http://www.ip-super.org/

TOGAF. (2008). *Framework*. Retrieved on January 11, 2008, from http://www.togaf.org/, http://www-128.ibm.com/developerworks/ibm/library/ar-togaf1/

Uschold, M., King, M., Moralee, S., & Zorgios, Y. (1998). The enterprise ontology. [from http://www.aiai.ed.ac.uk/project/enterprise/enterprise/ontology.html]. *The Knowledge Engineering Review, 1998*, Retrieved August 1, 2008.

Van Buuren, R., Hoppenbrouwers, S., Jonkers, H., Lankhorst, M., van Zanten, & Veldhuijzen van Zanten, G. (2006). *Architecture language reference manual*. (ArchiMate Deliverable 2.2.2b v4.1. Telematica Institute. 2006. TI/RS/2003/030).

Van Dongen, B. F., de Medeiros, A. K. A., Verbeek, H. M. W., Weijters, A. J. M. M., & van der Aalst, W. M. P. (2005). The ProM framework: A new era in process mining tool support. In *Applications and Theory of Petri Nets 2005. 26th International Conference, ICATPN 2005, Lecture Notes in Computer Science Volume 3536*, pp. (444–454). Miami, USA, June 2005. Springer-Verlag.

Warmer, J., & Kleppe, A. (2003). *The object constraint language* (2nd ed.). Addison Wesley.

WSBPEL. (2007). *OASIS Web services business process execution language (WSBPEL) TC. Web services business process execution language version 2.0 committee specification*. Retrieved from http://docs.oasis-open.org/wsbpel/2.0/CS01/wsbpelv2.0- CS01.pdf

WSMO. (2010). *WSML language reference*. Retrieved March 1, 2010, from http://www.wsmo.org/TR/d16/d16.1/v1.0/

Yun, L. (2008). *Semantic annotation for process models: Facilitating process knowledge management via semantic interoperability*. PhD dissertation. Department of Computer and Information Science. Norwegian University of Science and Technology. 2008. Trondheim, Norway.

Zachman, J. A. (1987). A framework for information systems architecture. *IBM Systems Journal, 26*(3), 276–292. doi:10.1147/sj.263.0276

Zachman, J. A. (1992). Extending and formalizing the framework for Information Systems architecture. *IBM Systems Journal, 31*(3).

Chapter 17
A Broader View on Context Models towards Supporting Business Process Agility

Barbara Thönssen
University of Applied Sciences Northwestern Switzerland, Switzerland

Daniela Wolff
University of Applied Sciences Northwestern Switzerland, Switzerland

ABSTRACT

Today's enterprises need to be agile, to be able to cope with unexpected changes, to increasingly be dynamic, and to continually deal with change. Change affecting business processes may range from ad hoc modification to process evolution. In this chapter we present dimensions of change concentrating on a specific ability of an enterprise to deal with change. To support business in being agile we propose a semantically enriched context model based on well known enterprise architecture. We present a context aware workflow engine basing on the context model and on rules which trigger process adaptations during run time.

INTRODUCTION

Continuously changing challenges, like shorter product cycles, increasing customer expectations, changing regulations, forces today's enterprises to be more agile (Allweyer, 2007; Scheer, 2003). Henbury regards agile enterprises as capable of rapid adaptation in response to unexpected and unpredicted changes and events, market opportunities and customer requirements (Henbury, 2006). So enterprises have to constantly rethink, optimize and modify their business processes and effectively arrange their information flow (Schwarz, 2001). Modification is difficult, complex and risky according to unintended side effect. Every change has an impact on other parts of the enterprise, which leads to the choice, whether to make

DOI: 10.4018/978-1-60960-126-3.ch017

a change or abandon the competitive benefits of innovation because of the risk (Mitra et al. 2006).

To handle the complexity of an enterprise and its objects, e.g. people, ICT infrastructure, organization structure, information resources etc. often Enterprise Architecture Frameworks (EAF) are used. One well-known example is Zachmann's Framework (Zachman, 1987), or the ARIS house (Scheer, 2000), EA are made for use by humans not by machines. Therefore to deal with changes Enterprise Architectures (EA) are consulted by humans, for example to identify dependencies between business processes and ICT resources. In case a process model needs to be modified, e.g. because of organizational restructuring, in best case an EAF is available to support the business engineer's task.

On the other hand side semantic technologies has been researched amongst others by (Hepp et al., 2005) for process implementation and querying by (Jennings et al., 2000) to build their 'agent based business process management system' or already by (Abecker et al., 1998) to model Organizational Memories.

Following (Winograd, 2001), who defines context as an "operational term: something is context because of the way it is used in interpretation, not due to its inherent properties" we regard enterprise objects as context in which change happens. To improve dealing with change, we model Enterprise Architecture as ontology, based on well-known Enterprise Architecture Frameworks. With that machines can be enabled to identify and deal with changes in order to improve 'time to act' and to reduce the risk of missing (unwanted) effects.

Business Process Management is one approach to make business more agile by making business processes more transparent through the use of process models. To increase the control of business processes, the quality, communication and the information flow and to shorten processing time workflow management systems are used (Galler & Scheer, 1995). However, this approach fails when supporting dynamic and variable processes execution (van der Aalst & Jablonski, 2000; Reichert & Dadam, 1998). An alternative approach towards agility takes into account that every business application is based on rules to conduct the business logic. When compliance requirements increased, along with other demands for business flexibility the business rules approach emerged. Combining these approaches allows supporting enterprises in being agile (Faget et al., 2003).

To identify the requirements for supporting agile enterprises we made a literature review. These requirements are taken to draft an ontology for semantically enriched representation of enterprise architecture and to evaluate current existing workflow management systems supporting agility of enterprises. After it, we developed our approach and implemented a prototype.

To better understand agility, the definition of agility is discussed in the next section. After it, the requirements are listed, which are necessary to fulfil if agility should be supported. Existing systems which wants to support parts of agility are evaluated. For the description of our approach, we introduce in section 4 the term context and context-awareness. In section 5 we describe our approach and present our prototype. After all we conclude this chapter and present presents future research directions.

Background

Today enterprises face increasingly dynamic and competitive environment with continuously changing customer interests and markets. The ability to cope rapidly and efficiently with unexpected and sudden change, uncertainty and unpredictability is called "agility" or "agile business" (Henbury, 2006).

Agility as a concept was firstly introduced by a group of scholars at Iacocca Institute of Leigh University in USA in 1991 (Iacocca, 1991). In their report they described practices observed and considered as important aspects of manufacturing during their investigation. They defined agility as "A manufacturing system with extraordinary capabilities (Internal capabilities: hard and soft technologies, human resources, educated management, information) to meet the rapidly changing needs of the marketplace. A system that shifts quickly among product models or between product models/lines, ideally in real-time response to customer demand". Due to Burgess' objection that this concept has been ill-defined and more work has to be done to refine the concept (Burgess, 1994), various definitions followed which expressed agility in different ways.

Dove (1994) was one of the first to discuss agility as the capability of a process to respond to the unanticipated change. An agile enterprise must be able to continuously adapt (Kidd, 1994) and respond quickly to changing customer requirements (Goldman et al., 1995). Dove (1999) states that an agile enterprise "can quickly satisfy customer orders; can introduce new products frequently in a timely manner; and can even get in and out of its strategic alliances speedily."

Therefore, "an agile process requires responsive people and organizations" (Cockburn et al., 2001) and needs highly skilled and knowledgeable people who are flexible, motivated and responsive to change (Kidd, 1994). For that new forms of organizational structures that engender non-hierarchical management styles and stimulate and support individuals, as well as cooperation and team working are needed. Kidd (1994) adds that agile manufacturing enterprises also need advanced computer based technologies. To support collaborative work Business Process Management systems were developed, dealing well with routine procedures to be accomplished many times but not suited to automate knowledge intensive tasks dealing with continuously changing requirements. Therefore, Feldkamp et al. (2007) suggest a new approach to support agility of knowledge intensives processes and tasks combining processes with business rules.

Yusuf et.al. (1999) considered all the definitions in order to gain a better understanding of what constitute agility, which leads to the following definition: "Agility is the successful exploration of competitive bases (speed, flexibility, innovation proactivity, quality and profitability) through the integration of reconfigurable resources and best practices in a knowledge-rich environment to provide customer-driven products and services in a fast changing market environment" (Yusuf et al. 1999).

The main driving force behind agility is change. Changes can be triggered outside a system, i.e. the context is the primary driver for change or inside a system due to detected problems. So, change may range from ad-hoc modifications of a single process instance to a complete restructuring of the process definition (van der Aalst & Jablonski, 2000). According to Sadiq et al. (2001), change in processes can be divided into the three dimensions: dynamism, adaptability and flexibility. (Sadiq et al., 2001; Lu et al., 2007).

- **Dynamism:** Dynamsim is the ability to change the process definition. The need to change a process definition may result from process improvements to process innovation or process reengineering.
- **Adaptability:** Adaptability is the ability to react to exceptional circumstances or unexpected events during the performance of a process instance, which may or may not be foreseen.
- **Flexiblity:** The third dimension is the flexibility is the ability to deal with a fair degree of uncertainty. This flexibility is often necessary in knowledge-intensive tasks, where people require applying and bringing together their experience, training, expertise and judgments (Heravizadeh et al., 2008). Depending on their experiences and the situation the employee have individual work routines (Kidd, 1994; Richter von Hagen et al., 2005; Davenport et al., 1996).

Every change in one part of an enterprise has an impact on other parts of the enterprise. Effect uncertainty is the inability to predict what the nature of the impact (effects) of a change will be. Response uncertainty is defined "as a lack of knowledge of response options and/or inability to predict the likely consequences of a response choice" (van Oosterhout et al., 2007). To express the ability to know which effect and consequence a change has, we add the following fourth dimension:

- **Awareness:** Awareness, as the ability to detect opportunities and risks. To identify the need of changes the organization has to continuously monitor itself as well as to be prepared to quickly take actions to change (Schatten & Schiefer, 2007).

The support of all three dimensions requires different requirements which are described in the next section.

Requirements

To support the four dimensions of agility we look at literature dealing with agility or a specific dimension of agility.

To ensure the changeability of a process definition, business process modelling should be kept simple. Therefore a process modelling language should provide an appropriate syntax and semantics, so that the process modeller can specify tasks and their order to support automated process verification, validation, simulation and process automation (Lu and Sadiq, 2007).

An exception is a situation that is not modelled in the process model or deviations between what is planned and what actually happens (Luo et al., 2000). To support adaptability exception handling mechanisms must be defined, or if no exception handling can be found for the current situation, the user must be able to obtain help in

determining how to proceed, when an exceptional situation occurs (Abbott & Sarin, 1994; Klein & Dellarocas, 2000). So, information artefacts or relevant experts which may help in the situation should be suggested.

For the support of flexibility it must be possible to start the execution of a partially defined and inconsistent process models. During run time depending on the situation the process should be fully specified (Sadiq et.al.,2001; Schwarz et.al., 2001; Jorgenson & Steinar, 1999). This functionality is called Lazy/Late Modelling. It must be possible that the employee is able to add and modify the workflow instance (Schwarz et.al., 2001; van der Aalst & Jablonski, 2000; Faustman, 1998). However, modification can be time consuming and complex (van der Aalst & Jablonski, 2000), so an assistant system is necessary which suggest possible modification depending on the current situation (Schwarz et.al., 2001). Due to the fact, that the employee reuses knowledge from experts or documents, the assistant system should be able to suggest also depending on the situation expert profiles and documents (Abecker et al., 2002). Additionally, the experts mentioned that they have to fulfil business rules and general regulations, like deadlines, and it is helpful if the assistant can indicate violated rules.

To be able to detect opportunities and risks, dependencies between sets of resources have to be retrieved, analyzed and interpreted. For instance if a regulation changes, the effects on products, processes have to be analyzed. To be able to retrieve the impacts the changing resources and their relationships to other resources have to be made explicit.

To sum up, the following requirements have to be kept to support the flexibility of a process:

- **Simple modelling and effective execution of process definitions:** To support the dimension of dynamism the user must be able to model a process in a simple way.

The system should be able to execute the process definition.

- **Lazy/Late modelling:** A system should be able to start with a partial model of a business process and refine this model later on during run time.
- **Modification of workflow instance:** To support the flexibility and adaptability the user must be able to adapt a process model during run time depending on the situation.
- **Assistant system for suggesting possible sub tasks:** To support the user in modifying the workflow instance, possible sub tasks should be suggested.
- **Assistant system for suggesting relevant experts and other information artifacts:** Because experts reuses knowledge from other experts or documents, expert profiles and knowledge artefacts should be suggested depending on the situation.
- **Assistant systems for indicating violated rules:** The knowledge worker has to keep deadlines, regulations and business rules, a user must be pointed to violated rules.
- **Assistant system for detecting dependencies between resources:** To support the awareness, the system must indicate impacts of changes.

There are two predominant formalism to express the logic of a business process, namely graph-based and rule based formalism. Whereas the rule-based formalism has the advantage of higher expressiveness and better support of flexible process models, the process models are visual and hence intuitive and therefore useful for all kinds of workflow designers (Lu & Sadiq, 2007). As mentioned in the introduction, typically, for the automation of a business process a WfMS forces a predefined process model, specifying the order of tasks, assigning people to roles or defining APIs to other systems, often based on the reference model provided by the WfMC (WfMC, 1995). Due to the predefined model, this approach supports the ability to change the process definition, but lacks in supporting adaptability and flexibility.

Figure 1 gives an overview of existing systems which wants to support specific dimensions of agility. POWM (Fünffinger et al., 2002), OpenWater (Whittingham et al., 2000), Adapt2 (Reichert & Dadam, 2007), InConcert (van der Aalst & van Hees, 2002) and Chameleon (Sadiq et al., 2005) allow ad hoc changes during run time of an workflow instance. The systems CPEF (Myers, 1999) and PMA (Pollack & Horty, 1999) combine planning algorithms and workflow management systems to support flexibility in workflow instances. Case Based Reasoning systems, like WorkBrain (Wargitsch et al., 1997), CBRFlow, Cake, Frodo, and AWD, store historical cases to provide adaptation of the current workflow instance by comparing the current workflow data with the historical cases. Rule based Systems allow adaptations depending on the actual workflow data through the use of predefined rules. Such rule base Systems are AgentWork, METEOR and AgFlow. All theses systems focus on the support of the flexibility and adaptability of the workflow instance itself. However, they lack in providing relevant information, like expert profiles and documents. Knowledge management systems focus on this part in supporting flexibility and adaptability. KnowMore, KontextNavigator, ExperKnowledge and DYONIPOS are systems which provide depending on the task the user has to perform relevant information artifacts.

Up to now, detecting opportunities and risks is a task, performed by humans. As enterprise objects are not modelled formally and described semantically, means of changes can not be identified automatically.

To effectively support agility the situation and therefore the need of the employee has to be indicated. Context is any information which can be used to characterize a specific situation (Dey & Abowd, 2000).

Figure 1. Evaluation

Requirements	Prozessportal (POWM)	OpenWater	ADAPT2	FLOWer	InConcert	Chameleon	Continuous Planning and Execution Framework	Plan Management Agent (PMA)	WorkBrain	CBRFlow	CAKE	FRODO	AIS Workware Demonstrator (AWD)	AgentWork	METEOR	AgFlow	Kombination von BPEL und Regeln	KnowMore	KontextNavigator	ExperKnowledge	DYONIPOS
	Flexible Workflow Management Systeme						Plan		Case-Based					Rule Based				Knowledge Management			
Lazy/Late Modeling	x	x	x	(x)	x	x	(x)	x	x	-	x	x	x	-	x	x	x	-	-	-	-
Modification of worklfow instance	x	x	(x)	x	x	x	(x)	-	x	-	x	x	x	-	-	(x)	-	-	-	-	-
Efficient support of structured workflows	x	-	x	-	(x)	x	x	x	x	x	x	x	-	x	x	x	x	-	-	-	-
Assistant System for suggesting possible sub tasks	(x)	(x)	-	x	-	-	(x)	x	(x)	x	(x)	(x)	(-)	-	(x)	-	(x)	-	-	-	-
Assistant System for indicating violated rules	-	-	-	-	-	-	x	(x)	-	-	-	-	-	-	-	-	-	-	-	-	-
Assistant System for suggesting relevant experts and information artifacts	-	-	-	-	-	-	-	-	-	-	-	-	-	-	-	-	-	x	x	x	x
Assistant system for detecting dependencies between resources	-	-	-	-	-	-	-	-	-	-	-	-	-	-	-	-	-	-	-	-	-

Context Aware Business Process Execution

Business Process Management Systems (BPMS) are available since the early 80s[1] supporting the definition, administration, customizing and evaluation of tasks evolving from business processes and organizational structures (Karagiannis, 1995). Business Process Management Systems like ADONIS[2] or ARIS allow explicitly modelling business processes, organizational structure, products and information technology and their interdependencies. Those elements can be considered as enterprise context, in fact explicitly described within the BPMS, but understandable only to humans, as they are not semantically described (Cacciagrano et al., 2009).

Whereas BPMS focus on business modelling, Workflow Management Systems (WfMS) support automatic execution and control of the processes; some of them offering APIs to BPMS. WfMS use context to assign tasks to the right people at the right time using the right information resource (Karagiannis, 1995; Aalst et al., 2004). In this sense context is used 'by machine' but limited to the process perspective, i.e. what is not necessary for execution is not modelled. Furthermore context information is only available within the WfMS. Thus, Saidani & Nurcan (2007) regard context as "*the collection of implicit assumptions that is required to activate accurate assignments in the BP model at the process instance level*" (original emphasis by the authors).

However, according to Smith et al. (2003) the third wave of Business Process Management is "not about business-process reengineering, enterprise application integration, workflow management or another packaged application - it is the synthesis and extension of all these technologies and techniques into a unified whole". For this, modelling context to serve one application or application has to be replaced by generic context models that "are of interest since many applications can benefit from these" (Linnhoff-Popien et al., 2004).

ENTERPRISE CONTEXT

In the late Eighties/early Nineties, research started on formal theory of context e.g. by McCarthy (1993). "The goal was to explain the properties of the context and the contextual reasoning in a systematic way" (Mena et al., 2007).

According to Dey et al. (2000) context is each information, which can be used to characterize the situation of an entity and that a system is context conscious if it uses context, in order to offer to the user independence of its activity information or services. Although that definition is very general, it is the most widely accepted (Zimmermann et al., 2007) and reflects the fact that context is considered in very different disciplines like natural language processing, cognitive psychology, artificial intelligence and more recently in ubiquitous and mobile computing (e. g. Schmidt, 2002). It is agreed that giving an universally valid definition of context is hard to reach (e. g. Mena et al., 2007; Baldauf et al., 2007). They state that "they [the context definitions] vary according to the framework of context use, the nature of the future use of context and of the future developed system." Mena et al. (2007) conclude that "defining and studying [context] content depend closely on the domain, and application nature" and that "we cannot speak about context in an absolute way". With respect to context-aware systems context can be considered as those elements of an user's environment the system is able to 'understand' (Brown, 1998).

The Workflow Management Coalition distinguishes between three types of data: application data, workflow relevant data and workflow control data. Often, the systems supporting the flexibility and adaptability use the last kind of data, to adapt the process execution. Workflow relevant data is data which can be manipulated by the workflow engine or by applications. Systems providing relevant information artefacts use additionally context data, like organizational context describing the user and his surrounding, business process,

to describe the activity the user is working on. DYNOPISUS uses in addition the behavioural context, to express how the user is working on the task, resource context, to describe which documents she uses to perform the task and the social context, describing with which people the user is collaborating.

Particular, mobile computing and web services provide individual services and information by reacting on the user's current location, used device, time, and organizational and action context (Baldauf et al, 2007; Rittwik & Chen, 2005).

Enterprise architecture wants to handle the complexity of an enterprise and its objects, by using Enterprise Architecture Frameworks (Zachman, 1987). The Zachman framework distinguishes between perspective and aspects. Aspects describe the application fields. The following aspects are used in the Zachman framework:

- **Data:** This aspect describes the data being used.
- **Function:** Processes coordinate the tasks of a company and explain how and in which order tasks have to be performed.
- **People:** People act in an organizational environment.
- **Network:** This aspect describes the location in which a business operates.
- **Time:** The time aspect contain a list of events or cycles, which are significant for an enterprise.
- **Product:** this aspect describe the features of products and services of an enterprise.
- **Motivation:** The motivation aspect describe why an enterprise acts in a predefined manner.

Figure 2 gives an overview of the mentioned systems and approaches, which uses context data.

It can be easily seen that the enterprise architecture provides the biggest overview of the enterprise context data.

Figure 2. Context data

Kontextdaten	Flexible Workflow Management Systems						Plan		Case-Based					Rule Based			Knowledge Management						
	Prozessportal (POWM)	OpenWater	ADAPT2	FLOWer	InConcert	Chameleon	Continuous Planning and Execution Framework	Plan Management Agent (PMA)	WorkBrain	CBRFlow	CAKE	FRODO	AIS Workware Demonstrator (AWD)	AgentWork	METEOR	AgFlow	KnowMore	KontextNavigator	ExperKnowledge	DYONIPOS	Enterprise Architecture	Mobile Computing	Web Services
Business process			x				x										x	x	x	x	x	x	
Organizational context			(x)														x	x		x	x	x	x
Workflow relevant data	(x)	x		x	x				x	x	x	x	x	x	x	x	x	x		x			
Application context																					x	x	x
Ressource context																				x	x	x	x
Social context																					x	x	
Business constraints																					x		
Geographical context																					x	x	x

How to model context - either to serve a specific purpose or not - is another topic of research (Linnhoff-Popien et al., 2004) addresses. They give an overview on context modeling approaches, e.g. the Key-Value-Models, Markup Scheme Models, Graphical Models like UML, Object Oriented Models, Logic Based Models and Ontology Based Models and evaluate the models with respect to the requirements they defined. They conclude "that the most promising assets for context modelling for ubiquitous computing environments [...] can be found in the ontology category"

The advantage of using an ontology to model context has been seen since long (Guha, 1991) and is now agreed widely. Schulz (2003), for example, stresses the understandability ontologies for modelling whereas Linnhoff-Popien et al. (2004) outline that "to develop a context model based on ontologies because of its knowledge sharing, logic inferencing and knowledge reuse capabilities". Context ontologies are introduced, amongst others, by Chen et al. (2003), Schulz (2003), Wang et al. (2004) or Jonsson (2007).

Using semantic technologies to describe an enterprise is an approach which is, amongst others, introduced by Abecker et al. (1998), Dietz (2006), Fox and Gruninger (1998), Leppänen (2007), Uschold et al. (1998). However, to have a formal model describing context and reasoning about it requires a common understanding of meaning based on shared vocabulary. Linnhoff-Popien and Strang (2004) state: "to describe contextual facts and interrelationships in a precise and traceable manner. [...it] is highly desirable, that each participating party [...] shares the same interpretation of the data exchanged and the meaning 'behind' it (so called shared understanding)" Kang et al., 2010), as well as Hinkelmann et al. (2010) already suggest relating enterprise ontologies to an enterprise architecture model to ensure completeness. Such a relation can ensure a common understanding, too.

Picking the (right) vocabulary to represent the knowledge of the domain is a challenge (Guha, 1991) as well as to find a good intermediate-granularity to model context (Lenat, 1998). Too coarse-grained would be too general for inferencing and too fine-grained would be too maintenance intensive and error prone. Building on well-known Enterprise Architecture Frameworks, for example the one by Zachman (Zachman, 1987), could help to deal with the balancing act.

Solutions and Recommendations

Figure 3 depicts parts of Zachman's framework as an example of the various types of enterprise objects represented in the enterprise context ontology. Using (existing) enterprise architecture framework (not necessarily Zachman's), formal representation of enterprise objects is related to aspects and perspectives, business users understand.

Following (Winograd, 2001) defining context as 'an operational term' we consider *context* as 'everything that is not *text*' as it depends on the point of view what is considered context is and

what is not. In an enterprise objects like business processes, organizational structure, personnel, information resources and their relations constitute the enterprise architecture. Each enterprise object is context for another one. For example: in case a process' activity is instantiated that activity becomes the subject using (other) enterprise objects, e.g. resources, rules etc. as context for its agile execution. Whereas for tagging a document, the activity in which it is used (created, modified) is context and the document is the subject.

In this sense business processes are not regarded as outside the context, using context for execution but as part of the context. What context is and what context needs depends on its use.

To give an example, in the following we introduce the application scenario of a manufacturer of espresso machines. As she highly relies on the suppliers for the various parts needed to produce the machines, supply-chain-management is vital

Figure 3. Enterprise architecture scaffolds the context ontology

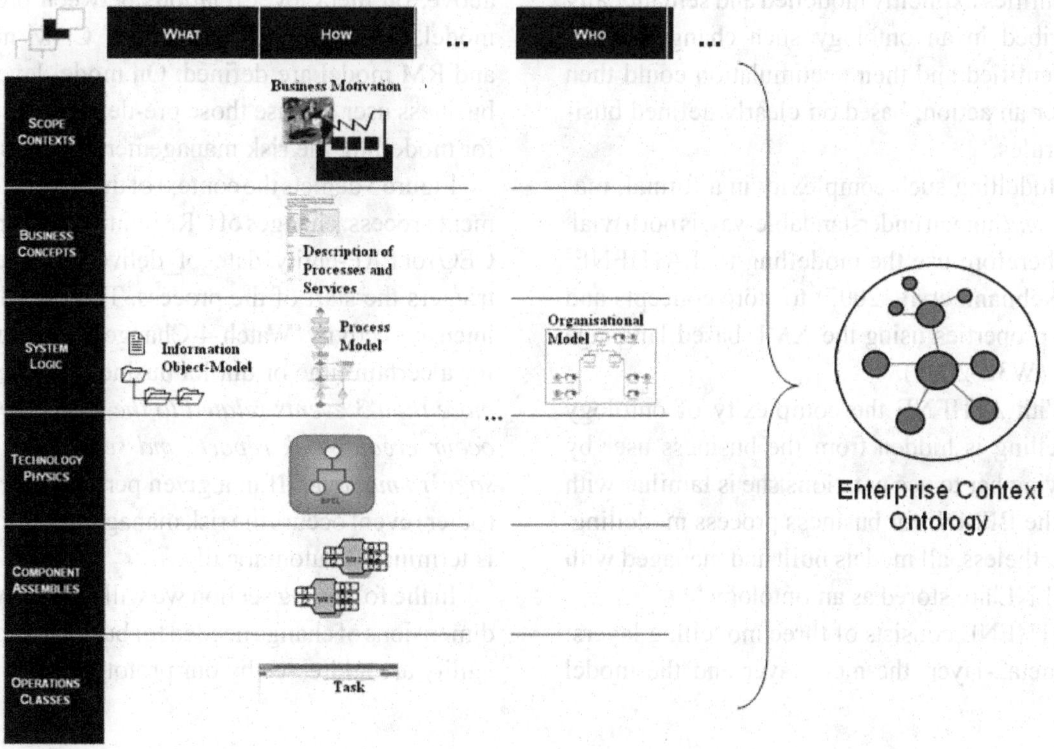

for the company's survival. The manufacturer therefore implemented a knowledge process for monitoring, identification and validation of changes related to suppliers (e.g. an activity to scrawl a supplier's website and trade register entry and to give a brief summary in a monthly report). However, changes relevant for supply-chain-management not only occur on the supplier's side, e.g. replacement of a CEO or merging with another company but as well internally, for example by delayed delivery or delivery of minor quality. Those changes are registered in an Enterprise Resource Planning (ERP)-System. As the delay affects the manufacturing process the delay reported in the monthly 'Suppliers Monitor' and stored in the Records Management (RM) System. In parallel the supplier's entry in the CRM-System is updated with the information about the new CEO and the possible merger. As long as these changes take place in isolation the risk may remain undiscovered as no single incidence is strong enough to raise a red flag.

Having instead the relations between the various entities explicitly modelled and semantically described in an ontology such changed could be identified and their accumulation could then trigger an action, based on clearly defined business rules.

Modelling such complexity in a formal, machine *and* human understandable way, is not trivial. We therefore use the modelling tool ATHENE[3] (Hinkelmann et al., 2007) to store concepts and their properties using the XML based language RDF (W3C 2004).

With ATHENE the complexity of ontology modelling is hidden from the business user by allowing her to use notations she is familiar with like the BPMN[4] for business process modelling. Nevertheless, all models built and managed with ATHENE are stored as an ontology.

ATHENE consists of three modelling layers: the meta2-layer, the meta layer and the model

layer. On the meta2-layer the ATHENE system architecture is defined, for example definitions of the super classes like object types or attributes. Building sub-classes on the meta layer the various model types are defined. Those meta models are than used by business engineers to build the business models, e.g. the specific process model of the espresso machine manufacturer.

Figure 4 shows print screens of the two modelling environments of ATHENE. The left screenshot shows the meta modelling environment (❶ repository of object types, ❷ attributes of object types, ❸ properties and characteristics). The right screenshot depicts the modelling environment for process models (❹ meta objects, ❺ model objects, ❻ attribute characteristics).

Relations between enterprise objects are described on meta model level and can be used on model level. Thus, again the user is not bothered with the complexity of semantic description but can simply relate enterprise objects like attaching an information object to a process task.

Regarding the applications scenario described above, on meta level relations between process model, CRM model, ERP model, CAM model and RM model are defined. On model level the business user can use those pre-defined relations for modelling the risk management process.

Figure 5 depicts the context of the risk management process: changes of CRM-entity (e.g. update CEO) or ERP-entity (date_of_delivery_exceeded) triggers the start of the process. The knowledge intensive activity 'Watch-4-Changes' is performed for a certain time or until a business rule, e.g. *if more than 3 events related to the same supplier occur create 'risk report' and send 'risk message' to manager.* If in a given period of time no (other) event occurs the risk management process is terminated automatically.

In the following section we will show how the dimensions of change needed for business process agility are addresses by our prototype.

Figure 4. ATHENE modelling environment

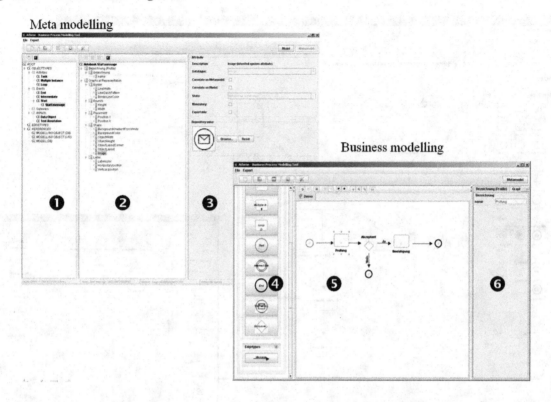

Prototype

A prototype was developed supporting flexibility, adaptability and dynamism. As indicated by the experts, the following requirements have to be fulfilled:

- Lazy/Late Modelling
- Modification of workflow instance
- Efficient support of structured workflows
- Assistant system for suggesting possible sub tasks
- Assistant system for suggesting relevant experts and other information artefacts
- Assistant systems for indicating violated rules

Current Workflow Management Systems efficiently support the structured workflows. Our approach combines therefore existing Workflow Management Systems with a Framework which is responsible for the dynamic part of the process. For the dynamic part we developed the so called KIT-Engine, which is implemented as a web service which can be easily integrated into existing internet based workflow engines.

The resulting overall architecture bases on the three layer architecture provided by Geminiuc (2007), who separates the rules from a BPEL model and a five layer architecture provided by Evans, who separates the domain knowledge from the application (Evans, 2004). This separation increases the flexibility, because rules and domain knowledge can be modified independently from the process model.

Figure 6 gives an overview of the whole architecture.

Depending on the context relevant information, possible sub tasks and violated rules must be suggested. To read out the context the semantic web framework JENA2 is used, with which the KIT-framework is able to read and modify the

Figure 5. Relating knowledge intensive activities to business rules using ATHENE

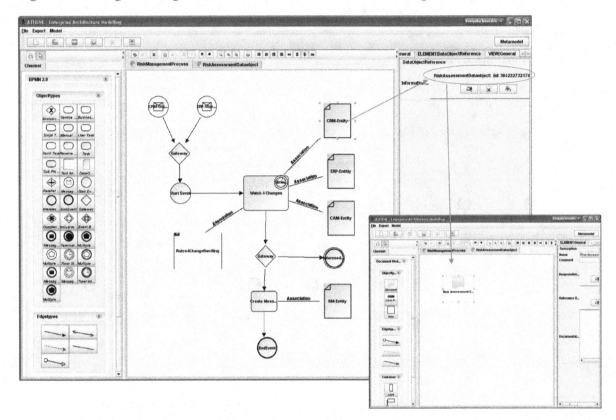

Context Ontology. Rules are used to automatically suggest depending on the context relevant information, experts, possible sub tasks and violated rules. On the condition part of the rule the context is specified and in the conclusion part the relevant information, sub tasks and violated rules are defined. If the user wants to perform other sub task, the current context data is stored to the conditioning part of the rule and the created task is saved to the consequence part. So, if a similar context is provided in new cases the new created task is shown as a possible sub task.

Therefore the rules engine and the JENA2 framework are basic components which are related to the infrastructure layer. According to Evans the Domain layer contains the context model. This provides the advantage of modifying the context ontology independently from the process model.

The KIT engine itself consists of the two components controller and user interface. The user interface shows the tasks, which have to be performed, and the relevant information to the user. The controller is responsible for the execution of the dynamic process part. If the KIT engine is invoked by the BPEL engine the context data is retrieved from the Context Ontology. This context data is given to the knowledge base of the rules engine. After it, the rules engine is executed and the data is provided to the user. If he changes context data the rules engine is invoked again.

According to the application scenario of a manufacturer of espresso machines, assume the task to find an appropriate supplier is embedded in a structured production process. For this knowledge intensive task the KIT Engine is invoked. The controller of the KIT Engine calls the JENA2 framework to retrieve information of

Figure 6. Overall architecture

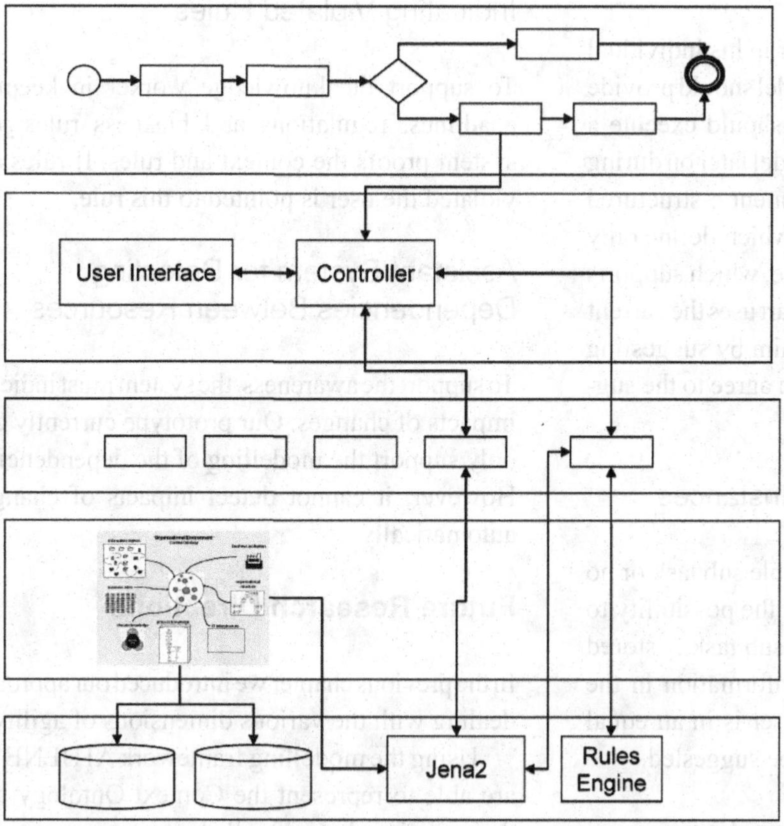

the current production process. This information is forwarded by the controller to the rules engine. Additionally, the set of rule is retrieved from the Context Ontology and is forwarded to the rules engine. The controller invokes the rules engine, which results are analysed by the controller. If the supplier with delayed deliveries or delivery of minor quality delivers the actual needed products, the information is given to the knowledge worker to support his decision finding the appropriate supplier.

Evaluation

In the requirements section we introduced requirements which have to be fulfilled if all dimensions of agility have to be supported. Using the Context Ontology allows defining all knowledge artefacts of an enterprise. The semantics helps to make the

relations between the knowledge artefacts explicit. The prototype allows modelling the Context Ontology and helps to support the execution of dynamic business processes.

Simple Modelling and Effective Execution of Process Definitions

To support dynamism we use traditional process models. This helps to easily modify process models due to its familiarity to process modeller. The execution is done by traditional workflow management systems, which are efficient for structured process parts. However, if larger sets of rules must be checked within a business process and if changes in regulations occur often it makes more sense to separate the rules from the business logic (Lienhard & Künzi, 2005).

Lazy/Late Modelling

To support a knowledge worker in his individual working routine the process model should provide more flexibility. So, a system should execute a partial model and refine this model later on during run time. To fulfil this requirement a structured process model contains parts, which define only the invocation of the KIT engine, which supports the dynamic process part. This part uses the current context of the user to support him by suggesting possible sub tasks. The user can agree to the suggestion or he can ignore it.

Modification of Workflow Instances

If the system provides no possible sub task or no relevant sub tasks, the user has the possibility to add individual sub tasks. This sub task is stored together with the contextual information in the Context Ontology. So, if the user is in an equal situation, the added tasks can be suggested.

Assistant System for Suggesting Possible Sub Tasks

The ad hoc modification of workflow instances is not an easy task. To support him in finding an appropriate sub task, the KIT engine provides him with a list of sub tasks which can be executed depending on his context.

Assistant System for Suggesting Relevant Experts and Other Information Artefacts

Because experts reuse knowledge from other experts or documents, the system provides depending on the context relevant expert profiles and knowledge artefacts.

Assistant Systems for Indicating Violated Rules

To support the knowledge worker in keeping deadlines, regulations and business rules, the system proofs the context and rules. If rules are violated the user is pointed to this rule.

Assistant System for Detecting Dependencies Between Resources

To support the awareness, the system must indicate impacts of changes. Our prototype currently can only support the modelling of the dependencies. However, it cannot detect impacts of changes automatically.

Future Research Directions

In the previous chapter we introduced our approach dealing with the various dimensions of agility.

Using the modelling framework ATHENE we are able to represent the Context Ontology and their relations between all elements semantically.

Instead of having different (parts of) context models embedded in the various applications enterprises run, knowledge is made explicit and managed purpose independent. On the basis of (Mitra et al., 2005) we state that "if knowledge is extracted and formalized [in an application independent context model] it can then be used in as many different [applications] as necessary, whenever and wherever it is needed".

However, currently the Context Ontology is not fully developed yet. During the European funded research projects FIT[5] and plugIT[6] we have implemented models for process knowledge, based on BPMN and BPMS[7], SWRL rules, organizational structure, IT system model, business motivation model of BPMS. Models for information objects and domain knowledge are in early stage of development. Hence, the relations between the various context models and their elements are still in its early stages and changes cannot be retrieved automatically.

As ATHENE was first implemented as a development framework only, the run time component to execute a business process is still under construction. During the FIT project we tested the described functionality of agile process management with demonstrators. We exported the executable process model out of ATHENE and imported it into the open source ActiveBPEL[8] engine.

As the development and implementation of context models in a company is time and therefore cost-intensive enterprises should cooperate with other enterprises. This cooperation allows various knowledge workers of different domains to coordinate for manufacturing products and services very quickly. It allows small companies, for instance, to "come together and deliver quality, scope and scale of products and services which they would not have been able to provide individually" (Yusuf et al., 1999). ATHENE supports the cooperation currently through the export and import of models. However, it is intended to extend the modelling environment for cooperative ontology development building up on experiences of the MyOntology project [9] (Hepp et al., 2005).

CONCLUSION

There is an increasing recognition that agility is a necessary condition for competitiveness, because today's enterprises need to be responsive to competitors, the market, organizational changes and changing customer requirements and need to be agile to continually deal with change. Focusing on one business application, e.g. the agility of business processes is not enough to deal with all changes necessary to make an enterprise agile.

Although with the KISS approach (Feldkamp et al., 2007) process agility has been reached, combining processes and context through the use of rules, only the dimensions of flexibility and adaptability can be supported. To deal with all four dimensions of changes a comprehensive context model is suggested. With that approach not only business *process* agility can be better supported but also other application domains like Business-IT-Alignment or Organizational Learning.

Using ATHENE for context modelling graphically represented meta-models for each context area can be provided. With that the complexity of ontologies can be hidden from the business user and enables her to adapt the context to the company's needs without involving a knowledge expert or loosing the semantic richness. Providing Reference Models she does not have to start from scratch but can build on existing models thus reducing time and effort for context modelling. That approach is especially interesting for small and medium sized companies with limited resources.

REFERENCES

W3C. (2004). *RDF primer*. Retrieved April 15, 2010, from http://www.w3.org/TR/rdf-primer/

Abecker, A., Bernardi, A., et al. (2000). Information supply for business processes: Coupling workflow with document analysis and information retrieval. In *Knowledge-Based System, Special Issue on AI in Knowledge Management, 13*, 271-284. Elsevier

Abecker, A., Hinkelmann, K., Maus, H., & Müller, H. J. (2002). Integrationspotenziale für Geschäftsprozesse und Wissensmanagement . In Abecker, A. (Eds.), *Geschäftsprozessorientiertes Wissensmanagement* (pp. 1–22). Berlin, Germany: Springer. doi:10.1007/978-3-642-55921-1_1

Allweyer, T. (2007). *Die Organisation des Wissens, Wie japanische Unternehmen eine brachliegende Ressource nutzbar machen*. Witten, W3L GmbH, 2. Nachdruck.

Baldauf, M., Dustar, S., & Rosenberg, F. (2007). A survey on context-aware systems. *International Journal Ad Hoc and Ubiquitous Computing, 2*(4), 263–277. doi:10.1504/IJAHUC.2007.014070

Brown, P. J. (1998). Triggering information by context. [London, UK: Springer.]. *Personal and Ubiquitous Computing, 2*(1), 18–27. doi:10.1007/BF01581843

Burgess, T. F. (1994). Making the leap to agility. *International Journal of Operations & Production Management, 14*(11), 23–34. doi:10.1108/01443579410068620

Cacciagrano, D., Corradini, F., et al. (2009). Resourceome: A multilevel model and a Semantic Web tool for managing domain and operational knowledge. In *Proceedings of the Fifth European Conference on Universal Multiservice Networks - ECUMN 2009.* Sliema, Malta.

Chen, H., Finin, T., et al. (2003). *Using OWL in a pervasive computing broker.* Workshop on Ontologies in Open Agent Systems (AAMAS 2003).

Cockburn, A., & Highsmith, J. (2001). Agile software development: The people factor. *Computer, 34*(11), 131–133. doi:10.1109/2.963450

Davenport, T., Jarvenpaa, S., & Beers, M. (1996). Improving knowledge work processes. *Sloan Management Review.*

Dey, A. K., & Abowd, G. (2000). Towards a better understanding of context and context-awareness. In *Proceedings of CHI2000: Conference on Human Factors in Computing,* The Hague, The Netherlands.

Dove, R. (1999). Knowledge management, response ability, and the agile enterprise. *Journal of Knowledge Management, 3,* 18–35. doi:10.1108/13673279910259367

Evans, E. (2004). *Domain-driven design, tackling complexity in the heart of software.* Boston, MA: Addison-Wesley.

Faget, J., Marin, M., Mégard, P., Owens, V. J., & Tarin, L.-O. (2003). Business processes and business rules: Business agility becomes real . In Fischer, L. (Ed.), *Workflow handbook* (pp. 77–92). Pompano Beach, FL: Future Strategies Inc.

Feldkamp, D., Hinkelmann, K., et al. (2007). KISS – Knowledge-intensive service support: An approach for agile process management. In A. Paschke & Y. Biletskiy (Eds.), *Proceedings Advances in Rule Interchange and Applications. International Symposium* (RuleML). Orlando, Florida, Springer, LNCS 4824.

Feldkamp, D., & Hinkelmann, K. (2010). Ontologies for e-government . In Healy, M., Kameas, A., & Poli, R. (Eds.), *TAO - Theory and applications of ontology.* Heidelberg, Germany: Springer.

Feldkamp, D., & Singh, N. (2010). Making the business process execution language (BPEL) flexible . In Alkhalifa, E. M. (Ed.), *E-strategies for resource management systems: Planning and implementation.* Hershey, PA: IGI Global.

Fünffinger, T. R., Rupprecht, C., Schott, H., & Sieper, A. (2002). Management von Prozesswissen in projekthaften Prozessen . In Abecker, A. (Eds.), *Geschäftsprozessorientiertes Wissensmanagement* (pp. 293–320). doi:10.1007/978-3-642-55921-1_12

Galler, J., & Scheer, A.-W. (1995). Workflow-Projekte: Erfahrungen aus Fallstudien und Vorgehensmodell. *Veröffentlichungen des Instituts für Wirtschaftsinformatik,* 117.

Geminiuc, K. (2007). A service-oriented approach to business rules development. Retrieved April 15, 2010, from http:// www. oracle. com/ technology/ pub/ articles/ bpel_cookbook/ geminiuc. html

Goldman, S. L., Preiss, K., et al. (1995). *Agile competitors and virtual organizations: Strategies for enriching the customer.* New York.

Guha, R. V. (1991). *Contexts: A formalization and some applications. Computer Science Department.* Stanford University.

Henbury, C. (2006). *Two definitions of agility.* Retrieved February 24, 2010, from http://www.cheshirehenbury.com/agility/twodefinitions.html

Hepp, M., Bachlechner, D., et al. (2005). *OntoWiki: Community-driven ontology engineering and ontology usage based on wikis.* International Symposium on Wikis (WikiSym 2005), San Diego, California, USA.

Hepp, M., & Leymann, F. (2005). *Semantic business process management: Using Semantic Web services for business process management.* Beijing, China: IEEE ICEBE.

Heravizadeh, M., & Edmond, D. (2008). *Making workflows context-aware: a way to support knowledge-intensive tasks.* APCCM.

Iacocca, I. (1991). *21st century manufacturing enterprise strategy: An industry-led view of agile manufacturing.* Bethlehem, PA: Leigh University.

Jennings, N. R., & Norman, T. J. (2000). Autonomous agents for business process management. [Taylor and Francis Ltd.]. *Applied Artificial Intelligence, 14,* 145–189. doi:10.1080/088395100117106

Jonsson, M. (2007). *Sensing and making sense. Designing middleware for context aware computing. Department of Computer and Systems Sciences.* Stockholm, Sweden: The Royal Institute of Technology. PhD.

Karagiannis, D. (1995). BPMS: Business process management systems. *ACM SIGGROUP Bulletin, 16*(1), 10–13. doi:10.1145/209891.209894

Kidd, A. (1994). *The marks are on the knowledge worker.* In Conference on Human Factors in Computing Systems, (pp. 186-191). Boston, MA: ACM.

Kidd, P. T. (1994). *Agile manufacturing: Forging new frontiers.* Reading, MA: Addison-Wesley.

Kidd, R. D. T. (1994). *The meaning of life & the meaning of agility. Agile manufacturing: Forging new frontiers.*

Klein, M., & Dellarocas, C. (2000). A knowledge-based approach to handling exceptions in workflow systems. *Journal of Computer Supported Collaborative Work . Special Issue on Adaptive Workflow Systems, 9*(3-4), 399–412.

Lenat, D. (1998). The dimensions of context-space. Retrieved April 20, 2010, from http://www.cyc.com/doc/context-space.pdf

Leppänen, M. (2007). *A context-based enterprise ontology business Information Systems* (pp. 273–286). Poznan, Poland: Springer.

Linnhoff-Popien, C., & Strang, T. (2004). A context modelling survey. 1st International Workshop on Advanced Context Modelling, Reasoning and Management, Nottingham.

Lu, R., & Sadiq, S. (2007), A survey of comparative business process modeling approaches. In *Proceedings of Business Information Systems: 10th International Conference* (BIS2007), (pp. 82-94).

Luo, Z., Sheth, A., Kochut, K., & Miller, J. (2000). Exception handling in workflow systems. *Applied Intelligence, 13*(2), 125–147. doi:10.1023/A:1008388412284

McCarthy, J. (1993). Notes on formalizing contexts. *Proceedings of the 13th International Joint Conference on Artificial Intelligence,* Chambery, France: Morgan Kaufmann.

Mena, T. B., Saoud, N. B.-B., et al. (2007). Towards a methodology for context sensitive systems development. 6th International and Interdisciplinary Conference CONTEXT 2007, Roskilde, Denmark, Springer.

Meyers, K. L. (1999). CPEF: A continuous planning and execution framework. *AI Magazine, 20*(4), 63–69.

Mitra, A., & Gupta, A. (2005). *Agile systems with reusable patterns of business knowledge: A component-based approach*. Norwood, MA: Artech House.

Mitra, A., & Gupta, A. (2005). *Agile systems, with reusable patterns of business knowledge, a component-based approach*. Norwood, MA: Artech House.

Mitra, A., & Gupta, A. (2006). *Creating agile business systems with reusable knowledge*. Cambridge, UK: Cambridge University Press.

Pollack, M. E., & Horty, J. F. (1999). *Adjustable autonomy for a plan management agent*. (AAAI Technical Report, SS-99-06).

Reichert, M., & Dadam, P. (1998). Adept flex - Supporting dynamic changes of workflows without losing control. *Journal of Intelligent Information Systems, 10*, 93–129. doi:10.1023/A:1008604709862

Reichert, M., & Dadam, P. (2007). Enabling Adaptive process aware Information Systems with ADEPT2 . In Cardoso, J., & van der Aalst, W. (Eds.), *Handbook of research on business process modeling* (pp. 173–203). New York, NY: Information Science Reference.

Richter von Hagen, C., Ratz, D., & Povaley, R. (2005). Towards self-organizing knowledge intensive processes. *Journal of Universal Knowledge Management, 2*, 148–169.

Riss, U. V., & Rickayzen, A. (2005). Challenges for business process and task management. *Journal of Universal Knowledge Management, 0*(2), 77–100.

Rittwik, J., & Chen, Y.-F. (2005). Context-aware mobile computing . In Ilyas, M., & Mahgoub, I. (Eds.), *Mobile computing handbook*. Florida: CRC Press.

Sadiq, S., Orlowska, E., & Sadiq, W. (2005). Specification and validation of process constraints for flexible workflows. *Information Systems, 30*.

Sadiq, S., Sadiq, W., & Orlowska, M. (2001). Pockets of flexibility in workflow specification . In *Proceedings Conceptual Modeling, ER2001*. Berlin, Germany: Springer.

Sadiq, S. W., Sadiq, W., et al. (2001). *Pockets of flexibility in workflow specification*. Conceptual Modeling - ER 2001, 20th International Conference on Conceptual Modeling, Yokohama, Japan, Springer.

Saidani, O., & Nurcan, S. (2007). Towards context aware business process modelling. In *Proceedings of BPMDS07*, Trondheim, Norway.

Schatten, A., & Schiefer, J. (2007). *Agile business process management with sense and respond*. IEEE International Conference on e-Business Engineering and the Workshops SOAIC 2007, SOSE 2007, SOKM 2007. Hong Kong, China, IEEE Computer Society.

Scheer, A.-W., Adam, O., Hofer, A., & Zangl, F. (2003). Nach Cost Cutting. Aufbruch durch Innovation . In *IM Fachzeitschrift für Information Management and Consulting* (*Vol. 18*). Sonderausgabe.

Schmidt, A. (2002). *Ubiquitous computing - Computing in context*. Computing Department, Lancaster University.

Schulz, S. (2003). *Kontext als Beziehung: Ein Kontextmodell für Mobiles Wissensmanagement*. *Informatik 2003*. Frankfurt am Main: Köllen Druck & Verlag GmbH.

Schwarz, S., & Abecker, A. (2001). *Anforderungen an die Workflow-Unterstützung für wissensintensive Geschäftsprozesse. Geschäftsprozessorientiertes Wissensmanagement auf der WM2001*. Baden-Baden.

Schwarz, S., Abecker, A., Maus, H., & Sintek, M. (2001). Anforderungen an die Workflow-Unterstützung für wissensintensive Geschäftsprozesse. In *Proceedings für die 1. Konferenz für Professionelles Wissensmanagement-Erfahrungen und Visionen*, WM2001, Baden-Baden.

Sharifi, H., & Zhang, Z. (2001). Agile manufacturing in practise - Application of a methodology. *International Journal of Operations & Production Management, 21*(5/6), 772–794. doi:10.1108/01443570110390462

Smith, H., & Fingar, P. (2003). BPM's third wave. Retrieved January 17, 2010, from http://www.bptrends.com/publicationfiles/bpm%20third%20wave%20smith%20fingar%20apr2003.pdf

van der Aalst, W., & Jablonski, S. (2000). Dealing with workflow change: Identification of issues and solutions. *International Journal of Computer Science and Engineering, 15*(5), 267–276.

van der Aalst, W., & van Hee, K. (2002). *Workflow management models, methods and systems*. Cambridge, MA: MIT Press.

van der Aalst, W. M. P., & Jablonski, S. (2000). Dealing with workflow change: Identification of issues and solutions. *International Journal of Computer Systems Science and Engineering, 5*, 267–276.

van Oosterhout, M., Waarts, E., van Heck, E., & van Hillegersberg, J. (2007). Business agility: Need, readiness and alignment with IT strategies . In Descouza, K. (Ed.), *Agile Information Systems: Conceptualization, construction, and management* (pp. 52–69).

von Halle, B. (2001). *Business rules applied: Building better systems using the business rules approach*. Wiley.

Wang, X. H., Gu, T., et al. (2004). *Ontology based context modeling and reasoning using OWL*. Communication Networks and distributed Systems Modeling and Simulation Conference (CNDS2004), San Diego, CA, USA.

Wargitsch, C., Wewers, T., & Theisinger, F. (1997). *WorkBrain: Merging organizational memory and workflow management systems*. In Workshop of Knowledge Based Systems for Knowledge Management in Enterprises at the 21st Annual German Conference on AI (KI-97), (pp. 214-219).

Whittingham, K., Stolze, M., & Ludwig, H. (2000). *The OpenWater project - A substrate for process knowledge management tools*. (AAAI Technical Report SS-00-03).

Winograd, T. (2001). Architectures for context. *Human-Computer Interaction*, 16.

Yusuf, Y. Y., & Sarhadi, M. (1999). Agile manufacturing: The drivers, concepts and attributes. *International Journal of Production Economics, 62*(3), 33–43. doi:10.1016/S0925-5273(98)00219-9

Zimmermann, A., Lorenz, A., et al. (2007). *An operational definition of context*. 6th International and Interdisciplinary Conference, CONTEXT 2007, Roskilde, Denmark, Springer.

ADDITIONAL READING

Alavi, M. and Leidner, D. E. (2001). Review: Knowledge Management and Knowledge Management Systems: Conceptual Foundations and Research Issues, in MIS Quarterly vol. 25(1): 107-136.

Areta, B.M. and Giachetti, R.E. (2004), A measure of agility as the complexity of the enterprise system, in Robotics and Computer-Integrated Manufacturing, 20, pp. 495-503.

Budzik, J., & Hammond, K. J. (2000). User Interactions with Everyday Applications as Context for Just-in-time Inforamtion Access. International Conference on Intelligent User Interfaces, New Orleans, Louisiana, United States.

Chen, H. (2003). *An Intelligent Broker Architecture for Context-Aware System*. Computer Science Baltimore County, University of Maryland PhD.

Faustmann, G. (1999). Enforcement vs. freedom of action an integrated approach to flexible workflow enactment, in SIGGROUP Bull. vol. 20(3): 5-6.

Giunchiglia, F. (1993). Contextual Reasoning. Proceedings of the IJCAI'93 Workshop on Using Knowledge in its Context, LAFORIA.

Gwizdka, J. (2000). What's in the Context? CHI 2000 Workshop 11. The What, Who, Where, When, Why and How of Context-Awareness.

Hammer, M., & Champy, J. (1993). *Reengineering the Corporation*. New York: Haper Collins Publisher.

Hinkelmann, K., & Probst, F. (2005). *Explizierung von Prozesswissen auf der Basis von Ontologien. WM2005 - Professional Knowledge Management*. Kaiserslautern.

Hinkelmann, K., Probst, F., et al. (2006). Agile Process Management Framework and Methodology. AAAI Spring Symposium on Semantic Web Meets e-Government. Stanford University.

Jorgensen, H. D., & Steinar, C. (1999). Emergent Workflows: Planning and Performance of Process Instances. In Becker, J. Mühlen, M. z. and Rosemann, M. (eds.) Proceedings 1999 Workflow Management Conference - Workflow-based Applications, Münster.

Jung, J., Choi, I., et al. (2007). An integration architecture for knowledge management systems and business process management systems. in Computers in Industry, vol. 58. pp. 21-34.

Keidl, M., & Kemper, A. (2004). Towards context-aware adaptable web services, In Proceedings of the 13th international World Wide Web conference on Alternate track papers and posters, pp. 55-65, New York, USA.

Laura, M. Meade and K.J. Rogers, (1997), Enhancing A Manufacturing Business Process For Agility, in: Innovation in Technology Management – The Key to Global Leadership. PICMET '97: Portland International Conference on Management and Technology, pp. 638-641.

Lautenbach, F., & Bauer, B. (2007). A Survey on Workflow Annotation & Composition Approaches. Workshop on Semantic Business Process and Product Lifecycle Management (SBPM 2007) in conjunction with the 3rd European Semantic Web Conference (ESWC 2007), Innsbruck, Austria, CEUR Workshop Proceedings series.

Lienhard, H., & Künzi, U.-M. (2005). Workflow and Business Rules - a Common Approach . In Fischer, L. (Ed.), *Workflow Handbook 2005* (pp. 129–139). Lighthouse Point, FL, USA: Future Strategies Inc.

Ching-Torng Lin, Hero Chiu and Yi-Hong Tseng (2005), Agility evaluation using fuzzy logic, in International Journal of Production Economics, 101 (2), pp. 353-368.

List, B., Schiefer, J., et al. (2001). Measuring Knowledge with Workflow Management Systems. 12th International Workshop on Database and Expert Systems Applications (DEXA 2001). Munich, Germany, IEEE Computer Society.

Maamar, Z., & Benslimane, D. (2006). (*12*) (*Vol. 49*). What Can Context Do for Web Services. In Communications of the ACM.

Mitra, A., & Gupta, A. (2006). *Creating Agile Business Systems with Reusable Knowledge*. Cambridge: Cambridge University Press.

Ploesser, K., & Peleg, M. (2009). Learning from Context to Improve Business Processes. *BP Trends*, *6*(1), 1–7.

Prekop, P., & Burnett, M. (2003). Activities, context and ubiquitous computing. *Computer Communications*, *26*(11), 1168–1176. doi:10.1016/S0140-3664(02)00251-7

Rosemann, M., & Recker, J. (2006). Context-aware Process Design: Exploring the Extrinsic Drivers for Process Flexibility. 18th International Conference on Advanced Information Systems Engineering. Workshops and Doctoral Consortium.

Rosemann, M., Recker, J., et al. (2006). Understanding Context-Awareness in Business Process Design. 17th Australasian Conference on Information Systems, Adelaide, Australia.

Schilit, B. N. (1995). *System architecture for context-aware mobile computing*. Columbia University. PhD.

Schönherr, M. (2004). Enterprise Architecture Frameworks. Enterprise Application Integration - Serviceorientierung und nachhaltige Architekturen. M. Schönherr and S. Aier. Berlin, Gito, pp- 3-48.

Soffer, P. (2005). On the Notion of Flexibility in Business Processes. CAiSE'05 Workshops., Porto, Portugal

Uschold, M., & King, M. (1998). The Enterprise Ontology. [Special Issue on Putting Ontologies to Use]. *The Knowledge Engineering Review*, *13*, doi:10.1017/S0269888998001088

van der Aalst, W. M. P., & Weske, M. (2005). Case Handling: A New Paradigm for Business Process Support. *Data & Knowledge Engineering*, *53*, 192–162.

Wonneberger, H. (2007). *Ableitung komplexer Kontextinformationen und deren Anreicherung aus externen Quellen. Seminar on Mobile and Context-aware Database Technologies and Applications*. Kaiserslautern.

KEY TERMS AND DEFINITIONS

Adaptability: Adaptability is the ability to react to exceptional circumstances or unexpected events.

Agility: Agility is the ability to cope with increasing changes.

Awareness: Awareness is the ability to detect opportunities and risks.

Context: Context is the conceptualization of all elements constituting and affecting an enterprise.

Dynamism: Dynamism is the ability to change the process definition.

Flexibility: Flexibility is the ability to deal with a fair degree of uncertainty.

Workflow Management System: A Workflow Management System is an information system that manages and executes business processes.

ENDNOTES

[1] ARIS, the BPMS developed by IDS Scheer, entered the market in 1984. URL: http://www.ids-scheer.com/en/index.html (February 14, 2010)

[2] ADONIS is the BPMS of BOC. URL: http://www.boc-group.com/ (February 14, 2010)

[3] ATHENE is an open source modeling framework developed by the University of Applied Sciences Switzerland.

[4] http://www.omg.org/spec/BPMN/1.1/ (retrieved 1.5.2010)

[5] FIT - Fostering self-adaptive e-government service improvement using semantic Technologies. Website of FIT: http://www.fit-project.org/.

[6] plugIT - Business and IT Alignment using a Model-Based Plug-In Framework. Website of the plugIT: www.plug-it.org/

[7] Allowing for more than one meta-model to represent a context area (here: process knowledge) is a strength of ATHENE. As there is a strict separation between concepts and their graphical representation, and all concepts are stored in the same ontology semantical description can be inherit and used in several models.

[8] http://www.activevos.com/community-open-source.php

[9] "The project is funded by the Oester-reichische Forschungsförderungsgesell-schaft GmbH (FFG) and the Bundes-ministerium für Verkehr, Innovation und Technologie (BMVIT) under the FIT-IT "Semantic Systems" program (contract number 812515)", URL: http://www.myon-tology.org/index.html (February 16, 2010)

About the Contributors

Stefan Smolnik is an Assistant Professor of Information and Knowledge Management at the EBS Business School in Germany. He holds a doctoral degree from University of Paderborn, Germany. Before joining EBS Business School, he worked as a Research and Teaching Assistant at the university's Groupware Competence Center. Stefan Smolnik has done research on the success and performance measurement of information and knowledge management systems, which has included several benchmarking studies. In addition, he is interested in the successful organizational implementation of social software. His work has been published in well reputed international journals and conference proceedings such as *Journal of Strategic Information Systems, Business & Information Systems Engineering, International Journal of Knowledge Management, Business Process Management Journal, the proceedings of the Annual Hawaii International Conference on System Sciences,* and *the proceedings of the Annual International Conference on Information Systems.*

Frank Teuteberg has, since 2008, held the Chair in Accounting and Information Systems, which is part of the Institute of Information Management and Corporate Governance (IMU) at the University of Osnabrück. In 1996 he received his degree in Business Administration with focus on Information Systems from Georg-August-Universität Göttingen/Germany. From 1996 to 2001, he worked as a Research Assistant to Prof. Dr. Karl Kurbel (holder of the Chair in Information Systems) at Europa-Universität Frankfurt (Oder), where he took up a postdoctoral position after his doctoral graduation in May 2001. From April 2004 to October 2007 Frank Teuteberg held a junior professorship of Business Administration/E-Business and Information Systems at the University of Osnabrück. He teaches at Virtual Global University (www.vg-u.de) and is a regular Visiting Professor at ESCEM (www.escem.fr) in Tours/Poitiers (France). Frank Teuteberg was the leader of a subproject on Mobile Supply Chain Management (run from April 2004 to the end of 2007) as part of the joint project "Mobile Internet Business" (www.mib.uni-ffo.de) which was funded more than 2 million Euros by the Federal Ministry of Education and Research. Currently he is the leader of a subproject in the joint project "IT-for-Green" (www.ertemis.eu; from April 2011 to October 2014) which is funded with more than 2 million Euros by the European Regional Development Fund (ERDF). He has published more than 120 scientific papers, many of which have appeared in leading German and international journals (e.g. Electronic Markets, International Journal of Project Management, International Journal of Computer Systems Science & Engineering, Corporate Social Responsibility and Environmental Management (formerly Eco-Management and Auditing)). His main research interests are Semantic Business Process Management, Sustainable Supply Chain Management, Green IT, Cloud Computing and IT Risk Management.

Oliver Thomas has, since 2009, held the Chair in Information Management and Information Systems, which is part of the Institute of Information Management and Corporate Governance (IMU) at the University of Osnabrück. In 1999, he received his diploma in Business Administration from the University of Saarland/Germany. From 1999 to 2002 he worked at the Institute for Information Systems (IWi) of the University of Saarland. Later, this institute has been integrated into the German Research Center for Artificial Intelligence (DFKI), and Oliver Thomas was a deputy head and a senior researcher from 2003 to 2009. Since 2004, Oliver Thomas is a Visiting Associate Professor at the Aoyama Gakuin University in Tokyo (Japan). His fields of research are business process management, enterprise modeling, product-service systems, enterprise architecture management, semantic technologies in information systems, and mobile information systems.

* * *

Witold Abramowicz is a Full Professor and the Chair of Department of Information Systems at The Poznan University of Economics, Poland. His particular areas of interest are information retrieval and filtering and knowledge management in MIS. He received his M.Sc. from The Technical University of Poznan, Poland, Ph.D. from The Wroclaw Technical University, Poland, and habilitation from The Humboldt University Berlin, Germany. He worked for three universities in the Switzerland and Germany for twelve years. He is an editor, author, or co-author of thirty two books (published mostly by Springer and Kluwer Academic Publishers) and over 200 book chapters, articles in various journals and conference proceedings. He chaired 20 scientific international conferences and was a member of the program committees of over 280 other conferences. He is member of the editorial boards in some international journals like *Wirtschaftsinformatik (A list), Comparative Technology Transfer, International Journal of Web Services Practices, International Journal of Web-based Learning and Teaching Technology,* and *Business & Information Systems Engineering*. Currently, Professor Abramowicz is and was involved in many research projects in the 6th and the 7th Framework Program EU. Professor Abramowicz is Vice President of the Polish Association of Management Information Systems, member of Polish Governmental Informatics' Council, and member of board of Semantic Technology Institutes International.

Alexey Alishevskikh started his professional career of a software developer in the web and e-commerce industry in 1998. Later Alexey focused his interests onto the emerging area of content management and professional web-publishing technologies. Since the very founding of the ViceVersa Company in 2003, Alexey has held the position of the technology director (CTO), in charge of defining the corporate technological strategy, as well as technical management of all solutions and projects the company carries out. Alexey is an early open source software adopter, and an initiator and major contributor of a number of open software projects. The technology, developed within the SCAN Semantic Desktop project, launched by Alexey in 2007, is at the heart of the technology solution, currently provided by the ViceVersa Technologies Company. Alexey is a participant of several international research and software development projects; currently he collaborates as a researcher and a software engineer with the University of Nottingham in the framework of the project in the Semantic Web and social networks research area.

Mauricio B. Almeida has, since 2004, been acting as Full Professor in the Department of Information Theory and Management at the Federal University of *Minas Gerais* (www.ufmg.br/english/). From 2000 to 2004, he worked in the Institute of Computer Science at Catholic University of *Minas Gerais* (www. pucminas.br). He acquired his PhD in Information Science at UFMG in 2006, also obtained a Master's degree in Information Science, a Postgraduate Certificate in Software Engineering, a Postgraduate Certificate in Business Administration, and an Engineering Degree. In 2010, he took up a postdoctoral position at State University of New York at Buffalo (www.buffalo.edu), with the team Ontology Research Group (http://org.buffalo.edu/) in the New York State Center of Excellence in Bioinformatics and Life Sciences (www.bioinformatics.buffalo.edu/). The project, developed during this sabbatical leave, is related to a vocabulary in the domain of human blood, in partnership with Brazilian healthcare institutions. His main research interest is knowledge representation, applied ontologies. He also develops research in information organization in companies, document management, and information security.

Jörg Becker is a Full Professor of Information Systems and holds the Chair of Information Systems and Information Management at the Department of Information Systems at the University of Münster, Germany. He is Managing Director of the Department of Information Systems and of the European Research Center for Information Systems (ERCIS), an international research network of outstanding researchers in IS. Since 2008, he is Vice-Rector for strategic planning and quality management of the University of Münster. In 2007, he was invited as a member of the North-Rhine Westphalian Academy of Sciences. He is Editor-in-Chief for the *Information Systems and e-Business Management* journal and is editor of several other IS journals. Jörg publishes his scientific papers in leading national and international journals and proceedings. Furthermore, he is editor of several monographs and edited books. His research interests incorporate business process management, conceptual modeling, data management, retail Information Systems, ERP systems, business intelligence, and e-government.

Andreas Bögl received his Mag. degree from Johannes Kepler University, Linz, Austria, in 2002. Afterwards, he worked as a Research Assistant at the Department of Business Informatics – Data & Knowledge Engineering at the University of Linz for four years. From 2004 to 2008, Andreas Bögl was a member of the Business Project Improvement (BPI) project, which was funded by Siemens AG. Within this project, he was responsible for the development of the pModeler prototype that facilitates automated detection of common modeling practices in EPC models. He is currently preparing a Ph.D. on the topic of modeling practices. His research interests include semantic business process management, process mining, process model quality, and semantic process model analysis.

Farid Bourennani is Lecturer and Research Associate at the University of Ontario Institute of Technology (UOIT). He received his Master's from UOIT and his B.Sc. from University of Sherbrooke.

Patrick Delfmann has, since 2006, been the Head of the Competence Center for Reference Modeling at the European Research Center for Information Systems (ERCIS) of the University of Münster, Germany. In 2001, he graduated in Information Systems with the focus on computer science in industry at the University of Münster. From 2001 to 2007, he worked as a Research Assistant at the chair of Prof. Jörg Becker at the University of Münster. In 2006, he received his doctoral degree in Information Systems and took up a postdoctoral position in 2007. In early 2011, Patrick was awarded his postdoctoral degree (venia legendi) in Information Systems. He was the coordinator of several research projects, funded by the German Research Foundation (DFG), the German Ministry of Education and Research (BMBF), and the European Union. He teaches at the University of Münster and has been a Visiting Professor at Moscow State University, at SAP Business School Vienna and Swiss Marketing and Advertising Institute (SAWI). He has published more than 60 scientific papers, many of which have appeared in high ranked national and international proceedings and journals. His main research interests are conceptual modeling, reference modeling, conceptual model analysis, semantic standardization and business process compliance management.

Timo von der Dovenmühle is studying Business Computer Science at the University of Oldenburg. Accompanying his studies, he successfully attends various competitions within the field of software engineering. In 2009 he published his first scientific paper within the area of Semantic Web service architectures. His main research interests are service oriented architectures, mobility, and efficiency improvements in computer systems based on green computing concepts.

Marwane El Kharbili is a Junior Researcher of the model driven engineering group at the Laboratory for Advanced Software Systems (LASSY) at the University of Luxemburg since August 2009. His work focuses on building a framework for regulatory compliance management for processes. He is under supervision of Prof. Pierre Kelsen from the University of Luxemburg and Prof. Elke Pulvermüller from the University of Osnabrück (Germany). Prior to joining LASSY, Marwane El Kharbili spent two years as a Research Engineer at the IDS Scheer in Saarbruecken (Germany), the world's leading business process analysis software company. He worked there on the business rule management capabilities of the ARIS platform. He also took part in the SUPER project where he did research on semantic process management and focused on semantic compliance. He graduated in computer science and holds a Master of Science from both the Universities of Karlsruhe (Diplom-Informatiker) in Germany, and the Grenoble INP (Ingenieur ENSIMAG) in France. Marwane El Kharbili's research focuses on compliance modeling and verification and covers a variety of fields: software language engineering, model driven engineering, policy and rule management, and the Semantic Web.

Tatiana Emshanova is a system software engineer in computer networks and development tools for multimedia environments. Since 1998 she has participated in a number of projects in content management, intranet and extranet system designing, and web-site developing both as a manager and a system analyst. For the most part she was responsible for customer relationship management, project management, design of information system architecture, information modeling, ontologies and taxonomies development, user requirement analysis, and user testing. Concurrently she has been involved in several projects as a consultant in business and knowledge management strategic planning, business processes optimization and quality control; as well as a researcher in information architecture, knowledge and innovation management, development, and facilitating of communities of practice. Tatiana is experienced in an organisation of regional and international round tables, research and business seminars, face-to-face, and teleconferences. She also took part in the similar events as a participant and a speaker. Currently Tatiana is interested in issues of Semantic Web, namely in semantically-based social desktop and collaborative environment development, linked open data, knowledge representation, information mapping, and ontologies development.

Michael Fellmann is currently working on his PhD thesis at the Institute of Information Management and Corporate Governance, University of Osnabrueck. He has been a Research Assistant at the Institute for Information Systems at the German Research Center for Artificial Intelligence (DFKI). Michael Fellmann received a Master of Arts in Information Science, Computer Science and Information Systems from the Saarland University. His fields of research are business process management, enterprise modeling, and semantic technologies.

Peter Fettke obtained a Master's Degree in Information Systems (Diplom-Wirtschaftsinformatiker) from the University of Münster, Germany, and a PhD Degree in Information Systems from the Johannes Gutenberg-University Mainz, both Germany. Since April 2006 he is a Senior Researcher in Information Systems at the Institute for Information Systems (IWi) at the German Research Center for Artificial Intelligence (DFKI), Saarbrücken. Peter has taught and researched previously at the Technical University of Chemnitz and the University Mainz, both in Germany. His research interests include Information Systems analysis and design, especially the use of conceptual modeling and component-based system paradigm. Peter has published numerous articles on reference modeling, conceptual modelling, and component-based engineering in both national and international journals and conference proceedings. Furthermore, he is a member of the editorial board of the *Journal of Cases on Information Technology* (JCIT) as well as the *Journal of System and the Management Sciences* (JSMS) and serves as a regular reviewer for the *Information Resources Management Journal* (IRMJ), *Data & Knowledge Engineering* (DKE), and *International Journal of Interoperability in Business Information System*s (IBIS). Recently, he has finished his Habilitation thesis on empirical Business Engineering.

Hans-Georg Fill has been, since 2006, an Assistant Professor at the Department of Knowledge and Business Engineering, part of the Faculty of Computer Science of the University of Vienna, Austria. In 2010, he was awarded an Erwin-Schrödinger Fellowship for conducting a one year research project at Stanford University, USA in the context of semantic-based modeling for Information Systems. In 2002 he received a degree in International Business Administration (equiv. BSc & MSc) with a focus on business informatics and human resource management from the University of Vienna, and in 2006 he graduated summa cum laude with a Doctorate in Business Informatics also from the University of Vienna. Besides his research and teaching activities at the University of Vienna he has been teaching at the École Nationale Supérieure des Mines de St-Étienne, France and the University of Regensburg, Germany. In 2009 he acted as Organization Chair for the 9th International Conference on Business Informatics which attracted more than 1000 participants. He is an active member of the Open Model Initiative (www.openmodels.at) where he maintains the Semantic-based Modeling Framework for Information Systems (SeMFIS). His research interests include semantic-based conceptual modeling and visualization, semantic business process and performance management, and the application of these approaches in the health care sector and the banking industry.

Agata Filipowska is an Assistant Professor at Poznan University of Economics, Department of Information Systems. She teaches courses on business process modeling, e-government, software engineering, and management Information Systems. Agata Filipowska has a Master of Science from Poznan University of Economics (received in 2004, Summa Cum Laude) and PhD from Poznan University of Economics and Macquarie University in Sydney (received in 2010, Summa Cum Laude). Since 2004 she has been involved in projects funded by European Commission under 6 and 7 Framework Programme: ASG, Insemtives, Service Web 3.0, SUPER and USE-ME.GOV. In SUPER and Service Web 3.0, Agata Filipowska coordinated dissemination activities. Moreover, Agata Filipowska chaired Organizing Committee of the International Conference on Business Information Systems from 2004 to 2006. Currently, Agata is involved in 3 externally funded research projects, namely semantic monitoring of cyberspace, advanced data extraction methods for the needs of expert search, and FP7 INSEMTIVES. She is a member of PC of several workshops and conferences and author (and lecturer) of few tutorials on semantic business process management. She is an author of numerous conference and journal papers. Her main areas of interest include information retrieval and filtering, information extraction, and business process management.

Jorge Marx Gómez studied Computer Engineering and Industrial Engineering at the University of Applied Sciences Berlin (Technische Fachhochschule Berlin). He was a Lecturer and Researcher at the Otto-von-Guericke-University Magdeburg (Germany) where he also obtained a PhD degree in Business Information Systems with the work "Computer-based Approaches to Forecast Returns of Scrapped Products to Recycling." From 2002 till 2003 he was a Visiting Professor for Business Informatics at the Technical University of Clausthal (TU Clausthal, Germany). In 2004 he received his habilitation for the work "Automated Environmental Reporting through Material Flow Networks" at the Otto-von-Guericke-University Magdeburg. In 2005 he became a Full Professor and Chair of Business Information Systems at the Carl von Ossietzky University Oldenburg (Germany). His research interests include very large business applications, federated ERP-systems, business intelligence, data warehousing, interoperability, and environmental (sustainability-oriented) management Information Systems.

José Manuel González Vázquez has, since January 2008, been Research Assistant and PhD candidate at the OFFIS – Institute for Information Technology –an affiliated Institute of the University of Oldenburg. He is member of the group Interoperability and Standards of Mathias Uslar at OFFIS Energy division. In 2004 he received his degree in Business Information Systems from the University of Hamburg / Germany. From 2004 to 2007 he worked as IT-Consultant at Lufthansa Systems Energy division where he was involved within several projects at the energy trading branch of a major European utility company. His research is on reference models and IT systems in the utility domain (electricity and gas). This includes semantic modeling, classifying and adding meta-data at information models to support requirement analysis within software product development at utilities and vendors. His PhD is supervised by Prof. Dr. Hans-Jürgen Appelrath at the Carl von Ossietzky University Oldenburg. Further on he is actively involved in national and international standardization and is member of the IEC German mirror committee DKE K 952 and IEC TC 57 Working Group 14, where he is part of the Common Information Model (CIM) modeling team.

Liane Haak studied Business Economics with major in Computer Science before she worked many years in the Department of Computing Science at University of Oldenburg in teaching and research. She operated industrial technology transfer projects in cooperation with the OFFIS Institute for Information Technology in the area of Enterprise Systems (ES). In 2007 she received her PhD in Computer Science at the University of Oldenburg and became Assistant Professor in the working group of Business Information Systems / Very Large Business Applications. Besides her teaching activities in Germany, she was a regular visiting lecturer at Wadi International University (Syria) and was involved in many international project activities, mainly with Syria and Latin America. From 2008 to 2010 Liane Haak was the project leader of the bi-national PhD-net DEEBIS-Net, which was funded by the Germany Academic Exchange Service (DAAD) to build up a research network with Cuba. She published numerous scientific national and international papers and was chair of several workshops, e.g. International ACM Workshop on Interoperability of Heterogeneous Information Systems 2005 and ES in Higher Education 2009 & 2010. Her main research interests focuses on knowledge management and semantic integration, enterprise systems (mainly ERP-systems and e-business), teaching methods in higher education, and mobile business solutions.

Bernd Heinrich has, since February 2009, been a Full Professor for Information Systems at the Department of Information Systems, Production and Logistics Management at the University of Innsbruck. He received his diploma in Information Systems from the University of Regensburg in 1999 and specialized in the fields of Information Engineering, Information Systems in the Financial Services industry, and Operations Research. From 1999 to 2002, he worked as a Research Assistant at the Chair of Information Management of Prof. Dr. Robert Winter at the University of St. Gallen. From 2002 to 2008, Bernd Heinrich worked as an Assistant Professor for Information Systems at the Department of Information Systems Engineering & Financial Management of Prof. Dr. Hans Ulrich Buhl at the University of Augsburg. During this time, he was project leader of several research groups and conducted a number of applied research projects (e.g. together with Siemens AG, Fujitsu Siemens Computers GmbH, HypoVereinsbank AG, and Allianz AG). Moreover, he had the leading responsibility for requesting and managing the fundamental research projects SEMPRO and the follow-up project, which are funded by the German Research Foundation. In 2007, he habilitated ("venia legendi") in the fields of Information Systems architectures, data quality, semantic-based process management, and standardization. Bernd Heinrich serves as a Reviewer and Associate Editor for several international journals and conferences. He has published numerous articles in books and journals as for example *Zeitschrift für Betriebswirtschaft, Business & Information Systems Engineering (Die Wirtschaftsinformatik), Information Systems and E-Business Management, Business Process Management Journal, Academy of Marketing Science Review, ACM Journal of Data and Information Quality,* and *Journal of Information Science.* Moreover, he presented his research at renowned international conferences such as International Conference on Information Systems and European Conference on Information Systems. His main research interests are semantic-based process management, data quality, IT portfolio management, and decision models for an economic-oriented standard adoption.

Sebastian Herwig holds a Diploma degree in Information Systems from the University of Münster, Germany. He studied Information Systems at the Technical University of Ilmenau, Germany, and at the University of Münster. Since 2007 he is a PhD student and Researcher at the European Research Center for Information Systems (ERCIS) at the University of Münster. Sebastian's current research interests include all aspects of conceptual modeling, in particular distributed modeling, standardization efforts in the modeling process, and the analysis of conceptual models. His publications appear in major international conferences and journals.

Frank Hogrebe holds a chair in Business Administration at University of Applied Administrative Sciences, Wiesbaden. He received diploma in Business Administration, Political Economics and Public Administration. From 2004 to 2010, Frank Hogrebe was the head of department of the administration at the capital city of Dusseldorf and led several projects. In parallel, he did his doctorate at the University of Hamburg and received his degree in 2011. His fields of research are Information Systems in public administration, e-government, and the reduction of bureaucracy.

Monika Kaczmarek, since 2010, has been an Assistant Professor at the Department of Information Systems, Faculty of Electronic Commerce and Informatics, Poznan University of Economics, Poland. Monika received her PhD in 2010 from Poznań University of Economics (PUE), Poland and Macquarie University in Sydney, Australia (Summa Cum Laude). Since 2004 she has been involved in projects funded by European Commission - Adatpive Services Grid (ASG), Semantics Utilised for Process Management Within and between Enterprises (SUPER) and Knowledge Web. She is currently involved in the realization of. Advanced Data Extraction Methods for the Needs of Expert Search as well as FP7 research project, INSEMTIVES. She also lectures in Artificial Intelligence Systems, IT Infrastructure Management, as well as Computer Science at PUE. She has published a number of scientific papers, many of which have appeared at leading international conferences and in journals. Her research interests include, among others, service ecosystems, business process management, knowledge representation, Semantic Web, and artificial intelligence methods.

Tomasz Kaczmarek is an Assistant Professor in the Department of Information Systems at Poznań University of Economics. He received his MSc in Economics (Information Systems) in 2002 and PhD in Economics (Information Systems) in 2006 from Poznan University of Economics. His professional interests include data integration, knowledge representation, information retrieval and filtering, markup languages, and web development. From 2003 to 2006 he was involved in the Adaptive Services Grid (ASG) project funded by the European Commission. Since 2006 he participated in two other research projects funded under 6th Framework Programme: SUPER (Semantics Utilised for Process Management within and between Enterprises) and TOWL (Time-determined Ontology Web Language). Currently, he works on advanced deep Web extraction methods in the Advanced Data Extraction Methods for the Needs of Expert Search project. He has also been working for two months in the School of Information Technology & Electrical Engineering at the University of Queensland in 2003 as visiting student, and for half a year in SAP Research CEC Karlsruhe in 2008 as a visiting researcher. He published several conference papers, journal papers, and book chapters in the area of information integration, information retrieval and Semantic Web services.

Michael Karlinger is a Research Assistant at the Department of Business Informatics – Data & Knowledge Engineering at Johannes Kepler University, Linz, Austria, since 2005. He received his Mag. degree from Johannes Kepler University in 2004. Before starting his academic career in 2005, he worked for one year as System Developer of the online tutoring system eTutor. In 2010 he received his Doctorate from Johannes Kepler University for his work on integrity constraints in XML. Beside XML integrity constraints, his research concentrates on security and privacy in outsourced databases and electronic health applications, including his participation in related research projects. Currently, he is the leader of an applied research project aiming at secure online file storage.

Mathias Klier has been an Assistant Professor at the Department of Information Systems, Production and Logistics Management at the University of Innsbruck since March 2009. He received his diploma in Business Mathematics from the University of Augsburg in 2005 and specialized in the fields of Optimization and Operations Research. For his diploma thesis, he received the Award from the Vodafone Research Foundation in the field of market and customer orientation. From June 2005 to January 2009, he worked as a Research Assistant at the Department of Information Systems Engineering & Financial Management of Prof. Dr. H. U. Buhl. During this time, he was leader of a research group and conducted several applied privately funded research projects (e.g. at MLP AG). He received his doctor's degree in February 2008 from the University of Augsburg. His doctoral thesis is on Designing Customer-Centric Information Systems - Research Contributions to Planning and Evaluating Data Quality Measures and Communication Standards. In 2008 he received the Research Award of Mercedes Benz for this work. He has published several articles in a number of international journals, such as *Journal of Information Science* or *ACM Journal of Data and Information Quality*. Moreover, he presented his research at international conferences such as European Conference on Information Systems and International Conference on Information Systems. His main research interests are semantic-based process management, data quality, and online social networks.

Yun Lin is working at the world's 4th largest ERP company, Unit 4 Agresso R&D, as a system design architect and researcher since 2007. She received her PhD degree at Norwegian University of Science and Technology in 2008. She earned her Master's degree from Zhongnan University of Economics and Law in China in 2001. She actively participated in EU research projects, some of which were in collaboration with Norway's largest research institute SINTEF. She has published articles in international refereed books, journals, conferences, and journals. She also supervised Master theses and projects for university students and industry internship students. Her main research interests are Information System modeling, ontology, Semantic Web, Web services, and Information System integration.

Łukasz Lis has been a PhD student and researcher at the European Research Center for Information Systems (ERCIS) at the Department for Information Systems at the University of Münster, Germany, since 2006. Beforehand, he worked as a Freelancer on the development of Web-based information systems. Łukasz holds a Master's degree in Information Systems from the Poznań University of Economics, Poland. His current research activities focus on conceptual modeling and research Information Systems.

Peter Loos is Director of the Institute for Information Systems (IWi) at the German Research Center for Artificial Intelligence (DFKI) and head of the chair for Business Administration and Information Systems at Saarland University. His research activities include business process management, information modeling, enterprise systems, software development as well as implementation of information systems. He wrote his PhD thesis on the issue of data modeling in manufacturing systems – awarded with the Dr.-Eduard-Martin-Preis – in 1991. In 1997, Prof. Loos received the Venia Legendi in Business Administration. During his earlier career Prof. Loos had been Chair of Information Systems & Management at University of Mainz, Chair of Information Systems & Management at Chemnitz University of Technology, Deputy Chair at University of Muenster, as well as Lecturer (Privatdozent) at Saarland University. Furthermore, he had worked for 6 years as Manager of the software development department at the software and consulting company, IDS Scheer. Prof. Loos has written several books, contributed to 30 books and published more than 100 papers in journals and proceedings.

Daniela Lucas da Silva is PhD student in Information Science at the Universidade Federal de Minas Gerais since 2009. She holds a Master's in Information Science from Universidade Federal de Minas Gerais. In 2002 she has got a Specialization Degree in Strategic Information Management from Universidade Federal de Minas Gerais, and in 2001 she graduated in Management Information Systems at the Faculty of Management Information Systems, UNA. She is a Professor at the Department of Library Science at the Universidade Federal do Espírito Santo and is a Researcher in the field of Ontological Engineering with interest in the topics: ontology, methodology for building ontologies, and controlled vocabularies.

Tariq Mahmoud studied Information Engineering at Al-Baath University in Syria. In 2007, he started his PhD at the Department of Computer Science in Carl von Ossietzky University of Oldenburg (Germany). He is currently a Research Assistant at the working group of Business Information Systems at the Carl von Ossietzky University of Oldenburg (Germany). His research interests include very large business applications, semantic enterprise SOA, information security, business intelligence, data warehousing and Semantic Web.

Simon Nikles has, since 2006, been Research Assistant at the Institute for Business Information Systems of the University of Applied Sciences North Western Switzerland. During this time, he was involved in several EU founded projects, such as FIT (Foresting self adaptive E-Government), MATURE (Continuous Social Learning in Knowledge Networks), and plugIT (Business and IT Alignment using a Model-Based Plug-in Framework), where his major focus has been ontology based modelling. In 2005 he received his degree in Business Information Systems from FHNW. Before and partially during his study, Simon Nikles worked as application Developer in the field of business applications.

Gustav Pomberger is Full Professor for Software Engineering and head of the Department of Business Informatics Software Engineering at the Johannes Kepler University of Linz since 1987. His resume begins with a degree in electrical engineering. After nine years of experience in industry, he made a career change to academia. After his dissertation he transferred to a postdoctoral position with Professor Niklaus Wirth at ETH Zurich. In 1983 he was appointed Professor of Computer Science at the University of Zurich. In 1987 he was simultaneously offered positions at ETH Zurich, the Technical University of Vienna, and Johannes Kepler University of Linz. From 1992 to 1999 he led the Christian Doppler Research Laboratory for Software Engineering. He is member of the senate of the Christian Doppler Research Society. He received the following awards: Austrian Computer Society Award for Particular Scientific Achievement (1985), Fellow of the Christian Doppler Research Society (2002) and the Upper Austrian Science Award (2006). His basic research focuses on the design of high-quality software architectures and the systematic organization of software development processes, his applied research currently concentrates on the design of software architectures for augmented and virtual reality based embedded systems (such as navigation systems, local and context-based services), and the design and implementation of real-time systems. In the broader field of business informatics, his current research emphases are the design and implementation of quality management systems, the diagnosis of the effectiveness and economy of IT systems, and the development of methods for business process improvement.

Elke Pulvermueller holds a Junior Professorship in the Department of Mathematics & Computer Science at the University of Osnabrück (Germany). There, she is head of the Software Engineering research group. Between September 2009 and March 2010 she has been temporarily appointed as an Acting Full Professor of the Institute of Software Technology and Programming Languages at the University of Luebeck (Germany). Previous to her appointments at Luebeck and Osnabrueck she has been a senior researcher / research assistant at the University of Luxembourg (2006 - 2007), at the Friedrich Schiller-University of Jena (Germany) and at the Universitaet Karlsruhe (Germany). She received her doctoral degree from the Friedrich Schiller-University of Jena in 2006. Her research focuses on new approaches in software and quality engineering. Elke Pulvermueller is a member of the German Computer Society (GI) and the ACM.

Shahryar Rahnamayan received his B.Sc. and M.S. degrees both with honors in software engineering. He received his Ph.D. degree in the field of evolutionary computation from University of Waterloo (UW), Canada. The opposition-based differential evolution (ODE) was proposed in his PhD thesis. Since August 2007, he has been a Chief Research Manager at OMISA Inc. (Omni-Modality Intelligent Segmentation Assistant); a company that develops innovative software for medical image segmentation. Before joining to Faculty of Engineering and Applied Science, University of Ontario Institute of Technology (UOIT), Canada, as a faculty member, he was a postdoctoral fellow at Simon Fraser University (SFU), Canada. His research includes evolutionary algorithms, opposition-based computation, and image processing. Dr. Shahryar was awarded the Ontario Graduate Scholarship (OGS), President's Graduate Scholarship (PGS), NSERC's Japan Society for the Promotion of Science (JSPS) Fellowship, NSERC's Industrial R&D Fellowship (IRDF), NSERC's Visiting Fellowship in Canadian Government Laboratories (VF), NSERC Discovery Grant, and the Canadian Institute of Health Research (CIHR) Fellowship twice.

Ilona Reischl joined the Austrian Medicines and Medical Devices Agency AGES/PharmMed in March 2006, as Head of the Division in charge of Clinical Trial Assessment, now the Department for Clinical Trials, Preclinical and Statistical Evaluation in the Institute for Marketing Authorization of Medicinal Products & Lifecycle Management. She transitioned from practical research to the regulation of medicines at the US Food and Drug Administration (FDA) assessing the quality of biotech investigational new drug applications (INDs) and working on a research project on T cell signaling. Her initial training comprised a degree in pharmacy, a PhD in immunology/allergology and postdoctoral experience at an industrial research institute, the University of Southampton (UK) and the National Institutes of Health (USA). Her interest in Information Systems arose from the managing requirements of her current position.

Michael Schrefl received his Dipl.-Ing. degree and his Doctorate from Vienna University of Technology, Vienna, Austria, in 1983 and 1988, respectively. During 1983 and 1984 he studied at Vanderbilt University, USA, as a Fulbright scholar. From 1985 to 1992 he was with Vienna University of Technology. During 1987 and 1988, he was on leave for participating in research projects at GMD IPSI, Darmstadt. He was appointed Professor of Business Informatics at Johannes Kepler University of Linz, Austria, in 1992, and Professor in Computer and Information Science at University of South Australia in 1998. He has published more than 100 scientific papers and participated in a range of national and international collaborative research projects. He currently leads the Department of Business Informatics – Data & Knowledge Engineering at the University of Linz, with projects in data warehousing, semantic systems, and web engineering. Prof. Dr. Michael Schrefl is a member of ACM and IEEE Computer Society.

Renato R. Souza has been working since 2010 as Researcher and Professor at Fundação Getulio Vargas, Brazil, and since 2003 has been either Adjoint or Collaborator Professor at the Universidade Federal de Minas Gerais, Brazil. Since 2009 he holds a visiting fellowship in the Glamorgan University, UK. He holds a graduate degree in Systems Engineering, a Master's degree in Production Engineering, a PhD in Information Science and a Postdoc in Computer Science. Since 2010 he is Associate Editor of the *New Review of Hypermedia and Multimedia Journal*. He was awarded in 2010 with the productivity scholarship of the CNPq, the Brazilian Federal Research Agency for three years. He has published many scientific in both national and international journals. His main research interests are natural language processing, knowledge organization systems, ontologies, and information retrieval.

Darijus Strasunskas is a Postdoc Researcher at NTNU. He received his PhD in Information Systems from the Norwegian University of Science and Technology (NTNU) in 2006. He has Master degree from Vilnius University (2000). From 1997 to 2001 he was employed by Kraft Foods International in Lithuania as Finance Analyst and was responsible for financial control of major capital project and ERP system implementation, later he became a key user of ERP system manufacturing module. For his performance he received a commendation award in 2001. His main research interests include, but are not limited to quantitative and qualitative evaluation of novel and traditional business models, intelligent information retrieval, and ontology quality aspects, as well as deployment of semantic technologies for information management. His publication list includes over 40 articles in international refereed books, journals, conferences, and workshops. He has been awarded for his contribution to science (best paper awards at the BIS 2009 and WSKS 2008 conferences) and practice (award for an outstanding performance at Kraft Foods International in 2001).

Rainer Telesko has, since 2007, been Professor for Business Informatics at the University of Applied Sciences North Western Switzerland, Institute of Information Systems. He received a PhD in Business Informatics from the University of Vienna. From 1993 to 2002 he was Research Assistant at the Institute of Information Systems of the University of Vienna (Department of Knowledge Engineering). From 2002 to 2007 he worked for the Corporate Research (Area: Software-intensive Systems) of Robert Bosch GmbH in Stuttgart. He was there engaged in projects for Knowledge Management for product development processes and Business Process Management (Member of the Corporate Systems Engineering Process Group). His main interests are business process management (compliance management), process-oriented knowledge management, business service management, and software engineering. Rainer Telesko was involved in several EU- and national funded projects in the field of knowledge engineering, knowledge management and business process management.

Barbara Thönssen has, since 2009, been co-heading the Competence Center Information and Knowledge Management, which is part of the Institut für Wirtschaftsinformatik (IWI) at the University of Applied Sciences Northwestern Switzerland (FHNW). In 1984 she received her Master degree in Information Science at the University of Saarland, Germany. She worked for Softex AG in Saarbruecken (Germany) from 1984–1987, and was responsible for the development of electronic dictionaries to be used for spelling checking and automatic indexing. After that Barbara Thönssen was lecturer at the Lehramt fuer Dokumentation in Frankfurt a.M. (Germany) teaching in the fields of information and documentation and information retrieval. In 1989 she joined the Swiss Bank Corporation in Basel (Switzerland) and worked as Business Analyst and Project Manager for electronic archives until 1995. From 1995–1997 she was Project Manager at Systor AG in Basel (Switzerland) leading projects in the area of electronic archiving, document management, and workflow management. From 1997–2000 Barbara Thönssen was Senior Project Manager for an international project on CRM at the United Bank of Switzerland (UBS) in Zurich (Switzerland). After that, she was Head of Department for E-Government and electronic archiving solutions for the Zurich City Council in Zurich (Switzerland). In 2004 she joined the FHNW in Olten, Switzerland. She is Lecturer in the Bachelor program Business Information Systems and responsible for the Certificate of Advanced Studies for "Records Management." Barbara Thönssen is engaged in several national and international research projects. Her current research is focussed on bringing semantic technologies into practise.

Mathias Uslar has studied computer science with a minor in legal informatics at the University of Oldenburg, Germany form 1999 till 2004. In October 2004, he started working as a Scientific Assistant at OFFIS -Institute for Information Systems in Oldenburg, later on working there as project leader and now as Group Manager in the Energy branch of the institute, leading the largest group in OFFIS. Since 2008, he is Head of the CISE, the Centre for IT Standards in the Energy Sector. In October 2009, he successfully defended his PhD thesis on the integration of heterogeneous standards in the electric utility domain and smart grids. Mr. Uslar is leading OFFIS' national and international work packages with the scope of standardisation and interoperability. He is member of German GI, IEEE, ACM, and IEC German mirror committee member DKE K 952, 952.0.10, 952.0.17, and international member of IE TC 57 WG 14 and 16. His research interests are with semantic modeling and technical interoperability in smart grid architectures. Currently, he is working on modeling DER, like CHP or PHEV, using the CIM (IEC 61968), and creating control structures for virtual power plants.

Daniela Wolff received her Diploma degree in Information Technology in 2006 from the University of Oldenburg, Germany. Since 2006 she has been working as a Researcher at the Competence Center Information and Knowledge Management, which is part of the Institute für Wirtschaftsinformatik (IWI) at the University of Applied Sciences Northwestern Switzerland (FHNW). She is Lecturer in the Bachelor program Business Information Systems and involved in the European funded projects FIT (Fostering self-adaptive e-government service improvement using semantic technolgies) and plugIT (Business and IT Alignment using A Model-Based Plug-In Framework). She is writing her dissertation about flexible process execution using a business rules approach.

Steffen Zimmermann has, since March 2009, been an Assistant Professor at the Department of Information Systems, Production and Logistics Management at the University of Innsbruck. He studied Business Administration at the University of Augsburg in the specialized fields of Information Systems, Financial Engineering and Economics of the Information Society. After his studies, he was Research Assistant at the Department of Information Systems Engineering & Financial Management of Prof. Dr. H. U. Buhl and received his Doctor's degree in February 2008. During this time, he was leader of a research group and he applied successfully for a publicly funded fundamental research project on the topic IT Portfolio Management at the German Research Foundation. Concurrently, he conducted several applied privately funded research projects (e.g. at MLP AG and WestLB AG). He has published several articles in a number of international journals, such as *DATA BASE for Advances in Information Systems* or *Business and Information Systems Engineering* (Die Wirtschaftsinformatik). Moreover, he presented his research at international conferences such as European Conference on Information Systems and International Conference on Information Systems. His main research interests are semantic-based process management, IT portfolio management, and global sourcing of IT.

Index